Essential Articulate® Studio '09

Patti Shank, Ph.D., and Jennifer Bircher

Wordware Publishing, Inc.

Library of Congress Cataloging-in-Publication Data

Shank, Patti, 1954-
Essential Articulate Studio '09 / by Patti Shank and Jennifer Bircher.
  p. cm.
  Includes index.
  ISBN-13: 978-1-59822-058-2 (pbk.)
  ISBN-10: 1-59822-058-6 (pbk.)
  1. Articulate Studio. 2. Computer-assisted instruction--Authoring programs.
  3. Web-based instruction--Design. I. Bircher, Jennifer. II. Title.
  LB1028.66.S53 2009
  371.33'44678--dc22   2009011115

© 2009, Wordware Publishing, Inc.

An imprint of Jones and Bartlett Publishers

All Rights Reserved

Jones and Bartlett Publishers, LLC
40 Tall Pine Drive
Sudbury, MA 01776
978-443-5000
info@jbpub.com
www.jbpub.com

No part of this book may be reproduced in any form or by any means
without permission in writing from Wordware Publishing, Inc.

Printed in the United States of America

ISBN-13: 978-1-59822-058-2
ISBN-10: 1-59822-058-6

10 9 8 7 6 5 4 3 2 1
0905

Dedication

For Greg, friend, sherpa, and fellow book lover, who slays dragons and keeps the troll under the stairs at bay so I can write.
— Patti

For Bailey and Will, who bring immeasurable joy to my life every day.
— Jennifer

Contents

About the Authors

Patti Shank is the president of Learning Peaks, an internationally recognized instructional design consulting firm. She has worked on a wide range of corporate training, higher education, and professional development information and instruction projects. Patti was an award-winning contributing editor for *Online Learning* magazine, and edited Training Media Review's *Authoring Tools Report*. She has authored, co-authored, or edited three online learning-related books, including *Making Sense of Online Learning* (with Amy Sitze, Pfeiffer, 2004), *The Online Learning Idea Book* (Pfeiffer, 2007), and the *E-Learning Handbook* (with Saul Carliner, Pfeiffer, 2008). She is regularly asked to speak at trade and academic conferences related to training, instructional design, and instructional technology. Patti lives just outside of Denver, Colorado, and her favorite flavor of ice cream is Phish Food.

Jennifer Bircher launched into the computer-based training (CBT) world during its infancy by developing courses for the U.S. Army Corps of Engineers. Specializing in applications training, her career has evolved over the past 19 years into designing, writing, and programming a variety of CBT, web-based training (WBT), and e-learning courses, both retail and custom. She has provided instructional design and content authoring services to numerous clients in the business and academic realms. Jennifer lives in Longmont, Colorado, and her favorite flavor of ice cream is dependent on her mood: either mint chocolate chip or coffee.

Doug Wagner (who is not on the cover as an author but helped us so much that we want to include him here) comes to computer-based training from an academic and journalistic background, having taught and written extensively in the areas of media history, media industries, and the political economy of information/communication technology. Doug discovered electronic learning during the mid-1990s, at the height of the Internet boom years, since which time he has worked as an instructional designer, course author, content writer, editor, and project manager for a wide variety of clients. Doug lives in Boulder,

Colorado, and his favorite flavor of ice cream is carob tofutti. (We try not to hold that against him.)

Patti, Jennifer, and Doug have worked together on numerous Learning Peaks (and other) projects so the team effort felt natural. Because of Patti, Jennifer, and Doug's wealth of experience, they are able to provide real-world perspectives, which should be especially valuable to anyone who is just starting to build information and instruction.

Acknowledgments

We want to acknowledge some folks who helped us get this book into your hands as quickly as possible.

Dave Mozealous, Articulate QA Manager (http://www.mozealous.com), was our guardian angel throughout the project. He made himself available to us on a moment's notice, including holidays, weekends, and while watching football games. He went above and beyond, again and again. Doug Wagner, our colleague, was initially roped into reading all of the chapters, editing the text for clarity and completeness, and trying all of the "how-tos." We then roped him into writing some of the Quizmaker content and the Video Encoder content. We literally couldn't have done this without Dave and Doug's help.

We had help from other Articulate staff as well. Tom Kuhlmann, the author of the Rapid E-Learning blog (http://www.articulate.com/rapid-elearning), read all of the chapters and answered numerous how-to questions. Both Gabe Anderson, director of customer support and author of the Word of Mouth blog (http://www.articulate.com/blog), and Magnus Nirell, QA Manager for Engage, answered numerous questions.

We also want to thank Rosie Piller, the OUR Center, and Sean Johnson. Sean's very cool Hand of Sean font is used for our screenshot callouts.

And finally, we want to thank Tim McEvoy, our publisher, for his support. Working with a good publisher is a wonderful experience.

```
   dP    dP                        dP                                                dP 1
   88    88                        88                                                88
d8888P 88d888b.  .d8888b. 88d888b. 88  .dP    dP    dP .d8888b. dP    dP 88
   88  88'  `88 88'  `88 88'  `88 8888"      88    88 88'  `88 88    88 dP
   88  88    88 88.  .88 88       88 88 `8b.  88.  .88 88.  .88 88.  .88
   dP   dP    dP `88888P8 dP      dP dP  `YP  `8888P88 `88888P' `88888P' oo
                                                  .88
                                              d8888P
```

---

1 ASCII art from ASCII Generator: http://www.network-science.de/ascii

About This Book

This book is designed to help novice to intermediate users of Articulate Studio '09 get the most from using these tools—Presenter, Engage, Quizmaker, and Video Encoder—to develop quality informational and instructional materials. It was written with the following goals in mind:

- Help new users get up to speed as quickly and painlessly as possible

- Assist users of previous versions of Articulate Studio (and previous versions of Presenter, Engage, and Quizmaker) in capitalizing on improvements made to these tools in the '09 versions

- Provide tips and tools to make building information and instruction using these tools faster, easier, and better

- Help new and previous users develop information and instruction that is more valuable for the intended audience(s)

Why It's Unique

This book is unique, from the standpoint of applications books. It serves as both a tutorial for the Articulate Studio '09 products and also as a primer on designing and building good information and instruction. The advice and insights are practical and take into account the we-need-it-yesterday environments that most people who use these tools operate in. The book can also serve as documentation, to be used whenever a question arises while using the Articulate Studio '09 products.

The book includes hundreds of screen captures, many with callouts, to reinforce the discussions and how-to steps provided throughout the book. Screen captures show a wide variety of topics to help readers see how what is being discussed applies to various content areas. Many online learning books talk about how to build good instruction, but this book actually *shows* you how to build it, using some of the best authoring tools in the industry.

The book is written so that each chapter stands alone but can also be used as a progressive "course" in using the Articulate Studio '09 tools. Readers can pick up the book, look for information on a specific topic (such as how to edit audio or what graphic formats can be imported), and find it quickly. Most information related to each tool is provided within the same section, but it is also easy to find similar information (for example, importing graphics) for each of the tools. Additional chapters and information is provided on building rapid e-learning and instructional design basics. Planning guides and other tools to make building information and instruction easier are provided throughout. Many chapters contain scripted or general practices and all contain a final recap of the most important points and insights from the chapter.

Intended Audience

This book is especially tailored for the needs of novice to intermediate developers of online information and instruction. This includes trainers, instructional designers and developers, teachers, instructors, content experts, and others involved in the process of building online information and instruction.

Organization

The book is designed for new and previous users of the Articulate Studio authoring tools. It has 27 chapters, covering most of the functionalities of the Articulate Studio '09 tools. It is organized into three main sections: Presenter (chapters 3-7), Quizmaker (chapters 8-13), and Engage (chapters 14-25). The final two chapters of the book cover publishing your project and using Video Encoder.

Each of the main sections—Presenter, Quizmaker, and Engage—include an introductory chapter that will help you plan the materials you want to build and describes the most commonly performed tasks using the tool.

Chapter 1, "Introduction to Articulate Studio," describes uses for each tool and how they can be used together. It is especially written for readers who have not used these tools previously or who are new to instructional authoring. Chapter 2, "Rapid E-Learning," discusses rapid development, including when and how to use rapid development processes, and how to determine what is needed before you dive into any project.

Book Conventions

Boldface text indicates a button, link, or menu item used to complete tasks inside each of the authoring tools.

Tips provide a helpful hints or insights from actual practice.

Notes provide cautionary information that you should be aware of.

Screenshots are based on the appearance of Articulate Studio '09 products at the time of this writing. Some minor features may have changed (because of product updates) since that time, so the current products might look slightly different from some of the screenshots in this book.

CD Files and Errata

The companion CD-ROM includes a 30-day trial version of Articulate Studio '09, Articulate Studio documentation, and links to helpful content on the Articulate Studio web site. The files are organized as follows:

- Studio-09-Update-4.exe: The 30-day trial version of Articulate Studio '09.

- Articulate-REL-Blog-ebook-8-page-excerpt.pdf: An excerpt from *The Insider's Guide to Becoming a Rapid E-Learning Pro* in PDF format.

- links.doc: Contains links to various articles on the Articulate Studio web site.

- Documentation: Articulate documentation files for the Articulate Studio authoring tools in PDF format.

Send errata to EAS09errata@learningpeaks.com, and look for errata updates at www.learningpeaks.com/EAS09errata.

Uses for This Book

This book is designed to be used as a tutorial and as a support tool for anyone who wants or needs to build quality online information or instruction quickly. Each chapter stands alone and references other chapters that have related information.

This is an excellent book to add to a library of books for teachers, trainers, instructional designers, instructors, and faculty involved in building online information and instruction. It is a good text to use in instructional authoring courses and multimedia authoring courses, especially early in the program, because the Articulate Studio tools have a relatively short learning curve and can help learners feel successful early on. It also makes an excellent text to support professional development courses for teachers, trainers, instructional designers, instructors, and faculty, or provide as a reward for creative online teaching.

Chapter 1

Introduction to Articulate Studio

Chapter Snapshot

In this chapter, you will learn about the Articulate Studio '09 authoring tools. We'll describe what each tool does and how it works and then we'll walk you through how the tools can be used together in more complex information or instruction. If you're new to Articulate authoring tools or instructional authoring, this chapter will get you off to a good start in thinking about how to use these tools to create good information or instruction.

> **?** Should I read this chapter if I'm a more experienced developer?

> **i** There certainly is information in this chapter that pertains to anyone using these products. And if you're trying to get your organization to pay for Articulate Studio, you'll find some good ammo for that discussion.

What Is Articulate Studio?

Articulate Studio '09 (Figure 1.1) contains three or four authoring tools (depending on whether you purchased Articulate Studio '09 Professional or Articulate Studio '09 Standard), including Presenter, Quizmaker, Engage, and Video Encoder. These tools can be used together or separately to create professional-looking online information or instruction. Outside elements (such as audio, video, and web pages) can be pulled in. It's easy to build attractive content that looks like it took a long time to build and coordinate the look and feel of content built in all of the tools. It's almost scary-wonderful how easy it is to change settings that make the output look and feel just the way you want.

Figure 1.1. The Articulate Studio '09 product suite (source: http://www.articulate.com/products/studio.php)

The primary output that you create when using the Articulate Studio authoring tools is *Flash* content. Flash content is a self-contained portable format that can be easily integrated into web content. Flash content from Articulate Studio tools technically plays in a Flash *player* (the background application that "plays" Flash content), but the Flash player is "invisible" to the viewer. Viewers see and interact with the Presenter, Engage, or Quizmaker player (which is visible, as you can see from the screenshots throughout this chapter). If this seems confusing (it is kind of confusing!), you can pretty much ignore this except to realize that in order to play Flash content you must have the Flash player installed.

Presenter installs a plug-in in PowerPoint that lets you create simple but not simplistic Flash content. Presenter's easy-to-use features (such as narrating your slides) are, well, easy to use. Presenter's more complex features let you go hog-wild with creativity. Articulate Engage lets you build exploration-oriented Flash content. Quizmaker, Articulate's quiz and survey and test development tool, has been redesigned from the ground up and rounds out your ability to author Flash content without being a Flash programmer.

In the not-too-distant past, creating attractive and engaging online information and instruction required the use of complex authoring tools and programming skills. Or it meant having a development team with these skills. Building courses took months (or more). And the whole process was expensive and intimidating for anyone new to the process. You can still build information or instruction that way, but in many cases, there's no need to. And that's terrific.

If you're new to building online content, chances are you purchased Articulate Studio '09 because the learning curve for the commonly used features (such as narrating slides and building content interactions) is reasonable and the output (what viewers see) can look like it took a lot of work to create.

If you've used more complex authoring tools and are now using rapid development tools instead of or in addition to more complex tools, we're guessing you like how streamlined the new development process is. The things that took days of scripting can now be done in hours. The freedom of creating anything is replaced with the thrill of making what's needed come to fruition quickly, and with great results, leaving you more time to attend to the million other things that need to get done.

The work I (Patti) have done with Training Media Review (http://www.tmreview.com) in reviewing authoring tools and working on their Authoring Tools Report has helped me appreciate the pain folks go through in trying to use tools that promise the moon but can't deliver. In the last few years instructional authoring has been approaching a "sweet spot" where we can develop what is needed without spending a fortune and without slaving for months to learn how to make the tool do what you want. Things that used to be hard, like video, have become easier as well. You can buy a low-end digital video camera, shoot some video, and have it on YouTube in a half hour!

What does all this have to do with Articulate Studio? A lot. These tools are certainly in the "sweet spot" of easy to learn and use while still allowing lots of flexibility in what you can develop. It's a great first authoring tool(set), but it's also good for folks who have more experience and simply don't need the hassle and expense of complex authoring for most of the projects they work on.

What's the big deal about Flash? Adobe Flash has long been the standard for creating engaging and interactive web content. Why aren't we using Flash to build online content instead of authoring tools that produce Flash content? The answer to that question is easy: In most cases, it's too hard and too time consuming. Flash has a steep learning curve, including learning its programming language, ActionScript. The typical online instruction project is needed yesterday. And many of the folks who build online instruction don't have the time to gain the skills needed to be a crackerjack Flash programmer. They may work with Flash developers, but if those developers are like most Flash developers, they are super busy with the stuff that really *needs* a Flash programmer.

As you use more and more of the features of each of the Articulate Studio tools to build projects, it gets harder and harder to tell what authoring tool was used to build it. Was it built with Flash or Articulate Engage? Articulate Presenter or Flash? Flash or Quizmaker? We won't tell if you won't.

If you can spend less time and still have quality Flash content, why spend the extra time? Exactly.

Using Articulate Studio

Articulate Studio '09 contains authoring tools that have different niches but are also made to work well together. Table 1.1 shows some primary uses for each tool.

Table 1.1. Typical uses for the Articulate Studio '09 tools

Tool	Uses
Presenter	Simple narrated PowerPoint presentations
	Presentations with added media (audio, video, Engage interactions, Quizmaker quizzes, other Flash files such as Captivate)
	Complex instruction with complex content, interactions, media, branching, quizzes, and almost anything else
Engage	Exploration and discovery content such as:
	Explanations
	Descriptions
	Process and procedures
	Conceptual overviews
	Instructions
	Terminology
	Media presentations
	Introductions and summaries
Quizmaker	Graded and ungraded questions and quizzes, including:
	Check-your-understanding questions
	Surveys
	Branched scenarios
	Quizzes and tests
Video Encoder	Convert video formats into the FLV Flash video format for use in Presenter, Engage, and Quizmaker

Next we'll provide a quick overview of each tool. We'll describe how the tool works and what you can do with it.

Presenter

Presenter is an authoring tool that works directly with Microsoft PowerPoint. Presenter has become well known for creating easy-peasy narrated PowerPoint presentations that are typically published as Flash (SWF) content. But Presenter is able to do much more than this and is extremely flexible. It can certainly be used to build narrated PowerPoint presentations, but it can also be used to build instructional sequences with branching, embedded Engage interactions and Quizmaker quizzes, Learning Games, audio, video, and more. You choose how much to include and the end result can be very simple, quite complex, and anything in between.

Figure 1.2 shows an example of content produced using Presenter.

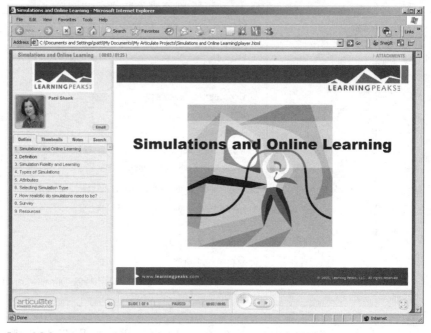

Figure 1.2. Presenter project

To build a Presenter project, you first build slides in PowerPoint. The slides contain the text and graphics that you want viewers to see when each slide is displayed. You can then add a variety of media and interactions and make your project as simple or complex as you want. You can also customize how the output looks and feels.

Once your project is complete, you'll publish it so intended viewers can view it. Publishing creates Flash content and other needed files. Viewers interact with the project in the Presenter player, the interface that displays the content.

Quizmaker

Quizmaker lets you quickly build graded quizzes and nongraded surveys using predefined question types. A graded quiz can contain both graded questions and nongraded questions, which are called survey questions in Quizmaker (see Figures 1.3 and 1.4 for a graded question example). Surveys contain only survey questions. To build a question slide, you select from 20 prebuilt question types, such as Multiple Choice, Matching Drag and Drop, and Likert Scale, and then input needed content. There are two ways to build questions. The easy-to-use Form view lets you input text into placeholders for quick content development. The PowerPoint-like Slide view lets you customize questions by adding text, pictures, video, audio, and hyperlinks and formatting these elements. You can also include customized non-question slides to provide additional content, such as an introduction.

Once you build your questions, you can arrange them within a quiz by creating customized groups. Quizmaker also provides branching functionality, so you can create branched scenarios based on viewer responses. Once you build a quiz, you'll publish it so intended viewers can view it. Publishing creates Flash content and other needed files. Viewers interact with the quiz in the Quizmaker player, the interface that displays the quiz slides. Figure 1.3 shows a simple question in Quizmaker's Form view. The content represents part of the development of the Wonders of the World question slide shown in Figure 1.4.

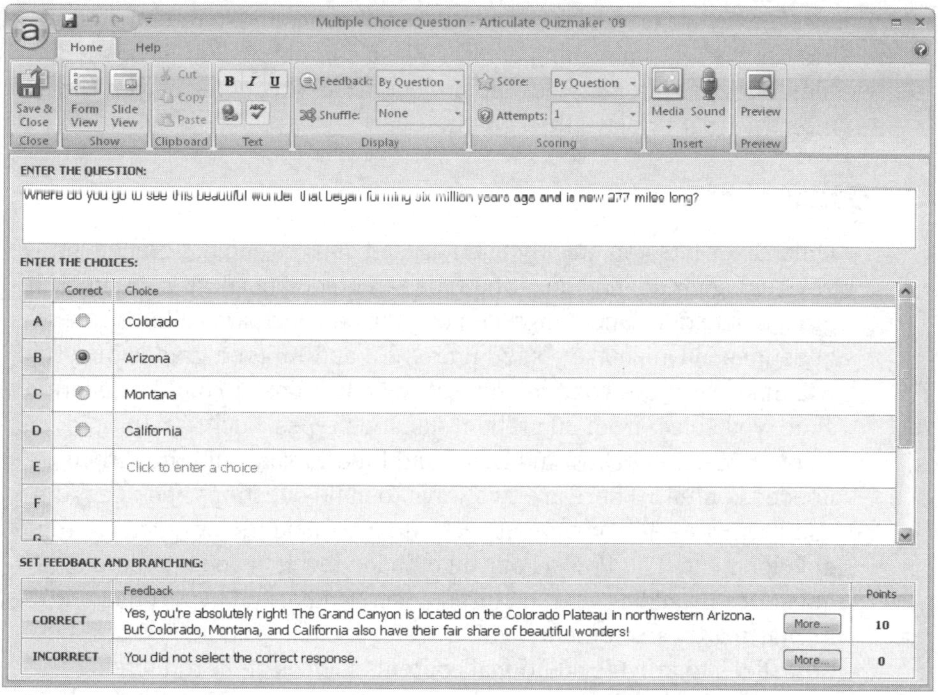

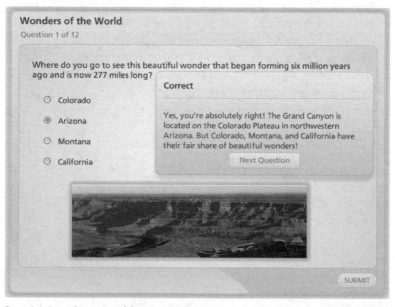

Figure 1.3. Quizmaker question slide in Form view

Figure 1.4. Quizmaker question slide in Preview window

Engage

Engage lets you create self-contained "discovery" experiences for viewers, called Engage *interactions*. You've probably seen online instructional materials where you roll over or click some part of the screen and additional information is shown. That's the type of content you can develop in Engage, but without having to build it in Flash.

To create an Engage interaction, you select an interaction template (for example, a Process or Timeline interaction template). Once your template is selected, you add the text, audio, and other media. You can change how your interaction looks and works or use the default settings. When you are done, you'll publish it so the intended audience can view it. Publishing creates Flash content and other needed files. The audience views the interaction through the Engage player, the interface that displays the interaction.

Figure 1.5 shows the Timeline interaction window, which is used to build this type of interaction. The content represents the early part of development of the An Early History of Computing Timeline interaction shown in Figure 1.6.

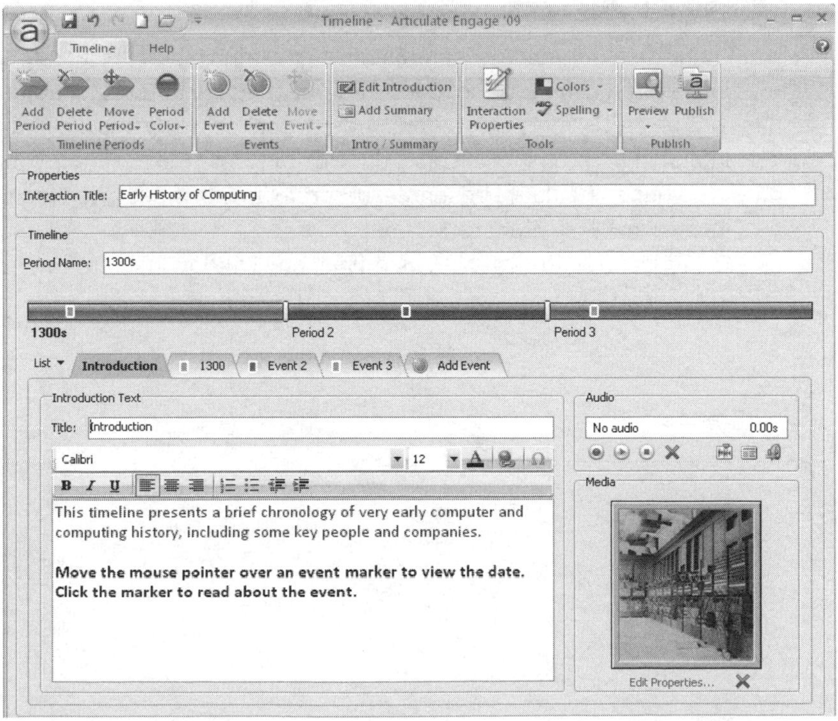

Figure 1.5. Engage Timeline interaction window

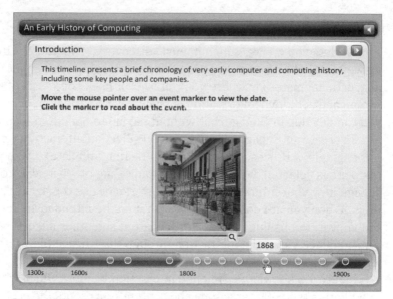

Figure 1.6. Engage Timeline interaction in Preview window

Video Encoder

Video Encoder converts almost any video into the FLV Flash video format. You can crop the video and only use certain parts, adjust the volume and brightness, add images, logos, or watermarks, and select publishing options for bitrate, dimensions, and more. Then you can add it to your Articulate Presenter '09 project or bring it into Quizmaker quizzes and Engage interactions.

Figure 1.7 shows the Video Encoder window used to import and edit video files.

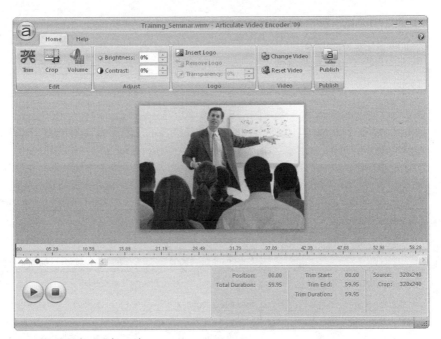

Figure 1.7. The Video Encoder window

All Together

The description of each tool in the previous section was meant to give you a feel for how the tool works and the end result. You can certainly use any of the Articulate Studio tools on their own, but we'd be remiss in not reminding you how well they work together.

To illustrate how the Articulate Studio '09 tools might be used together in a Presenter project, we'll take a look at two projects that use three or four of the Articulate Studio authoring tools. We'll start with a risk assessment module in a project management course (Table 1.2). Notice how the Articulate Studio tools are used to create a more engaging and comprehensive learning experience than could be created with only one tool.

Table 1.2. Presenter project module elements

Course: Project Management 101 Module: Project Risk Assessment		
Topic	Content	Elements
Introduction	Presentation	Narrated PowerPoint slides Engage FAQ interaction
Project risk overview	Presentation	Narrated PowerPoint slides Engage Pyramid interaction
	Self-check questions	Flash video (Video Encoder) Quizmaker multiple-choice questions
Risk evaluation process	Presentation	Narrated PowerPoint slides Engage Process interaction
	Self-check questions	Presenter choices Learning Game
Risk measurement	Presentation	Narrated PowerPoint slides
	Risk calculations	Excel workbook and PDF answer sheet
	Self-check questions	Presenter choices Learning Game
Risk communication and negotiation	Presentation	Narrated PowerPoint slides
	Self-check questions	Quizmaker multiple-choice questions
Communication	Web Object Q&A discussion forum	
Resources	Risk process job aid (PDF) Risk measurement job aid (PDF) Risk calculation tool (Excel spreadsheet)	
Glossary	Engage Glossary interaction	

Figure 1.8 shows the Project Management 101 module after being published. Figure 1.9 shows the Engage Pyramid interaction open in this module, and Figure 1.10 shows one of the Quizmaker self-check questions open in the module.

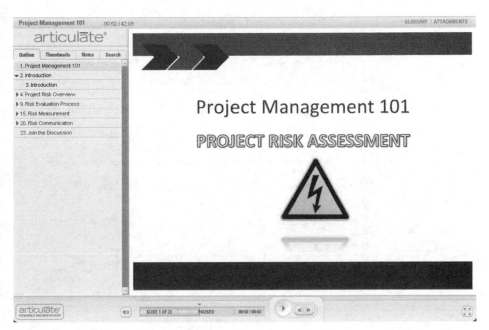

Figure 1.8. Project Risk Assessment module

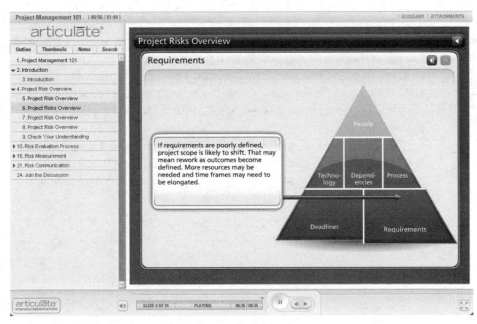

Figure 1.9. Engage Pyramid interaction in Project Risk Assessment module

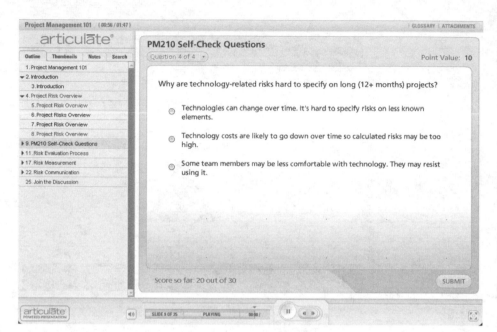

Figure 1.10. Quizmaker question used in Project Risk Assessment module

This Presenter project pulls together all the learning elements, which come from a variety of sources, including PowerPoint slides, Presenter Learning Games, Presenter Web Objects, Engage interactions, Quizmaker questions, and attachments. The narrator discusses the slide content and talks about the other resources. The viewer has plenty of opportunity to interact with content (and with other people through the discussion forum Web Object) and to practice.

Now we'll look at another module about how to sort data in Excel 2007 (Table 1.3). Notice how the Articulate Studio tools are used together with another authoring tool (Captivate) that creates application demos.

Table 1.3. Presenter project module elements

Course: Excel 2007 Basics		
Module: Sorting Data		
Topic	**Content**	**Elements**
Sorting Data	Presentation	Narrated PowerPoint slides
		Engage Process interaction
Sorting (one column, two to three columns, more than three columns)	Presentation	Narrated PowerPoint slides
		Captivate application demo
	Simulation	Captivate application interactive simulation
Review	Presentation	Narrated PowerPoint slides
		Engage FAQ interaction
		Captivate application demo (same as Sorting)
	Self-check review questions	Quizmaker drag and drop questions
Test	Simulation	Captivate application interactive simulation
Resources	Sorting job aid (PDF)	

Figure 1.11 shows the Sorting Data module after being published. Figure 1.12 shows the Engage Process interaction open in this module, and Figure 1.13 shows one of the Quizmaker questions open in this module.

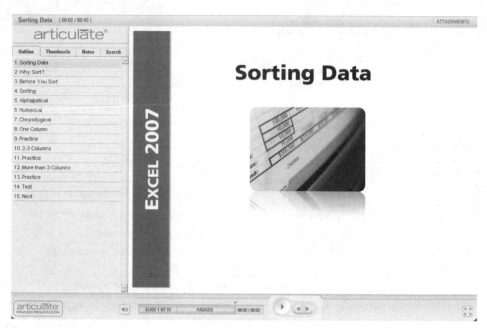

Figure 1.11. Sorting Data module

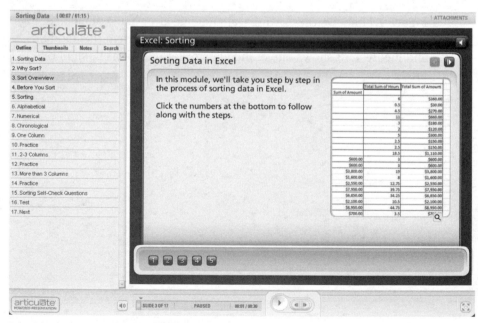

Figure 1.12. Excel Process interaction in Sorting Data module

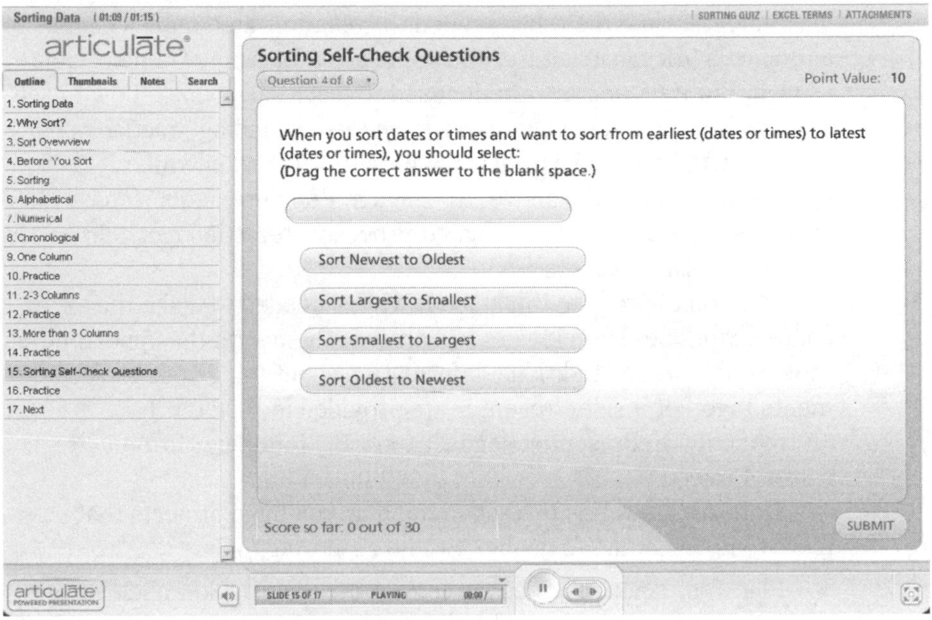

Figure 1.13. Quizmaker question in Sorting Data module

This Presenter project pulls together all the learning elements, which come from a variety of sources, including PowerPoint slides, Engage interactions, Captivate application demos and simulations, Quizmaker questions, and an attachment. When teaching how to use an application, it is beneficial to include demos (watch me) and simulations (you try). I (Patti) used Captivate to build these because that is the application demo/simulation tool that I normally work with. (There are numerous application demo/simulation authoring tools.) All of these elements can be embedded in Presenter so the viewer sees a seamless module, with everything in one place.

Figuring out how to best integrate these tools (and others, if needed) to build information or instruction starts with answering some simple questions:

1. What's needed to make this content clear and engaging?

2. Do viewers need practice opportunities? How will they be provided?

As you read through the rest of the chapters of this book, you will see tips and advice on ways to use these tools. Presenter can be a simple vehicle for delivering an online presentation with slides and narration.

That might be just the thing needed to communicate simple changes to a product's pricing structure. You could add a Learning Game or quiz as well. But if Presenter is being used to teach salespeople how to sell that product, more elements may be needed, including practice opportunities with branched scenarios built with Quizmaker, video, hyperlinks, or all of the above. An Engage FAQ interaction can be added as a glossary. And an Engage Process interaction can help explain the sales process.

The point here is to think about what's needed to make the content work best for viewers and provide them with the opportunities they need to learn. Additional information about tying your project elements together inside Presenter are provided in Chapter 3, "Introduction to Presenter," and Chapter 6, "Pumping Up Your Presenter Projects."

Here are a few tips to keep in mind as you build projects that use more than one of the Articulate Studio authoring tools:

- Plan your color schemes for consistency. Quizmaker and Engage contain many of the same built-in color schemes that are included in Presenter, so you can maintain a consistent look and feel across all slides. (Note that you can also create your own color schemes in all three products.)

- Use consistent fonts in Presenter, Quizmaker, and Engage for the same project.

- Look at the Engage interactions and see if there's a natural fit between what you need to explain and a specific interaction type. For example, the Process interaction is a natural fit for explaining how a given process works.

- Use Presenter Learning Games and Quizmaker quizzes to build self-check exercises that help the viewers figure out if they understand the content.

- Consider adding Engage interactions and simple video clips to *show* rather than *tell*. It's often hard for viewers to understand long or complex explanations without seeing appropriate visual content.

- When you think of using a variety of tools, think beyond Articulate Studio, too. For example, consider connecting viewers to outside content and social interaction through Presenter Web Objects.

- If you're new to authoring web content, start with simpler projects and fewer elements, such as narrated PowerPoint slides with an Engage interaction.

Installing Articulate Studio

You can install the entire Articulate Studio package together or you can install each Articulate Studio '09 application (Presenter, Quizmaker, Engage, and Video Encoder) separately. Following are instructions for installing the entire package. If you've purchased an application separately, installation instructions are available by searching the online help docs for that application using the keyword "install."

Installation Instructions

1. Previous versions of Articulate Studio applications will be uninstalled when you install Articulate Studio '09.

2. Download the Articulate Studio '09 installer.

3. Double-click **Studio'09 installer** to run the installation program.

4. After accepting the license agreement, review the four applications to be installed. Clear the check box next to any application you do not want to install at this time. Complete the installation process.

5. Launch an Articulate Studio '09 application by double-clicking its icon on the desktop or by selecting it from the Articulate Studio '09 submenu when you choose All Programs from the Start menu.

6. The first time you run an application, select **Activate Now With Your Serial Number** and enter your serial number. (If you are using a free trial, select **Continue trial.**)

Authoring Requirements

To build content using any of the Articulate Studio '09 applications, the following minimum system requirements apply:

Table 1.4. Authoring requirements

Hardware/Software	Requirement
CPU	500 megahertz (MHz) processor or higher
Memory	256 MB minimum

Hardware/Software	Requirement
Available disk space	100 MB minimum (per product being installed)
Display	800 x 600 screen resolution minimum (1,024 x 768 or higher is recommended)
Multimedia	Sound card and microphone (for recording narration)
Operating System	Microsoft Windows 2000 SP4 or later, XP SP2 or later, 2003, or Vista (32- or 64-bit)
.NET Runtime	.NET 2.0 or later (will be automatically installed if not present)
Microsoft PowerPoint (for Presenter projects)	PowerPoint 2000, PowerPoint 2002 (PowerPoint XP), PowerPoint 2003, or PowerPoint 2007
Adobe Flash Player	Adobe Flash Player 6.0.79 or later

Articulate Studio '09 will work with content created in previous versions, but previous versions cannot open content created in Articulate Studio '09.

Viewing Requirements

To view published content created by any Articulate Studio '09 application, you must have Flash Player 6.0.79 or later (Flash Player 7 or later recommended) and one of the following browsers:

■ Windows: Internet Explorer 6, Internet Explorer 7, Firefox 1.x and later, Safari 3, Google Chrome, Opera 9.5

■ Macintosh: Firefox 1.x and later, Safari 3

■ Linux: Firefox 1.x

Getting Help

Articulate provides numerous resources to help you use the Articulate Studio '09 applications. The tutorials, help documents, knowledge base articles, blogs, and community forums cover a wide range of topics to keep you up to speed. Best of all, they are constantly updated with new information. All of these resources are on the Articulate web site, and can be accessed directly from your browser or from within the applications. Keep in mind that you'll need an Internet connection to access all help information on the web site. Articulate also offers downloadable help files, which you can print or store on your computer for quick offline access.

Help Options

Each application contains options to access specific help resources on the web. Help options are available on the opening screen of each application, on the ribbon, and in dialog boxes.

Help Options on the Start Screen

When you first open Presenter, Quizmaker, or Engage, the start screen for that application is displayed. Each application (except Video Encoder) contains the same four help options at the bottom of the screen, as highlighted in Figure 1.14. These options give you one-click access to tutorials, Articulate community resources, support materials, and blogs. Table 1.5 describes each option.

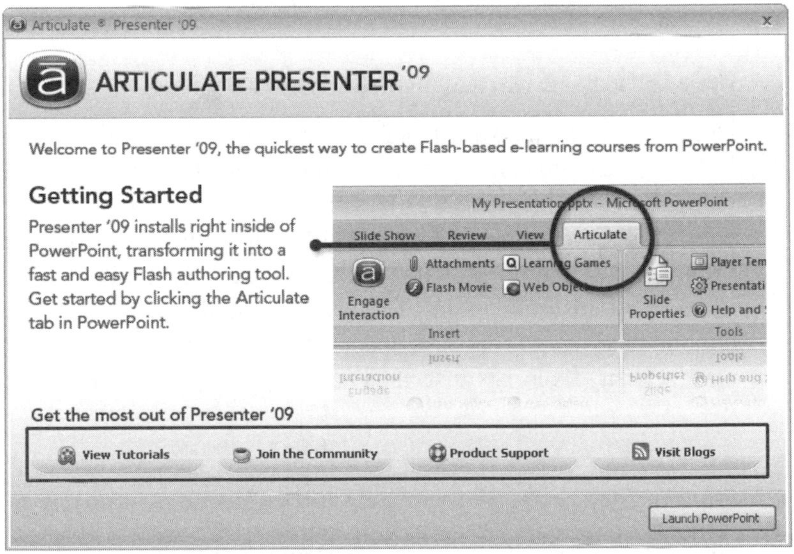

Figure 1.14. The four help options are View Tutorials, Join the Community, Product Support, and Visit Blogs.

Table 1.5. Help options on the start screen (Presenter, Quizmaker, and Engage)

Help option	Description
View Tutorials	Provides links to online application demos that show you how to perform common tasks related to the application; for example, how to add annotations in Presenter
Join the Community	Provides links to Articulate's terrific community resources: the Rapid E-Learning blog, Community Forum providing community discussions that take place using asynchronous discussion forums, Community Showcase of sample projects, and the Word of Mouth blog, which provides news on Articulate products and updates
Product Support	Opens the Product Support page for the application, which contains tabs for different support options, including tutorials, knowledge base questions, and help documents. The Product Support page is covered in more detail later in this chapter.
Visit Blogs	Opens the Rapid E-Learning blog. We highly recommend that you subscribe to this blog so you get all new postings via email. It provides a wealth of ideas that can increase your skills and the value of the projects you produce.
And you can press F1	Pressing the F1 key from the start screen opens the Product Support page for that application and displays the Help Docs tab.

Help Options in the Application Window

Help options are also available once you open the application's window. In Presenter, you can access a menu of options from the Articulate tab on the PowerPoint ribbon, as shown in Figure 1.15. (If you're working with an earlier version of PowerPoint, help options are contained on the Articulate menu.) In Quizmaker and Engage, the Help tab of the ribbon contains help options (Figures 1.16 and 1.17). Many of these options take you to the same place as the options on the application's start screen. Table 1.6 describes each help option for Presenter.

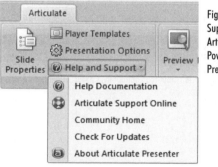

Figure 1.15. Help and Support menu on the Articulate tab of the PowerPoint 2007 ribbon in Presenter

Table 1.6. Presenter help options on the Help and Support menu

Help option	Description
Help Documentation	Opens the Product Support page for Presenter and displays the Help Docs tab
Articulate Online Support	Opens the Product Support page for Presenter, where you can choose from several help tabs
Community Home	Provides links to the Rapid E-Learning blog, Community Forum, Community Showcase, and the Word of Mouth blog
Check For Updates	Checks your version of Presenter against the latest update available from Articulate. Gives you the option to download the most recent update or informs you that no updates are required.
About Articulate Presenter	Opens a dialog box displaying the version of Presenter you are using, the serial number for your copy of the application, and links to the Articulate web site and end-user license agreement

Figure 1.16. Help tab on the Quiz window ribbon in Quizmaker

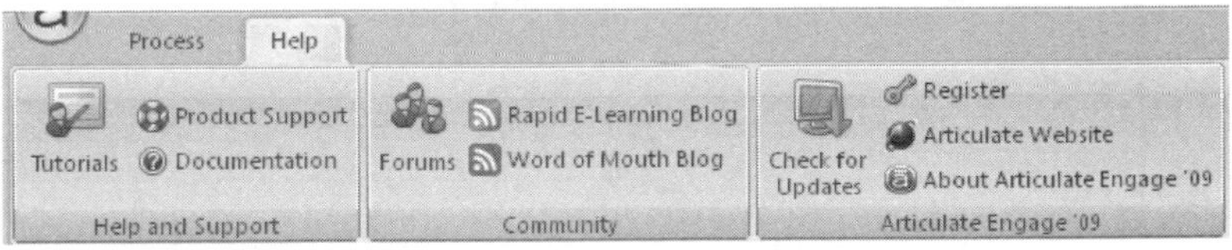

Figure 1.17. Help tab on the Process interaction window ribbon in Engage

The options on the Quizmaker and Engage ribbons are similar to those on the Help and Support menu for Presenter. Each group contains options that link directly to a specific resource.

Tip: Clicking the Help button on the far right side of the Engage window and Quizmaker window opens the Help Docs tab on the Product Support page for that application.

Help Options in Dialog Boxes

When you build projects using Presenter, Quizmaker, and Engage, you'll often work with dialog boxes to perform tasks such as setting properties and inserting components. Many dialog boxes contain a help link related to the task you are performing. Clicking this link opens the related topic in the Help Docs section of the Product Support web page. For example, the Attachments dialog box in Presenter enables you to attach files and links to your presentation. The help link Learn more about attachments appears in the lower-left corner of the dialog box, as highlighted in Figure 1.18. Clicking this link opens the Help Docs tab of the Product Support page and displays the help topic "Adding Attachments." From there, you can get more information about the task and can link to other help topics.

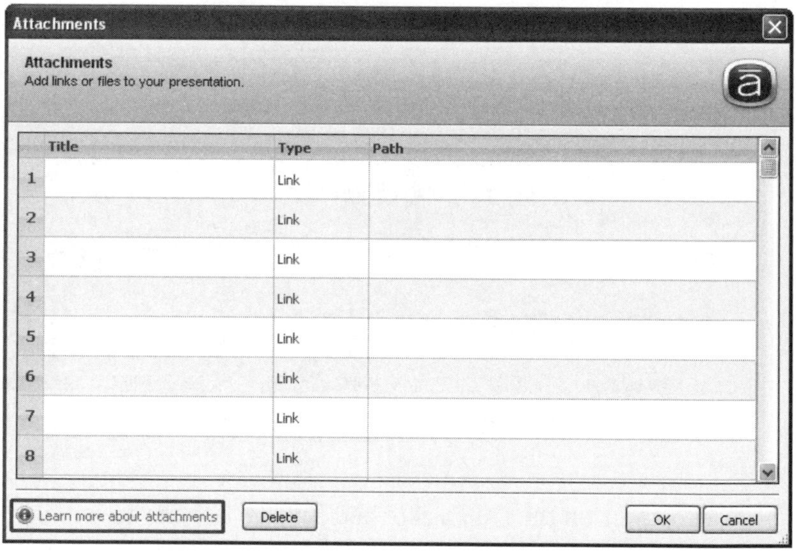

Figure 1.18. Attachments dialog box in Presenter

Product Support Page

The Product Support page is "help central" for each Articulate Studio '09 application. This application-specific page is accessible from any application by using options such as Product Support, Articulate Online Help, or Documentation, as described earlier in this section. You can also access this page from the home page of the Articulate web site by selecting Support and then selecting a product.

The Product Support page groups help options into tabs, as shown in Figure 1.19. Most of these options are also available on the first tab, named for the specific application. Table 1.7 describes each tab.

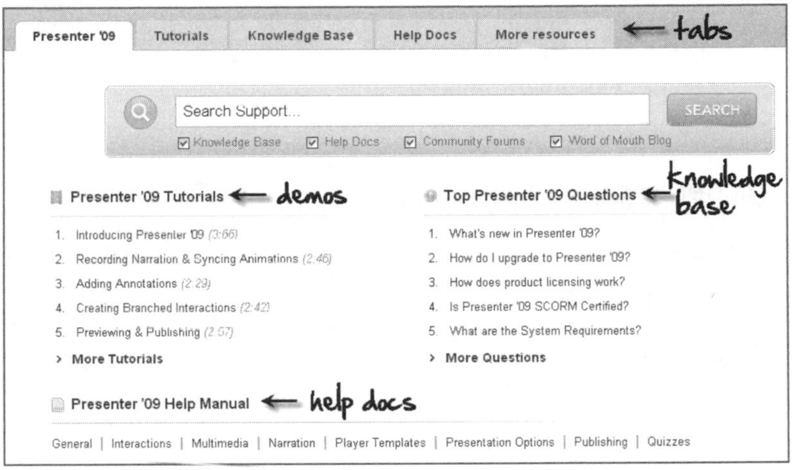

Figure 1.19. Product Support page for Presenter

Table 1.7. Product Support page tabs

Tab	Description
Application name (e.g., Presenter '09)	Contains most of the help options contained in the other tabs, including links to tutorials, knowledge base questions, and help docs
Tutorials	Contains links to all the tutorial demos related to the application
Knowledge Base	Contains frequently asked questions (FAQs) related to the application
Help Docs	Contains links to help topics about the application
More resources	Contains links to discussion forums and blogs. Also contains a link to submit a support question

Search for Help

You'll probably get the most out of the Product Support page by using its Search function. After all, many of us have specific questions when we're looking for help. Just enter a keyword or phrase in the Search Support box and check the areas you want to search: Knowledge Base, Help Docs, Community Forums, and Word of Mouth Blog. For example, to search for information about customizing the player template, type "customize player template" in the Search Support box, select the areas to search, and click Go. Articulate will then display a series of related links, and you're on your way.

Tip: For information about a simple how-to, consider selecting Help Docs and clearing the other options. The search results will be more manageable that way.

Downloadable Help Files

Articulate has packaged all of the Help Doc files into convenient downloadable PDF (portable document format) files. You can print them out or just store them on your computer for quick offline access. There are downloadable .pdf files available for each product (Presenter, Engage, Quizmaker, and Video Encoder), and there's also one downloadable .zip (compressed) file that contains all the Articulate Studio '09 help documents.

The files are accessible from the Help tab of the Product Support page for each tool. Figure 1.20 shows the documents available for Presenter: the Presenter manual and the manual for all Articulate Studio '09 applications.

Figure 1.20. The Help tab of Presenter allows you to download printed documentation.

Clicking the Presenter '09 Manual link opens the Presenter09_Documentation.pdf file in your web browser, where you can save and/or print the document. Clicking the All Studio '09 Manuals link prompts you to save or open the Studio09_Documentation.zip file. You then extract all of the .pdf files that are contained in the .zip file. Keep in mind you'll need Adobe Reader to view .pdf files on your computer. The free download for the reader is available from www.adobe.com.

Additional Resources

Hopefully this section has given you an idea of the help available on the Articulate web site. After you are somewhat comfortable with the tools, we recommend that you settle down with your favorite hot beverage and spend some quality time looking through Articulate blogs, reading discussions, and exploring the tutorial demos. Even if you're not looking for something specific, you'll be pleasantly surprised at the ideas that will jump out at you.

Articulate has a few resources that you may find especially useful when you are new to using these tools, including:

- 29 Really Useful Articulate Tutorials (http://www.articulate.com/blog/29-really-useful-articulate-tutorials)
- The Insider's Guide to Becoming a Rapid E-Learning Pro (http://www.articulate.com/rapid-elearning/downloads/Insiders_Guide_To_Becoming_A_Rapid_E-Learning_Pro.pdf)

Getting Started

Presenter, Quizmaker, and Engage can be used for both simple and complex projects—it all depends on your purposes. Before you start building anything, we recommend that you analyze the need and then determine what to include in your project. Our experience is that analysis and planning saves time and aggravation and typically provides better outcomes. Chapter 2, "Rapid E-Learning," and Chapter 3, "Introduction to Presenter," provide details about preparing for and planning your projects. The Quizmaker and Engage sections of the book also include sections on planning.

If you are new to using authoring tools, you might enjoy working with Engage first. It's easy to get started, and you can create something nifty in no time.

Because it's often helpful to see examples before getting started, consider reviewing demos for Presenter (http://www.articulate.com/products/presenter-demos.php), Quizmaker (http://www.articulate.com/products/quizmaker-demos.php), and Engage (http://www.articulate.com/products/engage-demos.php). Then jump into the Introduction chapters in this book.

Chapter Recap

The most important things to remember from this chapter:

■ The authoring tools in Articulate Studio '09 are in the "sweet spot" of easy to learn while still allowing lots of flexibility in what you can develop.

■ These tools are great for folks just starting out building online information and instruction, but they are also good for folks who have more experience and simply don't need the hassle and expense of complex authoring for most of the projects they work on.

■ As you use more of the features of each of the Articulate Studio tools, it gets harder to tell what authoring tool was used to build the project. Was it built with Flash or Engage? Presenter or Flash? Flash or Quizmaker? We won't tell if you won't.

■ Presenter works directly with Microsoft PowerPoint. Although Presenter is well-known for creating narrated PowerPoint presentations, it is able to do much more than this.

■ Quizmaker lets you quickly build graded quizzes and nongraded surveys using predefined question types.

■ Engage lets you create self-contained "discovery" experiences for viewers, called Engage interactions.

■ Video Encoder converts almost any video into the FLV Flash video format. You can crop the video and only use certain parts, adjust volume and brightness, add images, logos, or watermarks, and select publishing options for bitrate, dimensions, and more.

■ Presenter can pull together a variety of learning elements including slides, narration, video, Quizmaker questions, Engage interactions, and more.

■ Presenter, Quizmaker, and Engage can be used for both simple and complex projects—it all depends on your purpose.

■ Before you start building anything, we recommend that you analyze the need and then determine what to include in your project.

■ Articulate provides numerous resources to help you use the Articulate Studio '09 tools. The tutorials, help documents, knowledge base, blogs, and community forums cover a wide range of topics to keep you up to speed.

Chapter 2

Rapid E-Learning

Chapter Snapshot

In this chapter, we'll discuss effective ways to think through your projects before starting to build them.

Knowing when to use a rapid e-learning approach and thinking through your projects can save you time and aggravation and provide better outcomes.

> **?** With rapid e-learning, I don't have to do tons of thinking beforehand, right? I mean, isn't the point to build it fast?

> **i** Rapid projects benefit from planning, too. It's important to make sure that you're building what's needed.

Considering Rapid Approaches

"Rapid" e-learning, in a nutshell (preferably macadamia or pistachio), refers to online information and instructional materials that don't take a long time to build so they can be put into play fairly quickly. Traditional instructional design and development processes often require months or even years to create complex and critical instruction (such as flight instruction). If you have ever built storyboards (which describe what is to be built in detail) and waited for subject matter expert (SME) feedback, or slogged through rounds of revisions with SMEs and developers, you know how much time and energy these things can take.

Rapid e-learning uses design and development processes that facilitate building and delivering instructional content in days or weeks, rather than months or years. It is best used for instruction that focuses on lower-tier learning objectives (discussed next) and for information that requires very rapid dissemination.

If you are familiar with ADDIE, a systematic process for building instructional materials, you'll notice that all the steps (**A**nalyze, **D**esign, **D**evelop, **I**mplement, and **E**valuate) are still completed, but analysis is done quickly and typically the middle steps—design, development, and implementation—are done somewhat concurrently. If you're not familiar with instructional design or the ADDIE process, there's no need to worry about it. We've distilled the critical principles within the advice given throughout the book.

When Rapid Makes Sense

Benjamin Bloom, of Bloom's taxonomy fame, along with a group of educational psychologists, developed a classification system for cognitive outcomes (what trainers and others call learning objectives). They identified six levels of cognitive outcomes from simple recall or recognition of facts, at the lowest level, through increasingly more complex and abstract cognitive levels (see Figure 2.1). Although the names and order of these categories are argued in academic circles, it is very useful to think of learning objectives in a hierarchy from less complex (list, identify, classify, and so on) to more complex (solve, recommend, design, evaluate, and so on).

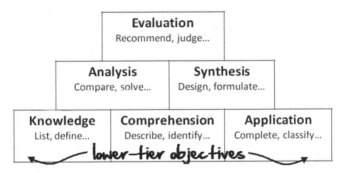

Figure 2.1. Pyramid of instructional objectives, adapted from "Bloom's Taxonomy" (Benjamin S. Bloom, Bertram B. Mesia, and David R. Krathwohl, Taxonomy of Educational Objectives, New York, Longmans, Green, 1956)

Rapid approaches often work well for lower-tier learning objectives. For example, *List the benefits of a Roth IRA* is a far easier task (for learners) than *Determine what percentage of IRA funds to put into a traditional IRA and what percentage of IRA funds to put into a Roth IRA*. The former is a lower-tier instructional objective and the latter is a higher-tier instructional objective. The former requires the ability to recall benefits but the latter involves analysis and evaluation of alternatives.

A rapid approach is best used for information and instruction that can be considered more or less disposable. But disposable doesn't mean not worthwhile! It means that the instruction either doesn't merit the intense design effort needed for higher levels of skill or mastery, or that the content is extremely time sensitive, changes rapidly, or goes out of date quickly.

Figure 2.2 shows various types of informational or instructional content and where they would typically fall on a continuum from information to instruction. Instruction generally requires far more effort to design than information because it typically requires additional elements, such as practice and assessment.

information ◄───────────────────────────────────► instruction

what's new   demo   job aid   tutorial   simulation   assessment

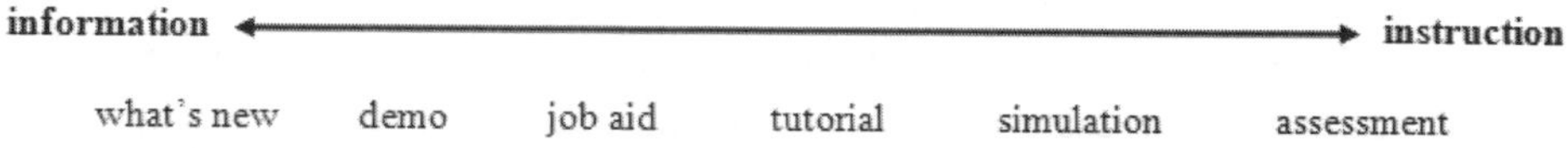

Figure 2.2. Information-instruction continuum

Let's consider examples of information and instruction developed for field sales staff who sell computer hardware. Information might include PDF files describing features, specifications, and benefits, and demos viewable on handhelds that can be used as product knowledge refreshers. Instruction might include self-paced modules on each piece of hardware, Q&A sessions through webinars, and hands-on practice handling common questions.

Instruction has a specific purpose—to change knowledge and skills for a particular reason. In a training environment, instruction is built to change what workers do on the job and should be designed to have a positive impact on business goals. Instruction typically includes activities that help learners practice and assessments.

Even though it may make sense to use a rapid approach for developing content on the information end of the information-instruction continuum, the ability to use a rapid approach depends on other factors as well. One big factor is availability of existing content. Content development often takes a great deal of time, so rapid design and development is best used when needed content is already available or easily obtained. Lack of available content is one of the single biggest risk factors associated with rapid e-learning. Even if a rapid approach makes sense (lower-tier objectives, information end of the information-instruction continuum), make sure adequate content is available before agreeing to tight deadlines.

A more rigorous design and development approach makes sense in certain circumstances, such as when learners *must* be able to perform critical skills with *great accuracy*. Examples of these types of skills include carrying out emergency procedures and flying a plane. And there are many types of instruction that require more effort than most rapid e-learning approaches allow. For example, we don't need supervisors to simply recall what policies apply to time off; we need them to be able to apply those policies fairly and consistently. We don't need information technology workers to simply list the benefits of different operating systems; we also need them to be able to recommend operating systems for a variety of situations. Higher level learning objectives typically merit more stringent instructional design approaches than lower level learning objectives.

This isn't an either/or situation. It often makes sense to use a rapid approach followed by less rapid approaches. In other words, we use rapid approaches to get quickly needed information out and then follow up with materials that may take more time. (We can think of this as "blended" instructional design.) A more rigorous design process produces instruction relatively slowly and can cost quite a lot. Still, it makes sense to use that process when learners must be able to perform critical skills with great accuracy.

What's the Rush?

We've seen a lot of emphasis lately on rapid learning. Why? Many jobs have become more complex in the past few decades. Not only do most jobs require more skills, but the skills needed to do any job are quickly outdated so there's need for continual updating. And information used to perform most jobs changes rapidly.

As a result, information and instruction needs to occur whenever it's needed and not just when there's a class available. It also needs to happen wherever it's needed, not just at headquarters or 1,000 miles away from the job. So there's a place for rapid approaches in almost all parts of teaching and learning.

When jobs are complex and information changes rapidly, the need for information and instruction often outpaces the ability to address them. In these environments, which are becoming more the norm than the exception, fast and adequate often beats out slow and close-to-perfect. It's important to understand that the choice of design and development approach (rapid or less rapid) isn't an all-or-nothing proposition. Rapid approaches can be used for portions of a course or curriculum, even if it isn't appropriate for the entire course or curriculum. Instructional objectives for a given course are typically a mix of less complex and more complex objectives. So, for example, for a business ethics course, a rapid approach might be used for an overview and a lesson on ethics terminology. Then a more rigorous approach could be used for scenario-based lessons that allow learners to practice in a variety of realistic situations.

 Takeaway: Instructors, trainers, and learners need to deal with the realities of today's world. We need to meet the most critical informational and instructional needs and usually, we don't have tons of time because as we're designing, the needs are shifting.

Terminology

Throughout this book we'll be using some terms that you may be unfamiliar with, so here are some definitions:

ADDIE is an instructional design model that includes these steps: analysis, design, development, implementation, and evaluation.

Assessment is how learners show they met the course learning objectives. Common methods of assessment in online courses include multiple-choice questions, Learning Games, and simulated tasks.

Asynchronous learning means people use online information, instruction, or communication tools (such as discussion forums) materials from wherever they are (assuming that they have an Internet connection) and whenever they want.

The **audience** is the group of intended users of specific information or instructional materials. We also call them "viewers" throughout this book.

Authoring means developing information and instruction using tools, proprietary systems, and/or programming. Some authoring tools are specifically made for instructional use and others are more generic and can be used for any type of web authoring.

Blended learning refers to a combination of delivery methods or strategies, including, but not limited to, online and face-to-face instruction, print and web materials, self-check questions and online discussions, wikis and blogs, and so on. The advantage of blended learning is that it can use the best features of each delivery method and strategy. For example, the ease of person to person practice in a classroom and the learn-from-anywhere-at-any-time of some types of online learning.

Discussion forums are online tools that allow people to communicate with each other by posting messages and replying to messages in an asynchronous manner.

e-Learning or online learning uses technology to deliver learning content, activities, and interactions. Typically used when delivery is via the Internet, CD-ROM, and through mobile devices such as PDAs and cell phones.

Feedback includes comments and other types of help provided to learners after they submit answers or select choices to tell them if their answers or choices are correct. This may also include remediation, which points to existing content or to new resources.

Flash is an authoring tool that is typically used to develop animations and simulations. Increasingly, it's also being used to develop web sites and web applications. Flash is a complex authoring tool. It isn't easy to become an expert with Flash unless you work with the program regularly. Articulate develops Flash content for you. Yes, you give up the ability to do anything you want, but you gain the ability to create valuable Flash materials without needing to have the skills you would need to develop using Flash itself.

Interaction refers to learner actions that impact what learners see and do with the materials. This can be low-level interaction, such as selecting which link to click, or higher levels of interaction, such as answering questions and making decisions about a scenario. Interaction can also occur between or among people (other learners, instructors, and experts).

The graphical **interface** of a computer screen consists of the screen elements and placement of those elements that make it easier (or harder) for users to do what they want to do. The goal of web interface design is to make the user's interaction (with online content) as simple and efficient as possible

A **job aid** is typically an electronic or print document that helps workers perform step-by-step tasks. These documents can also be developed to help people make decisions or understand a process.

JPEG (.jpg) is a graphics format typically used for photographs and other complex pictures.

An **LMS**, or learning management system, is an application that automates the tracking and administration of training. An LMS typically manages course registration and course catalogs, tracks learners and learning data (such as test scores), and provides reports about learners and usage.

Learning objectives are specific descriptions of what learners should be able to do as a result of the instruction.

Media include text, images, illustrations, simulations, audio, video, and other elements used to provide content and interactions. It can also mean online tools used to provide content and interactions (with content or people). The applications in Articulate Studio typically use the term "media" to refer to images, audio, and videos.

A **plug-in** (also called **player**) is software that adds functionality to a web browser, such as the ability to play animations, audio, or video. (For example, the Flash "player" is needed to view Flash content.)

PNG (.png) is a newer graphics format that was designed to replace the GIF format. The chief advantages are that .png file sizes are typically much smaller than .gif and bitmapped image files and they have excellent resolution and transparent backgrounds. One downside is that some older browsers don't recognize them.

SCORM is an acronym for Sharable Content Object Reference Model. It consists of a group of standards that help make course materials usable in various standards-compliant learning management systems.

SMEs, or subject matter experts, are people who are knowledgeable experts in the content area for which materials are being developed.

Synchronous learning means using online information, instruction, or communication tools at the same time as others, even though learners may be in different locations. This allows people to ask questions and react to what is occurring in real time. Webinars and conference calls are examples of synchronous learning.

Usability measures how easily a person can use something and achieve his or her goals. Good usability implies low frustration and the ability to do common tasks without excessive effort.

Articulate Studio '09—Rapid or Not?

Some people divide authoring tools into those that are good for rapid e-learning and those that aren't. Some authoring tools do have a steep learning curve, so if you aren't proficient with such a tool at the beginning of a rapid e-learning project, it's unlikely to be your tool of choice. But if you know how to use a specific tool, complex or not, or have a team member who knows how to use it, any tool can be used for rapid e-learning.

Some tools lend themselves to rapid e-learning by their nature. They are easy and intuitive to use and work as expected. The learning curve is typically lower for such tools, and novices can build something simple with relative ease.

Articulate Studio provides a set of tools that are well suited to rapid design and development by novice developers but are flexible enough to be used in unique ways by more experienced developers. So Articulate Studio gets high marks from us, and not because we're writing this book! These are tools that are not only fairly easy to use, but they also have flexibility to be used in a variety of ways.

Presenter is a very flexible authoring tool. It is commonly used to develop narrated online PowerPoint slide presentations and the default output (what the viewer sees) is attractive and intuitive to use, as you can see in Figure 2.3.

But Presenter output can look like many other types of instructional output, as well. You can see one example of this in Figure 2.4.

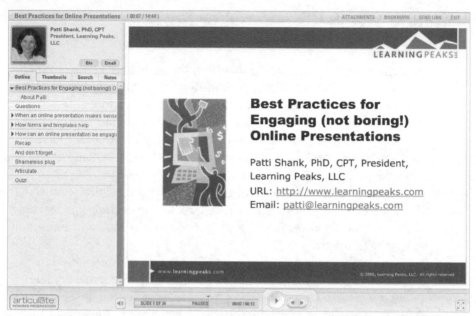

Figure 2.3. Default Presenter output

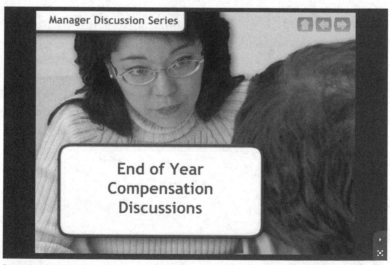

Figure 2.4. Customized Presenter output (source: http://www.articulate.com/products/demos/guru/
Weyerhaeuser/player.html)

And additionally, Presenter can display content other than PowerPoint
slides and narration, such as Articulate Engage interactions and

Articulate Quizmaker quizzes. You can also use Flash objects developed in other tools (such as Flash, Raptivity, and Captivate).

This kind of flexibility provides an advantage for Presenter that is hard to beat. The ability to customize output combined with the ability to deliver different kinds of content and media means you can use Presenter as the delivery mechanism for all kinds of rapid and not-so-rapid information and instruction.

Quizmaker can be used flexibly as well. You can quickly build a set of questions using the placeholders in Form view. You can get away with just entering a question and some answer choices and you're done. Default feedback is already provided. On the flip side, you can build complex question slides using graphics, hyperlinks, video, audio, and even branching. It just depends on how much time you want to spend and the results that you want to achieve.

Although we won't call Engage "inflexible," creating interactions is pretty straightforward. Engage does not contain all the customization features offered by Presenter and Quizmaker, but that's okay. The purpose of Engage is to let you use prebuilt templates to create interactions that would take hours to develop in Flash. Most of the elements and design features are already created for you, so you just need to add the text, audio, video, and graphic elements.

So are Presenter, Engage, and Quizmaker rapid e-learning tools or tools for less rapid development? The answer is "Yes."

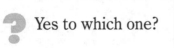 Yes to which one?

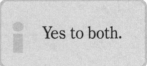 Yes to both.

In the next section, we'll look at critical steps that should be taken when you are asked to build (rapid or less rapid) information or instruction so that what you produce is worth the time required to build it and view it.

Determining What Is Needed

Building information and instruction requires time and effort, whether rapidly developed or not. In order to reduce the amount of rework and resources needed to do that rework, it's a very good idea to gather some information up front to reduce the amount of rework needed. (Notice that we didn't say eliminate.)

If you take a bit of time to gather information on the front end, you'll likely save time, effort, and aggravation all along the way. At a minimum, you'll want to know about the problem background, target audience, needed outcomes, content availability, deadlines, and resources. Table 2.1 describes rationales for gathering this information up front, while you can negotiate what will be built and the resources and time to build it.

Table 2.1. Information to be gathered up front and rationale

Information category	Rationale
Problem background	Gaining background on the problem to be prevented or resolved helps you understand the nature of the problem. Understanding how the desired information or instruction fits within the overall tactics that will be used to prevent or resolve a problem allows you to produce information or instruction deliverables that play nice with related deliverables (such as changes to policies, memos, all-hands meetings, and so on). This information can be used to negotiate your role and the role of the information or instruction you build so your work can be successful.
Target audience	Knowing who your audience is makes it possible to target their needs. A one-size-fits-all approach works at times (and is assumed to be needed for many rapid information or instruction projects), but in too many cases, these "solutions" become one-size-fits-nobody.
Access	You'll need to know if the target audience can access and view the media you want to use. Better to know up front what technology constraints you need to work within. Also, you'll want to know that the target audience will be able to use the materials.
Needed outcomes	Understanding what outcomes stakeholders are trying to achieve is critical. Sometimes stakeholders only care whether the information or instruction has been viewed. Other times, they want to reduce the incidence or severity of specific problems. This typically means that more thought and effort is needed. You may need to negotiate expected outcomes when they aren't attainable with the requested information or instruction or are impossible to produce given current deadlines and resources.

Information category	Rationale
Content availability	An e-learning project without ready-to-use content is likely to take much longer than an e-learning project with ready-to-use content. If there is little content or the content that is available isn't really usable as-is (for example, PowerPoint slides without slide notes or other detailed explanations), folks who can write and vet new content become critical. And that takes more time—period.
Deadlines	You will likely need to manage expectations when deadlines are tight. In some cases, you may need a phased approach, wherein less complex deliverables are delivered quickly and more complex deliverables are delivered later.
Resources	Stakeholders often ask for more than can be delivered with the available resources. Negotiating what is possible with given resources on the front end is wise.

Let's look at each of these information needs in more detail by exploring a case study in which a human resources director, Lynn, asks Marie and her learning technologies group to build a short online training module about vacation leave.

Problem Background

Problem background is critical if you want to build and deliver something of value. No matter what you are asked to build, you will likely need information about why the project you have been asked to build is necessary. Otherwise, your idea of the purpose of the project and the deliverables that are needed are likely to be different from that of the person who has engaged your help. Why? The person asking you to build something probably knows a whole lot about the problem that needs to be prevented or solved. When you know a lot about something, you sometimes forget that others don't know what you know. Plus the words and sentences can mean one thing to one person and something totally different to another.

So Marie's team needs to know more about the problem before building information or instruction on the topic of vacation leave. If Lynn's department is implementing a new vacation leave policy, the information or instruction to be developed may be quite different than if there are problems caused by employees not following the existing policy. And if managers are not enforcing the vacation policy, the information or instruction may be different yet.

After some questioning, Lynn explains to Marie that there are two common misconceptions about the existing vacation leave policy and these misconceptions cause some workers to apply for and use vacation leave inappropriately. When that happens, payroll processes the vacation leave as unpaid time off and workers are quite unhappy about not being paid when they expected to be paid. Lynn suggests building a short training module that allows viewers to deal with a variety of scenarios so they can see how to apply for leave in a variety of situations.

Target Audience

Knowing who the audience is makes it possible to target information/instruction to their needs. Even if you use a one-size-fits-all approach for the bulk of the materials you build, you may choose to build some of the materials for a specific audience. For example, online instruction for all staff on the topic of business ethics might include discussion of the ethics policy and how it applies to a variety of situations. Then a supervisory lesson might be added to help supervisors intervene on ethics-related issues that come up in their departments.

Lynn tells Marie that the audience is everyone in the company. Marie asks if management and staff should get the same course and a discussion takes place about the needs of these two groups. It looks like they can both use the same basic instruction, but the human resources department will present some lunch-and-learns for supervisory staff on applying the policy correctly once everyone has taken the training.

Marie also asks whether the instructional module should be provided in multiple languages, since the company operates in four countries. While most employees speak English, English is not the primary language for a small subset of employees. Lynn asks Marie to gather some information and make a recommendation about whether to provide the instructional module in languages other than English. (Add time.)

Access

When using technology to teach and learn, any number of technical access issues can arise. If learners don't have access to the materials or cannot access the media that is used (because they don't have needed players or a needed connection), they're not going to benefit from the training. And if they have adequate access but don't know how to use it, they're likely to be resistant. It's also important to know whether learners will be given time to use the materials. Learning by osmosis (a common expectation when e-learning was in its infancy) doesn't work. It's best to know what access issues you may be facing before you get started building information or instructional materials.

Marie knows that some manufacturing workers don't have access to the network, so she asks Lynn how to reach these workers. Lynn asks Marie to make a recommendation about how to provide the module to workers who do not have ready access to the network. (Add time.) Marie also isn't sure that all networked computers have audio cards and needs to check that out because she is planning to use Presenter and wants to be able to add narration. (Add time.)

Needed Outcomes

Learning about the problem's background usually gives you a good idea of the problem the stakeholder is trying to solve. But it pays to get specific here about the outcomes stakeholders expect from your work.

Lynn tells Marie that the human resources group is handling more than 50 problems related to this policy. Marie asks if she can view the cases to get a better sense of the problems and Lynn asks Manuel to help her. (Add time.)

Marie searches the intranet for the vacation leave policy and sees that two versions are out there. She also sees that the policy isn't very clear. Next steps? Tell the human resources department about the version problem and find out whether policy language is a problem. (Add time.)

Content Availability

Lack of content is a primary hold-up on many information/instruction projects. No matter what anyone tells you to the contrary, there's a really, *really* good chance that the content that is "available" is inadequate. Lack of clear/sufficient/compelling content means you have to fix/develop/scrounge around for content and beg subject matter experts (SMEs) to help you. (Add time.) Here are some content-oriented caveats to remember when starting an information/instruction project:

■ If someone tells you there is adequate content, ask to see the content before agreeing that there is adequate content. What is deemed adequate and what you need to complete the project are often quite different.

■ If there isn't adequate content, deadlines need to be longer because the content will need to be developed.

■ Unless you are an SME on the topic of the project you are building, it's hard to build adequate content without SME help. You could research the topic and come up with content but this takes *lots and lots of time*. (Getting the "add time" theme here?) And you'll likely need an SME to verify that the content is adequate and accurate. Like we said, time consuming...

■ Whether or not the person tasking you with the project says there is adequate content, obtain agreement for access to an SME. Then make sure the SME has time before you commit to specific timeframes. Too many people make commitments for SMEs without even checking with them. No wonder SMEs sometimes hate working with us.

Access to adequate content is a common factor limiting how quickly you can build a project. Marie asks about content and Lynn tells her that the only content she has is the policy. Marie doesn't groan because she's used to this. Marie makes a note to read the policy again and determine what other content and content help she'll need. She gains commitment from Lynn for SME time to develop additional content.

Deadlines

Typically, information and instructional projects are needed yesterday. Why? Don't tell anyone we said this, but it often takes a while for stakeholders to make decisions and when they decide that they need you to build information or instruction, they needed it last month. Or last year. So stakeholders think asking for it yesterday is giving you a break because they really want it last month, or earlier. We recommend that you view deadlines as a negotiation because you will often need to negotiate the mix of speed and quality. Some folks overpromise because they are being pressured, but this doesn't usually work out well. (You will likely not do a good job if you haven't slept for the last six days.) Better to under-promise and over-deliver.

Lynn wants the module completed in two weeks, but Marie negotiates for time to do a bit of extra analysis before she commits to a deadline. Lynn balks at first, but when Marie explains what she is going to do and how it will impact the desired outcomes, Lynn sees that this is a good plan. Two days later, Marie explains to Lynn that she thinks a three-pronged approach will work best. Someone on her team will begin developing a short information module about how to interpret the existing policy. At the same time, the version problem should be fixed and steps should be taken to write the policy more clearly. When the policy is rewritten, Marie's team will write a more comprehensive instructional module about how to interpret the policy, which will include scenario practice. Lynn is pleased by Marie's initiative and recommends that Marie gets a raise that will double her salary. (We made up the salary part.)

> Actually, you made up the whole scenario.

Resources

E-learning can be produced with a team or a team of one. Team members require extra time and iterations. But wait... is it possible to build good e-learning with one person's skills? Sure, it's possible and it happens regularly. But almost all e-learning projects *really* require at least two people—a subject matter expert/reviewer and a designer/developer. And some projects require additional specialized skills. If those skills aren't available, the materials and outcomes are likely to suffer or take longer to build (to acquire the skills or to work with additional team members who have the needed skills).

Marie's group has one good content developer and two multimedia developers. She knows she will also need a subject matter expert/reviewer and Lynn says Manuel can help. Marie asks Manuel if he has time and he says he's pretty booked up with this year's salary survey but will try hard to help. Marie is worried about whether she has adequate resources and access to an SME to get the project done as quickly as promised.

Thinking Through What Is Needed

Here's what we hope you will take away from the Marie/Lynn vacation time policy training scenario:

- Understanding the need is critical. There is an existing policy and it is not being followed. Before jumping in, Marie needs to understand the role that training will play in preventing or resolving the problem at hand.

- Thinking through the needs of the target audience, including access issues, helps Lynn and Marie consider what to do about workers with no access to the network and those who speak other languages.

- It's hard to commit to specific outcomes until you gather enough information to tell you what direction is appropriate.

- Deadlines and resources should be negotiated after you understand the nature of the problem!

Now let's look at a couple of practice scenarios. Practice 1 lists the questions you want to remember to ask when someone asks you to build information or instruction. Practice 2 lets you see if you remember the key points in this chapter.

Practice 1

Project Background Questions List

Instructions: For each information category in the table below, list questions you want to remember to ask before getting started on an upcoming e-learning project. (Some initial questions have been added to help you get started. Feel free to discard or rewrite these!)

Information category	Specific questions to ask	Who to ask
Problem background	What happened or is expected to happen that makes this training needed?	
Target audience	Who will be using this information or instruction?	
Access	Does the intended audience have network access, players for the media we want to use, and time to use the materials?	
Needed outcomes	What results do you want to obtain?	
Content availability	Can you show me the content that is available?	
Deadlines	When do you want/need this deployed? How much wiggle room do we have?	
Resources	What people/skills/tools can be used to get this accomplished?	

Practice 2

Instructions: Answer the following multiple-choice questions to see if you remember some key points in this chapter. The answers are provided following this list of questions.

1. SME is an acronym for
   a. System and methods expert
   b. Systematic modeling expert
   c. Subject matter expert

2. The recent emphasis on rapid e-learning comes from (select all that apply)
   a. The need to get urgent information and instruction out quickly
   b. The realization that traditional approaches are not worth the time that they take
   c. The need to expend less effort when designing disposable instruction

3. Information is different from instruction in that (select all that apply)
   a. Information is generally disposable but instruction rarely is
   b. Instruction often requires more effort to build than information
   c. Instruction is more important than information

4. Presenter, Engage, and Quizmaker can be authoring tools of choice for (select all that apply)
   a. Rapidly designed information
   b. Rapidly designed instruction
   c. Traditionally designed information and instruction

5. Some critical things to find out before committing to a project and deadlines include (select all that apply)
    a. Whether there is adequate content
    b. What outcomes project stakeholders need
    c. How the desired information or instruction fits into the wider scheme of problem resolution steps

6. Too many informational and instructional projects do not have the desired result because (select all that apply)
    a. They are developed without knowing what is really needed
    b. The people building them must build what they are told to build
    c. No one really cares about the results

Answers for Practice 2

Question	Answer/Discussion
1.	c. By the way, SMEs rarely like being called SMEs. We're just saying…
2.	a. and c. Traditional instructional design approaches are often worth the time for instruction on critical skills that must be performed very accurately.
3.	b. Both information and instruction can be disposable. And information and instruction can be equally important.
4.	a., b., and c. These tools are flexible and can be used in rapid and less-rapid approaches to building information and instruction.
5.	a., b., and c. If there isn't adequate content, building information or instruction will take longer than expected. It is critical to understand what outcomes are needed and how the information or instruction fits into the wider scheme of problem resolution steps so what is built is designed for the actual need.
6.	a., b., and c. This is a trick question, but in our experience, they're often all true. None of them *should be* true. And that's all we'll say about that (for now).

Chapter Recap

Here are the main points presented in this chapter:

- Rapid approaches are faster than traditional design and development approaches. They are often a good strategy for lower-level instructional objectives and when there simply is no time for a more lengthy process.

- Analyzing information and instructional needs takes time, but it often saves far more time than it takes.

- When skills mastery and evidence of real-life skills are needed, a more rigorous and time-consuming design approach is usually warranted.

- There's no need to select either a rapid or a less-rapid approach. It often makes sense to do both. That is, start with a rapid approach to get critical information out and follow up with a less-rapid approach to make sure that critical skills are gained.

- Presenter, Engage, and Quizmaker can be used for rapid and less-rapid approaches.

- Before getting started, it's extremely wise to learn about the problem background, target audience, access to the materials you are going to build, needed outcomes, content availability, deadlines, and resources.

Chapter 3

Introduction to Presenter

Chapter Snapshot

In this chapter, you will be introduced to Presenter.

Chapter Topics

You might be tempted to skip this chapter if you have used previous versions of Presenter or are an expert at building information and instructional projects. Because of my (Patti) many years building information and instruction, I wanted to add words of wisdom about making sure what you build is actually valuable for those who are going to use it. As a result, there's quite a bit of instructional design advice in the section titled "Planning Your Presenter Project."

What Is Presenter?

Presenter is an authoring tool that can be used to build a wide variety of informational and instructional outputs. At the less complex (easier to build) end of the spectrum, it can easily build narrated online PowerPoint presentations, and at the more complex end of the spectrum, it can build instructional sequences with interactions, branching, quizzes, embedded Flash objects, audio, and video. And it can build lots in between.

Presenter can be used as a rapid authoring tool (see Chapter 2, "Rapid E-Learning," for a discussion of rapid versus less rapid approaches) or as the container that holds and delivers more complex instructional sequences. How it's used is up to you and should be guided by potential viewers' needs.

> Might be smart to start with something simple if you are new to authoring.

Presenter is not a standalone authoring tool. That is, you can't build information or instruction with Presenter alone. You need to use PowerPoint to make Presenter work its magic.

> Isn't it weird to talk about PowerPoint in a book that is about other tools?

> Yes and no. Yes, Presenter and PowerPoint are different applications. Made by different companies, actually. But Presenter is designed to work *with* PowerPoint much like online banking applications are often meant to work with home finance applications such as Quicken. One difference though. Presenter works *inside* PowerPoint.

In fact, when you install Presenter, Presenter places either a tab (PowerPoint 2007) or a menu (PowerPoint 2000-2003) labeled "Articulate" inside PowerPoint that you can use to add media, interactions, narration, and annotations. The tab or menu that is installed in PowerPoint is shown in Figures 3.1 and 3.2.

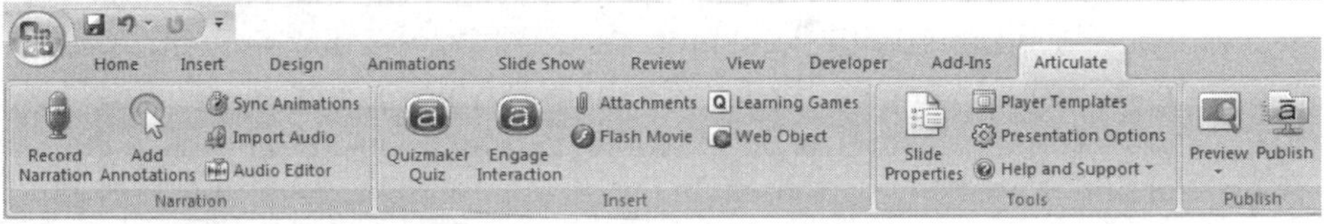

Figure 3.1. The Articulate tab in PowerPoint 2007

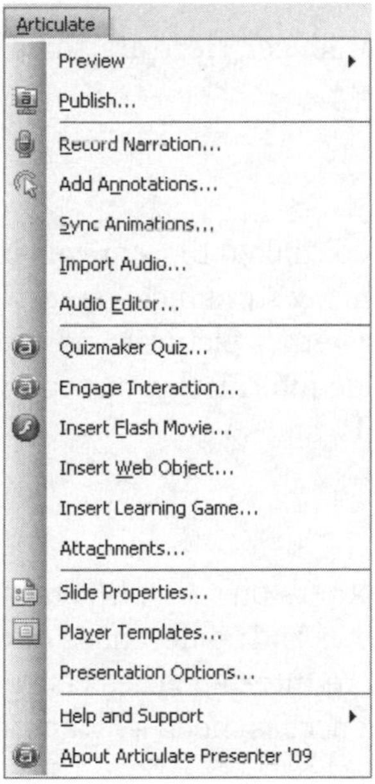

Figure 3.2. The Articulate menu in PowerPoint 2000-2003

So it's not weird to talk about PowerPoint in this book because PowerPoint is the canvas you'll use to "paint" the information or instruction you will build using this authoring tool. So you'll want to make sure it's a good canvas. One that won't rip with heavy use or topple over when used. (Enough canvas metaphors already...)

Best Uses of Presenter

Presenter is well known for producing narrated PowerPoint sequences that can be viewed online. Narrated PowerPoint sequences can also be produced using PowerPoint alone, so this isn't the main benefit of using Presenter. With Presenter, narrated PowerPoint sequences can be published as much smaller Flash files, which generally require less bandwidth. Presenter is *very* flexible and can be used to produce information or instruction that includes attachments, images, audio, Flash video, Engage interactions, Quizmaker quizzes, and links. Other Flash objects (such as software demos and Learning Games) can also be added to a Presenter project.

So what can *you* use Presenter to produce? Here are some ideas to get you started.

On the Web

Presenter projects can be embedded in or linked to from web pages. They can be added to explain your company's products or services, present case studies, tell stories, pull together pictures and commentary from events (like weddings), provide information on topics of interest, present FAQs, provide tutorials, and so on.

On a CD, DVD, or Flash Drive

Presenter projects can be provided to others on a CD, DVD, or flash drive. This might be useful at trade shows and conferences or during presentations to clients and others where Internet access isn't available or worries about available Internet access mean a "Plan B" is a good idea.

You'll see numerous examples of Presenter projects throughout the book, so hopefully you'll see that the sky is the limit!

Presenter 1-2-3-4-5 Workflow

Presenter projects are built using a minimum of two tools: PowerPoint and Presenter. Typically, PowerPoint slides are created and a narration script is written in the PowerPoint notes field for each slide. Then Presenter is used to add media and interactions, such as narration and attachments. The final project is then published so it can be viewed by others.

Figure 3.3 shows the typical 1-2-3-4-5 workflow process for building a Presenter project.

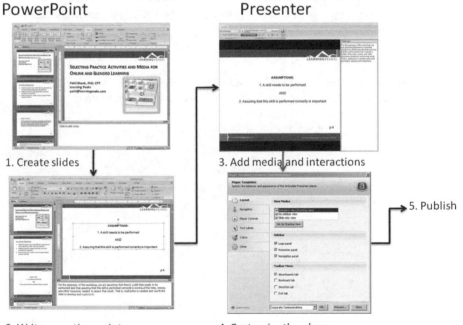

Figure 3.3. Typical Presenter high-level workflow

Look at steps 1 and 2. They are done in PowerPoint. Once the slides are completed, the next three steps in Presenter can be done using the Articulate tab or menu that is embedded in PowerPoint when Presenter is installed. Almost all Presenter projects include narration, so steps 1, 2, and 3 (narration) are common to most Presenter projects. If you want to add additional media, interactions, annotations, and so on, step 3 is expanded to include those tasks. If you decide to keep the default player (the window look and feel that the viewers see when they use the project), step 4 is skipped. When the project is complete, step 5, publishing, allows the final output to be accessed and used by the intended audience.

Let's break down this 1-2-3-4-5 workflow a bit further. Table 3.1 describes the substeps that are typically performed in each of the 1-2-3-4-5 steps, plus a list of tasks that should be accomplished before development and after the project is completed.

---

66 **Note:** See Chapter 4 for how-tos for the PowerPoint steps listed in the table, and Chapters 5-7 for how-tos for the Presenter steps.

Table 3.1. Typical Presenter detailed workflow

Before development: Determine what's expected, decide which elements to include, and build a storyboard (maybe).

Using PowerPoint		Using Presenter	
1. Create slides.	a) Create slides. b) Add text. c) Add graphics. d) Add animations.	**3. Add media and interactions.**	a) Add media and interactions (narration, attachments, Engage interactions, Quizmaker questions, Web Objects, Flash video, etc.). b) Review and revise narration script to go along with media, interactions, and annotations and record or rerecord, if needed. c) Preview and fix (throughout).
2. Write narration script.	a) Write narration script.	**4. Customize the player.**	a) Customize player templates.
		5. Publish.	a) Test and fix problems. b) Publish the project. c) Test the output.

After the project is completed: Keep an eye on the project and be prepared to fix any problems that arise as it is used. Also, set up a maintenance schedule for updating the project if project content will need to be changed over time.

> Folks often forget that they will need to maintain the project over time if content changes.

You can see from the detailed workflow that there is plenty to do to get your project from inspiration to completion. You may be wondering if the rapid approach discussed in Chapter 2 is possible, given all the substeps in Table 3.1. The answer depends on how complex your project is. A quick set of narrated PowerPoint slides output as Flash could take very little time from start to finish. A longer module with embedded Engage and Quizmaker interactions will take longer. Adding other media (such as Captivate demos or video) may require more time still, especially if you need to create (or wait for others to create) media elements before adding them to your Presenter project.

If your project is complex but you need it done quickly, you can include fewer interactions and media. Another alternative is to build a less complex project such as an introduction or awareness-level module, deliver it quickly, and then add additional elements and deliver the more complex portions later.

Planning Your Presenter Project

You can simply jump in and start building your project without doing much planning. And, truth be told, this is an approach that many take. But if your project is the least bit complex, you'll soon be frustrated with keeping track of the changes that need to be made, what has and hasn't been changed, and what you need to do to make changed content and unchanged content consistent. Exasperating.

One way to reduce this frustration is through planning. In this section, we'll describe what you can do to reduce the annoying and time-consuming back and forth that occurs when planning is not done. Some back and forth is inevitable. Even with the best planning, you'll have some aha moments while developing that will likely cause changes in the project. But you can reduce this quite a bit by thinking through what's needed before you begin.

Is there time for planning when information or instruction needs to be developed very rapidly? Gaining adequate information up front is often the difference between a fast-but-adequate rapid e-learning project and a fast-but-not-worth-the-time rapid e-learning project. It seems like planning takes up precious time, but it almost always saves much more time than it takes.

Without planning, most projects, even ones that require speed, are chaotic, like the scenario just described. Jumping in and winging it may seem like the best approach under tight deadlines (and there are certainly times when this is what needs to occur), but you'll find that even a small amount of planning usually pays off in fewer hassles, better outcomes, and less stress all around.

Deciding What to Include

What should you include in your Presenter project? If your viewers don't need to practice or gain specific job skills, good content and perhaps some Quizmaker questions to help the viewers determine if they understood the message might be enough. In that case, you'll want to make sure your Presenter project and content is user-friendly and worthwhile for the intended audience. That means that the content is clear and understandable, answers to typical viewer questions about the content are provided, and the project is easy to navigate. Some things you can do to make primarily informational content more user-friendly and worthwhile to viewers include:

- Write content at an appropriate reading level.
- Explain acronyms.
- Define words that viewers may not know.
- Describe the big picture, perhaps on an introductory slide.
- Use graphics such as graphs, flowcharts, and pictures to make content clearer.
- Sequence the content in an order that makes sense to viewers.
- Answer typical viewer questions.
- Make sure navigation makes sense to viewers (the default Presenter navigation that shows the slide titles and proceeds in a linear fashion meets this standard for smaller projects).
- Test the project before distributing it to make sure it works as expected.

Determining the Skill Goals

But what if the project's viewers need to practice or gain specific skills? That is, the purpose of the project is more instructional and viewers should be able to DO something as a result of viewing and interacting with the project? We capitalize DO here because the DOs are very important—the instruction should prepare learners to DO something. (See Chapter 2, "Rapid E-Learning," for a discussion of informational and instructional projects.) In that case, you'll want to make sure the project is user-friendly, worthwhile, *and* provides adequate practice. That means that it should contain good informational content and also opportunities for meaningful practice. Table 3.2 shows a list of typical skill types and examples of each.

Table 3.2. DO types and examples

DO type	Example
Recall facts.	Know the hours when the business is open and closed. Remember pay dates.
Find and make sense of information.	Determine whether the caller's service plan covers labor and parts. Calculate when timesheets are due on weeks with a holiday.
Understand underlying concepts.	Know how databases work. Understand how the likelihood of melting means that certain products need to be shipped overnight.
Understand how a process works.	Follow the travel expense reimbursement process. Describe how much time each step of the shipping process takes.
Complete needed steps.	Complete a new hire request. Check in new stock.
Determine which course of action is needed.	Ascertain the malfunction cause(s) and contact the appropriate department. Determine whether a refund or credit should be given.
Create a product or produce a specific result.	Write a discrepancy report. Transfer callers to the appropriate extension.
Troubleshoot and fix problems.	Find the damaged part and replace it. Analyze the reason for the delay and suggest solutions.

Knowing what learners need to be able to DO with the instruction helps you select instructional interactions and media to help them practice DOing it.

Selecting Appropriate Content, Interactions, and Media

If the project's viewers should be able to DO something as a result of viewing and interacting with the project, once you have determined the DOs, you'll need to select content, interactions, and media to be included in the project.

Content

Content may include onscreen text, documents, links, presentation sequences with slides and audio, videos, animations, simulations, archived online meetings and webinars, and so on. In Presenter, text and graphics are typically placed onto PowerPoint slides. Additional content may be produced in other applications (such as Engage and Quizmaker) and then brought into the Presenter project.

Interactions

There are three types of interactions to consider adding to your project: content interactions, social interactions, and assessment interactions.

Content Interactions

Content interactions can let the learner determine the direction and flow of content (for example, rollovers on a picture of a car prototype that show the inside of the car at that spot) or practice what is being learned by playing games, answering questions, using simulations, planning next steps, and so on. Since practice is such an important part of instruction, content interactions that provide practice opportunities are often critical to online instruction.

Content interactions can be produced using Engage, Presenter Learning Games, Quizmaker, or other tools that produce Flash animations, simulations, or games (which can be embedded in your Presenter project). They can also be provided through links to content on the Internet or within a corporate or organizational intranet. (Warning: Links can and do change, so they need to be maintained.)

Social Interactions

Social interactions help learners think through content, ask questions, get help, and figure out how the content applies to a variety of situations. In many cases, content is made generic so it can be viewed and used by many different users. A potentially large and important problem with generic content is that it may be hard for each viewer to determine how it applies in his or her own (often unique) situation.

Social interactions typically occur through emails, phone calls, meetings, online discussions, or Q&A sessions. These can be done online or offline, including on the job. Social interactions can be facilitated within your project through links to email addresses and phone numbers, chat sessions, discussion boards, online meetings, webinars, calendars with dates and times of face-to-face meetings, and so forth. Many social web applications, including wikis, blogs, and link sharing, can be excellent tools to add social interactions to information and instruction.

Assessment Interactions

Practice and social interactions allow learners to practice and hopefully apply the content to their own needs. Assessment interactions determine if the learner can actually perform as needed, in either a real or realistic way. Often, assessment interactions are similar to practice interactions but they are "graded."

Online instruction commonly includes practice and/or assessment interactions but often doesn't include social interactions. Although beyond the scope of this book, we'd like to urge you to consider social interactions when possible and appropriate because they can be extremely powerful for promoting learning and helping learners determine how the content applies to them personally.

A list of typical interactions (and the media used to produce them) for each DO type are shown in Table 3.3. (DO types are discussed in Chapter 2, "Rapid E-Learning.")

Table 3.3. DO types, interactions, and typical media

DO type	Typical interactions allow learners to:	Typical media (used to facilitate interactions)
Recall facts.	Recall facts. Classify facts. Use facts.	Recall questions Puzzles or games Documents, graphics, audio, and video
Find and make sense of information.	Locate needed information. Interpret information. Apply information to a specific issue, scenario, or problem.	Links to resources Questions using resources Documents, graphics, audio, and video Interactive forms
Understand underlying concepts.	Identify examples and nonexamples. Apply concept properties in new situations.	Interactive graphics (rollovers, etc.) Interactive classification, pairing, or sequencing Questions about concept properties

DO type	Typical interactions allow learners to:	Typical media (used to facilitate interactions)
Understand how a process works.	Put the process in order. Interpret a model or map of the process. Analyze when the process does and doesn't apply. Analyze how the process applies in specific situations.	Graphical analogy or model of process Animation to show stages of process or changes over time Interactive classification, pairing, or sequencing Documents, graphics, audio, and video
Complete needed steps.	Sequence the steps. Perform the steps. Use a job aid/decision matrix to perform the steps. Determine when to perform the steps.	Demo of steps being performed Simulation of performing the steps Job aids Decision matrixes Interactive classification, pairing, or sequencing
Determine which course of action is needed.	Determine which policies, criteria, and guidelines apply. Analyze when to apply the policy. Apply policies, criteria, and guidelines to scenarios. Solve problems that occur when the right course of action isn't taken.	Decision tools (matrix, flowchart, etc.) Documents, graphics, audio, and video Charts, schematics, or other data representations Branched scenarios
Create a product or produce a specific result.	Create a product. Evaluate product examples. Determine if needed result has been achieved.	Graphics showing product, product elements, or results Evaluation checklists Documents, graphics, audio, and video
Troubleshoot and fix problems.	Troubleshoot information resources, processes, procedures (steps), and actions. Determine when and where to get help.	Decision tools (matrix, flowchart, etc.) Documents, graphics, audio, and video Branched scenarios

> **Note:** All (content, social, and assessment) interactions *do not* have to happen online. You should also consider real-world inter-actions such as putting new toner in the copier *on the job* or taking customer calls *on the job* and using real desktop applica-tions (instead of simulated applications) such as building a spreadsheet in Excel using a job aid, tutorial, or manual.

Media

What media should you use? In general, you will use tools that you have at your disposal (either in-house or through vendors) that will allow you to produce the interactions that are needed. In other words, if you want learners to be able to put a list of steps in the correct order, a Presenter sequence Learning Game would be useful. If learners need to see how different parts of a process fit together, an Engage Process interaction would be useful. You can refer back to Table 3.3 for a list of typical interactions and the media used to produce them for each DO type whenever you are trying to determine what interactions would be most beneficial.

In order to show you how a designer might select slide content, interactions, and media for an instructional Presenter project, Table 3.4 provides a high-level blueprint of the topics, slide content, and interactions and media to be used for an online module that will be developed using Presenter.

Table 3.4. High-level blueprint of topics, slide content, and interaction and media for an online payroll and pay Presenter module

Lesson or Module: Getting Paid (online portion)		
Topic/DO	Content on PowerPoint slides	Interactions/media elements added to Presenter
Introduction	• Welcome message • What's in this module and why this information is important to you • How long this module will take • Intro to flowchart	• Welcome audio • Flowchart graphic of online and onsite orientation process with callout for this step

Lesson or Module: Getting Paid (online portion)		
Topic/DO	Content on PowerPoint slides	Interactions/media elements added to Presenter
The payroll process	• Introduction to payroll process Engage interaction • How to use the job aid	• Engage interaction on payroll process • Payroll process job aid (PDF)
Use the human resources web site to obtain answers to frequently asked pay-related questions: • Pay frequency • Pay periods • Pay dates • When pay is deposited • Differences when pay date falls on a holiday week • Contact names and departments for help with problems or questions	• Introduction to quiz • How to use the job aid	• Quizmaker questions about frequently asked payroll and pay-related questions (using human resources web site) • Link to human resources web site • Printable questions/answers from quiz questions job aid
Use time tracking application in accordance with human resources policies.	• Introduction to time tracking process • Introduction to time tracking policies • Introduction to the time tracking questions • How to use the job aid • Introduction to the practice simulation	• Engage interaction on time tracking process • Link to human resources policy manual/time tracking policy • Quizmaker time tracking questions (using human resources policy manual/time tracking policy) • Time tracking job aid (PDF) • Captivate time tracking practice simulation
Wrap-up	• What you learned in this module • Next steps for orientation	• Flowchart graphic of online and onsite orientation process with callout for next step

Interactions and media often take time to design and build. So if your project needs to be out the door quickly, pick those that you can build quickly or build your project in phases. Get needed content out there ASAP and follow up soon thereafter with new and improved materials that provide needed interactions.

Tip: If you have Articulate Studio '09, you have a suite of tools at your disposal to build a variety of content and interactions! These are discussed in more detail in the Engage and Quizmaker sections of this book and in Chapter 6, "Pumping Up Your Presenter Projects."

Tip: See Practice 1 at the end of this chapter to build a high-level blueprint for a current or upcoming Presenter project.

Considering Frustration

None of us sets out to build frustrating information or instruction. Frustration needlessly reduces mental capacity that would otherwise be available for learning. (If you are wondering if there is such a thing as "useful frustration," the answer is yes and it is discussed shortly.) And using multiple media can result in even more frustration than usual, as we'll discuss momentarily.

Research in the last 25 years done by Richard Mayer, John Sweller, Allan Paivio, and others provides guidance on how to best design learning material that includes text, audio, animations, images, videos, and so on. Since Presenter allows you to incorporate media from many sources, it's important to understand how to do this without inadvertently adding in unnecessary frustration.

Guidance for designing multimedia is built on certain suppositions about how we think, remember, and learn. We know that working memory (mental processes used for brief storage and use of information, such as remembering a web address that you hear on the radio so you can write it down) has limited capacity and can be easily overwhelmed. When learners are trying to make sense of what is being presented and integrate it with what they know, they are often putting forth a great deal of mental effort. So it makes sense to eliminate as much unnecessary frustration as possible so they are able to attend to the real task at hand.

Table 3.5 lists some of this design guidance based on research by Mayer and others about how people learn from multimedia.

Table 3.5. Design advice for narration, images, learner control, and removing extraneous information when designing multimedia

Elements	Dos and don'ts
Narration	• **Narration should *not* read the text on the screen.** (This is bolded because it is regularly violated.) • Narration/explanations should be conversational and concise. • If narration is used, make sure a text script (transcript) is also available for anyone who will not be able to hear the narration or who prefers to read a transcript of the narration. • When explanations are needed, narration is usually better than text explanations because it allows the viewer to look at the image while the explanation is occurring. Reading the explanation makes it hard to look at the image, so the viewer is forced to go back and forth between them, which is frustrating and hard. (If you offer a text version of the narration, the text will be available but should not be intrusive.) • Don't add narration or text explanations (beyond a heading and a brief introduction) for images that are self explanatory (such as a diagram showing where to place the fork, spoon, and knife when setting the table). • Some images will be self-explanatory to experts but not novices, so determine who will be using the project and if the visuals need an explanation. • Corresponding images and explanations should occur on the same screen. • If things are changing or moving on the slide, sync the narration with screen changes. (See Chapter 5, "Presenter Basics," for how to record narration that goes along with PowerPoint animations.)
Images	• Don't add images just to make the slide more "interesting." • Include diagrams, charts, and other relevant images to show relationships, how things work, and to make data (such as sales figures) more comprehensible. • On screens with complex images, help viewers know what to focus on. (See Chapter 6, "Pumping Up Your Presenter Projects," for how to add annotations.)
Learner control	• Let learners control play, pause, replay, and go forward and backward. This is especially important when learners will find the content challenging. • If learners will need to reference onscreen text for an activity, make sure that needed text remains on the screen during the activity.
LESS!!!	• Remove unessential words, images, and narration. • When learners need to think, don't make it harder to learn by adding anything extraneous like background music or additional images.

When learning, it helps to have control over the flow of information. For example, if the viewer cannot move more or less quickly at will, based on what they already know or need to spend more time on, they may feel like they are being held hostage. If the viewer wants to take notes but cannot pause or otherwise control when to go to the next screen, taking notes may be hard to do.

See where we're going? How do we allow viewers to have the control they need? First of all, provide the learner with adequate control over the narration and progression of slides by providing player controls such as volume control, forward/back/pause controller, and seekbar. These are selected using the Player Templates dialog box (see Chapter 7, "Customizing Presenter Player Templates").

One of the earlier pieces of advice was to provide a transcript of the narration. Allow viewers the option of downloading the transcript before the narration starts. Although it is hard to read a transcript while watching the slides, if the viewer can choose when to proceed, reading the transcript is more manageable. In addition, make sure that the narrator's voice and speed are pleasing by testing some example narration audio clips to see what others think of them.

Narrated explanations have an advantage over text explanations in a number of ways. You can "fit" far more audio on a slide than text. If you actually put your narration script in text on each slide, it'd likely use up all of the space. And most folks really don't like reading that much text on each slide. (If you have lots of text to be read, consider providing a downloadable and printable document to read offline.) But you can go overboard on narration, too. So while you can "fit" more words using narration, don't take that too far. More than 10-20 seconds of narration is going to feel like it's taking too long for the slide to be "done."

Narration is particularly useful in certain situations. It's hard to connect with learners in text. A text-driven online course can feel dispassionate and cold. When you hope to make an appeal or influence how learners feel, narration can be especially powerful. It's also very hard for learners to look at complex graphics, such as animations and diagrams, while simultaneously reading an explanation of those graphics. Narration is typically the better choice for explaining complex graphics. In that case, the narration should be in sync with animations so it is appropriate to what is happening on the screen.

Many instructional designers think that you have to choose between narrated or text explanations, but we'd suggest that this not become a hard and fast rule. It is often possible to combine narration and text explanations—but again, don't read the text on the slide. You could explain a complex diagram using narration and then, on the next slide, provide a concise recap of the concepts just explained using bullet points (in text).

Learners get "trained" how to use your materials by using your materials. If they are used to narration on each page and there are pages with no narration, they may sit and wait for it to start or get frustrated because they think that the sound isn't working. So if you are going to combine slides with narration and slides without narration, you may want to cue learners when to expect audio and when to not expect audio.

Before leaving the topic of learner frustration, we promised earlier to address the idea of "useful frustration." Learning can be and often is frustrating, even if sources of unnecessary frustration are lessened. It takes effort to read, listen, think through, make connections, make sense of images, integrate what is being presented with what is already known, determine how the content applies to their work, and so on. So we can't remove all frustration because some frustration is built into the learning process (and is even a good thing). The goal is to remove frustration that gets in the way or adds nothing useful.

Building a Storyboard (Maybe)

If your Presenter project is small, simple, and informational, you might choose to jump in and get started building the PowerPoint slides and narration script. The high-level blueprint discussed previously can be used as a tool for planning a simple Presenter project. But Presenter projects can easily get more complex when interactions, graphics, and media are added, and it's a good idea to plan them out in more detail.

After completing the high-level blueprint, you may want to build a detailed blueprint, otherwise known by instructional designers and developers as a "storyboard." Storyboards can be very simple, like the following example, or much more complex.

Table 3.6 shows part of a storyboard designed for a Presenter project on the XYZ Expense Submission application.

Table 3.6. Part of a storyboard designed for the XYZ Expense Submission application

Lesson or Module: XYZ Expense Submission Application			
Screen	**Slide content**	**Interactions and media/links**	**Narration script**
1	How to use the XYZ Expense Submission system	Screenshot of application opening screen	Welcome to a short tutorial on the XYZ Expense Submission application. This system will help you get your expenses paid as quickly and painlessly as possible so learning how to use it is a good idea!
2	In this tutorial, you will learn to input and track your expenses. Roll over each of the tabs on the screen below to find out the function of each tab. When you are done, press [next button screenshot] to continue.	Engage Labeled Graphic interaction showing application tabs and functions Next button screenshot (see Slide content column)	In this tutorial, you'll learn how to input and track your business expenses. Follow the directions on the screen. When you are done, press the Next button to continue.
3	XYZ Expense Submission system demo	Captivate XYZ Expense Submission System demo	Let's jump in and see how the system works. Click the Play button and watch as Maria inputs her expenses from her recent business trip.

Storyboards take time, and in many cases you will probably have less time than you need. So taking the time to build a storyboard must offer benefits that are worth the time. Here are some benefits you may experience from building a storyboard before starting on your Presenter project. By building a storyboard, you can:

■ See content gaps that need to be filled.

■ Document the project scope, which can help you determine (and negotiate for) needed resources.

■ Communicate more clearly with a subject matter expert (SME). The SME can review content before you dive into development. You can also post notes to the SME on content you need but don't yet have.

- Get feedback from stakeholders before starting development, which can save time and hassles.
- Get sign-off on the storyboard so when stakeholders ask for more, you can discuss desired scope changes with greater authority.

> Scope shift is common and having a signed off storyboard helps you negotiate changes and additions. See the next section.

If you are an SME and are building a Presenter project yourself, developing a simple storyboard will help you think through what you are building and whether the content and sequencing makes sense.

What do you think? Is a storyboard worth the time? That depends, of course, on whether the benefits are worth the effort. The more complex the project, the more benefits you'll see from developing a simple storyboard.

Tip: See Practice 2 at the end of this chapter to build a simple storyboard for a current or upcoming Presenter project.

Documenting and Managing Scope

In Chapter 2, "Rapid E-Learning," guidance is provided on gaining information about the problem to be prevented or resolved. Once you gather and analyze that information and decide that building information or instruction makes sense, but before you jump into the project, it's often worthwhile to document the scope of the project.

A scope document lists the specifics of what you agree to deliver. It includes details that describe the elements to be built and who will do what. As an example, Table 3.7 shows a portion of a very simple scope document for a Presenter project.

Table 3.7. Simple scope document example

Task/Deliverable	Who	When	Notes
☐ 1. **Slide content completed**	Janet/Marshall	10/1	Waiting on Katrina to provide common misconceptions.
☒ CC provides graphics	Janet/Marshall	10/6	
⊔ First draft (one iteration)	Tomas	10/12	
☐ Second draft (one iteration)			
☐ Sign-off			
☐ 2. **Narration script completed**	Janet/Marshall	10/4	
☒ First draft (one iteration)	Janet/Marshall	10/8	
☐ Second draft (one iteration)	Tomas	10/14	
☐ Sign-off			
☐ 3. **Two Engage interactions completed**	Li/Marshall	10/1	
☐ Select Engage interactions	Li/Marshall	10/4	
☐ Add content (one iteration)	Li/Marshall	10/8	
☐ Build interactions	Li/Marshall	10/10	
☐ Add to Presenter/test	Tomas	10/12	
☐ Sign-off			

Scope creep, the tendency of projects to get larger over time, is a major cause of e-learning project problems. This may happen through numerous small changes or through additions of larger elements that were not included in the original scope. For example, adding an additional Engage interaction to the project in Table 3.7 may seem manageable on first consideration, but may cause havoc because of other issues that arise as a result of this change. For instance, the SME may not have time to complete additional content and begin to balk at the work she has already agreed to do. Other project deadlines may be jeopardized because of the additional iteration needed for this new content.

Most seasoned instructional designers and developers would agree, we think, that scope creep is the norm rather than the exception. Project management research shows that scope issues rank highly as obstacles to project success, right up there with unrealistic estimates of cost and time.

The reasons that scope is so often a problem vary, but three very common mistakes make dealing with scope changes more of a hassle than they already are: 1) no scope (requirements) document, 2) a scope document that is too vague, and 3) unwillingness to discuss impending scope creep while it is happening (also known as the bag-over-the-head approach to project management).

We recommend that you document scope at the outset of the project and discuss with stakeholders the changes that occur when they occur, including the impact they have on project resources, time, cost, and outcomes. It is often a good idea to have every requested change (to the original scope) documented on an updated version of the scope document, get approval for the changes, and list the impact of the changes.

> Stakeholders and clients sometimes get annoyed when I bring up scope. They just want me to get it done.

> True enough. But they like talking about less-than-optimal project results even less.

Managing Presenter Folders and Files

When you build Presenter projects, you'll likely be working with a number of different file types: PowerPoint files, media files (such as graphics, audio and video files, and Flash and Web Objects), and any PDF, Word, or Excel attachments you want included in the Presenter project. When your project is completed, you'll publish the Presenter project so viewers can view the project outside of Presenter.

For example, let's say you want to build a welcome module for a new hire orientation. You'll start by building your PowerPoint slides. Then you'll add narration in Presenter. You may want to add an audio clip with a welcome message from the company's CEO and bring in some photographs of company executives. When you're ready to publish the module so that it can be viewed by others, you'll select the output type (web, CD, podcast, etc.) and Presenter will create the files needed to display the finished project for viewers.

When you build and edit a Presenter project, you'll be creating and editing a Presenter working file that has the extension .ppta. The .ppta file is the file that holds all of the assets for your project. When you publish the file, Presenter creates files that are viewable outside of the Presenter application. This is described in more detail in Chapter 26, "Publishing."

If you work with electronic files, you know how difficult it can be to find what you are looking for if you don't have them organized. Electronic files such as documents, graphics, audio clips, presentations, and so on are like paper files. If you don't organize them, they are easily lost.

Organizing Presenter Project Files

Here are some generic tips on organizing your Presenter project files so you won't spend needless time trying to track them down. (These tips assume you are using a Windows operating system so you may need to translate slightly for Mac or Linux.)

- In your My Documents folder (or wherever you keep you work files, including a network drive), create a folder for each Presenter project and save all of the files you are using to build the project inside this folder.

- Name your project folder in such a way that you can easily tell what project this is. For example, rather than naming the project folder "Presenter Project 1," give it a descriptive name such as "Company Welcome."

Consider organizing versions by date. Appending dates to document versions will help them sort by date. (Thanks to Eric Replinger for pushing me to label files this way.) For example, catalog2007_0201.doc and catalog2007_0228.doc will sort in order of date. And that's seriously useful when you're looking for a specific version. Also consider keeping multiple versions of documents as you change them on the likelihood that you will sometimes need to retrace where you've been at an earlier time.

Practice 1

||||► High-level Blueprint for Presenter Project

Instructions: Using the following table, document the topics/skills, slide content, and interactions and media. You may want to reproduce this table in your word processing application to use with current and future projects.

Lesson or module:		
Topics/Skills:	Content on PowerPoint slides	Interactions/media elements added to Presenter
Recall facts.		
Find and make sense of information, often with the aid of tools, resources, etc.		
Understand underlying concepts.		
Understand how a process works.		
Complete needed steps.		
Determine which course of action is needed.		
Create a product or produce a specific result.		
Troubleshoot and fix problems.		

Practice 2

||||▶ Storyboard for Presenter Project

Instructions: Using the following blank storyboard, document the actual slide content, interactions and media/links, and narration for a Presenter project. You may want to reproduce this table in your word processing application to use with current and future projects.

Lesson or module:			
Screen	Slide content	Interactions and media/links	Narration script

Chapter Recap

Here are some of the most important points made in this chapter:

- Presenter can be used to build a wide variety of information and instruction.

- Presenter is not a standalone authoring tool. You use it with PowerPoint. Parts of each Presenter project will be built using PowerPoint and other parts will be built using Presenter.

- Planning your Presenter project can save lots of time and aggravation. (Read the "Planning Your Presenter Project" section!)

- There are numerous ways to make your content more user-friendly and worthwhile to viewers. One way is to make sure that you answer the questions that viewers are likely to have. (Read "Deciding What to Include" for more ways!)

- Good instruction allows learners to practice. But practice does not have to be online.

- There are many ways to needlessly frustrate learners when building a project that includes multiple media (and most Presenter projects contain multiple media). For example, you should *not* read the text on each slide in your narration. (Read "Considering Frustration" to learn how to prevent more needless frustration!)

- Storyboards help you think through your project, get adequate feedback, and scope the project. They're often worth the extra time they take to build.

- Scope creep is common in information and instructional projects and it's helpful to plan for this by documenting and maintaining a scope document.

Chapter 4

First, Your PowerPoint Slides

Chapter Snapshot

We can't say this too strongly: Well-executed PowerPoint slides are absolutely critical to the quality of each Presenter project.

The slides you use in your Presenter project are the foundation of the project. If the slides don't "work," your project will struggle to get beyond the problems with your slides.

The primary goal of this chapter is to discuss how to develop PowerPoint slides that will be good *for your Presenter projects* rather than how to use PowerPoint. (You can find many good books on using PowerPoint.)

Revisiting the Presenter 1-2-3-4-5 Workflow

In this chapter, we'll discuss the first two steps in the Presenter 1-2-3-4-5 workflow: 1. Create slides and 2. Write narration script. Those two sets are highlighted in Figure 4.1.

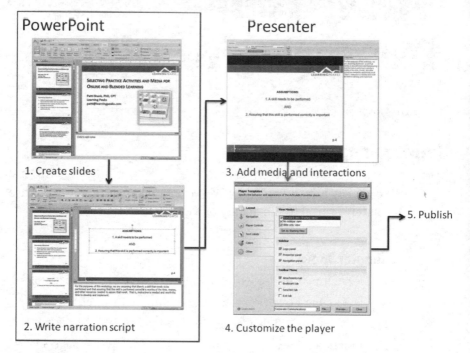

Figure 4.1. Presenter 1-2-3-4-5 workflow

Table 4.1 shows the typical substeps completed in steps 1 and 2 of the Presenter 1-2-3-4-5 workflow.

Table 4.1. Detailed workflow for steps 1 and 2

Using PowerPoint	
1. Create slides.	a) Create slides.
	b) Add text.
	c) Add graphics.
	d) Add animations.
2. Write narration script.	a) Write narration script.

Let's take a few steps back from the tasks required to build slides and a narration script to consider the bigger picture—the reason you are building a Presenter project in the first place. And why *are* you building a Presenter project? Here's a good big picture answer: To influence what viewers think and do.

> Never thought of it that way, but that's true.

So we'll start by considering the things you need to do to make your project influence people—to sell its intended message to its intended audience. You may not (yet) think that you need to *try* to influence your audience, but we want to convince you that you do. Consider the amount of time, effort, and money that goes into product packaging, corporate logos, and customer information materials. Why do organizations spend precious time and money in this way? Because it works. If you don't understand this principle, you can't make it work for you. So we're hoping to help you see the importance of designing your presentation with impact and influence in mind.

Once the important decisions have been made, the "Getting Your Slides Ready for Presenter" section is where we jump into the first two steps in the Presenter 1-2-3-4-5 workflow: 1. Create slides and 2. Write narration script.

This Chapter Is Different

This chapter is *not* a "how to build PowerPoint slides" book, so if you are new to using PowerPoint, you'll want to have access to the PowerPoint help documents and perhaps some good PowerPoint how-to books as well.

Why the big deal about this not being a how-to chapter? In subsequent chapters, we provide fairly detailed how-to steps for accomplishing Presenter, Engage, and Quizmaker tasks (for example, adding a logo, adding narration, customizing the player, and so on). We simply cannot do this in this chapter because 1) we aren't able to cram an adequate PowerPoint book into one chapter, and 2) PowerPoint 2000-2003 and PowerPoint 2007 are very different, so the steps for completing tasks using one version would not easily translate to the other. The tasks described in the later part of this chapter will be described generically. If you are unfamiliar with performing these tasks in your version of PowerPoint, you'll want to use the PowerPoint help documents. Click the question mark symbol in the upper-right corner of PowerPoint or press the **F1** key on the keyboard to open the help docs.

Designing PowerPoint Slides for Impact

You are promoting ideas and actions with every Presenter project you build. You may be shocked to learn that your project's intended audience probably isn't all that excited about viewing the Presenter projects you produce. (Well, they might be excited if your project is about how to get bathrooms to clean themselves or how to get free tickets to a sold-out concert or sporting event.) There's a good chance that viewers have too much to do and viewing your project is another to-do that needs checking off. If your project is seen by viewers as just another set of boring narrated PowerPoint slides, the attention they'll devote to it may be minimal. So this section discusses how to improve the impact of your Presenter projects.

If Your Slides Suck, Then...

It isn't possible to overstate how much the quality of your slides impact the perceived value of your Presenter projects—for better or worse. I (Patti) knew that this was true intellectually but recently had the occasion to see the impact of poorly executed slides in a Presenter project. Presenter worked well, but the final product felt unfinished. The content was good but the unattractive slides made it hard to recognize that it had good content. What's the point? If you do not have lots of experience with designing good slides, your Presenter projects may suffer. I'd like to recommend a couple of books that can help you with the "design" aspects of PowerPoint. They both assume that you know the mechanics of building PowerPoint slide decks (so if you're not there, start by getting some basic PowerPoint skills first).

Slide:ology: The Art and Science of Creating Great Presentations, by Nancy Duarte, O'Reilly Media, © 2008.

Beyond Bullet Points: Using Microsoft Office PowerPoint 2007 To Create Presentations That Inform, Motivate, and Inspire, by Cliff Atkinson, Microsoft Press, © 2008.

Also look through Garr Reynolds' blog on professional presentations: Presentation Zen (http://www.presentationzen.com).

Appropriate Design and Graphics

The first things you can do to better promote your project's ideas relate to design. The design of your slides needs to be appropriate for the topic and intended audience. What does that mean, exactly? Instead of answering the question directly, take a look at the following questions and at Figure 4.2 (the design examples use Microsoft's downloadable PowerPoint templates) and see how well your answers match ours. (Don't peek at the answers!)

1. Evaluate each of the three designs for a Presenter project that is about a company's products and services. Which slide design or designs would be most and least appropriate?

2. Evaluate each of the three designs for a Presenter project that concerns test scores. Which slide design or designs would be most and least appropriate?

3. Evaluate each of the three designs for a Presenter project that is for newly diagnosed cancer patients. Which slide design or designs would be most and least appropriate?

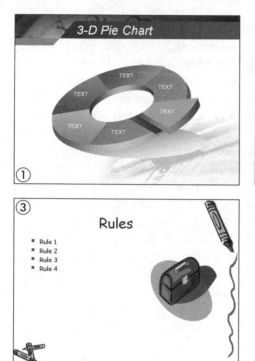

Figure 4.2. Example slide designs

Our answers:

1. Presenter project about a company's products and services: Design 1 has a professional look that is most appropriate for this kind of information. Design 2 might work as well if the graphics represent the subject or audience for the project, but a colored background makes the text harder to read. Design 3 is not the right look for this type of information unless the company sells products and services geared for school-aged children or teachers of those children.

2. Presenter project concerning test scores: All designs could be appropriate, depending on whose test scores are being discussed and the audience for the project. Design 1 would work best for a

business audience. Design 2 embeds pictures, making it more or less appropriate for some audiences, but the colored background makes the slides harder to read. Design 3 is appropriate if the project deals with children's test scores.

3.   Presenter project for newly diagnosed cancer patients: Design 2 has a "softer" design that is often used for health programs, but the colored background makes the slides harder to read so it might be a good idea to eliminate the background color in the bottom two-thirds of the slide. And the pictures in the template may not be representative of the patients who will be viewing the project, so those may need tweaking as well. Design 1 is general-purpose and professional, but might be too harsh. Design 3 is likely the wrong look for this audience, even if the intended audience is parents of children with cancer, because the design is too light for this topic.

So what's an appropriate design? An appropriate design looks professional, not homegrown (see Figure 4.3). It isn't hard to look professional, so there's rarely an excuse for not doing so. (Google "PowerPoint design templates" to see professional templates you can use or buy. You can also find templates to download at microsoft.com.)

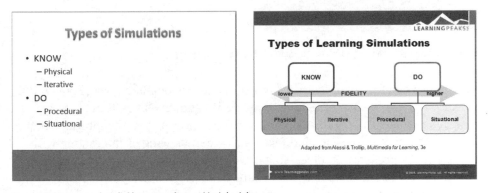

Figure 4.3. Homegrown look (left) versus professional look (right)

Appropriate designs are also tailored to the topic and the audience. If you were building a project for dieticians on dietary guidelines for kidney dialysis patients, you might want to make the design look and feel different than a project on dietary guidelines for kidney dialysis patients built for kidney dialysis patients and their families. The words you'd use would likely be different as well.

One of the great things about Presenter is that the end result doesn't have to look like PowerPoint. Take a look at Figure 4.4. All of these examples are Presenter projects but only one (the one at the top left) looks like a typical narrated PowerPoint slide project.

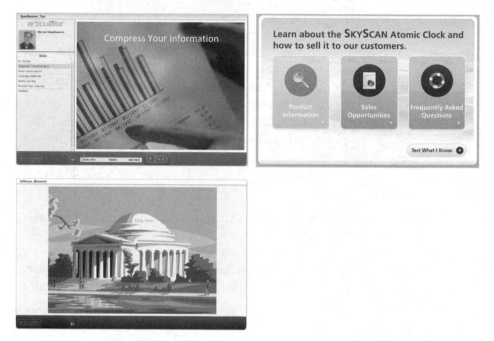

Figure 4.4. Examples of Presenter projects (source: Articulate Rapid E-Learning blog)

So don't assume that your project needs to look like PowerPoint at all! In fact, in Chapter 7, "Customizing Presenter Player Templates," you'll learn how to customize the Presenter player, the interface that the viewer sees and interacts with when viewing or interacting with your Presenter project, so it can look however you want it to look.

You'll also need to make sure that any graphics you use convey the tone and message you want to convey. If it is a serious topic, it needs a serious design and graphics. Resist the temptation to use humor unless it's appropriate and likely to be acceptable to all viewers. The bottom line is to make sure the design and graphics convey the right message. The opening music on the *Oprah!* show changes to match the tone for that day's subject (not that we are watching Oprah when we are supposed to be working), and we can learn from that.

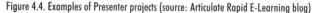

Tom Kuhlmann, who writes Articulate's Rapid E-Learning blog, has a terrific posting about making your e-learning courses look good (original posting: http://www.articulate.com/rapid-elearning/why-looks-matter-in-e-learning-courses). We totally agree that there's no reason to produce ugly information or instruction. He suggests that you learn about design, colors, fonts/type, and image quality. He also recommends looking at other designs to get ideas. Like Tom, I (Patti) recommend starting with Robin Williams' *Non-Designer's Design Book* (Peachpit Press, 2003) to get a feel for design concepts and terminology. Robin also has books on type and other more advanced design books. Tom also recommends Ellen Lupton's *Thinking with Type: A Critical Guide for Designers, Writers, Editors, and Students* (Princeton Architectural Press, 2004).

WIIFM?

Those viewing your project should be able to quickly answer the question "What's in it for me?" (WIIFM) so they can determine whether to pay more than limited attention to your project. Viewers' default position is almost always "Cursory attention is all that is needed," so you have to put some effort into changing that position. Some common approaches that can be used to engage viewers of online content include showing how the viewer will be able to:

- Do something he or she wants to do (such as increase sales).
- Avoid something he or she wants to avoid (such as reduced income).
- Solve a dilemma (such as why certain items are often on backorder).
- Answer a question (such as what a recent surveys says about customer needs).
- Get help (such as how to use the sales database to better target opportunities for repeat sales).

You need to understand your audience in order to figure out how to sell them on the project they are about to view. Figure 4.5 shows an example of a WIIFM slide I (Patti) designed to get my audience, instructional designers, thinking about the use of realism in e-learning simulations.

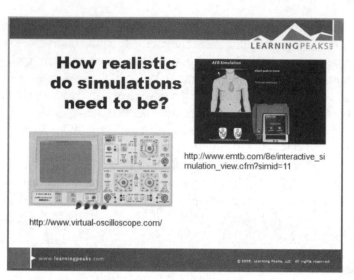

Figure 4.5. WIIFM slide in a presentation about simulations

If you are thinking "I'd like to know the answer to that question," the slide works for its intended purpose. What if you think you know your audience and cannot think of one reason they should want to view the project? That could mean you either don't know your audience well enough or the project isn't worth building. Of course, there are times when you may be told to build something you don't think should be built, but that's another subject entirely.

Word Surgery, Anyone?

Here's the most important advice in this section: *much less text*. And text that is displayed on each page should be readable and clearly organized. So what does *much less text* mean? It means that whatever text you start with, it's too much. Probably *way, way, way too much*. No long paragraphs of text. No bullet lists with full sentences. You need to be merciless in reducing the text on each slide. Think words and short phrases, not sentences. If you are too attached to the words, get someone else who is less invested in the words to get rid of those that aren't needed. To see what we mean, take a look at Figure 4.6, which shows two versions of the same slide—one with too much text and one with reduced text.

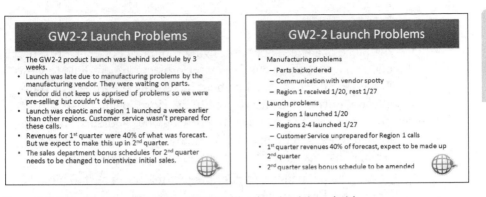

Figure 4.6. Bullet list slide with sentences (left) and bullet list slide with words and phrases (right)

The slide on the left has *way, way, way too much text*. How about the slide on the right? It only has *way too much text*. So it's better, but it could still use some skillful word surgery. Become a word surgeon or find someone who can do this for you.

So where does the extra (removed) text go? Here are some possible answers:

■ Use it for extra explanation in the narration. Narration should describe the details behind what appears on the screen. (But make sure that narration text is available for those who are unable to hear the narration.)

■ Provide links to more information.

■ Provide attachments with additional information.

■ Just get rid of it. Your Presenter projects are not meant to be exhaustive resources on a given topic.

The small amount of text displayed on any slide must be easy to read. Use common fonts and don't use more than two font families. Some research shows that sans-serif fonts, such as Arial or Helvetica, are easier to read onscreen than serif fonts, such as Times New Roman. Preview your project to see if the font size is large enough for audiences of all ages to read easily. And consider asking others to provide feedback on the text size. If you have sufficiently reduced the text on each screen, you should have no reason to use smaller text to cram everything in. And make sure there is enough contrast between the text and the background so that the text is readable against the background.

Establish Credibility

One last piece of advice about improving the impact of your Presenter projects: Make sure that your Presenter projects are credible to viewers. Everything discussed so far about increasing the impact of your project cannot overcome lack of credibility. How do you make sure your projects are credible? Start by knowing your audience. What do *they* need in order to feel that the information is credible? Here are some things that may improve the credibility of a given project:

- Provide the presenter's (and/or subject matter expert's) bio (see Chapter 5, "Presenter Basics").

- Support facts with simple tables and graphs.

- Answer questions viewers are likely to have and debunk common misconceptions about the topic.

- Supply credible sources of information (not Wikipedia or Uncle Joe's blog).

- Provide links to authoritative resources, or attachments with authoritative information.

- Describe the limits of the information you are providing and how to get additional information.

- Make sure that spelling and grammar are perfect, the reading level is correct, and jargon isn't used (unless intended viewers understand the jargon).

Getting Your Slides Ready for Presenter

Now it's time to discuss the first two steps in the Presenter 1-2-3-4-5 workflow: 1. Create slides and 2. Write narration script.

The tasks described in this section will be described generically. In case you are unfamiliar with performing these tasks in whatever version of PowerPoint you are using, make sure the help documents are nearby so you can look up the steps. Click the help symbol or press the F1 key on the keyboard to open the help documents. In PowerPoint 2007, you'll see this symbol on the far right corner of the ribbon. In PowerPoint 2000-2003, this symbol is on the standard toolbar, generally all the way to the right.

66 **Note:** As we said in the beginning of this chapter, the chapter does not provide step-by-step instructions. If you are new to using PowerPoint, you should ideally develop basic skills using the PowerPoint help, books, or classes.

We can't emphasize enough how important it is to have good PowerPoint skills before using PowerPoint for Presenter projects. It is far too easy to produce awful PowerPoint slides that then produce awful-looking Presenter projects.

Creating Slides

The first step in the Presenter workflow is to create the slides that will be used as the foundation of your Presenter project.

Creating Slide Masters

PowerPoint slide masters help you produce a set of slides for your Presenter project that let you globally apply a specific look and feel to all of the slides in your project. This way, the look of your slides will be consistent. You can format slide titles, fonts, formatting, graphics, backgrounds, colors, and headers and footers, and your settings will apply to all of the slides in your PowerPoint deck. In a nutshell, slide masters can make your presentation look better and reduce the amount of time you'll need to spend manipulating how individual slides look.

When you create or edit a slide master, you can select the elements that you want to appear on every slide, including:

- Heading style
- Text style
- Bullet style
- Text placeholders
- Borders
- Background
- Graphical elements to be included on all sides such as slide design, logos, and so on
- Header and footer elements including slide number, date, copyrights, and so on

> **66 Note:** Create the masters *before* adding content to slides. Otherwise, you may end up with a mishmash of styles on your slides. In PowerPoint 2007, you can develop masters for different layout types. You should determine what layouts you will be using and develop slide masters for each of these layouts.

Figure 4.7 shows how the slide masters look in PowerPoint 2007. They look very similar in PowerPoint 2000-2003.

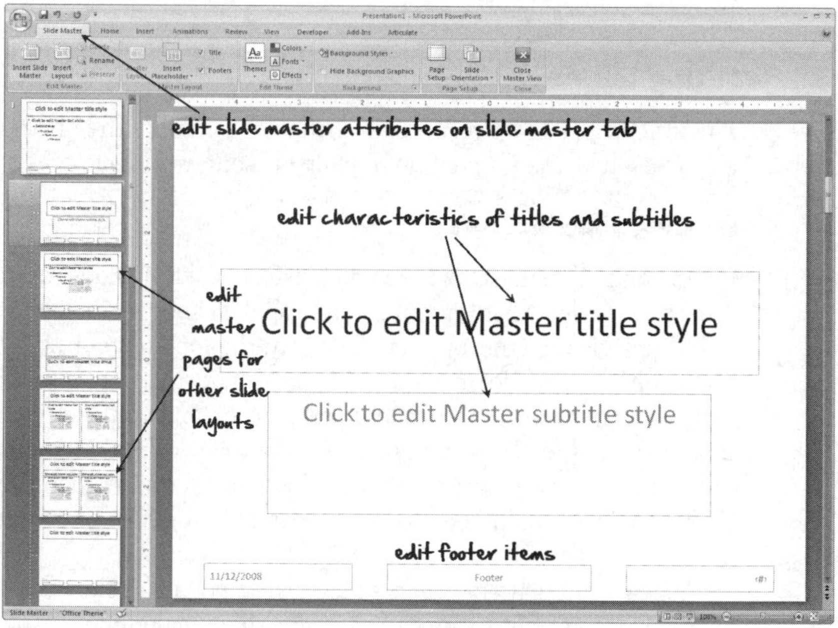

Figure 4.7. Slide masters in PowerPoint 2007

Search the PowerPoint help documents to find out how to create slide masters in your version of PowerPoint. Figure 4.8 shows the result of a search in the PowerPoint 2007 help documents using the search term "slide masters." In case you are unfamiliar with creating slide masters, we have highlighted the two topics you might find immediately useful.

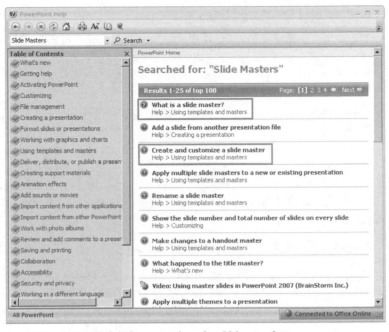

Figure 4.8. PowerPoint 2007 help documents with search on "slide masters"

Tip: Tom Kuhlmann, who writes Articulate's Rapid E-Learning blog, has a posting about creating PowerPoint templates to use in Presenter (original posting: http://www.articulate.com/rapid-elearning/secret-to-creating-powerpoint-templates-for-elearning). Rather than create "true" PowerPoint templates, he creates graphical images that he uses as PowerPoint backgrounds. And he creates variations on those backgrounds for different page types.

If you have minimal design "sense" and are too overwhelmed with all the other things you need to learn to build online information and instruction to get more (design sense) in a hurry, hire a graphic artist to build PowerPoint templates or backgrounds for you. One of the things I (Patti) learned a long time ago is that graphic designers are essential. Their services are typically reasonably priced and what they can do very quickly is amazing. After working with my designer friends Helen Macfarlane and John Patzman, I'll never again consider "hired" design help a luxury.

Adding and Deleting Slides

There are numerous ways to add and delete slides, but the following methods are convenient in all versions of PowerPoint.

Add Slides in Normal View or Slide Sorter View

Select the slide thumbnail that is *before* the slide you want to add. Right-click and then select **New Slide**.

To add a new slide with a specific layout in PowerPoint 2007, click the **New Slide** menu on the Home tab and select the desired slide layout. In PowerPoint 2000-2003, select **New Slide** from the **Insert** menu. If the Slide Layout pane isn't open, right-click the new slide and select **Slide Layout**.

Delete Slides in Normal View or Slide Sorter View

Right-click the slide thumbnail and then select **Delete Slide**. To delete multiple slides, hold down Ctrl while you click each slide that you want to delete and then right-click and select **Delete Slide**.

Selecting Objects on the Slide

Almost all of the how-to information in this chapter starts with "Select the…" You can select anything on the screen by clicking on it, but this doesn't always work as expected (for example, when you want to select a graphic but there is another object with a transparent background, such as a text box, on top of it). Table 4.2 describes how to select items on the slide normally and when objects (such as text and graphics) are stacked on top of each other.

Table 4.2. How to select objects on the screen

To Select	Do This
One object	Click it.
Multiple objects	Press and hold Shift or Ctrl while you click the objects.
A "grouped" object (multiple objects that behave as one object when moving, resizing, or rotating them)	Click the group.
An object that is under other objects and from the bottom object up	Select the top object, and then press Tab.
An object that is under other objects and from the top object down	Select the top object, and then press Shift+Tab.

More on Working with Slide Objects

In PowerPoint 2007, you can work with various items on the slide by using the **Select** menu on the Home tab. If you select **Selection Pane** from the **Select** menu, you will see all the objects on that slide. You can select objects on the Selection Pane to select them on the slide. This functionality becomes very useful with working with objects that are stacked on top of each other or when building complex animations in PowerPoint.

Adding Text

You can add text to the following slide elements:

- Text placeholders
- Text boxes
- Shapes

To locate more information on adding text, search your version of PowerPoint's help documents for "add text."

Inputting Text in Text Placeholders

Placeholders are boxes with dotted borders that you see in most of the preconfigured slide layouts (Figure 4.9). Title and content placeholders appear on most slide layouts.

Figure 4.9. Placeholders in PowerPoint slide layouts

To add text in a text placeholder: Click the placeholder and type the desired text. (As soon as you start typing, the placeholder text will disappear.)

Adding Your Own Placeholders

Search the PowerPoint help documents for "Add a text place-holder with custom prompt text" to see how to add your own placeholders and prompt text (such as the "Click to add title" text that appears in the title placeholder on most slide layouts) in slide masters to prompt developers to enter a certain type of content in that placeholder.

Inputting Text in Text Boxes

You can add text boxes to place text anywhere on a slide. First, create a text box by clicking the **Text Box** button in the Insert tab in PowerPoint 2007 or by selecting **Text Box** from the **Insert** menu in PowerPoint 2000-2003. Then type the desired text.

Adding Text to Shapes

When you add a shape such as a square, flowchart symbol, or block arrow to a slide, you can easily add text to it, as shown in Figure 4.10.

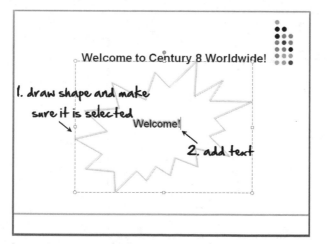

Figure 4.10. Adding text to a shape

First, add the shape by clicking the **Shapes** button on the Insert tab in PowerPoint 2007 or by selecting **Picture>AutoShapes** from the **Insert** menu in PowerPoint 2000-2003. Make sure the shape is selected, then right-click and select **Add Text** (PowerPoint 2000-2003) or **Edit Text** (PowerPoint 2007). Then type in the text. When you type text into a shape, the text attaches to the shape and moves with the shape if the shape is manipulated.

Tip: If you are having a hard time getting the text within a shape to fit the way you want it to, you can separately create a shape and a text box and then maneuver each so they are both where you want them to be.

Formatting Text

In PowerPoint, text is formatted using buttons on the Home tab (PowerPoint 2007) or Formatting toolbar (PowerPoint 2000-2003) (both are shown in Figure 4.11).

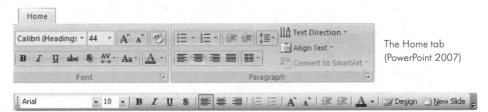

The Home tab (PowerPoint 2007)

The Formatting toolbar (PowerPoint 2000-2003)

Figure 4.11. Formatting text in PowerPoint

If you know how to format text in other Office applications, you should have no trouble formatting text in PowerPoint. To locate more information on formatting text, search your version of PowerPoint's help documents for "format text."

Tip: Make sure that the text you enter is readable for viewers. We recommend that you test different fonts and font sizes by entering them onto test slides. Then use the Articulate tab or the Articulate menu to preview the test slides in Articulate. (See Chapter 5, "Presenter Basics," for how to preview your slides in Presenter.)

> **Note:** Remember that your slides are going to be viewed in a *Presenter player*, not on a projection screen. Test read your slides as they will be used by viewers, not on a large projection screen (like those used for presentations) or full screen on a computer monitor.

> **Tip:** If you want to change fonts and font characteristics globally, that is, on *all* slides, make these changes to the slide masters (see the discussion about slide masters earlier in this chapter).

> **Note:** Working with slide masters can be tricky and operates differently in PowerPoint 2007 and PowerPoint 2000-2003. Use the help documents to find out how to work with slide masters in your version of PowerPoint.

Checking for Spelling and Grammar Mistakes

Correcting spelling and grammar mistakes is important! In PowerPoint 2007, you can check spelling and grammar by clicking the **Spelling** button on the Review tab. In PowerPoint 2000-2003, you can check spelling by selecting **Spelling** on the **Tools** menu. You can also press the **F7** button to perform this task in all versions of PowerPoint.

Inserting Symbols

The Symbol dialog box lets you insert symbols, such as ©, √, or ±, or special characters, such as an em dash (—), that are not on the keyboard in the text on a slide. You can use the Symbol font to input arrows, bullets, and scientific symbols. You may also have additional symbol fonts, such as Wingdings, Wingdings 2, and Wingdings 3, which include a variety of symbols. The fonts that you are using may also have some special characters such as fractions, international characters, and international monetary symbols.

In PowerPoint 2007, you can click the **Symbol** button on the Insert tab to get to the Symbol dialog box. In PowerPoint 2000-2003, you can open the Symbol dialog box by selecting **Symbol** from the **Insert** menu. If you need additional help with this task in your version of PowerPoint, search PowerPoint's help documents to find out how to add symbols.

Inserting Hyperlinks

The Insert Hyperlink dialog box lets you connect an object (text or graphics) on a slide to another slide in the same presentation, another slide in another presentation, an email address, a web page, or a file.

In PowerPoint 2007, you can open the Insert Hyperlink dialog box by clicking the **Hyperlink** button on the Insert tab. In PowerPoint 2000-2003, you can open the Insert Hyperlink dialog box by selecting **Hyperlink** on the **Insert** menu. You can also select the text you want to add a hyperlink to and use the shortcut **Ctrl+K** to open the Insert Hyperlink dialog box.

If you need additional help with this task in your version of PowerPoint, search PowerPoint's help documents to find out how to add hyperlinks. See Chapter 6, "Pumping Up Your Presenter Projects," for more information about using slide hyperlinks in your Presenter projects.

Adding Graphics

Graphics are often extremely valuable in Presenter projects, but it is not a good idea to load up your slides with extraneous graphics. (See Chapter 3, "Introduction to Presenter," for information about considering viewer frustration when adding content and media to slides.) It is extremely helpful to include diagrams, charts, and other relevant images to show relationships, to show how things work, and to make data (such as sales figures) more comprehensible.

In order to obtain additional advice about manipulating graphics in PowerPoint, we asked Jane Bozarth, a friend who published a book about using PowerPoint for e-learning, to provide some advice. As a result, some of the advice in this chapter about adding and manipulating graphics in PowerPoint comes from Chapters 5 and 6 in Jane Bozarth's book, *Better Than Bullet Points: Creating Engaging e-Learning with PowerPoint* (Pfeiffer, January 2008). You should consider adding this book to your library.

Figure 4.12. Jane Bozarth's *Better Than Bullet Points* (Reprinted with permission of John Wiley & Sons, Inc.)

Bitmapped vs. Vector Images

There are two kinds of images: bitmapped (also known as raster) and vector. Bitmapped images are made up of pixels, or small blocks of color, that when placed together make up the image. You can tell if an image is bitmapped by enlarging the image. The more you enlarge a bitmapped image, the more the edges start looking jaggedy or blocky. The types of bitmapped images you are likely to work with in PowerPoint are scanned images and photographs. Vector images are made up of lines and curves, not blocks. Vector images can be easily resized without looking jaggedy.

You will likely be working with both kinds of images when using graphics in PowerPoint. Vector images convert to Flash better because the lines are based on a mathematical formula and scale well. Bitmapped images do not scale well.

Working with (Auto)Shapes and Clip Art

PowerPoint makes it easy to add common shapes to your slides without having to draw them yourself. In PowerPoint 2007, you can select the **Shapes** button on the Insert tab and then select a shape (see Figure 4.13). In PowerPoint 2000-2003, you can do the same thing by selecting **Picture>AutoShapes** from the **Insert** menu.

Adding Shapes

To add the shape to your slide, select a shape from the options shown, and then click and drag it onto the slide. You can then manipulate the shape on the slide as desired.

Let's see if you remember the difference between bitmapped and vector graphics. Fill in the blank: (Auto)Shapes are vector graphics, so this means they can be resized...

The clip art that comes with PowerPoint (and additional clip art on the Microsoft site) may be bitmapped or vector , so you'll need to test whether the graphics you use can be resized without loss of quality.

Answer: ...without getting jaggedy.

Presenter

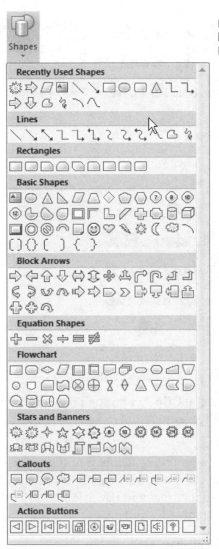

Figure 4.13. Shapes
button and shapes list in
PowerPoint 2007

Bozarth shows a good example of shapes and clip art used together (see Figure 4.14). Using shapes and clip art together makes it possible to develop many different types of images for your slides. You can also add graphs, organizational charts, flowcharts, and more. Use the help documents to find information on building and manipulating shapes, clip art, and graphs in your version of PowerPoint.

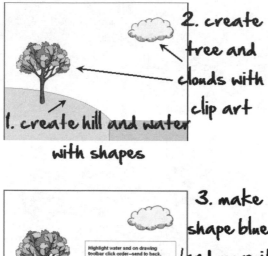

Figure 4.14. Using shapes and clip art to produce graphics (from *Better Than Bullet Points*, pp. 112-113; reprinted with permission of John Wiley & Sons, Inc.)

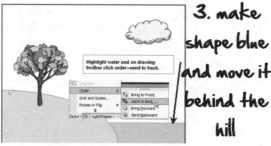

Adding Clip Art and Other Images (Such as Photographs) to Slides

To add clip art to slides: Click the **Clip Art** button on the Insert tab in PowerPoint 2007 or select **Picture>Clip Art** from the **Insert** menu in PowerPoint 2000-2003.

To add other images (such as personal photographs) to slides: Click the **Pictures** button on the Insert tab in PowerPoint 2007 or select **Picture>From File** from the **Insert** menu in PowerPoint 2000-2003, and then navigate to the location of the desired image.

Manipulating Clip Art Color and Attributes

To manipulate the color and other attributes of clip art in PowerPoint 2007, select the image and then right-click and select **Format Image**. The Recolor menu in the Format Picture dialog box provides a number of recoloring options for the picture. You can also add shadows and change the brightness and contrast.

In PowerPoint 2000-2003, you can do similar things using the Picture toolbar. Select the image and then use the Picture toolbar (which becomes visible when clip art is selected) to manipulate color and other attributes.

To locate more information on working with shapes and clip art, search PowerPoint's help documents for "shapes" and "clip art."

Editing Photos

PowerPoint provides a variety of tools for working with digital photographs. To use PowerPoint 2007's photo editing tools, place the desired digital photograph on the slide and make sure it is selected. The (Picture Tools) Format tab appears. This tab provides tools to adjust brightness, contrast, color, frames, and more. You can also crop and rotate photos. In PowerPoint 2000-2003, you can perform similar tasks using the Picture toolbar.

One especially important insight gained from Bozarth's discussion of cropping photos is this: When you are done cropping a picture, you'll want to remove the cropped areas to reduce the file size. In PowerPoint 2007, select the picture and then click the **Compress Pictures** button on the (Picture Tools) Format tab. In PowerPoint 2000-2003, right-click the picture and select **Format Picture**. The Format Picture dialog box opens. Click the **Picture** tab and then click the **Compress** button and check Delete cropped areas of picture so the cropped parts will be eliminated rather than hidden. Otherwise, the parts that you cropped out will not display on the slide but will continue to add to the project's file size.

Adding Charts

Graphics such as bar graphs and pie charts are used to display numeric data in a graphical format so it is easier to see what the numbers indicate. You can add charts in PowerPoint by clicking the **Chart** button on the Insert tab (PowerPoint 2007) or by selecting **Insert Chart** from the **Insert** menu (PowerPoint 2000-2003). When you add a chart, a spreadsheet will open where you can input the data. When you close the spreadsheet, PowerPoint will render the selected chart type.

To locate more information on working with charts, search PowerPoint's help documents for "create charts."

Adding SmartArt

Creating good images can be challenging if you aren't a graphic artist. The SmartArt feature in PowerPoint 2007 helps you build attractive graphical representations easily.

To add SmartArt: Click the **SmartArt** button on the Insert tab in PowerPoint 2007. Select the representation you want to use from the Choose a SmartArt Graphic dialog box (Figure 4.15). SmartArt graphics are available for a variety of representation types, such as processes, hierarchies, matrices, and so on.

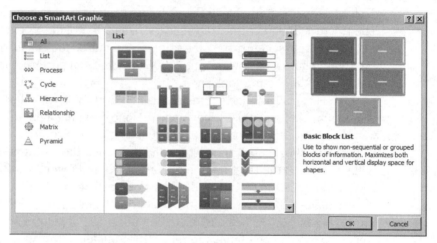

Figure 4.15. The Choose a SmartArt Graphic dialog box

After you select the SmartArt layout you want to use, you can replace the placeholder text with your own text (Figure 4.16).

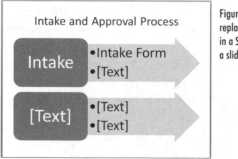

Figure 4.16. Example of replacing placeholder text in a SmartArt graphic on a slide

Converting Bullet Text to SmartArt

You can even convert existing bullet text to SmartArt. First, add your bullet points to a slide. Then click the text placeholder, the dotted box that surrounds the bullet text. Click the **Convert to SmartArt Graphic** button on the Home tab and select a desired SmartArt layout. Done! Figure 4.17 shows a slide with bullet points and text and Figure 4.18 shows the bullet text converted to SmartArt.

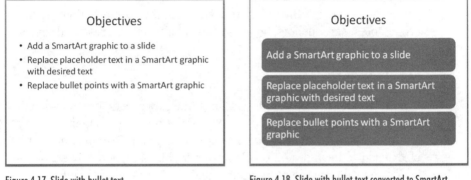

Figure 4.17. Slide with bullet text   Figure 4.18. Slide with bullet text converted to SmartArt

Manipulating a SmartArt Graphic

PowerPoint 2007 provides a number of tools for manipulating SmartArt graphics. When you select the SmartArt graphic, you can use the buttons on the (Smart Art) Design and Format tabs to manipulate the graphic. You can also use preconfigured SmartArt palettes by selecting the SmartArt graphic and clicking the **Change Colors** button on the (SmartArt) Design tab. You can also add or remove shapes in your SmartArt graphic if you need more or fewer shapes.

Before you create your SmartArt graphic, you should think about what type and layout are best for displaying your information. You can quickly switch layouts by selecting the SmartArt graphic and choosing another layout in the (SmartArt) Design tab so you can easily try out different layouts.

To locate more information about working with SmartArt in PowerPoint 2007, search PowerPoint 2007's help documents for "SmartArt." You can also download more SmartArt graphic temples from the Microsoft web site.

Note: SmartArt is a new, PowerPoint 2007 feature. Its conversion to Flash in Presenter varies. Be sure to preview SmartArt inside Presenter to make sure it looks the way you want it to.

Producing (Un)Fuzzy Graphics, Tables, and Screenshots

PowerPoint-to-Flash tools often produce fuzzy tables, screenshots, and graphics, and Presenter is no exception. They may look clear on your slides, but look less-than-okay in your Presenter project. If you want crisp tables, screenshots, and graphics, you'll want to read and maybe even dog-ear this section.

Simple Graphics

I (Patti) often develop simple graphics like flowcharts, organizational charts, and graphics made up of PowerPoint shapes to use in my Presenter projects. What works best for me to have them come out clearly is producing them on blank (white, blank layout) PowerPoint slides and then saving each graphic/slide as .png files. I then bring these files into an image editing program if there is too much white space around the image (SnagIt is my fave) to crop out excess white space. I then resave (still as .png). I then add these graphics to the appropriate project slide.

Tables

I like tables. Maybe I like them too much. But the tables I produce in PowerPoint don't look so hot when I publish slides with them in Presenter. What works best for me is building the tables in a Word document and then cutting and pasting the tables into an image editing program (SnagIt) and cropping, if needed. These are saved as .png files and then added to the appropriate project slides. One plus of building and using .png files this way is that you will have graphics and tables "source files" to edit and reuse in the future if you need them. (Chances are you'll need them.)

Screenshots

Dave Mozealous, Articulate QA Manager, wrote a blog posting (www.mozealous.com) about how to get great-looking screenshots (in other words, unfuzzy) in Articulate Presenter '09. Since this is an issue that concerns lots of Presenter users, we'll share the gist of it here.

Dave says that the crux of the fuzzy screenshot problem has to do with three things: scaling (changing the size of) bitmapped images, using the wrong image file type, and not un-scaling the images when they are placed on PowerPoint slides.

He says that no matter what program you use to resize screenshots, the result is a fuzzier screenshot. Not good. Getting around this problem requires making sure that the Presenter player is an optimal size, creating screenshots that are 720 pixels wide by 540 pixels high (or smaller), saving screenshots as .png files, and undoing the scaling that PowerPoint does automatically.

Getting Clear Screenshots

1. On the Articulate tab or menu (in PowerPoint), select **Player Templates**.

2. Click **Other.**

3. Select **Lock presentation at optimal size** from the Presentation size menu (the optimal size is 720 pixels wide by 540 pixels high).

4. Take your screenshots and save each in the PNG file format. Screenshots need to be smaller than or equal to 720 pixels wide by 540 pixels high (crop out extra space in an image editing program if needed, but don't resize the screenshot).

5. Note the size of each screenshot by right-clicking the saved image file (in the folder where you are saving screenshot files) and selecting the **Details** tab. The image dimensions in pixels are shown on this tab. (Write this information down.)

6. In PowerPoint, insert each screenshot on the desired slide.

7. Now we have a problem to solve. PowerPoint *automatically* scales inserted images, so we need to un-scale them. In addition, PowerPoint shows the size of images in inches, but we only know the size in pixels, so pixels need to be converted into inches.

Tip: Articulate has a pixels to inches conversion tool at http://www.articulate.com/blog/demos/pixel_form.html.

8. Now resize the image in PowerPoint so it is no longer scaled. Right-click the screenshot on the slide and select **Size and Position**. On the Size tab, enter the *non-scaled* picture size in inches (calculated from the original size in pixels in step 5).

9. Click the **Close** button.

Adding Animation

Animation in PowerPoint means adding visual or sound effects to objects on the slide. Animation effects often occur over time (for example, lines of bulleted text are added in succession). Having lines of bulleted text appear in sync with narration helps the viewer focus on narration rather than reading the rest of the bulleted text on the slide. Animated objects can also change in relationship to other objects on the screen (for example, as new objects are added to the screen, previously added objects can fade.

The good news is that you can create animations in PowerPoint and bring them into Presenter. This functionality brings a wonderful level of flexibility to graphic images and text on each slide.

This section is intended to help you develop PowerPoint animations that are useful for *learning*. Just because you can make things fly around on the slide doesn't mean you should. (You probably shouldn't.) You may want to reread the section in Chapter 3, "Introduction to Presenter," about viewer frustration to remind yourself of what *not* to do when adding objects to a slide.

Animations can be applied to objects (graphics and text) on the slide. There are four types of PowerPoint animations:

■ Entrance animations—to make objects appear on the slide

■ Emphasis animations—to change objects on the slide from one state to another (such as from not bold to bold or from green to orange)

■ Exit animations—to make objects disappear from the slide

■ Motion path animations—to make objects move along a specified path on the slide

There is a long list of custom animation effects that you can use in PowerPoint, but not all of them can be brought into Presenter. Tables 4.3 through 4.6 show which PowerPoint entrance, emphasis, exit, and motion path animations are supported in Presenter. Table 4.7 shows other PowerPoint animations that are *not* supported in Presenter. "Fully supported" means that the animation, when brought into Presenter, will act the same as it acts in PowerPoint. "Supported with changes" means that the animation, when brought into Presenter, will work but with some changes. "Not supported" means that the animation won't work in Presenter.

Support for PowerPoint Animations

Table 4.3. Presenter support for entrance animations

Entrance animations				
Fully supported	Appear	Ascend	Boomerang	Bounce
	Box	Center Revolve	Circle	Compress
	Crawl In	Credits	Curve Up	Descend
	Ease In	Expand	Fade	Fade Zoom
	Faded Swirl	Flash Once	Flip	Float
	Fly In	Fold	Glide	Grow & Turn
	Magnify	Peek In	Pinwheel	Random Effects
	Rise Up	Sling	Spinner	Spiral In
	Split	Stretch	Strips	Swish
	Swivel	Thread	Unfold	Whip
	Wipe	Zoom		
Supported with changes	*Fade animation is substituted:* Blinds Checkerboard Diamond	Dissolve In Plus Random Bars Wedge Wheel	*Edge does not skew:* Light Speed	
Not supported	Color Typewriter			

Table 4.4. Presenter support for emphasis animations

Emphasis animations				
Fully supported	Blast	Blink	Brush on Color	Color Blend
	Color Wave	Darken	Darken Desaturate	Flash Bulb
	Flicker	Grow/Shrink	Grow w/Color	Lighten
	Spin	Teeter	Transparency	Vertical Highlight
	Wave			
Not supported	Bold Flash	Bold Reveal	Brush on Underline	Change Fill Color
	Change Font	Change Font Color	Change Font Size	Change Font Style
	Change Line Color	Complementary Color	Complementary Color 2	Contrasting Color
	Shimmer	Style Emphasis		

Table 4.5. Presenter support for exit animations

Exit animations				
Fully supported	Ascend	Boomerang	Bounce Sink Down	Box
	Center Revolve	Circle	Collapse	Contract
	Crawl Out	Credits	Curve Down	Descend
	Disappear	Ease Out	Fade	Faded Swivel
	Faded Zoom	Flash Once	Flip	Float
	Fly Out	Fold	Glide	Grow & Turn
	Light Speed	Magnify	Peek Out	Pinwheel
	Plus	Random Bars	Random Effects	Sling
	Spinner	Spiral Out	Split	Stretchy
	Strips	Swish	Swivel	Thread
	Unfold	Whip	Wipe	Zoom
Supported with changes	*Fade animation is substituted:*	Diamond	Wedge	
		Dissolve Out	Wheel	
	Blinds			
	Checkerboard			
Not supported	Color Typewriter			

Table 4.6. Presenter support for motion path animations

Motion path animations (reverse direction and auto reverse only)				
Fully supported	4 Point Star	5 Point Star	6 Point Star	8 Point Star
	Arc Down	Arc Left	Arc Right	Arc Up
	Bean	Bounce Left	Bounce Right	Buzz Saw
	Circle	Crescent Moon	Curved Square	Curved X
	Curvy Left, Curvy Right	Curvy Star	Decaying Wave	Diagonal Down Right
	Diagonal Up Right	Diamond	Down	Draw Custom Path
	Equal Triangle	Figure 8 Four	Football	Funnel
	Heart	Heartbeat	Hexagon	Horizontal Figure 8
	Inverted Square	Inverted Triangle	Left	Loop de Loop
	Neutron	Octagon	Parallelogram	Peanut
	Pentagon	Plus	Pointy Star	Right
	Right Triangle	S Curve 1	S Curve 2	Sine Wave
	Spiral Left	Spring	Square	Stairs Down
	Swoosh	Teardrop	Trapezoid	Turn Down
	Turn Down Right	Turn Up	Turn Up Right	Up Wave
	Vertical Figure 8	Zigzag		

Table 4.7. Other unsupported animations

Unsupported animations		
Not supported	Transition effects between slides	Animation using a trigger "Start effect on click of…"
	Chart effects	Animations contained in the slide master
	Text "by letter" or "by word," and in reverse order	After animation effect options to "Hide After Animation" and "Hide on Next Mouse Click"
	Repeats	Timing option to "Rewind when done playing"
	PowerPoint sound effects	Animated GIFs (alternate recommendation is to convert to SWF format, then insert via Articulate> Flash Movie)

Animation Help

Animation is a hefty topic. In this book we are barely scratching the surface of what is possible, so you should use your help documents to find out how to create different types of animation in your version of PowerPoint. Figure 4.19 shows the result of a search of the help documents in PowerPoint 2007 using the search term "animations." In case you are new to creating PowerPoint animations, we have highlighted three topics you might find immediately useful.

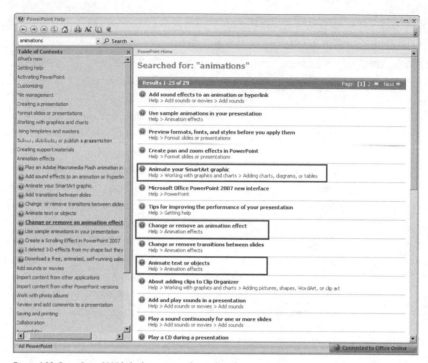

Figure 4.19. PowerPoint 2007 help documents with search on "animations"

Animating Objects

You can animate objects on the slide using built-in animations and custom animations. Although using built-in animations is simpler, we
recommend using custom animation because it allows more control.
The instructions below pertain to custom animation.

To animate an object, select the object to be animated and click the
Animations tab (in PowerPoint 2007) or select **Custom Animation**
from the **Slide Show** menu (in PowerPoint 2000-2003). Select the animation you want to use.

Once you have selected the animation, you can choose how the
animation will work using the Custom Animation pane, as shown on
the right in Figure 4.20.

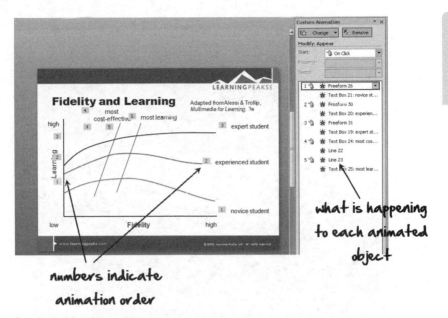

Figure 4.20. Slide and Custom Animation pane

All of the animations in Figure 4.20 are entrance animations. Each animation causes one line in the graph and a corresponding text box to appear on the slide in succession.

Tip: After you add an animation effect, make sure it works the way you want it to using the Preview button on the Articulate tab!

Appropriate Animations for Presenter Projects

Animations make screens more complex to process mentally, so they should be used for the right purposes (eye candy isn't the right purpose). Typically the right purpose is to focus viewers' attention or show how something works.

Focus Attention

Figure 4.21 shows an example from Bozarth's book *Better Than Bullet Points* that illustrates what parts of the body are affected when someone smokes a cigarette. In this animation, each body part is highlighted (emphasis animation) and explanatory text is displayed (entrance animation) as the animated dotted line moves from the mouth to the heart. In this animation, the focus is on one organ at a time.

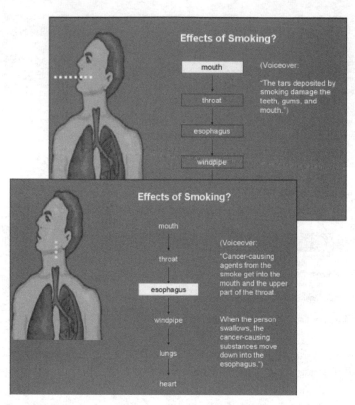

Figure 4.21. Animation showing body parts affected by cigarette smoke (from *Better Than Bullet Points*; reprinted with permission of John Wiley & Sons, Inc.)

Show How Something Works

An example from Bozarth's book of using animation to show how something works is shown in Figure 4.22. This animation shows the proper order for placing objects into a grocery bag, from heaviest to lightest. The animation was created using motion paths, which allow you to specify the route that objects take to get to their final destination on the slide. Right-clicking each object once it gets to the bag and choosing "Order—Send to Back" makes each item disappear behind the bag, as if it were placed in the bag.

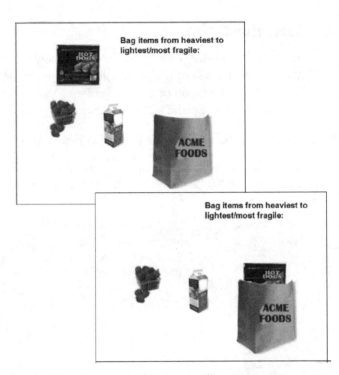

Figure 4.22. Animation showing how to bag groceries (from *Better Than Bullet Points*; reprinted with permission of John Wiley & Sons, Inc.)

Here are some ideas for using slide animations in your Presenter projects. Some of these are our ideas and others come from Bozarth's book.

- Illustrate changes over time, such as average budget in each block of five years since 1990.

- Show motion or direction, such as the direction in which ground water flows east of the Continental Divide and west of the Continental Divide.

- Demonstrate how to operate a piece of equipment, such as how to operate a waffle maker.

- Illustrate demographic differences, such as the median retirement age in a group of countries.

- Animate problem solving steps, such as the steps for calculating a 15% tip after a restaurant meal.

- Show how something looks up close, farther away, and very far away.

Writing the Narration Script

In this section, we'll discuss the second step in the Presenter workflow: Write the narration script. The narration script is what you want the narrator (who may be you or someone else) to say while recording the narration for a specific slide in Presenter.

Using the PowerPoint Notes Pane to Hold the Narration Script

The best way to build your narration script is to put the narration script for each slide in the Notes pane of each slide, as shown in Figure 4.23.

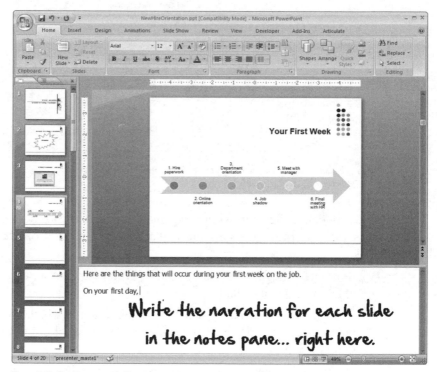

Figure 4.23. The Notes pane in Normal view

You can create the narration script as you create each slide or you can create the narration script after all the slides are created. There are plusses and minuses for both approaches.

If you create the script at the same time as you create the slides, it'll probably be easier to come up with the narration because you'll be fresh on the points that need to be made about each slide. You should also be able to see if additional slides or narration are needed or if there are gaps in information.

If you wait until you are done building the slides to create the narration script, you'll be able to monitor the flow of information as it proceeds from one slide to another. In the former case, problems with details may be more apparent. In the latter case, problems with the entire presentation may be more apparent. In either case, before recording you'll want to review the slides and narration from beginning to end to catch problems.

Tip: No matter how carefully you review the narration script, you are likely to catch even more problems while recording. It's the nature of the beast. The good news is that Presenter makes it extremely easy to rerecord the narration for one or many slides.

The advantage of entering the narration script for each slide into the Notes pane in PowerPoint, even if you build the narration script in another tool such as Word, becomes obvious in Figure 4.24.

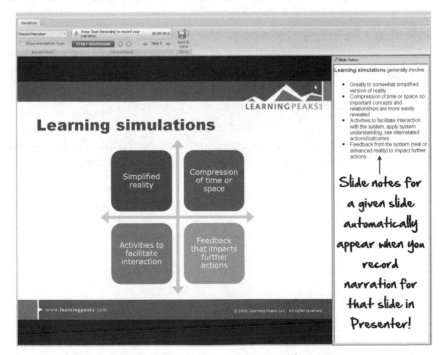

Figure 4.24. Text notes from PowerPoint are visible (when recording narration) in Presenter.

If the narration script that corresponds to each slide is entered in the Notes pane in PowerPoint, then these same notes will display when you are recording narration for that slide in Presenter. It's like a Presenter teleprompter!

Good Narration Scripts

In this section, we'd like to offer some rules of the road for writing a good narration script.

- Less is more. Your narration script for each slide should be concise and to the point.

- Know your audience. Narration should be easy to follow and understand *for the intended audience*.

- Write for hearing, not for print. Use short, conversational sentences, with natural breaks.

- Before recording, read your narration script for each slide out loud numerous times, making changes as needed, until the narration sounds conversational.

- Pause for effect if you are about to say, or have just said, something really important.

- Be aware of alliteration, the repetition of an initial consonant in words that are adjacent or close together. Alliteration makes the sentence hard to say and often hard to understand. (You already know this—remember trying to say "Peter Piper picked a peck of pickled peppers" several times in a row?)

- For a word that is hard to pronounce or that the narrator might not know how to pronounce, spell the word phonetically adjacent to the appearance of the word in the narration script.

Writing for reading aloud is a special skill. Most people aren't good at writing for hearing until they have practiced doing so over time.

Practice

To practice the skills described in this chapter, we recommend that you select a bite-sized project to practice with. Build the slides for that bite-sized project using this chapter and use the help documents, as needed, to add text, graphics, animations, and other objects. Then write, practice, and edit the narration script. When you are done, your slides can be augmented with narration in Presenter as you read the next chapter!

Check This Out

Tom Kuhlmann, the author of the Rapid E-Learning blog on the Articulate web site (http://www.articulate.com/rapid-elearning), has some great ideas about PowerPoint. Make a point to search for the following blog entries and sign up to get new ones automatically:

How Walt Disney Would Use PowerPoint to Create E-Learning Courses

January 15, 2008

The following articles are archived in Articulate's blog at http://www.articulate.com/blog. Just type a few of the key words in the search box to find the relevant topic.

Articulate 101: Add Animations to Your Next E-Learning Course

February 5, 2008

Build a Puzzle Animation in Just a Few Simple Steps

September 9, 2008

5 Must-Know PowerPoint Tips That Will Save You Time

September 16, 2008

The Hidden PowerPoint Shortcut Everyone Should Know

September 23, 2008

How to Be More Productive When Using PowerPoint to Create E-Learning Courses

September 30, 2008

5 Easy Tips to Whip Your Slides Into Shape

October 7, 2008

When It Makes Sense to Pay for Professional Narration

November 4, 2008

Chapter Recap

This chapter contains information about building the slides that you will use in your Presenter project. Here's our list of the most important things to remember from this chapter:

- The slides you use in your Presenter project are the foundation of the project. If they don't "work," your project will struggle to get beyond the problems with your slides.

- You are promoting ideas and actions with every Presenter project you build. Take care that the slides you develop promote the message you want viewers to receive.

- Appropriate designs are tailored to the topic and the audience. An appropriate design looks professional, not homegrown.

- Make sure the graphics you select convey the tone and message you want to convey. Serious topic, serious graphics. Resist the temptation to use humor unless it's appropriate and likely to be acceptable to all viewers.

- Those viewing your project should be able to quickly answer the question "What's in it for me?" so they can determine whether to pay more than very limited attention to your project.

- Use *much less text*—Whatever text you start with, it's too much. Probably *way too much*. No long paragraphs of text. No bullet lists with full sentences.

- PowerPoint slide masters should be used to globally apply a specific look and feel to all of the slides in your project.

- PowerPoint 2007 and PowerPoint 2000-2003 operate differently for some tasks. Use the help documents to find out how to do the tasks discussed in this chapter. That is especially true for creating slide masters and adding animation.

- There are a ton of things you can do with graphics and animation in PowerPoint. SmartArt is very cool! Many of these animations can be brought into Presenter—but check the tables in this chapter to be sure.

- Animations make screens more complex to process mentally, so they should be used for the right purpose (eye candy isn't the right purpose). Typically that purpose is to focus viewers' attention or show how something works. Resist the temptation to use lots of gratuitous graphics or animations!

- If the narration script that corresponds to each slide is entered in the Slide Notes pane in PowerPoint, then the slide notes from PowerPoint will display when you record narration for each slide in Presenter.

- You can create the narration script for each slide as you create each slide or you can create the narration script after all the slides are created.

- Writing for reading aloud is hard to do. We provide some insights about how to do this toward the end of this chapter in the section titled "Good Narration Scripts."

Chapter 5

Presenter Basics

Chapter Snapshot

In this chapter, you'll learn the basic skills that are common to building information and instruction using Presenter.

In the last chapter we discussed building good PowerPoint slides as the foundation of a Presenter project and completing the first two steps in the Presenter 1-2-3-4-5 workflow: 1. Create slides and 2. Write narration script. Now it's time to jump into the next three steps of the Presenter 1-2-3-4-5 workflow: 3. Add media and interactions, 4. Customize the player, and 5. Publish.

Dave Mozealous, Articulate QA Manager (blog: http://www.mozealous.com), and Tom Kuhlmann, the author of the Rapid E-Learning blog (http://www.articulate.com/rapid-elearning), contributed numerous tips to this chapter.

> I have never used an authoring tool. I'm feeling anxious!

> Chill... Start with a simple project— PowerPoint slides and narration.

Revisiting the Presenter 1-2-3-4-5 Workflow

In this and the next chapter we'll discuss the third step in the Presenter 1-2-3-4-5 workflow: Add media and interactions. This step is highlighted in Figure 5.1.

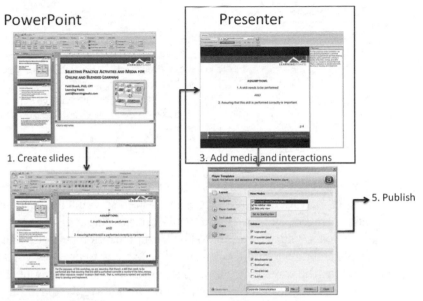

Figure 5.1. Presenter 1-2-3-4-5 workflow

Your Presenter project may include a wide variety of content and media. But almost all Presenter projects contain at least two items— PowerPoint slides (discussed in the last chapter) and narration. Narration is commonly used to:

■ Explain slide content.

■ Focus the viewer's attention on specific points or slide elements.

Narration typically explains the content on each slide, including specific areas of each slide or animations that may be occurring on the slide. (Notice that I said "explain slide content," not "read slide content." Reading slides to viewers often creates frustration and is more boring than watching paint dry. Don't do it.) Table 5.1 shows the typical substeps completed in step 3 of the Presenter 1-2-3-4-5 workflow. As you can see, narration is only one of the options you can add to a project.

Table 5.1. Detailed workflow for step 3

Using Presenter		
3. Add media and interactions	a)	Add media and interactions (narration, attachments, Engage interactions, Quizmaker questions, Web Objects, Flash video, other).
	b)	Review and revise narration script to go along with media, interactions, and annotations and record or rerecord, if needed.
	c)	Preview and fix (throughout).

You may think narration is too small of a step to take up an entire chapter, but narration is a big part of Presenter, so you'll be learning how to add narration, sync narration to any PowerPoint animations you included in your PowerPoint slides, edit narration, and edit slide notes while adding narration. We'll also discuss how to preview your project all along the way. We'll end with a very brief tutorial on publishing your project so you can see how publishing works. We'll expand upon adding media and interactions in Chapter 6, "Pumping Up Your Presenter Projects," and upon publishing your project in Chapter 26, "Publishing." And if you want to customize the player, the window that viewers see when they view a project, Chapter 7, "Customizing Presenter Player Templates," will help you do that.

At the end of this chapter, you'll have the skills to create a basic Presenter project.

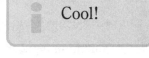

Cool!

Moving from PowerPoint to Presenter

In Chapter 4, "First, Your PowerPoint Slides," we discussed how to make sure that the PowerPoint slides you build for your Presenter project will have the desired impact. We then talked about getting your slides ready for Presenter. These two steps form the foundation of all Presenter projects and they should be completed before you start working with Presenter.

Once you have completed steps 1 and 2 in PowerPoint, you are ready to complete step 3, in Presenter.

As we've said before, working in Presenter means using the Articulate tab or menu (depending on the version of PowerPoint you are running) that was added when you installed Presenter to complete the Presenter tasks. So although we are now working with Presenter, you are doing this inside of PowerPoint.

In the sections that follow, we'll discuss the tab or menu that is installed in PowerPoint and how to complete the one task that is common to almost all Presenter projects: adding narration.

Launching Presenter

Presenter can be launched (opened) through either Presenter '09 or PowerPoint. You can launch Presenter using any of the following procedures:

- In Windows XP: Click the **Start** button, select **All Programs**, select **Articulate**, and select **Articulate Presenter '09**.

- In Windows Vista: Click the **Start** button, select **All Programs**, open the **Articulate** folder, and select **Articulate Presenter '09**.

- Double-click the **Articulate Presenter '09** shortcut icon on your desktop.

- Double-click a **PowerPoint** (.ppt or .pptx) or **Presenter** (.ppta) file.

Prior to this version, users produced the PowerPoint slides they wanted to use for a Presenter project and then used the Articulate menu installed in PowerPoint when Presenter is installed to add narration, interactions, and so on. In this new version of Presenter, users can launch Presenter by launching PowerPoint, as they did before (and use the installed tab—in PowerPoint 2007—or menu—in PowerPoint 2000-2003), or launch the Presenter application and then launch PowerPoint from the Presenter startup screen using the Launch PowerPoint button, highlighted in Figure 5.2.

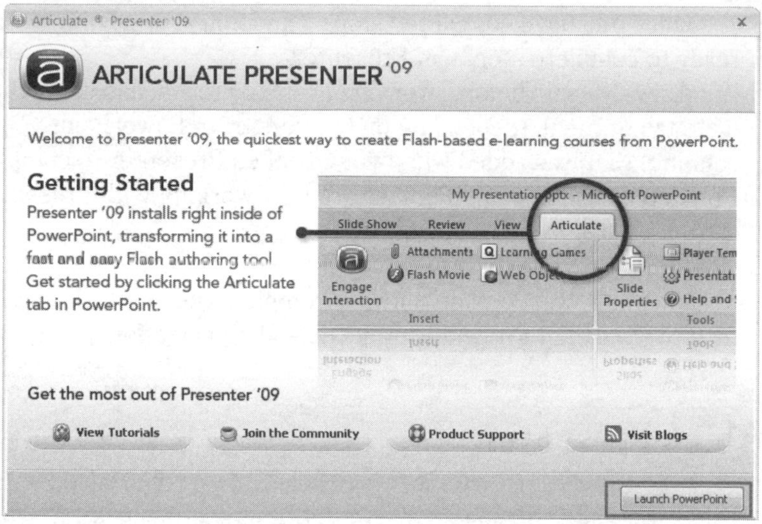

Figure 5.2. The Presenter startup screen with the Launch PowerPoint button highlighted in the bottom-right corner

If you are new to Presenter or to certain features, opening Presenter first provides ready links to some resources that may be very useful for beginners and anyone who needs help. When you launch PowerPoint from the Presenter startup screen, PowerPoint opens a blank presentation. To continue working on an existing presentation, navigate to the existing presentation and open it. Or you can simply open the existing presentation and click the Articulate tab or menu.

Tip: When working on an existing Presenter project, opening either the PowerPoint file (.ppt or .pptx) or the Presenter file (.ppta) will get you to the exact same place.

Exploring the Articulate Tab and Menu

Articulate works with PowerPoint 2000-2003, but it is designed to work especially well with PowerPoint 2007.

> ? Aaaahhhh! I don't have PowerPoint 2007!!!

> i It works with PowerPoint 2000-2003, too.

In PowerPoint 2007 (as in other Office 2007 applications), the familiar menus and toolbars have been replaced with the *ribbon*. The ribbon organizes PowerPoint buttons and menu items, such as bolding text and changing the slide layout, into logical groups, and the logical groups are arranged by tabs. Figure 5.3 shows the ribbon in PowerPoint 2007 with the Articulate tab of the ribbon selected.

Tab vs. Menu

When you install Presenter, the Articulate tab (in PowerPoint 2007) or the Articulate menu (in PowerPoint 2000-2003) is installed into the PowerPoint application. So the Presenter application "lives" inside PowerPoint. Whether you are using the Articulate tab (Figure 5.3) or the Articulate menu (Figure 5.4), the Articulate tasks and functions are identical.

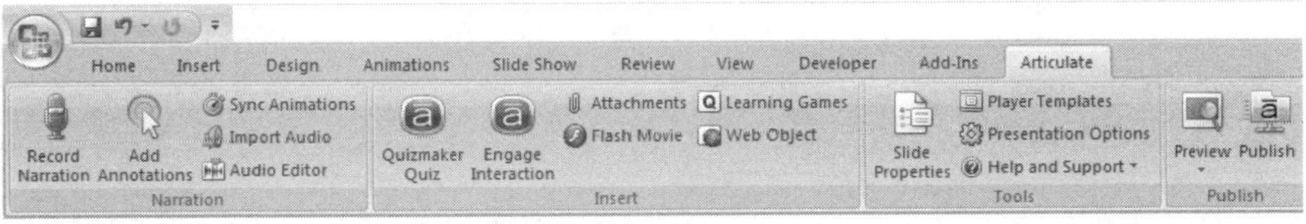

Figure 5.3. The Articulate tab on the PowerPoint ribbon in PowerPoint 2007

Figure 5.4. The
Articulate menu in
PowerPoint 2000-2003

Table 5.2 lists the button and menu items that appear on the Articulate tab in PowerPoint 2007 and the corresponding menu items on the Articulate menu for PowerPoint 2000-2003 in the order that they appear. Once again, you can see that the items are identical even though two of the items (Preview and Publish) appear last on the Articulate tab and first on the Articulate menu.

Table 5.2. Items on the Articulate tab and menu

Items on the Articulate tab (PowerPoint 2007)	Items on the Articulate menu (PowerPoint 2000-2003)
Narration group:	Preview
Record Narration	Publish
Add Annotations	Record Narration
Sync Animations	Add Annotations
Import Audio	Sync Animations
Audio Editor	Import Audio
Insert group:	Audio Editor
Quizmaker Quiz	Quizmaker Quiz
Engage Interaction	Engage Interaction
Attachments	Insert Flash Movie
Flash Movie	Insert Web Object
Learning Games	Insert Learning Game
Web Object	Attachments
Tools group:	Slide Properties
Slide Properties	Player Templates
Player Templates	Presentation Options
Presentation Options	Help and Support
Help and Support	About Articulate Presenter '09
Publish group:	
Preview	
Publish	

> ℹ See—they're the same!

Windows, Dialog Boxes, and Menus

After you build your slides in PowerPoint, the rest of the work you will do to build a Presenter project will be done using Presenter's task windows, dialog boxes, and menus. Figures 5.5 through 5.7 show examples of a Presenter task window, dialog box, and menu, respectively, that will open when you select the corresponding buttons or menu items on the Articulate tab or menu.

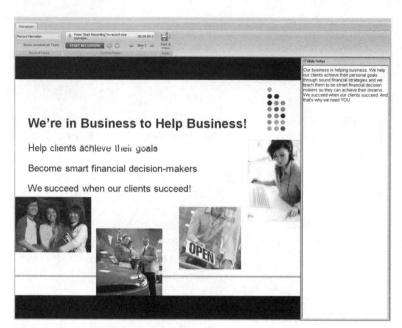

Figure 5.5. The Consolidated Recording window

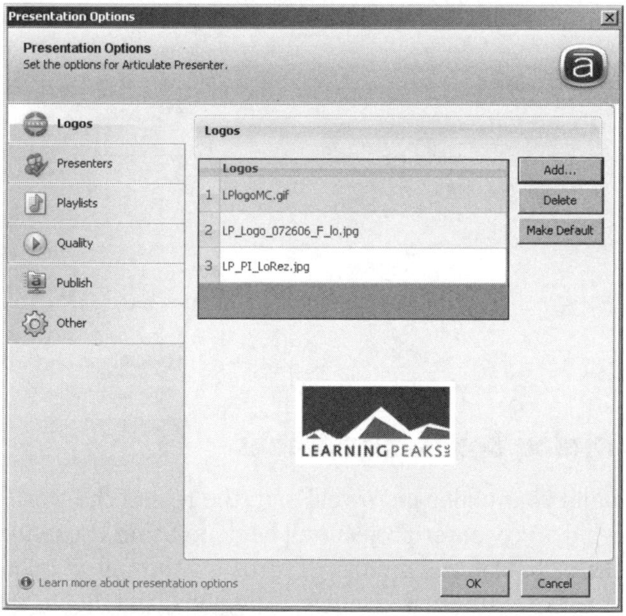

Figure 5.6. The Presentation Options dialog box

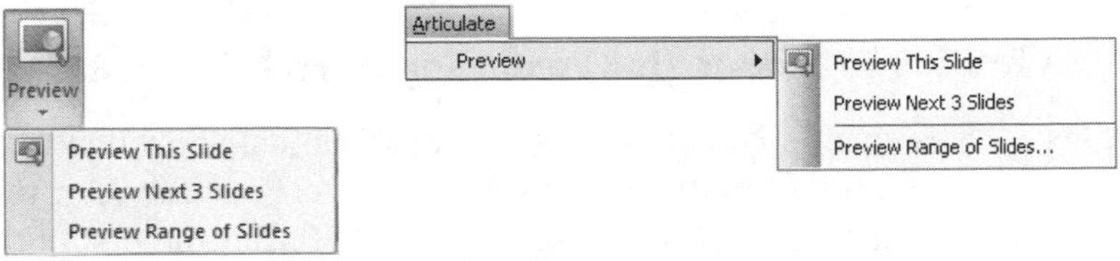

Figure 5.7. The Preview menu on the Articulate tab (left) and the Articulate menu (right)

Help from the Articulate Tab or Menu

Help options were discussed in Chapter 1, but it's helpful to know that they are available from the Articulate tab or menu (shown in Figure 5.8).

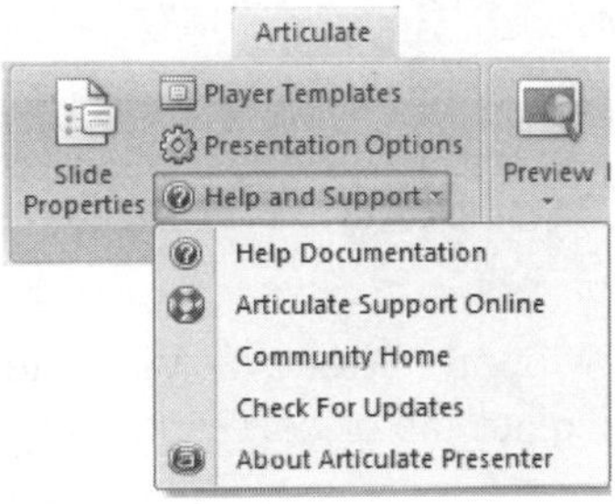

Figure 5.8. The Help and Support menu on the Articulate tab (above) and the Help and Support menu selection on the Articulate menu (right)

You Say To-may-to (tab) and I Say To-mah-to (menu)

This chapter contains many screenshots that show how each task is selected from the Articulate tab (PowerPoint 2007) or the Articulate menu (PowerPoint 2000-2003). But the rest of the Presenter chapters in this book typically show screenshots of the *button and menu items on the Articulate tab*. If you are using PowerPoint 2000-2003, don't let the differences in how the Articulate buttons and menu items are accessed (from a tab or menu) throw you. They are exactly the same items, accessed either from the Articulate tab or the Articulate menu. And no matter whether the tab or menu is used, they launch *identical* task windows, dialog boxes, and menus.

Exploring the Consolidated Recording Window

The Consolidated Recording window opens whenever you select one of the following buttons on the Articulate tab or corresponding menu selection on the Articulate menu.

■ **Record Narration:** Used to record narration that goes along with each slide. Can also be used to record narration that syncs with (PowerPoint) slide animations.

■ **Add Annotations:** Used to add annotations to slides.

■ **Sync Animations:** Used to synchronize *already recorded* narration with (PowerPoint) slide animations.

When the Consolidated Recording window opens, you can do any of these tasks by selecting it from the Record Mode group of the ribbon.

Figure 5.9. The Consolidated Recording window ribbon

Recording and Editing Narration

Recording and editing narration in Presenter is a very common task. In this section of the chapter, we'll help you get up and running on doing those tasks.

Getting Ready to Record Narration

Before you record narration, you'll need a microphone (unless you are lucky enough to have a sound studio that has the equipment that you'll need). Justin Wilcox, a senior support engineer at Articulate, provides some good advice on buying a microphone (the original article is here: http://www.articulate.com/blog/articulate-101-microphone-selection) that we are adapting in this section. You can use either a headset or a desktop microphone, and each has advantages and disadvantages.

Headset microphones require little effort to learn how to use and can generate acceptable audio quality. That's what I (Patti) use. But if your mouth is too close to the microphone, you may record some noises (often called "pop" noises). If you use a headset microphone, make sure you use a "windscreen" that goes over the end of the microphone to reduce pop noises. If your headset doesn't come with a windscreen, buy one that does or buy a windscreen for your headset microphone.

Desktop microphones also may require some effort to learn how to use and can also generate acceptable audio quality. It's more difficult to maintain a constant distance from a desktop microphone, which can affect volume and clarity. Desktop microphones don't come with windscreens, so the popping issue can arise here as well if the narrator is too close to the microphone. In another article on narration (the original article is here: http://www.articulate.com/blog/articulate-101-recording-tips), Justin says that the optimal distance between your mouth and the microphone is 8 to 12 inches. And the best placement of the microphone is slightly off to the side but pointing to your mouth. If you use a desktop microphone, get a stand for it rather than trying to hold it and use the computer at the same time.

Justin suggests not using the noise-cancelling feature on some microphones, but I haven't had any problems with that feature when I use my headset microphone. He also recommends a unidirectional microphone for recording narration because it isn't likely to pick up room noises. He recommends USB connections for your microphones.

Recording Narration

The Record Narration button on the Articulate tab and the Record Narration menu selection in the Articulate menu are shown in Figure 5.10. When you click the Record Narration button or select the Record Narration menu selection, the Consolidated Recording window is launched. You use the ribbon at the top to perform all narration tasks.

Figure 5.10. The Record Narration button (above) and the Record Narration menu selection (right)

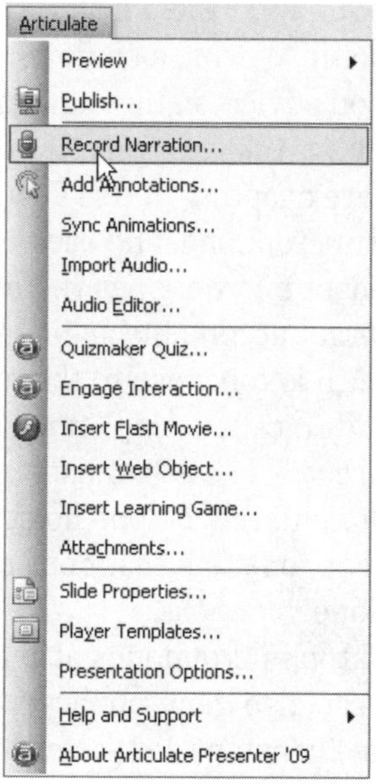

Figure 5.11 shows an example of a slide open in PowerPoint that contains animations. The numbers indicate the order in which the objects will appear on the screen. It is easy to record slides with animations (if you have any) and slides without animations in the same recording session.

If a slide has no animations, you record the narration, listen to the recording (and rerecord, if needed), and then move to the next slide. If a slide has animations, you record the narration that goes along with each animation segment, listen to the recording (and rerecord, if needed), and then move to the next slide.

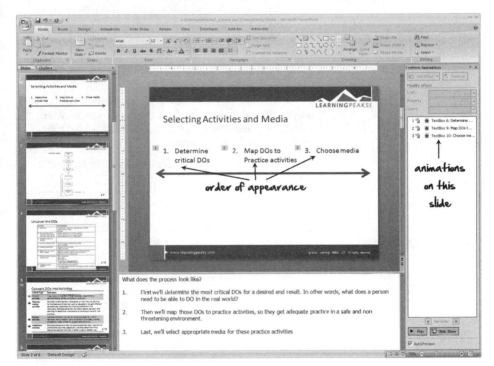

Figure 5.11. PowerPoint slides with animations

Table 5.3 describes the recording task options available in the ribbon of the Consolidated Recording window.

Table 5.3. Recording narration options

Task options	What happens
Start recording START RECORDING	Clicking the Start Recording button begins recording for the selected slide.
Stop recording STOP RECORDING	Clicking Stop Recording ends recording for the selected slide. The Start Recording button becomes a Stop Recording button as soon as recording begins if the selected slide has no PowerPoint animations or the last PowerPoint animation on the selected slide is being recorded.
Next animation NEXT ANIMATION	Clicking Next Animation begins recording for the next PowerPoint animation on the selected slide. The Start Recording button becomes a Next Animation button if the selected slide has PowerPoint animations left to be recorded. When all animation segments have been recorded, the Next Animation button becomes a Stop Recording button.
Play ▶	Clicking the Play button plays the narration recorded for the selected slide.
Pause ⏸	Clicking the Pause button pauses recording or playback for the selected slide.
Resume RESUME	Clicking the Resume button resumes recording or playback for the selected slide.
Slide selector ⬅ Slide 6 ➡	Clicking the forward and backward arrows navigates forward and backward to different slides. The forward arrow is commonly used to move to the next slide when you have completed recording the selected slide. You can also use the menu (click the down arrow under the slide number) to see slide thumbnails and additional information about each slide.
Save and close 💾 Save & Close	Clicking the Save & Close button saves your project and closes the Consolidated Recording window.

Recording Narration (Including Syncing Narration to PowerPoint Animations)

1. Open the PowerPoint slides you wish to narrate. Make sure that the slide notes (the narration script) are complete or complete them before recording so you can use them as a narration script.

2. Select the slide on which you want to start your narration.

3. Connect a microphone or headset with microphone to your PC.

4. Click the **Record Narration** button on the Articulate tab or select this option from the Articulate menu. The Consolidated Recording window opens.

5. Make sure that **Record Narration** is selected in the Record Mode menu.

6. For slides *without* animations:
   a. Click the **Start Recording** button. Read the slide notes to narrate that slide. You can tell that you are recording a slide without animations because the **Stop Recording** button appears, the microphone icon is flashing, and the time counter is counting (see Figure 5.12).

Figure 5.12. Microphone and time counter

   b. When you have completed narration for that slide, click the **Stop Recording** button.

7. For slides *with* animations:
   a. Click the **Start Recording** button. Read the slide notes to narrate the initial segment of that slide (what appears onscreen when the slide appears). You can tell that you are recording a slide with animations because the Next Animation button appears, the number of animations left to record is shown (see Figure 5.13), the microphone icon is flashing, and the time counter is counting.

Figure 5.13. Animations left to record

   b. Continue to click the **Next Animation** button until all anima-
       tions are on the screen and the narration for the selected slide
       is completed.

   c. When you have completed narrating all animation segments for
       that slide, click the **Stop Recording** button.

8. Click the **Play** button ⦿ to listen to the recording for that slide. If
    you are unsatisfied with it, you can rerecord it by clicking the
    Start Recording button and following the directions in step 6 or
    7. (You can also go back and do this later, if needed.)

9. Click the forward slide selector arrow to go to the next slide. You
    can also jump to any other slide by clicking the Thumbnails menu
    under the slide selector.

10. Click the **Save & Close** button when you are done.

---

66 **Note:** When you rerecord narration for a slide, the previous nar-
    ration is replaced by the new narration.

▶**Tip:** It is *extremely* easy to rerecord narration for a single slide
or numerous slides, so don't worry about changing your mind.

Getting Ready to Narrate

Practice reading your script from start to finish in advance of
recording because it will cut down on mistakes and tripping over
your words (it happens!) and give you an opportunity to change
the slide notes before recording. You can either record all the
way through or record, replay, and if necessary rerecord each
slide until you are satisfied with the recording.

   While recording narration, leave a second of silence before
and after the narration for each slide so that the narration doesn't
get cut off at the beginning or end.

Importing Audio

You may choose to import audio rather than record it in Presenter. For example, you may use professional voice talent to record audio for use in your Presenter projects (because it sounds, well, more "professional"). Or you may prefer to record narration using external applications with more audio editing options.

Importing "outside" audio files into your project is easy. Table 5.4 shows the audio formats that can be imported into Presenter:

Table 5.4. Audio formats that can be imported into Presenter

File type	Formats
WAV	• PCM (Microsoft Pulse Code Modulation)
	• Microsoft ADPCM (Microsoft Adaptive Delta Pulse Code Modulation)
	• GSM 6.10 (Microsoft Groupe Spécial Mobile)
	• IMA ADPCM (Microsoft Interactive Multimedia Association) (4 bits per sample)
	• CCITT A-Law/G.711 CCITT u-Law (Microsoft International Telecommunications Union)
MP3	• MP3 (MPEG-1 Audio Layer 3)

To import audio, click the **Import Audio** button in the Articulate tab or select the **Import Audio** menu selection in the Articulate menu (Figure 5.14). The Import Audio window (Figure 5.15) is launched.

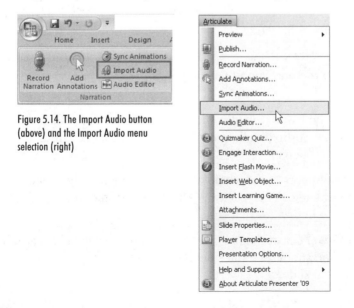

Figure 5.14. The Import Audio button (above) and the Import Audio menu selection (right)

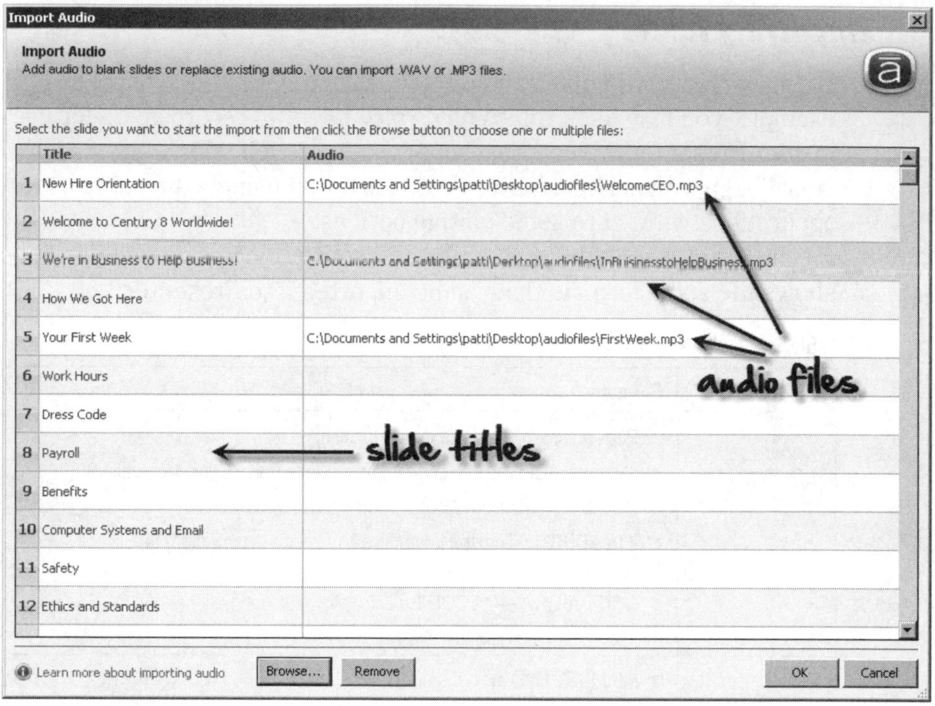

Figure 5.15. The Import Audio window

Importing Audio

1. Create .wav or .mp3 audio files to import or locate files that have already been created.

 Note: You can only import one audio file per slide.

---

2. Click the **Import Audio** button on the Articulate tab or select the **Import Audio** option from the Articulate menu. The Import Audio window opens.

3. In the Import Audio window, click the slide for which you want to import audio. Then click the **Browse** button to find the file you wish to import for that slide.

4. Once you select the file you want to import, click the **Open** button. You should see the selected file in the audio cell for the selected slide.

5. Continue to select slides and browse to the corresponding audio files until you are finished importing audio files.

6. If you made a mistake and put a file in the wrong location, you can remove the file by clicking the slide for which you want to delete audio and clicking the **Remove** button.

7. Click **OK** to close the Import Audio window.

8. Click **Preview** on the Articulate tab or **Preview** on the Articulate menu to hear the imported audio and note if any changes need to be made.

Importing Multiple Audio Files

If you want to import a series of files into your project, navigate to a folder that contains the files, select all of the files you want to include in your series, and click the **Open** button. The Confirm narration import order window will open and you can determine the order of the files or remove files, as needed. Click **OK** to close this window when sequencing is done. You will see that the files have been imported in the selected sequence.

Tip: Articulate says that imported .wav files are recommended over imported .mp3 files. The basic WAV settings that they recommend are:

- Bit rate: 16 bit
- Sampling rate: 44 kHz
- Encoding: PCM
- Format: WAV

Remember though that .wav files are typically larger than .mp3 files (for the same audio clip).

Importing .mp3 Files

If you decide to import .mp3 files rather than .wav files, you should make sure that they are Flash-supported files. If you choose to import .mp3 files, Articulate recommends using 192 Kbps .mp3 files. A full list of Flash-supported MP3 settings is provided here: http://www.articulate.com/blog/flash-supported-mp3-settings.

Editing Audio

Once you add audio, you may want to edit or "fix" parts of it. You may find, for example, that there's too much or too little silence before narration starts or there's a section of audio that needs to be deleted or the volume is too loud or too soft in places. The Audio Editor button in the Articulate tab and the Audio Editor menu selection in the Articulate menu (Figure 5.16) launches the Audio Editor (Figure 5.17), which you can use to make changes to audio you have recorded in Presenter or have imported.

Figure 5.16. The Audio Editor button (above) and the Audio Editor menu selection (right)

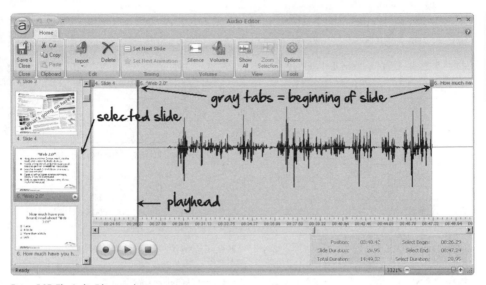

Figure 5.17. The Audio Editor window

At the top of the Audio Editor window is the ribbon, which contains buttons you will use to do the bulk of your editing work. The left pane shows a thumbnail of each slide from your PowerPoint file. The main area of the Audio Editor shows the waveform (the jagged line) of the audio that goes with the selected slide. The vertical line is the playhead, which marks the current location within the audio file being edited. At the bottom are player controls for Record (circle), Play/Pause (triangle), and Stop (square).

You can zoom in on the waveform by clicking and dragging a portion of the waveform (where you want to zoom in) and then clicking the **Zoom Selection** button in the ribbon. This is handy when you need to get very precise about where you want to start and stop the audio, add silence, and so on. You can use the **Show All** button to zoom back out.

What Else Does the Audio Editor Do?

The Audio Editor provides another way to record narration and import audio. This isn't covered here because we have already described how to record narration and import audio. But you may be interested in using the Audio Editor to record a word or sentence to insert into previously recorded audio clips.

Table 5.5 lists the buttons in the Audio Editor and describes each button's purpose.

Table 5.5. Audio Editor buttons and controls

Button	Purpose
Play	Plays the audio clip
Pause	Pauses the audio clip
Stop	Stops playing and resets the playhead to the beginning of the clip
Save & Close	Saves any changes you have made and closes the Audio Editor
Cut	Cuts the selected area from the waveform and puts it on the clipboard (so you can paste it elsewhere, if desired) (shortcut — Ctrl+X)
Copy	Copies the selected area on the waveform and puts it on the clipboard (so you can paste it elsewhere, if desired) (shortcut — Ctrl+C)
Paste	Pastes what is on the clipboard to the selected location
Import	Imports single or multiple files
Delete	Deletes the selected section of the audio clip (shortcut — Delete)
Set Next Slide	Sets next slide start point to the current point of the playhead on the waveform
Set Next Animation	Sets next animation start point to the current point of the playhead on the waveform
Silence	Opens the Insert Silence dialog box where a specified duration of silence can be added (at the playhead current position)
Volume	Opens the Change Volume dialog box where the volume of the selected portion of the waveform can be increased or decreased
Show All	Shows all audio (waveform for the whole project)
Zoom Selection	Zooms in on the selected portion of the waveform (waveform for selected portion)
Options	Sets playback and recording options

If the slide you are working on has animations, the animations appear in the Audio Editor as gray dots. Slide 6 in Figure 5.18 has two animations. You can also see where slides 6 and 7 begin because these are marked with gray tabs.

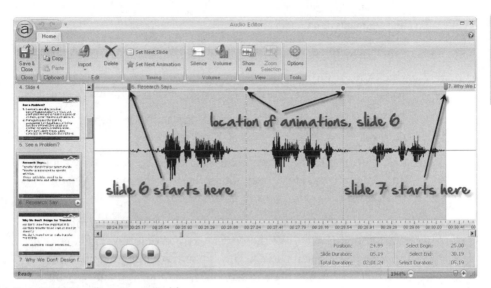

Figure 5.18. Location of animations in the slide

Selecting a Portion of the Waveform

A lot of the Audio Editor tasks involve acting on a "selected" portion of the waveform. You select a portion of the waveform by clicking inside the waveform and dragging to show the beginning and end points to be acted upon. This may require playing and pausing the clip and zooming in and out to make sure the starting and stopping locations are *exactly* where you need them to be. It pays to be exact.

Read this and commit it to memory—It will save you from screaming like someone stole your favorite pen! After you edit an audio clip, *listen to it immediately*. If you made a mistake (for example, you deleted a section of the clip you should not have deleted), click the **Undo** button at the top of the Audio Editor.

Deleting Segments of an Audio Clip

1. Make sure the slide containing the audio you want to edit is open.

2. Click the **Audio Editor** button on the Articulate tab or **Audio Editor** on the Articulate menu. The Audio Editor window opens.

3. Click the **Play** button to determine the approximate portion to be deleted.

4. Zoom in around the approximate section to be deleted by clicking and dragging to select a portion of the waveform and then clicking the **Zoom Selection** button in the ribbon.

5. Now play and pause the clip (as needed) to determine the exact start and stop points of the segment to be deleted. This may require playing and pausing the clip and zooming in and out to make sure the starting and stopping locations are *exactly* where you need them to be.

6. Select the segment to be deleted by clicking inside the waveform at the beginning of the section to be deleted and dragging to show the end of the section to be deleted.

7. Click the **Play** button to play the segment to be deleted to determine if the selection is accurate. If the beginning and end points of the segment need to be refined, they can be moved by clicking and dragging until the segment is just right.

8. Click the **Delete** button. The highlighted part of the clip is deleted.

9. Play the audio clip to be sure the delete is satisfactory. You can undo and repeat if necessary.

10. Click the **Save & Close** button.

Moving Audio

1. Make sure the slide containing the audio you want to edit is open.

2. Click the **Audio Editor** button on the Articulate tab or **Audio Editor** on the Articulate menu. The Audio Editor window opens.

3. Click the **Play** button to determine the approximate portion to be moved.

4. Zoom in around the approximate section to be moved by clicking and dragging to select a portion of the waveform and then clicking the **Zoom Selection** button in the ribbon.

5. Now play and pause the clip (as needed) to determine the exact start and stop points of the segment to be moved. This may require playing and pausing the clip and zooming in and out to make sure the starting and stopping locations are *exactly* where you need them to be. It pays to be exact.

6. Select the segment to be moved by clicking inside the waveform at the beginning of the section to be moved and dragging to show the end of the section to be moved.

7. Click the **Play** button to play the segment to be moved to determine if the selection is accurate. If the beginning and end points of the segment need to be refined, they can be moved by clicking and dragging until the segment is just right.

8. Click the **Cut** button. The highlighted part of the clip is cut from the existing clip.

9. Click in the waveform to the exact place to move the clip.

10. Click the **Paste** button. The clip is moved to the new location.

11. Play the audio clip to be sure the move is satisfactory. You can undo and repeat if necessary.

12. Click the **Save & Close** button.

Inserting Silence

1. Make sure the slide containing the audio you want to edit is open.

2. Click the **Audio Editor** button on the Articulate tab or **Audio Editor** on the Articulate menu. The Audio Editor window opens.

3. Listen to the audio clip (click the **Play** button and the **Pause** button to start and stop the clip) and make note of the place where silence is needed. You can listen to clips through headphones or your computer's speakers.

4. Place the playhead in the waveform where you want to insert silence.

5. Click the **Silence** button on the ribbon.

6. In the Insert Silence dialog box, input the number of seconds of silence to insert and then click **OK**.

7. Play the audio clip to be sure the silence is satisfactory. You can undo and repeat if necessary.

8. Click the **Save & Close** button.

Adjusting Volume (On a Single Slide)

1. Make sure the slide containing the audio you want to edit is open.

2. Click the **Audio Editor** button on the Articulate tab or **Audio Editor** on the Articulate menu. The Audio Editor window opens.

3. Click the **Play** button to determine the approximate portion where volume adjustments are needed.

4. Zoom in around the approximate section where volume adjustments are needed by clicking and dragging to select a portion of the waveform and then clicking the **Zoom Selection** button in the ribbon.

5. Now play and pause the clip (as needed) to determine the exact start and stop points of the segment where volume adjustments are needed. This may require playing and pausing the clip and zooming in and out to make sure the starting and stopping locations are *exactly* where you need them to be.

6. Select the segment where volume adjustments are needed by clicking inside the waveform at the beginning of the section and dragging to show the end of the section where volume adjustments are needed.

7. Click the **Play** button to play the segment where volume adjustments are needed to determine if the selection is accurate. If the beginning and end points of the segment need to be refined, they can be moved by clicking and dragging until the segment is just right.

8. Click the **Volume** button on the ribbon.

9. In the Change Volume dialog box, increase or decrease the volume and then click **OK**.

10. Play the audio clip to be sure the volume adjustment is satisfactory. You can undo and repeat if necessary.

11. Click the **Save & Close** button.

Adjusting Volume (Over More Than One Slide)

Open the Audio Editor and click the **Show All** button in the ribbon. You will see the audio for the entire project and you can zoom in on various sections and make volume adjustments.

Setting Slide and Animation Timing in the Audio Editor "On the Fly" While Listening to the Audio

1. Click the **Audio Editor** button on the Articulate tab or **Audio Editor** on the Articulate menu. The Audio Editor window opens.

2. Play the audio starting on the desired slide.

3. When you reach the place in the audio where the next slide should start, click the **Set Next Slide** button in the ribbon to set the next slide to start there.

You can also set the next animation start point by playing the audio and clicking the **Set Next Animation** button when you reach the place in the audio where the next animation should start.

Enhancing Existing Audio

Hiya, Phil!

Phil Corriveau, an Articulate MVP that you will see on Articulate's discussion boards, provides some good advice about making Presenter audio better (the original article is at http://www.articulate.com/blog/articulate-101-how-to-make-the-most-of-your-recorded-audio) that we are adapting in this section.

Tip: Consider manipulating duplicate copies of audio clips in case your experiments don't work out as desired.

Phil explains that when your audio files are published in Presenter, the files need to be reduced to a fraction of the original sizes. To work this magic, some frequencies are removed from audio clips and bass frequencies are reduced the most (especially with Articulate's quality settings of 32 Kbps and below). A considerable loss in quality occurs to reduce file size, but Phil recommends adding some bass back to your audio before you import it into Articulate to make the clips sound better. This is easy to do in audio editing applications using the graphic equalizer functions. Audacity (http://audacity.sourceforge.net) is a free audio editor that he says can easily do the trick. When you are done adding some bass, import the file into Presenter, preview the page, and listen to the file. Tweak again if needed.

In addition, you may find that some audio clips are louder than others, even after optimizing audio volume in Presenter's Audio Editor. Phil recommends a free tool that you can use to help with inconsistent volume levels across slides called The Levelator (http://www.conversationsnetwork.org/levelator), which reduces volume peaks and raises volume valleys.

According to Phil, "There is a great deal of subjectivity involved in audio enhancement, and it will require some trial and error on your part. But you'll find that by trying some of these tricks—and by having a little patience—you can take your audio to the next level."

Tip: You can also export audio in WAV or MP3 format from the Audio Editor so that you can work with it in an external editor. Then you can import the edited version. To do this while in the Audio Editor, click the Options button (the lowercase "a" with a line over it in the top-left corner) and select the Export option.

Syncing Animations

The Sync Animations button on the Articulate tab and the Sync Animations menu selection on the Articulate menu let you sync *previously recorded narration* (recorded in Presenter or brought into Presenter as imported audio) to slide animations. Why might you need to sync animations with existing audio?

■ You may not feel comfortable recording narration at the same time as syncing animations. You can record the narration first (using

Record Narration) and then use Sync Animations to set the animation timings for those slides that have animations.

■ You synced animations while recording narration previously but feel like you didn't sync the animations well. Sync Animations allow you to resync the animations without needing to rerecord the narration.

■ You imported narration and want to sync the narration with slide animations.

Whether you record narration for slides with animations alongside those slides without animations (as described earlier) or record narration for all slides without syncing and then go back to sync is up to you.

Syncing Audio to (PowerPoint) Slide Animations

1. Make sure that the audio narration for the applicable slide is recorded and "inside" Presenter (by importing audio or by recording narration).

2. Make sure that the applicable PowerPoint slides are open and the slide on which you want to sync animations is selected.

66 **Note:** Don't forget that for PowerPoint animations to be used in Presenter, they must be triggered by "on click."

3. Click the **Sync Narration** button on the Articulate tab or select this option from the Articulate menu. The Consolidated Recording window opens.

4. Make sure that **Sync Narration** is selected in the Record Mode menu.

5. Click the **Start Sync** button. The audio file for the selected slide will begin to play and the Start Sync button will change to a Next Animation button.

6. At the precise moment that you want the next animation to begin, click the **Next Animation** button.

7. Continue clicking the **Next Animation** button when you want the next animation to appear until all the existing audio is synced with slide animations.

8. When the audio file reaches the end, the Next Animation button will turn into a Start Sync button and the synchronization is complete.

9. Click the **Play** button ⊙ to listen to the recording for that slide.

    ■ If you are not satisfied with the synchronization, you can click the **Start Sync** button and redo these steps to replace previous syncing.

    ■ If you are unhappy with the recording, you can rerecord it by clicking **Record Narration** in the Record Mode menu and rerecording the narration. Then you can sync the slide again.

    ■ If you are happy with the narration and syncing, go to the next step.

10. Click the forward **slide selector** to go to the next slide. You can also jump to any other slide by clicking the Thumbnails menu under the slide selector.

11. Click the **Save & Close** button when you are done.

Tip: Sync Animations can also be used to set the timings for slide animations on slides that do not include audio.

Editing Slide Notes While Recording Narration or Syncing Animations

While you are narrating your slides, you may decide that the narration script needs to be edited. (In fact, this is likely.) You could go back to your PowerPoint slides and edit the script and then rerecord in Presenter, but there's an easier way. You can edit your notes in the Consolidated Recording window's Slide Notes pane (see Figure 5.19) and those edits will also change the slide notes in your PowerPoint slides! (Sweet!)

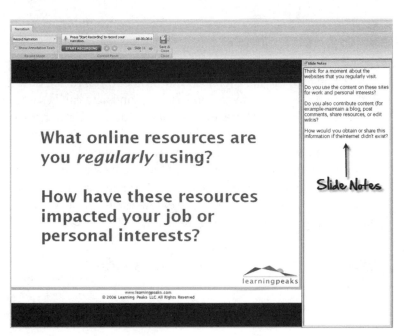

Figure 5.19. The Consolidated Recording window

Editing Slide Notes while Narrating

1. In the Consolidated Recording window, make changes to the narration script in the Slide Notes pane.

2. Rerecord the narration using the changed slide notes.

3. When you close the Consolidated Recording window, the changed slide notes are also changed in the Slide Notes pane of each PowerPoint slide.

Previewing Your Project

It's a good idea to take a look at your project often to see how it works. Publishing the course to see how it looks and acts can be time consuming, especially if there are a lot of animations. Rather than *publish* the course to see how the changes look, you can *preview* your course.

You can select how much you want to preview by clicking the Preview button on the Articulate tab or the Preview menu selection on the Articulate menu (Figure 5.20), and then choosing Preview This Slide, Preview Next 3 Slides, or Preview Range of Slides. This will open the Preview window (Figure 5.21).

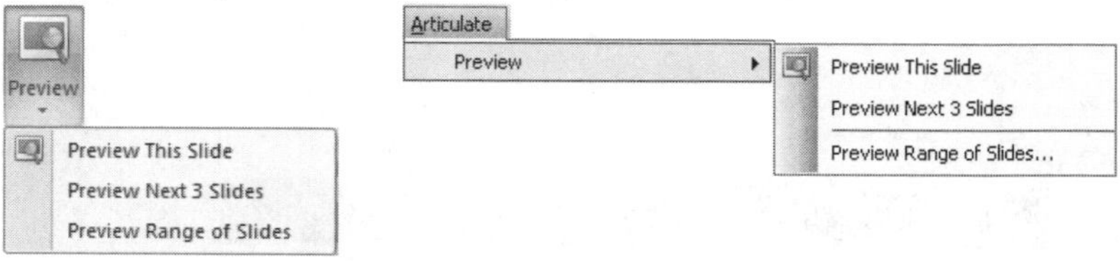

Figure 5.20. The Preview button (left) and the Preview menu selection (right)

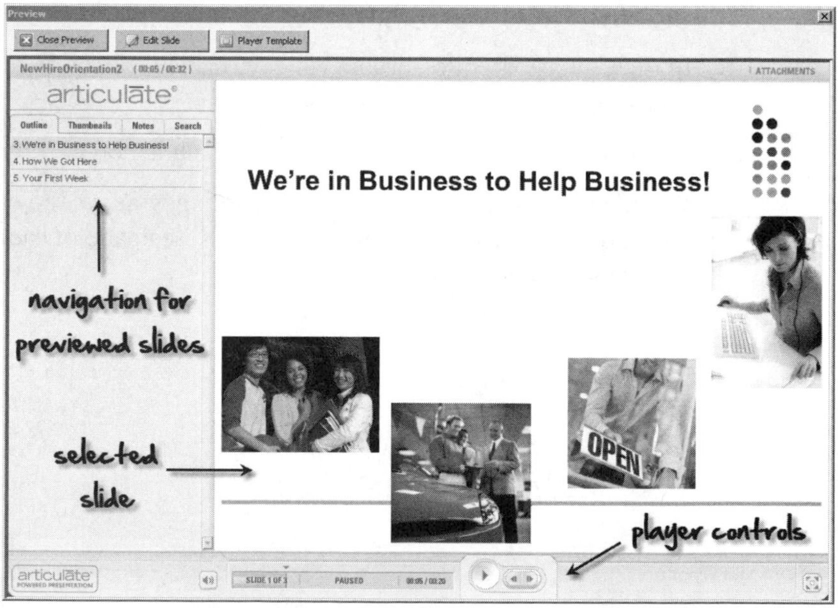

Figure 5.21. The Preview window with the default player

The Preview window shows your Presenter project embedded in either the last player template used when publishing this project or the default player template if this project has not yet been published. (Presenter player templates are discussed in Chapter 7, "Customizing Presenter Player Templates.") If narration is recorded for the slides selected for preview, the narration that goes with those slides will play.

To preview your project:

1. Click the **Preview** option on the Articulate tab or the Articulate menu.

2. Select the slides you want to preview, then choose one of the following:

   Preview This Slide   Preview the selected slide

   Preview Next 3 Slides   Preview the selected slide plus the next two slides

   Preview Range of Slides   Preview a range of slides of your choosing or preview all of the slides

   The Preview window opens.

3. If you would like to preview your project in another player template, click the **Player Template** button. You can select a player template, logo, or Presenter to use for the preview.

4. When you are done, close the preview window by clicking the **Close Preview** button at the top of the screen.

Setting Presentation Options

Presentation options are used to set up logos, presenters, and playlists, and specify quality settings, publishing settings, and other settings. This is important: When you are working with presentation options, you are setting up elements that can be selected for *any* Presenter project, not just the current project. Although the name of the button, "Presentation Options," makes it sound as though you are setting options for the current presentation, Program Options is really what the presentation options settings are all about.

The **Presentation Options** button on the Articulate tab or the **Presentation Options** menu selection on the Articulate menu (Figure 5.22) opens the Presentation Options dialog box (Figure 5.23), where you can select settings for Presenter.

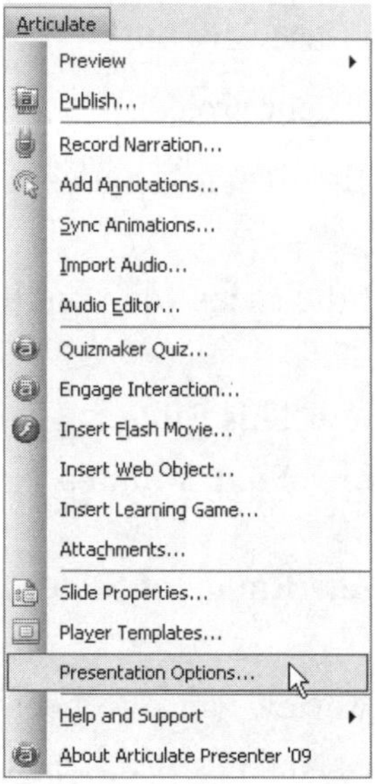

Figure 5.22. The Presentation Options button (above) and the Presentation Options menu selection (right)

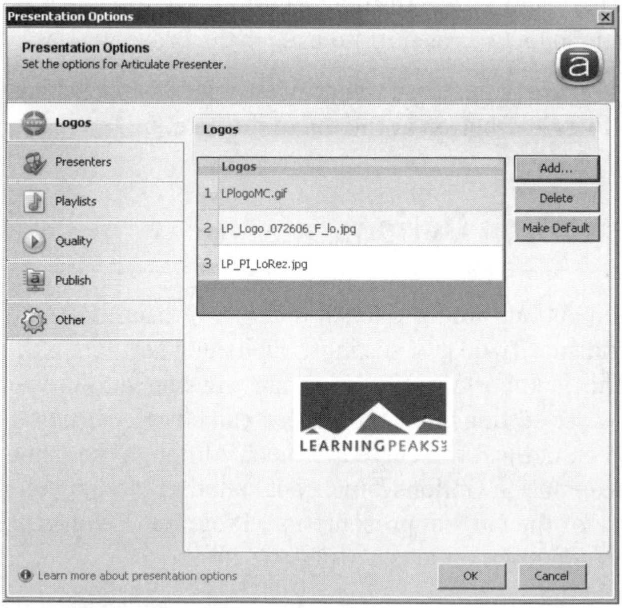

Figure 5.23. The Presentation Options dialog box

Table 5.6 describes the purpose of each tab in the dialog box.

Table 5.6. Presentation Options dialog box tabs

Tab	Purpose
Logos	Adds or deletes logos and sets a default logo
Presenters	Adds, edits, or deletes information for presenters (name, title, email, bio, photo, photo properties) and sets a default presenter
Playlists	Sets playlist and tracks for background music
Quality	Sets output compression/quality settings for images and audio (more compression means lower quality but less bandwidth needed to view)
Publish	Sets publishing options
Other	Sets recording, general, and proxy settings

Logos Tab

The Logos tab lets you add and delete logos that can be used in any Presenter project and set a default logo.

Adding or Deleting Logos and Selecting a Default Logo

1. Click the **Presentation Options** button on the Articulate tab or **Presentation Options** from the Articulate menu. The Presentation Options dialog box opens.

2. Click the **Logos** tab (Figure 5.24).

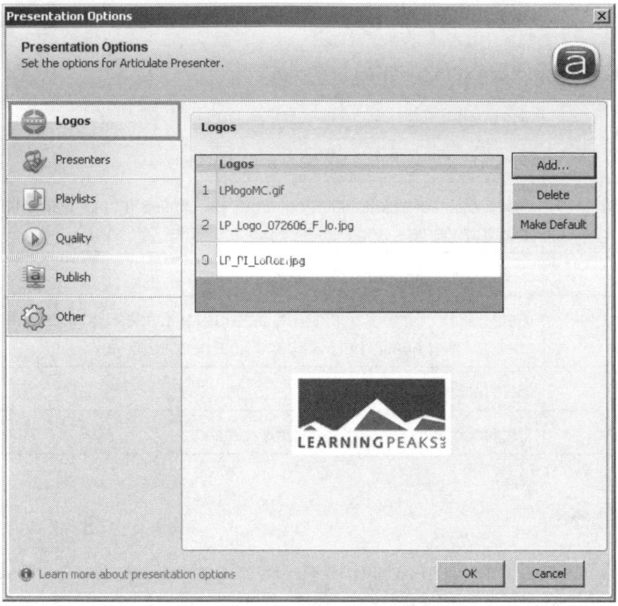

Figure 5.24. Presentation Options dialog box with the Logos tab highlighted

3. To add a logo, click the **Add** button. Supported image formats are SWF (Flash), JPG, GIF, BMP, EMF, and WMF. Optimal maximum width is 244 pixels.

4. To delete a logo, click the logo and click the **Delete** button.

5. To make a logo the default, click the logo and click the **Make Default** button.

6. When you are done, click the **OK** button.

Presenters Tab

The Presenters tab lets you add and delete presenters that can be used in any Presenter project and set a default presenter.

Adding, Editing, or Deleting Presenters, and Selecting a Default Presenter

1. Click the **Presentation Options** button on the Articulate tab or **Presentation Options** from the Articulate menu. The Presentation Options dialog box opens.

2. Click the **Presenters** tab (Figure 5.25).

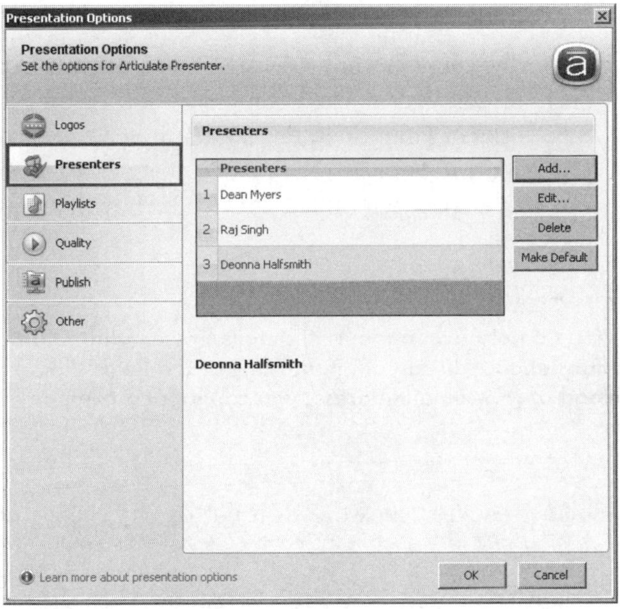

Figure 5.25. Presentation Options dialog box with the Presenters tab highlighted

3. To add a presenter, click the **Add** button and input desired details into the form fields. For example:

Name: The presenter's first and last names

Title: The presenter's title

Email: The presenter's email address

Presenter bio: Information about the presenter

Photo: Click **Browse** to add or edit a photo. Supported image formats are JPG, GIF, BMP, and EMF. Optimal image size is 73x85 pixels. If your image is not exactly 73x85 pixels, you have two options:

- **Maintain aspect ratio:** Maintains the original dimensions of your image
- **Stretch to fit:** Stretches the image to 73x85 (this may distort the image).

Typically, you will want to either select **Maintain aspect ratio** or edit your image in an image editing program such as Fireworks or Paint Shop Pro so that it is 73x85 pixels before you import it. For *best* results, edit to exactly 73x85 pixels so the image space isn't filled out to 73x85 with a gray background.

> **Tip:** You do not have to input all details. If you want to input other information, you can put it into any of the fields. For example, instead of your email address, you can input a company web address.

4. To edit a presenter, click the **Edit** button and change desired details.

5. To make a presenter the default presenter, click the presenter and click the **Make Default** button.

6. When you are done, click the **OK** button.

> **Tip:** You can assign presenters for different slides in the project using slide properties (discussed later in this chapter).

> **Tip:** You don't have to use presenter information just for presenter information. For example, you could put course information in the Presenter bio field and then, using the Text Labels tab of the Player Templates dialog box, change the text on the Bio button from Bio to Course info.

Playlists (Background Music) Tab

The Playlists tab lets you add and delete playlists that can be used in any Presenter project.

Creating and Editing Playlists

1. Click the **Presentation Options** button on the Articulate tab or **Presentation Options** from the Articulate menu. The Presentation Options dialog box opens.

2. Click the **Playlists** tab (Figure 5.26).

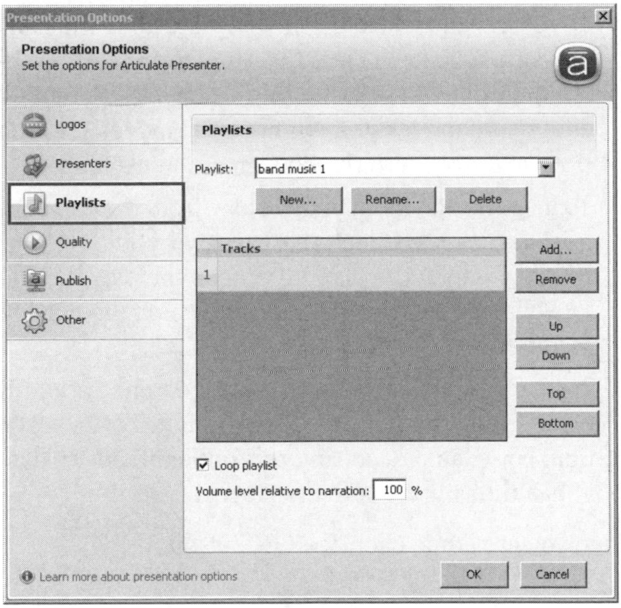

Figure 5.26. Presentation Options dialog box with the Playlists tab highlighted

3. To create a new playlist, click the **New** button. Enter a name for the new playlist and then click **OK** to save it.

4. If working with an existing playlist, select the name of the playlist you want to edit in the Playlist menu.

5. To edit a playlist name, tracks, sequencing, and volume:

  ▪ To rename a playlist: Click the **Rename** button to give it a new name. Click **OK** to save changes.

  ▪ To delete a playlist: Click the **Delete** button to delete it. Click **OK** to save changes.

  ▪ To add tracks to a playlist: Click the **Add** button, browse to desired audio file (.mp3 or .wav), and click **Open**. The track is added to the Tracks section of the dialog box.

  ▪ To remove tracks from a playlist: Click the name of a track in the playlist and click the **Remove** button.

  ▪ To reorder the tracks in the playlist: Click the name of a track in your playlist and click the **Up**, **Down**, **Top**, or **Bottom** button to change its position in the playlist. Up moves a track up one; Down moves it down one; Top moves it to the top; and Bottom moves it to the bottom of the playlist.

  ▪ To loop the playlist (songs replay from the top once the last track is played): Check the **Loop playlist** box. The playlist will loop only if the playing time of the playlist is less than the total playing time of the slides to which the playlist is assigned.

  ▪ To change the volume level relative to narration: Enter a percentage volume relative to the volume of the recorded narration. For example, setting this option to 50% plays the playlist at half the volume of the narration.

6. When you are done, click the **OK** button.

Quality Tab

The Quality tab lets you select default quality settings for publishing to the web, LMS, or Articulate Online (but not CD). If you want to change the quality settings for a specific Presenter project, use the Presentation Options tab to make the desired changes.

Selecting Quality Settings

1. Click the **Presentation Options** button on the Articulate tab or **Presentation Options** from the Articulate menu. The Presentation Options dialog box opens.

2. Click the **Quality** tab (Figure 5.27).

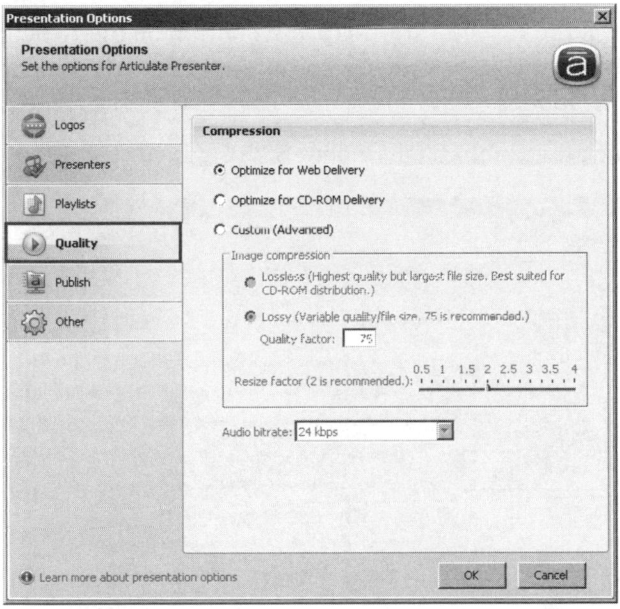

Figure 5.27. Presentation Options dialog box with the Quality tab highlighted

3. Set the desired compression settings:

   ■ **Optimize for Web Delivery:** Choose this option if you will be publishing presentations delivered on either the Internet or an intranet.

   ■ **Optimize for CD-ROM Delivery:** Choose this option if you will be publishing presentations delivered via CD-ROM.

   ■ **Custom (Advanced):** These settings should be used by advanced users only.

Publish Tab

The Publish tab lets you select default publishing settings. If you want to change the settings for a specific Presenter project, use Presentation Options to make the desired changes.

Selecting Publishing Options

1. Click the **Presentation Options** button on the Articulate tab or **Presentation Options** from the Articulate menu. The Presentation Options dialog box opens.

2. Click the **Publish** tab (Figure 5.28).

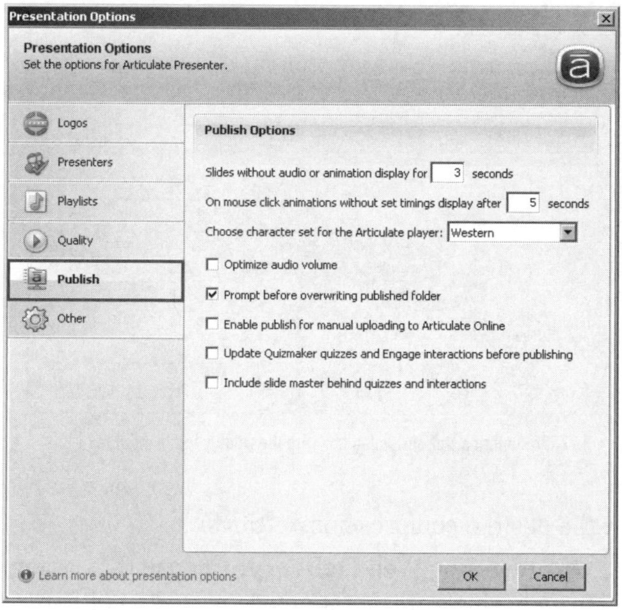

Figure 5.28. Presentation Options dialog box with the Publish tab highlighted

3. Select desired publishing options:

Table 5.7. Publish tab options

Option	What it does
Slides without audio or animation display for ____ seconds	Sets the duration, in seconds, for slides without any audio or animations (must be greater than 0).
On mouse click animations without set timings display after ____ seconds	Sets the duration, in seconds, for slides that contain PowerPoint animations that do not have set timings.
Choose character set for the Articulate player	Presentations published in English and most Western European languages should choose Western. Presentations published in Asian, Eastern European, or other languages, should choose Non-western.
Optimize audio volume	Normalizes audio files, which adjusts the height of the waveform to a consistent level without distortion.
Prompt before overwriting published folder	This setting provides a prompt when overwriting existing files with the same name.
Enable publish for manual uploading to Articulate Online	This setting allows you to publish locally to an output format that can be manually uploaded to Articulate Online. Typically used when a company firewall prohibits publishing directly to Articulate Online.
Update Quizmaker quizzes and Engage interactions before publishing	This setting updates embedded Quizmaker quizzes and Engage interactions to the latest version before publishing.
Include slide master behind quizzes and interactions	This setting inserts the project's slide master behind inserted Quizmaker quizzes/surveys and Engage interactions.

Other Tab

The Other tab lets you select default recording, general, and proxy settings. If you want to change the settings for a specific Presenter project, use Presentation Options to make the desired changes.

Selecting "Other" Settings (Recording, General, and Proxy)

1. Click the **Presentation Options** button on the Articulate tab or **Presentation Options** from the Articulate menu. The Presentation Options dialog box opens.

2. Click the **Other** tab (Figure 5.29).

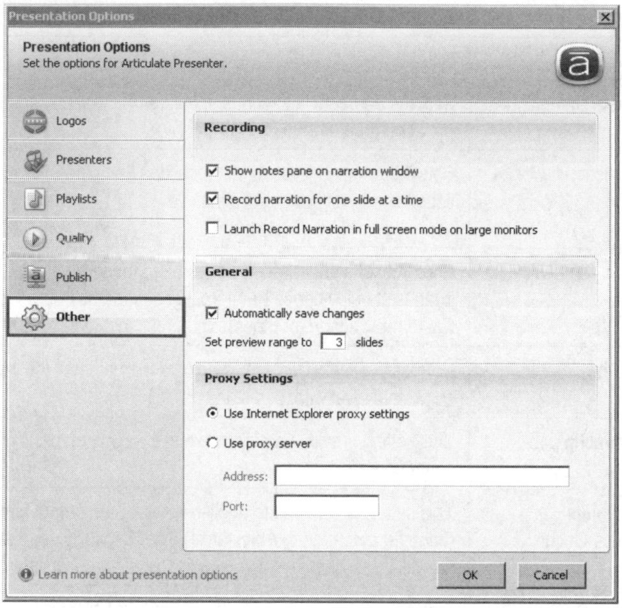

Figure 5.29. Presentation Options dialog box with the Other tab highlighted

3. Select desired options:

Table 5.8. Other tab options

Option	What it does
Recording	**Show notes pane on narration window:** Check this box to display the slide notes (narration script) while recording narration.
	Record narration for one slide at a time: Check this box to record narration for one slide at a time. Uncheck to record narration continuously across all slides in your presentation.
	Launch Record Narration in full screen mode on large monitors: Check this box to launch record narration in a screen maximized to take advantage of larger monitors. This can cause performance problems on slower machines.
General	**Automatically save changes:** Check this box to automatically save your work.
	Set preview range to ____ slides: Specify a value from 1 to 99 to determine the default number of slides to show when you select the option to Preview Next ____ Slides. The default value is 3.
Proxy Settings	Check with your IT department to determine what settings are needed. The default settings may work in many cases.

4. Click **OK** to save your changes or **Cancel** to exit without saving.

> **Note:** It's important to realize that the presentation options are *not* project specific. If you input specific options in the Presentation Options dialog box, they will become the default options for subsequent projects. (These settings can be changed as needed.) Table 5.9 lists the default for each of the Presentation Option dialog box tabs.

Table 5.9. Presentation Options dialog box defaults

Tab	Defaults
Logos and Presenters	• If you *have published the current presentation previously*, the default logo and presenter will be the ones set in the Presentation Options dialog box. If no logo or presenter are specified in Presentation Options, the last selected logo and presenter are used. • If you *have not published the current presentation before*, the default logo and presenter will be the ones set in the Presentation Options dialog box. If no logo or presenter are specified in Presentation Options, the logo and presenter are set to none/blank.
Quality	If you input quality options for one project, they will be the same for the next project unless you change them.
Playlists	You can select and use a playlist from another project and you can add a playlist for the current project. But if no playlist is selected for the current project, none will be used.
Publish	If you input publishing options for one project, they will be the same for the next project unless you change them.

Selecting Slide Properties

The Slide Properties window lets you specify how slides and slide titles appear in the player, whether slides branch (take the viewer to different slides) based on viewer action, which presenter (typically the narrator) is associated with each slide, and whether there is slide-level audio. It allows you to make powerful adjustments that can dramatically increase the impact of your presentation.

To work with slide properties, click the **Slide Properties** button on the Articulate tab or **Slide Properties** on the Articulate menu (Figure 5.30). This will open the Slide Properties window (Figure 5.31).

Articulate

Slide Properties	Player Templates
	Presentation Options
	Help and Support ▾

Tools

Articulate

Preview ▶

Publish...

Record Narration...

Add Annotations...

Sync Animations...

Import Audio...

Audio Editor...

Quizmaker Quiz...

Engage Interaction...

Insert Flash Movie...

Insert Web Object...

Insert Learning Game...

Attachments...

Slide Properties...

Player Templates...

Presentation Options...

Help and Support ▶

About Articulate Presenter '09

Figure 5.30. The Slide Properties button (above) and the Slide Properties menu selection (right)

Slide Properties

Slide Properties
Set properties like navigation title, branching and presenters.

Transfer_Shank   25 Slides, Total Duration: 00:02:01   Group By: Slide number

Slide	Navigation Title	Level	Change View	Branching	Lock	Presenter	Audio Playlist	Advance
1	Transfer of Learning	1	Slide only		🔒			Automatically
2		2	No sidebar					Automatically
3	Objectives	2						Automatically
4		2	No sidebar					Automatically
5	See a Problem?	1	No sidebar					By User
6	Research Says...	2						Automatically
7	Why We Don't Design fc	2						Automatically

ⓘ Learn more about Slide Properties   OK   Cancel

Figure 5.31. The Slide Properties window

At the top of your slide list, you will see the file name for the open project. To the right of the title are the total number of slides and the total duration of your project (based on actual length of narration and the time set for slides without narration).

The Slide Properties window has a Group By menu that you can use to sort the slides. Slides can be grouped by:

- **Slide number:** Slides appear in slide order. This is the default.
- **Presenter:** Slides are grouped by presenter.
- **Audio Playlist:** Slides are grouped by playlist.
- **Move to Next Slide:** Slides are grouped by the Move to Next Slide setting.

When Group By is set to Slide Number, you can select multiple slides by Shift-clicking (hold Shift and click) one or more rows. Then you can right-click to adjust some properties for the selected slides. For example, you can change the Advance for a selected group of slides to By User by Shift-clicking to select the slides to be changed, right-clicking and selecting Advance to Next Slide, and then selecting By User.

Let's take a look at each of the columns of the Slide Properties window.

Slide Number and Slide

The slide number in the leftmost column of the Slide Properties window reflects the chronological number of a slide (from PowerPoint). A tiny thumbnail of each slide is shown next to the slide number. If you click the thumbnail, a larger thumbnail is viewable. This is useful when you cannot remember what is on the slide while you are working in the Slide Properties window.

Navigation Title

The text shown in the Navigation Title column is the slide title that appears in the player navigation. It is called a *navigation* title in the Slide Properties window because the navigation title text appears in the sidebar of the Presenter player and clicking the title will take the viewer to that slide. The default title is the slide title entered on each PowerPoint slide or, if there is no slide title, the slide number. If the default title isn't desirable (because it's too long, isn't informative enough, or doesn't exist), you can change it in the Slide Properties window.

In Figure 5.32, you see five slides. Two of the titles shown might be too long and two of the titles are just "Slide #," which is never a good title to appear in navigation.

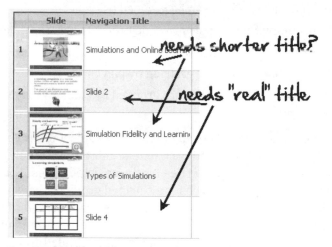

Figure 5.32. Slide titles in Slide Properties window

Figure 5.33 shows that the titles for slides that only had a number have been changed.

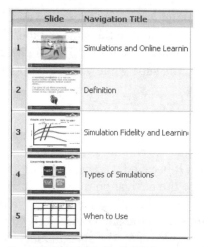

Figure 5.33. Revised slide titles in Slide Properties window

Figure 5.34 shows how these five slide titles look in the sidebar of the Presenter player.

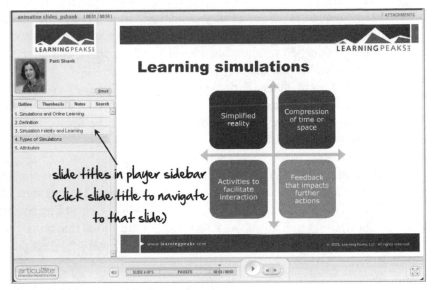

Figure 5.34. Slide titles in the sidebar of the Presenter player

Changing the Navigation Title

1. Click the **Slide Properties** button on the Articulate tab or **Slide Properties** from the Articulate menu. The Slide Properties window opens.

2. Click the cell in the Navigation Title column you want to change, delete the current slide title, and type the desired title. The changed title will appear as the Navigation Title in the Presenter player sidebar.

3. Click the **OK** button.

> **Tip:** Change all slide titles labeled "Slide #" to a "real" title!

Level

The slide level number shown in the Level column refers to each slide's indentation on the player sidebar. Level 1 is the highest level and is the default for all slides unless the slide level is changed in the Slide Properties window. Each level 1 slide appears unindented (all the way to the left) on the player sidebar.

Slides are changed to level 2 to indicate that they are "child" slides of the level 1 ("parent") slide immediately above it. Typically, the level 1 slide is used to introduce a new topic and all the level 2 slides below it are related to that topic.

For example, let's say you are developing a Presenter project to help the people in your organization use a new online travel system. The course contains the following main sections: 1) Overview of the New Travel System, 2) Air Travel, 3) Hotel, 4) Rental Car, 5) Upon Return. Figure 5.35 shows a selection of the slides that were developed for this project. Notice that they are all level 1 by default.

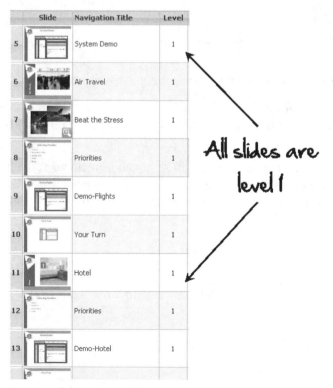

Figure 5.35. All slides in the Travel System project are level 1.

Figure 5.36 shows the same selection of slides but with child slides changed to level 2. Slides 6 and 11 are section introduction slides, so they remain at level 1, but the slides within each section have been changed to level 2.

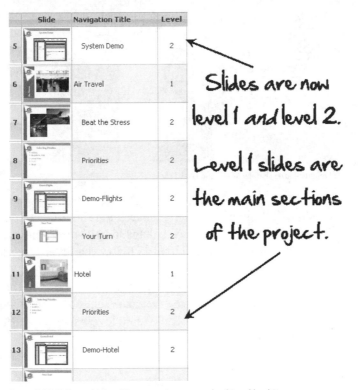

Slide	Navigation Title	Level
5	System Demo	2
6	Air Travel	1
7	Beat the Stress	2
8	Priorities	2
9	Demo-Flights	2
10	Your Turn	2
11	Hotel	1
12	Priorities	2
13	Demo-Hotel	2

Slides are now level 1 and level 2. Level 1 slides are the main sections of the project.

Figure 5.36. Slides in the Travel System project are now level 1 and level 2.

Figure 5.37 shows a portion of the navigation panel opened in the player. The navigation titles for level 1 slides are unindented and located on the far left of the sidebar. The navigation titles for level 2 slides are indented and open once the viewer navigates to that section of the project.

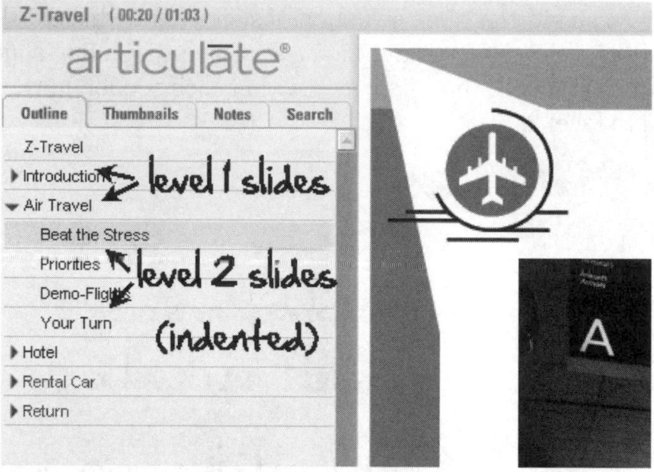

Figure 5.37. Presenter player showing level 1 and level 2 slides

All level 1 slides are shown on the sidebar when the project opens in the player, but the level 2 slides are collapsed below the relevant level 1 slide. The slides at level 2 are indented below the level 1 section slide that they belong to.

Figure 5.38 shows a portion of the navigation settings in the Player Templates dialog box where you can select how slide navigation should expand when there are multiple slide levels (see Chapter 7, "Customizing Presenter Player Templates").

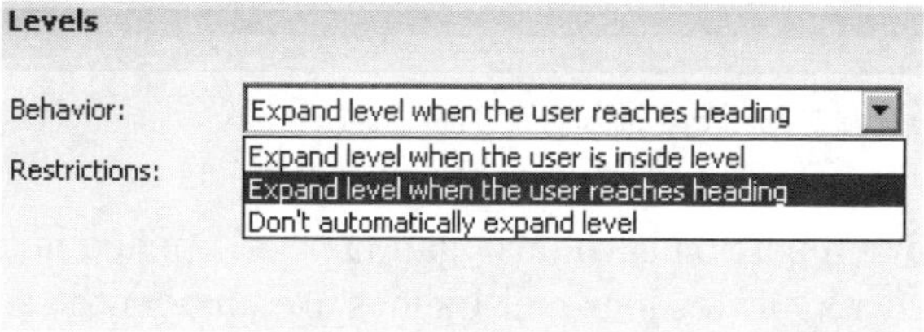

Figure 5.38. Slide level expansion behavior in the Player Templates dialog box

Note: The number of levels available to the developer increases by one when a new level is added. For example, when you change a slide at level 1 to level 2, level 3 is added and can be selected.

Changing Level

1. Click the **Slide Properties** button on the Articulate tab or **Slide Properties** from the Articulate menu. The Slide Properties window opens.

2. Click the cell in the Level column you want to change and select the desired level. The changed level will also be reflected in the player sidebar navigation.

3. Click the **OK** button.

Note: You can only change slide levels in the Slide Properties window when viewing the slides in the default Group By: Slide number view.

> ### Removing Slide Numbers to Reduce Confusion
>
> If you change the level of slides, consider removing the slide numbers that appear by default. This setting can be changed in the Player Templates dialog box (see Chapter 7, "Customizing Presenter Player Templates"). Otherwise, the slidebar will appear to have missing slides (because the child slides are hidden below the parent slides in the sidebar).

Change View

Change View allows you to select one of three views for how each slide appears in the player. There are three slide views: standard, no sidebar, and slide only.

Standard View (Default)

In standard view, the slide window shows the top bar, bottom bar, and sidebars, as shown in Figure 5.39.

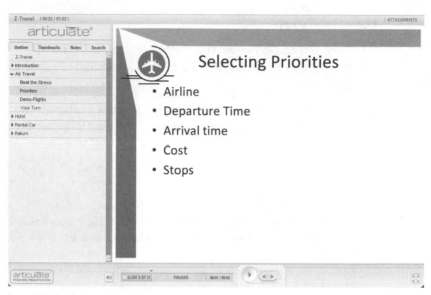

Figure 5.39. Standard view

No Sidebar View

If No sidebar view is selected, the sidebar is hidden but the top bar and bottom bar are shown (Figure 5.40).

Figure 5.40. No sidebar view

Slide Only View

In Slide only view, the top bar, bottom bar, and sidebar are hidden and the slide is larger, as shown in Figure 5.41. Notice the controls on the bottom right of the screen. These allow the viewer to play/pause and return to the standard view.

Figure 5.41. Slide only view

Changing View

1. Click the **Slide Properties** button on the Articulate tab or **Slide Properties** from the Articulate menu. The Slide Properties window opens.

2. Click the cell in the Change View column for the cell you want to change and select the desired view. The changed view will be reflected in the player.

3. Click the **OK** button.

> **Note:** Slide view "inherits" the same slide view as the slide before it if no view is selected.

Branching and Locking (and Hiding Slides)

Slides appear in order (slide 1, slide 2, slide 3, and so on) by default. Branching lets you customize the slide that viewers will see if they click the Next or Back buttons on the player. Although it might seem weird to go through the slides out of order, there are a number of reasons you might wish the viewer to see a slide other than the next slide.

For example, you might create a Presenter project that describes three new products. Figure 5.42 shows a flowchart of the different branches through this project. On the first slide (slide 1), using hyperlinks created in PowerPoint, the viewers can choose which product they want to learn about or view a welcome audio or download a sales kit. Clicking the product A hyperlink takes the viewer to slides 4-10. Clicking the product B hyperlink takes the viewer to slides 11-16, and clicking the product C hyperlink takes the viewer to slides 17-23. At the end of each branch, the viewers are taken to slide 24, which helps them plan their strategy for selling each of these products. And once they reach slide 24, there are links back to slide 1, so another product can be selected.

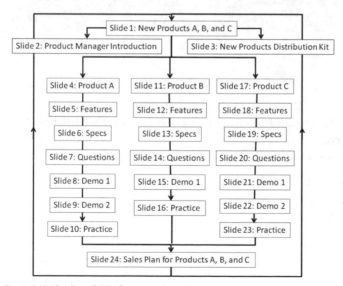

Figure 5.42. Flowchart of slides for new products sales training

Detailed how-tos associated with branching, locking slides, and hiding slides in the sidebar navigation will be provided in Chapter 6, "Pumping Up Your Presenter Projects." But for now, we do want you to understand what branching, locking, and hiding slides is all about.

"Locking" slides (by clicking in the Lock column in the Slide Properties window for slides you want to lock) means disabling player controls on that slide, including sidebar navigation, seekbar, and next/back controls. Disabling player navigation can be really useful when implementing hyperlink-based branching (where the branch taken is determined by the hyperlink each viewer clicks). If a slide is locked, viewers are forced to navigate using the hyperlinks on the slide.

Hiding Slides

Hiding slides (by right-clicking the title in the Slide Properties window and selecting **Hide in Navigation Panel**) allows you to keep a slide title from appearing in the sidebar navigation. When you select Hide in Navigation Panel, the Navigation Title field in the Slide Properties window will change to *(Hidden)*. Hiding slides is especially useful when implementing branched paths so the viewers don't get confused about where they are.

---

66 **Note:** Hiding slides in the Slide Properties window hides the slide from navigation but not from the project.

Presenter

Earlier in this chapter, we described how to add a presenter to a Presenter project. You can designate which presenter goes with a given Presenter project two different ways. If a project has only one presenter, you can select the presenter (or no presenter) during publishing (see Chapter 26, "Publishing"). If you have more than one presenter, you can select the presenter to be associated with each slide in the Slide Properties window.

Specifying a Presenter for Each Slide

1. Click the **Slide Properties** button on the Articulate tab or **Slide Properties** from the Articulate menu. The Slide Properties window opens.

2. Click the cell in the Presenter column for the slide on which you want to specify a presenter and select the desired presenter. (Presenters need to be set up in the Presentation Options dialog box before they will appear on the list of available presenters.)

3. Click the **OK** button.

Audio Playlist

If you want to specify a playlist for a given slide, it can be selected here.

Specifying an Audio Playlist for a Slide

1. Click the **Slide Properties** button on the Articulate tab or **Slide Properties** from the Articulate menu. The Slide Properties window opens.

2. Click the cell in the **Audio Playlist** column for the slide on which you want to specify a playlist. (Playlists need to be set up in the Presentation Options dialog box before they will appear on the list of available playlists.)

3. Click the **OK** button.

Advance

Advance indicates how each slide moves forward to the next slide. The default is Automatically. This means that when one slide ends, the next slide is presented. You can change this setting to By User if you want the viewer to have to click to advance the slide.

> **Tip:** If a slide has complex information such as charts or diagrams, it is often best to let the viewer determine when to move forward.

Specifying Advance Properties for Each Slide

1. Click the **Slide Properties** button on the Articulate tab or **Slide Properties** from the Articulate menu. The Slide Properties window opens.

2. Click the cell in the **Advance** column for the slide on which you want to modify the advance properties. The property will toggle from Automatically to By User.

3. Click the **OK** button.

> **Tip:** You can also access Slide Properties tasks by right-clicking inside the Slide Properties window.

Making Backups of Presenter Project Files

It's a good idea to create a backup or archive of Presenter files for a number of reasons, including saving project files in case they are needed in the future or gathering needed files so they can be worked with on another computer. The Send to Articulate Presenter Package feature creates a zipped folder that contains all needed Presenter files along with any embedded media files (such as Flash movies and Engage interactions).

> **Tip:** The Send to Articulate Presenter Package is also useful for sending all project files to collaborators.

Backing Up Presenter Project Files

1. Open the desired PowerPoint file.

2. In PowerPoint 2007: Click the **Office** button (top right-hand corner). Select **Send** and then select **Articulate Package**. In PowerPoint 2000-2003: From the **File** menu, select **Send to** and then select **Articulate Presenter Package**.

    The Articulate Presenter Package dialog box opens.

3. Input or browse to where you want the zip file to be created. You can optionally specify Package Notes, including the Project (name), Version (number), Author (name), Email (address of owner or author), and Special Instructions.

4. Click **Create Package**.

5. The Publish Successful dialog box tells you if the package was successfully created. You can click **Open Folder** to view the created folder and files.

Publishing Projects (Q&D)

Chapter 26, "Publishing," is devoted to publishing your Presenter projects, but we are going to end this chapter with a Q&D (quick and dirty) discussion of publishing your Presenter project for viewing through a web browser. If you are new to Presenter and want to get the flavor of working from beginning to end on a simple Presenter project, you can create and complete your project in this chapter.

Publishing to the Web

1. Complete your project. (Duh.)

2. Click the **Publish** button on the Articulate tab or choose **Publish** on the Articulate menu. The Publish window, shown in Figure 5.43, opens.

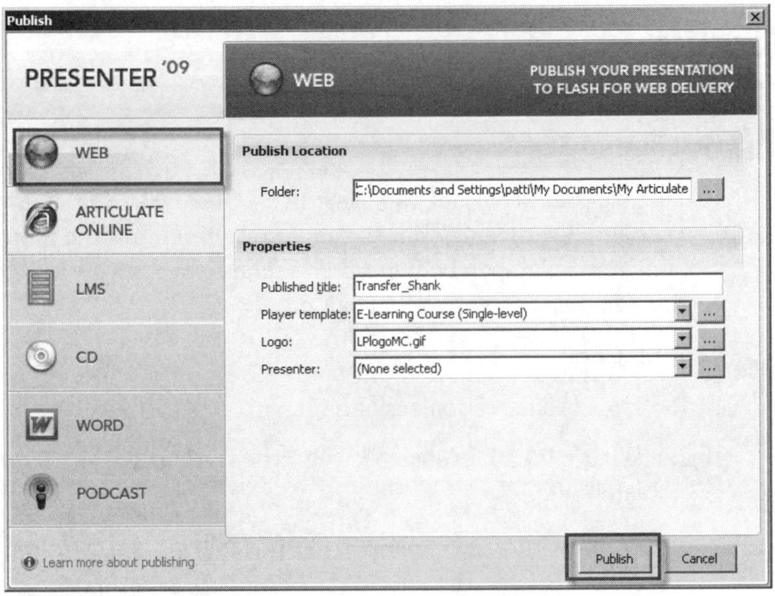

Figure 5.43. Publish window with Web tab and Publish button highlighted

3. Click the **Web** tab.

4. Specify where you want this Presenter project's files to be saved. The default location is My Documents\My Articulate Projects, but you can choose a different location by clicking the ellipsis button (...) or typing in a directory path for your computer or network drive.

5. Make sure the Published title is correct. (You can change it.)

6. Click **Publish**. When publishing is complete, the Publish Successful dialog box will open. Select **View Presentation** to see the final output in your web browser.

Practice 1

▶ What Do You Know?

This chapter describes the basic Presenter tasks that you will perform over and over again. Want to see if you remember the most important things? It's an open book quiz, so feel free to find the answers in this chapter. The answers follow but *don't peek*!

Questions

1. How is a narration script built?

2. What's the difference between the Articulate tab and the Articulate menu?

3. What tasks are done using the Consolidated Recording window?

4. How can you change the narration script while you are recording narration?

5. How can you be super precise when editing audio in the Audio Editor?

6. Why might you add silence to an audio clip?

7. While recording narration, how can you tell if there are PowerPoint animations in the slide you are narrating?

8. How do you rerecord the narration for a slide if you mess up the narration?

9. Why should you listen to each audio clip immediately after you record it?

10. What audio formats can be imported into a Presenter project?

11. How can you hide a slide title in the sidebar navigation?

12. In the Slide Properties window, if a cell is blank, what does that mean the property is set to?

Answers

1. How is a narration script built?

   By inputting the script into the slide notes in PowerPoint.

2. What's the difference between the Articulate tab and the Articulate menu?

   If you are using PowerPoint 2007, the Articulate tab is installed into PowerPoint. For earlier versions, the Articulate menu is installed. Whether you are using the Articulate tab or the Articulate menu, the Articulate tasks and functions are identical.

3. What tasks are done using the Consolidated Recording window?

   Recording narration, adding annotations, syncing narration, and adding or changing slide notes.

4. How can you change the narration script while you are recording narration?

   You change the slide notes in the Consolidated Recording window.

5. How can you be super precise when editing audio in the Audio Editor?

   You can zoom in on the portion you are editing.

6. Why might you add silence to an audio clip?

   Add silence if the narration for a slide begins too quickly or ends too abruptly.

7. While recording narration, how can you tell if there are PowerPoint animations on the slide you are narrating?

   You'll know that there are animations on that slide if the Next Animation button is displayed in the Consolidated Recording window.

8. How do you rerecord the narration for a slide if you mess up the narration?

   Click the Record Narration button in the Consolidated Recording window and the new narration will record over the old (messed up) narration.

9. Why should you listen to each audio clip immediately after you record it?

   If you made a mistake, you can use the Undo button at the top of the Audio Editor and rerecord.

10. What audio formats can be imported into a Presenter project?

    You can import .wav and .mp3 files.

11. How can you hide a slide title in the sidebar navigation?

    You can hide a slide title in the sidebar navigation by right-clicking the cell in the Navigation Title column for the slide to be hidden and selecting Hide in Navigation Panel.

12. In the Slide Properties window, if a cell is blank, what does that mean the property is set to?

    If a property cell is blank, it means that the property will be the same as the slide above it.

Practice 2

Narration, Syncing Narration, and Publishing

This practice consolidates many of the skills from this chapter and should be used with a PowerPoint slide deck of your choosing. (Note: Make a copy and *play with the copy!*) Another alternative is to search for PowerPoint slides online and use those to practice with or use examples and templates from Microsoft's web site (www.microsoft.com). Use a small slide deck with four to eight slides for this practice.

PowerPoint

1. Develop a narration script (using PowerPoint's slide notes) for a small set of PowerPoint slides that are suitable for a Presenter project (see Chapter 4, "First, Your PowerPoint Slides").

2. If you want to practice syncing narration with PowerPoint animations, make sure that at least one slide has animations.

3. Practice reading the narration script.

4. Save the slides.

Presenter—Narration

1. Open the slides selected for practice in PowerPoint, if not already open. Plug in your headset or microphone.

2. Click the **Record Narration** button on the Articulate tab or select **Record Narration** from the Articulate menu. The Consolidated Recording window will open.

3. Click the **Start Recording** button to record the narration for the first slide to be recorded, using the slide notes as a narration script.

4. If there are PowerPoint animations on the slide, click the **Next Animation** button and record the narration that goes along with that segment of the animation. Click **Next Animation** again and record the narration for the next segment and so on until you have recorded all the narration to go along with the animations on that slide.

5. When recording is complete for that slide, click the **Stop Recording** button.

6. Click the **Play** button ⏺ to listen to the recording. Rerecord the narration, if needed, by repeating steps 2-5.

7. Click the forward slide selector to go to the next slide and repeat steps 2-6.

8. When you have finished recording the narration, click the **Save & Close** button.

9. Click **Preview** on the Articulate tab or **Preview** on the Articulate menu to preview your slides with narration. You can start and stop as needed to note any changes that need to be made.

10. Make any changes necessary and preview the slides again. All done?

11. If yes, click the **Publish** button on the Articulate tab or select **Publish** from the Articulate menu.

12. Specify where you want this Presenter project's files to be saved. The default location is My Documents\My Articulate Projects, but you can choose a different location.

13. Click **Publish**. When publishing is complete, the Publish Successful dialog box will open. Select **View Presentation** to see the final output in your web browser.

14. Pat yourself on the back!

Chapter Recap

This chapter contains information about tasks that are common to most Presenter projects. Here's our list of the most important things to remember from this chapter:

- When you install Presenter, an Articulate tab (in PowerPoint 2007) or an Articulate menu (in PowerPoint 2000-2003) is installed into PowerPoint. Whether you are using the Articulate tab or the Articulate menu, the items on the tab and on the menu are identical, and they both launch identical windows, dialog boxes, and menus.

- Most Presenter projects contain, at a minimum, slides and narration. We discussed how to build your slides in the last chapter and this chapter discusses adding narration in detail.

- The Consolidated Recording window is opened whenever you select one of the following buttons on the Articulate tab or corresponding menu selections on the Articulate menu:
  - Record Narration
  - Add Annotations
  - Sync Animations

- If you use PowerPoint animations in your slides, you can record narration that syncs with each animation's appearance on the screen.

- If you have access to higher quality audio recording and editing equipment, you may want to develop your audio clips using that equipment and import them into Presenter.

- Presenter's Audio Editor will let you perform simple edits on your audio files, including deleting portions, adding silence, and increasing or decreasing the volume.

- Preview your project often so you can catch mistakes and fix them. It's usually easier and less of a hassle to correct mistakes immediately.

- You can select slide properties for each slide, such as navigation title, level, view, and advance method. This is a *very* powerful feature.

- Publishing your project to the web is very easy.

- You are going to be a very good Presenter project builder.

Chapter 6

Pumping Up Your Presenter Projects

Chapter Snapshot

In this chapter, you will learn how to add pizzazz to your Presenter projects.

The information in this chapter assumes a foundational understanding of how to build good PowerPoint slides and the functionalities and tasks presented in Chapter 5, "Presenter Basics."

Dave Mozealous, Articulate QA Manager (blog: http://www.mozealous.com), and Tom Kuhlmann, the author of the Rapid E-Learning blog (http://www.articulate.com/rapid-elearning), contributed numerous tips in this chapter.

Revisiting the Articulate Tab vs. Menu

In Chapter 5, "Presenter Basics," we discussed using the Articulate tab (in PowerPoint 2007) or the Articulate menu (in PowerPoint 2000-2003) that is installed into PowerPoint to accomplish Presenter tasks. In case you haven't read that chapter, we want to remind you that whether you are using the Articulate tab (Figure 6.1) or the Articulate menu (Figure 6.2), the Articulate tasks and functions are identical.

Figure 6.1. The Articulate tab in PowerPoint 2007

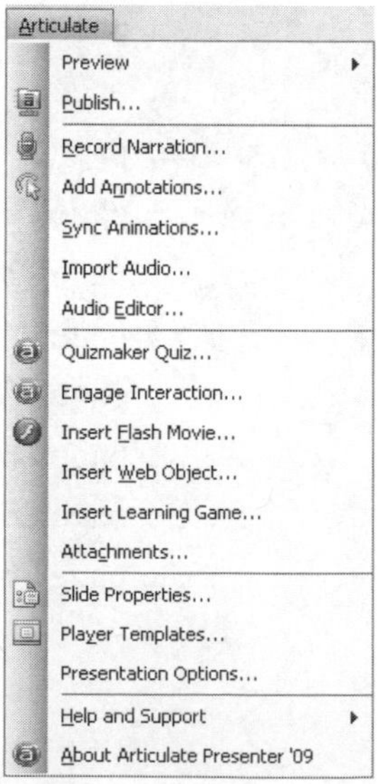

Figure 6.2. The Articulate menu in PowerPoint 2000-2003

Revisiting the Presenter 1-2-3-4-5 Workflow

In this chapter, we'll discuss the third step in the Presenter 1-2-3-4-5 workflow: 3. Add media and interactions. This step is highlighted in Figure 6.3.

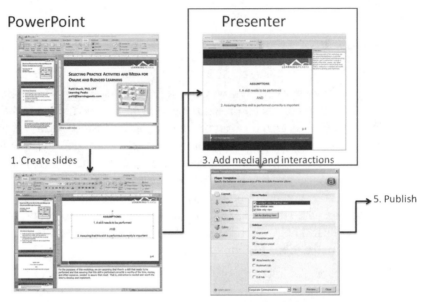

Figure 6.3. Presenter 1-2-3-4-5 workflow

Table 6.1 shows the typical substeps completed in step 3 of the Presenter 1-2-3-4-5 workflow.

Table 6.1. Detailed workflow for step 3

Using Presenter	
3. Add media and interactions	a) Add media and interactions: narration, attachments, Engage interactions, Quizmaker questions, Web Objects, Flash video, etc.
	b) Review and revise narration script to go along with media, interactions, and annotations and record or rerecord, if needed.
	c) Preview and fix (throughout).

In Chapter 5, "Presenter Basics," we discussed the most common "add media and interactions" task that occurs in step 3—adding narration to your slides. If you are new to Presenter or have limited experience with using it, we highly recommend that you work your way through Chapter 5 before diving into this chapter because many of the tasks described in that chapter are jumping-off points for the tasks in this chapter.

Ready for Fun?

If you have worked your way through Chapter 5, "Presenter Basics," or are an experienced Presenter user, you may be ready for the *really* fun stuff. This chapter contains lots of options for creating engaging and meaningful Presenter projects. In fact, if you are anything like me (Patti speaking), you may have fireworks going off in your head with new ideas as you use this chapter!

A recommendation, if I may… As you skim or read through this chapter, write the ideas that pop into your head as notes in the margins. That'll help you collect all of your ideas in the same place as the basic instructions for implementing them.

Adding Attachments

Attachments are additional resources you want to make readily available to anyone who is viewing your Presenter project. Depending on the topic of your project, you may wish to provide downloadable documents such as PDF files, Word documents, or Excel spreadsheets to viewers. If your project is about company financials, for instance, printable copies of the charts and graphs shown onscreen may be desirable. A module built as part of a new hire orientation may include forms and printable job aids for setting up direct deposit of paychecks.

Viewers access attachments by clicking the **Attachments** button on the top bar of the player, as shown in Figure 6.4. The Attachments button is included in the Presenter player by default, but it can be eliminated if there are no attachments by using the Layout tab of the Player Templates dialog box. (As you can see from the figure, other buttons can be placed on the top bar of the player as well.)

Figure 6.4. Top bar of the Presenter player with the Attachments button highlighted

You can add two types of attachments to your Presenter projects: hyperlinks to web pages and files attached to the project.

Tip: If viewers may not have network or Internet access while viewing the project, you should attach a file rather than a link if possible.

Adding Attachments to Your Project

1. Finalize any files you wish to attach to your project and get the URLs (web site addresses) for any links you want to provide.

2. Click the **Attachments** button on the Articulate tab (Figure 6.5) or the **Attachments** menu item on the Articulate menu. The Attachments window opens (Figure 6.6).

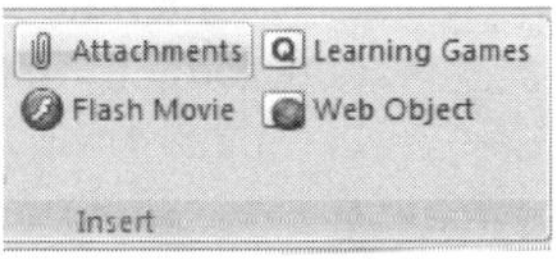

Figure 6.5. The Attachments button on the Articulate tab

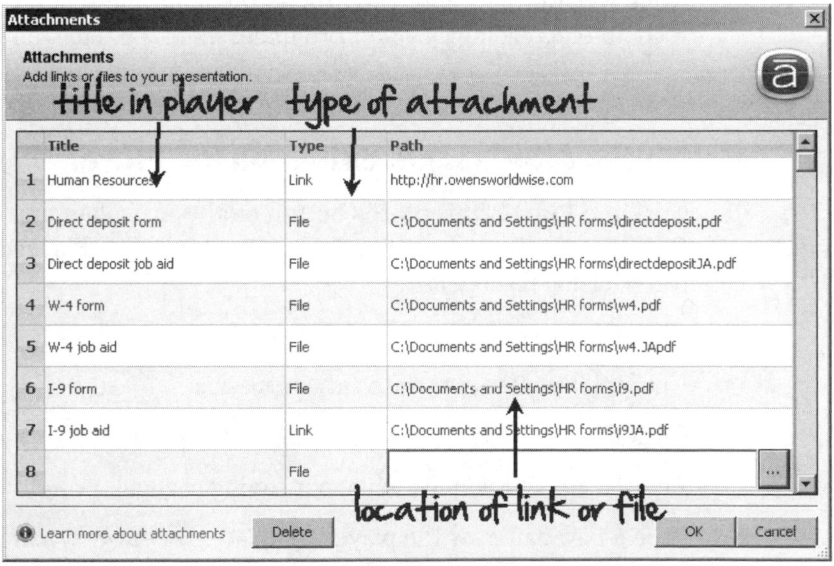

Figure 6.6. Attachments window

3. For each attachment that you wish to add to the project:
   a. Input a title for the attachment. This is the title that will appear when the viewer clicks the Attachments button on the player.
   b. Select an attachment type from the **Type** menu: **Link** or **File**. A link is a *hyperlink* that will open (if the viewer has network or Internet access) when the viewer clicks on it. A file is an *electronic file* that is attached to your project.
   c. Provide a path to the attachment. For a link, type the URL. For a file, type or browse to the file's location. Attached files become part of the supporting files for the project.

4. Click **OK** when you are done.

Removing the Default Attachments Button

If you don't have any attachments, you should remove the Attachments button so it does not appear on the player. Player navigation elements can be removed from a specific Presenter player template using the Player Templates dialog box. Chapter 7, "Customizing Presenter Player Templates," discusses customizing the player in detail. (Presenter's player customization functionalities are amazing but they are also complicated.) So while we are removing the button in the following section, we recommend reading Chapter 7 to understand the topic fully.

Deleting the Attachments Button on the Player

1. Click the **Player Templates** button on the Articulate tab or select **Player Templates** from the Articulate menu. The Player Templates dialog box opens.

2. Click the **Layout** tab.

3. Uncheck the **Attachments tab** check box.

4. Click **Close**.

5. Answer **Yes** to the question about saving changes.

6. Type a new name for the player template. We suggest using **[templatename]_noattachments**.

Deleting Attachments

1. Click the **Attachments** button on the Articulate tab or **Attachments** on the Articulate menu.

2. In the Attachments window, click the row containing the attachment to delete and click **Delete**.

3. Click **OK**.

Adding Annotations

Annotations are used to focus viewer attention on desired areas of the screen. This is especially useful when you want viewers to concentrate on a specific object on the screen, such as the account selection menu on a banking application screen or a specific bullet point that you are discussing.

In Chapter 3, "Introduction to Presenter," we discussed the notion of viewer frustration when dealing with complex screens. One of the points made in that chapter was helping viewers know what to attend to on complex screens. That's the primary purpose of using annotations, to point to what the viewer should be looking at on a given screen.

What's a complex screen? Well, that's a good question but there isn't a simple answer. Any screen that contains new information may feel complex to the viewer.

The Add Annotations button on the Articulate tab is shown in Figure 6.7. When you click the Add Annotations button or the Add Annotations menu selection, the Consolidated Recording window is launched (Figure 6.8). The ribbon at the top (Figure 6.9) of the Consolidated Recording window is used to perform annotation tasks.

Figure 6.7. The Add Annotations button on the Articulate tab

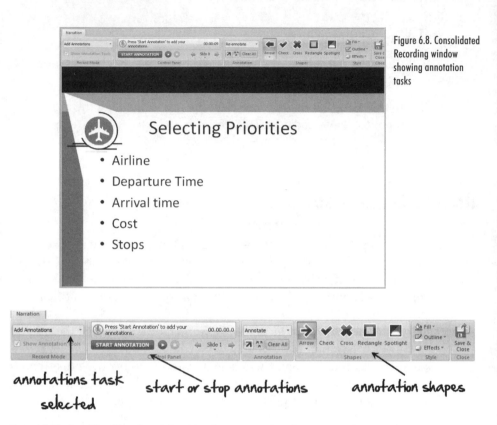

Figure 6.8. Consolidated Recording window showing annotation tasks

Figure 6.9. The Consolidated Recording window ribbon showing annotation tasks

Table 6.2 describes the annotation task options available in the ribbon of the Consolidated Recording window.

Table 6.2. Annotation options

Task options	What happens
Start Annotation START ANNOTATION	Clicking the Start Annotation button begins to sync annotation, using the selected shape, with recorded narration for the current slide.
Stop Annotation STOP ANNOTATION	Clicking the Stop Annotation button ends syncing annotations with recorded narration for the current slide. **Note:** Annotation automatically stops at the end of the audio clip.
Play ▶	Clicking the Play button plays the audio, animations, and annotations for the current slide.
Pause ⏸	Clicking the Pause button pauses annotation or playback.
Resume RESUME	Clicking the Resume button resumes annotation or playback.

Task options	What happens
Slide Selector ⇐ Slide 6 ⇒	Clicking the forward and backward arrows navigates forward and backward to different slides. The forward arrow is commonly used to move to the next slide when you have completed annotating the selected slide.
	You can also use the menu (click the down arrow under the slide number) to see slide thumbnails and additional information about each slide.
Save & Close	Clicking the Save & Close button saves your project and closes the Consolidated Recording window.

Annotations can be added to slides *while* recording narration or *after* you have recorded narration. We're going to discuss adding annotations *after* recording narration because we think that most people would have a hard time recording *and* adding annotations at the same time.

Adding Annotations to Your Project

1. Plan the annotations you wish to use for your project, including:

   ■ The parts of the slide to be annotated

   ■ When the annotations should start and stop (synced with narration)

   ■ The shape(s) to be used and, if using an arrow, the type of arrow to be used

   ■ Whether to move one instance of the shape when annotating different places on the slide (Show One) or show multiple instances of the shape when annotating different places on the slide (Show All)

   ■ Customization options for the selected shape

2. Select the slide on which you want to start your narration.

3. Click the **Add Annotations** button on the Articulate tab or **Add Annotations** from the Articulate menu. The Consolidated Recording window opens.

4. Select the shape to be used (Figure 6.10):

    ■ Arrow (select from arrow types)

    ■ Check

    ■ Cross

    ■ Rectangle

    ■ Spotlight

Figure 6.10. Annotation shapes

5. Select the number of annotations to show on the screen (Figure 6.11). If you want to show one instance of the shape at a time when annotating different places on the slide, select Show One. If you want to have all shapes remain on the screen, showing multiple instances of the shape, select Show All. (How the screen looks with Show One and Show All is illustrated at the bottom of Figure 6.11.)

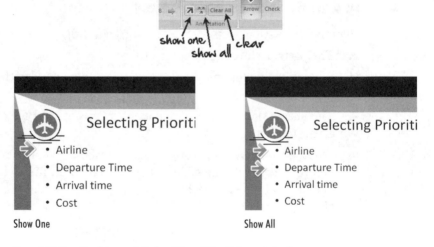

Figure 6.11. Show One (one annotation) and Show All (multiple annotations)

6. Customize the annotation shape, if desired. Table 6.3 shows the customization options for each annotation shape.

Table 6.3. Customization options for each annotation shape

Shape	Customization options
Arrow	Arrow types, fill, outline, effects
Check	Fill, outline, effects
Cross	Fill, outline, effects
Rectangle	Outline, animation, corners
Spotlight	Spotlight, outline, effects

Figure 6.12 shows examples of the customization option menus for each of the annotation shapes. Each shape has its own customization options so the options you see will depend on which shape is chosen.

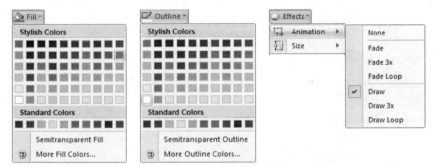

Figure 6.12. Annotation customization option menus: Fill (left), Outline (middle), Effects (right)

7.   When you have selected all desired options for the chosen annotation shape, click the **Start Annotation** button. Listen to the audio narration. Click the screen where you want the selected annotation to appear at the points in the narration where you want the annotation to appear. Annotation automatically stops at the end of the narration.

8. Click the **Play** button ▣ to listen to the narration and watch the annotations appear. If you are unsatisfied with when the annotations appear or what they look like, you can select other options (steps 2-6) and redo the annotations (step 7). (You can also go back and do this later, if needed.)

9. Click the forward slide selector to go to the next slide. You can also jump to any other slide by clicking the Thumbnails menu under the slide selector.

10. Click the **Save & Close** button when you are done.

11. Preview the annotations to make sure they work as desired (Figure 6.13).

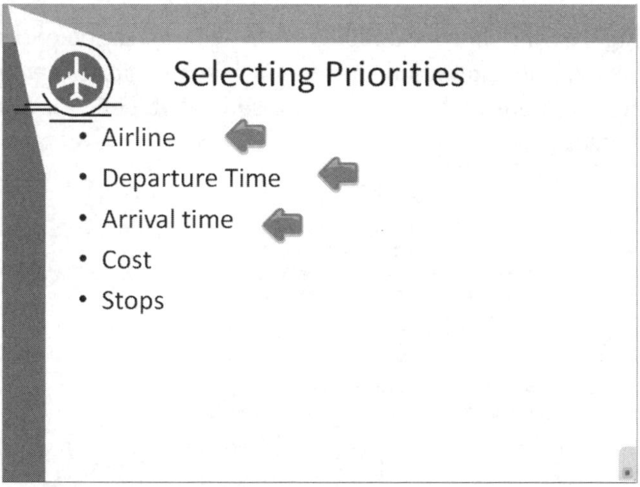

Figure 6.13. Preview the annotations.

Annotations can be powerful, but they can also muck up the screen. Figure 6.13 is going to end up with five copies of the arrow on the screen at once. Too many? Perhaps selecting Show One rather than Show All would have made more sense for this annotation. We think that Show One is often going to be a better option than Show All because the purpose of using annotations is to *focus* attention. But Show All could certainly make sense if your purpose is to point out disorder or too much of something.

Table 6.4 lists potential uses for the different annotation types.

Table 6.4. Potential uses for different annotation shapes

Shape		Potential uses
Arrow	→	Point out and discuss different objects, or point to bullet points as they are being discussed
Check	✔	Point to good examples or point to right answers
Cross	✖	Point to non-examples or point to wrong answers
Rectangle	☐	Focus attention on a specific rectangular area of the screen
Spotlight	◩	Highlight a specific area of the screen

Arrow, check, and cross annotation shapes are fairly easy to understand. But rectangle and spotlight shapes are a bit different. Figure 6.14 shows the rectangle annotation being used to point out the information needed on the top part of a travel expense report. The narration that goes along with the slide describes this section of the report and the annotation is used to help viewers focus on this section.

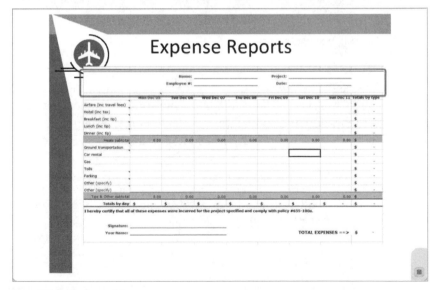

Figure 6.14. Rectangle annotation

Figure 6.15 shows the next slide, which discusses a set of travel-related expense categories. In this example, the spotlight annotation is used to focus on the top set of travel expense categories. The rest of the screen is grayed out so the viewer can more easily concentrate only on this section of the expense report.

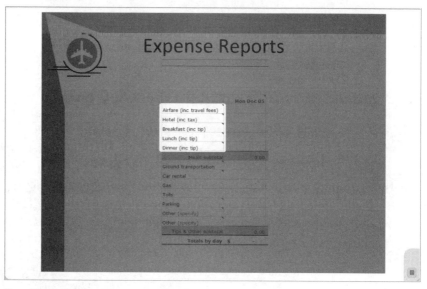

Figure 6.15. Spotlight annotation

You can make the annotation appear to zoom in on the spotlighted portion of the screen (not a feature of the spotlight annotation) by taking a screenshot of the spotlighted area and then enlarging it in the slide that follows the slide with the spotlight annotation (Figure 6.16).

Tip: The "zoom" effect could also be created using PowerPoint animations by switching the original spotlight annotation graphic for the "zoomed" graphic.

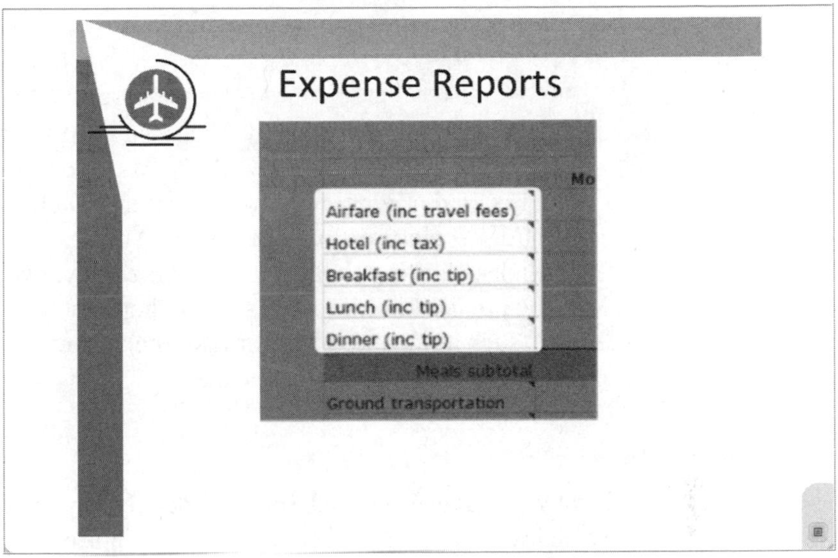
Expense Reports
Airfare (inc travel fees)
Hotel (inc tax)
Breakfast (inc tip)
Lunch (inc tip)
Dinner (inc tip)
Meals subtotal
Ground transportation

Figure 6.16. "Zoom" effect on spotlighted area

Removing Annotations

1. Click the **Add Annotations** button on the Articulate tab or **Add Annotations** from the Articulate menu. The Consolidated Recording window opens.
2. Select the slide on which you want to start your narration.
3. Click the **Start Annotation** button.
4. Click the **Clear All** button (Figure 6.17).
5. Click **Save & Close.**

Re-annotate
Clear All
Annotation

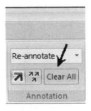

Figure 6.17. The Clear All button in the Consolidated Recording window

Adding Slide Hyperlinks

In addition to adding hyperlinks that can be accessed from the **Attachments** button on the player, you can also add hyperlinks on the slides themselves. Slide text and other objects on the screen (such as text boxes, hotspots, buttons, pictures, or other objects) can easily be turned into hyperlinks. Clicking these links can take the viewer to another slide in the project (also known as branching), open an object or media element (such as an audio file), or take the viewer to a network or Internet resource (such as a web page).

Branching

Branching involves a navigational scheme that doesn't proceed in a linear (slide 1→ slide 2 → slide 3, and so on) manner. Figure 6.18 shows a branching diagram where the viewer can select one of three branches (one branch for each product). On slide 1, the viewer can select a product to learn about, view a welcome audio, or download a sales kit. Clicking the product A hyperlink takes the viewer to slide 4 (which continues through to slide 10). Clicking the product B hyperlink takes the viewer to slide 11 (which continues through to slide 16), and clicking the product C hyperlink takes the viewer to slide 17 (which continues through to slide 23). At the end of each branch, the viewers are taken to slide 24, which helps them plan their strategy for selling each of these products. And once they reach slide 24, there are links back to slide 1, so another product can be selected.

Figure 6.19 shows the first screen of the New Products training project. You can see the options for navigating: the three new product "buttons" and the two links at the top of the screen. The Todd's Introduction link takes the viewer to slide 2. The New Product Distribution Kit link takes the viewer to slide 3. The Kell 1 button takes the viewer to slide 4. The Kell 2 button takes the viewer to slide 11. The Monett 4 button takes the viewer to slide 17.

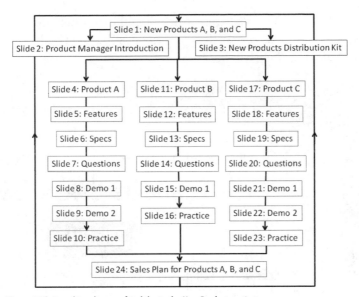

Figure 6.18. Branching diagram for slides in the New Products project

Figure 6.19. New Products slide with branched navigation

All the links on the first screen (including the buttons) are hyperlinked to specific slides. Figure 6.20 shows the first button (Kell 1) being hyperlinked to slide 4.

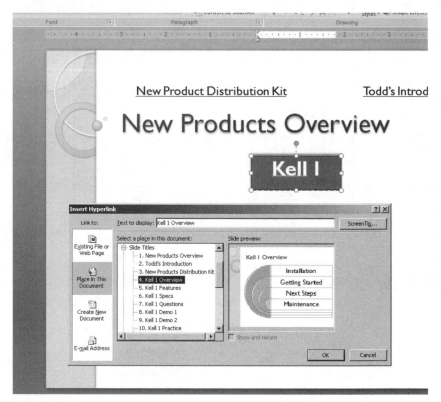

Figure 6.20. Creation of a hyperlink to another slide

Adding Slide Hyperlinks for Branching and Navigation

One reason for building navigation into the slides themselves, as shown in the last section, is to respond to different viewer needs. The viewer can choose the desired path without having to click through each slide to get where he or she wants to go. The branched navigation in the New Products Overview slide was designed to make it easy for viewers to come back and review one or more of the products as needed.

Another reason for building branching into the slides is to take viewers to specific slides based on their decisions on a current slide. Figure 6.21 shows a diagram of the branching implemented in a project about nutrition. The branching in this project is based on the answer that the viewer chooses.

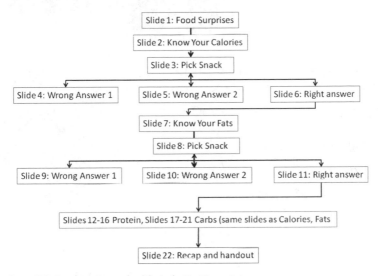

Figure 6.21. Branching diagram for slides in the Nutrition project

Figure 6.22 shows slide 3 of the Nutrition project in the Presenter player. On this slide, viewers are asked to click an answer (one of the snacks). Each snack picture is hyperlinked to a specific slide in the project. This works very similarly to the New Products project, which branched to a set of slides based on the path the learner decides to take. In the Nutrition project example, the viewer doesn't pick a path. The path is "chosen" for them based on the answers he or she selects.

Once viewers click an answer, they are taken to a custom feedback slide. Figure 6.23 shows the slide that appears next if the viewer selects the donut. If the viewers select the wrong answer, a Try again link brings them back to the slide with all three choices. Once they select the right answer, they move on to the next section.

Figure 6.22. Nutrition project with branched feedback

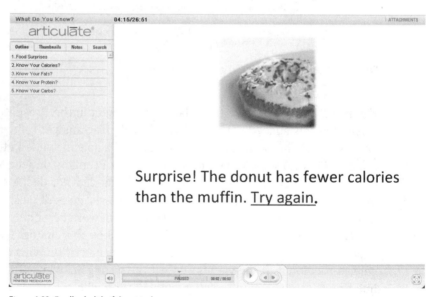

Figure 6.23. Feedback slide if donut is chosen

Branched navigation can be very powerful, but there are some "gotchas" to be aware of. Most of the fixes for these "gotchas" are made using the Slide Properties window. (The Slide Properties window is discussed in detail in Chapter 5, "Presenter Basics.") The following functionalities make branched navigation work: Lock (player navigation), Hide in (sidebar) Navigation Panel, and Branching (set next and previous slides). Figure 6.24 shows these settings in the Slide Properties window. In addition, *not* displaying slide numbers in the Presenter player slide title navigation makes it less obvious that slide titles are hidden. These functionalities will be described next.

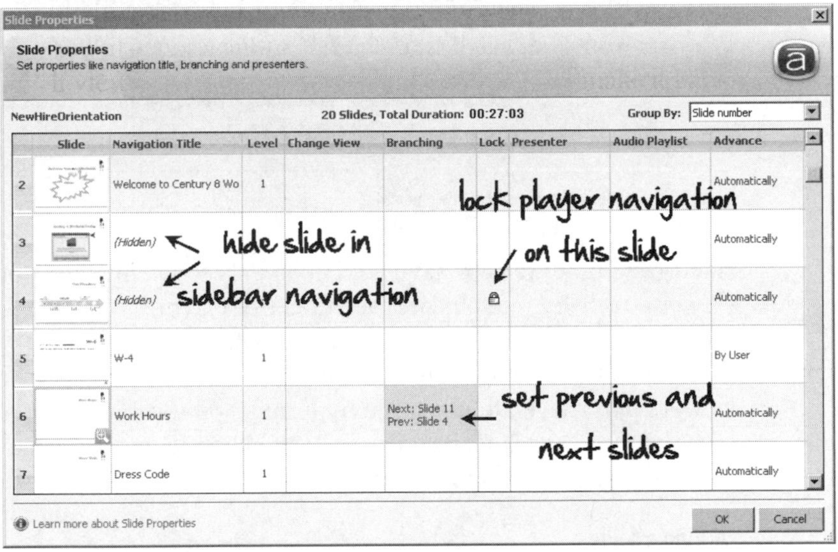

Figure 6.24. Branching functionalities in the Slide Properties window

Locking (Player Navigation)

The default Presenter player includes navigational elements. Which elements are included depends on the selected player template and the view chosen for each slide. (Player templates are discussed in Chapter 7, "Customizing Presenter Player Templates.") The default player template in Standard view contains the sidebar slide title navigation, the seekbar, and the forward/backward/pause controller, as shown in Figure 6.25.

Figure 6.25. Standard player navigation elements

Having multiple ways to navigate becomes a problem when you want viewers to click a slide link rather than use player navigation. Locking slide navigation is the solution to this problem. Locking means disabling the player navigation controls on that slide. If a slide is locked, viewers *must* navigate using the hyperlinks on the slide. The slide with the three snack foods above is locked so the viewer has to select one of the snack foods to continue.

Locking a Slide

1. Click the **Slide Properties** button on the Articulate tab or **Slide Properties** from the Articulate menu. The Slide Properties window opens.

2. Click the cell in the **Lock** column for the slide you want to lock. A lock icon will appear in that cell (Figure 6.26).

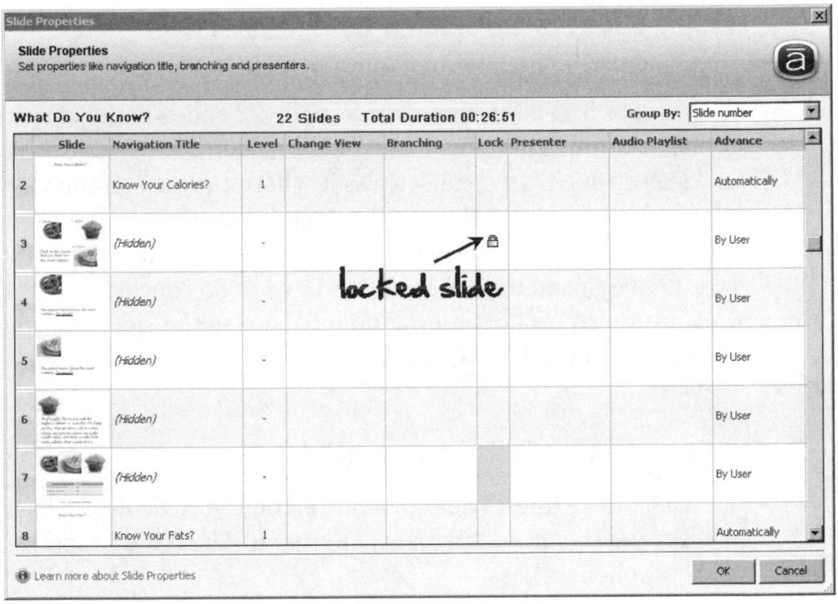

Figure 6.26. Locking slides in the Slide Properties window

3. Click the **OK** button.

Unlocking a Slide

1. Click the **Slide Properties** button on the Articulate tab or **Slide Properties** from the Articulate menu. The Slide Properties window opens.

2. Click the lock icon in the cell you want to unlock. The lock will disappear.

3. Click **OK**.

> **Note:** If the viewer tries to navigate to a locked slide, he or she will see a lock icon, as shown in Figure 6.27.

Figure 6.27. The lock icon shows that the navigation is locked.

Hiding Slides in the Sidebar Navigation Panel

The sidebar navigation in the Nutrition project shows five slide titles (see Figure 6.27). But there are actually 22 slides in the project. Some of the slide titles have been purposely hidden in the sidebar navigation so viewers don't get confused about where they are. If the viewer sees that he is on slide 3 and then slide 5 and then slide 13, he might think that something was very wrong. Viewers don't understand branching (nor do they need to) and shouldn't have to be concerned that they are viewing slides "out of order." Hiding slides in the sidebar navigation allows you to use branched navigation without causing concern for viewers.

Hiding Slides in the Sidebar Navigation Panel

1. Click the **Slide Properties** button on the Articulate tab or **Slide Properties** from the Articulate menu. The Slide Properties window opens.

2. Right-click the slide number for the slide you want to hide and select **Hide in Navigation Panel**. The text in the Navigation Title column will change to *(Hidden)*.

    The Navigation Title text for slides 3-7 in Figure 6.28 show *(Hidden)* because they are slides where branching occur.

Tip: If you want to hide more than one slide in the sidebar navigation, you can Shift-click the slide number cells to select more than one slide and then right-click and select Hide in Navigation Panel. All selected slides titles will change to (Hidden).

---

3. Click the **OK** button.

Note: Hiding slides in Slide Properties only hides the slide from navigation.

Unhiding Slides in the Sidebar Navigation Panel

1. Click the **Slide Properties** button on the Articulate tab or **Slide Properties** from the Articulate menu. The Slide Properties window opens.

2. Right-click the slide number for the slide you want to unhide and click **Hide in Navigation Panel** (which has a checkmark next to it when the title is hidden). *(Hidden)* will disappear and Navigation Title will show. You can click in the Navigation Title field and change the name, if desired.

3. Click **OK**.

Setting Branching (Next and Previous Slides)

The next branching navigation challenge to overcome is fixing what happens when the viewer is supposed to click a slide link but uses the player navigation instead. By default, if a viewer clicks the back button, he or she goes back to the previous slide number. If the viewer clicks the forward button, he or she goes forward to the next slide number. But we've already seen that when implementing branching, viewers may need to go to a different slide rather than the previous number (when going backward) or the next slide number (when going forward).

We have already discussed locking a slide when you want player navigation disabled for that slide. The Slide Properties window also allows you to set which slide the viewers go to when they click the forward and backward buttons.

Setting Previous and Next Slides

1. Click the **Slide Properties** button on the Articulate tab or **Slide Properties** from the Articulate menu. The Slide Properties window opens.

2. Click the cell in the **Branching** column for the slide where you want to set previous and next slides. The Branching dialog box opens (Figure 6.28).

3. In the Branching dialog box, select the slide to which the viewer should branch when the current slide is completed and the slide to branch to if the backward button is clicked.

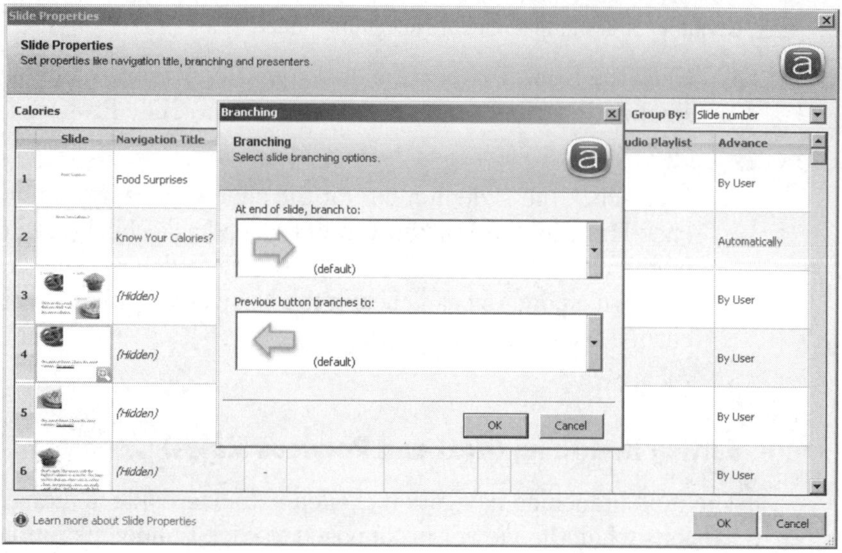

Figure 6.28. Slide Properties window and the Branching dialog box

4.   Click the **OK** button.

Changing Previous and Next Slides

1.   Click the **Slide Properties** button on the Articulate tab or **Slide Properties** from the Articulate menu. The Slide Properties window opens.

2.   Click the cell in the **Branching** column for the slide where you want to change previous and next slides. The Branching dialog box opens.

3.   In the Branching dialog box, select the slide to which the viewer should branch when the current slide is completed and a new slide to branch to if the backward button is clicked (Figure 6.28).

4.   Click **OK**.

Eliminating Slide Numbers

When using the default player in Standard view, a number appears next to each slide title on the Presenter player. If you hide slides to make branching less confusing to viewers, viewers may be confused because some slide title navigation numbers are missing (because they are hidden). You can easily remove slide numbers from the slide title navigation.

Tip: Unless your slides are all at the same level (see the "Slide Properties" section in this chapter), you should consider eliminating slide numbers so the lack of slide number continuity won't throw off viewers.

Player navigation elements can be removed from a specific Presenter player template using the Player Templates window. Chapter 7, "Customizing Presenter Player Templates," discusses customizing player attributes. (Presenter's player customization functionalities are amazing but they are also complicated. We recommend reading Chapter 7 before working with player templates.)

Eliminating Slide Numbers in Slide Title Navigation

1. Click the **Player Templates** button on the Articulate tab or **Player Templates** from the Articulate menu. The Player Templates window opens.

2. Click the **Other** tab.

3. Uncheck the **Display slide numbers in navigation tabs** setting.

4. Click **Close**.

5. Answer **Yes** to the question about saving changes.

6. Type a new name for the player template. We suggest using **[template name]_noslidenumbers**.

Eliminating Player Navigation Altogether

It may have occurred to you that you could create navigation using PowerPoint hyperlinks only, and not use Presenter player navigation. You can accomplish this by embedding navigation links in the slides themselves *and* using Slide only view (see Chapter 5, "Presenter Basics"). In Slide only view, the top bar, bottom bar, and sidebar are hidden and the slide is larger.

Figure 6.29 shows a Presenter project where the navigation is built into the slides. The buttons on the bottom of the slide are hyperlinked to the appropriate places in the presentation. In this project, all of the slides are shown in Slide only view.

Figure 6.29. Navigation built into the slides

Because we don't know what version of PowerPoint you are using (PowerPoint 2007 operates much differently than previous versions), we will provide general guidance about creating navigational hyperlinks on your PowerPoint slides but not step-by-step instructions.

To create navigation links in PowerPoint slides: Create text, shapes (with text or symbols), or other objects to be used as navigational links. Select the text, shape, or object you want to use as a hyperlink. Right-click and choose **Hyperlink** from the right-click menu. You can select:

- **Existing file or Web page:** To link to a file or site on the web
- **Place in This Document:** To link to a selected slide
- **Create New Document:** To link to a document that has not yet been created
- **E-mail Address:** To link to a specified email address with a specified subject line

Tip: You can create a navigation "menu" with shapes, buttons, or objects. First create the shapes, buttons, or objects and then hyperlink each of them to the appropriate slide. Then select the group of linked shapes, buttons, or objects and copy and paste them onto other slides. This way, you don't need to recreate these same navigation elements on every slide! (Way too tedious.)

Selecting Shapes on a Slide

If you develop navigation "buttons" using shapes with text, you can get mighty frustrated when trying to select the shape in order to make a hyperlink. As Figure 6.30 shows, if you select the shape, the hyperlink will be applied to the shape. But it's easy to think you have selected the shape when you have really selected the text *on* the shape. If you select the text by mistake, you will see that the *text* on the shape becomes the hyperlink, not the button. If this happens, undo and try again.

What is selected?   *How link looks on the slide*

Shape is selected   Can't "see" the link but it's there

Text is selected (doesn't   Shape text becomes the link ☹
look much different!)

Figure 6.30. How a shape and text look when selected and how the resulting hyperlink looks

Note: If you want viewers to navigate using slide hyperlinks *throughout the project*, make sure that player navigation elements (such as the sidebar slide title navigation and the forward/back/pause buttons) are removed from the player. Player navigation elements can be removed from a specific Presenter player template using the Player Templates window. Chapter 7, "Customizing Presenter Player Templates," discusses customizing player attributes. If you only want to force viewers to use slide hyperlinks *on certain slides*, use the Lock functionality described later in this chapter.

To wrap up our branching discussion, we'll look at a final example. In this example, the viewers branch to different slides based on the answer they select.

Figure 6.31 shows a slide in a performance management project where the viewers are asked to select the right next step after they have listened to an audio where they hear a supervisor and staff member discussing performance issues.

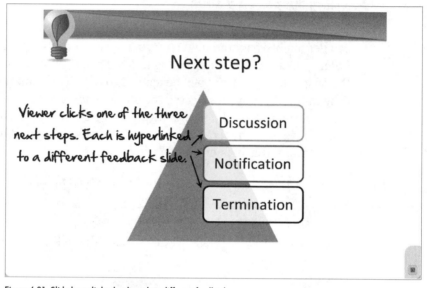

Figure 6.31. Slide hyperlinks that branch to different feedback pages

Figure 6.32 shows the slide that the viewers see if they select the wrong answer. It contains feedback about the answer they chose and a link back to the slide with the audio so they can listen to it once more.

Figure 6.32. Feedback slide for incorrect answer

Adding Slide Hyperlinks for Additional Content

Another reason for adding hyperlinks to slides is to link to additional content. This could be content that viewers are *expected* to read, view, or hear such as an audio or video clip, or content that is "extra" for those who want or need additional information, such as more details, definitions, references, and so on.

Figure 6.33 shows the first slide that viewers see in the branched scenario about Leanne's lateness problem. The "Listen" button is actually hyperlinked to a duplicate slide with an audio file, which lets viewers hear Leanne's supervisor discuss the facts of Leanne's lateness problems. After viewers hear the clip, they are asked (on the next slide) to determine what course of action should be taken (shown earlier).

Figure 6.34 shows an example of additional content or extra information that viewers can access, if they desire to do so. A list of links like this is typically provided at the end of a course. In Presenter, this list can also be accomplished by using the Attachments functionality (described earlier in the chapter). Plus, Presenter lets you bring in objects from the web (discussed later in this chapter) and that functionality provides another way of "linking" to outside resources.

Figure 6.33. "Listen" hyperlink in Presenter

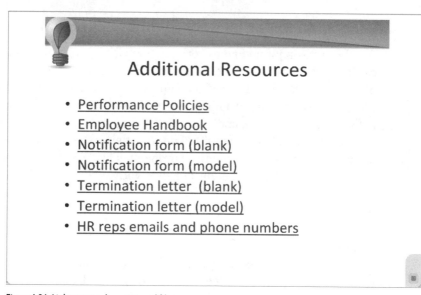

Figure 6.34. Links to extra documents and files

Adding Slide Hyperlinks for Navigation, Branching, or Additional Content

Note that the process may be slightly different depending on the version of PowerPoint you are using.

1. Plan out your links and the paths viewers take. Make sure any "branches" get to the end without confusion.

2. Create needed text or objects (such as text boxes, hotspots, buttons, pictures, or other objects) to be used as hyperlinks (and put them on the appropriate slide or slides).

3. Select the text or object, right-click, and choose **Hyperlink** from the right-click menu. You can select:

    ■ **Existing file or Web page:** To link to a file or site on the web

    ■ **Place in This Document:** To link to a selected slide

    ■ **Create New Document:** To link to a document that has not yet been created

    ■ **E-mail Address:** To link to a specified email address with a specified subject line

Removing or Editing Slide Links for Navigation

Right-click the linked text or object and select Edit Hyperlink or Remove Hyperlink.

 Note: If you link to a web page or file on the web that has a URL, use an absolute link, such as http://www.gotothislink.com or http://www.gotothislink/feedingfrenzy_jobaid.pdf. If you link to a document that is not on the web, use a relative link.

In order to determine the "path" for relative links for items that are attached (by adding Attachments), follow these steps:

1. Insert the file as an attachment and note the file name so you can input it in step 3.

2. Select the text or object to use for the link, right-click, and choose **Hyperlink** from the right-click menu.

3. Input this relative link: **data/downloads/<filename>**.

4. Click **OK**.

As a finale for this branching section, we'd like to show you another example of branching because it is bound to give you additional ideas about how to use the branching functionalities discussed in this section. Tom Kuhlmann, the author of the Rapid E-Learning blog, produced the branching example that you see in Figures 6.35 and 6.36.

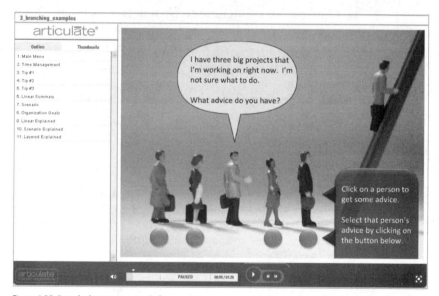

Figure 6.35. Branched scenario example (source: http://www.articulate.com/community/blogdemo/3_branching_examples/player.html)

Figure 6.36. Branched scenario example (source: http://www.articulate.com/community/blogdemo/
3_branching_examples/player.html)

In this example, when you click a "person," you branch to a duplicate
of the slide where the talk bubble has changed. This branching strategy makes it seem as if you are staying on the same slide but the
"person" speaking is changing.

The basics for accomplishing this are as follows:

1. Produce a set of duplicate slides with the same people and back-
    ground. There should be two slides for each person who offers
    advice. (One is used for each person's advice and one is used for a
    reaction to each person's advice.)

2. Each duplicate slide should have links from the person to the
    advice slide for that person and from something else (Tom used a
    number) to the reaction slide for each person's advice.

3. Create an advice talk bubble for each person on the slide desig-
    nated as their advice slide.

4. Create a reaction talk bubble for each person's advice on the slide
    designated as the reaction slide.

I asked Tom for additional hints on this approach and here's his advice:

"I create a master slide and then enough blank slides to accommodate the links. I build all of the links on the master because they need to work the same on all of the slides. Then I copy and paste onto all of the blank slides. After that, I change the feedback and in the case of the demo, the button color. You can also add unique animations or annotations to those slides."

I hope these branching examples have given you ideas for using branching in your Presenter projects.

Adding Learning Games

Engage interactions and Quizmaker quizzes can be added to Presenter projects to provide interactivity. But Presenter also offers a way to add interactivity through Learning Games.

The Learning Games button on the Articulate tab is shown in Figure 6.37. When you click the Learning Games button or select Learning Games from the Articulate menu, the Learning Games Wizard is launched.

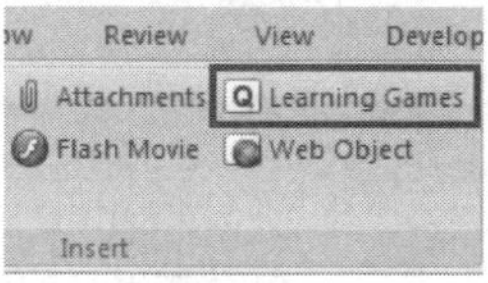

Figure 6.37. The Learning Games button on the Articulate tab

Learning Games can engage viewers as they are viewing and interacting with a Presenter project. They can be added to let viewers test their knowledge and break up sequences where viewers are primarily watching screens and listening to narration. Table 6.5 describes the three Learning Games that are available to insert into Presenter projects.

Table 6.5. Learning Games types and descriptions

Game type	Description
Choices	Choose the correct answer to multiple choice and true/false questions.
Word Quiz	Select letters that spell out the answer to a question.
Sequence	Arrange items in the correct order.

Each Learning Game is created by filling in forms in each Learning Games Wizard window. Figures 6.38 through 6.43 step you through a typical process of creating a Learning Game.

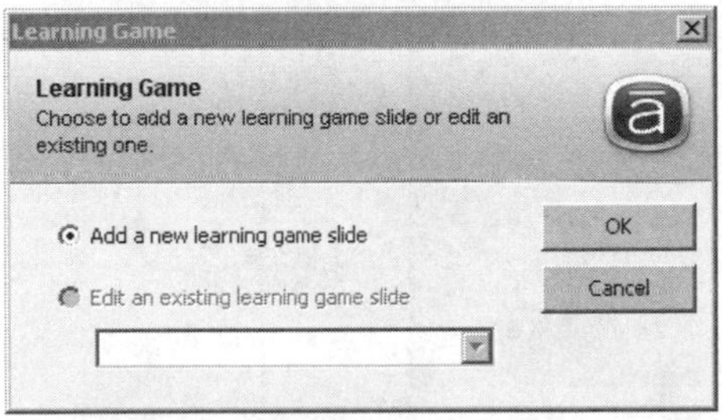

Figure 6.38. Step 1: Open the Learning Games Wizard and add a new game.

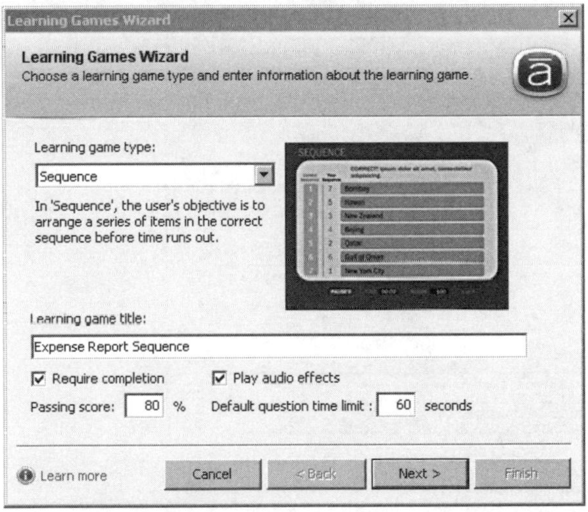

Figure 6.39. Step 2: Select the game type and input a game title.

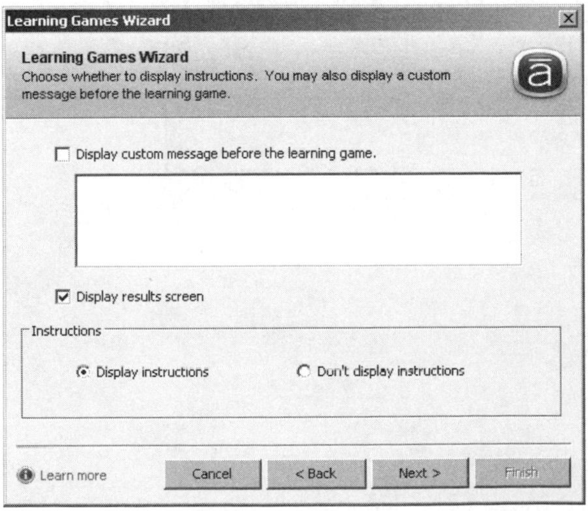

Figure 6.40. Step 3: Add message if desired and determine whether to show instructions.

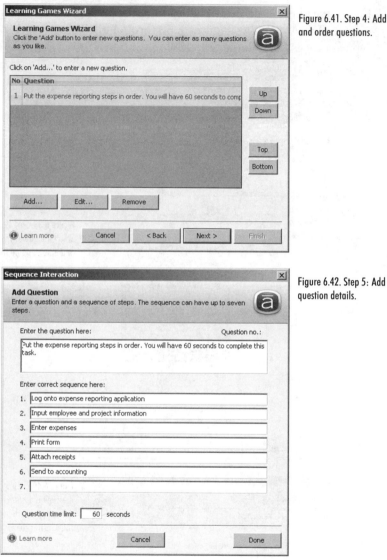

Figure 6.41. Step 4: Add
and order questions.

Figure 6.42. Step 5: Add
question details.

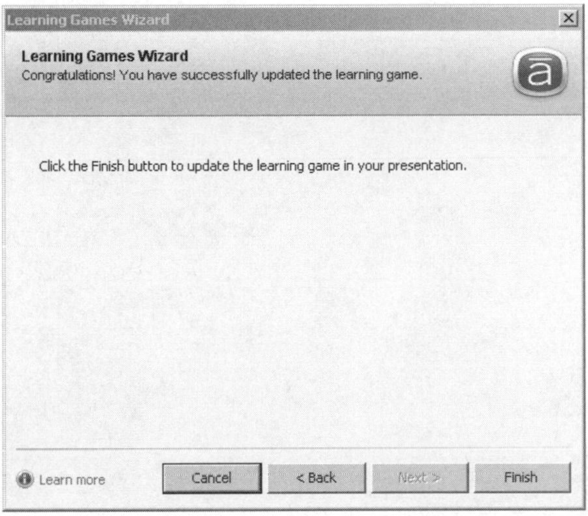

Figure 6.43. Step 6:
Finish the game.

Once you have created a Learning Game, a game placeholder slide is inserted into your Presenter project (Figure 6.44). To see the actual game that you created, you'll need to preview or publish your Presenter project (Figure 6.45).

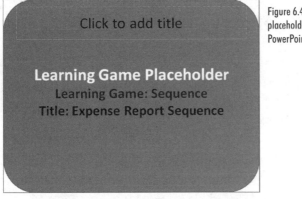

Figure 6.44. Game
placeholder in
PowerPoint slide

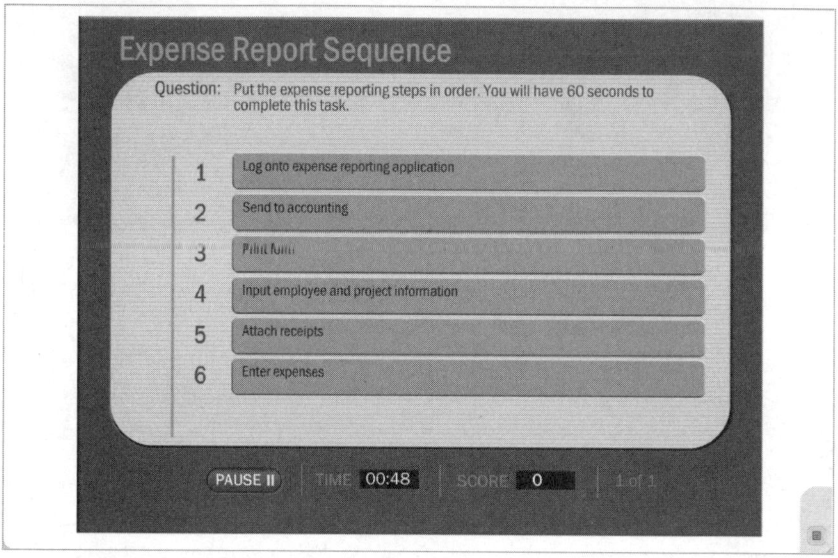

Figure 6.45. Game in Preview mode

Table 6.6 shows some potential uses for each game type. (You can probably think of others.)

Table 6.6. Potential uses for Learning Games

Game	Potential uses
Choices	Recall facts.
	Determine if a statement is correct or incorrect.
	Decide which decision/behavior/approach is correct/preferred.
	Select the appropriate item/resource to use in a given situation.
Word Quiz	Figure out the letters in the answer to a question by selecting letters.
Sequence	Order the steps to be followed.
	Arrange the list from most to least.
	Arrange the list from least to most.

Adding a Learning Game (or Editing an Existing Game)

1. Plan the game questions, including questions and answers.

2. Select the slide that appears *before* where you want the Learning Game slide(s) to appear.

3. Click the **Learning Games** button on the Articulate tab or **Learning Games** from the Articulate menu. The Learning Games Wizard opens.

4. Choose to **Add a new Learning Game slide** or **Edit an existing Learning Game slide**. If editing an existing game, select which one. Click **OK**.

5. If adding a new game, select the game type and input the game title (Figure 6.46).

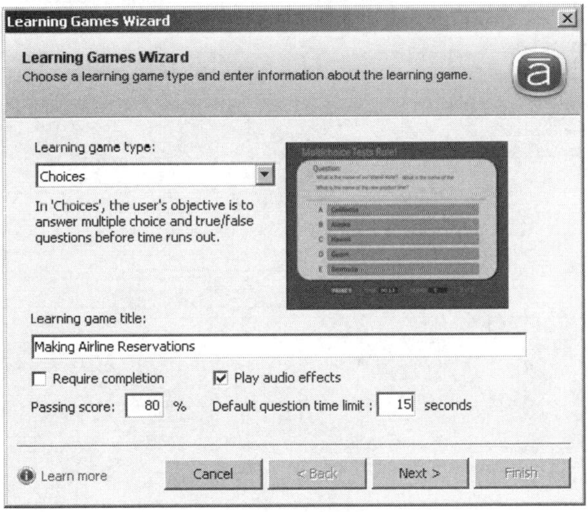

Figure 6.46. Selecting the Choices game type and inputting a title

---

|||||**Tip:** Use a unique title that identifies the specific game rather than a generic title such as "Choices game" or "Word Quiz Game 3."

6. Select or edit the game settings:

   ■ Choose whether to **Require completion**. If checked, viewers must complete the game before continuing.

■ Choose whether to **Play audio effects**. If checked, viewers will hear game sound effects.

■ Input the **Passing score**. 80% is the default.

■ Input the **Default question time limit** for each question. The time limit is the amount of time viewers are given to answer each question. The maximum time is 10 minutes (600 seconds).

7. Click the **Next** button.

8. Choose whether to **Display custom message before the Learning Game**. Type a custom pre-game message in the text box, if desired.

9. Choose whether to **Display instructions** and click **Next**. Note: Standardized instructions that describe how the game works (that cannot be edited) are put on a page before the game, as shown in Figure 6.47.

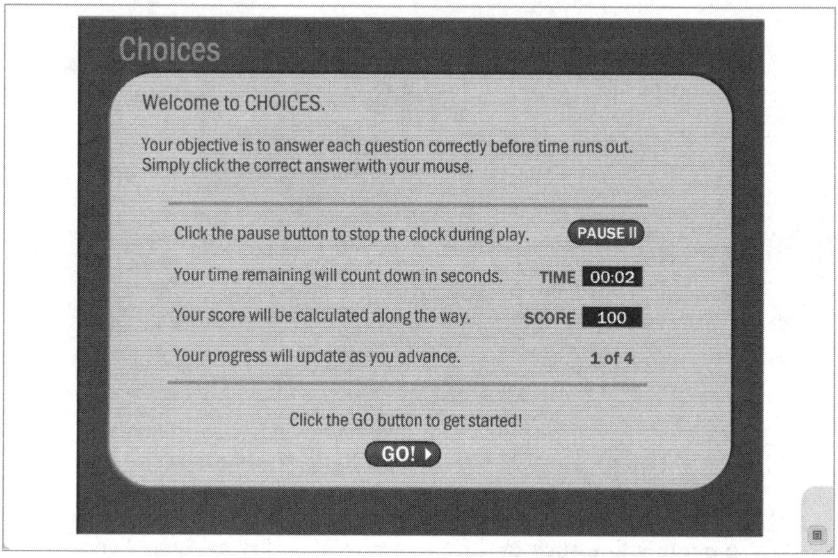

Figure 6.47. Learning Games instruction screen

10. Click **Add** to add a new question. Or click **Edit** to edit an existing question.

For a Choices game: In the Multiple Choice Interaction dialog box:

a. Select the Question type—Multiple choice or True/False.
b. Enter the question text in the Enter the question here text box.
c. Enter up to five answers. Note: 3-5 are grayed out until you put answers in the text boxes.
d. Select the Correct answer.
e. Enter the Question time limit in seconds.

For a Word Quiz game:

a. Enter the question text in the Enter the question here text box.
b. Enter the answer text in the Enter the answer here text box.
c. Enter the Question time limit in seconds.

 Tip: This game works best with short answers and a few words only.

For a Sequence game:

a. Enter the question text in the Enter the question here text box.
b. Enter the correct steps in the correct order in the Enter correct sequence here text boxes. You can enter up to seven steps.
c. Enter the Question time limit in seconds.

11. Click **Next Question** to add another question or click **Done** to stop adding or editing questions.

Note: You can edit questions by selecting the question from the Question list and clicking the Edit button. You can delete questions by selecting the question from the Question list and clicking the Remove button. You can change the order of a question by selecting the question from the Question list and clicking the Up, Down, Top, or Bottom button.

12. Determine whether to display a results screen and the pass and fail feedback to display on the results screen.

13. Click the **Finish** button.

Removing a Learning Game

Delete the game placeholder slide.

> **Note:** Deleting a Learning Game *permanently* removes it. If you unintentionally delete a Learning Game, you can undo the deletion by pressing Ctrl+Z.

Adding Engage Interactions

Engage interactions allow viewers to "discover" content in a way that is fun. Some of the Engage interactions are especially useful for answering viewers' questions, such as the FAQ interaction and the Glossary interaction. In this section, we'll discuss how to put an Engage interaction inside a Presenter '09 project. You can use Engage interactions created in Engage '09 and Engage 2 in your Presenter project. (If you need to learn to use Engage, there's an entire section of the book (Chapters 14-25) devoted to it. Check that out and then come back here!)

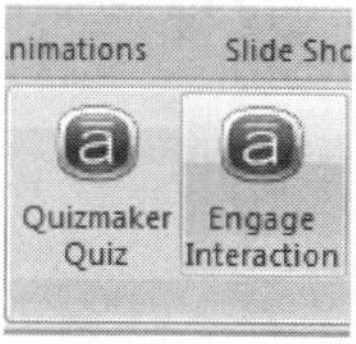

Figure 6.48. The Engage Interaction button on the Articulate tab

The Engage Interaction button on the Articulate tab is shown in Figure 6.48.

There are actually *three* ways to insert an Engage interaction into your Presenter project:

- Embedding an existing Engage interaction from within Presenter
- Creating a new interaction by launching Engage from Presenter
- Publishing an interaction from Engage to a Presenter project

In this chapter, we are focusing on inserting an existing Engage interaction from within Presenter and will also discuss how to launch Engage from Presenter to create a new interaction. The steps to create an Engage interaction are covered in Chapters 14-25. The last method, publishing an interaction from Engage to a Presenter project, is covered in Chapter 26, "Publishing."

From Presenter, you can embed an Engage interaction into a Presenter project as a *slide* or as a *tab*.

Embedding an Engage Interaction as a Slide

When an Engage interaction is embedded into a Presenter project as a slide, the interaction fills an entire slide and is treated like any other slide in the project. Figure 6.49 shows the Engage interaction after it has been embedded into a PowerPoint slide presentation.

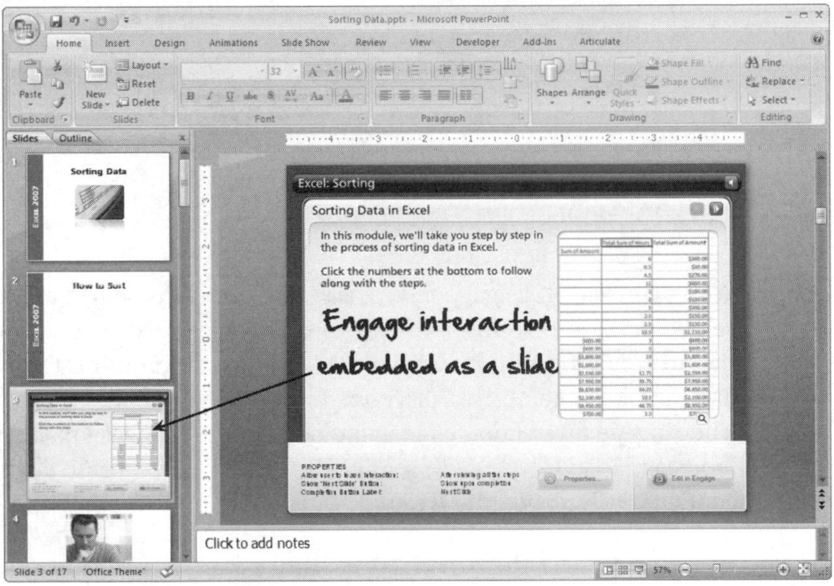

Figure 6.49. Engage interaction embedded as a slide

Figure 6.50 shows the same Engage interaction in the Presenter player.

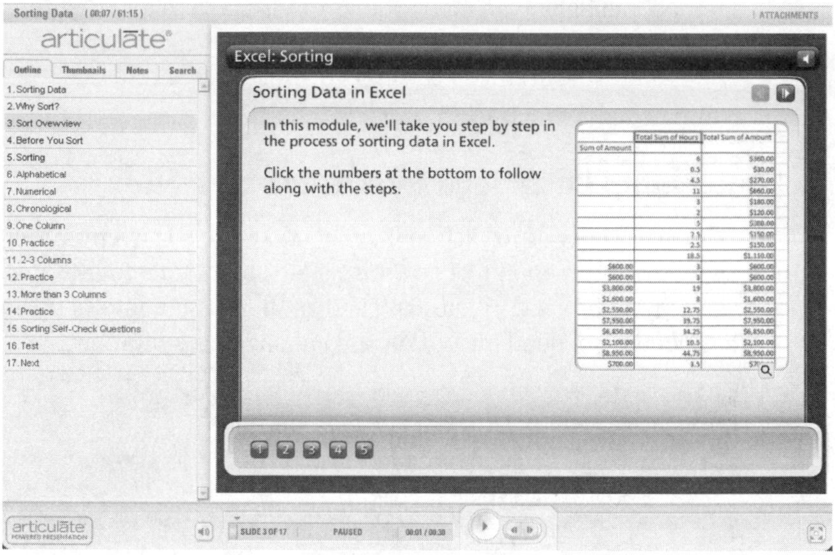

Figure 6.50. Sorting Process interaction in Presenter player

When you add an Engage interaction as a slide, Presenter automatically creates a new slide with the interaction and places it at the end of the presentation. You can move the slide to a different location by dragging it to the desired place in Normal view or Slide Sorter view. The Engage interaction slide is included in the standard navigation. (You cannot add anything else, such as text or graphics, to a slide that contains an Engage interaction.)

Embedding an Interaction as a Slide

1. Click the **Engage Interaction** button on the Articulate tab or **Engage Interaction** on the Articulate menu.

2. In the Quizzes and Interactions dialog box, select the **Engage Interactions** tab (Figure 6.51).

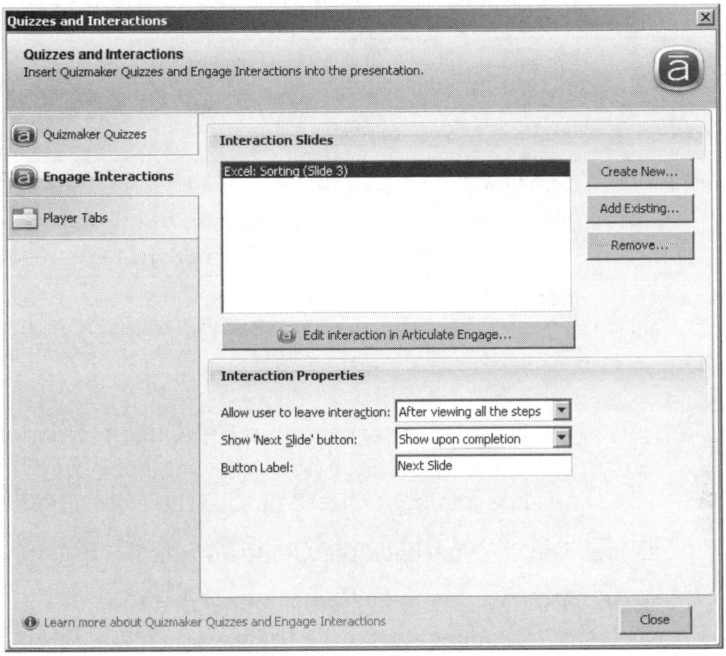

Figure 6.51. Quizzes and Interactions dialog box

3. Choose whether to create a new interaction or insert an existing interaction.

   ■ **To create a new interaction:** Click the **Create New** button. This launches the Engage program, where you create the interaction. When your interaction is complete, click the **Save and Return to Presenter** button that appears on the Engage ribbon.

   ■ **To insert an existing interaction:** Click the **Add Existing** button. The Select Engage Interaction dialog box opens. Navigate to the desired interaction. (Engage interaction files use the file extension .intr.) Click the **Open** button to insert the interaction. If previous versions of the interaction exist, a message will ask if you want to update the interaction.

66 Note: You cannot insert *published* Engage interactions from here.

4. Set the desired interaction properties:

Table 6.7. Interaction properties

Property	Options	Recommendations
Allow user to leave interaction	Anytime After viewing all the steps	Most of the time
Show 'Next Slide' button	Don't show Show always Show upon completion	If viewer should use player navigation to move forward If player navigation isn't available When "After viewing all the steps" is chosen
Button Label	Next Slide	If you choose to display the Next Slide button, keep the default label or delete it and input the desired button label.

5. After you create or insert an interaction, the interaction title is displayed in the Interaction Slides list in the Engage Interactions tab. The slide number is listed next to the interaction title.

6. When you're done, click the **Close** button.

Figure 6.52 shows a close-up of the embedded Engage interaction in PowerPoint. Presenter shows the first screen of the interaction on the slide. The lower section of the slide displays interaction properties, which you can edit by clicking the Properties button. You can also edit the interaction itself using the Edit in Engage button. To see the entire interaction, you can use the Preview button on the Articulate tab.

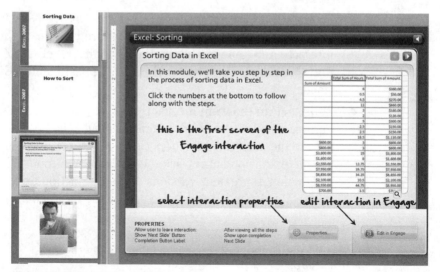

Figure 6.52. Close-up of Engage interaction in PowerPoint

Embedding an Engage Interaction as a Tab

When an Engage interaction is embedded into a Presenter project as a tab, it acts like a button on the Presenter player. (We actually prefer to refer to this as embedding an Engage interaction as a player *button* because it doesn't look or act like a tab.) Engage interactions that are embedded as a tab are accessible anytime from the player (Figure 6.53). Viewers can click the tab and open the interaction from anywhere in the project.

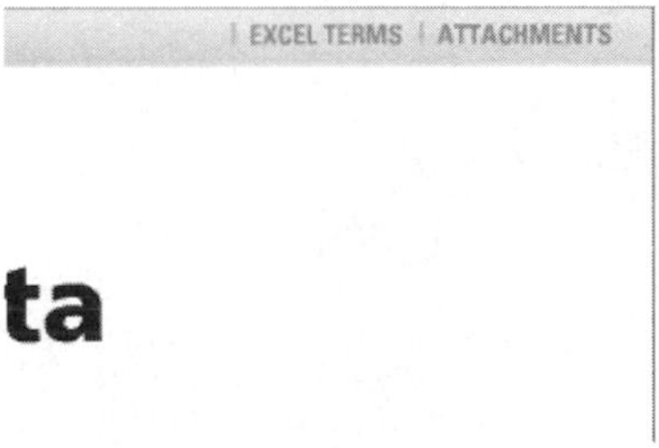

| EXCEL TERMS | ATTACHMENTS

ta

Figure 6.53. Engage interaction embedded as a tab

By adding an interaction as a tab, viewers have the flexibility to access the interaction anytime and from any slide. This would be especially beneficial if there are interactions that you want viewers to use throughout the project. For example, a Glossary interaction would likely be used anytime and it would be best to not "hide" it on a slide.

Embedding an Interaction as a Tab

1. Click the **Engage Interaction** button on the Articulate tab or **Engage Interaction** on the Articulate menu.

2. In the Quizzes and Interactions dialog box, select **Player Tabs** (Figure 6.54).

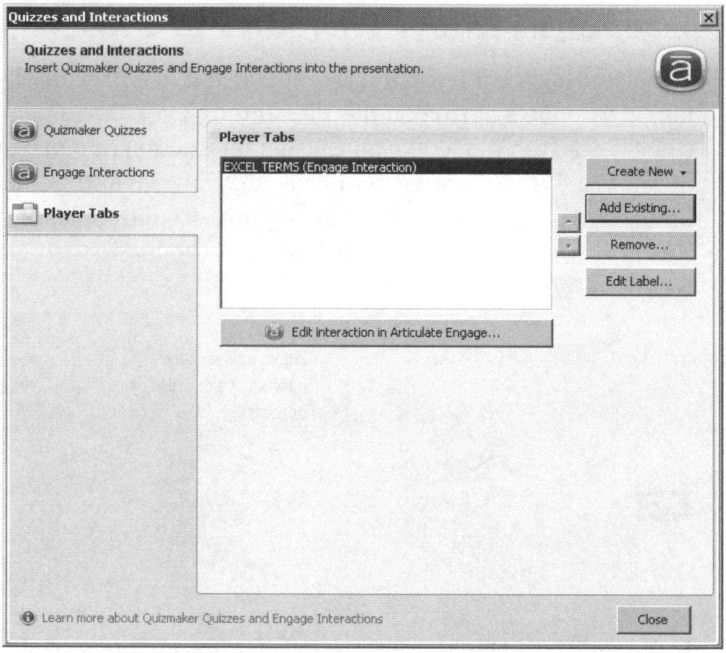

Figure 6.54. Quizzes and Interactions dialog box

3. Choose whether to create a new interaction or insert an existing interaction.

    ■   **To create a new interaction:** Click the **Create New** button, then select **Engage Interaction**. This launches the Engage program, where you create the new interaction. When the interaction is complete, click the **Save and Return to Presenter** button that appears on the Engage ribbon.

    ■   **To insert an existing interaction:** Click the **Add Existing** button to open the Select Engage Interaction dialog box. Navigate to the desired interaction. (Engage interaction files use the file extension .intr.) Note: You cannot insert *published* Engage interactions from here. Click the **Open** button to insert the interaction. (If previous versions of the interaction exist, a message will ask if you want to update the interaction.)

4. After you create or insert an interaction, the interaction title is displayed in the list in the Player Tabs tab of the Quizzes and Interactions dialog box. This title will be used as the label on the

tab menu. To change the label, click the **Edit Label** button, enter a new name in the Edit Tab Label dialog box, and click **OK**.

5.   When you're done, click the **Close** button.

Figure 6.55 shows a close-up of the Engage interaction tab in the Presenter player.

Figure 6.55. Glossary interaction tab

Figure 6.56 shows the "opened" Glossary interaction (Excel Terms) embedded as a tab in the Presenter player. Interactions that are embedded as a tab in the Presenter player, like the Excel Terms glossary interaction shown, open *outside* of the Presenter player (in their own window) when they are clicked.

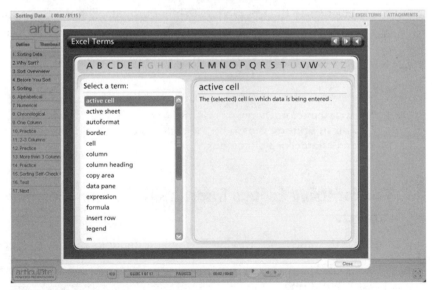

Figure 6.56. The Engage Glossary interaction opened

Deleting or Editing an Engage Interaction

If you change your mind about using an Engage interaction that you have previously added as a slide or tab, it can easily be deleted.

Deleting or Editing an Interaction (Slide or Tab)

1. Click the **Engage Interaction** button on the Articulate tab or **Engage Interaction** on the Articulate menu.

2. In the Quizzes and Interactions dialog box, select **Engage Interactions** if the interaction is a slide or select **Player Tabs** if the interaction is a tab.

3. Select the interaction from the Interaction Slide list (for slides) or the Player Tabs list (for tabs).

4. **To remove an interaction:** Click the **Remove** button, then click **Yes** to confirm, and close the Quizzes and Interactions dialog box. (You can also delete the slide as you would delete any slide to remove the interaction.)

   To edit an interaction: Click the **Edit interaction in Articulate Engage** button in the Quizzes and Interactions dialog box. Presenter opens the Engage program, where you can make changes to the interaction. When finished, click the **Save and Return to Presenter** button that appears on the Engage ribbon. The interaction will be saved and reinserted into your presentation. Then click the **Close** button.

> **Tip:** If the interaction was inserted as a slide, you can also click the **Edit in Engage** button on the slide instead of using the Quizzes and Interactions dialog box.

Tips for Using Engage Interactions in Your Presenter Projects

Here are some tips for using Engage interactions in your Presenter projects.

- **Color schemes:** Consider the color scheme used in the selected Presenter player template when creating Engage interactions that will be embedded in a Presenter project. Presenter '09, Quizmaker

'09, and Engage '09 have color schemes that are designed to look good together. For example, if you use the "Blue Dark" color scheme in Presenter, you can also use the "Blue Dark" color scheme in Engage.

■ **Fonts:** Use the same fonts in Presenter, Quizmaker, and Engage when they will be used for the same project.

■ **Navigation:** If you insert an Engage interaction as a slide and keep the Next Slide button that is embedded in the slide as a default, you may want to lock player navigation on that slide so viewers are not confused about how to navigate. (See this chapter's branching section for information about how to lock player navigation in the Slide Properties window.)

■ **Using slide and tab interactions in the same project:** For a good example of a presentation that uses both slide interactions and tab interactions, check out David Moxon's article on the Word of Mouth blog, "Articulate 101: Engage Slides and Tabs" (http://www.articulate.com/blog/articulate-101-engage-slides-and-tabs).

Adding Quizmaker Quizzes

When people think of instruction, quiz and test questions often come to mind. Quizmaker questions can be used to help learners check whether they understand the content. Quizzes and tests are commonly used to assess whether the learner has met the learning objectives. In this section, we'll discuss how to put Quizmaker quizzes and questions into a Presenter project. (If you need to learn to use Quizmaker, there's an entire section of the book (Chapters 8-14) devoted to it. Check that out and then come back here!)

Figure 6.57. The Quizmaker Quiz button on the Articulate tab

The Quizmaker Quiz button on the Articulate tab is shown in Figure 6.57.

There are actually *three* ways to insert a Quizmaker quiz into your Presenter project:

■ Embedding an existing Quizmaker quiz from within Presenter

■ Creating a new quiz by launching Quizmaker from Presenter

■ Publishing a quiz from Quizmaker to a Presenter project

In this chapter, we are focusing on inserting an existing Quizmaker quiz from within Presenter and we will also discuss how to launch Quizmaker from Presenter to create a new interaction. The steps to create a Quizmaker quiz are covered in Chapters 8-14. The last method, publishing a quiz from Quizmaker to a Presenter project, is covered in Chapter 26, "Publishing."

From Presenter, you can embed a Quizmaker quiz into a Presenter project as a *slide* or as a *tab*.

Embedding a Quizmaker Quiz as a Slide

When a Quizmaker quiz is embedded into a Presenter project as a slide, the quiz fills the entire slide and is treated like any other slide in the project. Figure 6.58 shows the Quizmaker slide after it has been embedded as a PowerPoint slide.

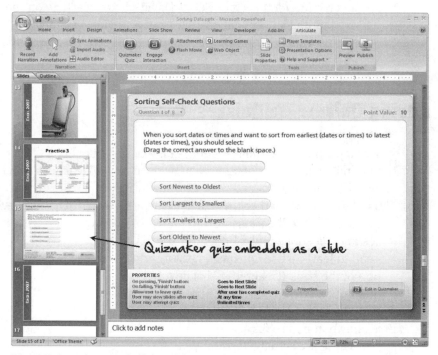

Figure 6.58. Quizmaker quiz embedded as a slide

Figure 6.59 shows the same Quizmaker quiz in the Presenter player. When you add a Quizmaker quiz as a slide, Presenter automatically creates a new slide with the quiz and places it at the end of the presentation. You can move the slide to a different location by dragging the slide to the desired location in Normal view or Slide Sorter view. The Quizmaker slide is included in the standard navigation. You cannot add anything else, such as text or graphics, to a slide that contains a Quizmaker quiz.

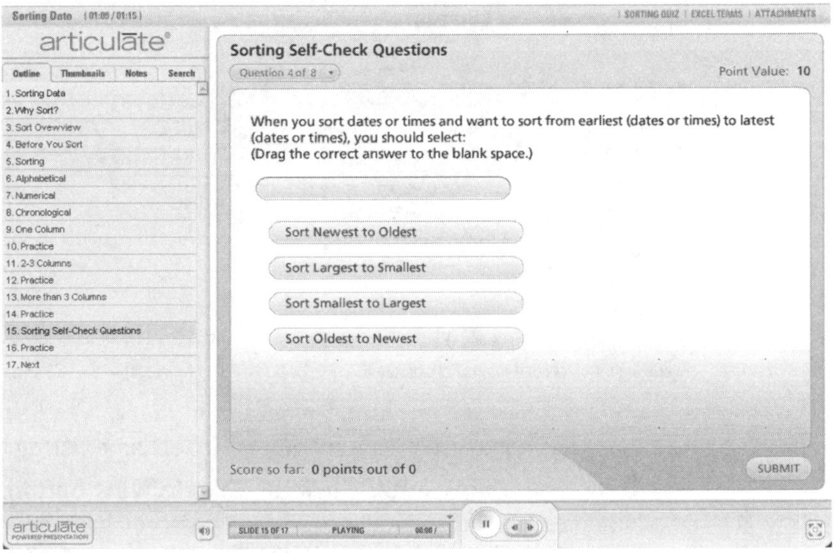

Figure 6.59. Quizmaker quiz in Presenter player

Embedding a Quiz as a Slide

1. Click the **Quizmaker Quiz** button on the Articulate tab or **Quizmaker Quiz** on the Articulate menu.

2. In the Quizzes and Interactions dialog box, select the **Quizmaker Quizzes** tab.

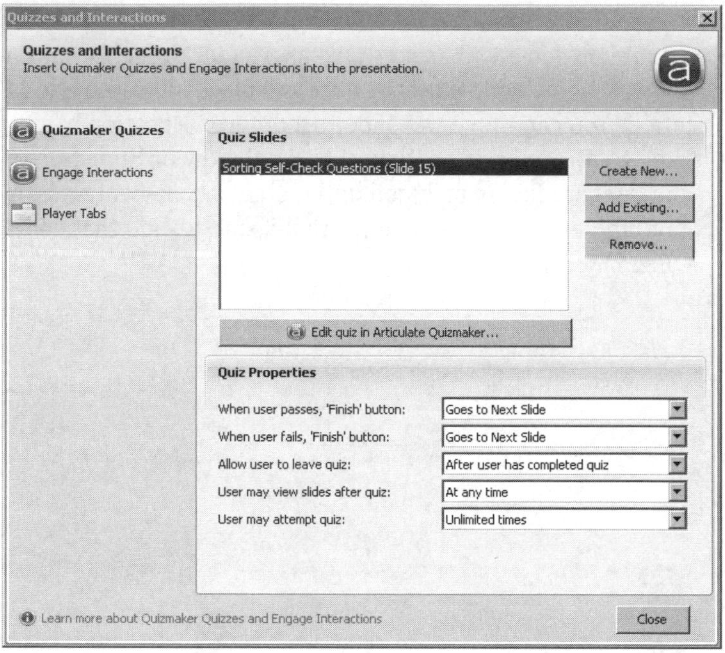

Figure 6.60. Quizzes and Interactions dialog box

3. Choose whether to create a new quiz or insert an existing quiz.

■ **To create a new quiz:** Click the **Create New** button. This launches the Quizmaker program, where you create a quiz. When your quiz is complete, click the **Save and Return to Presenter** button that appears on the Quizmaker ribbon.

■ **To insert an existing quiz:** Click the **Add Existing** button. The Select Quizmaker Quiz dialog box opens. Navigate to the desired quiz. (Quizmaker files use the file extension .quiz.) (You cannot insert *published* Quizmaker quizzes from here.) Click the **Open** button to insert the quiz.

4. Select the desired quiz properties:

Table 6.8. Quiz properties

Property	Options	Recommendations
When user passes, 'Finish' button:	Goes to Next Slide Goes to Previous Slide Goes to (select slide)	Select the slide that the viewer should see next
When user fails, 'Finish' button:	Goes to Next Slide Goes to Previous Slide Goes to (select slide)	Select the slide that the viewer should see next
Allow user to leave quiz:	At any time After user has completed quiz	Nongraded quizzes Graded quizzes
User may view slides after quiz:	At any time After attempting quiz After passing quiz	Nongraded quizzes Nongraded quizzes Graded quizzes
User may attempt quiz:	Unlimited times Just once Select number of tries	Nongraded quizzes Match to circumstances Match to circumstances

5.   After you create or insert a quiz, the quiz title is displayed in the Quiz Slides list on the Quizmaker Quizzes tab. The slide number is listed next to the quiz title.

6.   When you're done, click the **Close** button.

Figure 6.61 shows a close-up of the embedded Quizmaker quiz slide in PowerPoint. Presenter shows the first screen of the quiz on the slide. The lower section of the slide displays the quiz properties, which you can edit by clicking the Properties button. You can also edit the quiz using the Edit in Quizmaker button. To see the entire quiz, you can use the Preview button on the Articulate tab.

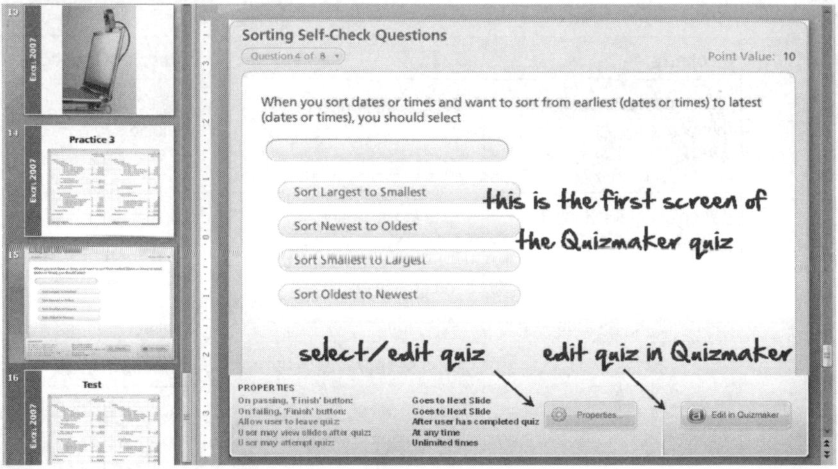

Figure 6.61. Close-up of Quizmaker quiz in PowerPoint

Embedding a Quizmaker Quiz as a Tab

When a Quizmaker quiz is embedded into a Presenter project as a tab, it acts like a button on the Presenter player. (We actually prefer to refer to this as embedding a Quizmaker quiz as a player *button* because it doesn't look or act as a tab.) Quizmaker quizzes that are embedded as a tab are accessible anytime from a tab on the player (Figure 6.62). Viewers can click the tab and open the quiz from anywhere in the project.

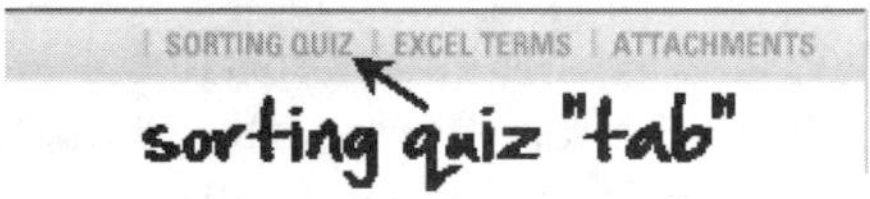

Figure 6.62. Quizmaker embedded as a tab

By adding a quiz as a tab, viewers have the flexibility to access the quiz anytime and from any slide. Although you might think that all quizzes would typically be embedded as slides so that they are delivered after related content, there are circumstances where you might choose to add a Quizmaker quiz as a tab. For example, you might place an end-of-module survey (with questions asking the viewer to provide feedback on specific aspects of the module) on the player as a tab so the viewer can use it anytime. You might develop a bank of questions that viewers could use anytime they want to be sure they understand the content (a study test for a certification exam, for instance) and place that quiz as a tab on the player. In addition, you might choose to have an "open book" test. Putting the test tab (button) on the player makes it much easier for viewers to use course content while taking the test.

Embedding a Quiz as a Tab

1. Click the **Quizmaker Quiz** button on the Articulate tab or **Quizmaker Quiz** on the Articulate menu.

2. In the Quizzes and Interactions dialog box, select **Player Tabs** (Figure 6.63).

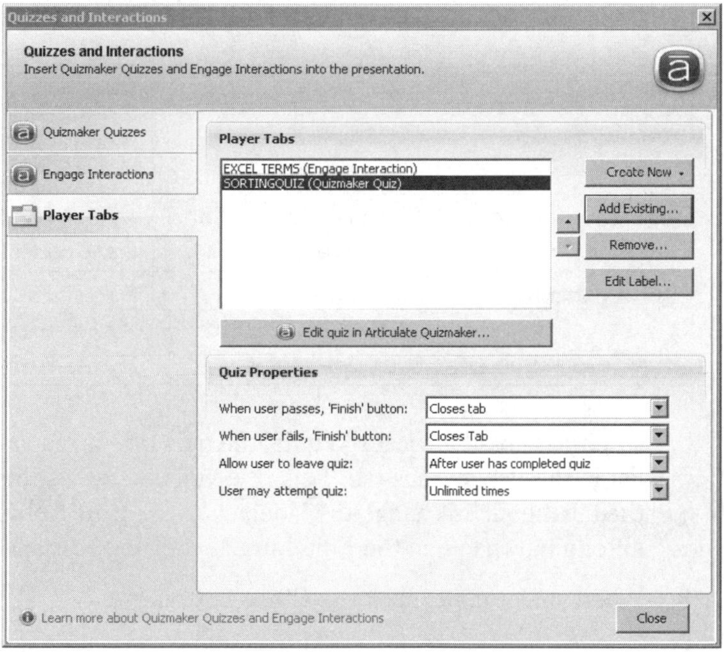

Figure 6.63. Quizzes and Interactions dialog box with Player Tabs selected

3. Choose whether to create a new quiz or insert an existing quiz.

    ■ **To create a new quiz:** Click the **Create New** button, then select **Quizmaker Quiz**. This launches the Quizmaker program, where you can create the new quiz. When the quiz is complete, click the **Save and Return to Presenter** button that appears on the Quizmaker ribbon.

■ **To insert an existing quiz:** Click the **Add Existing** button. The Select dialog box opens. Navigate to the desired quiz. (Quizmaker quizzes use the file extension .quiz.) Note: You cannot insert *published* Quizmaker quizzes from here. Click the **Open** button to insert the quiz. (If previous versions of the quiz exist, the Open button will contain an arrow, which you can use to select a previous version.)

4. Select the desired quiz properties:

Table 6.9. Quiz properties

Property	Options	Recommendations
When user passes, 'Finish' button:	Closes tab Goes to URL	Closes tab would work in most situations
When user fails, 'Finish' button:	Closes tab Goes to URL	Closes tab would work in most situations
Allow user to leave quiz:	At any time After user has completed quiz	Nongraded quizzes Graded quizzes
User may attempt quiz:	Unlimited times Just once Select number of tries	Nongraded quizzes Match to circumstances Match to circumstances

5. After you create or insert a quiz, the quiz title is displayed in the list in the Player Tabs tab. This title will be used as the label on the tab menu. To change the label, click the **Edit Label** button, enter a new name in the Edit Tab Label dialog box, and click **OK**.

6. When you're done, click the **Close** button.

Figure 6.64 shows a close-up of the embedded Quizmaker tab in the Presenter player. To see the entire quiz, you can use the Preview button on the Articulate tab (Figure 6.65).

Figure 6.64. Quiz tab

Figure 6.65 shows the quiz opened.

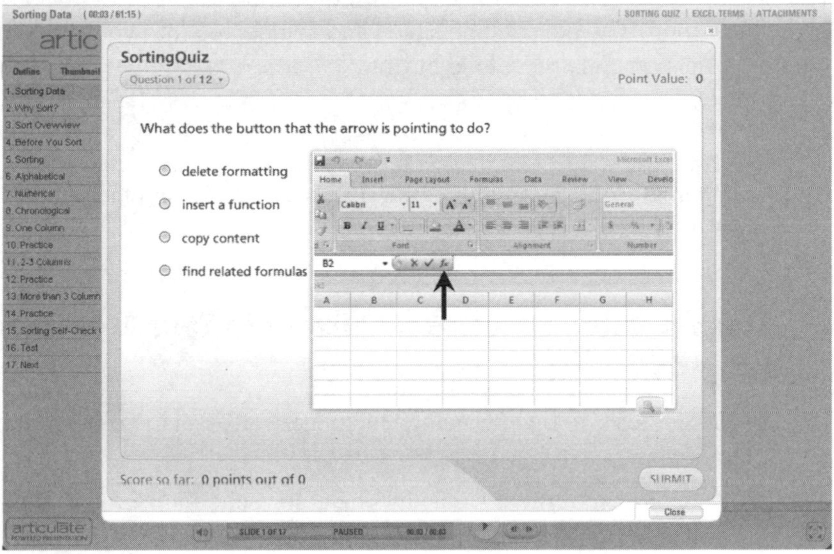

Figure 6.65. Quizmaker quiz opened

Deleting or Editing a Quizmaker Quiz

If you change your mind about using a Quizmaker quiz that you have previously added as a slide or tab, it can easily be edited or deleted.

Deleting or Editing a Quiz (Slide or Tab)

1.   Click the **Quizmaker Quiz** button on the Articulate tab or **Quizmaker Quiz** on the Articulate menu.

2.   In the Quizzes and Interactions dialog box, select **Quizmaker Quizzes** if the quiz is a slide or select **Player Tabs** if the quiz is a tab.

3.   Select the quiz from the Quiz Slides list (for slides) or the Player Tabs list (for tabs).

4.   **To remove a quiz:** Click the **Remove** button and close the Quizzes and Interactions dialog box. (You can also delete the slide as you would delete any slide to remove the quiz.)

     To edit a quiz: Click the **Edit quiz in Articulate Quizmaker** button. Presenter opens the Quizmaker program, where you can make changes to the quiz. When finished, click the **Save and Return to Presenter** button that appears on the Quizmaker ribbon. The quiz will be saved and reinserted into your presentation. Then click the **Close** button.

> **Tip:** If the quiz was inserted as a slide, you can also click the Edit in Quizmaker button on the slide instead of using the Quizzes and Interactions dialog box.

Tips for Using Quizmaker Quizzes in Your Presenter Projects

Here are some tips for using Quizmaker quizzes in your Presenter projects.

- **Color schemes:** Consider the color scheme used in the selected Presenter player template when creating Quizmaker quizzes that will be embedded in a Presenter project. Presenter '09, Quizmaker '09, and Engage '09 have color schemes that are designed to look good together. For example, if you use the "Blue Dark" color scheme in Presenter, you can use the "Blue Dark" color scheme in Quizmaker.

- **Fonts:** Use the same font in Presenter, Quizmaker, and Engage when they will be used for the same project.

Adding Web Objects

Adding a Web Object to a Presenter project means making use of "outside" web content. The content resides outside of Presenter but is "called up" inside of Presenter. The content can reside at a specific web address (such as http://www.dietfacts.com) or on HTML pages that reside on an internal storage medium (such as the network drive).

For example, if you develop a Presenter project on nutrition, you might want viewers to interact with a web site that has nutritional information. Or if you develop a Presenter project on maximizing your 401(k), you might want viewers to interact with a mutual funds research site.

The primary reasons for adding Web Objects is to take advantage of outside sources of web content and leverage content created for other purposes. You can also use Web Objects to show media elements (such as a QuickTime video) that can't be brought into Presenter directly. Figure 6.66 shows a YouTube video that is playing inside a Presenter project.

Figure 6.66. Presenter project with embedded YouTube video (source: http://www.articulate.com/community/blogdemo/wo_demo/player.html)

Note: Don't forget that outside content that is not under your control may be moved or removed at any time.

The Web Object button on the Articulate tab is shown in Figure 6.67. When you click the Web Object button or select Web Object from the Articulate menu, the Insert Web Object dialog box is launched.

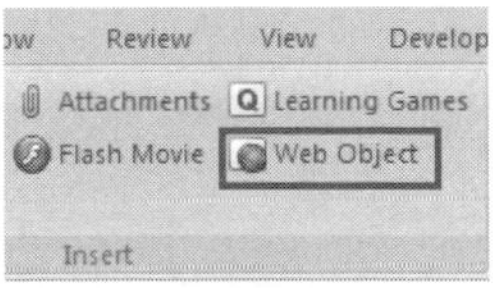

Figure 6.67. The Web Object button on the Articulate tab

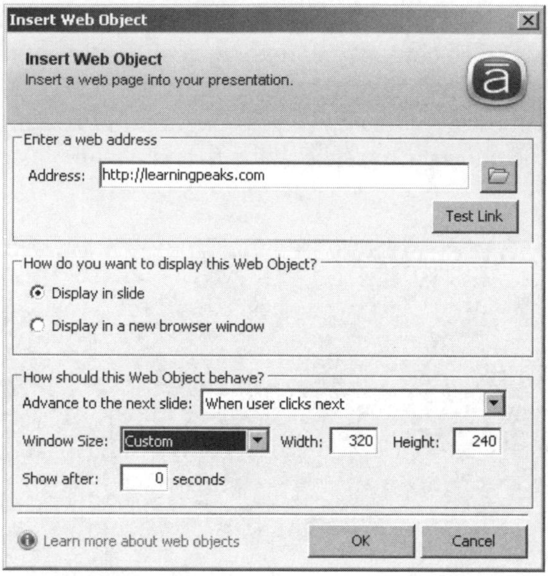

Figure 6.68. The Insert Web Object dialog box

There are two ways to display a Web Object in a Presenter project:

■ **Display in slide:** This method places the Web Object on a slide. The Web Object can take up the entire slide or only a portion of the slide. When the published project is open, the Web Object will appear where it was placed on the slide.

■ **Display in a new browser window:** This method opens a new browser window (outside of the Presenter player) that contains the Web Object. A Web Object placeholder icon appears on the slide where the Web Object will open. When the published project is open and the viewer reaches the slide with the Web Object, the new browser window opens with the Web Object displayed.

Tip: You may need to warn viewers that a pop-up blocker may stop the new browser window from opening.

Figure 6.69 shows an example of the placeholder that is put on the slide when Display in slide is chosen. Figure 6.70 shows how the Web Object actually looks inside the Presenter player. This Presenter project is on simulations and the Web Object shown is an example of an online simulation.

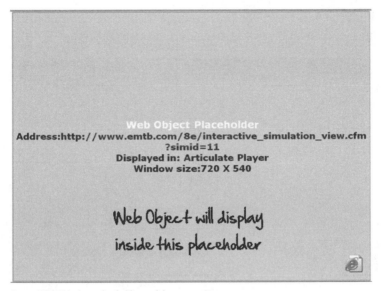

Figure 6.69. Web object placeholder on slide

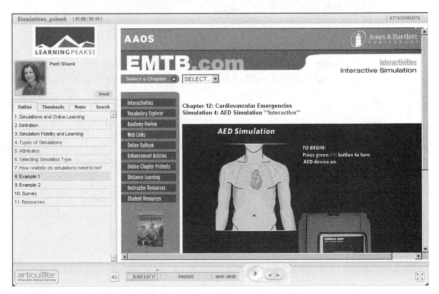

Figure 6.70. Web object in Presenter player

Figure 6.71 shows an example of the icon that is put on the slide when Display in a new browser window is chosen. Figure 6.72 shows how the Web Object actually looks outside of the Presenter player. This is another simulation example inside the same project.

Figure 6.71. Web Object icon on slide

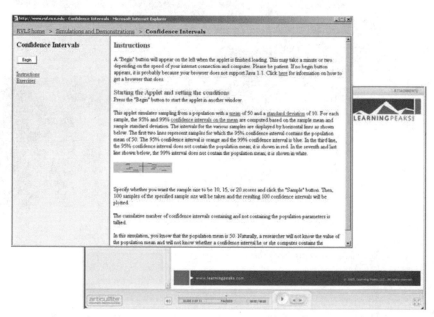

Figure 6.72. Web Object open in new browser window

Adding a Web Object

1. Select the slide where you want a Web Object to appear.

2. Click the **Web Object** button on the Articulate tab or **Web Object** from the Articulate menu. The Insert Web Object dialog box opens.

3. Enter the **address** of the Web Object using either of the following methods:

   ■ Input the web address (URL) if the desired Web Object is a web page on the Internet (you can click **Test Link** to open the link in your browser to make sure that the web address works)

   ■ Browse for the folder that contains the Web Object you want to use. Note: The folder *must* contain either an *index.htm* or an *index.html* file. Make sure that related files such as graphics and media are in the same folder. (This folder is added to the Presenter project files.) The index file is the file that will display in the slide or browser window.

4. Specify how the Web Object should be displayed by choosing one of the following:

   ■ **Display in slide:** The Web Object will display as *part* or *all of a slide* inside your Presenter project

   ■ **Display in a new browser window:** The Web Object will display in a new browser window when viewers arrive at the slide containing the Web Object.

5. Specify how the Web Object should behave.

   If **Display in slide** was chosen:

   ■ **Advance to the next slide:** Choose whether users should advance to the next slide automatically or when the user clicks Next.

   ■ **Window size:** Choose whether your Web Object should take up the full slide (720 pixels x 540 pixels), or specify custom width and height dimensions (in pixels, with a maximum of 720 pixels x 540 pixels) for your Web Object. After your Web Object placeholder is created, you can also resize it on your PowerPoint slide.

Tip: It's easiest to choose Full Slide and then manipulate the size on the slide.

■ **Show after _____ seconds:** Specify when the Web Object should appear. The default is 0 seconds, which means that the Web Object will appear immediately. If you want the Web Object to open after the slide loads, input the number of seconds to delay before the Web Object displays.

If **Display in a new browser window** was chosen:

■ **Browser controls:** Specify whether you want the browser window with the Web Object to display **All browser controls**, **No address bar**, or **No browser controls**.

■ **Window size:** Choose whether your Web Object should display at the default size (current browser window size), full screen (browser window maximized), or a custom size (specify width and height dimensions in pixels).

■ **Show after _____ seconds:** Specify when the Web Object should appear. The default is 0 seconds, which means that the Web Object will appear immediately. If you want the Web Object to open after the slide loads, input the number of seconds to delay before the Web Object displays.

6. Click **OK** to add the Web Object to your slide. Note: You can only add one Web Object to a slide.

7. A Web Object placeholder or Internet Explorer icon will appear on the slide.

If you chose **Display in slide**, you will see a placeholder for it on the slide. When the slide opens, the Web Object will show inside the placeholder area. You may position or resize this placeholder anywhere on the slide. To see the Web Object on the slide, preview or publish the slide.

If you chose **Display in a new browser window**, you will see only an Internet Explorer icon at the bottom right-hand corner of the slide. This is meant to indicate (to you) that a Web Object that displays in a new browser window has been added to the slide. The icon is not visible to the viewer. To see the Web Object in the new browser window, preview or publish the slide.

Deleting a Web Object

Delete the slide with the Web Object placeholder.

Tips for Using Web Objects in Your Presenter Projects

■ Make sure that the viewer has Internet access before using Web Objects that require it. Also, remember that web resources may not be there in the future.

■ Don't use Web Objects that contain media that require plug-ins (for example, PDF Reader or QuickTime player) that viewers don't have, don't want, or can't download.

■ You may not want to launch Web Objects in a new browser window if viewers have small monitors (which would make it hard to view the Presenter project and the browser window at the same time).

■ Web Objects that are displayed in a new browser window may distract or pull away some viewers and may trigger viewers' pop-up blockers.

The following are some good uses for Web Objects:

■ Web-based activities (for example, a "scavenger hunt" on the company intranet to find answers to questions)

■ Web-based resources (for example, the policy manual in a sexual harassment course)

■ Interact-with-people activities using discussion forums, wiki pages, or del.icio.us resources

Adding Flash Video

Adding video to your Presenter project is similar to adding an Engage interaction or a Quizmaker quiz. Create the Flash video file (Video Encoder will help you convert your video files to Flash video if you have other video files) and add it to Presenter.

The Flash Movie button on the Articulate tab is shown in Figure 6.73. When you click the Flash Movie button or select Flash Movie from the Articulate menu, you can navigate to find the Flash video file (with either a .swf or .flv file extension) to add to the project.

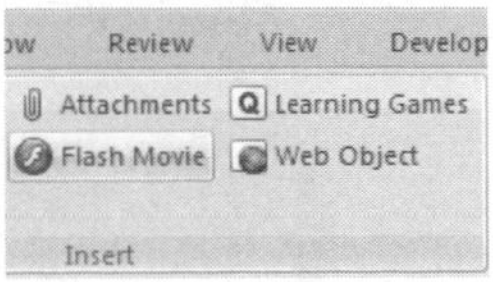

Figure 6.73. The Flash Movie button on the Articulate tab

Presenter lets you add Flash video in one of three ways:

■ **Display in slide:** Displays the Flash video on a slide

■ **Display in presenter panel:** Displays the Flash video in the pre-senter panel of the Presenter player

■ **Display in new browser window:** Displays the Flash video in a new browser window

You can insert up to three existing Flash videos (in SWF or FLV for-mat) per slide—using each of the display methods (Display in slide, Display in presenter panel, and Display in new browser window). Pre-senter '09 supports Flash movies created using ActionScript 2.0 or earlier. ActionScript 3.0 is not supported.

Adding a Flash Video

1. Click the **Flash Movie** button on the Articulate tab or select **Flash Movie** from the Articulate menu.

2. Navigate to the Flash movie you want to include. Select the desired .swf or .flv file and click **Open**. The Insert Flash Movie dia-log box opens (Figure 6.74). You can preview the Flash video by click-ing the Play button underneath the first video frame.

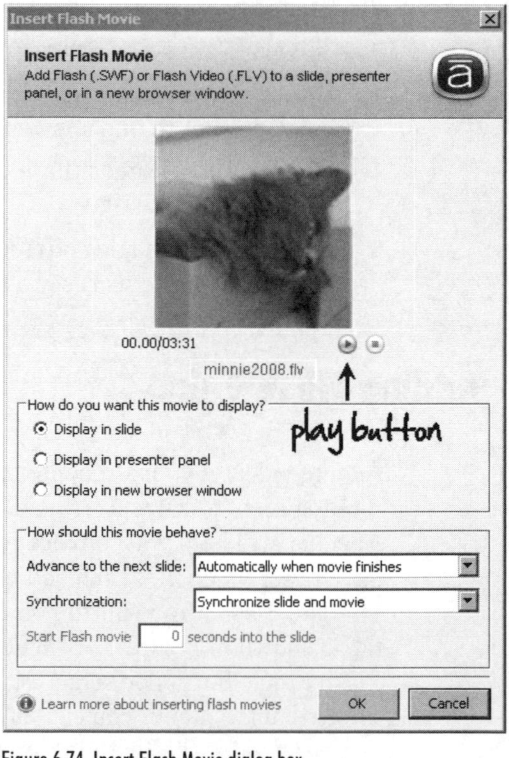

Figure 6.74. Insert Flash Movie dialog box

3. Choose how you want the movie to display:

    ■ Choose **Display in slide** to display the Flash video in a slide.

    ■ Choose **Display in presenter panel** to display the Flash video in the presenter panel of the Presenter player.

    ■ Choose **Display in new browser window** to open a new window with your Flash video embedded in it.

4. Select behaviors for the selected Flash video. Available options are dependent on the display method (Table 6.10).

Table 6.10. Flash movie behavior settings

Display method	Behaviors	Options
Display in slide	Advance to the next slide:	Automatically when movie finishes
		When user clicks next
	Synchronization:	Synchronize slide and movie
		Movie plays independently of slide
Display in presenter panel	Advance to the next slide:	Automatically when movie finishes
		When user clicks next
Display in new browser window	Browser controls:	All browser controls
		No address bar
		No browser controls
	Start Flash movie ____ seconds into the slide	Input the desired number of seconds

5. Click **OK**.

You will see the first frame of the Flash movie as a placeholder in the PowerPoint slide (if Display in slide is selected) or presenter panel (if Display in presenter panel is selected). If Display in new browser window is selected, a Flash icon will appear in the lower-right corner of the slide. Figure 6.75 shows the FLV placeholder if the Flash video is displayed in a slide and Figure 6.76 shows the Flash icon that appears if the Flash video is displayed in a new browser window.

Figure 6.75. FLV placeholder on slide—Flash video will display in the player

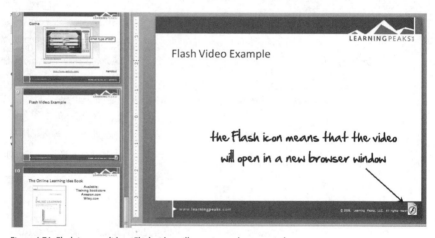

Figure 6.76. Flash icon on slide—Flash video will open in new browser window

If you've chosen Display in slide, you can adjust the placement and size of the Flash movie by clicking and dragging the placeholder image to move it or resize it. To maintain the aspect ratio, hold down the Shift key while resizing.

Note: Presenter '09 produces Flash 6.0.79 output.

Removing a Flash Video

Click the placeholder or icon on the slide and delete it.

Tips for Using Video in Your Presenter Projects

Here are a few tips for shooting video for your Presenter projects:

- Get a tripod and use it.
- Don't overuse the zoom. Viewers should notice what's happening onscreen, not what the camera is doing.
- Make sure that the people in the video aren't wearing busy patterns. Patterns and lines can look wavy or worse on video.
- Need cheap (or free) actors? Check out the drama department of a local college or university.
- This article explains how to set up a low-budget video studio: http://www.bmyers.com/public/869.cfm?sd=30

Here are some tips for using Flash video in your information and instruction:

- Use Flash FLV video (rather than Flash SWF video) for video that is more than a minute long.
- Talking heads aren't the best use for video bandwidth except when what the speaker has to say is extremely meaningful or insightful. (Randy Pausch's "Last Lecture" is a great example of this: http://www.youtube.com/watch?v=R9ya9BXClRw.)
- Some talking head video may be useful for helping learners feel connected to the instructor or expert. This type of talking head video can be placed in the presenter panel of the sidebar. That way, viewers can see who is talking as he or she narrates the slides.
- For other talking heads, consider audio or audio+picture.
- Video can be stopped or slowed to explain a concept that is hard to see or understand at normal speed.
- Keep video clips short. Five minutes is about as long as any viewer can be expected to watch. One minute is better still.

Grainy, non-professional video can feel more "real" than professional video. "Real" people are often far more interesting than scripted performers.

Practice

No need for me to tell you this, but here goes anyhow....

> Play with this stuff! Check out examples in the Articulate blogs too!

Chapter Recap

Here's our list of the most important things to remember from this chapter:

- You can provide downloadable documents, such as PDF files, Word documents, or Excel spreadsheets, or provide URLs to viewers by adding attachments.

- Annotations can help viewers focus their attention on specific areas of the screen.

- Slide text and other objects on the screen (such as text boxes, hotspots, buttons, pictures, or other objects) can easily be turned into hyperlinks. Clicking these links can take the viewer to another slide in the project (also known as branching), open an object or media element (such as an audio file), or take the viewer to a network or Internet resource (such as a web page).

- Branching (using a nonlinear path through the content) can be very powerful but comes with some "gotchas." The following slide properties functionalities available on the Slide Properties window make branched navigation work: Lock (player navigation), Hide in (sidebar) Navigation Panel, and Branching (set next and previous slides). In addition, *not* displaying slide numbers in the Presenter player slide title navigation makes it less obvious that some slide titles are hidden.

- Learning Games can engage viewers as they are viewing and interacting with a Presenter project. They can be added to let viewers test their knowledge and break up sequences where viewers are primarily watching screens and listening to narration. Learning Games come with Presenter and are easy to add to Presenter projects.

- Engage interactions allow viewers to "discover" content. They are easy to create in Engage and easy to add to Presenter projects. They can be added as slides or as tabs.

- Quizmaker questions can be used to help learners check whether they understand the content. Quizzes and tests are commonly used to assess whether the learner has met the learning objectives. They can be added as slides or as tabs.

- Adding a Web Object to a Presenter project allows you to call up "outside" web content. The content can reside at a specific web address or on HTML pages that reside on an internal storage medium (such as a network drive).

- Adding video to your Presenter project is similar to adding an Engage interaction or a Quizmaker quiz. Create the Flash video file (Video Encoder will help you convert your video files to Flash video if you have other source files) and add it to Presenter.

> Your head might explode from all this fun if you aren't careful. ☺

Chapter 7

Customizing Presenter Player Templates

Chapter Snapshot

This chapter explores ways to create and work with customized Presenter player templates. The primary reason to customize player settings is to make the player look and act a certain way. You may wish to "brand" the player so it looks like your company's print and web media, or customize certain course types with a set of global player settings.

Dave Mozealous, Articulate QA Manager (blog: http://www.mozealous.com), and Tom Kuhlmann, the author of the Rapid E-Learning blog (http://www.articulate.com/rapid-elearning), contributed numerous tips in this chapter.

Revisiting the Articulate Tab and Menu

In Chapter 5, "Presenter Basics," we discussed using the Articulate tab (in PowerPoint 2007) or the Articulate menu (in PowerPoint 2000-2003) that is installed into PowerPoint to accomplish the Presenter tasks. In case you haven't read that chapter, we want to remind you that whether you are using the Articulate tab (Figure 7.1), or the Articulate menu (Figure 7.2), the Articulate tasks and functions are identical.

Figure 7.1. The Articulate tab in PowerPoint 2007

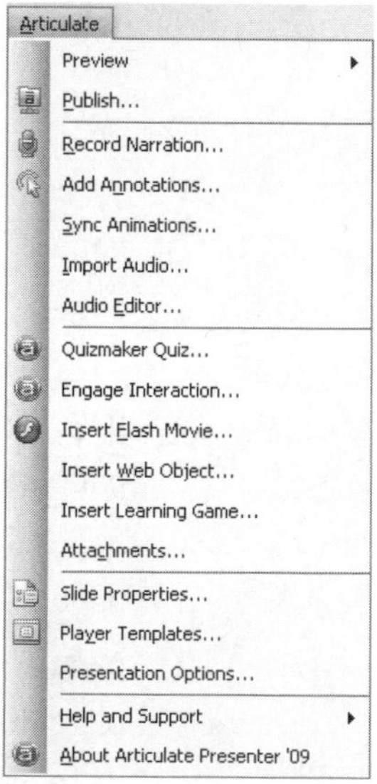

Figure 7.2. The Articulate menu in PowerPoint 2000-2003

Revisiting the Presenter 1-2-3-4-5 Workflow

In this chapter, we'll discuss the fourth step in the Presenter 1-2-3-4-5 workflow: 4. Customize the player. This step is highlighted in Figure 7.3.

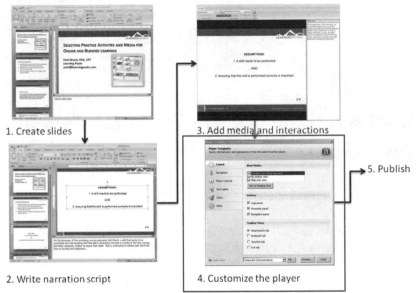

Figure 7.3. Presenter 1-2-3-4-5 workflow

Table 7.1 shows the typical substep completed in step 4 of the Presenter 1-2-3-4-5 workflow.

Table 7.1. Detailed workflow for step 4

Using Presenter	
4. Customize the player	a) Customize player templates

? Do I have to customize the player? I mean,
I have to get this project done quickly.

i Nope. This step is optional. But come back
here when you have more time to see how
easy it is to "brand" your projects.

What Is a Player and Why Would You Want to Customize It?

The player is the interface in which the output of a Presenter project plays. It includes graphical elements, such as navigational tools, player controls, and colors that the viewer sees and can interact with. Figure 7.4 shows the default player (not customized). Notice that it contains two ways to navigate the content: screen titles on the left sidebar and player controls on the bottom to move forward and backward. The color scheme is dull but not unattractive. Figure 7.5 shows a player that has been customized. The sidebar is gone, and this makes it look very different from the default player. All in all, the two players look and feel very different, don't they?

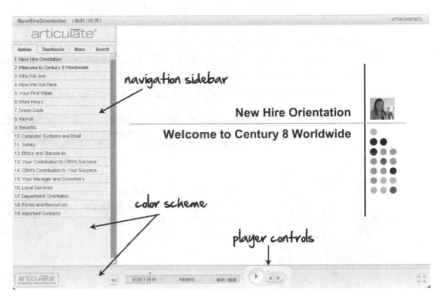

Figure 7.4. Default Presenter player

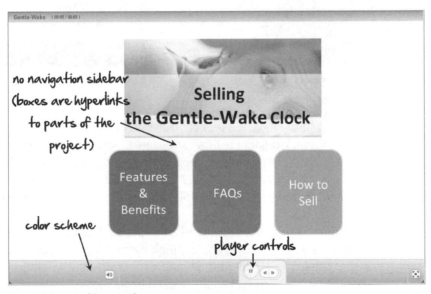

Figure 7.5. Customized Presenter player

Figure 7.6 shows another customized player. Customizations in this example are less dramatic than the customization shown in Figure 7.5. They include making slide notes available at the bottom of the player (shown in open state) and applying a preconfigured color scheme (Blue Deep). These changes literally took only seconds to make.

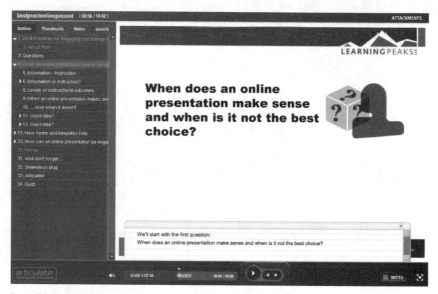

Figure 7.6. Customized Presenter player

Customizing the look and feel of your Presenter projects allows you to "brand" them. Branding is how companies make their products look uniquely theirs. For example, the "swoosh" on a running shoe tells you it's a Nike running shoe. The logo and color scheme on FedEx trucks set them apart from the logo and color scheme on United Parcel Service trucks.

Although you can certainly use the default Presenter player, at some point you're likely going to think to yourself, "I wonder how I can get the player to (fill in the blank)." This chapter will help you answer that question and make desired changes to the player.

Working with Player Templates

One of the most amazing things about Presenter is that it is so easy to change how the player looks and acts. Almost every element of the Presenter player can be customized. In fact, it can be pretty darn hard to tell what authoring program made Presenter output because customization of the player can make the project look like it was built using any number of authoring tools.

Player Templates

A *player template* is a collection of settings for player layout, navigation, player controls, text labels, color schemes, and other settings that are saved with a specific player template name. Presenter comes with a set of preconfigured player templates such as E-Learning Course (Single-level), Tradeshow Loop, and Corporate Communications. You can use these player templates and you can also create and use your own player templates. The ability to create player templates (and use them for your Presenter projects) is a nothing-short-of-amazing feature. Once you get the hang of working with player templates, you'll appreciate how powerful they are and how much time they can save.

Figure 7.7 shows the Player Templates dialog box. The settings for the Selling2 player template (which was created to be used with a certain group of online courses) is being edited. Any changes made to the settings are being made to the Selling2 player template because this is the template that is "open" for changes in the Player Templates dialog box.

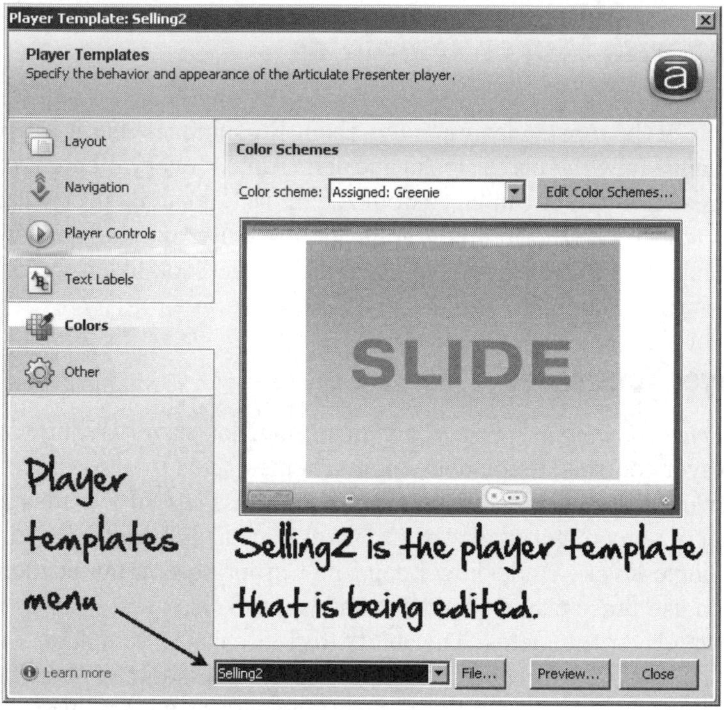

Figure 7.7. Player Templates dialog box with the Selling2 player template being edited

Player Templates Dialog Box

The Player Templates dialog box is used to edit, create, and save player templates. Use the Player Templates button on the Articulate tab (Figure 7.8) or the Player Templates selection on the Articulate menu to open the Player Templates dialog box (Figure 7.9).

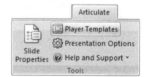

Figure 7.8. Player Templates button on the Articulate menu

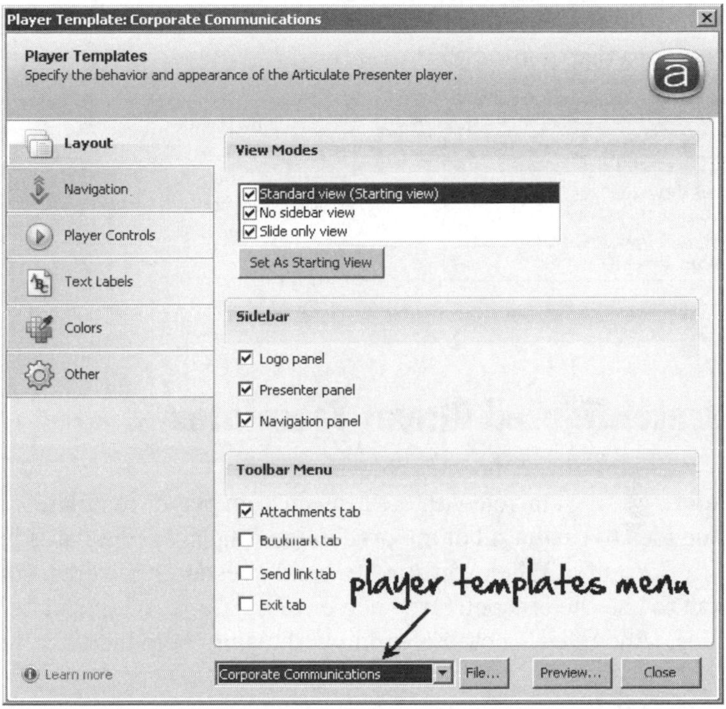

Figure 7.9. The Player Templates dialog box

The tabs on the left side of the Player Templates dialog box allow you to edit settings for a specific group of player elements. So, for example, the Layout tab lets you select and edit layout settings. The Colors tab lets you modify and create color schemes.

The player templates menu at the bottom of the Player Templates dialog box shows a list of available player templates. You can use any of the preconfigured player templates or create your own player templates by selecting player settings and saving these with new player template names. Once saved, they will be added to the player templates menu. Creating and editing player templates makes it easy to apply the same settings to multiple Presenter projects.

Figure 7.10 is an example of preconfigured and created player templates in the menu at the bottom of the Player Templates dialog box. The last three player templates shown in the menu—Product Update 1, Product Update 2, and FAQs—are newly created. The first three player templates—E-Learning Course (Single-level), E-Learning

Course (Multi-level), and Tradeshow Loop—are preconfigured player templates that come with Presenter.

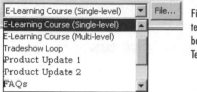

Figure 7.10. The player templates menu at the bottom of the Player Templates dialog box

Using Preconfigured Player Templates

Before getting started with creating custom player templates, it's a good idea to review all of the preconfigured player templates that come with Presenter. When you start to build Presenter projects, you may wish to use the preconfigured player templates that Articulate provides. (And there's nothing wrong with using them indefinitely.)

Reviewing Preconfigured Templates

1. Make sure that PowerPoint is open.

2. Click the **Player Templates** button on the Articulate tab or **Player Templates** from the Articulate menu. The Player Templates dialog box opens.

66 **Note:** The Player Templates dialog box opens with the settings for the template that you used last.

3. Select a player template from the player templates menu at the bottom of the dialog box.

4. Click the **Preview** button. A preview window opens, showing the selected template.

5. Close the preview window when you are done previewing that player template.

6. Select another player template to preview and repeat.

7. Click the **Close** button.

> **Tip:** See the section titled "What about Applying a Player Template to a Presenter Project?" later in this chapter for more information.

Customizing Player Settings

In this section, we'll discuss each of the tabs on the Player Templates dialog box and the settings that can be modified on each tab.

Layout Tab

A layout is an arrangement of items (such as tabs, panels, and toolbars) on a page. The Layout tab on the Player Templates dialog box allows you to make changes to the player layout settings shown in Table 7.2.

Table 7.2. Layout settings

Layout setting	Description	
View Modes	Sets the view modes that may be used in the project. (Different modes may be selected for different slides using the Slide Properties window.)	
	Standard view	All default player elements are included (unless turned off elsewhere), including navigation at the bottom and sidebar on the left.
	No sidebar view	Sidebar elements, including the logo, presenter, and navigation panels are hidden, but the bars at the top and bottom of the player remain visible.
	Slide only view	Only the slide is visible and it zooms to the size of the player.
Set As Starting View	To change the starting view, select the view that should show when the project is launched and press the Set As Starting View button.	

Layout setting	Description	
Sidebar	Sets the sidebar elements that are visible.	
	Logo panel	Show/hide the logo panel.
	Presenter panel	Show/hide presenter's name, title, and company.
	Navigation panel	Show/hide the navigation panel, including • Title: Slide titles (configured using the Slide Properties button or menu selection) • Thumbnails: Slide thumbnails • Search: Search slides and speaker notes • Notes: Presenter notes
Toolbar Menu	Sets the toolbar elements that are visible.	
	Attachments tab	Show/hide the Attachments tab.
	Bookmark tab	Show/hide the Bookmark tab.
	Send link tab	Show/hide the tab that allows viewers to send an email with a link to the project.
	Exit tab	Show/hide the Exit tab.

Changing a Player Template's Layout Settings

1. Make sure that PowerPoint is open.

2. Click the **Player Templates** button on the Articulate tab or **Player Templates** from the Articulate menu. The Player Templates dialog box opens.

 Note: The Player Templates dialog box opens with the settings for the template that you used last.

3. Select the template name whose layout settings you wish to edit from the player templates menu at the bottom of the Player Templates dialog box.

4. Click the **Layout** tab (Figure 7.11).

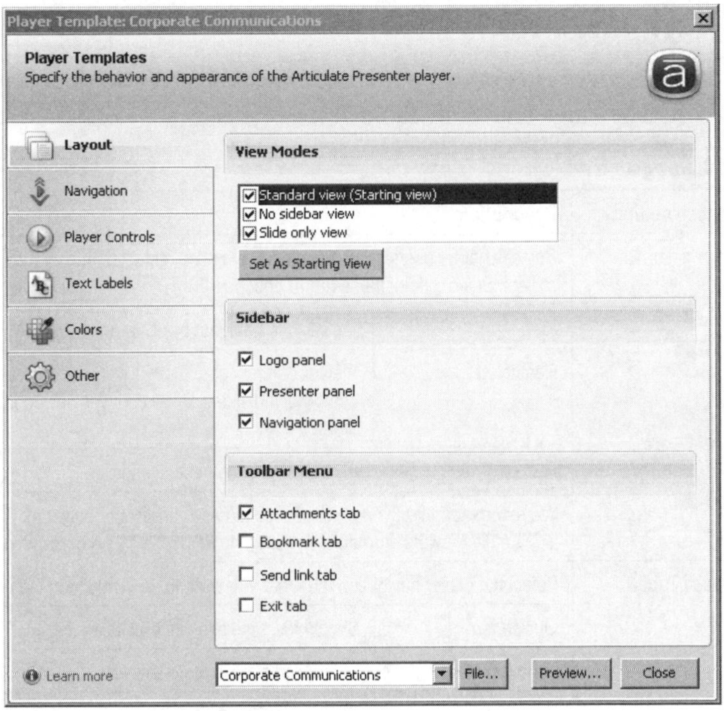

Figure 7.11. Player Templates dialog box, Layout tab

5. Edit the view modes, sidebar, and toolbar menu settings for this template. (See Table 7.2 for a description of each of these elements.)

6. Click the **Close** button. When prompted whether to save the changes, select **Yes**. (If you select **No**, your changes will be lost.) When prompted to enter a name for your new template, type the new name in the text box.

66 **Note:** The layout settings you select apply *only* to the *specific player template* being modified in the Player Templates dialog box.

Navigation Tab

The Navigation tab allows you to make changes to the player navigation settings shown in Table 7.3.

Table 7.3. Navigation settings

Navigation setting	Description	
User navigation is:	Select whether users can navigate freely or are restricted in how they can view the project. Select *one* of these menu options:	
	Free	Viewer can navigate freely to any slide.
	Restricted	Viewer can navigate freely to current slide and any previously viewed slides. Slides not yet viewed must be viewed in order.
	Locked	All slides must be viewed in order.
	We recommend that you *don't* use locked and *rarely* use restricted. See "(Not) Creating Cranky Viewers" immediately following this table for an explanation.	
Navigation Tabs	Select the player navigation tabs that you want to be included in the player:	
	Outline tab	Show/hide slide titles in the Outline tab.
	Thumbnails tab	Show/hide slide Thumbnails tab.
	Notes tab	Show/hide Slide Notes tab.
	Search tab	Show/hide Search tab.
	You can change the order of the selected tabs by selecting a tab name and using the up/down arrows to move the tab up or down in the list. The tab in the top position will appear as the first tab at the top of the navigation panel of the player, looking left to right. Other tabs will appear in the order they appear in the list.	
Set As Starting Tab	Select the tab that is active (open) when the project is opened by selecting the desired starting tab name and clicking the Set As Starting Tab button.	
Automatic scroll navigation	Select whether the slide navigation should automatically scroll so that the current slide title is always visible in the slide title navigation.	

Navigation setting	Description		
Levels	Select how slide levels expand in slide title navigation. Slides can be set to different levels in the Slide Properties windows. Lower-level (child) slides can be set to expand below higher-level (parent) slide titles in the navigation.		
	Behavior	Select when to expand slide level in the slide title navigation.
		• Expand level when the user is inside level: Automatically expands child slide title navigation when the viewer reaches the first child slide beneath a parent slide.
		• Expand level when the user reaches heading: Automatically expands child slide title navigation when the viewer reaches the parent slide immediately above it.
		• Don't automatically expand level: Child slide titles are displayed in the slide title navigation along with parent slide titles, but the viewer has to manually expand the level to view the child slide titles.
	Restrictions	Select slide title navigation expansion restrictions. These settings are only relevant if your project contains more than one level, as set in the Slide Properties window.
		• Only expand once the user is inside the level: Viewer can manually expand slide title navigation levels only when viewing a parent slide's child slides.
		• Only expand after the user reaches heading: Viewer can manually expand slide title navigation levels only when viewing the parent level.
		• Levels can be expanded at any time: Viewer can manually expand slide title navigation levels any time.

(Not) Creating Cranky Viewers

Give viewers as much control as possible. You may think you have a good reason to restrict navigation, but adults are pretty cranky about having control taken away from them for silly reasons (such as someone thinking the slides must be viewed in a certain order) and they may want to come back to view a specific slide later without hassles. Make it hard for them and they'll opt out mentally even if they click through to make it *look* like they viewed the entire thing.

Changing a Player Template's Navigation Settings

1. Make sure that PowerPoint is open.

2. Click the **Player Templates** button on the Articulate tab or **Player Templates** from the Articulate menu. The Player Templates dialog box opens.

 Note: The Player Templates dialog box opens with the settings for the template that you used last.

3. Select the template name whose navigation settings you wish to edit from the player templates menu at the bottom of the Player Templates dialog box.

4. Click the **Navigation** tab (Figure 7.12).

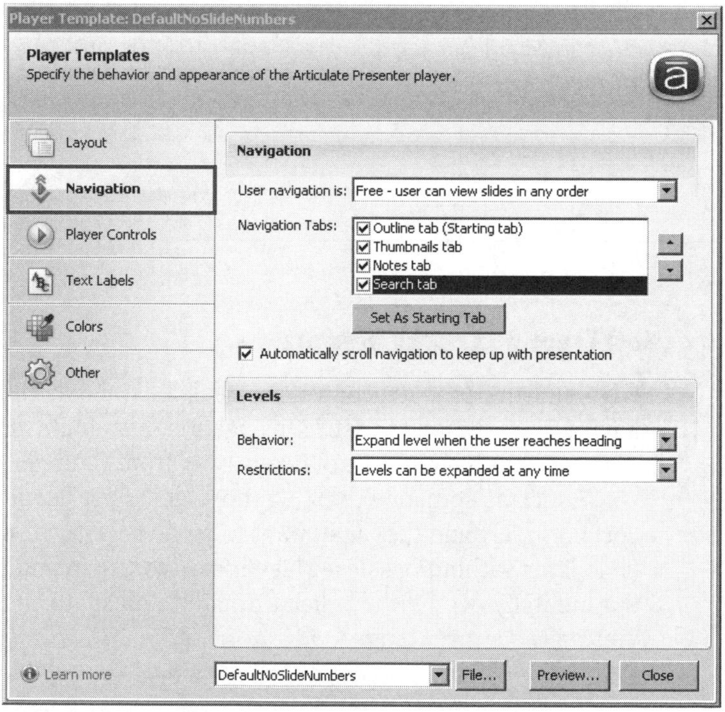

Figure 7.12. Player Templates dialog box, Navigation tab

5. Edit the user navigation, navigation tabs, navigation scrolling, and navigation levels behavior and restrictions settings for this template. (See Table 7.3 for a description of each of these settings.)

6. Click the **Close** button. When prompted whether to save the changes, select **Yes**. (If you select **No**, your changes will be lost.) When prompted for the name, type a new name in the text box.

> 66 **Note:** The navigation settings you select apply *only* to the *specific player template* being modified in the Player Templates dialog box.

Player Controls Tab

You can determine which controls are available to viewers and how those controls will act. The Player Controls tab in the Player Templates dialog box allows you to make changes to the player control settings shown in Table 7.4.

Table 7.4. Player control settings

Player control setting	Description	
Player Controls	Select the player controls that you want to be included in the player:	
	Volume control 🔊	Show/hide the volume control.
	Forward/back/pause controller	Show/hide the forward/back/pause control.
	Seekbar SLIDE 9 OF 14 PLAYING 00:01 / 00:05	Show/hide the seekbar.
	Change view mode button	Show/hide the change view mode button.
	Elapsed and total presentation time	Show/hide the elapsed time/total time on the seekbar.
	Show slide notes button at bottom 📄 NOTES	Show/hide slide notes at the bottom of the player.
	Display powered-by logo articulate POWERED PRESENTATION	Show/hide the Powered by Articulate logo.
	Tip: Opt for giving as much control over viewing as possible. Controls that we think should always be available include volume control (if there is audio), forward/back/pause controller, elapsed and total presentation time, and show slide notes.	

Player control setting	Description	
Miscellaneous	Select other viewer control settings:	
	Prompt to resume on presentation restart	If checked, user is prompted whether to resume where he or she stopped the last time the project was viewed.
	When running in LMS, ignore Flash cookie	If checked, the project will use bookmarking from LMS (if supported). If unchecked, project resumes using LMS resume data, if supported. Otherwise the Flash cookie is used.
	Enable keyboard shortcuts	If checked, keyboard shortcuts (see Table 7.5) will be available to viewers.
	Allow user to seek within seekbar	If checked, viewers can navigate *within each slide* using the seekbar.
	Loop presentation	If checked, project automatically starts over from the beginning after the last slide is completed. **Tip:** This functionality is good for kiosks and trade shows.
	Open slide notes when presentation starts	If checked, slide notes are open and at the bottom of the player when the project is launched.

Table 7.5. Keyboard shortcuts

Shortcut	Action
Arrow right, Arrow down	Go to next slide
Arrow left, Arrow up	Go to previous slide
Home	Go to first slide
Spacebar	Play/Pause
O, T, N, S	Go to tab—Outline, Thumbnails, Notes, Search
V	Toggle display modes (normal, no sidebar, full screen)
B	Toggle presenter bio button
E	Toggle presenter email button
M	Toggle audio mute

Changing a Player Template's Player Control Settings

1.   Make sure that PowerPoint is open.

2.   Click the **Player Templates** button on the Articulate tab or **Player Templates** from the Articulate menu. The Player Templates dialog box opens.

> 66 **Note:** The Player Templates dialog box opens with the settings for the template that you used last.

3.   Select the template name whose player control settings you wish to edit from the player templates menu at the bottom of the Player Templates dialog box.

4.   Click the **Player Controls** tab (Figure 7.13).

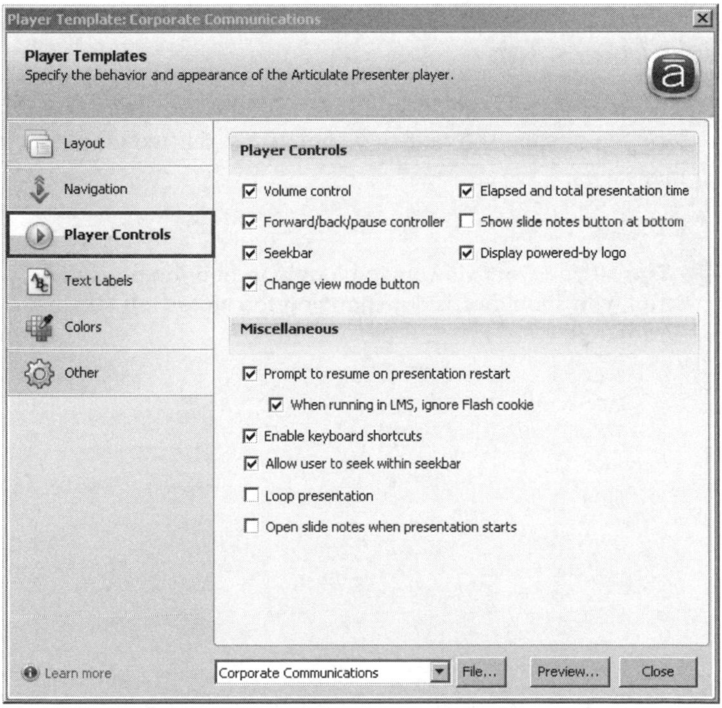

Figure 7.13. Player Templates dialog box, Player Controls tab

5. Edit the player controls and miscellaneous settings. (See Table 7.4 for a description of each of these settings.)

6. Click the **Close** button. When prompted whether to save the changes, select **Yes**. (If you select **No**, your changes will be lost.) When prompted for the name, type a new name in the text box.

> **Tip:** It's a good idea to include the seekbar when you are allowing viewers to navigate freely. This way, viewers can search for content *within* a specific slide without having to view the entire slide.

> **Note:** The player control settings you select apply *only* to the *specific player template* being modified in the Player Templates dialog box.

Text Labels Tab

The Text Labels tab of the Player Templates dialog box (Figure 7.14) lets you change the text that appears on 64 (wow!) player buttons and messages.

> **Tip:** If you want viewers to be able to find the narration transcript, you should consider changing the Notes tab text (Notes) to "Transcript."

Player Template: Corporate Communications   ✕

Player Templates
Specify the behavior and appearance of the Articulate Presenter player.   ⓐ

| Layout |
| Navigation |
| Player Controls |
| **Text Labels** |
| Colors |
| Other |

Click a cell to enter custom text.

	Buttons/Messages	Custom text
1	Bio Button	Bio
2	Email Button	Email
3	Email Text Message	To send a message, please click the link below.
4	Outline Tab	Outline
5	Thumbnails Tab	Thumbnails
6	Search Tab	Search
7	Notes Tab	Notes
8	Search: Search For	SEARCH FOR:
9	Search: Search In	SEARCH IN:

Language: [Use existing labels ▾]

ⓘ Learn more   [Corporate Communications ▾] [File...] [Preview...] [Close]

Figure 7.14. Player Templates dialog box, Text Labels tab

For example, Figure 7.15 shows the default bio and email buttons on the default player template.

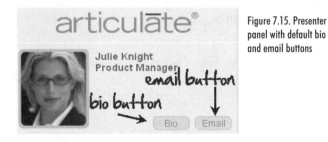

Figure 7.15. Presenter panel with default bio and email buttons

Figure 7.16 shows the same buttons after substituting "About me" for bio and "Contact me" for email using the Text Labels tab of the Player Templates dialog box.

Figure 7.16. Presenter panel with customized bio and email buttons

Changing a Player Template's Text Label Settings

1. Make sure that PowerPoint is open.

2. Click the **Player Templates** button on the Articulate tab or **Player Templates** from the Articulate menu. The Player Templates dialog box opens.

 Note: The Player Templates dialog box opens with the settings for the template that you used last.

3. Select the template name whose text label settings you wish to edit from the player templates menu at the bottom of the Player Templates dialog box.

4. Click the **Text Labels** tab.

5. Edit the desired button and message settings by clicking inside the **Custom text** column and typing the text you want to appear in place of the default text.

6. Click the **Close** button. When prompted whether to save the changes, select **Yes**. (If you select **No**, your changes will be lost.) When prompted for the name, type a new name in the text box.

 Note: The text label settings you select apply *only* to the *specific player template* being modified in the Player Templates dialog box.

Localizing (Changing the Language of) Text Label Settings

If you want the text labels to be in another language, you can select from one of these pre-installed languages:

- Brazilian Portuguese
- Dutch
- English
- French
- German
- Italian
- Japanese
- Korean
- Simplified Chinese
- Traditional Chinese
- Universal Spanish

When you select one of these languages, you will see that the text labels are translated into the chosen language (Figure 7.17).

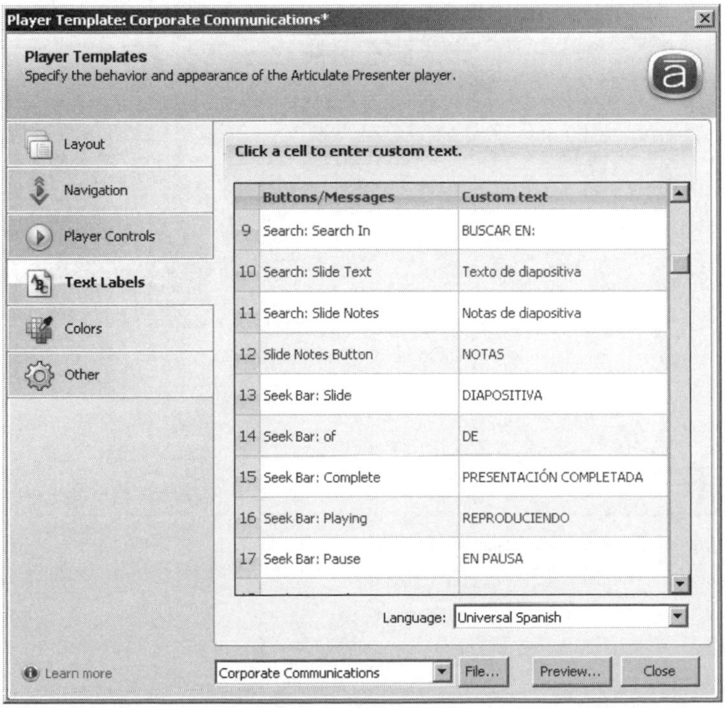

Figure 7.17. Text labels in Universal Spanish

> 66 **Note:** The text label settings you select apply only to the specific
> player template being modified in the Player Templates dialog
> box.

Colors Tab

The Colors tab of the Player Templates dialog box lets you change the
default color scheme and apply any of twenty additional preconfigured
color schemes that come with Presenter. It also lets you create and
save your own color schemes. You can change the colors used for buttons, tabs, scroll bars, playback controls, and other player elements.
Figure 7.18 shows the Player Templates dialog box with the Color
scheme menu open.

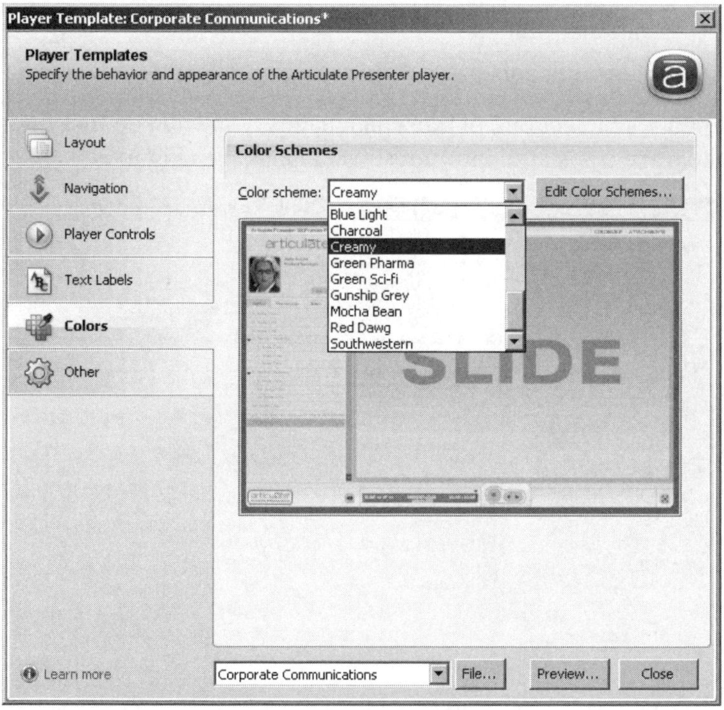

Figure 7.18. Player Templates dialog box, Colors tab

You can modify the color of selected player elements either by clicking on a color palette or by inputting RGB, Hex, or HSL numbers or letters. RGB numbers specify the intensity of each color component (red, green, and blue) on a scale from 0 to 255, where 255 represents full intensity. So full-intensity red with no green or blue would be represented by 255, 0, 0. Hex (hexadecimal) uses six numbers or letters to specify the intensity of the colors red, green, and blue. The first two numbers or letters represent the intensity of red, the second two numbers or letters represent the intensity of green, and the last two numbers or letters represent the intensity of blue. So full-intensity red with no green or blue would be represented by #FF0000. HSL stands for hue, saturation, and luminosity. Hue specifies the base color, and the other two values specify the saturation of the base color and how bright the base color should be.

Tip: The web site On The Matrix has a good description of these color naming schemes (http://www.on-the-matrix.com/webtools/HtmlColorCodes.aspx). There are numerous web sites that can help you make good color choices. One favorite is Adobe's Kuler (http://kuler.adobe.com).

Creating a New Color Scheme By Editing an Existing Scheme

1. Make sure that PowerPoint is open.

2. Click the **Player Templates** button on the Articulate tab or **Player Templates** from the Articulate menu. The Player Templates dialog box opens.

Note: The Player Templates dialog box opens with the settings for the template that you used last.

3. Select the template name whose color scheme you wish to edit from the player templates menu at the bottom of the Player Templates dialog box.

4. Click the **Colors** tab (Figure 7.19).

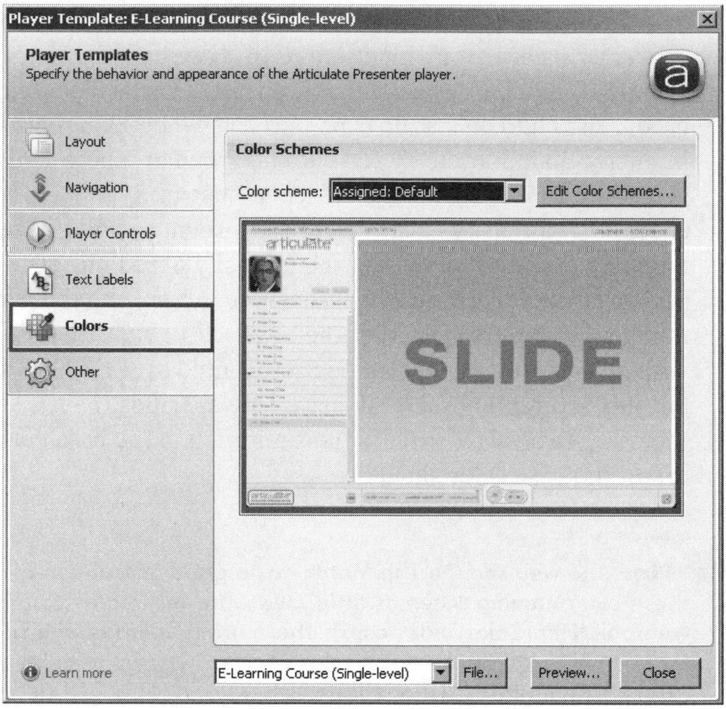

Figure 7.19. Player Templates dialog box

5. Select the color scheme you wish to edit from the Color scheme menu.

6. Click the **Edit Color Schemes** button. This will open the Color Schemes window (Figure 7.20).

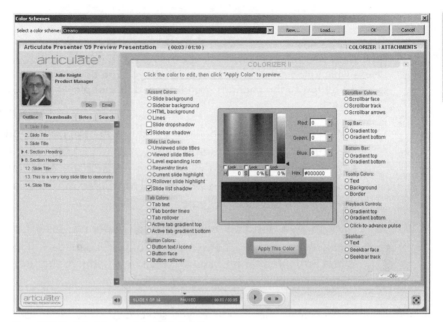

Figure 7.20. The Color Schemes window (Colorizer II)

7. To change the color of a specific player element, select the check box or radio button corresponding to that player element. The bottom rectangle in the center of the Color Schemes window shows the current color (Figure 7.21). Enter the new color in one of these ways:

■ Click the new color on the color palette.
■ Specify the new color using RGB numbers.
■ Specify the new color using HSL numbers.
■ Specify the new color using the Hex color code.

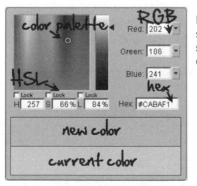

Figure 7.21. Ways to select new colors for specified player elements

Tip: To help you figure out what each player element in the Color Schemes window is, click one element in the window, choose a very bright color, and click the Apply This Color button. Note which element changed color. When you are done, click the Cancel button so the changes aren't applied to that player template.

8. (If you closed the Color Schemes window in the previous step, click the **Edit Color Schemes** button again to reopen the window.) Select or input the desired color for each player element you wish to change and click the **Apply This Color** button to apply the new color to the color scheme.

9. Click the **OK** button. When prompted whether to save the changes, select **Yes**. (If you select **No**, your changes will be lost.) When prompted for the name, type a new name in the text box.

Note: The color scheme settings you select apply *only* to the *specific player template* being modified in the Player Templates dialog box.

Creating a New Color Scheme

1. Make sure that PowerPoint is open.

2. Click the **Player Templates** button on the Articulate tab or **Player Templates** from the Articulate menu. The Player Templates dialog box opens.

Note: The Player Templates dialog box opens with the settings for the template that you used last.

3. Click the **Colors** tab.

4. Click the **Edit Color Schemes** button on the Player Templates dialog box.

5. Click the **New** button on the Color Schemes window.

6. Input the name for the new color scheme.

7. To change the color of a specific player element, click the check box or radio button corresponding to that player element. The color palette will reflect the current color. Change the color in one of these ways:

   ■ Click the new color on the color palette.

   ■ Specify the new color using RGB numbers.

   ■ Specify the new color using HSL numbers.

   ■ Specify the new color using the Hex color code.

Tip: To help you figure out what each player element in the Color Schemes window is, click one element in the window, choose a very bright color, and click the Apply This Color button. Note which element changed color. When you are done, click the Cancel button so the changes aren't applied to that player template.

8. (If you closed the Color Schemes window in the previous step, click the **Edit Color Schemes** button again to reopen the window.) Select or input the desired color for each player element you wish to change and click the **Apply This Color** button to apply the new color to the color scheme.

9. When you are satisfied with the color scheme, click **OK** to save the settings.

Note: The color scheme settings you select apply *only* to the *specific player template* being modified in the Player Templates dialog box.

> **?** These two ways of developing new color schemes seem like they're the same.

> **i** Good catch. They really only differ in whether you input the new color scheme name at the end or the beginning of the process.

Other Tab

The Other tab in the Player Templates dialog box (Figure 7.22) allows you to make changes to the browser window and slide title settings shown in Table 7.6.

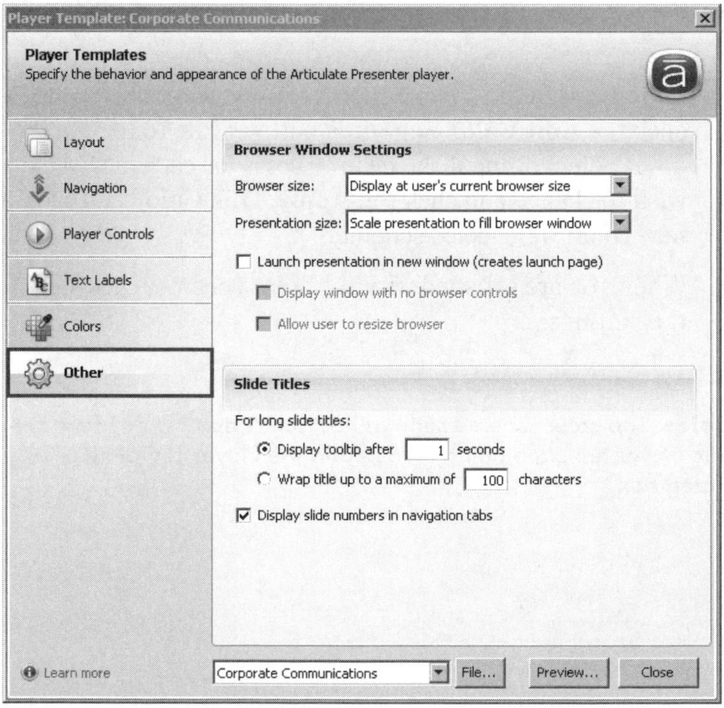

Figure 7.22. Player Templates dialog box, Other tab

Table 7.6. Other settings

Other setting	Description		
Browser Window Settings	Select desired browser window settings:		
	Browser size (browser plus player inside browser)	Display at user's current browser size (default): Browser window will remain the same size and player size will depend on presentation size selection:
		• Scale to fill: Player adjusts to fit in browser window.
		• Lock at optimal size: Player is locked at optimal size.
		Resize browser to optimal size: Browser window will resize to 980 pixels wide by 640 pixels tall and player size will depend on presentation size selection (same as above).
		Resize browser to fill screen: Browser window will resize to full screen and player size will depend on presentation size selection (same as above).
	Presentation size (player size only)	Scale presentation to fill browser (default): Player will adjust to the user's browser.
		Lock presentation at optimal size: Player will resize to 980 pixels wide by 640 pixels tall regardless of the browser size (see tip that follows this table).
	Launch presentation in new window	If checked, project will launch in a new window via a launch page.
	Display window with no browser controls	If checked, browser window will open without browser controls (stop, refresh, forward, backward, etc.).
	Allow user to resize browser	If checked, the browser window can be resized by the viewer.
Slide Titles	Select desired slide title settings:		
	Display tooltip after ___ seconds	If the slide title extends beyond available space in the sidebar, a tooltip with the full title will appear after the mouse hovers over the title for input number of seconds.
	Wrap title up to a maximum of ___ characters	Specify the maximum number of title characters that should be shown in the sidebar view.
	Display slide numbers in navigation tabs	Show/hide slide numbers in the sidebar. If you show slide numbers, those characters will count toward the maximum number of characters.

 Note: The other settings you select apply *only* to the *specific player template* being modified in the Player Templates dialog box.

||||▶**Tip:** Slides typically look best if you lock the presentation at the optimal size.

Creating New Player Templates

New player templates are created in the following ways:

■ Editing the settings on any or all of the Player Templates dialog box tabs (Layout, Navigation, Player Controls, Text Labels, Colors, and Other) for an existing player template and saving the modified player template with a new name (as described throughout the "Customizing Player Settings" section of this chapter).

■ Selecting desired settings on any or all of the Player Templates dialog box tabs (Layout, Navigation, Player Controls, Text Labels, Colors, and Other) and then saving these settings with a new player template name (described next).

Creating a New Player Template

1. Make sure that PowerPoint is open.

2. Click the **Player Templates** button on the Articulate tab or **Player Templates** from the Articulate menu. The Player Templates dialog box opens.

 Note: The Player Templates dialog box opens with the settings for the template that you used last.

3. Click the **File** button at the bottom of the dialog box and select either:

■ **New:** To modify the player template that is currently open (in the menu at the bottom of the Player Templates dialog box) with a new name.

■ **New from existing:** To select and modify any existing player template with a new name.

4. Input the name for the new player template and click **OK**.

5. Select the desired settings on all of the Player Templates dialog box tabs (Layout, Navigation, Player Controls, Text Labels, Colors, and Other).

6. Use the **Preview** button to view the results. Continue to make settings changes as desired.

7. When you are satisfied with the new player template settings, click **Close** to save the settings.

Sharing Your Project Files

If you are collaborating on a project and want to give your player template customizations to your collaborators, give them the PowerPoint source document (.ppt or .pptx file) and the associated Presenter .ppta file. When they open the project, they'll have access to your custom player templates.

The Presenter .ppta file is produced and updated whenever you preview or publish your project. If you want more information on these files, the following discussion thread may be useful: http://www.articulate.com/forums/articulate-presenter/8335-what-exactly-ppta.html.

What about Applying a Player Template to a Presenter Project?

You may wonder why this chapter describes how to customize Presenter player templates but doesn't describe how to *apply* a player template to a specific Presenter project. That's because player templates, like presentation options, allow you to create elements that can be used in *any* Presenter project. You will select the player template to be applied to your project when you publish it, as shown in Figure 7.23.

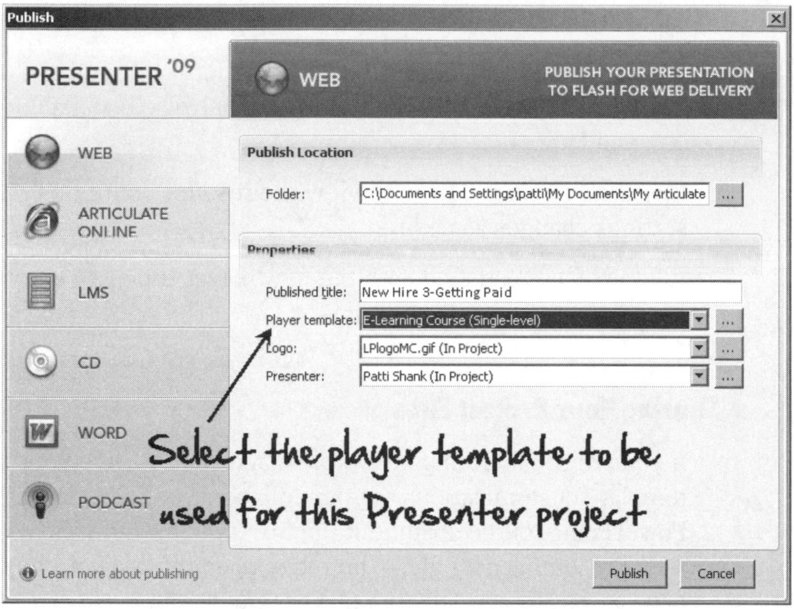

Figure 7.23. Player template selection when publishing

If you want to see how a given project looks inside a specific player template, preview the project. When the preview opens, click the Player Template button and select a player template. Your preview will be shown with the selected template.

Practice

In this practice, you'll create a new player template. The purpose of this practice session is to gain experience with changing player settings and viewing those changes.

1. Make sure that PowerPoint is open.

2. Click the **Player Templates** button on the Articulate tab or **Player Templates** from the Articulate menu. The Player Templates dialog box opens.

3. Click the **File** button and select **New**.

4. Type **Test** for the new player template name and click **OK**.

5. Click the **Preview** button. Notice the elements in the sidebar (logo, presenter, and slide list) and the Attachments button. Notice the tabs (Outline, Thumbnails, Notes, Search) on the left side (sidebar) of the player. Close the Preview window.

6. On the **Layout** tab of the Player Templates dialog box, uncheck Logo panel, Presenter panel, and Attachments tab. Click the **Preview** button and notice the effects of these changes on the player. Close the Preview window.

7. On the **Navigation** tab of the Player Templates dialog box, uncheck Thumbnails tab. Click the **Preview** button and notice the effects of these changes on the player. Close the Preview window.

8. On the **Colors** tab of the Player Templates dialog box, select the **Blue Medium** color scheme from the Color Schemes menu. Click the **Preview** button and notice the effects of these changes on the player. Close the Preview window.

9. (Still on the Colors tab) Click the **Edit Color Schemes** button. Select **Lines** in the Accent Colors group. Select a bright green color from the color palette. Click the **Apply This Color** button and notice what changed. Click **OK**.

10. When prompted whether to save the changes to the color scheme name, select **Yes**.

11. Click **Close**.

12. When prompted whether to save the changes to the player template name, select **Yes**.

13. To delete the Test player template, click the **Player Templates** button on the Articulate tab or **Player Templates** from the Articulate menu. The Player Templates dialog box opens. Select the **Test** player template in the menu at the bottom of the Player Templates dialog box. Click the **File** button and select **Delete**. When prompted whether to delete, click **Yes**.

Chapter Recap

This chapter contains information about working with Presenter player templates. Here's our list of the most important things to remember from this chapter:

■ The *player* is the interface in which a given Presenter project plays.

■ Each player template is a selection of settings for player layout, navigation, player controls, text labels, color schemes, and other settings that are saved with a specific player template name.

■ Presenter comes with a set of preconfigured player templates. You can use these player templates in their current state or edit their settings to meet your needs. You can also create your own player templates.

■ The player settings you select apply *only* to the *specific player template* being modified in the Player Templates dialog box.

■ The ability to edit, create, and save player templates (and use them as desired for your Presenter projects) is an amazing feature. This functionality makes it easy to apply the same settings to other Presenter projects.

■ New player templates are created by selecting desired settings on any or all of the Player Templates dialog box tabs (Layout, Navigation, Player Controls, Text Labels, Colors, and Other) and then saving these settings with a new player template name.

■ You will select a player template to use when publishing your project. But if you want to see how the project looks in a specific player template right now, preview the project. When the preview opens, click the Player Template button and select a player template. Your preview will be shown with the selected template.

Chapter 8

Introduction to Quizmaker

Chapter Snapshot

In this chapter, you'll get a feel for the Quizmaker program and how to prepare to build your quizzes and questions.

> **?** Developing questions looks like it requires some thought.

> **i** It does require thought. It's important to develop *good* questions, not just any questions!

What Is Quizmaker?

Quizmaker '09 lets you quickly build Flash-based quizzes and surveys using predefined question types. Its interface makes it easy to build graded quizzes, which are scored, and surveys, which are not scored. Select a question type, add your content and media, format the design, and you have a professional-looking question in minutes. Add additional questions and then publish the quiz or survey as Flash content.

Graded quizzes can contain both graded (scored) questions and survey (unscored) questions. Surveys can contain only survey questions. All quizzes consist of a series of *slides* that are displayed in the Quizmaker *player*. A slide can contain either a question or informational content, such as an introduction.

Viewers navigate through the quiz by answering the question on each question slide or by clicking the Next button on an information slide. Feedback can be provided. At the end of the quiz, a Results slide displays the viewer's quiz score (for graded quizzes) or a thank you message (for surveys). The Results slide can also include the option to review the quiz questions, responses, and correct answers.

66 **Note:** Because surveys are not really "quizzes," Articulate typically refers to a survey quiz as just a survey.

Quizzes and surveys are built using predefined question slides and created-from-scratch information slides (called "blank" slides). The following is a brief description of the slide types that you can include in your quizzes:

- **Graded questions:** Quizmaker provides 11 predefined question types that can be scored as correct or incorrect, such as Multiple Choice, Matching Drag and Drop, and Fill in the Blank.

- **Survey questions:** Quizmaker provides nine predefined question types that are not scored, such as Likert Scale, Ranking Drag and Drop, and Pick One.

- **Results slide:** Quizmaker provides a predefined Results slide that shows the viewer's score for graded quizzes and a thank you message for surveys.

- **Blank slide:** You can use blank slides to add "non-question" information such as a quiz introduction, instructions, or additional content used to answer the question.

Although the 20 question types are predesigned and prebuilt, Quizmaker lets you customize and format each question type. Through a combination of question slides and blank slides, you can build a variety of quizzes and surveys. Figure 8.1 shows a flowchart of a graded quiz that contains a mixture of graded questions, survey questions, and informational blank slides. The blank slides are shaded in the diagram. A survey flowchart would look similar but with all survey questions instead of both graded and survey questions.

66 **Note:** You cannot create your own question types, but you can customize and format many features of Quizmaker's built-in questions.

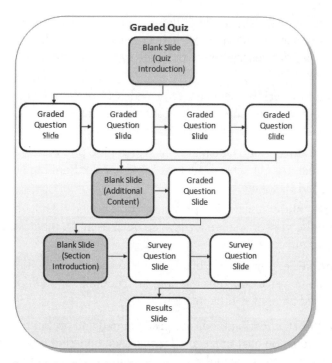

Figure 8.1. Sample graded quiz flowchart showing graded questions, survey questions, and blank slides

The Quizmaker *player* serves as the interface or "container" for each quiz. The player includes the navigation controls for the viewer and can be customized by modifying or creating *player templates*. Each player template determines the quiz attributes, such as what elements are displayed, how the questions are submitted, and the color scheme. Quizmaker comes with four preconfigured templates, and you can also create your own customized templates. Figure 8.2 shows the Quizmaker player using the default template, where the viewer submits answers one at a time. Feedback (if included) is displayed after each question is answered. The Question list navigation panel lets the viewer jump to different questions in the quiz.

Depending on the player template you choose for each quiz or survey, the features will vary. For example, the preconfigured template for a survey does not display the point value and score because surveys are not graded.

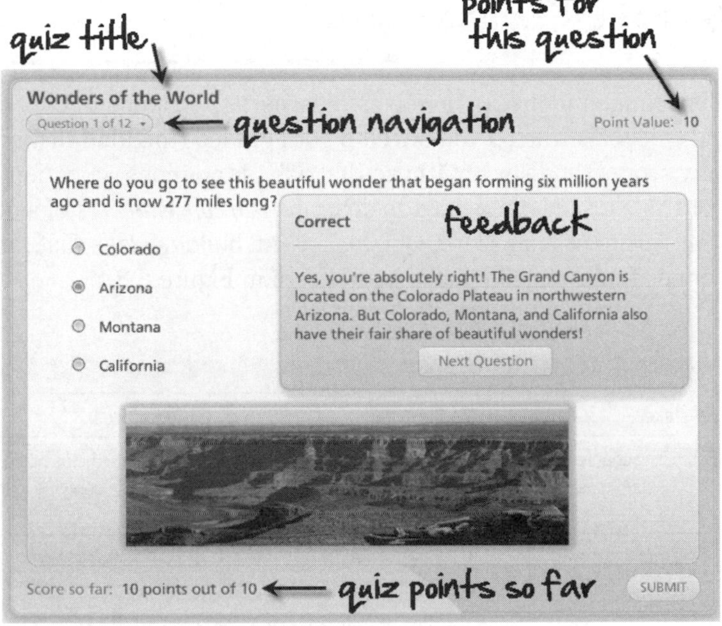

Figure 8.2. Typical Quizmaker player for a graded quiz

Once you complete your quiz, you *publish* it as Flash output that can be used in a variety of places, such as in a Presenter project or on a web page. If you publish the quiz (or the Presenter project containing the quiz) to a learning management system (LMS) or to Articulate Online, you can track quiz results. Even if you publish to a format other than an LMS or Articulate Online, you can still track quiz activity by having the results emailed at the end of a quiz.

Because of the built-in question types and player, what could take days to build in Flash can now take just hours to build in Quizmaker. And the portability of the Flash files opens up a range of great uses for your quizzes.

Best Uses of Quizmaker

It is common in instruction to ask learners to respond to questions, and Quizmaker helps you develop both graded (the kind that are typically scored) and survey (those that ask for opinions) questions. The word "stakes" is often used to describe the *consequences* of a quiz, test, or assessment final score. Quizmaker can build quizzes that range from no stakes to high stakes, as shown in Figure 8.3.

No stakes	Medium stakes	High stakes
Score isn't counted or has no consequences	Score determines if learner can proceed to the next unit of instruction	Score determines placement or ability to continue to the next step

Figure 8.3. Stakes for graded questions

Survey questions are not shown in the figure because they aren't scored and typically have no consequences for the respondent. No-stakes quizzes may include self-check questions that let learners assess their knowledge, get feedback, and make use of additional resources or help. These exercises can be optional, and they can be very powerful and useful learning tools. Medium-stakes quizzes are often placed at the end of a lesson or module. The score may be used to determine whether the learner can move on to the next lesson or module. High-stakes tests are typically used to determine if the learner qualifies for or can continue in a specific position or program.

In this section of the book, we discuss surveys and low- to medium-stakes quizzes because the issues for building and assuring the validity of higher stakes tests is beyond the scope of this book. We are using the term "quiz" because that is what Articulate calls a group of graded questions, but don't let that trip you up. Groups of graded questions are more commonly called tests or assessments.

Quizmaker surveys and quizzes can be used by themselves (standalone), inside a Presenter project, or along with other web or instructional authoring tools. Inserting or embedding Quizmaker surveys and quizzes into a Presenter project is easy because they are made to work optimally together. Quizmaker surveys and quizzes can also be used with other authoring tools or with standard web development tools. For example, you may wish to develop a survey that is used after a webinar to solicit topics for additional webinars. Since Quizmaker publishes Flash content, the content can be used anywhere a Flash file can be inserted or embedded, including in a web page.

 Note: Chapter 6, "Pumping Up Your Presenter Projects," explains how to insert or embed Quizmaker quizzes into a Presenter project. Chapter 26, "Publishing," explains how to "publish" a Quizmaker quiz.

Quizmaker 1-2-3-4-5 Workflow

The typical workflow for building a quiz involves creating the *quiz* itself and building the *questions* inside the quiz. Figure 8.4 shows the typical 1-2-3-4-5 workflow process for building any Quizmaker quiz. Before the process begins, you'll need to plan your quiz and questions. And throughout the process, you'll be previewing, testing, and fixing the quiz and questions.

Let's break down this 1-2-3-4-5 workflow a bit further. Table 8.1 provides a brief description of each step in the process. Notice that steps 2 and 3 are repeated for each question to be included in the quiz. Also keep in mind that you can customize the quiz (step 4) at various times during development.

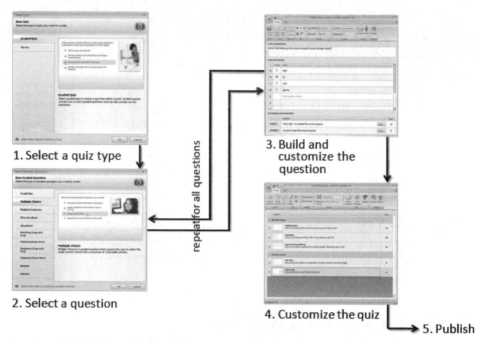

1. Select a quiz type

2. Select a question

repeat for all questions

3. Build and customize the question

4. Customize the quiz

5. Publish

Figure 8.4. Typical Quizmaker high-level workflow

Table 8.1. Typical Quizmaker typical detailed workflow

	Step	Description
	1. Select a quiz type.	a) Determine whether to build a graded quiz (graded questions and nongraded survey questions) or a survey (only nongraded survey questions).
		b) Use the New Quiz dialog box to start the new quiz.
		c) Select the appropriate player template for the quiz.
		d) Set the quiz properties.
R E P E A T	2. Select a question.	a) Decide on a graded or survey question (depending on the quiz type) to build.
		b) Use the New Graded Question dialog box and New Survey Question dialog box to view samples and start the new question.
	3. Build and customize the question.	a) Add the content elements required by the selected question such as question text, answer choices, and feedback.
		b) Customize the question by adding a variety of other features such as images, audio, and animation effects.

Step	Description
4. Customize the quiz.	a) Add informational ("blank") slides, such as introduction, review, and transition slides. b) Customize features of the quiz by grouping questions, randomizing questions, and modifying the Results slide. c) Customize the Quizmaker player by modifying the color scheme and changing navigation options. d) Create quiz templates for future use.
5. Publish the quiz.	a) Test and fix the quiz (again). b) Determine how you want to deliver the quiz, such as in Presenter, on the web, or on a CD. c) Create the appropriate output files.

The remaining chapters in this section of the book (Chapters 9-13) step you through this workflow. Chapter 9, "Quizmaker Basics," explains the essential tasks you'll need to perform all five steps. Chapter 10, "Creating Graded Questions," and Chapter 11, "Creating Survey Questions," focus on the first part of step 3 by explaining how to build each of Quizmaker's 20 question types. Chapter 12, "Pumping Up Your Questions," describes the second part of step 3—how to customize questions as you build them. Chapter 13, "Pumping Up Your Quizzes," describes some cool ways you can customize the quiz (step 4). In Chapter 26, "Publishing," we cover step 5 in the workflow.

A Quick Look at Graded Quizzes and Surveys

As we've mentioned, you can use Quizmaker to build both graded quizzes and nongraded surveys. A graded quiz can contain both graded questions and survey questions, whereas a survey can contain only survey questions. Let's take a look at both quiz types and the questions you can build for each.

Graded Quizzes

You'll typically create a graded quiz when you want to provide feedback and score the results. Graded quizzes are commonly used to:

- Select lessons that are needed (pretest)
- Provide feedback to help the learner overcome misconceptions

■ Tell the learner if he or she needs to review the content or get additional help

■ Determine if the learner has met learning objectives

■ Determine if the learner can go to the next lesson or module

When building a graded quiz, you can choose from the 11 built-in graded questions as shown in the New Graded Question dialog box (Figure 8.5). You can also include survey questions in a graded quiz. For example, a quiz designed to test whether customer service representatives know how to input each of the backorder options might contain eight graded questions, followed by a few survey questions that gather information about the experience level of the rep and collect feedback about backorder options.

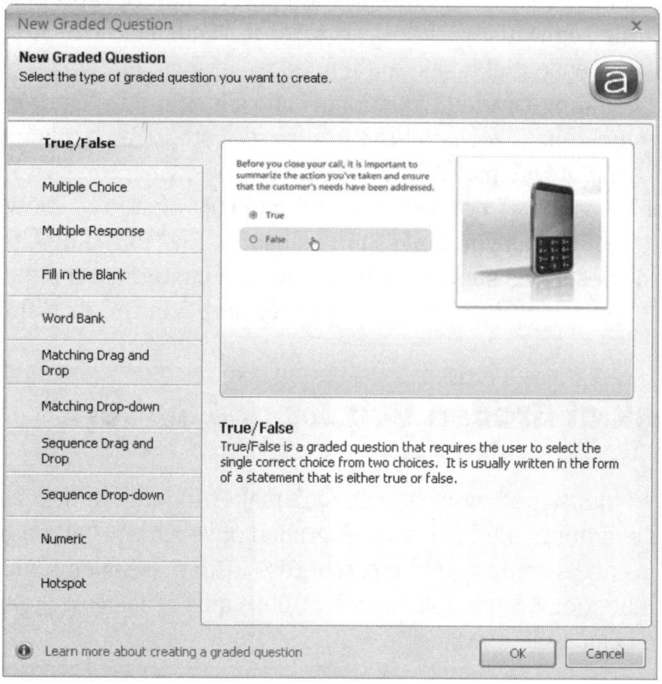

Figure 8.5. New Graded Question dialog box

Each graded and survey question type is covered in detail in Chapter 10, "Creating Graded Questions," and Chapter 11, "Creating Survey Questions."

Table 8.2 provides an at-a-glance reference of the graded question types and what they are typically used for.

Table 8.2. Graded question types and uses

Graded question type	Description	Typical (good) uses
True/False	Choose whether a statement is true or false.	Self-check questions, debunking myths or misconceptions
Multiple Choice	Choose one correct answer out of several choices.	All kinds of questions, from recalling facts to scenarios
Multiple Response	Choose one or several correct answers out of several choices.	All kinds of questions, from recalling facts to scenarios
Fill in the Blank	Type the correct answer into a text box.	Questions where recalling a specific phrase or word is needed (terminology, definitions, rule, policy, translation)
Word Bank	Drag one correct answer out of several choices and drop to an answer placeholder.	Questions where the viewer must determine which short answer is correct (similar to Multiple Choice)
Matching Drag and Drop	Drag and drop each item in one column to its matching description in another column.	Questions where understanding pairings (this goes with that) is needed (classification, Q and A, symbols, what to do, who to contact, applies/doesn't apply)
Matching Drop-down	Select one item in a drop-drown list of items that matches its description. Each drop-down list contains the same item choices for all descriptions listed.	Questions where understanding pairings is needed (classification, Q and A, symbols, what to do, who to contact, applies/doesn't apply)
Sequence Drag and Drop	Place a series of items in the correct order by dragging and dropping each item.	Questions about order and sequence (processes, procedures, timeframes, priorities)
Sequence Drop-down	Using a series of drop-down lists with the same items, place the items in order.	Questions about order and sequence (processes, procedures, timeframes, priorities)
Numeric	Type the correct numeric answer into a text box.	Questions where a specific number is critical (speed, time, distance, days, date, calculation, etc.) or where performing a calculation is needed
Hotspot	Identify the correct area of a graphic by clicking it.	Questions about visual information (flowchart, components, location, screenshot, group of people, etc.)

Surveys

A survey is an information-gathering tool that you can use for a variety of purposes. For example, a survey can collect learner opinions about the course. Because surveys are not scored, only survey questions can be included. Quizmaker offers nine common survey question types. Figure 8.6 shows these question types and Table 8.3 provides a brief description of each for quick reference.

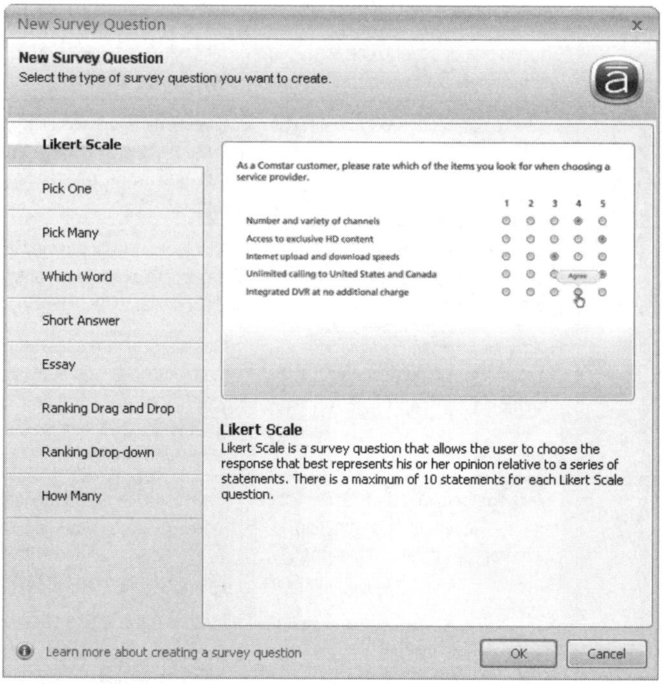

Figure 8.6. New Survey Question dialog box

Table 8.3. Survey question types and uses

Survey question type	Description	Typical (good) uses
Likert Scale	Use a rating scale to specify opinions based on a series of statements or questions.	Determine agreement/disagreement, gauge opinions, ascertain level of satisfaction/dissatisfaction
Pick One	Select one choice out of several choices. (Similar to graded Multiple Choice.)	Determine the *most* important part, need, problem, or issue

Survey question type	Description	Typical (good) uses
Pick Many	Select several choices out of several choices. (Similar to graded Multiple Response.)	Determine the *most* important parts, needs, problems, or issues
Which Word	Drag one choice out of several choices and drop to a placeholder. (Similar to graded Word Bank.)	Determine the *most* important part, need, problem, or issue
Short Answer	Type a response of up to 256 characters into a text box.	Obtain limited opinions, thoughts, experiences, explanations in respondent's own words
Essay	Type a lengthy response into a text box.	Obtain detailed opinions, thoughts, experiences, explanations in respondent's own words
Ranking Drag and Drop	Place a series of items in order of preference by dragging and dropping each item. (Similar to graded Sequence Drag and Drop.)	Determine order of importance, usefulness, effectiveness, difficulty
Ranking Drop-down	Using a series of drop-down lists with the same items, place the items in order of preference. (Similar to graded Sequence Drop-down.)	Determine order of importance, usefulness, effectiveness, difficulty
How Many	Type a numeric response into a text box. (Similar to graded Numeric.)	Gather demographic information (age, income, zip code, etc.), occurrences (orders, complaints), and wishes (response time, evening hours, available openings)

Surveys can be designed with closed-ended questions and open-ended questions.

Closed-ended Survey Questions

Closed-ended questions have a fixed set of answers. For example, on the question "How would you rate the content in this module?" the respondent may choose from among the following closed-ended answers: unsatisfactory, satisfactory, and excellent. The data from closed-ended questions is easy to analyze statistically. But they are difficult to write because the author must determine what range of answers are likely to be selected by respondents. You have probably answered closed-ended survey questions that you felt didn't include the answer you wanted to provide, so you know how important it is to produce an adequate set of answers.

Open-ended Survey Questions

Open-ended questions allow respondents to answer in their own words. For example, "What other topics would you like to see offered in our webinar series?" is an open-ended question. Open-ended questions are useful for gaining unsolicited answers, which may be more accurate than the answers selected on closed-ended questions. They are also useful for asking for information not already answered in closed-ended questions. For example, the question "Is there anything else you would like to tell us about the module?" is commonly used after a series of closed-ended questions. The responses to open-ended questions can often provide very important and insightful information, but the responses can be more difficult to analyze. Table 8.4 describes when to use closed-ended and open-ended questions.

Table 8.4. When to use closed-ended and open-ended questions

Question type	When to use
Closed-ended	When statistical analysis is needed, to understand how respondents rank various items, and when likely response choices are known
Open-ended	To get more information than can be contained in closed-ended questions, to get "deeper" information when likely response choices are unknown, and to get additional information

Because closed-ended and open-ended questions provide different types of information, it is often worthwhile to include both types of questions. Quizmaker provides nine survey question types. Two of the nine survey questions types, Short Answer and Essay, are open-ended. The rest are closed-ended.

Planning Your Quizzes and Questions

Planning your questions and quizzes usually translates into better quizzes and questions. Which translates into better information. You may feel that you don't have time to plan, especially if you are working on a rapid design project. But planning typically saves far more time than it takes. Unclear or problematic quiz and survey questions are frustrating or worse, especially if decisions are being made based on the score. And unclear or problematic survey questions are unlikely to give you the information you want.

Choosing the Quiz Type and Question Type(s)

If you are trying to measure content knowledge, you will probably be using graded quiz questions. If you are simply looking for information or feedback, you'll likely be using nongraded survey questions. If you want to do both, you'll build a graded quiz because it can contain both graded and survey questions.

Quiz questions are commonplace in learning-related content. But does that automatically mean you should include one (or more)? No. Quizzes take time (your time to build and each viewer's time to take) and should be built to either provide the viewer or you (or both) with useful information. Table 8.5 lists some of the more common goals for quiz and survey questions that are provided as part of a lesson or module and also lists the Quizmaker question type that is most appropriate for each goal.

Table 8.5. Quiz goal and question types

Goal	Type of Quizmaker questions
Gather information about learner wants and needs.	Survey question
Solicit opinions about the course content, instruction, or activities.	Survey question
Determine if the learner understands the content.	Graded question
Determine if learning objectives have been met.	Graded question + ?
Determine if the learner can progress.	Graded question + ?
Provide interactive activities so the learner is doing something other than reading or listening.	?
Provide practice opportunities.	?
Determine if the learner is able to perform as needed.	?

The question marks in the table indicate there are some important caveats in those circumstances. We'll discuss those caveats next.

Determining If Learning Objectives Have Been Met

Well-written learning objectives are specific statements about what the learner should know or be able to DO as a result of the instruction. DO is capitalized because the DOs are very important. Instruction should ideally prepare learners to DO what they need to be able to do in the real world.

Graded questions can be used to assess whether learners have met *some* learning objectives but not all. They can measure "thinking about" far better than they can measure "doing." Thinking tasks such as deciding or selecting can be measured by questions that require those tasks. But it's not as easy to measure actual doing with quiz questions because the questions themselves are typically more about "thinking about doing" than actually doing. Quiz questions usually require selecting a correct answer among given answers, which is much easier than actually having to figure out what to do. This distinction may not matter for less complex instruction, but it definitely matters for very critical tasks such as giving the correct medication or landing an airplane in heavy fog. You can't measure whether a learner can do these critical tasks with quiz questions alone.

Determining If the Learner Can Progress

Using a test score to determine if a learner can progress (to the next module or course, to the pool of applicants for a specific program or job, to a higher position at work, and so on) increases the consequences of the test score. The greater the consequences, the higher the stakes of the test. There are many considerations when developing higher stakes tests and those are beyond the scope of this book. But if you are developing higher stakes tests you'll want to consult with a test expert who can assure that you are measuring the right things in the right way. The type of expert you would want to consult would typically have a doctorate in educational psychology or educational measurement. Two places to find these kinds of experts are in a school of education in a local college or university or through the National Council on Measurement in Education (http://www.ncme.org).

Providing Interactive Activities so the Learner Is Doing Something Other Than Reading or Listening

There isn't anything inherently wrong with using questions as interactive activities to break up the reading and listening in a typical online module. But you'll want to make sure that the questions are pertinent and that the feedback is useful. Adults get annoyed when they feel that their time is being wasted, so develop valuable questions or make them optional if they aren't really needed. For example, questions with realistic scenarios and feedback help viewers use the content. Questions that ask viewers to recall module facts (that they don't need to commit to memory) are less valuable and less worthy of the time it takes to develop and answer them.

Providing Practice Opportunities

Learners should practice if they are expected to use what they are learning in the real world, so practice questions are good. But it's also important to realize the limitations of using practice questions. Practice questions can only prompt viewers to remember content or *think through* a given situation or issue. In real life, situations do not come with a limited context and three to five possible choices like questions do. In all of these ways, practice questions are simplified from reality. When learners must be able to perform a specific skill in real life, it is often critical that they *also* get the opportunity to practice in a more realistic manner. This may involve simulations (which may include complex scenario-based questions) and on-the-job practice.

Determine If the Learner Is Able to Perform as Needed

If you want to determine whether learners can actually *perform* in a given situation, questions are often not enough, for the same reasons they are not enough for practicing. When it is important to determine if learners can perform, a performance assessment will likely be needed (instead of or in addition to quiz questions). Performance assessments assess actual or simulated performance.

Planning Graded Questions

Graded questions used to determine if the learner has met the learning objectives should be written so they actually *do* measure the learning objective. For example, an objective that states "The learner will be able to write a legally defensible performance appraisal" cannot be measured with a multiple-choice test because the learner *can't* write a performance appraisal on a multiple-choice test. But "The learner will be able to tell the difference between a legally defensible performance appraisal and a performance appraisal that is not legally defensible" *can* be measured on a multiple-choice test. This is *not* a reason for writing dumbed-down objectives, however. The point here is that knowing what the learner should know and be able to do (specific and measurable learning objectives) points you to what assessments are needed. Quiz questions simply cannot measure all objectives.

In Chapter 3, "Introduction to Presenter," we described a method for selecting appropriate content, interactions, and media. We'll briefly review that methodology next because it is also useful for determining appropriate assessments.

Good instruction allows learners to practice doing what they need to be able to DO in real life, in a safe environment, with meaningful feedback and help, until they are able to DO what they need to be able to DO effectively. Table 8.6 shows the most typical DO types and some examples of each.

Table 8.6. DO types and examples

DO types	Examples
Recall facts.	Know the hours when the business is open. Remember pay dates.
Find and make sense of information.	Determine whether caller's service plan covers labor and parts. Calculate when timesheets are due on weeks with a holiday.
Understand underlying concepts.	Know how databases work. Understand that overnight shipping is needed for perishable items.
Understand how a process works.	Be able to follow the travel expense reimbursement process. Be aware of the hiring process.
Complete the needed steps.	Complete a new hire request. Check in new stock.
Determine which course of action is needed.	Ascertain the malfunction cause(s) and contact the appropriate department. Determine whether a refund or credit should be given.
Create a product or produce a specific result.	Write a discrepancy report. Transfer callers to the appropriate extension.
Troubleshoot and fix problems.	Find the damaged part and replace it. Analyze the reason for the delay and suggest solutions.

If the purpose of graded questions is to determine if learners can, in fact, do something as a result of viewing and interacting with the information or instruction, assessments should match the DOs that the learner needs to be able to do in real life. Table 8.7 shows the most typical DO types and typical assessment options.

Table 8.7. DO types and assessment options

DO types	Assessment options
Recall facts.	• Recalling, classifying, or using facts
Find and make sense of information.	• Locating, interpreting, or applying information
Understand the underlying concepts.	• Identifying appropriate examples • Applying concept properties
Understand how a process works.	• Sequencing process elements • Analyzing when the process applies and doesn't apply • Analyzing how the process applies in specific situations
Complete needed steps.	• Sequencing the steps • Analyzing when to perform the steps • Performing the steps*
Determine which course of action is needed.	• Determining which policies or guidelines apply • Analyzing when to apply the policy or guidelines • Applying policies and guidelines to scenarios • Solving problems that occur when the right course of action isn't taken
Create a product or produce a specific result.	• Creating a product or result* • Determining if needed result has occurred • Solving problems that happen when the needed result hasn't occurred
Troubleshoot and fix problems.	• Determining what is wrong • Determining what fix is needed • Determining how to get help • Fixing problems*

The items that are starred (*) typically require a level of DOing that cannot be assessed with questions. Many of the others can be assessed with well-written questions, but remember that you can only assess "thinking about doing" and not actual doing. (And *actual* doing is typically a lot harder than selecting an answer from among three to five possible answers.)

> 66 **Note:** The more complex the assessment, the harder it is to write good questions. Well-written questions may involve scenarios, media, and using real resources (such as a policy manual or job aid). For very critical or complex tasks, you should consider assessing actual doing instead of, or in addition to, using questions.

See the Practice at the end of this chapter to build an assessment blueprint for a current or upcoming project. Chapter 10, "Creating Graded Questions," contains specific advice about designing graded questions.

Planning Survey Questions

Surveys are commonly used as data collection tools for improving instruction because they are easy to administer. But the value of survey data is highly dependent on the design and implementation of the survey and the willingness of the survey takers to answer honestly and completely. Surveys are used for opinion-oriented information (for instance, "Was the glossary helpful?"), to ask questions about potential improvements ("What would make the resource links more useful?"), or to confirm problems and the reason for them ("Please explain any problems you have experienced.").

Figuring Out What You Want to Know

Planning your survey starts with figuring out what information you want. (Yeah, duh. But you'd be amazed at how many survey developers don't figure out what they want to know first.) Don't start writing survey questions until you have listed the questions you want to answer. Make those questions as specific as you can. For instance, "Do you think we should keep doing webinars?" is too general. What do you want to know? Here are some specific things you might want to know about webinar offerings:

- Are the webinars too long, the right length, or too short?
- Are they held at a time of day that works with your work schedule?
- Is there enough time for questions?
- Does the speaker involve the audience enough?

Even though these questions are more specific, you may need to also include some open-ended questions that allow respondents to describe things in their own words rather than selecting an answer that may not provide enough detail. So judiciously adding "Explain: _____" to a closed-ended question in which the respondent picks one option from a list can yield information of significantly higher value.

The more specific you are about what you want to know, the easier it will be to write questions that target this information. Make sure that each question asks one thing at a time. For example, "Yes" or "No" answers to the question "Were the links and examples useful tools?" won't tell you if the links *and* examples were both useful or not useful or if one was useful but not the other.

Make sure your language is precise and as clear as possible. The word "valuable" might mean very different things to different people. One learner might reply "No" to the question "Was [resource name] valuable?" because he didn't know it was there and another might answer similarly because it didn't provide the information he needed. Having an open-ended "Explain:____" after the question may help you understand what each respondent thinks.

Planning Quiz and Question Elements

We'll now take a look at the visual and structural elements you'll want to think about while planning your quizzes and questions. Quizmaker provides a great set of tools to help you add content elements, customize design elements, and structure the quiz. We'll briefly discuss those elements here, so that you have a general idea of what to plan for before starting to build a quiz. If some elements don't mean a whole lot to you right now, don't worry. The remaining chapters in this Quizmaker section provide additional details about working with all of them.

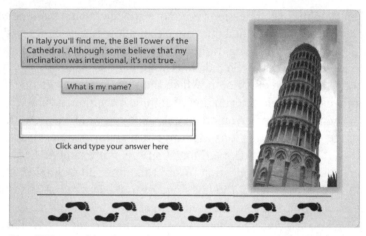

Figure 8.7. Question slide with text and graphics

Content

Question slides and blank slides can contain text, audio, video, and a variety of graphic elements, such as pictures and shapes. Figure 8.7 shows a slide with text and graphics.

- ■ **Text:** Okay, pretty obvious. Use text to state the question and answer choices, provide feedback, and include additional information. You can customize the text in a variety of ways using Quizmaker's formatting tools.

- ■ **Audio:** Include audio on a slide to expand on the question text, narrate an introduction, or complement the feedback text. You can also use audio for questions related to listening skills, such as identifying a musical instrument. Quizmaker supports .mp3 and .wav audio files.

- ■ **Video:** Add a video to provide context for a question. For example, show a movie of a technical procedure and ask a question about the procedure. Videos can also be used on slides to provide additional information. Quizmaker lets you insert .swf (Flash) and .flv (Flash video) files. (You can use Video Encoder '09 to convert most video formats to .flv files.)

- ■ **Graphics:** Use pictures to provide context for a question or to serve as answer choices. Avoid using graphics as "eye candy" and remember that graphics should have a purpose other than to "dress up" slides. Quizmaker supports graphic files in these formats: JPG (or JPEG), EMF, WMF, TIF, BMP, GIF, and PNG. You can also insert shapes, lines, and callouts using Quizmaker's built-in tools.

Design Elements

Quizmaker lets you customize the design of the slides and the design of the player, which contains the slides.

- **Slide design theme:** A slide design theme is a collection of visual properties, such as background pattern and color, text colors, and fonts that can be applied to just one slide or to all slides in the quiz. You can use the default design theme, select another predefined theme, or create your own theme. For example, the slide in Figure 8.7 uses a custom theme, which includes the Articulate font style, the Office color theme, and the Style 9 background. Although the slide design theme is separate from the color scheme used for the player, you'll want to make sure that the colors and fonts you use in your slides don't "clash" with the colors and fonts you choose for the player.

- **Quizmaker player features:** The features of the player depend on the player template you select for the quiz. (Refer back to Figure 8.2 for an example of a typical player.) Player design features include the color scheme, the font style of the text on the player, and the types of information displayed, such as the cumulative score. As mentioned earlier, the color scheme used by the player is separate from the design theme used by the slides. So as you plan the color scheme for the player, make sure it's consistent with the slide design theme (which is pretty easy to do because Articulate provides compatible colors for slides and the player). One more consideration: If you're planning to insert your quiz into a Presenter project, consider the color scheme used by the Presenter player. You want to make sure the Quizmaker player colors and the Presenter player colors are compatible.

Structure

Quizmaker gives you lots of flexibility for structuring the slides in a quiz and controlling how your viewers answer the questions.

- **Question groups:** You can organize questions into separate groups within one quiz. For example, you may want to group

questions by topic, such as sales-related questions, customer ser-
vice-related questions, and personnel-related questions. A very
common way to organize graded questions is by learning objectives. Figure 8.8 shows an example of a quiz divided into two
groups: one group of graded questions and one group of survey
questions.

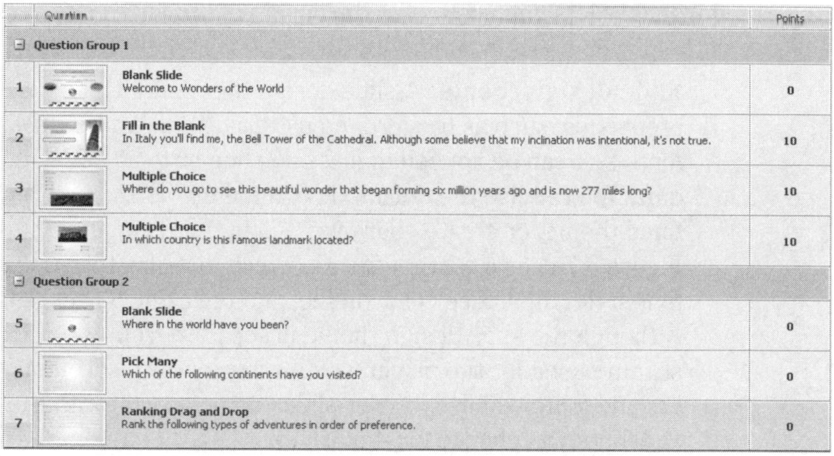

Figure 8.8. Quiz with question groups

- **Blank slides:** Blank slides let you include "non-question" information in a quiz, such as an introduction, instructions, transitions
  between question groups, and content used to answer a question
  (for example, a video to be viewed before answering a question
  about the video content).

- **Question submission:** The Quizmaker player template determines how viewers submit the questions. They can answer and
  submit questions one at a time (which can include feedback for
  each question), or they can answer all of the questions and then
  submit them at once (no feedback for specific questions). As you
  plan your quiz, think about the structure that makes the most
  sense.

Delivery Method

Quizzes can be "delivered" to viewers in several different ways,
depending on how you publish the quiz. A quiz can be published to be
used in a Presenter project, on a web page, on a CD, and even in a

Word document. You can also publish quizzes to a learning management system (LMS) and to Articulate Online (Articulate's online e-learning tracking service).

The delivery method you choose determines whether the learners' quiz results can be tracked. If you plan to track quiz results, you'll need to publish to an LMS, to Articulate Online, or to a Presenter project that will be published to an LMS or Articulate Online. If you publish to a web page or CD, you can still obtain a summary of quiz results via email, but they won't include the detailed tracking provided by the other delivery methods.

Chapter 26, "Publishing," provides details about how to publish your quizzes. We mention it here so you can start thinking about the best delivery method for your quizzes. The selection of publishing output type strongly depends on whether you want to track the quiz results. For example, a quiz that provides self-check questions for reinforcement doesn't necessarily need to be tracked, but a quiz that determines employee placement is likely to be tracked.

Managing Quizmaker Files

When you build and save a new quiz, Quizmaker creates a working file using the extension .quiz. This file is usable only by the Quizmaker program—it's the file you work with to create or modify the quiz. (Note that specific questions inside a quiz are not saved as files.) After you finish building the quiz, you *publish* the output to a .swf file (plus other supporting files), which is viewable to learners outside the Quizmaker program.

For example, let's say you start a graded quiz (WondersQuiz.quiz) and save it in the default My Documents\My Articulate Projects folder, as indicated in Figure 8.9. Every time you want to edit the quiz, you open the WondersQuiz.quiz file in Quizmaker, make the changes, and then save it. When you're satisfied with the quiz, you publish it so that it can be used on a web site. After you use the Publish to Web option, Quizmaker creates a folder containing a set of files required to display the quiz on the web. Figure 8.10 shows the high-level set of files generated during publishing.

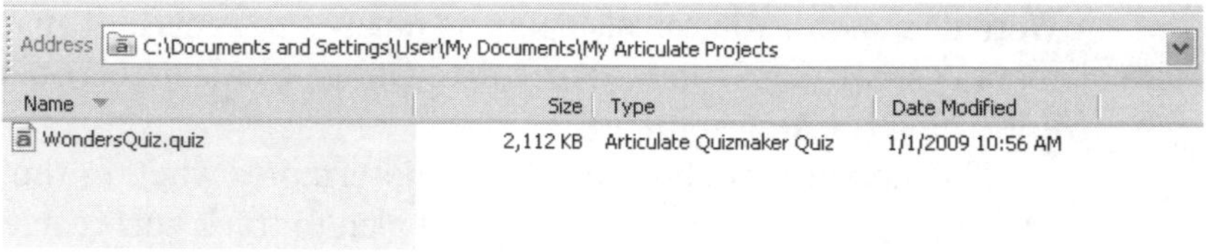

Figure 8.9. Quizmaker working file

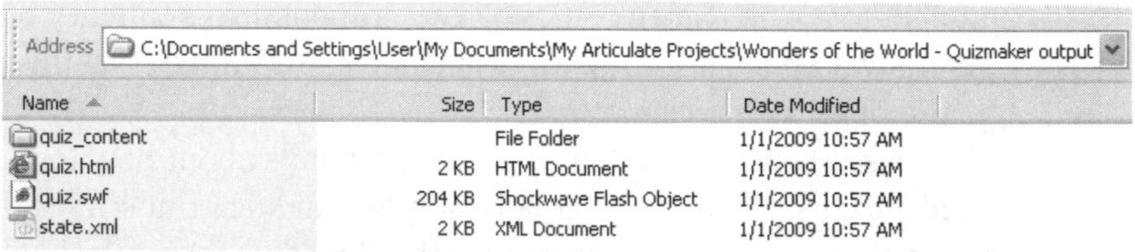

Figure 8.10. Quizmaker published files

Quizmaker also lets you create a *quiz template* from an existing quiz. A quiz template stores the slide design features and whatever content you want to keep from an existing quiz. You can then create a new quiz using the quiz template. The file name extension for a quiz template is, quite simply, .quiztemplate. By default, quiz template files are saved in the My Articulate Projects folder. Chapter 13, "Pumping Up Your Quizzes," provides details on working with quiz templates.

Note: Quiz templates are different from player templates. Player templates determine how the quiz looks inside the player, whereas quiz templates determine how the slides look.

You can store files with the .quiz and .quiztemplate extensions in other folders besides the default My Articulate Projects folder. In fact, it's a good idea to create an easily recognizable folder for each of your quizzes. You can use that folder to store the .quiz file and other files used to create the interaction, such as audio and graphics. We also suggest setting up a new folder to store the quiz templates that you create so that they are easily retrievable.

Practice

Using the following table, document the topics/DOs for a specific instructional project, then match those DOs to appropriate assessments. (Consider using the DO types and assessment options presented in Table 8.7 while completing this table.)

You may want to reproduce this table in your word processing application to use with current and future projects.

Quizmaker

Lesson or module:		
DO types	DOs	Assessment options
1. Recall facts.		
2. Find and make sense of information, often with the aid of tools, resources, etc.		
3. Understand underlying concepts.		
4. Understand how a process works.		
5. Complete the needed steps.		
6. Determine which course of action is needed.		
7. Create a product or produce a specific result.		
8. Troubleshoot and fix problems.		

Chapter Recap

Here's our list of the most important things to remember from this chapter:

■   Quizmaker '09 lets you quickly build Flash-based quizzes and surveys using predefined question types.

■   Graded quizzes can contain both graded (scored) questions and survey (unscored) questions. Surveys can contain only survey (unscored) questions.

■   The Quizmaker player serves as the interface or "container" for the quiz. The player template determines the quiz attributes, such as what elements are displayed, how the questions are submitted, and the color scheme.

■   Once a quiz is completed, it can be published as Flash output that can be used in a variety of places, such as in a Presenter project or on a web page.

■   The 1-2-3-4-5 workflow for developing a quiz includes selecting a quiz type; selecting a question; building and customizing each question; customizing the quiz; and publishing the quiz.

■   You'll typically create a graded quiz when you want to provide feedback or score the results. Quizmaker provides 11 predefined graded question types, and you can also include survey questions.

■   You'll typically create a survey when you want to gather information or opinions. Quizmaker provides nine predefined survey question types. Seven of these types are closed-ended (contain a fixed set of answers), and two types are open-ended (allow respondents to answer in their own words).

■   Planning your quizzes involves choosing the appropriate quiz type, selecting the right graded question to meet the learning objective, and selecting the right survey question to gather the desired information. When planning, also consider what quiz and question elements to include, such as text, audio, videos, graphics, design themes, and player features.

- If you plan to track quiz results, you'll need to publish to an LMS, to Articulate Online, or to a Presenter project that will be published to an LMS or Articulate Online.

- Working files in Quizmaker use the file name extension .quiz. These are the files you create and modify in Quizmaker. You can also create quiz templates, which use the file name extension .quiztemplate.

- A published quiz results in a .swf (Flash) file, along with supporting files. These are the files that viewers need to interact with the quiz.

> Now get ready to start building your quizzes!

Chapter 9

Quizmaker Basics

Chapter Snapshot

In this chapter, you'll learn the essential tasks required to create a quiz and build questions.

One of the beauties of Quizmaker is that you can spend an hour building a simple quiz with simple questions (that look great), or a couple
days building a sophisticated quiz with richly formatted questions.
Either way, you'll need to perform the essential tasks for creating a
quiz and its questions. We've tried to identify those tasks in this chapter so that after reading it, you'll be well equipped to jump in and start
building your quizzes. Chapters 10-13 give you more details for working with each question type and pumping up your questions and
quizzes. Most of our design advice about specific question types is in
Chapter 10, "Creating Graded Questions," and Chapter 11, "Creating
Survey Questions," so we recommend that you work with those
chapters next.

Revisiting the Quizmaker 1-2-3-4-5 Workflow

In Chapter 8, "Introduction to Quizmaker," we discussed the workflow
of developing a quiz and its questions. In this chapter, you'll get a feel
for the essential tasks needed to perform all five steps, plus preview
and save your quiz (Figure 9.1). Specifically:

■ **Step 1:** Selecting a quiz type involves identifying the right quiz for
your needs, opening it using the New Quiz dialog box, optionally
selecting a player template, and setting quiz properties.

■ **Step 2:** Selecting a question involves identifying the right graded
question or survey question and then opening it using either the
New Graded Question dialog box or the New Survey Question
dialog box.

■ **Step 3:** Building and customizing the question involves entering
the content elements into the provided placeholders and then customizing it with features such as images and audio. Repeat steps 2
and 3 for each question in the quiz.

■ **Step 4:** Customizing the quiz involves modifying default elements
of the quiz, such as grouping questions, customizing the player
template (or creating a new one), and modifying the Results slide.
You can also add non-question ("blank") slides to the quiz.

■ **Step 5:** Publishing the quiz involves creating the final output files
that viewers will use to take the quiz.

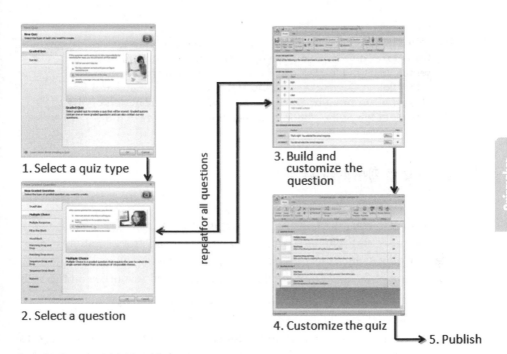

1. Select a quiz type

2. Select a question

3. Build and customize the question

repeat for all questions

4. Customize the quiz

5. Publish

Figure 9.1. Quizmaker 1-2-3-4-5 workflow

Launching Quizmaker

Quizmaker is a separate application installed on your computer. You can start Quizmaker using any of the following procedures:

- In Windows XP: Click the **Start** button, select **All Programs**, select **Articulate**, and select **Articulate Quizmaker '09**.

- In Windows Vista: Click the **Start** button, select **All Programs**, open the **Articulate** folder, and select **Articulate Quizmaker '09**.

- Double-click the **Articulate Quizmaker '09** shortcut icon on your desktop.

- Double-click an existing quiz file or quiz template file in Windows Explorer.

IIII**►Tip:** If you are building a Presenter project that has a
Quizmaker quiz in it, you can open Quizmaker from within Presenter. Just double-click a slide containing a Quizmaker quiz and
select Edit in Quizmaker. The Quizmaker program opens and displays the current quiz. Or click the Quizmaker Quiz button on the
Articulate tab of the ribbon and click the Create New button.

Selecting a Quiz Type

After you start the Quizmaker program, the start screen is displayed
(Figure 9.2). From here, you can start a new quiz from scratch, start a
new quiz using a quiz template, or open an existing quiz. The lower
section of the screen offers links to tutorials and resources on the web.

■ To start a new quiz from scratch, click Create a new quiz on the
left side.

■ To start a new quiz from a template that you have created, click its
name in the New from quiz template section.

■ To open an existing quiz, click its name in the Open a recent quiz
section. (Note that moving the mouse pointer over an existing quiz
name displays a thumbnail preview of the quiz, as well as its file
location.) Use the Browse button to locate quizzes that don't
appear in this list.

IIII**►Tip:** You can remove a quiz from the Open a recent quiz list by
right-clicking the quiz name or icon and selecting Remove from
List.

Selecting an existing quiz immediately opens the quiz file, where you
can make changes. Selecting a quiz template opens the template,
which you can use to build and save a new quiz. Selecting Create a
new quiz opens the New Quiz dialog box (Figure 9.3), where you can
select a quiz type.

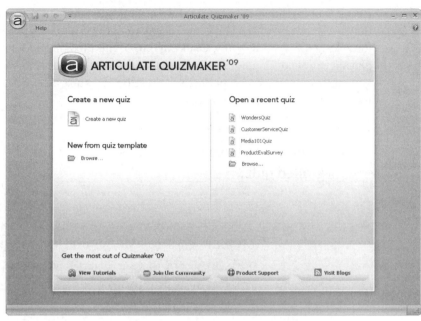

Figure 9.2. Quizmaker start screen

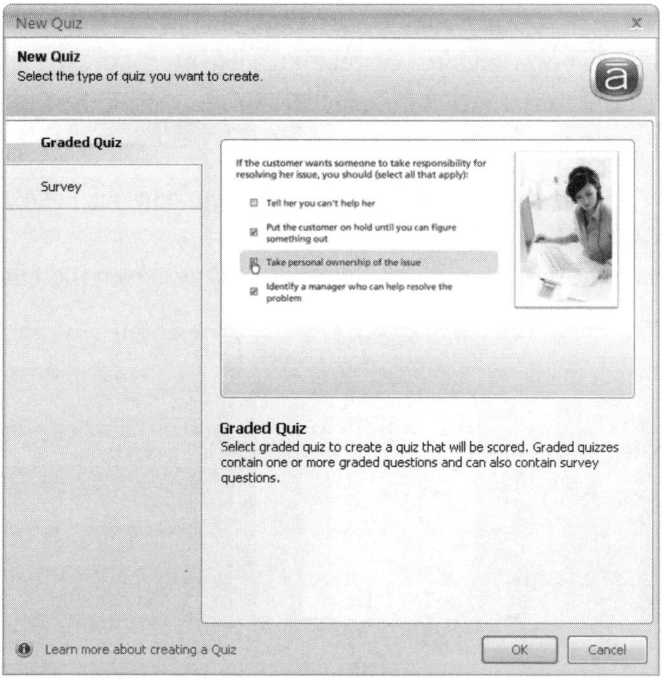

Figure 9.3. New Quiz dialog box

Recall that a graded quiz can contain both graded and survey questions. A survey can contain only survey questions and is typically used for asking for opinions only. Clicking one of the tabs on the left displays a panel containing information about the quiz type and an image showing an example of a published question. To start a new quiz, click its tab and then click the OK button.

> **?** Why would I use survey questions in a graded quiz?

> **i** You may want to ask opinion-oriented questions about the quiz or lesson or ask for insights about the knowledge or skills covered in the quiz.

You can open a new or existing quiz from the current quiz. To start a new quiz while working in a current quiz, use one of these methods:

- Click the **Articulate** button and select **New** from the File menu.
- Press **Ctrl+N**.

To open an existing quiz while working in a current quiz, use one of these methods:

- Click the **Articulate** button and select **Open** from the File menu.
- Press **Ctrl+O**.

Exploring the Quizmaker Interface

The window shown in Figure 9.4 represents the Quiz window that is displayed after you start a new graded quiz. It is similar to the window used for surveys. (We'll take a look at the Quiz window for a survey later in this chapter.) The Quiz window contains tools to both manage the questions in the quiz and work with features of the quiz. Let's take a closer look at each of the elements in this window.

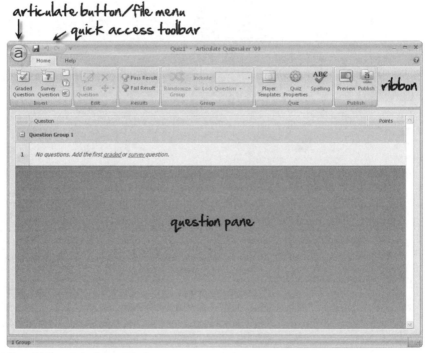

Figure 9.4. Quiz window for graded quiz

Articulate Button/File Menu (Quiz Window)

Clicking the Articulate button opens the File menu (Figure 9.5), which contains commands to work with the quiz file. As you'll see later, the options on the File menu change when you are working with a specific question in the Question window. Table 9.1 describes the commands in the Quiz window's File menu.

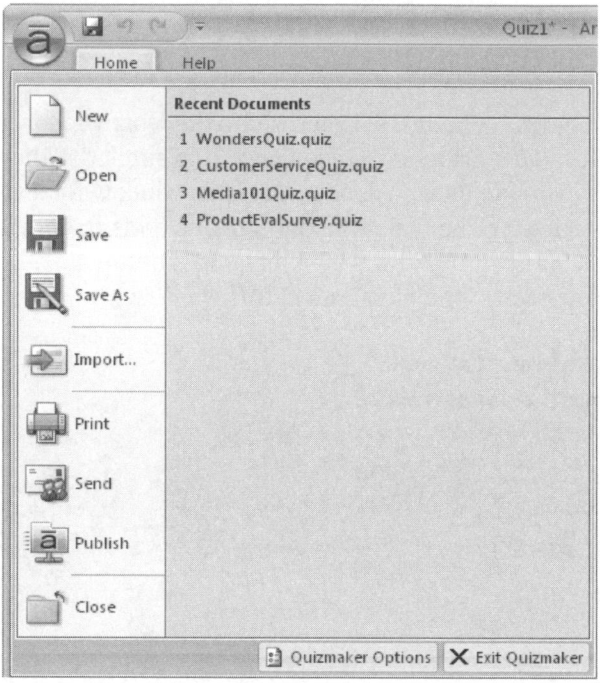

Figure 9.5. Quiz window File menu

Table 9.1. Quiz window File menu commands

Command	Description
New	Displays the New Quiz window, where you can select a quiz type (shortcut — Ctrl+N)
Open	Displays the Open dialog box, where you can select an existing quiz (shortcut — Ctrl+O)
Save	Saves the current quiz using the current file name and location (shortcut — Ctrl+S)
Save As	Displays the Save As dialog box, where you can save the quiz using a different file name and location. You can also save the quiz as a template.
Import	Displays the Open dialog box, where you can select a quiz to import into the current quiz. After you select a quiz, the Import Quiz dialog box lets you choose the questions to import.
Print	Opens the Word tab of the Publish dialog box, where you can publish the quiz to a Word document and then print it (shortcut — Ctrl+P)
Send	Displays the message window of your default email program, where you can send the current (unpublished) quiz as an email attachment
Publish	Displays the Publish dialog box, where you can publish the quiz using a specific output format (shortcut — F10)

Command	Description
Close	Closes the current quiz and displays the Articulate Quizmaker start screen
Quizmaker Options (button)	Opens the Quizmaker Options dialog box, where you can set global preferences for working with the program. (This dialog box is covered later in this chapter.)
Exit Quizmaker (button)	Closes the Quizmaker program

Quick Access Toolbar

The Quick Access toolbar (Figure 9.6) contains buttons that activate common commands. Table 9.2 describes what each button does.

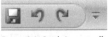

Figure 9.6. Quick Access toolbar

Table 9.2. Quick Access toolbar buttons

Button	Description
Save	Saves the current quiz using the current file name and location (shortcut — Ctrl+S)
Undo	Reverses the effects of your most recent action; becomes active only after you perform an action (shortcut — Ctrl+Z)
Redo	Restores the most recent action that you've undone; becomes active only after you undo an action (shortcut — Ctrl+Y)
Customize	Displays a menu of options, where you can hide buttons on the Quick Access toolbar and control the ribbon display

Tip: You can add almost any tool from the Quizmaker ribbon to the Quick Access toolbar. Just right-click the tool (such as the Edit Question button) and select Add to Quick Access Toolbar.

Ribbon (Quiz Window)

Quizmaker uses an Office 2007-style *ribbon* to organize most of the tools used to work with quizzes and questions. The ribbon is divided into *tabs*, which contain tools related to specific tasks. The ribbon tabs in Quizmaker vary depending on what you are working on, but the Help tab is always available. The tabs on the Quiz window ribbon for a graded quiz are shown in Figures 9.7 and 9.8.

Tip: You can hide the ribbon by right-clicking it and selecting Minimize the Ribbon. Just the ribbon tabs are displayed. Redisplay the ribbon by right-clicking a tab and selecting Minimize the Ribbon again.

Why Does My Ribbon Look Different from the Pictures in this Book?

The screenshots shown in the chapters on Quizmaker are based on the smallest (non-maximized) Quizmaker windows. If your Quizmaker windows are configured for a larger display size, you'll notice that more of the button icons are accompanied by text labels. For example, the **Delete Question** button looks like ✕ in the smaller Quiz window, and looks like ✕ Delete Question in a larger Quiz window. In addition, more button labels are displayed in a survey Quiz window than in a graded Quiz window.

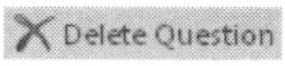

Home Tab

The Home tab tools consist of buttons and menus used to work with the current quiz (Figure 9.7). These tools are organized by groups, which are briefly described in Table 9.3. You will work with these groups in more detail in Chapters 10-13.

Figure 9.7. Quiz window Home tab

Table 9.3. Quiz window Home tab groups

Group	Description
Insert	Contains tools to add new questions and blank slides to the quiz
Edit	Contains tools to edit, delete, and move specific questions in the quiz
Results	Contains tools to customize the Results slides that are shown at the end of the quiz
Group	Contains tools to organize the quiz questions into groups

Group	Description
Quiz	Contains tools to customize the Quizmaker player, set general default properties of the quiz, and run a spell check on all questions
Publish	Contains tools to preview the entire quiz and to publish it using a specific output format

Help Tab

The Help tab in Quizmaker (Figure 9.8) is similar to the Help tab in the Engage ribbon and the Help and Support menu in Presenter. A few items are Quizmaker-specific, such as the tools in the Articulate Quizmaker '09 section. The Documentation button in the Help and Support group leads directly to Help topics for Quizmaker. Chapter 1, "Introduction to Articulate Studio," describes how to use the help system from any Articulate Studio program.

Figure 9.8. Quiz window Help tab

Question Pane

The Question pane in the Quiz window displays all of the questions in the current quiz. You use this pane to organize the questions in various ways, such as by grouping them. Figure 9.9 shows a quiz with two groups of questions.

Question			Points
⊟ **Question Group 1**			
1		**Multiple Choice** Which of the following is the correct command to access the login screen?	10
2		**Word Bank** Which of the following promotions will Two-Plus customers qualify for?	10
3		**Sequence Drag and Drop** Below are the steps to completing the customer checklist. Place these steps in order.	10
⊟ **Question Group 2**			
4		**Pick Many** What features do you think are marketable to Two-Plus customers? Check all that apply.	0
5		**Likert Scale** Rate the importance of each feature listed below	0

Figure 9.9. Quiz window Question pane

Selecting a Player Template

The Quizmaker player displays the quiz slides and contains the navigation controls for your viewers. The way the player looks and acts depends on the *player template* selected for the quiz. Quizmaker comes with four preconfigured player templates and automatically assigns the Quiz - Submit one at a time template to a new quiz. The template determines a number of features, such as how the questions are submitted, whether a running score is displayed, and the color scheme used by the player. You can keep the default template for the quiz, select a different template, customize an existing template, or create a new template. Chapter 13, "Pumping Up Your Quizzes," describes all the features of player templates, but it's helpful to have a general idea of what each template offers when you begin creating your quiz.

You can certainly keep the default template for the quiz, but if you want to select a different player template (or just look at the options), click the Player Templates button on the Home tab of the Quiz window ribbon. The Player Template Manager dialog box opens and displays the four preconfigured templates provided by Quizmaker (Figure 9.10). The currently selected template is highlighted and is identified by the words "(In use)". Table 9.4 provides a brief description of each template.

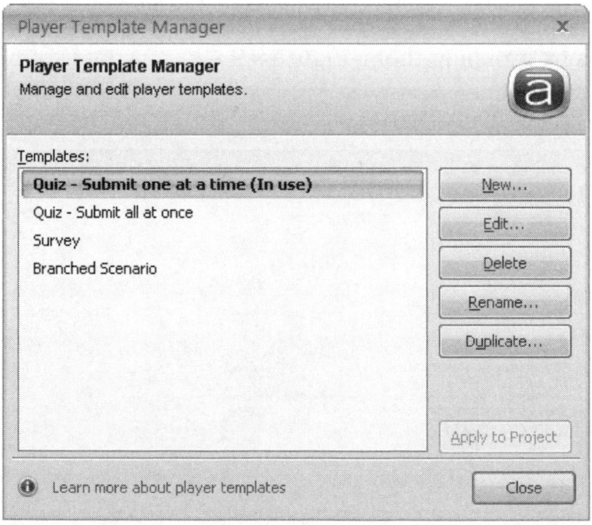

Figure 9.10. Player Template Manager dialog box

Table 9.4. Preconfigured templates

Template	Description
Quiz - Submit one at a time	Structures the quiz so that viewers answer a question, submit it, and receive feedback (if provided) for each question. The Question list navigation panel is included, allowing viewers to jump to specific questions. A cumulative score for graded quizzes is also included.
Quiz - Submit all at once	Structures the quiz so that viewers answer all questions and submit them together. (No feedback can be displayed for individual questions.) The Question list navigation panel is included, allowing viewers to jump to specific questions. A cumulative score cannot be displayed because the questions are graded together at the end of the quiz.
Survey	Structures the quiz based on the features of a typical survey. Questions are answered and submitted one at a time, but scoring and point values are not included. The Question list navigation panel is not included.
Branched Scenario	Structures the quiz based on the features of a typical branched scenario, which displays specific slides based on how the viewers answer a question. *Note that the branching itself is not part of the template; you implement the branching functionality as you build the slides.* The template structures the player so that viewers answer and submit questions one a time. The Question list navigation panel is omitted so that viewers cannot jump to different questions.

If you want to use a different template, select it and click the Apply to Project button. You can change your mind and apply a different template at any time. As mentioned earlier, you can modify various options of the existing templates or create a new template. Chapter 13, "Pumping Up Your Quizzes," explains how to customize template settings and create new player templates.

Setting Quiz Properties

Quizmaker lets you set general *properties* of the current quiz, such as the passing score and the default feedback text used for questions. These options are contained in the Quiz Properties dialog box (Figure 9.11), which is accessible by clicking the Quiz Properties button on the Home tab of the Quiz window ribbon. Although you can work with these properties at any time, it's generally helpful to set them *before* you begin creating your questions. Many of the options affect the default features of new questions, so it's more efficient to customize these options up front. We realize that if you're new to Quizmaker, these options may not mean much to you right now. But after you've built a few questions, the options will make more sense and you'll see why you should work with them up front rather than later.

> **Note:** The properties you set apply only to the current quiz, not to other quizzes.

The Quiz Properties dialog box contains two panels of options, which are described next. Note that some options do not apply to surveys, so if you open this dialog box from a survey, some options will not be included. The examples in Figures 9.11 and 9.12 represent the options for graded quizzes.

Setting Quiz Info

The Quiz Info panel of the Quiz Properties dialog box (Figure 9.11) lets you set the options described in Table 9.5.

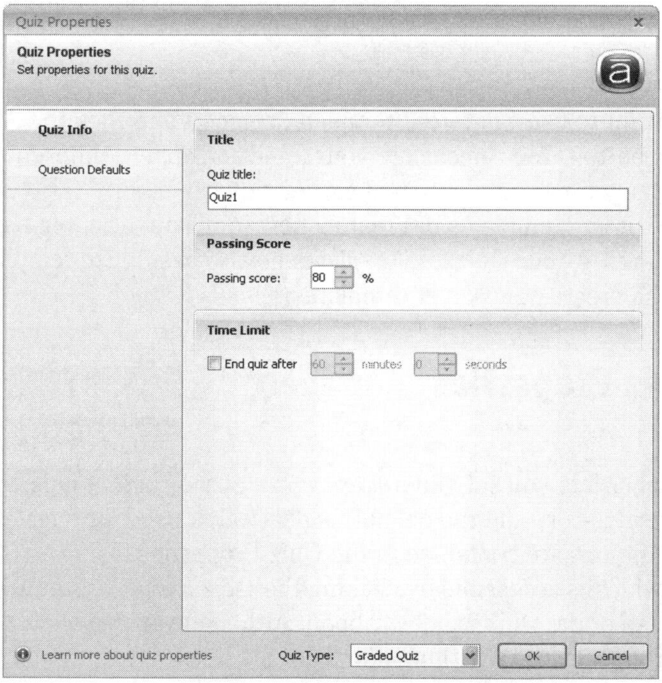

Figure 9.11. Quiz Properties dialog box Quiz Info panel for graded quiz

Table 9.5. Quiz Properties dialog box Quiz Info panel options

Option	Description
Title	The quiz title appears at the top of the Quizmaker player. By default, Quizmaker enters the file name of the quiz for the quiz title, you can (and probably should) change it. For example, the file name of the quiz can be CSQuiz001.quiz, and the Quiz title can be Customer Service Quiz.
Passing Score	The default passing score for a quiz is 80%, meaning 80% of the questions need to be answered correctly to pass. Use this option to change the score to any value from 0% to 100%. **Note**: This option applies only to graded quizzes.
Time Limit	By default, there is no time limit for the quiz, meaning viewers can take as much time as needed to complete it. You can set a time limit by selecting the check box and entering the hour and minute values, but we recommend keeping the default unless there is a compelling reason to impose a time limit.

Setting Question Defaults

The Question Defaults panel of the Quiz Properties dialog box (Figure 9.12) lets you change the default values that are used for each new question. Note that you can still change these values in the question itself, once you start building the question. Table 9.6 describes these options.

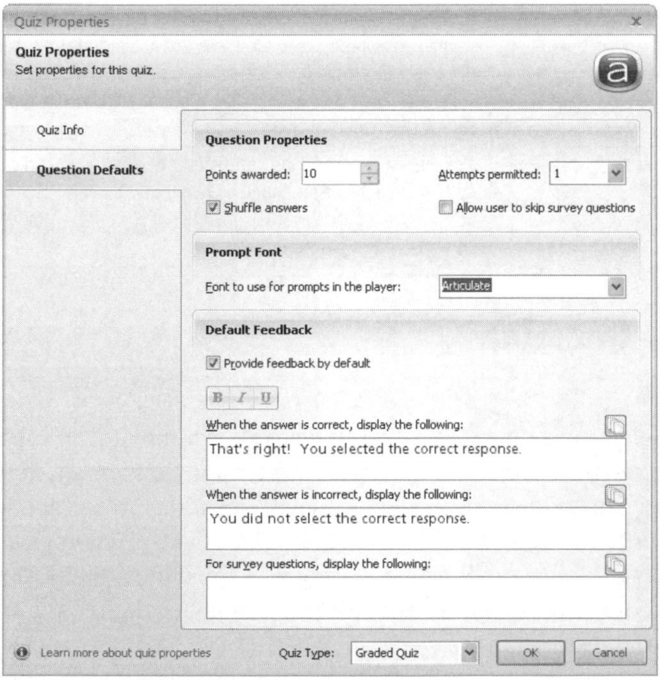

Figure 9.12. Quiz Properties dialog box Question Defaults panel for graded quiz

Table 9.6. Quiz Properties dialog box Question Defaults panel options

Option	Description
Points awarded	Use this option to set the default number of points awarded to each correct answer. **Note**: This option applies only to graded quizzes.
Attempts permitted	Use this option to set the number of times the viewer can try to answer the question before the next question is displayed. **Note**: This option applies only to graded quizzes.
Shuffle answers	By default, the answer choices are shuffled (the order is randomized) each time the question is displayed. Deselect the check box to keep the answers in the order in which you build them in the question.
Allow user to skip survey questions	Select this option if you want viewers to be able to skip over survey questions. Although this option is available for both surveys and graded quizzes, it is most applicable when you have a graded quiz that includes both graded and survey questions.
Fonts to use for prompts in the player	Use this option to control the font that is used for all prompts that Quizmaker displays during the running quiz. These prompts include question feedback messages and error messages, such as when the viewer clicks Submit before answering the question.
Provide feedback by default	Select this option to provide the ability to include feedback for every question. You can turn off feedback for specific questions using the Feedback list on the Question window ribbon.
Feedback text boxes	Use these text boxes to revise the default feedback text that is used for incorrect, correct, and survey answers in new questions. If you want to apply the revised feedback text to the questions that have already been created, click the Apply to All button 📋 . Use the Bold, Italic, and Underline buttons **B** *I* <u>U</u> to apply these formats to the default feedback text.
Quiz Type	Use this list to convert the current quiz to either a graded quiz or a survey. Note, however, that if a graded quiz contains graded questions (which it probably will!), you cannot convert the graded quiz to a survey.

Selecting a Question

After selecting a quiz type, selecting a player template, and setting quiz properties, your next step is to start adding questions. Remember that you can add both graded and survey questions to a graded quiz, but a survey is limited to survey questions. If you are going to use survey questions in a graded quiz, it may be a good idea to put those at the end of the quiz so the respondent will answer the most important (graded) questions first.

66 **Note:** You can also add a blank slide to the quiz, which can then be customized to provide an introduction to the quiz or to present additional content within the quiz. Chapter 13, "Pumping Up Your Quizzes," provides details on working with blank slides.

Adding a Graded or Survey Question

To add a new question, you can click the Graded Question or Survey Question button on the Home tab of the Quiz window ribbon (Figure 9.7). Alternatively, you can click the **graded** or **survey** links that appear at the top of the Question pane when a new quiz is started (Figure 9.4). The New Graded Question dialog box (Figure 9.13) or the New Survey Question dialog box is then displayed.

Figure 9.13. New Graded Question dialog box

Each question is represented by a tab on the left side of the dialog box. Clicking a tab displays a sample and additional information about the question. To start a new question, click its tab and then click the OK button.

If you are new to using Quizmaker, looking at the sample question that is shown can be very helpful. It can give you an idea about which question type to use and how to set up that type of question.

Form View vs. Slide View

After you select a question, the Question window for that question type opens. By default, the question is displayed in Form view. This view provides placeholders for each element of the question. It's an easy way to add the content elements quickly to the question. Slide view also lets you add content elements along with modifying the layout and formatting other features of the question. Figure 9.14 provides a comparison of these two views.

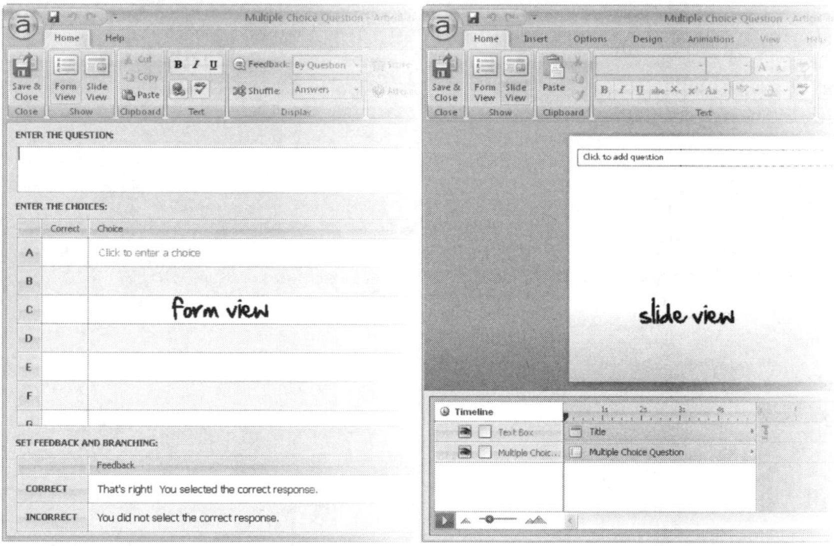

Figure 9.14. Question window in Form view and Slide view

A common approach to question building is to add the basic content elements using Form view. Then switch to Slide view to customize the layout, add media objects, create animations, and time the display of specific objects of the question. Following is a summary of what you can do in each view.

Form View

- Enter the question and answer choices.
- Customize default feedback text.
- Add branching.
- Format text (limited).
- Add one media file (image or movie), which is placed by default next to the question.
- Record or import one sound clip.
- Set display options, such as shuffling the answer choices.
- Modify scoring options.
- Preview, save, and close the question.

Slide View

- Perform everything you can do in Form view, with a few exceptions.
- Customize the layout by rearranging objects.
- Format text (extended).
- Format question and answer areas, such as adding borders and colors.
- Apply design themes and background graphics.
- Work with the slide master.
- Insert and format multiple media files, shapes, and text boxes.
- Record and import multiple audio clips.
- Animate objects and add slide transitions.
- Add slide notes.
- Use the timeline to make objects appear/disappear at different times.

Here's what you cannot do in Slide view:

- Customize default feedback text.
- Add branching.
- Add answer choices for *some* types of questions.

The next two sections in this chapter describe how to build a question using each of these views. Note that just the basic steps will be covered. Chapters 10-13 provide more details about creating and formatting your questions.

Building Questions in Form View

Form view allows you to quickly build questions. Following are the basic tasks you'll perform to create a question in this view:

■ Enter the question text.

■ Enter the answer choices.

■ Set feedback and branching, if needed.

■ Customize display and scoring options.

■ Preview and save the question.

In this section we step through each of these tasks, and at the end of the section you'll have a chance to practice building a simple question in Form view from start to finish. Let's start by taking a quick look at the Question window interface in Form view.

Exploring the Form View Interface

Form view provides placeholders that you can use to create the question, and the ribbon at the top of the Question window provides tools to work with the question (Figure 9.15). Notice that these tools are different from the ones on the Quiz window ribbon. The ribbon changes depending on the available features. And the ribbon for survey questions is slightly different from the one for graded questions, displayed here. We'll focus on the graded question ribbon for now and take a look at the survey question ribbon later in the chapter.

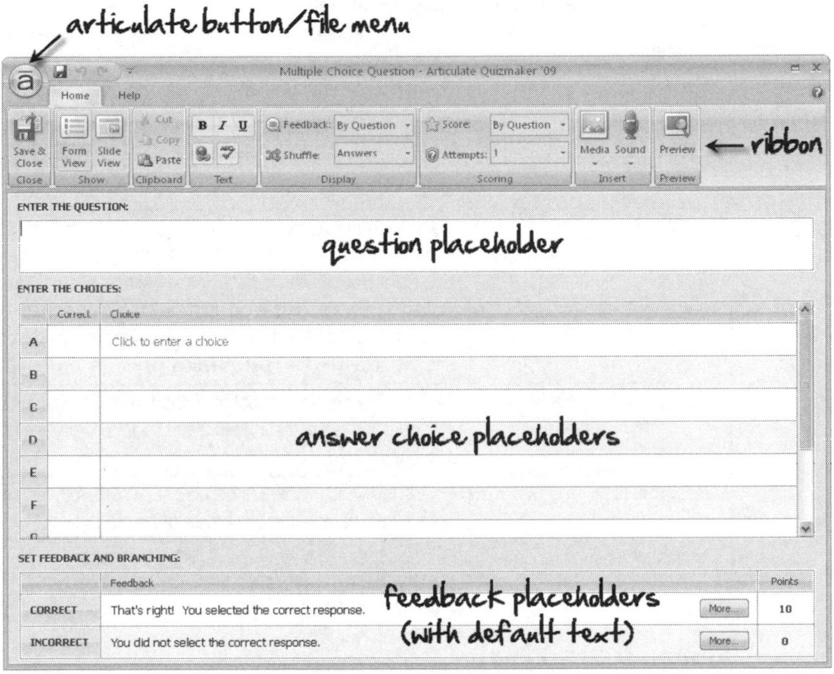

articulate button/file menu

Figure 9.15. Question window in Form view showing Multiple Choice question

Articulate Button/File Menu (Question Window)

Although the function of the Articulate button on the Question window is the same as that on the Quiz menu, the File menu on the Question window (which is displayed when you click the Articulate button) is different (Figure 9.16). This menu contains commands to work with the current question and to navigate to other questions in the quiz. Table 9.7 describes the commands in the Question window File menu.

Figure 9.16. Question window File menu

Table 9.7. Question window File menu commands

Command	Description
Save & Close	Saves the current question and closes the Question window
Cancel	Closes the Question window without saving your changes
Delete Question	Deletes the current question from the quiz and closes the Question window
Edit Next Question	Displays the next question in the quiz in the Question window. If the current question is the last one in the quiz, this command is Edit Pass Result, which displays the Results slide of the quiz for editing. (This feature is a big time saver, as you can move right to the next question to edit it instead of closing the current question and then opening the next question.)
Edit Previous Question	Displays the previous question in the Question window. If the current question is the first one in the quiz, this command is dimmed and unavailable.
Quiz Properties	Opens the Quiz Properties dialog box, where you can change default quiz values and customize other properties
Quizmaker Options (button)	Opens the Quizmaker Options dialog box, where you can set preferences for working in Quizmaker

Ribbon (Form View)

The ribbon on the Question window in Form view contains the Home tab (Figure 9.17) and standard Help tab. The tools on the Home tab are used to work with the current question. Table 9.8 provides a brief description of each group on the Home tab for graded questions.

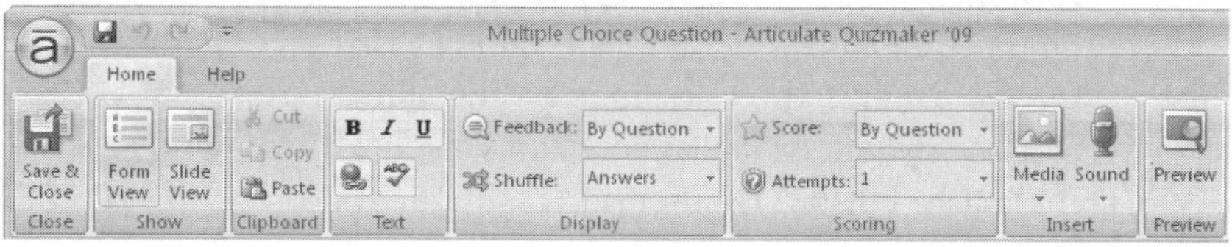

Figure 9.17. Question window ribbon Home tab in Form view

Table 9.8. Question window ribbon Home tab groups in Form view

Group	Description
Close	Contains the button to save the current question and close the Question window
Show	Contains the buttons to switch between Form view and Slide view
Clipboard	Contains tools to cut, copy, and paste text in the question
Text	Contains tools to format text, add hyperlinks, and check spelling
Display	Contains tools to select the level of feedback and shuffle the order of the answer choices

Group	Description
Scoring	Contains tools to select whether the question is scored by question or answer, and how many times the viewer can try to answer the question
Insert	Contains tools to add a picture, movie, or sound clip to the question
Preview	Contains the button to preview the current question in the Quizmaker player

Placeholders

The placeholders (shown in Figure 9.15) are used to enter the content for your question, answer choices, and feedback. The Set Feedback and Branching placeholders already contain some default text. The More button leads to additional feedback options.

Now that you've explored the Form view interface, let's look at the tasks for building a simple question. Keep in mind that Chapter 12, "Pumping Up Your Questions," provides more details on formatting and customizing your questions. We'll cover just the basics here.

Entering the Question Text

The Enter the Question placeholder contains the text used to prompt an answer. It may be a question (such as "How many...?") or a statement (such as "Select the answer that best describes..."). Figure 9.18 shows an example of completed question text. You can use the tools on the ribbon (Figure 9.17) to copy and paste text from other sources, add hyperlinks, and add limited formatting (bold, italic, and underline). The question text can be as long as necessary because the Quizmaker player is scrollable. (If the content length exceeds the height of the slide area, scroll bars are added to the player so that viewers can scroll down to view more content.) However, it is better to be concise if possible. If you find that a lot of background is required for the question, consider creating a separate information slide to present the additional material.

Tip: If you do use an information slide for additional information, you may need to concisely restate the important points on the question slide so that viewers do not need to remember everything on the previous information slide. Another possibility is to prompt the viewer to use the Question list navigation panel in the Quizmaker player to return to the information slide.

ENTER THE QUESTION:
Which of the following theories of media effects asserts that heavy viewing causes viewers to see the world as it is portrayed on television?

Figure 9.18. Question text in Form view

Note: Entering question text is mandatory. You cannot leave it blank.

Entering the Answer Choices

The answer choices section will vary, of course, depending on the question type. But the placeholders are basically the same. Figure 9.19 shows the answer choices for a completed Multiple Choice question. Each row (generally labeled A, B, C, etc.) is a placeholder for one answer choice. You enter the text for the answer in the Choice column and indicate the correct answer by clicking its radio button in the Correct column. For some question types, more than one answer choice can be correct. You can use the tools on the ribbon (Figure 9.17) to cut, copy, and paste text, as well as add limited formatting.

ENTER THE CHOICES:

	Correct	Choice
A	○	Agenda setting
B	●	Cultivation analysis
C	○	Uses and gratifications
D	○	Spiral of silence
E		Click to enter a choice
F		
G		

Figure 9.19. Answer choices in Form view

Note: At least one answer choice must be entered, and at least one answer has to be identified as correct.

Tip: You can use the Tab key to move from field to field.

Setting Feedback and Branching

A feedback pop-up box is displayed by default after the viewer completes a graded question. The Set Feedback and Branching placeholders contain default feedback text for correct and incorrect answers (Figure 9.20). The Feedback placeholder locations will vary, depending on whether you set feedback at the question level or the answer level (more on that later.) You can modify the feedback text for the current question here or delete it entirely.

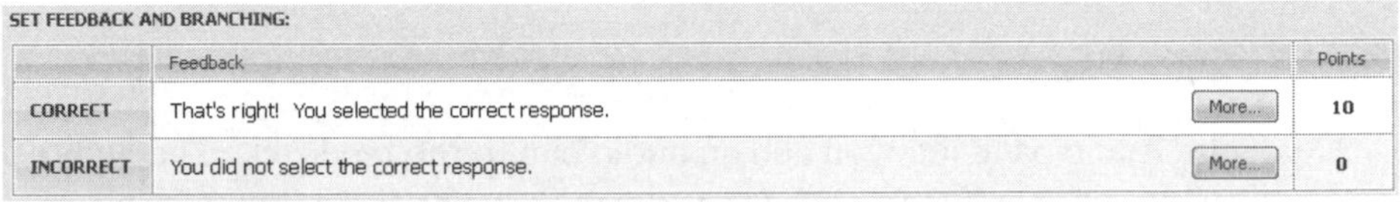

SET FEEDBACK AND BRANCHING:		
	Feedback	Points
CORRECT	That's right! You selected the correct response. [More...]	10
INCORRECT	You did not select the correct response. [More...]	0

Figure 9.20. Set Feedback and Branching placeholders in Form view

> **Note:** The default feedback is based on the default feedback specified in the Quiz Properties dialog box. The section titled "Setting Quiz Properties" earlier in this chapter explains how to change the default feedback that appears in every quiz question. Typically, it is best to provide feedback that explains why the answer selected was correct or incorrect so you can reinforce the right answer.

For additional feedback options, click the More button. This opens the Question Feedback dialog box (Figure 9.21), which contains the Text pane, Audio pane, and Branching pane.

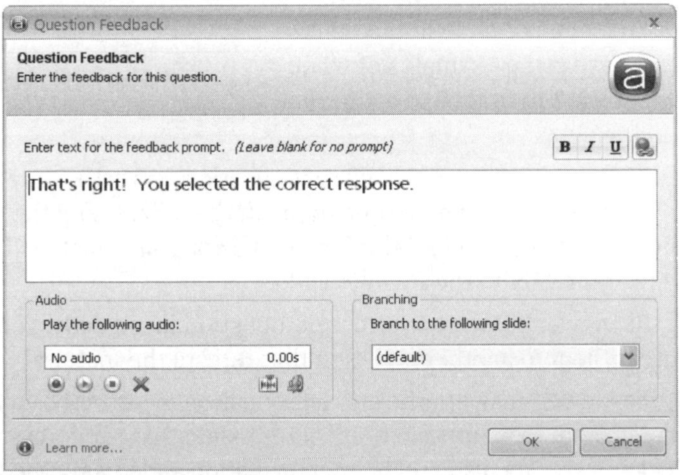

Figure 9.21. Question Feedback dialog box

Text Pane

The top pane of the Question Feedback dialog box lets you customize the feedback text, just as you can in the Question window. You can format text using the Bold, Italic, and Underline buttons **B** *I* <u>U</u>, and add a hyperlink using the Hyperlink button 🔗. Hyperlinks in feedback are valuable for directing the viewer to a web site containing information related to the question. Note, however, that hyperlinks are *not* used to link to other questions in the quiz. To do that, you use the Branching pane, which is covered below.

Audio Pane

The Audio pane lets you add an audio clip to the feedback. The audio can accompany feedback text, or it can serve as the only feedback if you delete the feedback text. All of the tools you need to record and import audio are available here. These tools are covered in Chapter 12, "Pumping Up Your Questions."

Branching Pane

The Branching pane (Figure 9.22) lets you change the navigation of the quiz based on how the viewer answers the current question. The default navigation for both correct responses and incorrect responses is to continue to the next question. However, you can modify this navigation by selecting another question or slide in the quiz. Following are some examples of when you might want to branch to a different slide in the quiz:

Figure 9.22. Question Feedback dialog box Branching pane

■ If the viewer answers the current question correctly, they may not need to answer any more questions in the quiz. Using the Branching pane, you can select the Finish Quiz option, which will take the viewer directly to the Results slide.

■ If the viewer answers the current question incorrectly, you can direct them to another question that retests the material.

■ If the viewer answers the current question incorrectly, you can direct them to an information content slide that reinforces the correct answer. You can create an information slide using the Blank

Slide feature, which is covered in Chapter 13, "Pumping Up Your Quizzes."

■ Instead of using the standard pop-up feedback text (which can contain only text and audio), you can direct the viewer to a comprehensive feedback slide. You can create a feedback slide using the Blank Slide feature, which is covered in Chapter 13, "Pumping Up Your Quizzes."

■ In a survey, you can direct the viewer to a specific question based on how he or she answers the current question. For example, a Pick One survey question may ask the viewer's age range. For the answer choice 55-65, you can branch to a different question or slide. (Note that this requires feedback to be set for specific answer choices, which is covered in the following section titled "Customizing Display and Scoring Options.")

■ Create a branched scenario in which certain slides are displayed based on how the viewer answers a question. Chapter 13, "Pumping Up Your Quizzes," provides an example of a branched scenario.

When you choose to branch to another slide based on the viewer's response, you can choose one of the following:

■ Include the standard feedback pop-up and then branch to the slide.

■ Skip the standard feedback pop-up and immediately branch to the slide.

To branch and *include* the standard feedback pop-up:

1. Make sure the feedback prompt contains text.

2. Select the slide from the Branching list.

When the viewer clicks Submit to answer the question, the feedback pop-up box will be displayed. After the viewer clicks the Next Question button to proceed, the branched slide will be displayed.

To branch and *skip* the standard feedback pop-up:

1. Delete the text in the feedback prompt.

2. Select the slide from the Branching list.

Immediately after the viewer clicks Submit to answer the question, the branched slide will be displayed.

When a feedback item branches to a different slide, the branching icon ◀ is placed next to the More button in Form view. You can reset the feedback item so that it does not branch by selecting (default) from the Branching list.

Customizing Display and Scoring Options

Now that you've entered the question text, answer choices, and feedback text, let's look at a few of the options you can select for feedback display, answer display, and scoring. Figure 9.23 shows the tools in the Display and Scoring groups on the Home tab of the ribbon. Depending on the question type, some of these options might be unavailable or limited.

◔ Feedback:	By Question ▾		☆ Score:	By Question ▾
✄ Shuffle:	Answers ▾		◉ Attempts:	1 ▾
	Display			Scoring

Figure 9.23. Display and Scoring groups on Question window ribbon

Displaying Feedback by Question or Answer

By default, feedback is displayed at the question level, meaning that if the viewer answers the question incorrectly, the same incorrect feedback message is displayed regardless of which incorrect answer was selected. In other words, by default, there is just one correct feedback response and one incorrect feedback response for the question. The default option of displaying feedback by question is indicated in the Feedback list box on the ribbon as By Question (Figure 9.23).

You can create unique feedback for each answer choice by changing the feedback display to By Answer. Quizmaker then moves the Feedback placeholders next to each answer choice (Figure 9.24), where you can enter text tailored to that answer. If you do not want to display feedback after the question, then select None from the Feedback list on the ribbon.

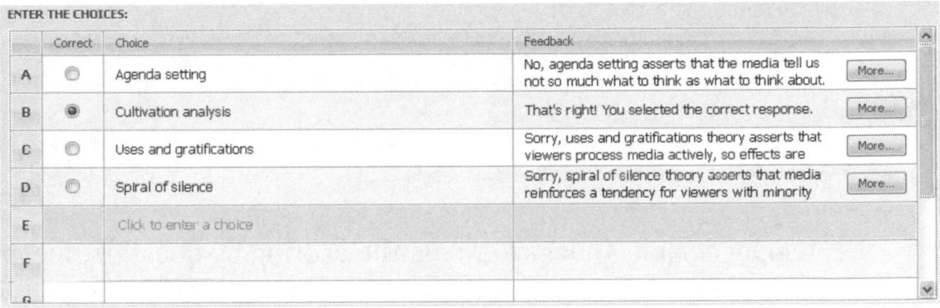

Figure 9.24. Feedback set to By Answer

Shuffling Answers

The Shuffle list box on the ribbon lets you control whether the answer choices are shuffled (the answer order is randomized) when the question is viewed. By default, shuffling is set to Answers, meaning the answers are displayed in random order. You can specify that the answer choices are always displayed in order by selecting None from the Shuffle list.

If you choose to shuffle the answers, you can still anchor any of the answer choices to a specific slot. This is helpful if you want to make sure an answer choice always appears first (or last) in the list. To anchor an answer choice, right-click the choice and select Anchor Choice from the shortcut menu.

Scoring by Question or Answer

Before getting into the options to score by question or by answer, let's take a general look at how Quizmaker scores questions. Keep in mind that different question types may have different types of scoring. We'll use the Multiple Choice question type as the example here. In later chapters, we'll point out unique scoring options for each question type.

By default, Quizmaker assigns a 10-point value when a question is answered correctly, with no points awarded for incorrect answers. These point scores are displayed in the Points column of the Set Feedback and Branching section. You can change the values for either response by clicking in the Points field and entering a new value, as shown in Figure 9.25.

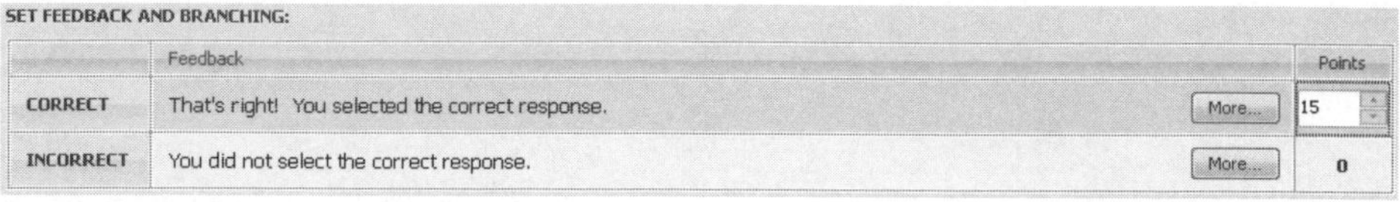

Figure 9.25. Points column in Set Feedback and Branching section

Also by default, Quizmaker sets the scoring by question, meaning there is just one score for the correct answer and one score (which may be zero) for any incorrect answer. The default option of scoring by question is indicated in the Score list box on the ribbon (Figure 9.23). You can assign a specific score for each answer choice by changing the score display to By Answer. Quizmaker then moves the Points column to the Enter the Choices section (Figure 9.26), where you can assign specific scores to each answer choice.

Figure 9.26. Points column in Enter the Choices section

Setting Number of Attempts

The Attempts list box on the ribbon (Figure 9.23) lets you specify how many times the viewer can try to answer the question correctly before being forced to move to the next question. By default, this value is set to 1. You can change this to a value of 2 through 10, or set the attempts to Unlimited.

The tasks we have just discussed are sufficient to create a simple question. Your next steps are to preview and save the question.

Previewing Questions

You can preview what the question will look like inside the Quizmaker player anytime after you have entered the question text and the minimum number of correct answer choices (depending on the question type). Most features of the slide will be active, including any animation effects and object timings. Note that previewing a single question from the Question window is slightly different from previewing the entire quiz from the Quiz window. Previewing the quiz is covered later in this chapter.

To preview the current question, click the Preview button on the Home tab of the Question window ribbon. The Preview window is then displayed (Figure 9.27). You can verify that the question works as desired by selecting a correct or incorrect response. After selecting a response and clicking Submit, you can verify that the scoring works as expected for that response by checking the score display at the bottom of the Preview window.

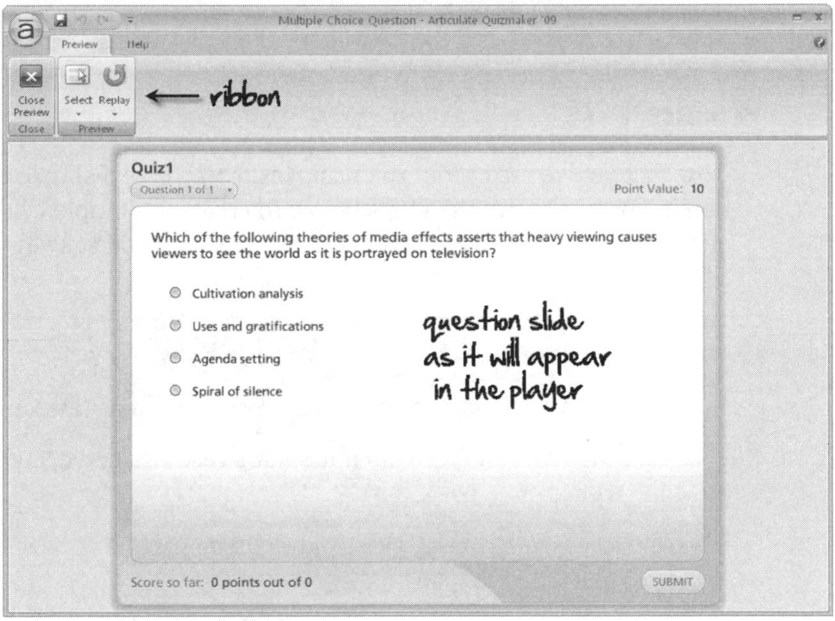

Figure 9.27. Preview window for a single question

The ribbon on the Preview window contains the Preview tab and the standard Help tab. The Select menu lets you preview another question in the quiz. The Replay menu lets you repeat the preview of the current question, preview the questions in a specific group, or preview each question in the quiz.

After previewing the question, you can use the Close Preview button to close the preview and return to the Question window, where you can make changes to the question if needed.

Saving Questions

You can save the current question and leave the Question window open by pressing the keyboard shortcut Ctrl+S. Clicking the Save & Close button on the ribbon saves the current question, closes the Question window, and returns you to the Quiz window. If you want to close the Question window without saving the changes, just click the Close button on the title bar or select Cancel from the File menu.

> 66 **Note:** Individual questions are not saved using a specific name. In other words, you won't see the Save As dialog box when you save a question to the quiz.

Practice 1

Now that you've read about the basic tasks to create a simple question in Form view, try the steps below to create a Multiple Choice question. We'll let you come up with the question and answer choices.

 Building a Multiple Choice Question in Form View

1.   From the Quizmaker start screen, click **Create a new quiz**.

2.   Click the **Graded Quiz** tab if it's not already selected, and click the **OK** button.

3.   Click the **Graded Question** button on the ribbon *or* click the **graded** link in the Question pane.

4.   Click the **Multiple Choice** tab and click the **OK** button.

5.   Enter the question in the **Enter the Question** box.

6.   Enter the answer choices in the **Enter the Choices** section. Indicate the correct answer by clicking the radio button in the Correct column.

7.   Click the **More** button in the Correct feedback placeholder.

8.   Select the text and replace it with a different message.

9. Select the revised text, click the **Bold** button B, and click **OK**.

10. Preview the question so far:
    a. Click the **Preview** button on the ribbon.
    b. Select the correct answer and click **Submit**.
    c. Note the score at the bottom of the window and click the **View Results** button.
    d. In the message that appears, click **Replay**.
    e. Select an incorrect answer and click **Submit**.
    f. Note the score at the bottom of the window and click the **Close Preview** button on the ribbon.

    Next you'll customize some of the feedback and scoring options.

11. Click the **Feedback** list box on the ribbon and select **By Answer**.

12. Click the **Score** list box on the ribbon and select **By Answer**.

13. In the **Feedback** column of the answer choices, enter a different feedback message for each answer choice.

14. In the **Points** column of the answer choices, assign a point value of **5** to one of the incorrect answers.

15. Preview the revised question:
    a. Click the **Preview** button on the ribbon.
    b. Select the incorrect answer with the score value of 5 and click **Submit**.
    c. Note the score at the bottom of the window and click the **View Results** button.
    d. In the message that appears, click **Replay**.
    e. Select another incorrect answer and click **Submit**.
    f. Note the score at the bottom of the window and click the **Close Preview** button on the ribbon.

16. Click the **Save & Close** button on the ribbon.

Quizmaker

Building Questions in Slide View

As we discussed earlier, Slide view offers a freeform environment to build your questions. Even if you choose to build the question content using Form view, you can customize and "pump up" the question using the expanded formatting and layout tools in Slide view. This section covers just a few of the basic tasks you can perform to build a question in Slide view. Chapter 12, "Pumping Up Your Questions," covers more Slide view options. Here are the tasks you'll learn about in this section:

- Enter the question text.
- Add answer choices (for some, but not all, question types).
- Insert additional objects.
- Modify the layout of objects.
- Use the timeline to time the appearance of objects.
- Format objects.
- Customize the Slide view workspace.

At the end of the section you'll have a chance to practice building a simple question in Slide view from start to finish. Let's start by taking a quick look at the Question window interface in Slide view.

Exploring the Slide View Interface

Clicking the Slide View button on the Question window ribbon displays the current question in Slide view, where you can build content, change the layout, and format objects. This view contains a ribbon with seven tabs, the slide, slide notes, and the timeline (Figure 9.28). The File menu (accessed through the Articulate button) contains the same options as the File menu in Form view.

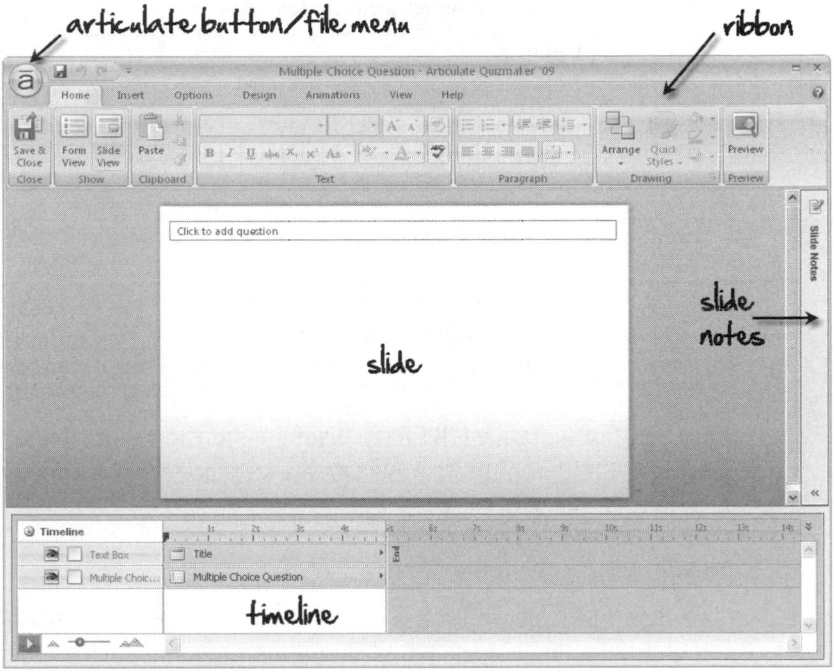

articulate button/file menu *ribbon*

slide notes

slide

timeline

Figure 9.28. Question window in Slide view

Ribbon (Slide View)

The ribbon on the Question window in Slide view (Figure 9.29) is different from the ribbon in Form view. The Slide view ribbon contains the Home tab, the standard Help tab, and five tabs containing tools to customize and format the question elements and objects. If you're familiar with PowerPoint 2007 and other Office 2007 programs, you'll notice that many of the tools on this ribbon are similar to the ribbon tools in those programs. Table 9.9 provides a brief description of each group on the Home tab.

Figure 9.29. Question window ribbon Home tab in Slide view

Table 9.9. Question window Home tab groups in Slide view

Group	Description
Close	Contains the button to save the current question and close the Question window
Show	Contains the buttons to switch between Form view and Slide view
Clipboard	Contains tools to cut, copy, and paste text in the question
Text	Contains tools to format text, add hyperlinks, and check spelling
Paragraph	Contains tools to format paragraphs, such as changing alignment, adding indents, and creating bulleted lists
Drawing	Contains tools to format specific objects in the content slide, such as rearranging objects, adding colors, and adding effects
Preview	Contains the button to preview the current question in the Quizmaker player

Later in this section we'll take a brief look at the other ribbon tabs. Chapter 12, "Pumping Up Your Questions," covers working with those tabs in more detail.

Slide

The slide in the center of the window will, when done, contain all of the elements and objects comprising the question, such as the question text, answer choices, images, movies, and shapes. You can think of the slide as the canvas or "stage" for creating the question. Depending on the question type, Quizmaker adds default elements on the slide, such as the question text placeholder.

Slide Notes

The slide notes on the right side of the window can be used to enter notes about the current question (Figure 9.30). These notes are for the developer's use and are not seen by the viewer when the question is launched. You can expand and collapse the slide notes by clicking the double-arrow button.

Figure 9.30. Slide Notes expanded

Timeline

The timeline lets you time objects on the slide to appear (and disappear) at specific time intervals (Figure 9.31). For example, you can display the question ("Title") immediately, and then display the answers ("Multiple Choice Question") a second or so later. You can also hide and unhide objects. Every object on the slide is listed in the timeline, so you can work with each object individually.

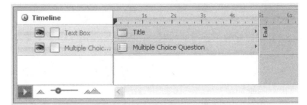

Figure 9.31. Timeline

Now that you've explored the Slide view interface, let's look at just a few of the basic tasks for building a question in Slide view.

Entering the Question

Quizmaker always provides a placeholder for the question, which is contained in a text box. So this part is pretty easy. Just click inside the placeholder and either type the question text or copy/paste it from another source. Later we'll discuss ways to format the question text and the text box that contains it.

Note: Adding question text is required. Quizmaker won't let you remove the question text box, and you cannot leave the question text empty.

Entering the Answer Choices

Depending on the question type, you may or may not be able to add answer choices using Slide view. For example, many of the matching types of graded questions require that you enter the answer choices and matches in Form view. In those cases, you will need to add the answer choices in Form view and then switch to Slide view to format and customize them, if needed.

If you are able to add answer choices in Slide view, the Add Choice button will be active on the Insert tab (Figure 9.32). For example, if you're building a Multiple Choice question, you can click the Add Choice button to insert the first answer choice. Quizmaker then creates two text boxes: one for the new answer choice and another that will contain all answer choices. These separate text boxes come into play later if you want to format the answer choices as a group or separately.

Home
Insert
Options
Design
Animations
View
Help
Save & Close
Form View
Slide View
Add Choice
Picture
Shapes
Text Box
Hyperlink
Symbol
Flash
Sound
Preview
Close
Show
Choices
Illustrations
Text
Media Clips
Preview

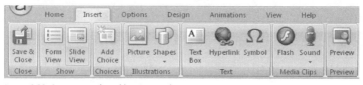

Figure 9.32. Question window ribbon Insert tab

Each text box for an individual answer choice contains an area for the answer text and an icon used to indicate the correct answer(s) depending on the question type. After completing the first answer choice, click the Add Choice button again to add the next choice and so forth. Figure 9.33 shows the completed answer choices in Slide view.

Note: For most question types, at least one answer choice must be entered, and at least one answer has to be identified as correct.

Tip: You can use graphics instead of (or along with) text for the answer choices in some question types. This is covered in Chapter 12, "Pumping Up Your Questions."

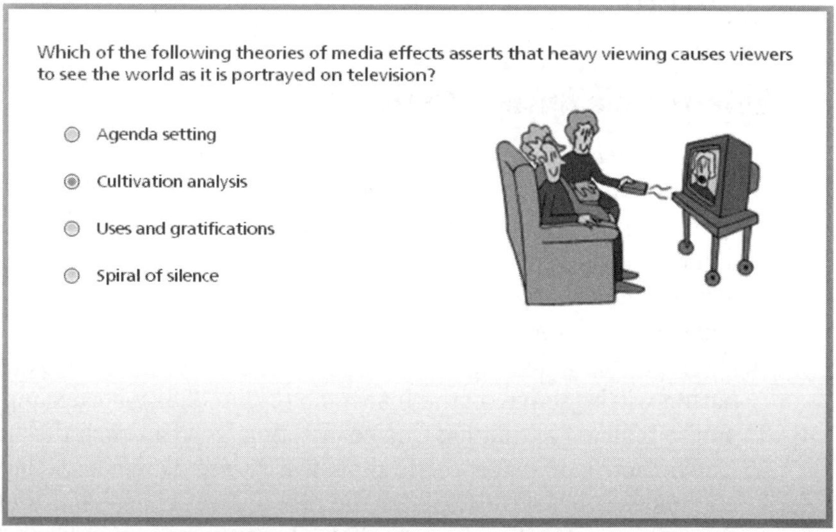
Which of the following theories of media effects asserts that heavy viewing causes viewers to see the world as it is portrayed on television?
Agenda setting
Cultivation analysis
Uses and gratifications
Spiral of silence

Figure 9.33. Completed question text, answer choices, and inserted image in Slide view

Inserting Additional Objects

One of the advantages of building a question in Slide view is that you can add a variety of objects to the slide. The Insert tab on the ribbon (Figure 9.32) contains tools to add pictures, shapes, and other objects directly on the slide. Note that Form view only lets you add one picture or movie, which is placed by default next to the question. Slide view lets you add multiple objects to the question and you can put them anywhere on the slide. Table 9.10 provides a brief description of each group on the Insert tab.

Table 9.10. Question window ribbon Insert tab groups in Slide view

Group	Description
Close	Contains the button to save the current question and close the Question window
Show	Contains the buttons to switch between Form view and Slide view
Choices	Contains the button to add an answer choice to the content slide. This button is available only for some question types.
Illustrations	Contains tools to add images and shapes, such as rectangles, lines, arrows, and callout boxes
Text	Contains tools to add text boxes, hyperlinks, and symbols
Media Clips	Contains tools to add Flash movies and audio clips
Preview	Contains the button to preview the current question in the Quizmaker player

Chapter 12, "Pumping Up Your Questions," covers the tools on the Insert tab in more detail. But here's a quick explanation of how to add an image to a question in Slide view:

1. Click the **Picture** button on the Insert tab of the ribbon.

2. Browse to the picture file you want and double-click it.

3. Using the mouse, size the picture if desired and drag it to the correct location.

Figure 9.33 shows an inserted image.

Modifying the Slide Layout

Another advantage of working in Slide view is that you can modify the layout of the slide by moving objects that are on the slide. For example, you can place the question text on the left side and group the answer choices on the right side. You can also arrange the answer choices individually. Figure 9.34 provides an example of a modified slide layout.

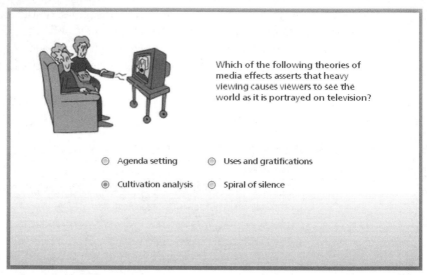

Figure 9.34. Modified slide layout

To modify the layout, select, resize, and drag objects around the slide. Typically, that means you click the object to select it, drag a handle on its selection border to resize it, and then drag the object's border to move it. Keep these points in mind as you change the layout:

- You can move multiple objects as a group by Ctrl+clicking each object to select it.

- You can select, resize, and move answer choices as a group. Click any answer choice and then click the dashed border that appears around the group. Drag a handle on the outside border to resize the answer choice area and drag the outside border to move all choices together.

- You can select, resize, and move specific answer choices within a group by Ctrl+clicking the desired choices. In Figure 9.34, we created two columns of answer choices by selecting the first two choices and moving them, then selecting the second two answer choices and moving them.

Formatting Objects

Slide view provides a rich assortment of tools to format objects placed on the slide, as well as to apply global formats to all objects on the slide. If you're familiar with PowerPoint 2007 or other Office 2007 applications, you'll notice that many of the formatting tools on the Quizmaker ribbon are the same as those on the PowerPoint 2007 ribbon. Most of these ribbon tools are also contained in dialog boxes and shortcut (right-click) menus.

Formatting Using the Ribbon Tools

To format any object in Slide view, such as the question text box, answer text box, or images, first select the object by clicking it. The tools in the ribbon's Home tab become active and the *context-sensitive tab(s)* for that specific object also become available (Figure 9.35). Context-sensitive ribbon tabs contain additional tools for working with a selected object. For example, when you select a drawing object, such as a text box, the Drawing Tools Format tab becomes available (Figure 9.36). Table 9.11 briefly describes each group in the Drawing Tools Format tab.

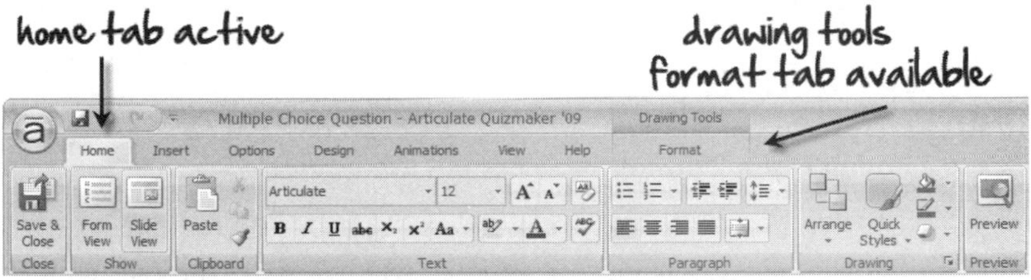

Figure 9.35. Question window ribbon in Slide view (after selecting a drawing object) with the Home tab active

Figure 9.36. Question window ribbon in Slide view (after selecting a drawing object) with Drawing Tools Format tab active

66 Note: All of the tools in the Drawing group of the Home tab are also on the Drawing Tools Format tab.

Table 9.11. Drawing Tools Format tab groups

Group	Description
Close	Contains the button to save the current question and close the Question window
Show	Contains the buttons to switch between Form view and Slide view
Insert Shapes	Contains tools to add more shapes to the question, such as rectangles, lines, arrows, callout boxes, and text boxes
Shape Styles	Contains tools to apply a predefined shape style to the selected object(s) and apply individual style properties to the selected object(s). Style properties include the shape fill (e.g., background color), shape outline (e.g., color and weight), and shape effects (e.g., shadow).
Arrange	Contains tools to control the position of the selected object(s) on the slide, such as bringing a specific object in front of others, aligning a group of objects, and rotating the object(s)
Size	Contains tools to change the width and height of the selected object(s) by entering pixel values. Note that you can also resize objects by dragging a handle on the selected object.
Preview	Contains the button to preview the current question in the Quizmaker player

Tip: Quizmaker Help provides detailed descriptions of each option in the Drawing Tools Format tab.

For the example shown in Figure 9.37, we used the following ribbon tools to format the Question text box:

- Home tab: Text group:
  - Font = Calibri
  - Font Size = 14
  - Font Color = White
  - Bold
- Drawing Tools Format tab:
  - Shape Fill color: Green (yes, we know the book is in black and white…)
  - Shape Outline color: Dark green

- Shape Outline weight: 4 pixels
- Shape Effects: Glow

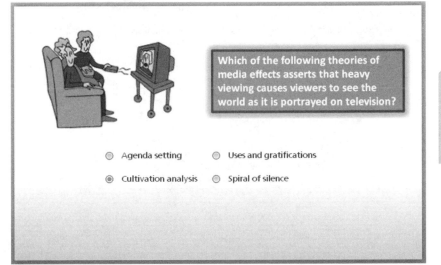

Figure 9.37. Formatted question text

Formatting Using Dialog Boxes and Shortcut Menus

All of the formatting tools on the Quizmaker ribbon are also accessible from various dialog boxes. Whether to use the dialog boxes or the ribbon is a matter of personal preference. Dialog boxes generally contain groups of related options. You can choose a number of options and then apply them to the selected object all at once.

Many dialog boxes are accessible from the ribbon by clicking the diagonal arrow button ⬓ that appears on the right side of the related group name. For example, clicking the diagonal arrow button on the Shape Styles group on the Format tab (Figure 9.38) opens the Format Shape dialog box (Figure 9.39), where you can apply several formatting options to the selected object.

Tip: Quizmaker Help provides detailed descriptions of each option in the Format Shape dialog box.

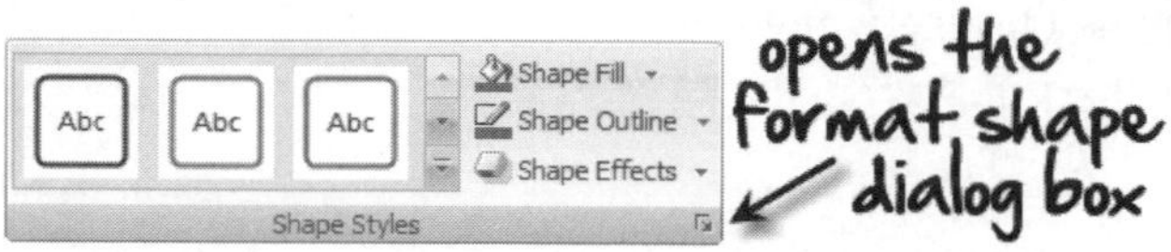

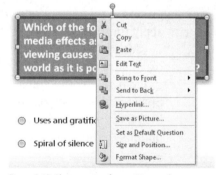

Figure 9.38. Question window ribbon in Slide view showing the Shape Styles group of the Drawing Tools Format tab

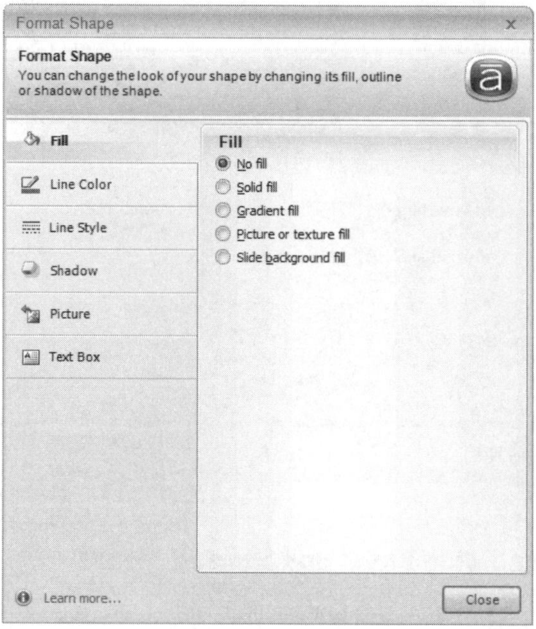

Figure 9.39. Format Shape dialog box

You can also access formatting options for an object by displaying its shortcut menu. First, select the object, and then right-click any of the object's borders. The options on the shortcut menu will vary depending on the type of object. The example in Figure 9.40 shows the options for a question text box.

Figure 9.40. Shortcut menu for question text box

We've just scratched the surface of the many formatting options you can use to customize questions in Slide view. Chapter 12, "Pumping Up Your Questions," describes additional ways to format objects, including pictures, movies, and sounds.

Timeline Basics

Although Chapter 12, "Pumping Up Your Questions," covers working
with the timeline in detail, we'll discuss the basics of timing objects
here. Figure 9.41 shows the timeline for the completed example used
in this chapter. Each object on the content slide (question, answer
choices, picture) has a corresponding item, or *layer*, in the timeline.

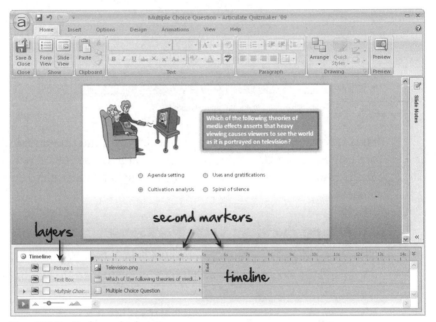

Figure 9.41. Timeline for completed question

The timeline layers appear in the order they are "stacked" on the content slide. If you have stacked objects on top of each other on a
PowerPoint slide (Bring to Front, Send to Back, etc.), stacking order
should be familiar. Since the picture layer in this example appears at
the top of the timeline, that means it appears on top (in front) of the
other objects that are on lower layers on the timeline, no matter where
you move it. You can change which objects are on top by dragging the
layer to a lower position in the timeline.

The numbers at the top of the timeline represent seconds. These
numbers serve as a guide for controlling when an object appears on
the slide and how long it remains there. By default, all objects appear
immediately and they remain on the slide until the viewer has finished
the question. (Don't be misled by the End marker on the timeline—it

doesn't mean the question ends there. We'll discuss this in detail in Chapter 12.)

To time an object to appear at a specific time during the question, just drag the object on the timeline to the appropriate second marker. Figure 9.42 shows the Television.png picture timed to appear two seconds after the question and answer choices are displayed on the slide.

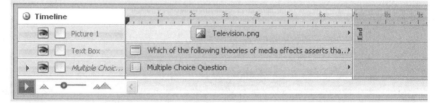

Figure 9.42. Picture object timed to appear after two seconds

So that's our quick explanation of working with the timeline. In Chapter 12, "Pumping Up Your Questions," you'll learn more about all the features of the timeline, including how to synchronize audio and hide objects.

Customizing the Slide View Workspace

The View tab on the ribbon (Figure 9.43) includes the Show/Hide group and the Zoom group, which let you customize the features that appear as you work in Slide view.

Figure 9.43. Question window ribbon View tab in Slide view

By selecting or clearing any of the check boxes in the Show/Hide group, you can display or hide workspace features. By default, Quizmaker displays the slide notes and the timeline. The Zoom group lets you adjust the display size of the content slide within the stage. Table 9.12 describes the options in these two groups.

Table 9.12. Show/Hide and Zoom groups options

Option	Description
Ruler	Displays a horizontal ruler and a vertical ruler, which can help you measure and line up objects on the slide
Gridlines	Adds horizontal and vertical gridlines to the slide, which can help you align objects along the same horizontal and/or vertical positions
Notes	Displays the slide notes on the right side of the window. You can expand and collapse the slide notes by clicking the double-arrow on the Slide Notes pane.
Timeline	Displays the timeline at the bottom of the window. You can expand and collapse the timeline by clicking the double-arrow on the Timeline pane.
Player	Displays the slide as it will appear in the Quizmaker player. If the Gridlines option is selected, the gridlines will also be displayed, but will not appear in the running question. Also note that the Player option is just for display purposes. To test the question in the Quizmaker player, use the Preview button on the ribbon.
Zoom	Displays the Zoom dialog box, which you can use to increase or decrease the display size of the slide in the window
Fit to Window	Adjusts the display size of the slide so that all of it fits in the window

Figure 9.44 shows the Slide view when all of the options, except the Timeline option, in the Show/Hide group are selected.

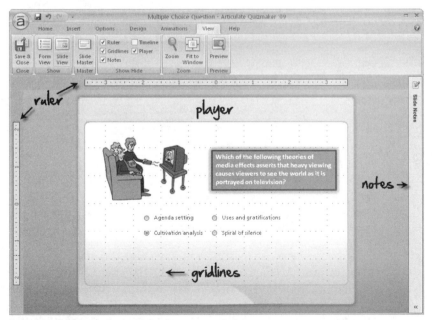

Figure 9.44. Slide view displaying ruler, gridlines, notes, and player

Note that the View tab also contains the standard Close, Show, and Preview groups, which contain the same tools as those groups in other ribbon tabs. The Master group contains a button that switches to Slide Master view. This view lets you work with the slide master to apply formatting properties and objects to all slides in the quiz. Chapter 12, "Pumping Up Your Questions," describes how to work with the slide master.

Other Slide View Tools

The Design tab, Animations tab, and Options tab on the Slide view ribbon contain additional tools to format and customize the current question. The Design tab (Figure 9.45) lets you apply an entire theme and background style to the question. The Animations tab (Figure 9.46) lets you animate specific objects in the question and add transition effects when the question is displayed. The Design and Animations tabs will be covered in detail in Chapter 12, "Pumping Up Your Questions."

Figure 9.45. Question window ribbon in Slide view, Design tab

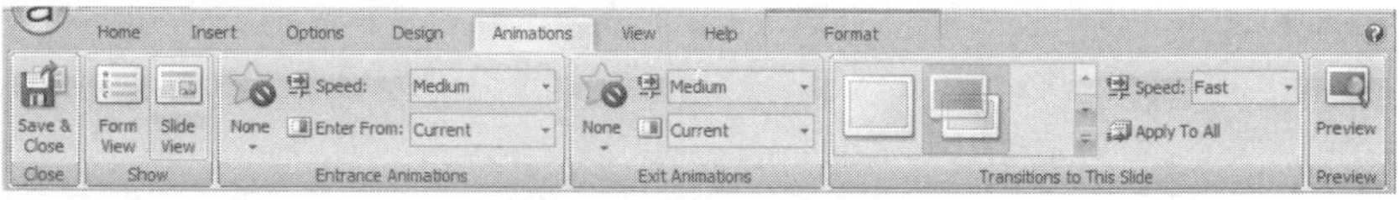

Figure 9.46. Question window ribbon in Slide view, Animations tab

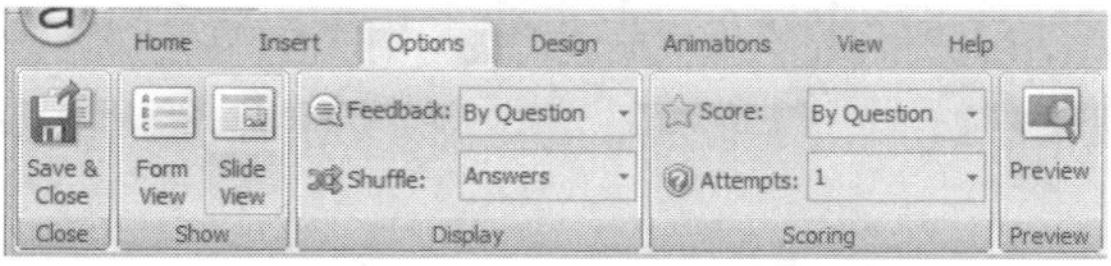

Figure 9.47. Question window ribbon in Slide view, Options tab

The Options tab (Figure 9.47) contains the same options as those found on the Form view ribbon. For example, the Save & Close button is used to save the current question and close the Question window. The Preview button lets you preview the current question. You can use the Display group to control feedback options and the Scoring group to control the scoring of the current question. For more information about these options, refer to the section titled "Building Questions in Form View" earlier in this chapter.

Practice 2

Now that you've read about the basic tasks to create a simple question in Slide view, try the steps below to create a Multiple Response question. This question is very similar to the Multiple Choice question type. We'll let you come up with the question and answer choices. Note that if you still have Quizmaker open from the previous Practice ("Building a Multiple Choice Question in Form View"), you can skip the first two steps below and just add the new question to the current quiz.

▶ Building a Multiple Response Question in Slide View

1. From the Quizmaker start screen, click **Create a new quiz.**

2. Click the **Graded Quiz** tab, if it's not already selected, and click the **OK** button.

3. Click the **Graded Question** button on the ribbon.

4. Click the **Multiple Response** tab and click the **OK** button.

5. Click the **Slide View** button on the Home tab of the ribbon.

6. Click in the **Click to add question** placeholder and type the question text.

7. Click the **Insert** tab on the ribbon.

8. Click the **Add Choice** button.

9. Type the first answer choice in the text box provided. If this is a correct answer, click the check box to the left of the answer choice.

10. Repeat steps 8 and 9 to add the remaining answer choices.

11. On the Insert tab, click the **Picture** button.

12. Browse to an image file and double-click it.

13. If necessary, resize the image by dragging a handle on its selection border.

14. Using the mouse, drag the image to the appropriate location on the slide.

15. Click anywhere in the Question text box.

16. Click the Drawing Tools **Format** tab on the ribbon.

17. Apply a few format options as follows:

    a. Click the arrow on the **Shape Fill** button and select a light color.

    b. Click the arrow on the **Shape Outline** button and select a dark color.

    c. Click the arrow on the **Shape Outline** button, select **Dashes**, and select a dash style.

    d. Click the arrow on the **Shape Effects** button, select **Shadow**, and select one of the shadow styles.

18. Preview, save, and close the question:

    a. Click the **Preview** button on the ribbon.

    b. Select the correct answers and click **Submit**.

    c. Click the **Close Preview** button on the Preview window ribbon.

    d. Click the **Save & Close** button on the Question window ribbon.

Options for Surveys and Survey Questions

So far in this chapter, we have used a graded quiz and graded questions to explore the steps to build a question. Although most of the tasks and tools are the same for building a survey and survey questions, some of the options on the ribbon are different. This section takes a quick look at these different options.

Survey Quiz Window

Figure 9.4 showed the Quiz window for a graded quiz. The Quiz window for a survey is shown in Figure 9.48 and looks very similar. The ribbon contains the Home tab and the Help tab. The only difference on the ribbon is that the survey Quiz window contains the Survey Result button instead of the Pass Result and Fail Result buttons on the graded Quiz window. Because surveys are not scored, the results screen displays a summary of the survey results. Also, some of the button icons have accompanying labels because the ribbon on the survey Quiz window has more room.

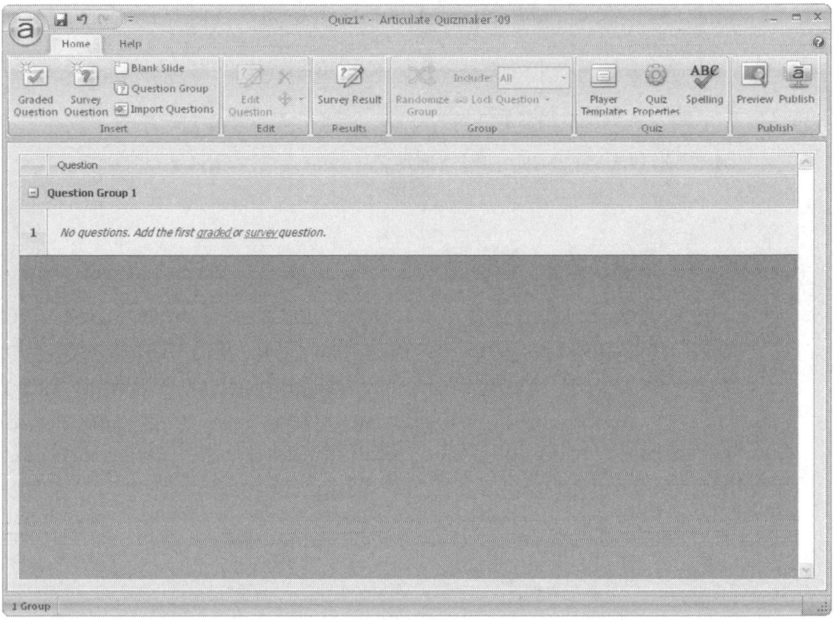

Figure 9.48. Quiz window for survey

Graded Questions in a Survey?

You may notice that the survey Quiz window contains the "graded" question link for new quizzes and the Graded Question button (Figure 9.49). You may also recall that surveys cannot contain graded questions. If you click either of these items, Quizmaker reminds you that you can't have graded questions and gives you the option of converting the survey to a graded quiz. So you cannot have graded questions in a survey, but you can change your mind and build a graded quiz instead.

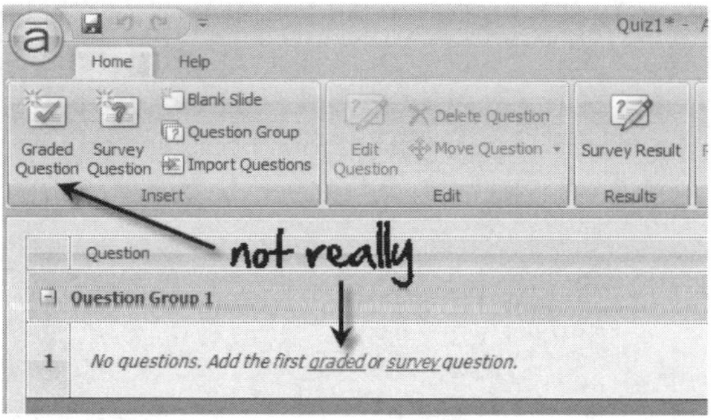

Figure 9.49. Close-up of the survey Quiz window

Survey Question Window

The Question window for a survey question (Figure 9.50) is very similar to the Question window for a graded question. Depending on the question type, the placeholders are used for the question/instructions, answer choices, and feedback. Since there are no correct and incorrect answers, there is no scoring. Consequently, the Home tab on the ribbon does not contain a Scoring group (Figure 9.51).

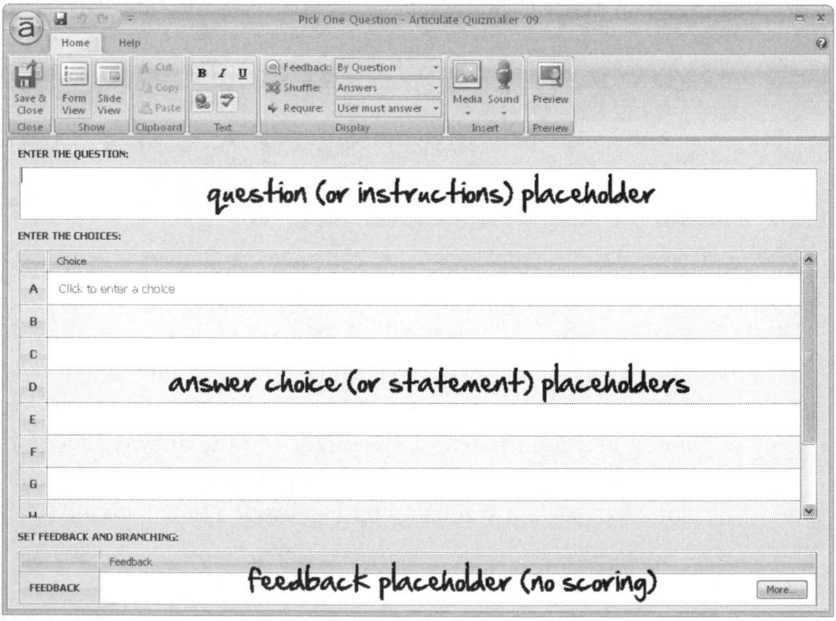

Figure 9.50. Question window for survey question

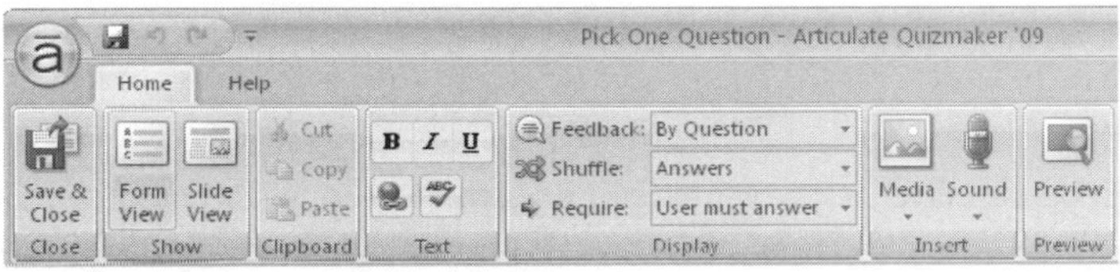

Figure 9.51. Question window ribbon Home tab for survey

Following is a summary of the options and tasks for surveys and survey questions that are different from the options and tasks for graded questions:

- Answer choices do not contain an icon for "correct" or "incorrect" because there are no correct or incorrect answers.

- When you add a survey question to a survey, the feedback is set by default to None and the feedback placeholder does not appear. However, as with graded questions, you can use the Feedback list on the Home tab of the ribbon to change the feedback to By Question (Figure 9.51) or to By Answer (if applicable to the question type). Note that when you add a survey question to a graded quiz, the feedback is set by default to By Question.

- The feedback placeholder does not contain a Points column because survey questions are not scored.

- The Home tab on the ribbon contains a Require option, which lets you specify whether viewers must answer the question or they may skip it.

With the above exceptions, building a survey question is like building a graded question. The Slide view for survey questions contains the same options as Slide view for graded questions, except that the Options tab on the ribbon does not contain a Scoring group.

Now that we've explored various ways to build questions, the next section takes us back to the Quiz window, where you can organize all the questions in your quiz.

Working with the Question List

The Quizmaker 1-2-3-4-5 workflow presented at the beginning of this chapter shows the tasks required to build the quiz and build the questions. Step 4 of this process is to customize the quiz as a whole by organizing the questions and modifying various properties of the quiz. Chapter 13, "Pumping Up Your Quizzes," covers many of these options. In this section, we'll look at just a few of the basic tasks you'll want to do after you've built some of the questions in a quiz.

The Question list in the Quiz window displays all the questions in the current quiz in the default order they will appear in the quiz (Figure 9.52). You can use this list to organize and edit questions. The Home tab on the ribbon contains several tools to work with the Question list (Figure 9.53).

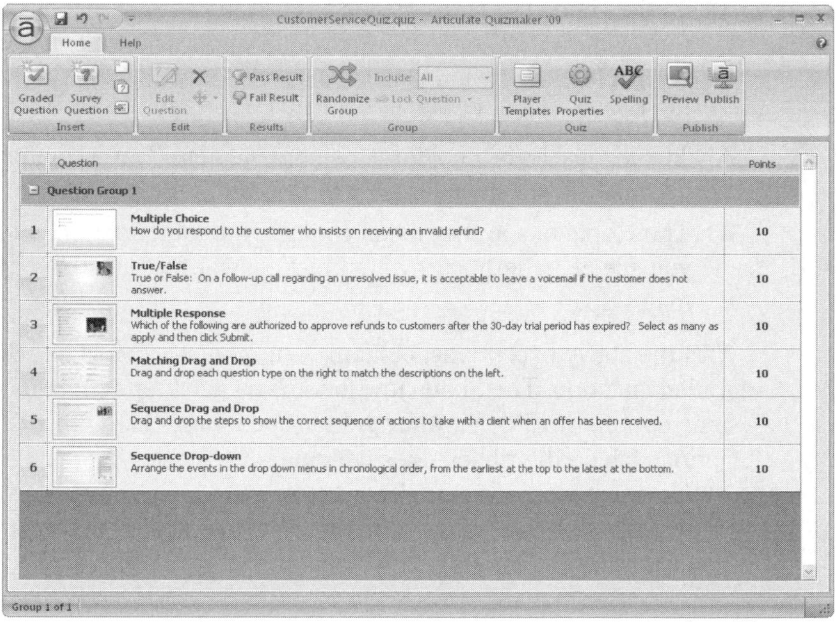

Figure 9.52. Quiz window Question list

Figure 9.53. Quiz window ribbon Home tab (graded quiz)

Following are a few of the tasks you can do with the Question list:

Open a question to edit it:

- Double-click the question.
- Select the question and click the Edit Question button on the ribbon.

Delete a question:

- Select the question and click the Delete Question button ☒ on the ribbon.
- Select the question and press the Delete key.

Move a question:

- Drag a question using the mouse.
- Select the question, click the Move Question button ✛▾ on the ribbon, and select Up or Down.

Change the question's score value:

- Click the number in the Points column of the Question list and enter a new point value. (Note that the point value for survey questions is always 0 and cannot be changed.)

Organize questions into groups:

- Click the New Question Group button ⧉ on the ribbon, and then create new questions or move existing questions into the group. (Details are covered in Chapter 13, "Pumping Up Your Quizzes.")

Randomize question order:

- Click the Randomize Group button on the ribbon. (Details are covered in Chapter 13, "Pumping Up Your Quizzes.")

You can also use a question's shortcut (right-click) menu to manipulate it in the Question list. Note that the commands on the shortcut menu vary, depending on the question type. Figure 9.54 shows the shortcut menu for a Multiple Choice question, and Table 9.13 describes the commands.

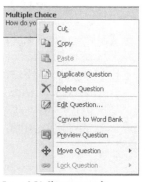

Figure 9.54. Shortcut menu for Multiple Choice question

Table 9.13. Shortcut menu commands for a Multiple Choice question

Command	Description
Cut, Copy, Paste	Moves or copies the selected question to a different location in the current quiz or to another quiz
Duplicate Question	Adds a copy of the selected question to the current quiz
Delete Question	Removes the question from the quiz
Edit Question	Opens the question in the Question window, where you can make changes
Convert to [...]	This command varies depending on the question type, and it is not available for all question types. It converts the selected question to a different question type, using the same question text and answer choices. For example, you can convert a Multiple Choice question to a Word Bank question.
Preview Question	Previews the current question in the Quizmaker player
Move Question	Displays the Move Question submenu, where you can move the question up or down in the Question list
Lock Question	This option is available only when the question group is randomized. It locks the selected question into a specific location in the quiz, so that it is not randomized with the other questions.

Previewing and Saving Quizzes

If you've read the two sections on building questions in Form view and Slide view, you know that you can preview and save individual questions from the Question window. You can also preview the entire quiz and save the entire quiz at any time from the Quiz window.

Previewing Quizzes

By previewing a quiz, you can work with the quiz the way your viewers will work with it in the Quizmaker player (almost). The questions are presented in the specified order. You can verify that the question text, answer choices, layout, scoring options, and Results slide work as expected. To start the preview, click the Preview button on the Home tab of the Quiz window ribbon. The Preview window (Figure 9.55) displays the first question in the quiz unless you have randomized the question order.

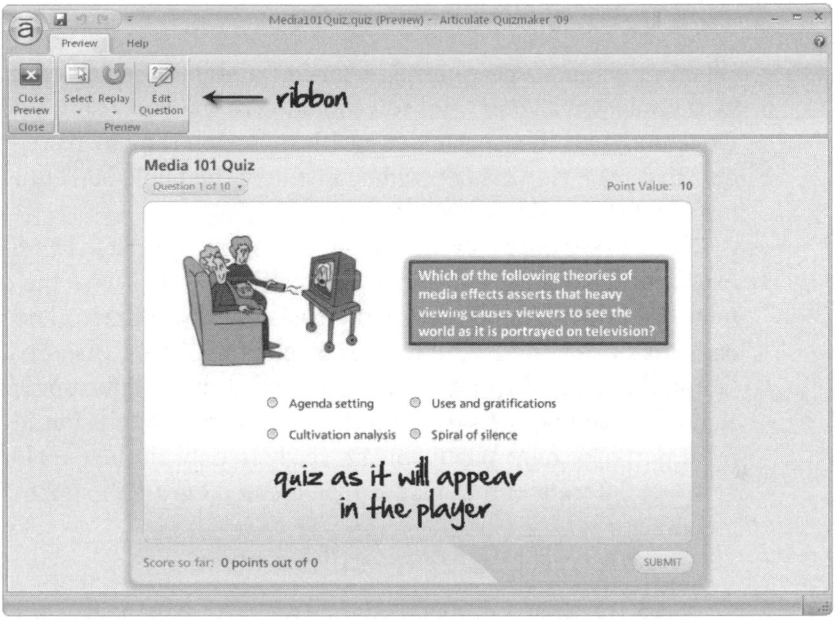

Figure 9.55. Preview window for quiz

The ribbon on the Preview window contains the Preview tab and the standard Help tab. The Preview tab is similar to the Preview tab on the ribbon that is displayed when you preview a specific question from the Question window. In the quiz Preview tab, however, the Edit Question button is included, which lets you open and edit the current question. The Select menu lets you preview another question in the quiz. The Replay menu lets you repeat the preview of the current question, preview the questions in a specific group, or preview the entire quiz again from the beginning. You can leave the preview at any time using the Close Preview button.

If you preview the quiz to the end, the Results slide is displayed last. There, you can verify the scoring results and then preview the quiz review. The quiz review displays each question with the correct answer and indicates whether the viewer answered it correctly or incorrectly.

Saving Quizzes

When you create a new quiz, Quizmaker assigns a default file name of Quiz1.quiz, Quiz2.quiz, etc. You should save the quiz using a different file name, then choose a folder location to store the file. Note that the quiz that your viewers see will be in one of the published output formats, not the QUIZ format.

Quizmaker quizzes are saved in one of two formats. The file name extension for regular quiz files is .quiz. You may also save the quiz as a template, which can be used as the basis for new quizzes. The file name extension for quiz templates is .quiztemplate. (Chapter 13, "Pumping Up Your Quizzes," covers how to create quiz templates.) Keep in mind that the saved quiz file or quiz template is for development purposes only. When you are ready to publish the quiz for your viewers, different output files will be created during the publishing process.

To save a regular quiz file for the first time:

1. Click the **Save** button 🔲 on the Quick Access toolbar, *or* click the **Articulate** button ⓐ and select **Save** or **Save As** from the File menu.

2. In the Save As dialog box, enter a new name in the File name box.

3. By default, Quizmaker stores new quiz files in the My Articulate Projects folder. In Windows XP, this is a subfolder under the My Documents folder. To store the file in a different location, browse to the folder using the Save in list or the icons on the left side of the Save As dialog box.

4. Click the **Save** button.

As you continue developing the quiz, you should save it frequently by clicking the **Save** button on the Quick Access toolbar. You can also use the shortcut keys **Ctrl+S**. If you want to save the file later using a different file name or location, select the **Save As** command from the File menu, which opens the Save As dialog box.

Publishing Quizzes

The last step in the Quizmaker workflow is to *publish* your quiz. Publishing means creating the output files that viewers use to work with the quiz. Chapter 26, "Publishing," provides details on the various output file formats you can create. But here's a quick explanation of publishing to the web, in case you want to create a complete quiz from start to finish while working through this chapter.

Figure 9.56. Publish dialog box Web panel

To publish a quiz to the web:

1. Click the **Publish** button on the ribbon.

2. In the Publish dialog box, click the **Web** tab (Figure 9.56).

3. In the Publish Location section, use the Folder box to enter the full path name of the folder to contain the published quiz.

4. In the Properties section, verify that the properties are appropriate for the quiz. You may change the Quiz Title, Passing Score, Player Template, and Quality properties by clicking the current

value (blue text link). Note that the Quality value should be set to **Optimized for Web delivery** or a custom setting.

5. At the bottom of the Publish dialog box, click the **Publish** button.

6. In the Publish Successful dialog box, choose whether to view the quiz, send as email, send to an FTP site, create a Zip file, or open the folder containing the published files.

When you publish a quiz to the web, Quizmaker creates a folder called [Name of Interaction] - Quizmaker output. This folder contains all of the files required to post the quiz to a web site.

Printing Your Quiz

If you want to print a copy of your quiz, first publish it to Microsoft Word using the Publish dialog box. The output file is a Word document, which you can then print.

Setting Quizmaker Options

Quizmaker offers several global preferences that affect your (the developer's) experience with the program. These options are contained in the Quizmaker Options dialog box, which is accessible from the File menu.

To open the Quizmaker Options dialog box:

1. Click the **Articulate** button ⓐ.

2. In the lower right section of the File menu, click the **Quizmaker Options** button.

The Quizmaker Options dialog box contains three categories of options: Options, Spelling, and Proxy Settings. The default selections are shown in Figure 9.57, and Table 9.14 provides a brief description of each option. For a complete description of each item, click the Learn more about Quizmaker options link at the bottom of the Quizmaker Options dialog box.

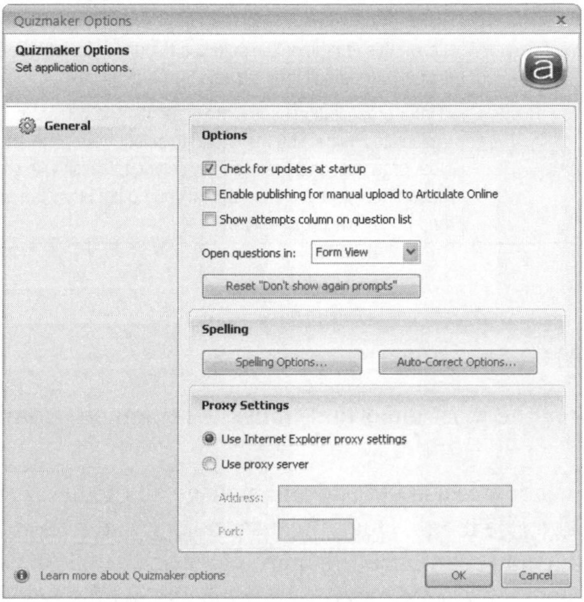

Figure 9.57. Quizmaker Options dialog box showing default selections

Table 9.14. Quizmaker Options dialog box options

Option	Description
Check for updates at startup	Check this option if you want Quizmaker to look for program updates once a week. (You can always manually check for updates using the Check for Updates button on the ribbon's Help tab.)
Enable publishing for manual upload to Articulate Online	Check this option if you want to manually upload a published quiz to your Articulate Online account.
Show attempts column on Question list	Check this option if you want to include the Attempts column in the Quiz window, which displays the number of attempts allowed for each question.
Open questions in	Select Form View or Slide View as the default view when you start a new question or open an existing question.
Reset "Don't show again prompts"	Click this button to ensure that all prompts are shown until you click the "Don't show again" check box in a prompt. An example of a prompt is the confirmation message that is displayed when you delete a question.
Spelling Options	Click this button to configure how Quizmaker checks the spelling in a quiz. Note that this option is similar to the spelling options used in Microsoft Office 2007.
Auto-Correct Options	Click this button to configure how Quizmaker automatically enters or corrects text entries. Note that this option is similar to the autocorrect options used in Microsoft Office 2007.

Option	Description
Use Internet Explorer proxy settings	Leave this default option selected to publish to Articulate Online using your default Internet settings (in most cases).
Use proxy server	If your organization uses a proxy server and you are publishing to Articulate Online, you may need to select this option and input your organization's proxy server settings. Check with your IT department if you're unsure, or if you do not know the address and port of the proxy server.

Chapter Recap

Here's our list of the most important things to remember from this chapter:

- The Quiz window is used to add and manage all the questions in the quiz. The File menu, Quick Access toolbar, and ribbon contain tools to build and customize the quiz. The ribbon tools are basically the same for graded quizzes and surveys, with a few differences.

- The Question window is used to build a specific question, such as a Multiple Choice or True/False question. The ribbon contains different tools, depending on whether you are working with the question in Form view or Slide view.

- Form view provides structured placeholders that you can use to enter the basic content elements of the question, such as the question text, answer choice, and feedback text. You can also add one media file or sound file in Form view.

- Slide view provides a freeform environment where you can enter content elements, add multiple media and sound files, change the layout of the slide, format objects, time objects, and apply design themes.

- Many of the tools on the Slide view ribbon are similar to the tools on the PowerPoint 2007 ribbon.

- Each question must contain question text and the minimum number of correct answer choices (depending on the question type).

- Using Form view, you can customize the feedback that is displayed after the viewer answers the question. You can set feedback for the correct and incorrect answers, as well as assign unique feedback for each incorrect answer.

■ Use the branching feature in Form view to select a specific slide to display depending on how the viewer answers a question. For example, branch to the end of the quiz or to a review slide.

■ Set scoring options, shuffle the answer order, and set the number of attempts using the ribbon tools in Form view or Slide view.

■ Preview the current question using the Preview button on the Question window ribbon in Slide view or Form view. Preview the entire quiz using the Preview button on the Quiz window ribbon.

■ To save the question and return to the Quiz window, use the Save & Close button on the Question window ribbon.

■ After building a few questions, you can use the Question list in the Quiz window to open, move, delete, reorder, randomize, and group questions. You can also change the scoring of specific questions.

■ The Quizmaker Properties dialog box lets you customize general properties of the current quiz, such as the quiz title, passing score, time limit, and the default values used for questions.

■ Save your quiz using the Save button on the Quick Access toolbar or the Save and Save As commands on the File menu. Quiz files are saved using the file name extension .quiz. You can also save the quiz as a template, which uses the file name extension .quiztemplate.

■ Publish your quiz using the Publish dialog box. After you select the type of output (e.g., Web), the location of the files, and properties, Quizmaker creates an output folder containing the appropriate files to run the interaction.

■ Check out the Quizmaker Options dialog box to set global preferences while working with Quizmaker, such as opening questions in Form view or Slide view by default.

> Come back to this chapter as needed! The remaining chapters in the Quizmaker section build on this chapter by describing how to create different question types and pump up your questions and quizzes.

Chapter 10

Creating Graded Questions

Chapter Snapshot

In this chapter, you'll learn how to add different types of graded questions to a graded Quizmaker quiz in order to test and score viewers' knowledge and competency in a range of areas.

If you're an e-learning developer, there's a good chance you've developed assessments using graded quiz questions, such as multiple-choice, fill-in-the-blank, true/false, drag and drop, and essay. Each section in this chapter shows you how to design and build a different type of Quizmaker graded question. Tips are provided at the end of each section to help you think about the question type and apply some of the formatting options that are covered in other chapters.

Revisiting the Quizmaker 1-2-3-4-5 Workflow

Chapter 9, "Quizmaker Basics," discussed the essential tasks for creating a quiz, adding questions, and publishing the quiz. All steps in the Quizmaker workflow were covered at a basic level. This chapter, as well as Chapter 11, "Creating Survey Questions," and Chapter 12, "Pumping Up Your Questions," focus on step 3 of the workflow, as shown below. Table 10.1 shows all of the substeps typically completed in step 3 of the Quizmaker 1-2-3-4-5 workflow.

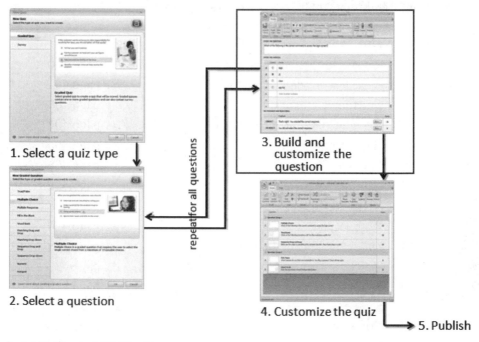

Figure 10.1. Quizmaker 1-2-3-4-5 workflow

Table 10.1. Detailed workflow for step 3

Step	Description
3. Build and customize the question	a) Add the content elements required by the selected question, such as question text, answer choices, and feedback. b) Customize the question by adding a variety of other features, such as images, audio, and animation effects.

Although this chapter touches on substep b) Customize the question, most of the nitty-gritty details for customizing questions are described in Chapter 12, "Pumping Up Your Questions." In this chapter (and the next), our focus is on describing each of the question types provided by Quizmaker. And we've kept the step-by-step details short, since most of those were already covered in Chapter 9, "Quizmaker Basics."

What Is a Graded Question?

Articulate defines a graded question as a question that has a correct or incorrect response(s) and a defined point value. Graded questions are used to create graded quizzes to determine if the viewer understands the content or whether some or all of the learning objectives have been met. Point values for each question add up to a final score, or grade, which is typically used to determine if the content has been adequately mastered. If it has been mastered, the viewer usually is done with the lesson or module. If not, the viewer typically can either retake the lesson or module or be given additional help if "passing" the lesson or module is deemed critical. A graded quiz is typically given *after* a lesson or module is completed and these kinds of graded quizzes are sometimes referred to as post-tests. Graded questions can also be used to determine what lessons or modules are needed. When used in this way, a graded quiz is commonly referred to as a pre-test.

Remember that Quizmaker allows you to create two types of quizzes—graded quizzes and surveys. Graded quizzes can contain both graded and survey questions, but a survey can contain only survey questions. Quizmaker offers 11 types of graded questions. We'll discuss all of these types in this chapter.

Tip: Quizmaker provides an option to convert some question types to another, similar question type. For example, you can convert a Multiple Choice question to a Word Bank question. Just right-click the Multiple Choice question in the Quiz window and select Convert to Word Bank.

The tasks for building each question type are similar, but there are differences among the questions. These differences affect various features of the questions, such as scoring, answer shuffling, and feedback responses. Where appropriate, we have identified these features. If you read about all 11 questions from start to finish, you'll also find some redundancy among the information. Our goal is to keep all pertinent information about each question type together in each section. So if you jump to any question type, all the information you need to build it will be there.

Tip: Chapter 8, "Introduction to Quizmaker," provides some insights about graded questions that you may wish to review.

Although Chapter 9, "Quizmaker Basics," explains how to start a graded quiz and select a question, here's a quick recap on starting a new graded question:

1. From the Quizmaker start screen, click **Create a new quiz**.

2. In the New Quiz dialog box, click the **Graded Quiz** tab.

3. In the Quiz window, click the **Graded Question** button on the Home tab of the ribbon.

4. In the New Graded Question dialog box (Figure 10.2), select the question type.

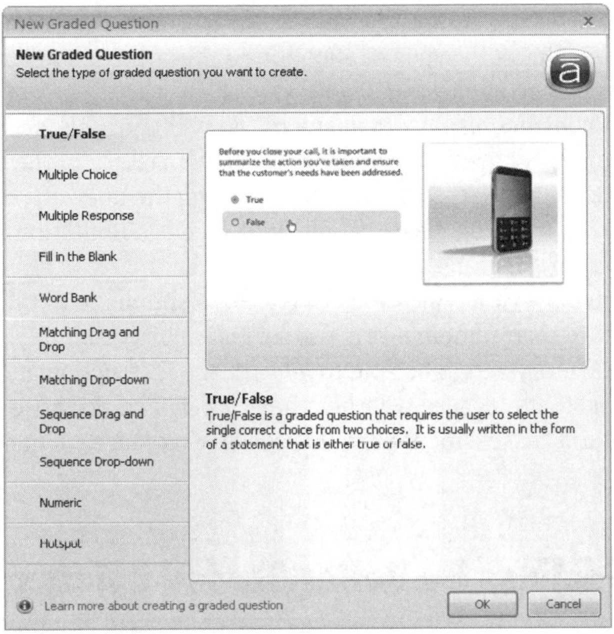

Figure 10.2. New Graded Question dialog box

Question Categories

Quizmaker contains a variety of graded question types. These question types can be categorized into one of two categories: recall questions and application questions.

Recall questions require the viewer to remember specific content, either word for word, paraphrased, or in a summarized format. Most of the Quizmaker graded question types can be written as recall questions.

Application questions require *using* the content and then either selecting or inputting a correct answer(s). These are typically more complex than recall questions and should be written so that learners apply what they have learned in a real or realistic way. They often use resources (such as a manual or guidelines) and may include media (such as an audio file or video) in a realistic scenario. Multiple Choice and Multiple Response (which is a variation on Multiple Choice) questions are commonly the question types that are written as application questions.

Recall questions are typically easier to answer than application questions. But both types of questions suffer from a similar problem. Most recall and application questions ask viewers to select the correct answer from among a list of answers. They do not ask viewers to provide the answer, perform the task, or show mastery of the skill. Selecting an answer is easier than providing the answer, performing the task, or showing mastery of a skill. This is a limitation of most test questions in general.

To avoid writing questions that are too simplistic to measure anything more than remembering factual content, we should consider what learners need to be able to *do* with the instruction and construct questions that measure whether they can, in fact, do those things. In other words, assessments should assess what learners need to be able to do.

Design Guidelines for Better Graded Quizzes

Two goals you should have when building a graded quiz are to make sure it is user-friendly and that it adequately assesses the learning objectives the questions are written to assess. Table 10.2 provides some guidelines that can help you build a graded quiz that meets these goals.

Table 10.2. Guidelines for writing a better quiz

Quiz element	Guidelines
Interface	Be consistent in placement of instructions, questions, answers, and other elements when designing a quiz or survey so that learners only have to figure out how the quiz works once.
Instructions	At the beginning, concisely explain how the quiz works (how many questions, approximate amount of time the quiz will take). If the directions aren't concise, it's likely that viewers will not read them. Repeat important directions throughout (such as "Select all that apply") as needed.
Language	Provide clear, concise instructions and make sure the wording is precise, clear, and non-ambiguous. Make sure that the instructions and questions are written so that viewers do not need to figure out what the words mean.

Quiz element	Guidelines
Learning objectives	Write questions that adequately cover the learning objectives. Don't dumb down the objectives so you can write less complex questions. Consider using actual performances for learning objectives that cannot be assessed with Multiple Choice questions. To weight the quiz toward the more important learning objectives, use relatively more questions about the most important learning objectives.
Test	Test the quiz before using it and fix wording and other problems.

True/False

The True/False question, which is among the simplest of graded questions, presents the viewer with a statement and prompts him or her to choose whether the statement is correct (true) or incorrect (false).

The True/False question is a quick and simple way to test a range of factual knowledge that can be expressed as two mutually exclusive alternatives or which represent opposed, either-or qualities. The two choices do not have to be "true" and "false." Some examples of True/False questions are:

- Evaluating a statement as correct or incorrect.

- Evaluating an action as appropriate or not, based on company practice and/or on a fictional scenario.

- Classifying an item into one of two opposing categories, such as possible/not possible, increasing/decreasing, interior/exterior, or Republican/Democrat.

- Creating a branched scenario in which viewers are directed to a different slide based on their responses.

True/False questions have an obvious downside with only two answer choices. The viewer has a 50 percent probability of *guessing* the correct answer. As a result, True/False questions should generally not be used in questions designed to measure achievement of a learning objective. Here's an exception: They may be used as part of a branched scenario question meant to measure achievement of a learning objective. They can also be used in self-check questions, which are questions that are built for the viewer to check their understanding but the score is irrelevant. (You can set the point value of self-check questions to 0.)

Building the True/False Question

After you select the True/False tab and click OK from the New Graded Question dialog box, Quizmaker displays the True/False Question window. To build the question in Form view:

1. Enter the question.

2. Click the radio button to specify the correct response: True or False.

3. If you want to edit the answer choices, click the text in the Choice column and type in the answer choices you want.

4. If desired, insert media or audio and/or modify the default feedback, branching, display options, and scoring options. (See Chapter 9, "Quizmaker Basics," for details.)

5. If desired, switch to Slide view to customize the question, such as by formatting the question text box and animating the screen text or graphics. (See Chapter 12, "Pumping Up Your Questions," for details.)

Figure 10.3 shows an example of a completed True/False question in Form view, and Figure 10.4 shows the same question as it appears in the Preview window.

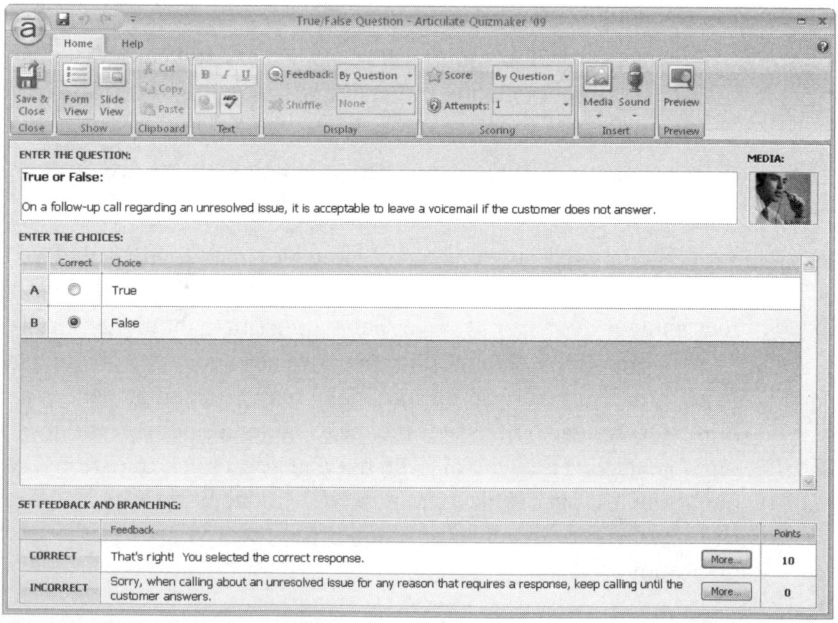

Figure 10.3. True/False question in Form view

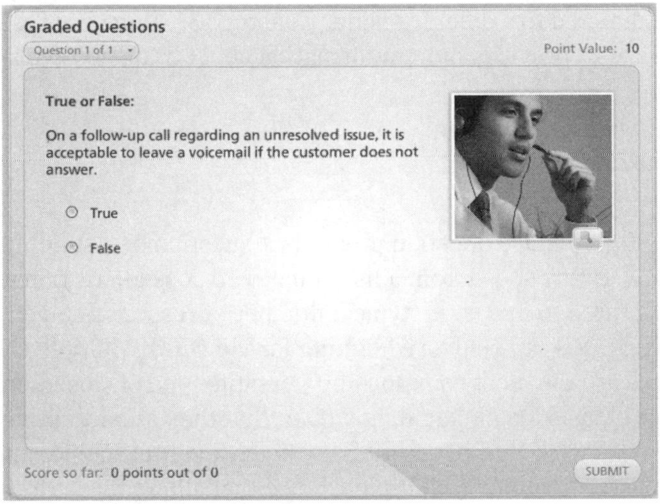

Figure 10.4. True/False question in Preview window

Tips

- When considering using a closed-ended objective question type such as the True/False question, remember to keep the question content clear and simple with unambiguously correct and incorrect choices.

- Don't make the correct and incorrect choice obvious from the wording of the question. But on the other hand, don't try to "trick" the viewer by diverting his or her attention with extraneous information.

- Although the answer choices of "True" and "False" display by default, you can adopt the true/false format to other two-choice question types by editing the terms to show different choices, such as yes/no, acceptable/not acceptable, or positive/negative.

- Quizmaker allows you to choose whether to provide feedback to the viewer by question (providing one response for the correct answer and one response for all incorrect answers) or by answer (providing different feedback for each answer choice) using the Feedback list on the ribbon.

- You can use the True/False question to create a branched scenario. For example, present a situation and ask viewers to respond in one of two ways. If they respond "True" (or "Yes"), then they are directed to the next slide. If they respond "False" (or "No"), they are directed to a different slide. Chapter 13, "Pumping Up Your Quizzes," provides more information about branched scenarios.

Multiple Choice

The Multiple Choice question presents a question or a statement and asks viewers to choose from a list of up to 10 possible responses, although three to five is the typical number of responses (and more than five is likely to be overwhelming for viewers). Multiple Choice questions are the most common and versatile type of closed-ended question types. Keep in mind, however, that they are deceptively difficult to write well. Because Multiple Choice and Multiple Response questions (a variation of Multiple Choice that allows more than one correct answer) are used so often, we are going to provide extra guidance on writing them in this section.

Multiple Choice Question Parts

A Multiple Choice question has two parts: the question text (sometimes called the "stem") and the alternative answers. The question text initiates the question with a question, incomplete statement, or situation. The alternative answers are a list of possible answers or solutions. They include the correct answer(s) and incorrect or inferior answer(s), which are called distractors (guess why).

Table 10.3. Parts of a Multiple Choice question

Part	Description	Common problems
Question text	Describes the: • Question to be answered • Incomplete statement to be completed • Decision to be made • Problem or situation to be resolved	• Confusing, long-winded, or ambiguous language • Inadequate instructions
Alternative answers (correct answers and incorrect answers, or distractors)	The alternatives from which the viewer selects the correct answer(s)	• Confusing or ambiguous language • No clear, right answer(s) • Poorly written or implausible alternative answers

Creating Good Multiple Choice Questions

Multiple-choice tests can be developed for many different types of content and, if the questions are well-written, can measure achievement of multiple levels of learning objectives. The objectives can range from simple recall and comprehension to more complex levels, such as ability to analyze a situation, apply principles, discriminate, interpret, judge relevance, select the best solution, and so on. The Multiple Choice question is a good tool for testing factual, conceptual, or procedural information and is especially useful when you are testing online or administering to a large number of viewers because they can be evaluated automatically.

But (and this is a big but) Multiple Choice questions are difficult to write well and are therefore fraught with some common problems. The most common problems and solutions are listed in Table 10.4.

Table 10.4. Common multiple-choice problems and solutions

Problem	Solutions
Unclear, long-winded, and imprecise language	• Reduce the wordiness of answers by including words in the question text that would otherwise be repeated in each of the alternative answers.
	• Avoid technical language or jargon unless understanding technical language and jargon is the purpose of the question.
	• Avoid negatives (not, doesn't, won't) and these words: always, often, frequently, never, none, rarely, and infrequently.
	• When a negative is used, it should be CAPITALIZED, underlined, or **bolded** to call attention to it.
	• Don't provide unnecessary, superfluous information.
	• Don't try to trick the viewer.

Problem	Solutions

Confusing or ambiguous answers	• Make sure all distractors are plausible, especially to those with lower skills or lesser knowledge. These are the best types of plausible but incorrect distractors:*
	
	   ◦ Common errors and commonly held myths or misconceptions (for those with less knowledge or skill)
	
	   ◦ Statements that are true but do not answer this question
	
	   ◦ Content that is paraphrased incorrectly
	
	• You can vary the number of distractors, but they must all be plausible.
	
	• If answers include best and not-as-good alternatives ("Select the *best* answer…"), provide enough detail to differentiate best from not as good.
	
	• Keep all answers about the same length. (Longer answers are often the right answer.)
	
	• Avoid answers that combine answers ("b and c").
	
	• Don't use "all of the above," or "none of the above." The alternative answer "all of the above" is the correct response more than 50% of the time and "none of the above" is rarely the correct answer.
	
	• Make sure that wording or grammar doesn't give away the answer.
	
	• Make sure that there is one unambiguous right answer (or more than one answer for Multiple Response questions).

* This advice about writing plausible distractors is the most important piece of Multiple Choice question writing advice!

Let's see if you can tell what's wrong with each of the following questions. The answers follow, but don't peek!

1. A vendor offers a staff member two tickets to the World Series. Based on the rules listed in the Vendor Gift Policy, he/she cannot accept them:
   a) Unless the tickets have no street value
   b) If the vendor is expecting "quid pro quo"
   c) If the gift is worth more than $25 or is considered to be an inducement
   d) Unless the vendor is also a friend

2. The opposite of a strait is an
   a) peninsula
   b) continent
   c) isthmus
   d) bay

3. Cracking, blistering, and flaking are all examples of
    a) corrosion
    b) a corroded pipeline
    c) a really bad day
    d) pipeline failure

Answers:

Question 1 uses some terms that the viewer may not know: street value, quid pro quo, and inducement. Answer c has two answers in one.

The answers in Question 2 tell which answer is correct. Only one of the answers is *grammatically* correct when placed with the question text and that is c) isthmus.

Question 3 has two answers, a and b, that are too much alike and could be considered correct. Plus it has a silly, throwaway answer, c. (Add that to the list of things to not do.)

Another problem that occurs frequently when writing multiple-choice questions is that they are written at too low a level to match the objective. The multiple-choice questions in Table 10.5 provide examples of questions written for a broad range of objective levels.

Table 10.5. Multiple-choice questions written at different learning objective levels

Learning objective level	Example questions
Knowledge: Ability to recall content in exactly the same form	The A580 computer system is an appropriate choice for which customer? a) Small business b) Networked business office c) Home office d) Road warrior
Comprehension: Ability to restate, translate, apply rules, recognize unseen examples	A customer calls the billing services department at Jackson Companies. He asks about making an online bill payment. Customer service representative Cheryl should say, a) "I am sorry but we do not offer that service." b) "I can understand why that would be convenient. Let me check on whether we have any plans to introduce this." c) "I understand that you are disappointed. If you would like to make a complaint, I can transfer you to my supervisor." d) "This doesn't seem to be something most people would use." (This question would work well with audio.)

Learning objective level	Example questions
Application: Ability to determine which rules apply and use them to solve a problem	Marcus has been on staff for two months and has been late to work three times. You have not yet given him a warning or discussed his lateness because he is usually only 5 minutes late. He again arrives late, this time by 20 minutes. Which one of the following actions is the most appropriate? a) Discuss his problem with getting to work on time, and give him a verbal warning. b) Discuss his problem with getting to work on time, and give him the first written warning. c) Discuss his problem with getting to work on time, and give him a final written warning. d) Fire him because he is unreliable and is an at-will employee.

Building the Multiple Choice Question

After you select the Multiple Choice tab and click OK from the New Graded Question dialog box, Quizmaker displays the Multiple Choice Question window. To build the question in Form view:

1. Enter the question, including instructions, if needed. If the question has a "best" answer, the viewer should be told to pick the *best* answer.

2. Enter the answer choices. Quizmaker allows you to provide as many as 10 answer choices but more than five is likely to be too many.

3. Specify the correct answer by clicking the appropriate radio button in the Correct column.

4. If desired, insert media or audio and/or modify the default feedback, branching, display options, and scoring options. (See Chapter 9, "Quizmaker Basics," for details.)

5. If desired, switch to Slide view to customize the question, such as by formatting the question text box and animating the screen text or graphics. (See Chapter 12, "Pumping Up Your Questions," for details.)

Figure 10.5 shows an example of a completed Multiple Choice question in Form view, and Figure 10.6 shows the same question as it appears in the Preview window.

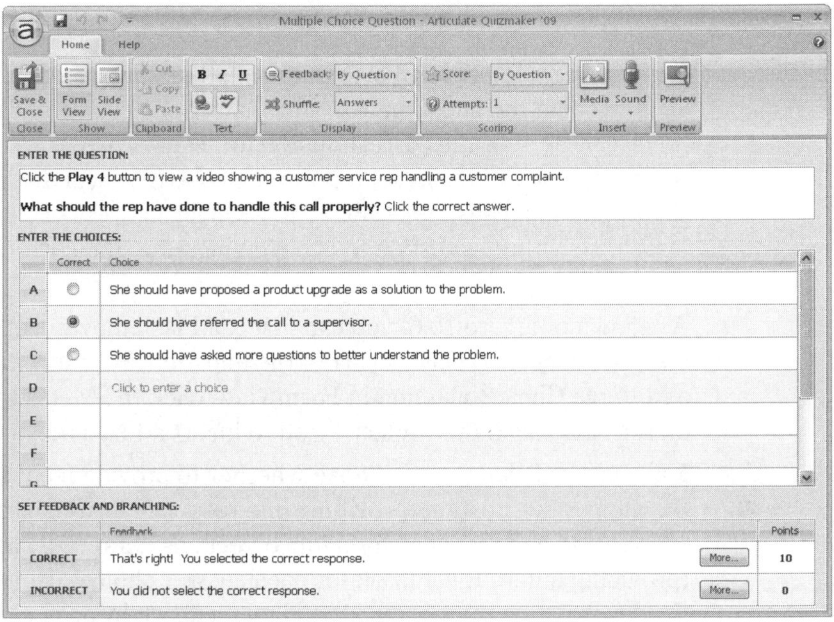

Figure 10.5. Multiple Choice question in Form view

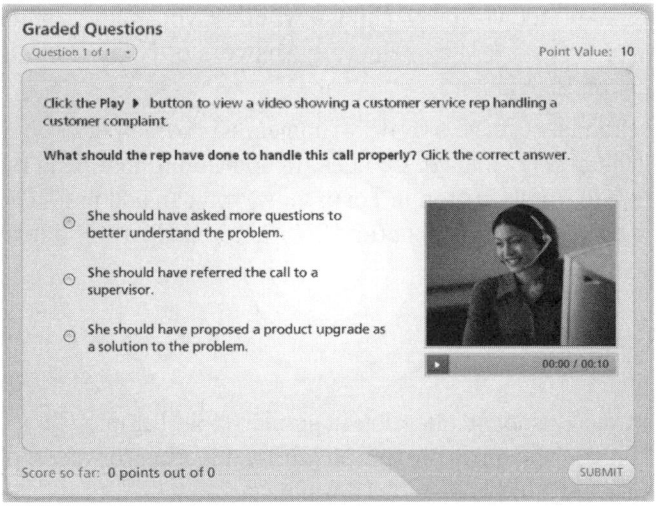

Figure 10.6. Multiple Choice question in Preview window

Tips

■ When using a Multiple Choice question, think first and foremost about writing the question text and answer choices carefully and precisely. Be sure the correct answer is clearly correct and that the distractors, or incorrect answers, are clearly incorrect but at the same time plausible. Also try to keep all answers of similar length, structure, and style to avoid giving away the correct choice.

■ As shown in Figure 10.6, you can insert a Flash movie that the viewer can click to play as part of the question. To insert media in a Multiple Choice question in Form view, click the Media button on the ribbon and then select Flash to insert a Flash movie.

■ Quizmaker allows you to choose whether to provide feedback to the viewer by question (providing one response for the correct answer and one response for all incorrect answers) or by answer (providing different feedback for each answer choice) using the Feedback list on the ribbon. Providing feedback by answer often makes sense for complex questions and when the viewer is told to select the "best" answer.

■ Quizmaker allows you to choose whether you want to shuffle the answer order or not by selecting Answers or None from the Shuffle list on the ribbon.

■ You can insert images or drawn objects as part of questions, or even as parts of answer choices. In addition to inserting media using the Media button in Form view, you can add media in Slide view as described in Chapter 12, "Pumping Up Your Questions."

Multiple Response

The Multiple Response question is similar to a Multiple Choice question in that the viewer is presented with a question (or incomplete statement) and a list of up to 10 possible responses. But in a Multiple Response question the viewer may select more than one correct answer. When designing a Multiple Response question, you may choose any number or combination of correct response options. Be sure to indicate in the question text that the viewer selects as many choices as apply, or tell the viewer to select a specific number of correct choices.

The Multiple Response question is a good tool for any type of question for which multiple correct responses are appropriate.

Tip: All of the guidance provided in the "Multiple Choice" section applies for Multiple Response questions as well. Because Multiple Response questions are typically harder to answer than Multiple Choice questions that have only one correct answer, it is even more important that the language be precise and unambiguous.

Building the Multiple Response Question

After you select the Multiple Response tab and click OK from the New Graded Question dialog box, Quizmaker displays the Multiple Response Question window. To build the question in Form view:

1. Enter the question, which should also indicate that viewers can click more than one answer ("select all that apply" works well for many Multiple Response questions) or should click a specific number of answers.

2. Enter the answer choices.

3. Specify all correct answers by clicking the appropriate check box or boxes in the Correct column.

4. If desired, insert media or audio and/or modify the default feedback, branching, display options, and scoring options. (See Chapter 9, "Quizmaker Basics," for details.)

5. If desired, switch to Slide view to customize the question, such as by formatting the question text box and animating the screen text or graphics. (See Chapter 12, "Pumping Up Your Questions," for details.)

Figure 10.7 shows an example of a completed Multiple Response question in Form view, and Figure 10.8 shows the same question as it appears in the Preview window.

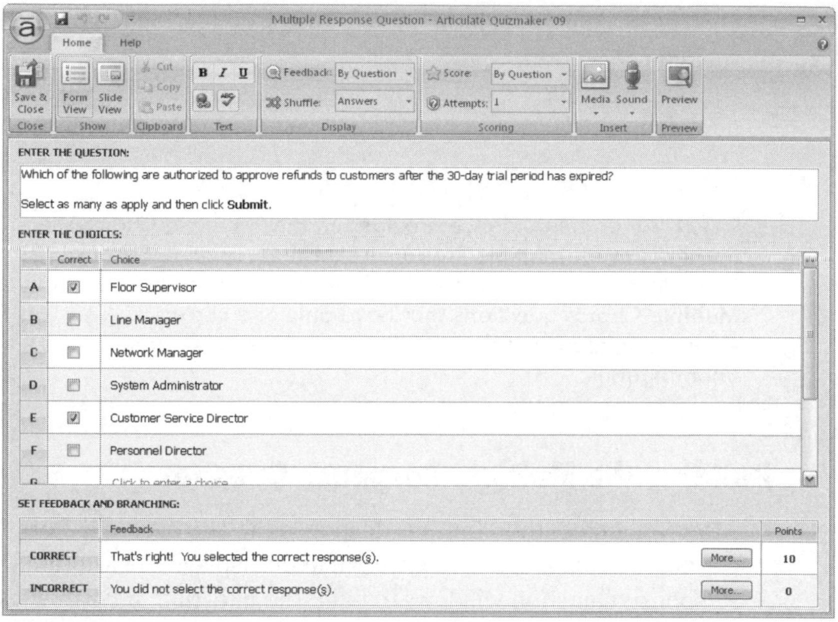

Figure 10.7. Multiple Response question in Form view

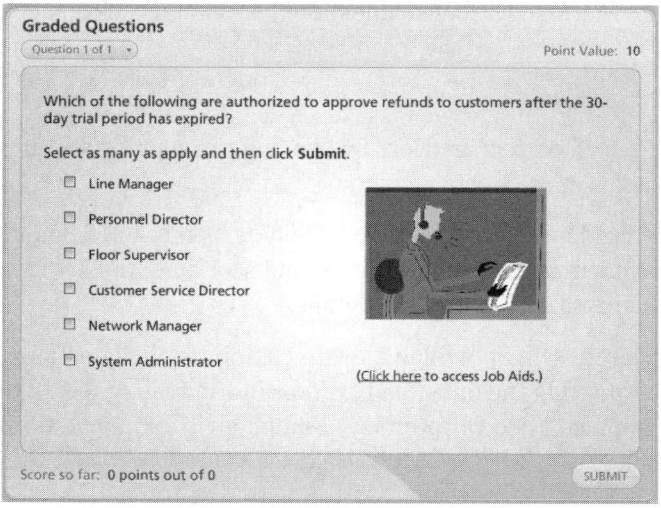

Figure 10.8. Multiple Response question in Preview window

Tips

- Because Multiple Response questions provide more complex combinations of correct and incorrect responses than do Multiple Choice questions, they can be even more difficult to write. So when using a Multiple Response question, be sure to clearly specify questions and answer choices and make sure that distractors are plausible but incorrect.

- Note that the only feedback options available for Multiple Response questions are None and By Question and that there is no By Answer option. Multiple Response questions have too many possible response combinations to make it practical to provide different feedback for each one. So make sure that the feedback you input clearly explains what the correct responses were and why. For the same reason, the only Score option is By Question because there are too many possible responses to assign a point value to each.

- As with any question type, Quizmaker allows you to insert hyperlinks into your Multiple Response questions. Taking as an example the Multiple Response question shown in Figures 10.7 and 10.8, you might want to insert a link to allow viewers to access a job aid or other tool. To insert a hyperlink, switch to Slide view, select the text you want to link, and then click Hyperlink on the Insert tab to open the Insert Hyperlink dialog box.

- As with the Multiple Choice question, Quizmaker allows you to choose whether or not you want to shuffle the answers by selecting Answers or None from the Shuffle list on the ribbon.

- By default, Quizmaker displays correct and incorrect feedback that displays the text "You selected the correct response" and "You did not select the correct response." Since the viewer does not always select a single response when responding to a Multiple Response question, you may want to pluralize the feedback text to reflect multiple correct responses.

Fill in the Blank

The Fill in the Blank option presents viewers with a statement that includes a blank space into which they must type text to enter a response and complete the statement. A Fill in the Blank question is a good tool for testing the viewer's ability to *recall* factual information. Some examples of Fill in the Blank questions are:

■ Asking viewers to recall a name, place, rule, concept, or any other quantity that can be unambiguously expressed as a specific word or short phrase.

■ Asking viewers to identify the correct spelling of a word or the correct translation of a word in a different language.

Building the Fill in the Blank Question

After you select the Fill in the Blank tab and click OK from the New Graded Question dialog box, Quizmaker displays the Fill in the Blank Question window. To build the question in Form view:

1. Enter the question.

2. Enter at least one and as many as 10 acceptable answers. By default, acceptable answers are not case sensitive, so when correct case is an essential part of the answer, click the Answers are case sensitive check box below the Acceptable Answers section.

3. If desired, insert media or audio and/or modify the default feedback, branching, display options, and scoring options. (See Chapter 9, "Quizmaker Basics," for details.)

4. If desired, switch to Slide view to customize the question, such as by formatting the question text box and animating the screen text or graphics. (See Chapter 12, "Pumping Up Your Questions," for details.)

Figure 10.9 shows an example of a completed Fill in the Blank question in Form view, and Figure 10.10 shows the same question as it appears in the Preview window.

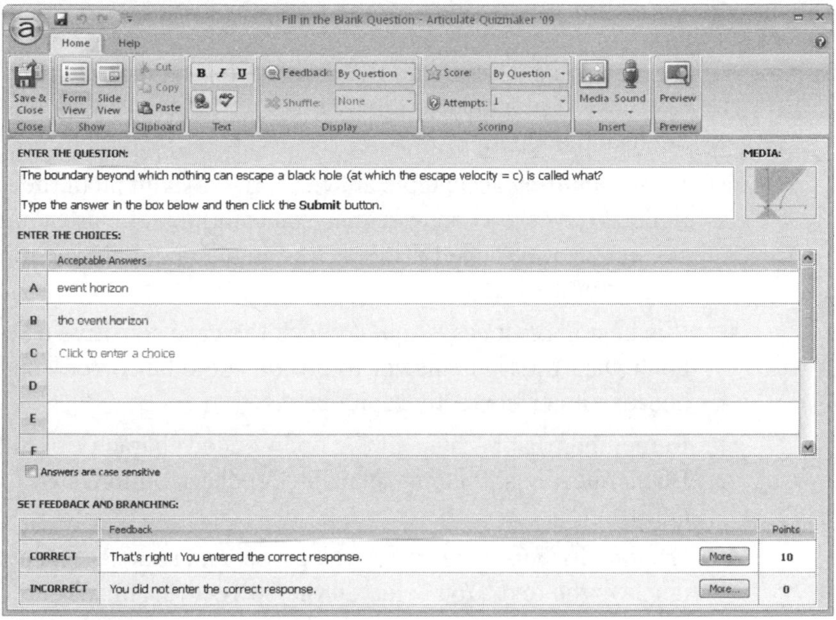

Figure 10.9. Fill in the Blank question in Form view

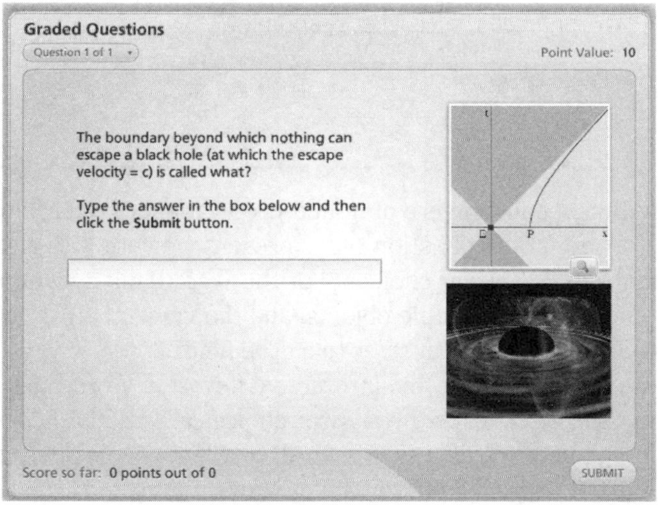

Figure 10.10. Fill in the Blank question in Preview window

Tips

- When writing a Fill in the Blank question, be sure the question text is precise enough so the viewer understands what answer needs to be input.

- When inputting acceptable answers, try to input all of the variations of the correct answer that you can think of. For example, the correct answer "The Battle of the Bulge" might also be input as "Battle of the Bulge."

- It is best in most cases to *not* check the case sensitive box. You don't want the right answer to be considered incorrect just because it is incorrectly capitalized.

- Remember that because of the open-ended character of Fill in the Blank questions, the only available feedback option is By Question.

- By default, Quizmaker displays correct and incorrect feedback that displays the text "You selected the correct response" and "You did not select the correct response." Since the viewer does not "select" a response when responding to a Fill in the Blank question, you may want to edit the feedback text to show something like "You entered the correct response."

Word Bank

The Word Bank question is a drag-and-drop variant of the Multiple Choice question. Both question types present viewers with a question and as many as 10 answer choices. For the Word Bank question, the answer choices are draggable objects, and the viewer is instructed to drag and drop the correct answer to a drop field.

Because of its graphic and interactive format, a Word Bank question is a good choice when the answer choices are relatively short (although not necessarily a single word) or when you decide that there is some instructional benefit to having viewers drag and drop the response.

Because Word Bank questions are similar to Multiple Choice questions, they have many of the same advantages and problems, and are similarly difficult to write. Most of the guidance provided in the Multiple Choice question section applies for Word Bank questions, too. So be sure to write and specify your Word Bank questions with caution and precision.

Building the Word Bank Question

After you select the Word Bank tab and click OK from the New Graded Question dialog box, Quizmaker displays the Word Bank Question window. To build the question in Form view:

1. Enter the question, which should specify that the viewer drag and drop the correct answer choice to the drop field.

2. Enter the answer choices.

3. Specify the correct answer by clicking the appropriate radio button in the Correct column.

4. If desired, modify the default feedback, branching, display options, and scoring options. (See Chapter 9, "Quizmaker Basics," for details.)

5. If desired, switch to Slide view to customize the question, such as by formatting the question text box and animating the screen text or graphics. (See Chapter 12, "Pumping Up Your Questions," for details.)

Figure 10.11 shows an example of a completed Word Bank question in Form view, and Figure 10.12 shows the same question as it appears in the Preview window.

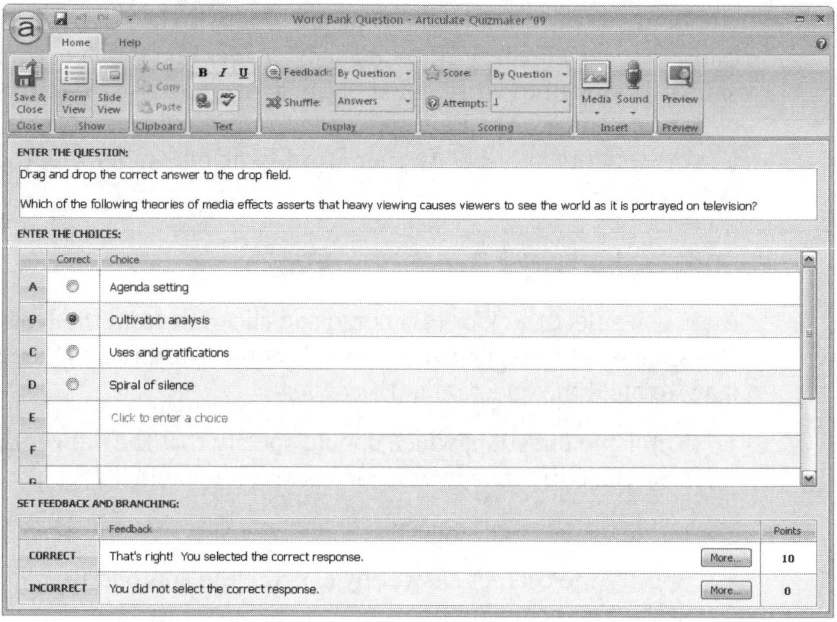

Figure 10.11. Word Bank question in Form view

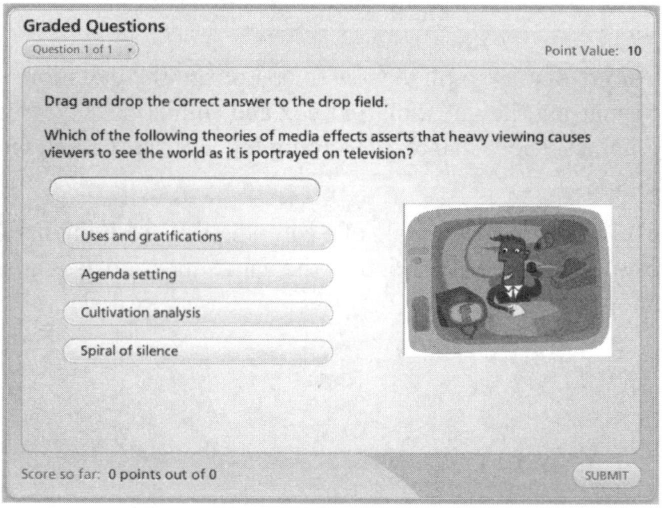

Figure 10.12. Word Bank question in Preview window

Tips

- As when using a Multiple Choice question, think first and foremost about specifying the questions and answer choices carefully and precisely. Be sure the correct answer is clearly correct and that the distractors, or incorrect responses, are clearly incorrect, but at the same time plausible. Also try to keep all answers of similar length, structure, and style to avoid giving away the correct choice.

- Providing By Answer feedback, which lets you specify different feedback for each answer choice, is often a good option for a Word Bank question. Taking the Word Bank question shown in Figures 10.11 and 10.12 as an example, the author might want to provide feedback that explains each incorrect response.

- As a general rule, you will want to keep Word Bank answer choices relatively short, but there may be exceptions for which you decide to create a Word Bank question with long answer choices. If you create answer choices that are long enough to wrap to a second or third line of text, be sure to preview your question to ensure the answers fit on the screen.

Matching Drag and Drop

A Matching Drag and Drop question presents the viewer with a question and instructions to drag items in the right column to match items in the left column. Each object in a column has only one correct match with an object in the other column, so to be graded as correct, a viewer has to correctly match all pairs. Quizmaker allows you to specify as many as 10 matched pairs, but you should probably use fewer pairs so viewers aren't overwhelmed.

A Matching Drag and Drop question is a good tool for testing the ability of viewers to recognize relationships and make associations. Some examples of Matching Drag and Drop questions are:

- Matching questions with answers.
- Matching terms with definitions or descriptions.

- Matching names with symbols or images.
- Matching specifications or calculations with the numerical values they define.
- Matching causes with effects.
- Matching procedures with operations.
- Matching principles with situations to which they apply.

Building the Matching Drag and Drop Question

After you select the Matching Drag and Drop tab and click OK from the New Graded Question dialog box, Quizmaker displays the Matching Drag and Drop Question window. To build the question in Form view:

1. Enter the question, which should include instructions to drag and drop each object in the right column to match an object in the left column.

2. Enter the fixed choices in the Choice column, and the draggable matching object for each in the associated row of the Match column. When the quiz is previewed or published, Quizmaker will display the choices in the order you enter them and will shuffle the order of the draggable matching objects.

3. If desired, insert media or audio and/or modify the default feedback, branching, display options, and scoring options. (See Chapter 9, "Quizmaker Basics," for details.)

4. If desired, switch to Slide view to customize the question, such as by formatting the question text box and animating the screen text or graphics. (See Chapter 12, "Pumping Up Your Questions," for details.)

Figure 10.13 shows an example of a completed Matching Drag and Drop question in Form view, and Figure 10.14 shows the same question as it appears in the Preview window.

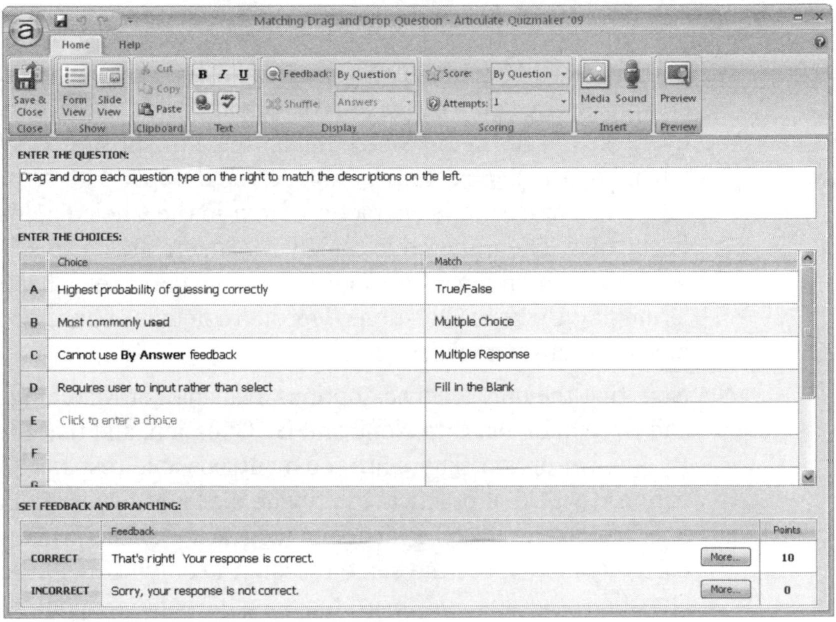

Figure 10.13. Matching Drag and Drop question in Form view

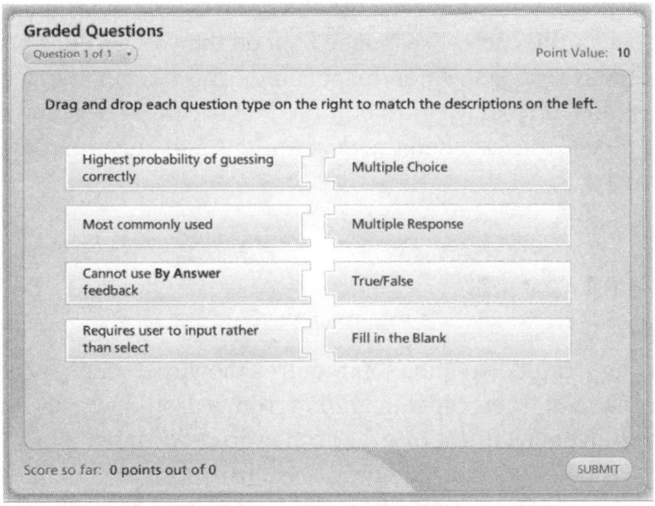

Figure 10.14. Matching Drag and Drop question in Preview window

Tips

■ You can use a Matching Drag and Drop question to match terms and images by using images in the Choice fields. (You cannot, however, use images in the Match fields, since the images won't move when the Match objects are dragged and dropped.) To create this effect, add at least one character of text in the Choice fields in Form view. Then, switch to Slide view, insert the images, and overlay them on top of the appropriate choices. (See Chapter 12, "Pumping Up Your Questions," for more details about using images as answer choices.)

■ Note that the only feedback options available for Matching Drag and Drop questions are None and By Question, and that there is no By Answer option. There are too many possible response combinations to make it practical to provide different feedback for each one. Make sure that the incorrect feedback explains what pairs correctly match. For the same reason, the only Score option is By Question—because there are too many possible responses to assign a point value to each.

■ By default, Quizmaker displays correct and incorrect feedback that displays the text "You selected the correct response" and "You did not select the correct response." Since the viewer does not "select" a response when responding to a Matching Drag and Drop question, you may want to edit the feedback text to show something like "You matched the descriptions and question types correctly."

Matching Drop-down

A Matching Drop-down question requires viewers to match each item in a column with a corresponding item from a drop-down list. Each drop-down list is identical to every other drop-down list, such that each item shown has one, and only one, correct match. To be graded as correct, a viewer has to correctly match all pairs. Quizmaker allows you to specify as many as 10 matched pairs.

A Matching Drop-down question is functionally equivalent to a Matching Drag and Drop question, and so comes with the same basic applications and recommendations. Like the Matching Drag and Drop question, the Matching Drop-down question is a good tool for testing viewers' abilities to recognize relationships and make associations. Some examples of Matching Drop-down questions are:

- Matching questions with answers.

- Matching terms with definitions or descriptions.

- Matching names with symbols or images.

- Matching specifications or calculations with the numerical values they define.

- Matching causes with effects.

- Matching procedures with operations.

- Matching principles with situations to which they apply.

Building the Matching Drop-down Question

Building the Matching Drop-down question is basically the same as building the Matching Drag and Drop question. After you select the Matching Drop-down tab and click OK from the New Graded Question dialog box, Quizmaker displays the Matching Drop-down Question window. To build the question in Form view:

1. Enter the question, which should also include instructions to click the drop-down lists to select the correct match for each item.

2. Enter the items to be matched in the Choice column, and the matching items for each Choice in the associated row of the Match column. When the quiz is previewed or published, Quizmaker will display the drop-down items in a random order that is the same for each Choice item.

3. If desired, insert media or audio and/or modify the default feedback, branching, display options, and scoring options. (See Chapter 9, "Quizmaker Basics," for details.)

4. If desired, switch to Slide view to customize the question, such as by formatting the question text box and animating the screen text or graphics. (See Chapter 12, "Pumping Up Your Questions," for details.)

Figure 10.15 shows an example of a completed Matching Drop-down question in Form view, and Figure 10.16 shows the same question as it appears in the Preview window.

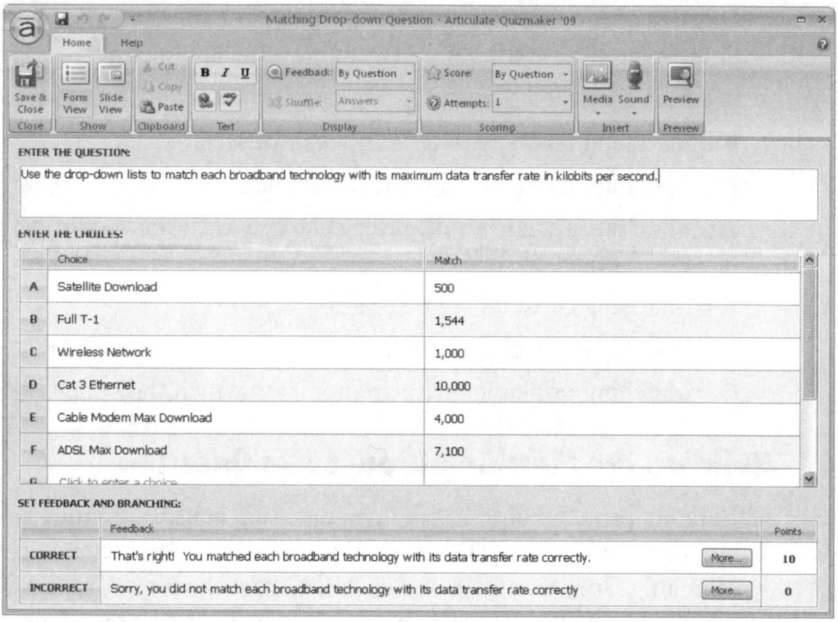

Figure 10.15. Matching Drop-down question in Form view

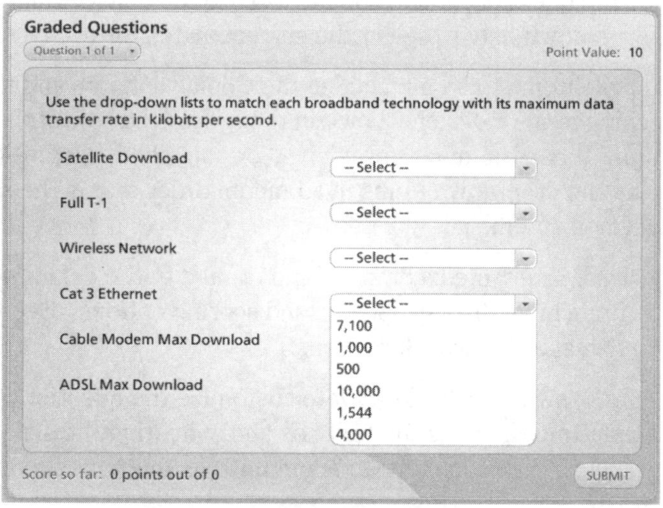

Figure 10.16. Matching Drop-down question in Preview window

Tips

■ You should remind the viewer that each match in the drop-down menu matches one and only one choice, since it is technically possible (but never correct) for the viewer to use the same match item twice. You can provide this reminder in the question or in a separate text box.

■ Although you can include up to 10 items in the drop-down menu, fewer items are less overwhelming to the viewer.

■ Note that the only feedback options available for Matching Drop-down questions are None and By Question, and that there is no By Answer option. There are too many possible response combinations to make it practical to provide different feedback for each one. Incorrect feedback should explain which pairs correctly match so the viewer knows the correct answer. For the same reason, the only Score option is By Question—because there are too many possible responses to assign a point value to each.

■ By default, Quizmaker displays correct and incorrect feedback that displays the text "You selected the correct response" and "You did not select the correct response." Since the viewer does not "select" a response when responding to a Matching Drop-down question, you may want to edit the feedback text to show something like "That's right! You matched each broadband technology with its data transfer rate correctly."

Sequence Drag and Drop

A Sequence Drag and Drop question requires the viewer to drag and drop items into a correct order, or sequence. Quizmaker allows you to include as many as 10 items in this type of question and requires that the viewer place all items in the proper sequence to be graded as correct.

A Sequence Drag and Drop question is a good tool for testing viewer knowledge of any information that can be arranged in a particular sequence, order, or hierarchy. Some examples of Sequence Drag and Drop questions are:

■   Ordering historical events.

■   Sequencing actions that comprise a process or procedure.

■   Ordering priorities.

Building the Sequence Drag and Drop Question

After you select the Sequence Drag and Drop tab and click OK from the New Graded Question dialog box, Quizmaker displays the Sequence Drag and Drop Question window. To build the question in Form view:

1.   Enter the question, which should include instructions to drag and drop the items to the correct sequence or order.

2.   Enter the items to be ordered or sequenced in the Correct Order column, in the correct order as indicated. You can add as many as 10 items. When the quiz is previewed or published, Quizmaker will shuffle the order of the draggable items.

3.   If desired, insert media or audio and/or modify the default feedback, branching, display options, and scoring options. (See Chapter 9, "Quizmaker Basics," for details.)

4.   If desired, switch to Slide view to customize the question, such as by formatting the question text box and animating the screen text or graphics. (See Chapter 12, "Pumping Up Your Questions," for details.)

Figure 10.17 shows an example of a completed Sequence Drag and Drop question in Form view, and Figure 10.18 shows the same question as it appears in the Preview window.

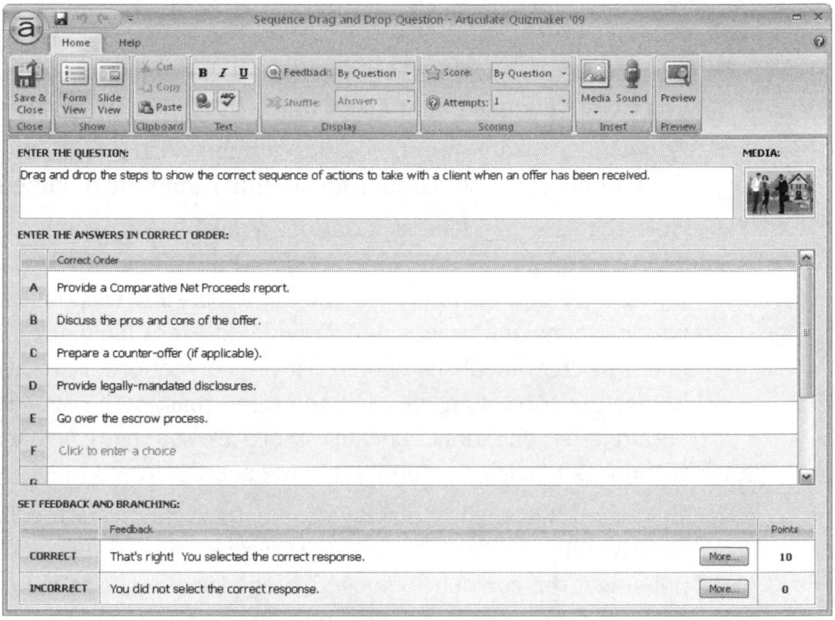

Figure 10.17. Sequence Drag and Drop question in Form view

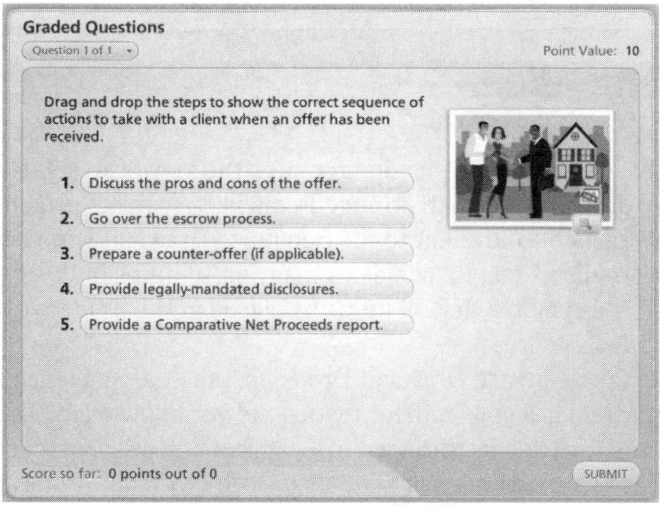

Figure 10.18. Sequence Drag and Drop question in Preview window

Tips

■ Keep in mind as you build a Sequence Drag and Drop question that you cannot control the order in which the items are displayed.

■ By default, the answer choices are numbered 1, 2, 3, 4, and so on. This numbering and number formatting cannot be modified.

■ Note that the only feedback options available for Sequence Drag and Drop questions are None and By Question, and that there is no By Answer option. There are too many possible response combinations to make it practical to provide different feedback for each one. Incorrect feedback should list the correct order so the viewer knows the correct answer. For the same reason, the only Score option is By Question—because there are too many possible responses to assign a point value to each.

■ By default, Quizmaker displays correct and incorrect feedback that displays the text "You selected the correct response" and "You did not select the correct response." Since the viewer does not "select" a response when responding to a Sequence Drag and Drop question, you may want to edit the feedback text to show something like "You put the items in the correct sequence."

Sequence Drop-down

A Sequence Drop-down question requires the viewer to select from a series of drop-down lists to arrange items into a correct sequence, and so is functionally equivalent to the Sequence Drag and Drop question. Quizmaker allows you to include as many as 10 items in this type of question and requires that all items be placed in the proper sequence to be graded as correct.

Like the Sequence Drag and Drop question, the Sequence Drop-down question is a good tool for testing viewer knowledge of any information that can be arranged in a particular sequence, order, or hierarchy. Some examples of Sequence Drop-down questions are:

■ Defining hierarchies, such as military ranks.

■ Ordering items that imply quantitative values, such as the highest mountains, the largest continents, or the fastest computer chips.

Building the Sequence Drop-down Question

Building the Sequence Drop-down question is basically the same as building the Sequence Drag and Drop question. After you select the Sequence Drop-down tab and click OK from the New Graded Question dialog box, Quizmaker displays the Sequence Drop-down Question window. To build the question in Form view:

1. Enter the question, which should include instructions to click the drop-down lists to arrange items in the correct sequence or order.

2. Enter the items to be ordered or sequenced in the Correct Order column, in the correct order as indicated. You can add as many as 10 items. When the quiz is previewed or published, Quizmaker will display the items in the drop-down lists in a random order that is the same for each list.

3. If desired, insert media or audio and/or modify the default feedback, branching, display options, and scoring options. (See Chapter 9, "Quizmaker Basics," for details.)

4. If desired, switch to Slide view to customize the question, such as by formatting the question text box and animating the screen text or graphics. (See Chapter 12, "Pumping Up Your Questions," for details.)

Figure 10.19 shows an example of a completed Sequence Drop-down question in Form view, and Figure 10.20 shows the same question as it appears in the Preview window.

Quizmaker

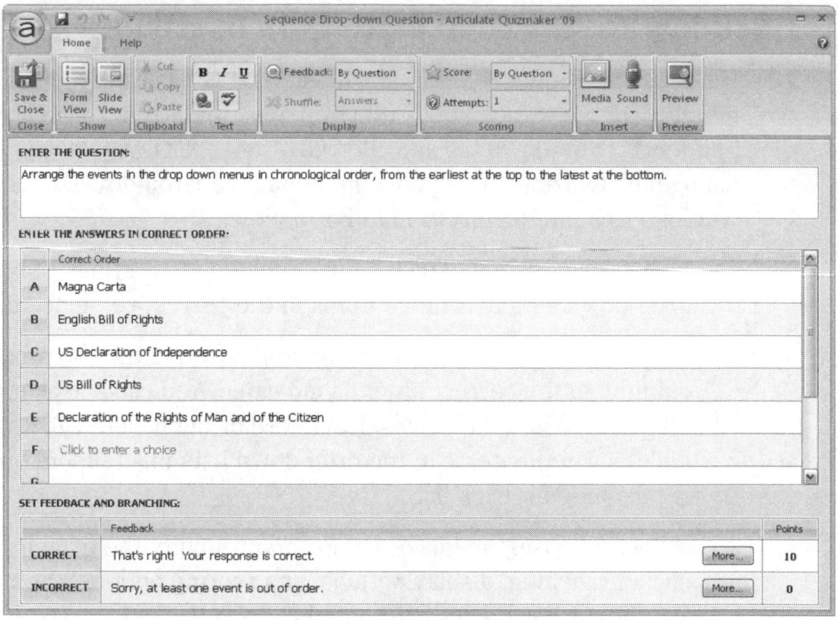

Figure 10.19. Sequence Drop-down question in Form view

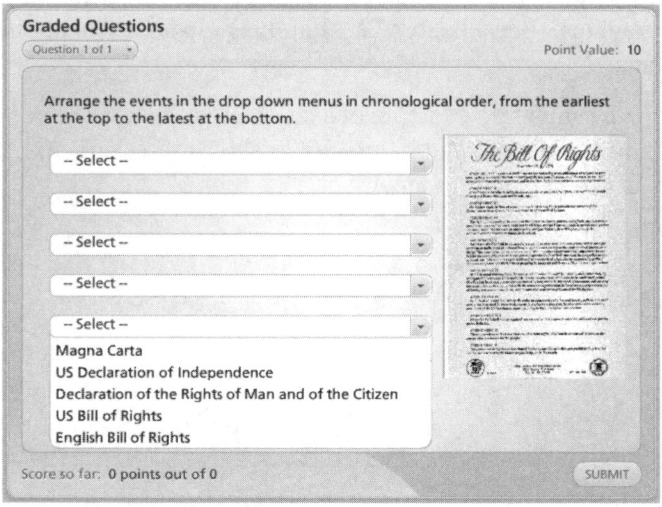

Figure 10.20. Sequence Drop-down question in Preview window

Tips

- Although functionally equivalent to the Sequence Drag and Drop question, the Sequence Drop-down question takes up less screen space and so may be a better choice when you want to show a graphic or add video media, or when there are a greater number of choices to rank.

- Like the Sequence Drag and Drop question, you cannot control the order in which the items display in the drop-down lists.

- Note that the only feedback options available for Sequence Drop-down questions are None and By Question, and that there is no By Answer option. There are too many possible response combinations to make it practical to provide different feedback for each one. Incorrect feedback should list the correct order so the viewer knows the correct answer. For the same reason, the only Score option is By Question—because there are too many possible responses to assign a point value to each.

Numeric

A Numeric question presents a question to the viewer that requires the inputting of a single numerical value into a text box. Accordingly, the Numeric question is essentially a Fill in the Blank question that accepts only one numerical value as the answer. The viewer can enter a few non-numerical characters, such as the comma and percent sign, but they are not part of the answer and are ignored by Quizmaker.

A Numeric question is, as you would expect, a good tool for testing viewers' ability to either recall or calculate a numerical value. Some examples of Numeric questions are:

- Recalling important numbers, such as the price of items for sale.

- Making calculations of any type, such as loan payments or pricing options.

Building the Numeric Question

After you select the Numeric tab and click OK from the New Graded Question dialog box, Quizmaker displays the Numeric Question window. To build the question in Form view:

1. Enter the question, which should also include instructions to type the correct value in the entry field.

2. Enter all acceptable values for the correct answer. The values can be identified by a single number, a range of numbers, or any combination of up to 10 numbers and/or ranges. For each acceptable value, click the drop-down list on the left to select a value option (such as Equal to, Between, Greater than, etc.). Then type or use the arrows to enter the numerical value or values in the field(s) in the center and right columns.

3. Using the drop-down list below the values section, specify whether *any* of the values you entered are acceptable answers, or if the value entered by the viewer must meet *all* of the criteria.

4. If desired, insert media or audio and/or modify the default feedback, branching, display options, and scoring options. (See Chapter 9, "Quizmaker Basics," for details.)

5. If desired, switch to Slide view to customize the question, such as by formatting the question text box and animating the screen text or graphics. (See Chapter 12, "Pumping Up Your Questions," for details.)

Figure 10.21 shows an example of a completed Numeric question in Form view, and Figure 10.22 shows the same question as it appears in the Preview window.

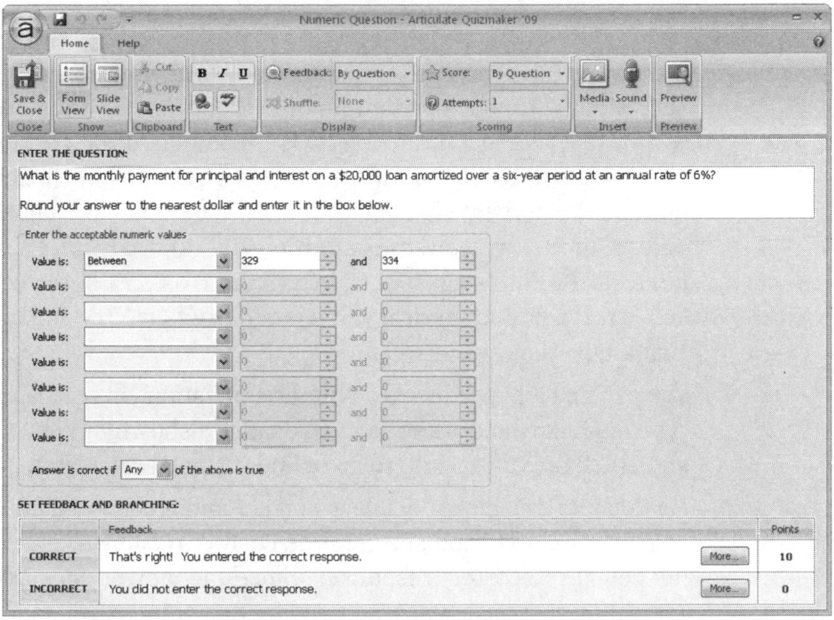

Figure 10.21. Numeric question in Form view

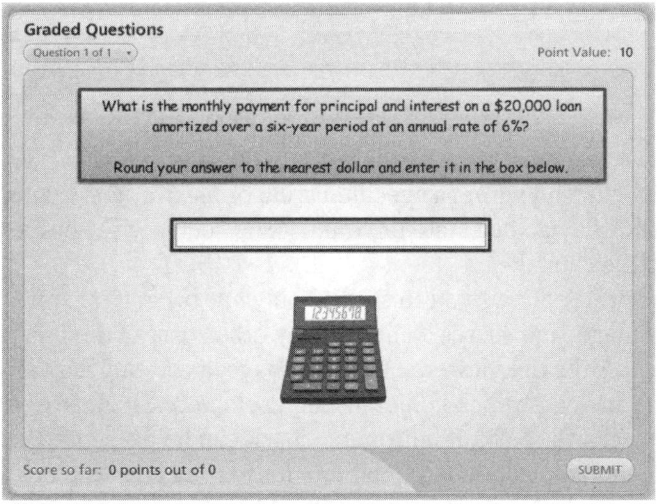

Figure 10.22. Numeric question in Preview window

Tips

■ Quizmaker does accept some non-numerical values in answers, such as the percent sign, but ignores these values when scoring a response as correct or incorrect. For example, if the viewer inputs as the answer to a Numeric question the value 10%, Quizmaker ignores the percent sign and evaluates the numerical value 10 as correct or incorrect. Because of this, you cannot *require* a non-numerical value (such as the percent sign) as part of the correct answer. If a non-numerical value is required, use the Fill in the Blank question type instead.

■ You can add a hyperlink to a Numeric question, as you can for any type of Quizmaker question. The example shown in Figures 10.21 and 10.22 provides a link to an online financial calculator.

■ By default, Quizmaker displays correct and incorrect feedback that displays the text "You selected the correct response" and "You did not select the correct response." Since the viewer does not "select" a response when responding to a Numeric question, you may want to edit the feedback text to show something like "You entered the correct value."

Hotspot

A Hotspot question requires viewers to identify an area within an image by clicking within a specified area, or *hotspot*. For example, you might show a map of a state or country and require viewers to click to identify the capital city.

Quizmaker allows you to specify only *one correct area* on a background image, and scores a click on any other part of the image as incorrect. After the viewer clicks the image, a rotating icon is displayed to indicate which point has been selected. Then, after the viewer clicks the Submit button, feedback can be presented.

A Hotspot question is a good tool for testing any type of knowledge that can be displayed and specified graphically. Some examples of Hotspot questions are:

■ Identifying a component of a machine or device, such as the correct switch on a control panel or the correct connection on the back of a computer.

■   Simulating action taken on a control panel or device.

■   Finding a location on a map.

■   Selecting the correct image among a group of images (that are merged into a single background graphic).

Building the Hotspot Question

After you select the Hotspot tab and click OK from the New Graded Question dialog box, Quizmaker displays the Hotspot Question window. To build the question in Form view:

1. Enter the question, which should also include instructions to click the correct area of the graphic and then click the Submit button.

2. Click the **Choose Image** button to open the Insert Picture dialog box, then browse and select the background graphic containing the hotspot. (Only the graphic file types supported by Quizmaker will be available in the dialog box.)

3. Click the **Add Hotspot** button to start the process of adding the correct hotspot area to the graphic.

4. You can choose the shape of the hotspot that will identify the correct area during feedback. Select **Add Oval**, **Add Rectangle**, or **Add Freeform**.

5. Using the mouse, draw the shape around the correct graphic area. Note that after you draw the shape, the Add Hotspot button changes to Remove Hotspot, which you can use to delete the hotspot and start over if necessary.

6. If desired, modify the default feedback, branching, display options, and scoring options. (See Chapter 9, "Quizmaker Basics," for details.)

7. If desired, switch to Slide view to customize the question, such as by formatting the question text box and animating the background graphic. (See Chapter 12, "Pumping Up Your Questions," for details.)

Figure 10.23 shows an example of a completed Hotspot question in Form view, and Figure 10.24 shows the same question as it appears in the Preview window.

Quizmaker

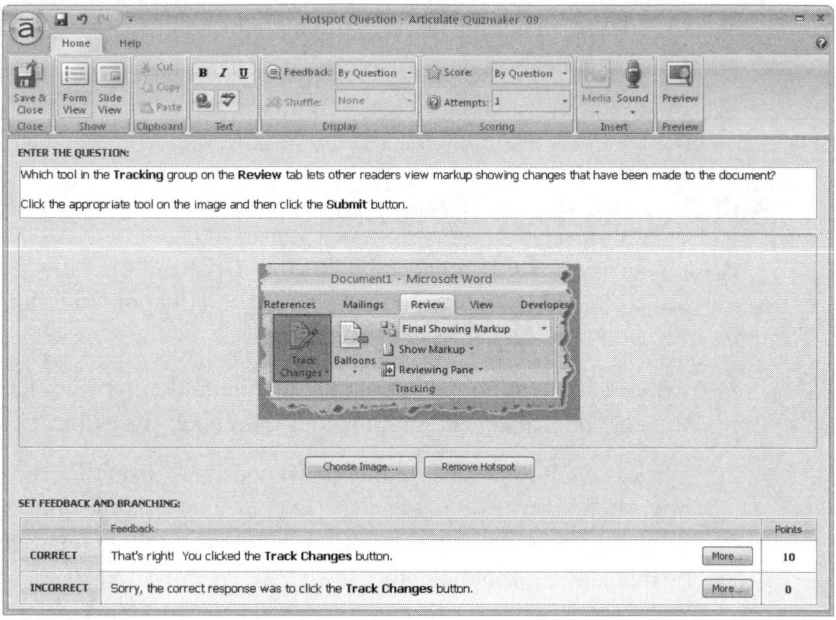

Figure 10.23. Hotspot question in Form view

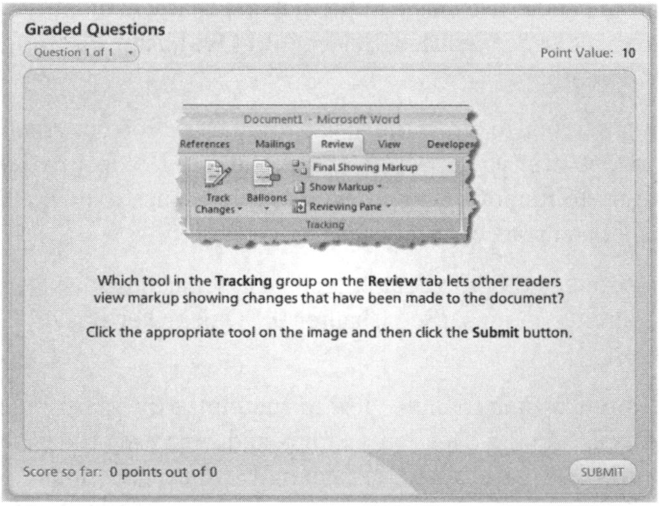

Figure 10.24. Hotspot question in Preview window

Tips

- Although you can have only one background graphic, you can have the viewer select from a number of different images by combining several images into one. For example, if you want the viewer to select among a series of musical instruments, create one graphic with all instruments.

- You can add additional images, illustrations, and text boxes to the question using Slide view. However, only the background graphic that you select using the Choose Image button serves as the hotspot image.

- Quizmaker will resize any background image to fit on the slide. However, the image will display best if the original is not too much larger or smaller than the size that displays on the screen. Keep in mind that the total Quizmaker slide area is about 686 x 424 pixels.

- You may want to use Slide view to modify the layout in order to accommodate images that are significantly taller or wider than the optimal aspect ratio. For example, if the background image tends toward vertical, you might display the question to the left of the image instead of above it. Switch to Slide view and click and drag to reposition the background image and question text.

- By default, Quizmaker displays correct and incorrect feedback that displays the text "You selected the correct response" and "You did not select the correct response." Since "response" is not a precise term for what a viewer does when responding to a Hotspot question, you may want to edit the feedback text to show something like "You selected the correct item."

Chapter Recap

Here's our list of the most important things to remember from this chapter:

■ A graded question has a correct or incorrect response(s) and a defined point value.

■ Graded questions can be used only in graded quizzes, not in surveys.

■ The tasks for building each question type are similar, but there are differences among the question types. These differences affect various features of the questions, such as scoring, answer shuffling, and feedback responses.

■ Graded questions are commonly used to determine if the learner has met the learning objectives.

■ There are two categories of graded questions: those that test whether the learner can recall content and those that test whether the learner can apply content in a realistic way. Question writers too often write recall questions when the learning objectives clearly call for application questions.

■ Two goals you should have when building a graded quiz are to make sure it is user-friendly and adequately assesses the learning objectives for which the questions are written.

■ When writing distractors for Multiple Choice and Multiple Response questions, make sure all distractors are plausible, especially to those with lower skills or lesser knowledge. These are the best types of plausible but incorrect distractors:

■ Common errors and commonly held myths or misconceptions (for those with less knowledge or skill)

■ Statements that are true but do not answer this question

■ Content that is paraphrased incorrectly

■ The True/False question presents viewers with a statement and prompts them to choose whether the statement is correct (true) or incorrect (false).

- The Multiple Choice question presents a question or a statement and asks viewers to choose from a list of possible responses.

- The Multiple Response question presents a question or a statement and asks viewers to choose from a list of possible responses, allowing them to choose more than one correct answer.

- The Fill in the Blank question presents viewers with a statement that includes a blank space into which they must type text to enter a response and complete the statement.

- The Word Bank question presents viewers with a question and as many as 10 answer choices and instructs them to drag and drop the correct answer to a drop field.

- The Matching Drag and Drop question presents viewers with a question and instructions to drag items in the right column to match items in the left column.

- The Matching Drop-down question requires viewers to match each item in a column with a corresponding item from a drop-down list.

- The Sequence Drag and Drop question requires viewers to drag and drop items into a correct order, or sequence.

- The Sequence Drop-down question requires viewers to select from a series of drop-down lists to arrange items into a correct sequence, and so is functionally equivalent to the Sequence Drag and Drop question.

- The Numeric question presents a question to the viewers, who respond by inputting a single numerical value into a text box.

- The Hotspot question requires viewers to identify an area within an image by clicking the image within a specified area, or *hotspot*.

Chapter 11

Creating Survey Questions

Chapter Snapshot

In this chapter, you'll learn how to add different types of survey questions to a Quizmaker survey in order to gather information from a group of individuals.

If you're an e-learning developer, you may need to develop survey instruments designed to gather opinion information, such as how company employees feel about the company's training programs. Each section in this chapter shows you how to design and build a different type of Quizmaker survey question. The sections follow the same structure as the sections in the previous chapter, which include basic steps for developing each question and helpful tips for each question type.

What Is a Survey Question?

A survey question collects opinion information, so there is no correct or incorrect response. A survey question, whether used in a quiz with graded questions or in a survey, with only survey questions, has no point value and is not scored.

The purpose of a survey is to gather information. A survey may be used to find out what viewers know about a topic, solicit opinions about courses or policies, or find out how they intend to act. A survey question can be closed-ended, where the respondent has to select from among listed choices, or open-ended, where the respondent can input his own answers into a text box.

Remember that both graded quizzes and surveys can contain survey questions. Quizmaker offers nine types of survey questions.

Tip: Quizmaker provides an option to convert some question types to another, similar question type. For example, you can convert a Pick One question to a Which Word question. Just right-click the Pick One question in the Quiz window and select Convert to Which Word.

Although Chapter 9, "Quizmaker Basics," explains how to start a quiz and select a question, here's a quick recap of starting a new survey question:

1. From the Quizmaker start screen, click **Create a new quiz**.

2. In the New Quiz dialog box, click the **Survey** tab or the **Graded Quiz** tab, depending on the type of quiz you want to create.

3. In the Quiz window, click the **Survey Question** button on the Home tab of the ribbon.

4. In the New Survey Question dialog box (Figure 11.1), select the question type.

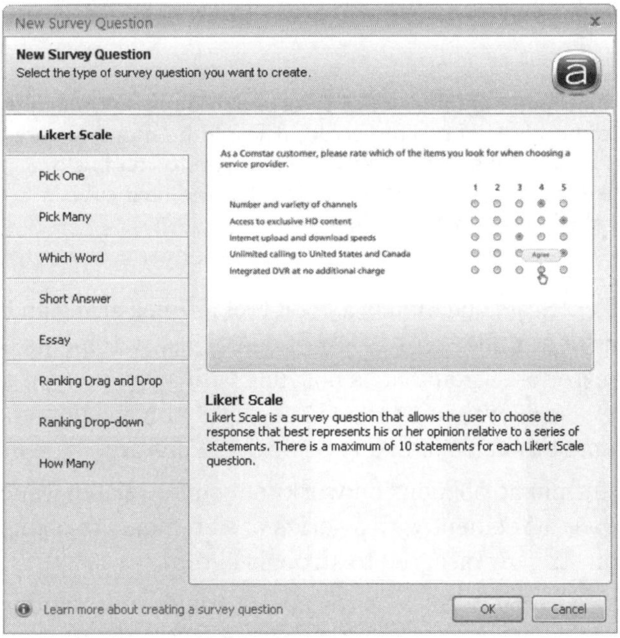

Figure 11.1. New Survey Question dialog box

Now let's learn how to create and build each type of survey question.

Likert Scale

The Likert Scale question asks viewers to use a rating scale to specify
how closely their thoughts, opinions, or feelings match a series of
questions or statements. By default, Quizmaker's Likert Scale questions provide a five-point Likert scale, which means viewers can select
a response along a five-point scale. One end of the scale represents the
most of the measured quality (such as "strongly agree") and the other
end of the scale represents the least of the measured quality (such as
"strongly disagree"). But Quizmaker allows you to modify your Likert
Scale questions to include as few as two points on the scale and as
many as 10 points.

> **Note:** Because the Quizmaker Likert scale does not match the
> rigid requirements of a Likert scale, it would be more correct to
> call this a Likert-like scale. (We're telling you to call this a
> Likert-like scale so the Ph.D. know-it-all in the next cubicle
> doesn't steal your lunch money.)

The Likert Scale question is a good tool for measuring and comparing
opinions or attitudes on a series of questions, statements or issues
with greater precision than is possible with a yes-no type question and
greater ease of evaluation than is possible with an open-ended question. Some examples of Likert Scale questions are:

- Determining opinions on work- or course-related issues by rating
  viewer agreement with a series of statements of opinion (rating
  from strongly disagree to strongly agree).

- Determining needs, desires, and attitudes toward programs, processes, and courses by rating agreement with statements about
  wants and preferences (rating from strongly disagree to strongly
  agree).

- Determining satisfaction with various aspects of programs, processes, and courses (rating from not at all satisfied to very
  satisfied).

Building the Likert Scale Question

After you select the Likert Scale tab and click OK from the New Survey Question dialog box, Quizmaker displays the Likert Scale Question window. To build the question in Form view:

1. Enter the instructions, which should tell viewers to respond to each question or statement by selecting from a five-point scale, specifying what the values at both ends of the scale represent.

2. Enter a series of as many as 10 statements about which you want to evaluate viewers' opinions or attitudes.

3. Click the **Scale** button to open the Likert Scale Labels dialog box to specify the labels to show on the Likert scale. By default, Quizmaker creates a five-point Likert scale with the labels ranging from "strongly disagree" to "strongly agree." You can edit the labels to show any values you wish. Additionally, you can create any number of value choices for the scale by creating the desired number of scale labels.

4. Also by default, the Show numbers on scale check box is selected, which specifies that the numbers 1, 2, 3, 4, and 5 display on the scale and that the scale labels do *not* display. If you want to display the scale labels, clear the Show numbers on scale check box.

5. If desired, insert media or audio and/or modify the default feedback and display options. (See Chapter 9, "Quizmaker Basics," for details.)

6. If desired, switch to Slide view to customize the question, such as by formatting the question text box and animating the screen text or graphics. (See Chapter 12, "Pumping Up Your Questions," for details.)

Figure 11.2 shows an example of a completed Likert Scale question in Form view, and Figure 11.3 shows the same question as it appears in the Preview window.

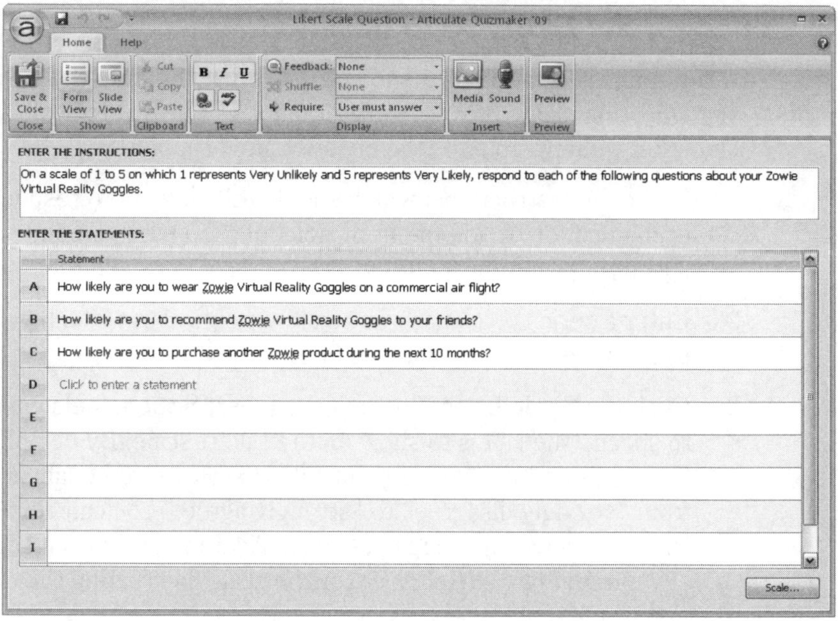

Figure 11.2. Likert Scale question in Form view

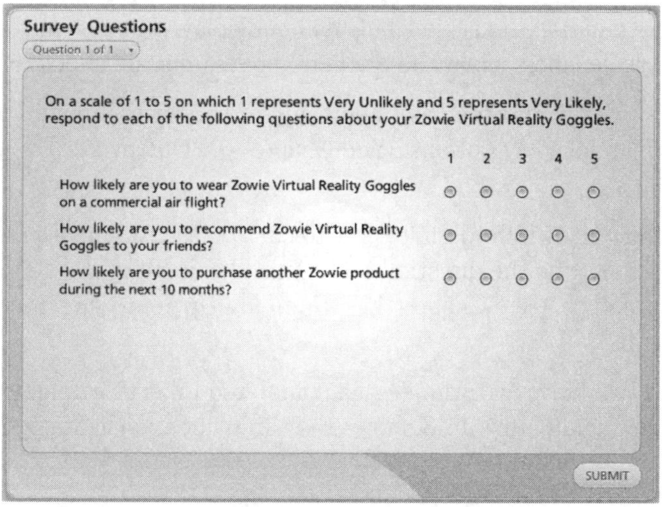

Figure 11.3. Likert Scale question in Preview window

Tips

■ Quizmaker allows you to display scale numbers or scale labels, *but not both*. If you want to display both numbers and labels, select the Show numbers on scale check box and then add text boxes in Slide view to display the labels. (See Chapter 12, "Pumping Up Your Questions," for details about adding text boxes.)

■ When you show scale labels, only the labels at the two ends of the Likert scale display when the question is previewed or published. Viewers can read the labels assigned for the remaining Likert values by moving the mouse pointer over the radio buttons.

■ Quizmaker by default does not show feedback for Likert Scale questions or for any survey question, but you can provide feedback if you select By Question from the Feedback list. Note that the only feedback options available for Likert Scale questions are None and By Question and that there is no By Answer option.

■ Note that the Shuffle list is disabled for Likert Scale questions, so the items in a Likert Scale question display in the order you list them in Form view.

Pick One

The Pick One question presents a question or statement and requires the viewer to choose *one* response from a list of up to 10 possible responses. This question type is good for determining which of a group of items is preferred, or for any comparison of responses to items that have varying degrees of correctness or value, because the viewer is forced to select only one response choice. Some examples of Pick One questions are:

■ Determining which qualities are most important.

■ Determining which problems are most difficult.

■ Determining which issues are most important.

■ Defining subgroups of viewers for branching. (See the tips later in this section.)

Building the Pick One Question

After you select the Pick One tab and click OK from the New Survey Question dialog box, Quizmaker displays the Pick One Question window. To build the question in Form view:

1. Enter the question, which may include instructions for the viewer to click the answer that best responds to the question.

2. Enter the answer choices. Quizmaker allows you to provide as many as 10 answer choices.

3. If desired, insert media or audio and/or modify the default feedback and display options. (See Chapter 9, "Quizmaker Basics," for details.)

4. If desired, switch to Slide view to customize the question, such as by formatting the question text box and animating the screen text or graphics. (See Chapter 12, "Pumping Up Your Questions," for details.)

Figure 11.4 shows an example of a completed Pick One question in Form view, and Figure 11.5 shows the same question as it appears in the Preview window.

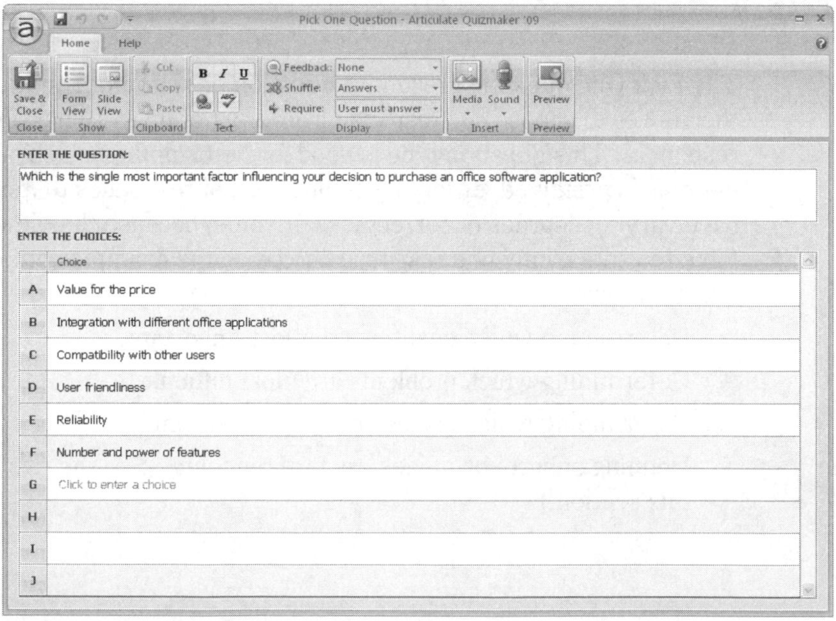

Figure 11.4. Pick One question in Form view

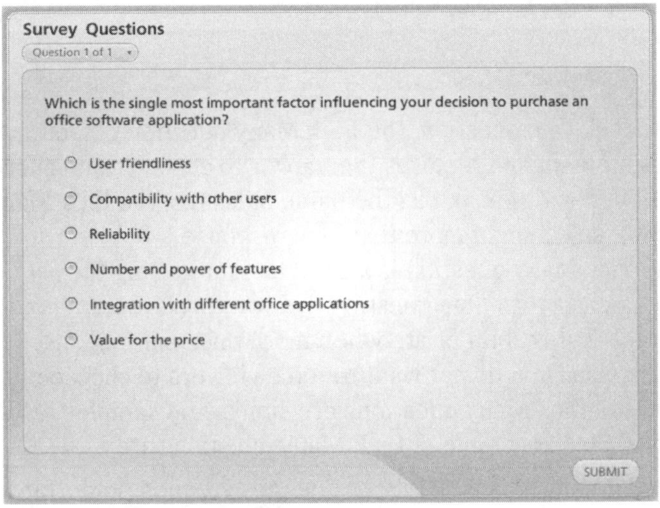

Figure 11.5. Pick One question in Preview window

Tips

■ Be sure to specify your question and answer choices carefully, so that viewer responses will provide the information you need.

■ A Pick One question with two answer choices is a good question type to divide viewers into two subgroups for branching. For example, if you want people who have taken a course to answer one group of questions and people who have not taken a course to answer another group, you could provide a Pick One question that asks whether the viewer has taken the course with the answers "yes" and "no." Then apply branching to direct each group of viewers to the desired set of questions. See Chapter 9, "Quizmaker Basics," and Chapter 13, "Pumping Up Your Quizzes," for details about branching.

Pick Many

Like the Pick One question, the Pick Many question presents a question or statement and requires the viewer to choose from a list of up to 10 possible responses, but as the name indicates, the Pick Many question allows selection of more than one response.

The Pick Many question is a good tool for getting the same type of information as a Pick One question—viewer preference among a group of choices—but is appropriate when more than one response may be appropriate and you do not want to force viewers to choose only one. Examples of Pick Many questions are similar to examples for Pick One questions. Some example of Pick Many questions are:

- Determining which quality or qualities are most important.
- Determining which problems are most difficult.
- Determining which issues are most important.

Building the Pick Many Question

After you select the Pick Many tab and click OK from the New Survey Question dialog box, Quizmaker displays the Pick Many Question window. To build the question in Form view:

1. Enter the question, including instructions for the viewers to select as many responses as apply.

2. Enter the answer choices in the Choice fields. Quizmaker allows you to provide as many as 10 answer choices.

3. If desired, insert media or audio and/or modify the default feedback and display options. (See Chapter 9, "Quizmaker Basics," for details.)

4. If desired, switch to Slide view to customize the question, such as by formatting the question text box and animating the screen text or graphics. (See Chapter 12, "Pumping Up Your Questions," for details.)

Figure 11.6 shows an example of a completed Pick Many question in Form view, and Figure 11.7 shows the same question in the Preview window.

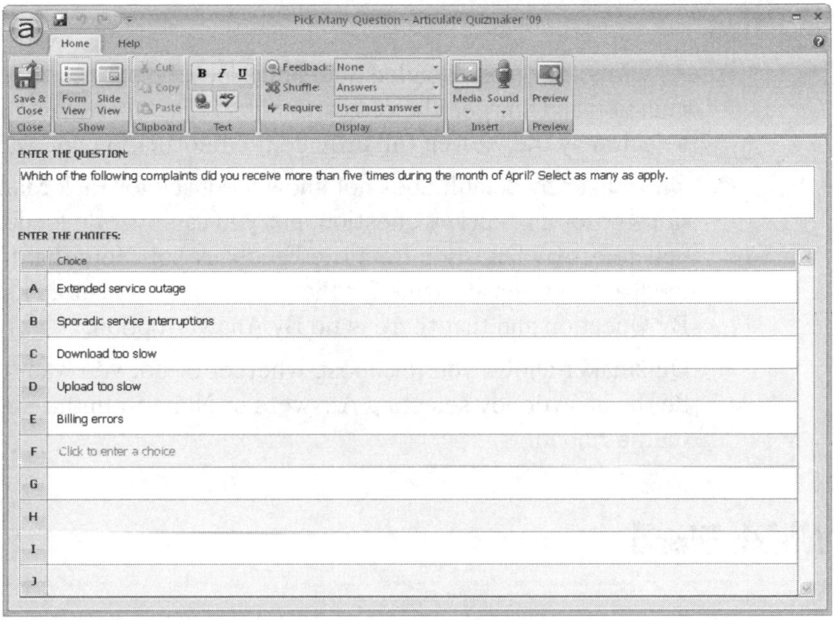

Figure 11.6. Pick Many question in Form view

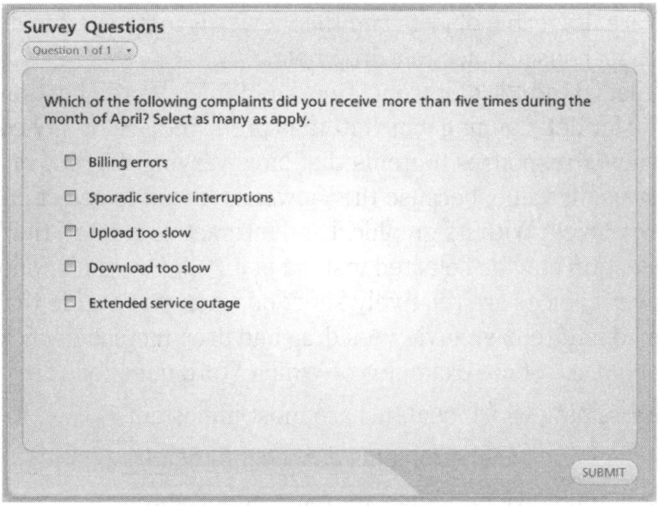

Figure 11.7. Pick Many question in Preview window

Tips

- As with other closed-ended question types, be sure to specify your question and answer choices carefully so that *all* answer choices selected by the viewer will provide the information you want.

- Quizmaker by default does not show feedback for Pick Many questions or for any survey question, but you can provide feedback if you select By Question from the Feedback list. Note that the only feedback options available for Pick Many questions are None and By Question and that there is no By Answer option.

- Quizmaker allows you to choose whether or not you want to shuffle the answers by selecting Answers or None from the Shuffle list on the ribbon.

Which Word

The Which Word question is a drag-and-drop variant of the Pick One question. Both question types present viewers with a question and as many as 10 answer choices. For the Which Word question, the answer choices are draggable objects and the viewer is instructed to drag and drop one response choice to a drop field.

Similar to the Pick One question, the Which Word question is a good tool for determining which item is preferred, or for any comparison of viewer responses to items that have varying degrees of correctness, or value, because the viewer is forced to select only one response choice. With its graphical and interactive format, the Which Word question may be selected instead of a Pick One question when the answer choices are relatively short or when you decide that there is some benefit to having viewers drag and drop instead of clicking answer choices. Some examples of Which Word questions are:

- Determining which qualities are most important.
- Determining which problems are most difficult.
- Determining which issues are most important.
- Defining subgroups of viewers for branching. (See the tips later in this section.)

Building the Which Word Question

After you select the Which Word tab and click OK from the New Survey Question dialog box, Quizmaker displays the Which Word Question window. To build the question in Form view:

1. Enter the question, which should include instructions to drag and drop the correct or preferred response to the drop field.

2. Enter the response choices in the Choice fields. Quizmaker allows you to provide as many as 10 response choices.

3. If desired, insert media or audio and/or modify the default feedback and display options. (See Chapter 9, "Quizmaker Basics," for details.)

4. If desired, switch to Slide view to customize the question, such as by formatting thc question text box and animating the screen text or graphics. (See Chapter 12, "Pumping Up Your Questions," for details.)

Figure 11.8 shows an example of a completed Which Word question in Form view, and Figure 11.9 shows the same question as it appears in the Preview window.

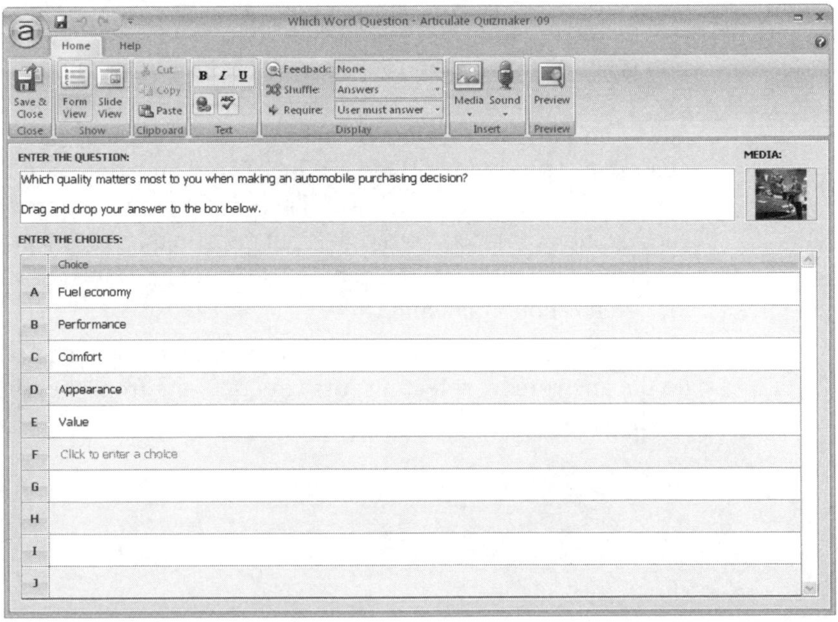

Figure 11.8. Which Word question in Form view

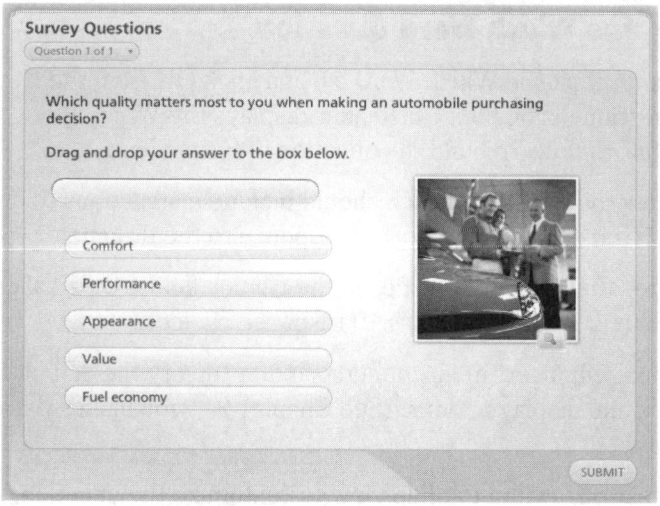

Figure 11.9. Which Word question in Preview window

Tips

- As with any multiple-choice or selection type questions, be sure to specify your question and answer choices carefully so that viewer responses will provide the information you want.

- A Which Word question with two answer choices is a good question type to specify subgroups of viewers for branching. For example, if you want to direct viewers who answer "yes" to one set of questions and the people who answer "no" to a different set of questions, you could provide a Which Word question with the answer choices "yes" and "no." Then apply branching to direct each group of viewers to the desired questions. See Chapter 9, "Quizmaker Basics," and Chapter 13, "Pumping Up Your Quizzes," for details about branching.

- Quizmaker allows you to choose whether or not you want to shuffle the answers by selecting Answers or None from the Shuffle list on the ribbon.

Short Answer

The Short Answer question presents a question or statement and asks the viewer to type a brief response (as many as 256 characters in length—a bit longer than this sentence) into a text box. Short Answer questions are one of the two open-ended question types in Quizmaker, so viewer responses are not limited to a finite number of choices. For this reason, Short Answer questions and other open-ended questions allow survey authors to gather a wider range of information, but are more difficult to interpret.

The Short Answer question is a good choice when the information you are seeking does not distill into 10 or fewer response choice categories, when you know too little about possible responses to provide explicit choices, or when you want viewers to explain their answers to another question. Some examples of Short Answer questions are:

■ Any type of opinion question to which viewers might respond with more choices than you can think of.

■ Gathering information about favorites and least-favorites.

■ Asking viewers to explain a closed-ended choice.

Building the Short Answer Question

After you select the Short Answer tab and click OK from the New Survey Question dialog box, Quizmaker displays the Short Answer Question window. To build the question in Form view:

1. Enter the question, which may include instructions to type a brief response in the text box. (In the example shown in Figure 11.11, we put the instructions in a separate text box.)

2. If desired, insert media or audio and/or modify the default feedback and display options. (See Chapter 9, "Quizmaker Basics," for details.)

3. If desired, switch to Slide view to customize the question, such as by formatting the question text box and animating the screen text or graphics. (See Chapter 12, "Pumping Up Your Questions," for details.)

Figure 11.10 shows an example of a completed Short Answer question in Form view, and Figure 11.11 shows the same question as it appears in the Preview window.

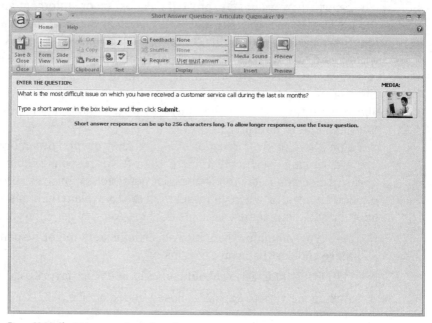

Figure 11.10. Short Answer question in Form view

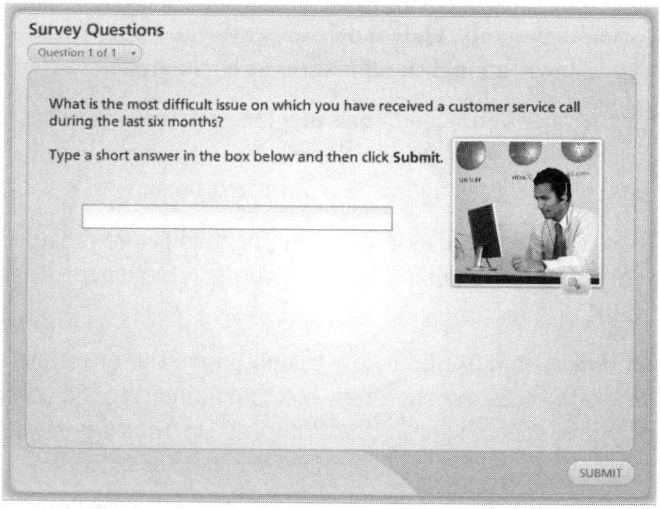

Figure 11.11. Short Answer question in Preview window

Tips

■ When writing a Short Answer question, be sure the question adequately specifies the information that you want to gather so the viewer knows what you are looking for.

■ Remember that because of the open-ended character of the Short Answer question, the only operative feedback option is By Question.

Essay

The Essay question is the other open-ended question that Quizmaker provides. But unlike the Short Answer question, the Essay question allows viewers to type a lengthy response—limited only by the author's choice of what to set as the word limit. By default, Quizmaker allows Essay question responses to be as long as 5,000 characters (several single-spaced typewritten pages), a generous allowance that will be more than adequate for most purposes. But you can set the limit for your question as low or high as you like.

The Essay question is a good tool when you want to gather complex or detailed information about viewers' knowledge, thoughts, opinions, feelings, or experience. Essay question data is difficult to interpret, but provides a depth and breadth of information beyond any other question type. Some examples of Essay questions are:

■ Asking about experiences.

■ Getting positions and opinions.

■ Understanding problems.

■ Obtaining information about preferences.

Building the Essay Question

After you select the Essay tab and click OK from the New Survey Question dialog box, Quizmaker displays the Essay Question window. To build the question in Form view:

1. Enter the question, which may include instructions to type a response of specified length in the text box.

2. If desired, insert media or audio and/or modify the default feedback and display options. (See Chapter 9, "Quizmaker Basics," for details.)

3. If desired, switch to Slide view to customize the question, such as by formatting the question text box and animating the screen text or graphics. (See Chapter 12, "Pumping Up Your Questions," for details.)

Figure 11.12 shows an example of a completed Essay question in Form view, and Figure 11.13 shows the same question as it appears in the Preview window.

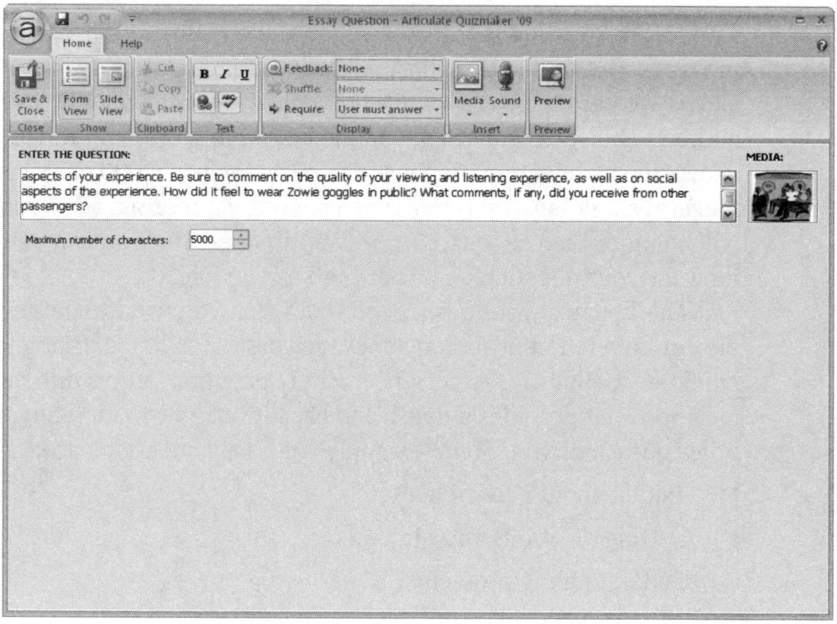

Figure 11.12. Essay question in Form view

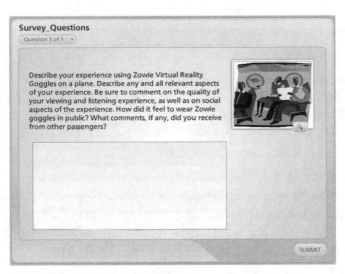

Survey_Questions

Question 1 of 1 ▾

Describe your experience using Zowie Virtual Reality Goggles on a plane. Describe any and all relevant aspects of your experience. Be sure to comment on the quality of your viewing and listening experience, as well as on social aspects of the experience. How did it feel to wear Zowie goggles in public? What comments, if any, did you receive from other passengers?

SUBMIT

Figure 11.13. Essay question in Preview window

Tips

■ Because responses to Essay questions can be lengthy and complex, be especially careful to write your question in a way that clearly specifies the information you want. Think carefully about balancing open-endedness (providing the question in an open and general way to avoid limiting the viewer's response) with specificity (which reminds the viewers to include certain items or to include responses to particular questions). The Essay question shown in Figures 11.12 and 11.13 illustrates one approach to obtaining this sort of balance.

■ Consider asking viewers to provide a certain *number* of examples, options, etc. Sometimes it is easier to get concrete information when viewers are told to provide a specific number.

Ranking Drag and Drop

The Ranking Drag and Drop question asks viewers to drag and drop up to 10 items to rank them in a preferred order. This question is a good tool for determining viewer priorities of various types. Some examples of Ranking Drag and Drop questions are:

■ Asking viewers to rank products or services.

■ Asking viewers to rank issues in terms of importance.

■ Asking viewers to evaluate items based on a specific attribute, such as ranking tasks on their perceived level of difficulty.

Building the Ranking Drag and Drop Question

After you select the Ranking Drag and Drop tab and click OK from the New Survey Question dialog box, Quizmaker displays the Ranking Drag and Drop Question window. To build the question in Form view:

1. Enter the question, which should include instructions to drag and drop the items to rank them according to specified criteria.

2. Enter the choices up to a maximum of 10.

3. If desired, insert media or audio and/or modify the default feedback and display options. (See Chapter 9, "Quizmaker Basics," for details.)

4. If desired, switch to Slide view to customize the question, such as by formatting the question text box and animating the screen text or graphics. (See Chapter 12, "Pumping Up Your Questions," for details.)

Figure 11.14 shows an example of a completed Ranking Drag and Drop question in Form view, and Figure 11.15 shows the same question as it appears in the Preview window.

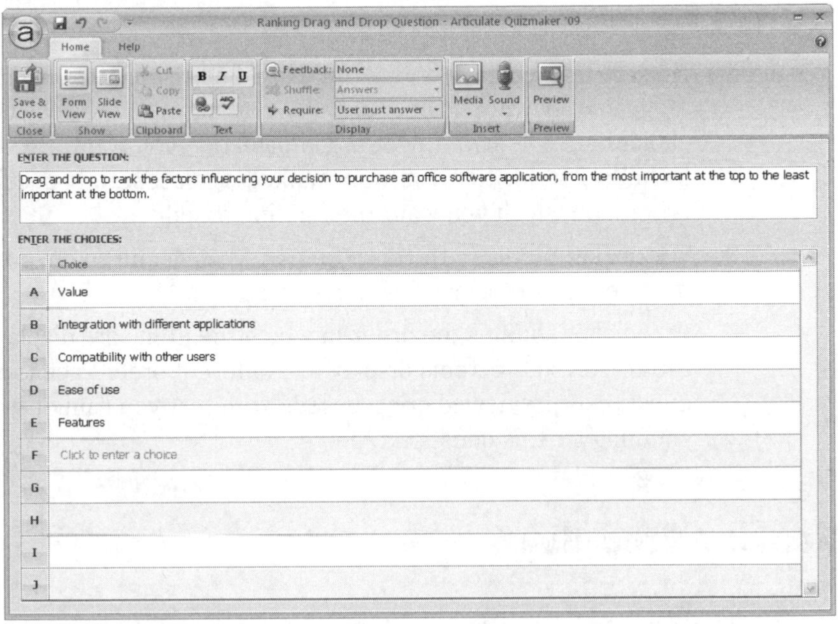

Figure 11.14. Ranking Drag and Drop question in Form view

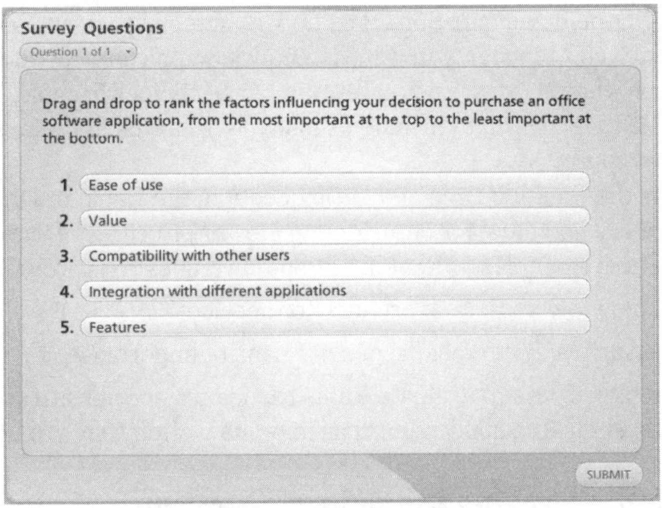

Figure 11.15. Ranking Drag and Drop question in Preview window

Tips

■ Be sure to specify your Ranking Drag and Drop question and draggable answer choices carefully, making sure the answer choices are adequate to get the information you want. Be sure to include all items that you want ranked, and accurately specify the criteria on which you want the ranking based.

■ Quizmaker numbers the drop fields 1, 2, 3, 4, and so on. You cannot override or format this numbering.

■ Quizmaker shuffles the order in which the items are displayed on the screen so the items display in a different order each time the question is previewed or accessed. Note that you cannot turn off shuffling for this question type.

Ranking Drop-down

The Ranking Drop-down question asks viewers to rank items in a preferred order by selecting from a series of drop-down lists. Although functionally equivalent to the Ranking Drag and Drop question, the Ranking Drop-down question takes up less screen space and so may be a better choice when you want to show a graphic or add video media, or when there are a greater number of choices to rank. Quizmaker allows you to include as many as 10 items in the ranking drop-down lists.

Like the Ranking Drag and Drop question, the Ranking Drop-down question is a good tool for determining viewer priorities of various types. Some examples of Ranking Drop-down questions are:

■ Asking viewers to rank products or services.

■ Asking viewers to rank issues in terms of importance.

■ Asking viewers to evaluate items based on a specific attribute, such as ranking applications based on how often they are used.

Building the Ranking Drop-down Question

Building the Ranking Drop-down question is essentially the same as building a Ranking Drag and Drop question. After you select the Ranking Drop-down tab and click OK from the New Survey Question dialog box, Quizmaker displays the Ranking Drop-down Question window. To build the question in Form view:

1. Enter the question, including instructions to use the drop-down lists to rank the items from top to bottom according to specified criteria.

2. Enter the choices up to a maximum of 10.

3. If desired, insert media or audio and/or modify the default feedback and display options. (See Chapter 9, "Quizmaker Basics," for details.)

4. If desired, switch to Slide view to customize the question, such as by formatting the question text box and animating the screen text or graphics. (See Chapter 12, "Pumping Up Your Questions," for details.)

Figure 11.16 shows an example of a completed Ranking Drop-down question in Form view, and Figure 11.17 shows the same question as it appears in the Preview window.

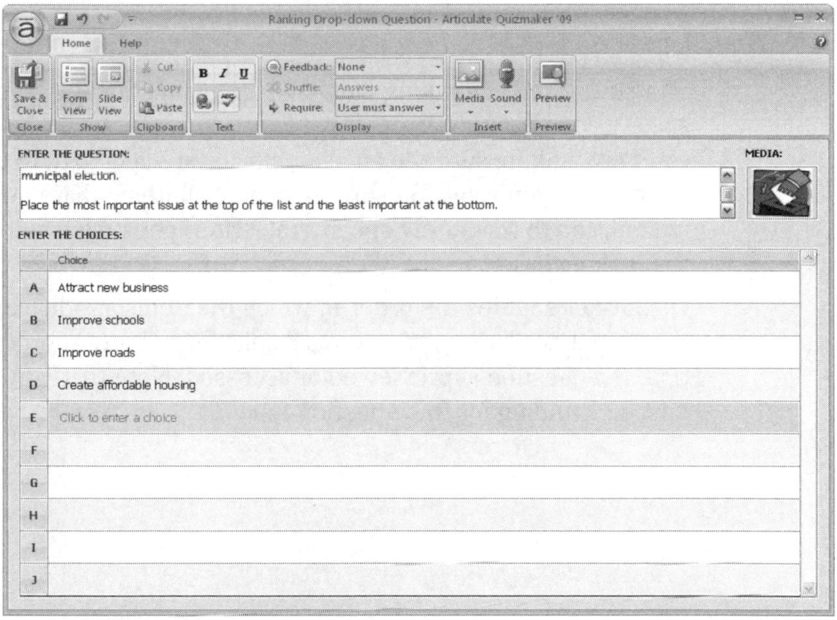

Figure 11.16. Ranking Drop-down question in Form view

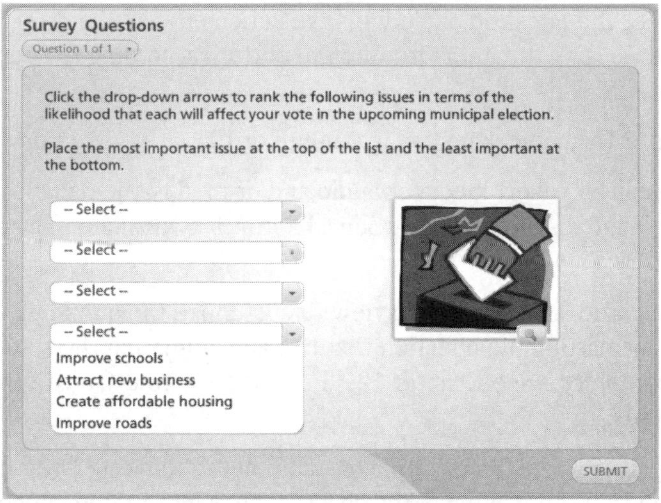

Figure 11.17. Ranking Drop-down question in Preview window

Tips

- Similar to using a Ranking Drag and Drop question, be sure to specify your Ranking Drop-down question and answer choices carefully, making sure the answer choices are adequate to get the information you want. Be sure to include all items that you want ranked, and to accurately specify the criteria on which you want the ranking based.

- Quizmaker shuffles the order in which the items are displayed in the drop-down lists, so the items display in a different order each time the question is previewed or accessed. Note that you cannot turn off shuffling for this question type.

How Many

The How Many question presents viewers with a question or statement and asks them to respond by inputting a single numeric value. This question type could be considered open-ended, but viewers can only input a numeric value. It can be a good tool for gathering quantitative information that cannot be reduced to 10 or fewer choices. Some examples of a How Many question are:

■ Getting demographic information from viewers such as age and years of service.

■ Determining how many occurrences of a specified circumstance have taken place, such as how many complaints they have received of a particular type.

Building the How Many Question

After you select the How Many tab and click OK from the New Survey Question dialog box, Quizmaker displays the How Many Question window. To build the question in Form view:

1. Enter the question, which should include instructions to enter a numeric response in the text box.

2. If desired, insert media or audio and/or modify the default feedback and display options. (See Chapter 9, "Quizmaker Basics," for details.)

3. If desired, switch to Slide view to customize the question, such as by formatting the question text box and animating the screen text or graphics. (See Chapter 12, "Pumping Up Your Questions," for details.)

Figure 11.18 shows an example of a completed How Many question in Form view, and Figure 11.19 shows the same question as it appears in the Preview window.

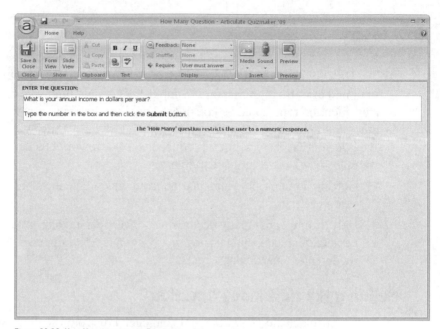

Figure 11.18. How Many question in Form view

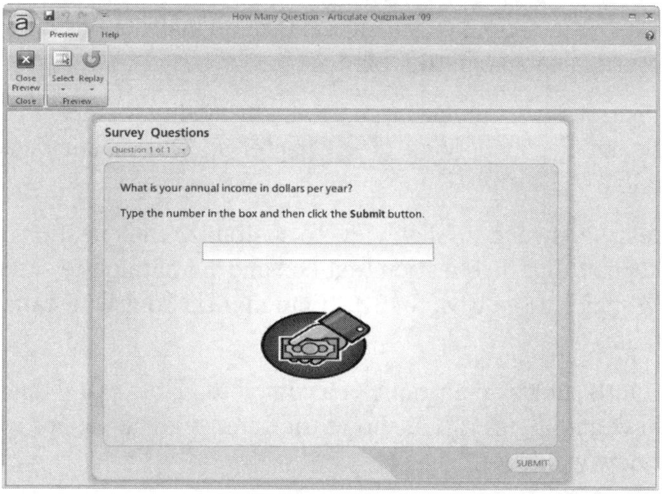

Figure 11.19. How Many question in Preview window

Tips

- If you are asking for personal information (such as age), explain how it will be used or make answering the question optional.

- If you are asking for a preference-oriented number, you may want to add some reality-based limits so the viewer knows the range of answers that might be considered "normal." For example, when asking how many hours people are willing to wait for a help desk return call, you may want to add that the range of possible hours is 4 to 24 hours.

Chapter Recap

Here's our list of the most important things to remember from this chapter:

- The purpose of a survey is to gather information. A survey question has no correct or incorrect response and no point value, and the viewer is not scored on the responses.

- Both graded quizzes and surveys can contain survey questions.

- The tasks for building each question type are similar, but there are differences among the question types. These differences affect various features of the questions, such as scoring, answer shuffling, and feedback responses.

- The Likert Scale question asks viewers to use a multi-point rating scale to specify how closely their thoughts, opinions, or feelings match a series of questions or statements.

- The Pick One question presents a question or statement and requires viewers to choose one response from a list of possible responses.

- The Pick Many question presents a question or statement and asks the viewer to choose one or more responses from a list of possible responses.

- The Which Word question presents viewers with a question and a series of answer choices, from which they can drag and drop one response to a drop field.

- The Short Answer question presents a question or statement and asks viewers to type a brief response into a text box.

- The Essay question is an open-ended question that asks viewers to type a lengthy response an essay in a text box.

- The Ranking Drag and Drop question asks viewers to drag and drop a series of items to rank them in a preferred order.

- The Ranking Drop-down question asks viewers to rank items in a preferred order by selecting from a series of drop-down lists.

- The How Many question is an open-ended question that presents viewers with a question or statement and asks them to respond by inputting a numeric value.

Chapter 12

Pumping Up Your Questions

Chapter Snapshot

In this chapter, you'll learn how to pump up your questions by moving beyond the default features of Quizmaker's built-in question types.

The question text, answer choices, and feedback text form the foundation of a Quizmaker question, but there's plenty more you can do to create a rich and engaging question. The Articulate web site and blogs provide some fantastic examples of sophisticated question slides that were built using Quizmaker's tools. Our goal in this chapter is to give you the skills to use these tools and to provide some ideas for making your questions more engaging. Once you have a handle on these tools, we expect you to visit the web site and dig deeper into those examples!

Revisiting the Quizmaker 1-2-3-4-5 Workflow

If you've read the previous chapters about Quizmaker, you should have a handle on starting a quiz and building basic questions—steps 1, 2, and 3 in the Quizmaker 1-2-3-4-5 workflow. Now we're going to focus on the second part (b) of step 3 in the workflow—customizing, or "pumping up," your question slides, as shown in Figure 12.1. Table 12.1 shows all of the substeps typically completed in step 3 of the Quizmaker 1-2-3-4-5 workflow.

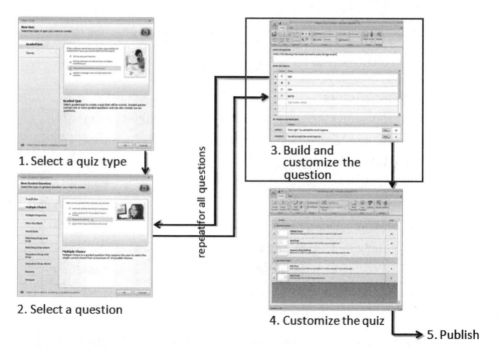

Figure 12.1. Quizmaker 1-2-3-4-5 workflow

Table 12.1. Detailed workflow for step 3

Step	Description
3. Build and customize the question	a) Add the content elements required by the selected question, such as question text, answer choices, and feedback. b) Customize the question by adding a variety of other features, such as images, audio, and animation effects.

Quizmaker lets you add images and movies to your slides, as well as add animation effects to objects. You can create your own graphic objects using shapes and text boxes, add a hyperlink on a slide that opens a web page, and change colors, fonts, and background using design themes. The Quizmaker timeline lets you bring your slides to life by having objects appear on (and disappear from) the slide at different times. In this chapter, we'll step through how to use each of these great features and provide some ideas for when to use them.

A Little Is Good, but Too Much Is...

Although it is possible to add media, animations, and timings to your question slides, always think first and foremost about what the person using the quiz needs. If the quiz is graded, don't add anything that distracts learners from the task at hand, which is passing the quiz. Research shows that learners can be easily overwhelmed when dealing with complex multimedia screens. So err on the side of caution, especially with graded quizzes.

Adding Media

Quizmaker uses the term *media* to refer to still images (pictures) and Flash movies. These graphic elements can help describe the question or answer choices on a question slide, as well as complement content on a non-question slide. Following are some ideas for using images and movies in quizzes:

- **Question text:** A media file can clarify the question or can be used as the question itself. For example, insert a movie showing a technical procedure and then ask a question about that procedure. Or insert a still image and ask the viewer to identify the image.

- **Answer choices:** Media files can be used instead of answer text or along with answer text. For example, insert images of four pieces of equipment and ask the viewer to identify the correct piece of equipment.

- **Results slide:** Media files can be added to the Results slide. (This slide also comes with a default image, which you can replace.) A media file can also serve as a hyperlink to related information or to a certificate.

- **Non-question slides:** You can use blank slides to build an introduction to the quiz or to provide additional information between questions in the quiz. Images or movies on these slides can act as graphic reminders. For example, add an image of a map to the introduction slide that you create for a geography quiz.

- **Surveys:** If you are building a survey, you may want to add media that provides additional information to help respondents form an opinion.

---

66 **Note:** Don't use media gratuitously. That is, media should always have a purpose other than to "dress up" slides and questions. If it doesn't have a clear purpose, viewers will wonder how the image or media relates to the question. Better to not confuse or overwhelm them with anything that is unrelated to the task at hand.

In case you're wondering, you *cannot* add an image or movie to the standard feedback pop-up box. You can, however, create a custom feedback slide using the Blank Slide feature. This slide can contain images and movies. Chapter 13, "Pumping Up Your Quizzes," explains how to work with blank slides.

Although you can add a media file in Form view, you have much more flexibility adding media files in Slide view. The following sections cover how to add images and movies in both views.

Video vs. Movie

If you've read the Engage sections of this book or have worked with Engage, you may have noticed that Flash movie files are referred to as *video* files in Engage. Although the terminology is different, the files are the same. You can insert .swf and .flv files into Engage interactions and Quizmaker questions.

Before You Add Any Media!!!

Many of the things you can do with questions that are discussed in this chapter are fun to play with (and fun is good). But some of these are inappropriate for graded tests because they can be distracting or frustrating or worse. In Chapter 3, "Introduction to Presenter," we discussed the topic of frustrating or confusing viewers. We recommend that you read that section before considering whether the things you wish to add are appropriate uses of media. For example, while it might be appropriate to develop study questions with sound effects and marching band music for your third-grade class to use to study American history, it would be far less appropriate to use that same media in a certification exam that determines who is eligible for the selection pool for a promotion. It might be fine to use crazy animations and sound effects on self-check questions to help students prepare for a music theory final, but it'd be less appropriate to use these same effects for the actual final.

We don't want to limit your fun, however. Go crazy building five will-you-marry-me quiz questions for your soon-to-be fiancée and the practice quiz you develop for your driver's ed students. But use restraint on a business ethics end-of-course quiz, and don't even think about using any gratuitous media for the certification exam.

Adding and Formatting Images

An image is a "still" picture and can be created using a variety of graphic programs, resulting in a variety of media file types. Quizmaker supports graphics in JPG (or JPEG), EMF, WMF, TIF, BMP, GIF, and PNG formats. For screenshots, the best file type to use in Articulate programs is PNG because it uses *lossless compression*—your file will look the same as the original image if it's not scaled (enlarged or reduced).

When creating or selecting graphics, keep in mind that the entire slide content area is about 686 x 424 pixels. Given that a significant portion of the slide will contain the questions and answer choices (or other content), the optimal graphic size should be much smaller. Although Quizmaker will scale down (reduce) graphics to enable them to fit on the slide, the best quality will result if you insert an image that does *not* need to be scaled down. When graphics are scaled down, quality is lost. So try to use graphics that are small enough to fit in the slide without having to be reduced by Quizmaker.

Once you have created or obtained the images for a quiz, you can insert them into your quiz slides (Figure 12.2). Although you can insert an image in Form view, you have more flexibility inserting images in Slide view. We'll cover both methods next.

Figure 12.2. Question slide with image

Adding an Image in Form View

Quizmaker lets you add just one media file in Form view, which is automatically inserted next to the question text. You can then move and customize the image or movie by switching to Slide view.

To add an image in Form view:

1. Open the question in Form view.

2. Click the **Media** button on the Home tab of the ribbon.

3. From the Media menu, select **Picture**.

4. In the Insert Picture dialog box, browse to the image file and then double-click it.

A thumbnail of the inserted picture is displayed to the right of the question text in the newly displayed Media pane (Figure 12.3).

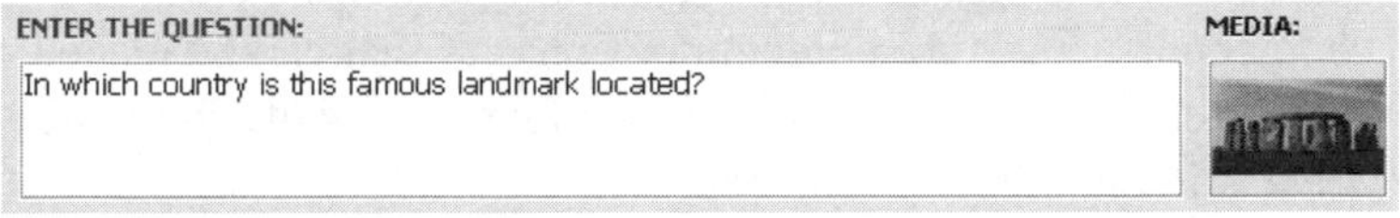

ENTER THE QUESTION: MEDIA:

In which country is this famous landmark located?

Figure 12.3. Form view showing media file inserted

If you want to replace an image with another picture or movie, double-click the thumbnail image in the Media pane and select another file from the Change Image dialog box. (Or just repeat the steps to add an image; Quizmaker will replace the old image with the new one.) To remove the image in Form view, click the Media button and select Remove Media.

Adding Images in Slide View

Because Slide view offers a freeform development environment, you can add multiple media files to the slide, position them where you want, and format them.

To add an image in Slide view:

1. Open a question in Slide view.

2. Click the **Picture** button on the Insert tab of the ribbon.

3. In the Insert Picture dialog box, browse to the image file and then double-click it.

By default, Quizmaker places the image in the center of the slide. If the size of the original image is larger than the slide, Quizmaker will reduce the image size to fit the slide. Once the image has been inserted, you can:

■ **Move the image** to another location on the slide by dragging it.

■ **Resize the image** by dragging any of its handles on the selection border. (Remember that scaling the image reduces quality.)

■ **Format the image** using the Picture Tools Format tab (covered shortly).

> **Tip:** To remove an image added in Slide view, you must delete it in Slide view. An image added in Slide view does not show up in Form view.

If you want to use images as answer choices in a question, keep in mind that the images are not technically part of the answer choice components. They are independent objects that can be placed over the answer choice text boxes. Due to this arrangement, you need to make a few adjustments to the answers.

To use images as answer choices:

1. When you build the question, create each answer choice using the text "a, b, c" or "1, 2, 3" etc.

2. In Slide view, insert each image as described earlier.

3. Position each image next to an answer choice.

4. Click the **Options** tab on the ribbon.

5. Using the Shuffle list, change the shuffle option to **None**.

It's important to turn off answer shuffling because the images are not "attached" to the answer choices. If the answers are shuffled during the quiz, then the answer choices will appear in a different order while the images will stay in the same place. Figure 12.4 shows an example of a question using images as answer choices.

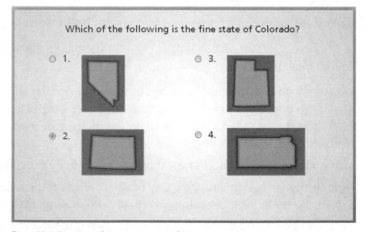

Figure 12.4. Question with images as answer choices

Formatting Images in Slide View

Once you add an image to a slide you can format it in a variety of ways using the Picture Tools Format tab on the ribbon (Figure 12.5). This context-sensitive tab becomes available after you select an image on the slide. Once the tab appears on the ribbon, you can click it to activate it.

Figure 12.5. Slide view Question window ribbon, Picture Tools Format tab

Formatting images in Quizmaker is very similar to formatting images in any Office 2007 application, such as PowerPoint. For that reason, we won't go into too much detail here. Table 12.2 describes the groups on the Picture Tools Format tab, which gives you an idea of how you can format an image after selecting it. Note that you can apply formats to multiple images at once by selecting the images together (Ctrl+click each image).

Table 12.2. Picture Tools Format tab groups on the Question window ribbon

Group	Description
Close	Contains the button to save the current question and close the Question window
Show	Contains the buttons to switch between Form view and Slide view
Adjust	Contains tools to adjust the brightness, contrast, and color of the image. The Change Picture button lets you swap the image for a different one while keeping the format properties. The Reset Picture button serves to undo many of the format properties you've applied to the image.
Picture Styles	Contains tools to apply a predefined style to the image and apply individual style properties to the image. Style properties include the picture shape (e.g., modify it so it appears as a triangle or other shape), picture border (e.g., color and weight), and picture effects (e.g., shadow).
Arrange	Contains tools to control the position of the image on the slide, such as bringing it in front of others, aligning it with a group of objects, and rotating it

Group	Description
Size	Contains tools to change the width and height of the image by entering specific pixel values. Note that you can also resize the image by dragging one of its selection border handles. The Zoom Picture button applies the Zoom feature to the image, which enables viewers to enlarge the image during the quiz. The Crop button lets you crop out (remove) parts of the image.
Preview	Contains the button to preview the current question in the Quizmaker player

Adding and Formatting Flash Movies

Quizmaker enables you to insert two types of Flash video (movie) files into questions: .swf (Flash) and .flv (Flash video). These movies can be produced using the Adobe Flash program, as well as by using many other programs. If you have Video Encoder '09, which comes with Articulate Studio '09, you can use it to convert most standard video formats to .flv files.

Tip: A video longer than 60 seconds should be in FLV format instead of SWF format. A video in a .swf file over 60 seconds in length will have audio synchronization issues in the Flash player when it is published.

As discussed in the section "Adding and Formatting Images," keep in mind that the slide content area is 686 x 424 pixels. However, you can specify that the movie is displayed in a separate browser window, which means movies with larger dimensions can be used. (But remember that if a video is launched in a new browser window, the video browser window could overlap or obscure the Quizmaker player window.) Figure 12.6 shows a movie on a question slide.

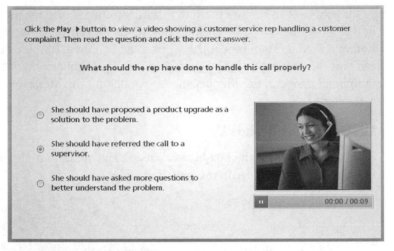

Figure 12.6. Question slide with a movie

Although you can insert a video in Form view, you have more flexibility inserting videos in Slide view. We'll cover both methods next.

Adding a Movie in Form View

Quizmaker lets you add just one media file in Form view, which is automatically inserted next to the question text. You can then move and customize the image or movie by switching to Slide view.

To add a movie in Form view:

1. Open the question in Form view.

2. Click the **Media** button on the Home tab of the ribbon.

3. From the Media menu, select **Flash**.

4. In the Insert Flash dialog box, browse to the movie file and then double-click it.

5. In the Flash Movie Properties dialog box, select the options you want and click **OK**. (These options are covered in just a bit.)

A thumbnail of the inserted video is displayed to the right of the question text in the newly displayed Media pane.

If you want to replace the movie with another movie (or picture), first remove the movie by clicking the Media button and selecting Remove Media. Then repeat the steps to add a movie (or picture). You can edit the properties of the current movie by double-clicking the thumbnail image in the Media pane or by clicking the Media button and selecting Flash.

Adding Movies in Slide View

Slide view gives you the flexibility to insert and position multiple Flash movies anywhere on the question slide.

To add a movie in Slide view:

1. Open a question in Slide view.

2. Click the **Flash** button on the Insert tab of the ribbon.

3. In the Insert Flash dialog box, browse to the movie file and then double-click it.

4. In the Flash Movie Properties dialog box, select the options you want and click **OK**. (These options are covered next.)

By default, Quizmaker places the movie in the center of the slide. Once the movie has been inserted, you can:

■ **Move the movie** to another location on the slide by dragging it.

■ **Resize the movie** by dragging any of its handles on the selection border.

■ **Customize the movie** using the Movie Tools Options tab (covered shortly).

Selecting Flash Movie Properties

When you insert a movie in either Form view or Slide view, the Flash Movie Properties dialog box is displayed immediately after you select the movie file. This dialog box lets you control how the movie functions. Figure 12.7 shows the default values selected, and Table 12.3 describes all the options on the dialog box.

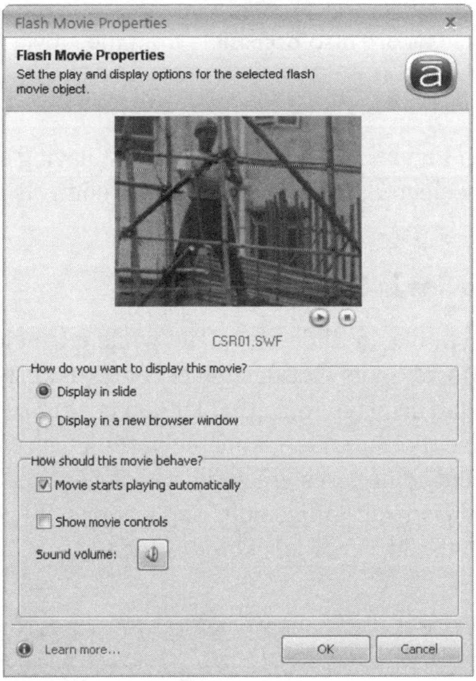

Figure 12.7. Flash Movie Properties dialog box

Table 12.3. Flash Movie Properties dialog box options

Option	Description
Display in slide	Displays the movie file in the slide instead of in a separate window
Display in a new browser window	Displays the movie file in a separate browser window after the viewer clicks the Play button or clicks the movie
Movie starts playing automatically	Starts the movie automatically when the question slide is displayed. Note that this option is not available if you have selected the Display in a new browser window option.
Show movie controls	Displays the Playbar on the movie, which includes the Pause/Play button and a progress bar
Browser controls	This option is available only when the Display in a new browser window option is selected. You can select whether browser features (menu bar, toolbar, address bar) are displayed when the movie is running in the browser window.
Sound volume	Click the sound icon to increase or decrease (or mute) the sound level of the movie.

66   Note: Some of these options are also accessible from the Movie Tools Options tab on the ribbon.

For the example used in Figure 12.6, the Movie starts playing automatically option was unselected, and the Show movie controls option was selected.

Customizing Flash Movies in Slide View

After you insert a Flash movie in Slide view (and while it is selected), the context-sensitive Movie Tools Options tab becomes available (Figure 12.8). Clicking this tab displays tools that let you customize the movie file. Some of these tools are also available in the Flash Movie Properties dialog box, and some tools are similar to the options you may be familiar with in Microsoft Office 2007 applications. Table 12.4 describes the groups on the Movie Tools Options tab.

Figure 12.8. Slide view Question window ribbon, Movie Tools Options tab

Table 12.4. Movie Tools Options tab groups on the Question window ribbon in Slide view

Group	Description
Close	Contains the Save & Close button, which saves the current question and closes the Question window
Show	Contains the buttons to switch between Form view and Slide view
Play	Contains the Preview button, which plays a preview of the movie on the slide
Movie Options	Contains options that are also accessible from the Flash Movie Properties dialog box. (See Table 12.3 for descriptions.) Note that you can click the diagonal arrow button 🔲 to the right of the Movie Options group name to open the Flash Movie Properties dialog box.
Arrange	Contains tools to control the position of the movie on the slide, such as bringing it in front of others and aligning it with a group of objects
Size	Contains tools to change the width and height of the movie by entering specific pixel values. Note that you can also resize the movie by dragging one of its selection border handles. Keep in mind that resizing the movie affects only its appearance on the slide. If you configure the movie to be displayed in a separate browser window, the movie will be played at full size.

Group	Description
Preview	Contains the button to preview the current question in the Quizmaker player. Note that if you configure the movie to be displayed in a separate browser window, you cannot preview that functionality.

Practice 1

If you have an image file and a movie file (.swf or .flv) handy, you can practice creating a question that contains both of these objects. Note that this practice relies on your knowledge of how to create a new question (covered in Chapter 9, "Quizmaker Basics").

Adding an Image and Movie

1. Create a new Multiple Choice question in Form view by adding a question and several answer choices.

2. Click the **Media** button on the Home tab of the ribbon.

3. From the Media menu, select **Picture**.

4. In the Insert Picture dialog box, browse to the image file and then double-click it.

5. Notice the thumbnail image to the right of the question text. Click the **Slide View** button on the Home tab of the ribbon to switch to Slide view.

6. Using the mouse, drag the image to the lower-left corner of the slide.

7. Click the **Format** tab under Picture Tools on the ribbon. (If the Format tab is not available, make sure the image is selected.)

8. Click the down-arrow button ⬇ next to the thumbnail icons in the Picture Styles group.

9. From the Picture Styles menu, select **Simple Frame, Black** (the tooltip displays the style name).

10. Click the **Picture Effects** button on the ribbon.

11. From the Picture Effects menu, select **Shadow**, and then select one of the effects in the Outer section.

12. Click the **Insert** tab on the ribbon and then click the **Flash** button.

13. In the Insert Flash dialog box, browse to the Flash movie file and then double-click it.

14. In the Flash Movie Properties dialog box, select the **Show movie controls** check box and click **OK**.

15. Using the mouse, drag the movie to the lower-right corner of the slide.

16. Click the **Options** tab under Movie Tools on the ribbon. (If the Options tab is not available, make sure the movie is selected.)

17. Click the **Movie Volume** button on the ribbon and select **Low**.

18. If necessary, resize the Flash movie by dragging its handles with the mouse or by entering new dimensions in the **Width** and **Height** boxes on the ribbon.

19. Preview the movie by clicking the **Preview** button in the Play group on the ribbon.

20. Preview the slide by clicking the **Preview** button in the Preview group on the ribbon.

Adding Audio

Quizmaker lets you add audio clips to slides and to feedback responses. You can record an audio clip or import one from another source. Here are some ideas for using audio in your quiz slides:

■ **Question slide:** Expand on the question text to give more background. (But don't read the question text verbatim.) Include additional instructions for selecting the correct answer(s). Use audio for questions related to listening skills.

■ **Non-question slide:** Provide a friendly narration on an introduction slide or give verbal pointers on review slides.

■ **Results slide:** Offer congratulations on the Pass Result slide or motivation on a Fail Result slide. You can even add sound effects, such as applause, just for fun.

■ **Feedback:** Complement the feedback text with additional information about the correct or incorrect response.

- **Any slide:** Play background music for quizzes that are not graded. For example, patriotic music for study questions in a third-grade history quiz.

- **Surveys:** Use a brief audio message to introduce a survey and describe how the survey information will be used.

> **Note:** An audio clip is attached to a specific slide or feedback pop-up, not to the overall quiz.

Can the Viewer Start or Stop the Audio?

The short answer is *no*, but there is a workaround to this. If you want your viewers to control the audio, you can insert a Flash movie that contains audio and a static image. Viewers can use the movie controls to start/stop the audio. This is helpful when you'd like viewers to listen to an audio clip, such as a customer service conversation, and then answer a question. Adding Flash movies was covered earlier in this chapter.

Quizmaker supports .wav and .mp3 audio files. (To learn more about these files types, refer to Quizmaker Help.) If you're importing audio, Articulate recommends .wav files because Articulate's compression technology is designed for speech; the .mp3 files you already have may not be designed this way. If you're recording your own audio, you'll need a good microphone. (Chapter 5, "Presenter Basics," provides more information about using microphones.)

Adding Audio to Slides

You can add one or more audio clips to question slides, non-question (blank) slides, and Results slides. The audio begins playing when the slide is displayed. You can add one clip using Form view, and add multiple clips using Slide view. The procedures are basically the same for both views, so we'll just cover how to add one audio clip in Form view now. Later, we'll cover switching to Slide view to customize the audio and add additional audio clips.

Quizmaker lets you record your own audio "on the fly" or import an existing audio clip using the Sound menu on the Form view ribbon (Figure 12.9). Let's look at both options.

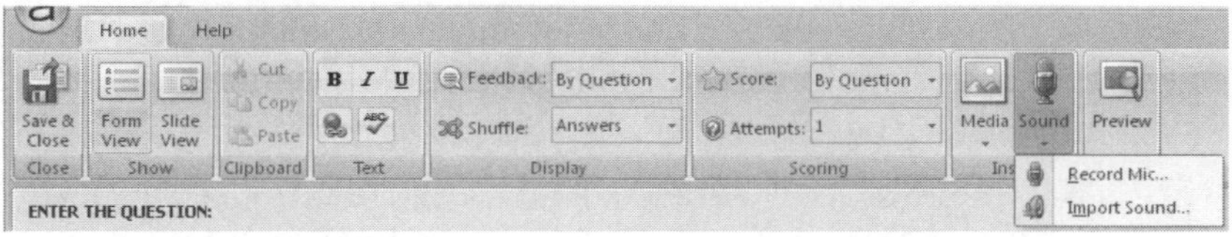

Figure 12.9. Form view Question window ribbon, Sound menu on the Home tab

Recording Audio

To add audio to a slide by recording it:

1. Open the slide in Form view.

2. Click the **Sound** button on the Home tab of the ribbon.

3. Select **Record Mic** from the Sound menu.

4. In the Record Microphone dialog box (Figure 12.10), click the **Record** button ⊙.

5. Now, just talk... The Audio control field displays a running count of the recording time, in seconds.

6. When you have finished, click the **Stop** button ⊙ in the Audio pane. The Audio control field then displays the text **Ready** and the length of the audio clip in seconds.

Figure 12.10. Record Microphone dialog box

7. To verify that the audio is correct, click the **Play** button ⊙.

8. If you need to revise or remove the audio, you have a few options:

   ■ Simply click the **Record** button ⊙ again to record over the existing clip.

   ■ Delete the clip by clicking the **Remove/Delete** button ✕.

   ■ Replace the clip by importing an existing audio file using the **Import audio file** button 🎤. (More on importing audio later...)

   ■ Edit the audio clip (remove "uhs", add silence, etc.) using the **Edit Audio** button 🎚. (More on that later, too...)

9. When you're satisfied with the audio, click the **Save** button to save the clip to the question.

After you add the clip, the icon on the Sound button on the ribbon changes to the loudspeaker 🔊 to indicate that the question slide contains audio. The menu options also change to Play Sound, Edit Sound, and Remove Sound.

Tip: If you want to prepare a script and read it while recording, use the Narration Script button 📄. The chapters on Engage and Presenter in this book explain how to use the Narration Script feature.

Tip: To control the type of input/output devices you're using to record, click the Recording Options link before you start recording.

Importing Audio

Although Quizmaker makes it easy to record your own audio, you can also import audio files. For example, you might hire a voice talent to narrate the scripts. Quizmaker supports .mp3 and .wav audio files.

To add audio to a slide by importing it:

1. Open the slide in Form view.

2. Click the **Sound** button on the Home tab of the ribbon.

3. From the Sound menu, select **Import Sound**.

4. In the Insert Sound dialog box, do one of the following:

   ■ Type the name of the audio file.

   ■ Browse to the folder containing the audio files and click the file. (In Windows XP, Engage displays the My Articulate Projects folder by default, which is contained in the My Documents folder.)

5. Click the **Open** button.

You can play the imported clip by clicking the Sound button on the ribbon and selecting Play Sound from the Sound menu. The menu also includes the Edit Sound and Delete Sound options.

Editing Audio

Quizmaker offers a tool that lets you modify audio files. The Audio Editor enables you to delete and move sections of an audio clip, as well as add silence and change the volume (Figure 12.11). This is the same Audio Editor used by Presenter and Engage.

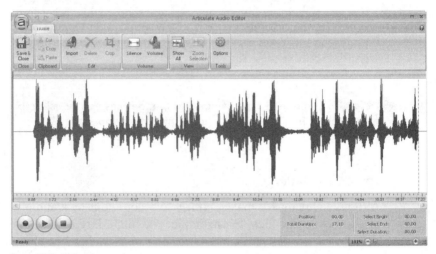

Figure 12.11. Audio Editor window

After adding an audio clip to a slide, you can use any of the following methods to open the Audio Editor window:

- In Form view, click the **Sound** button on the Home tab of the ribbon and select **Edit Sound**.
- From the Record Microphone dialog box, click the **Edit audio** button ▣.
- In Slide view, click the icon representing the audio clip ◀ , click the **Sound Tools Options** tab on the ribbon, and then click the **Audio Editor** button. (More on working with sound in Slide view later…)

The Articulate Audio Editor window displays a series of waveforms, which are visual representations of the sound. The waveforms correspond to time intervals, which are marked in seconds and fractions of seconds. Because Chapter 5, "Presenter Basics," covers working with the Audio Editor in detail, we won't cover it again here. You can refer to that chapter as well as the "Editing Audio" topic in the Quizmaker '09 Help documentation.

Adding Audio to Feedback

So far we've focused on adding an audio clip to a slide, which plays when the slide is displayed. You can also add an audio clip to one or more feedback responses, which is played when the feedback is displayed. By default, graded questions contain a correct feedback response and an incorrect feedback response. You can add audio to one or both of these responses. In addition, if you have specified feedback for all of the incorrect answers (if the question type permits), you can add audio to any or all of those feedback responses. Audio can only be added to feedback using Form view.

To add audio to feedback:

1. Open the question slide in Form view.

2. Click the **More** button next to the feedback response that will contain the audio.

3. In the Question Feedback dialog box, use the Audio pane to record or import the audio (Figure 12.12). The procedures to record, import, and edit audio clips are the same as the ones we covered in the sections titled "Recording Audio," "Importing Audio," and "Editing Audio," so we won't repeat them here.

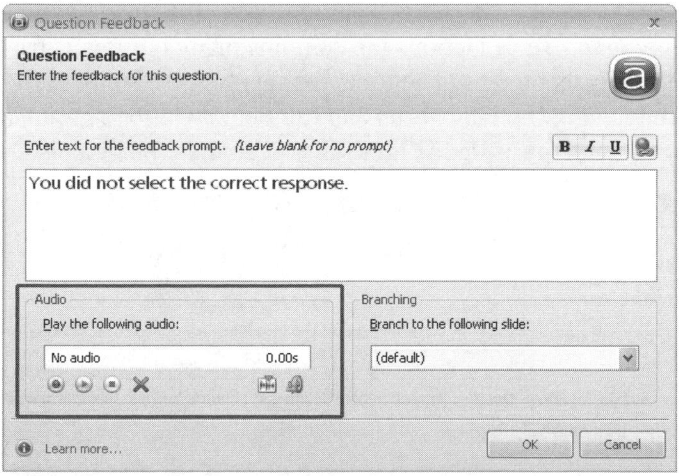

Figure 12.12. Question Feedback dialog box with Audio pane highlighted

4.   After adding the audio clip, click the **OK** button to close the dialog
     box. A sound icon appears next to the More button in the Feed-
     back section to indicate that the feedback response contains audio
     (Figure 12.13).

	Feedback		Points
CORRECT	That's right! You selected the correct response.	More...	10
INCORRECT	You did not select the correct response.	◊ More...	0

Figure 12.13. Incorrect feedback response with audio

Using Sound Tools in Slide View

After you've added an audio clip to a slide, it is represented by a sound
icon that appears by default to the left of the slide in Slide view (Figure
12.14). You can work with the audio clip using the Sound Tools Options
tab on the ribbon. This context-sensitive tab becomes available when
you click the audio clip's sound icon. After it is displayed in the ribbon,
just click the tab to make it active.

Figure 12.14. Sound icon (audio clip) in Slide view

The Sound Tools Options tab contains many of the standard tools found
in other ribbon tabs. The tools that apply specifically to the audio clip
are found in the Play group and the Sound Options group, as highlighted in Figure 12.15. Table 12.5 describes these tools.

Figure 12.15. Slide view Question window ribbon, Sound Tools Options tab with the Play and Sound
Options groups highlighted

Table 12.5. Slide view Question window ribbon, Sound Tools Options tab's Play group and Sound Options group tools

Option	Description
Preview	Plays the selected audio clip. The icon changes to a "Stop" button while the audio plays, which you can click to stop the preview. (Note that the other Preview button, located in the Preview group, shows the entire question in the Quizmaker player.)
Sound Volume	Displays a menu that lets you control the volume of the clip as it will be played in the Quizmaker player. Options are Low, Medium, High, and Mute.
Audio Editor	Opens the Audio Editor window, where you can modify the audio sound file
Change Sound	Opens the Change Sound dialog box, where you can select an audio file to import. Note that if the current clip is a recording that you created in Quizmaker and you want to rerecord it, you'll need to do that using the Record Microphone dialog box.
Export Audio	Opens the Export Audio dialog box, where you can export the selected audio clip as a .wav file, an .mp3 file, or both. This feature is helpful when you record the audio in Quizmaker and would like to save the recording locally as an audio file.
Reset Sound	Discards the changes you've made to the audio file, such as sound volume

 Note: Feedback audio is not accessible in Slide view and cannot be manipulated using these tools.

Inserting Additional Audio in Slide View

In the previous sections we described how to add one audio file to a question slide using Form view. Slide view lets you add multiple audio files to a question slide, if necessary. You might need more than one audio file, for example, if you want to play a brief music clip or sound effect, and then follow that with a clip of narration.

The procedures to add an audio file in Slide view are the same as those to add one in Form view. The only difference is that the Sound menu button is on the Insert tab on the Slide view ribbon (Figure 12.16). And because you can add more than one audio file in Slide view, you can use the Sound menu multiple times to insert additional audio files. (This is different from the Sound menu button in Form view, which changes after you add one audio file.)

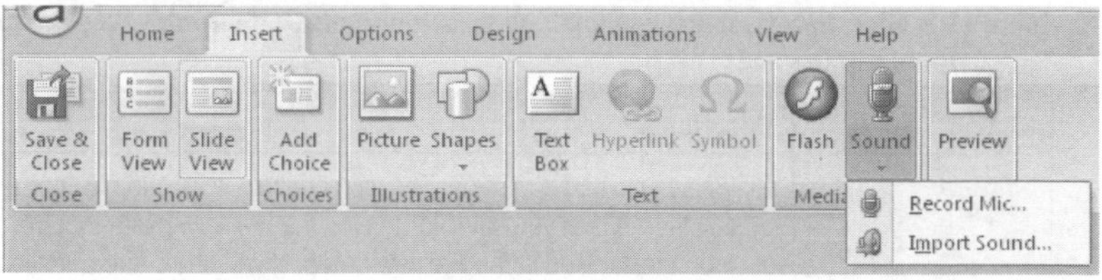

Figure 12.16. Slide view Question window ribbon, Insert tab Sound menu

Following are some points to keep in mind if you choose to add more than one audio file:

■ Each audio file will be represented by a separate sound icon next to the content slide. Click the sound icon to work with options for that audio clip.

■ If the audio files are located in the same position on the timeline, they will play at the same time. You'll need to control the timing of each audio file using the timeline, which is covered later in this chapter.

Using Audio Clips as Answer Choices

You can use audio clips as answer choices in questions requiring listening skills. For example, you might want to present responses from three customer service agents and have the viewer identify the agent who responded appropriately to the customer. Keep in mind, however, that Quizmaker does not enable the viewer to "click and replay" an audio clip. The clips are played one at a time, and then the viewer must answer. (However, the viewer can replay the question, which lets them hear all the audio clips again.) So think carefully about whether this approach is appropriate for your audience. If it is critical for your viewers to replay audio without replaying the question, then insert a Flash movie instead (see our earlier comment in this chapter about this workaround).

If you choose to use audio clips as answer choices, we strongly recommend that you preface the question with an introduction slide that prepares viewers for the question. On the introduction slide, you should explain that the next slide (the actual question slide) will play a number of audio clips. Explain that the viewer will listen to the clips and then answer a question about them. The introduction slide should also include the actual question, so that viewers have time to read and think about the question before hearing the audio clips. When viewers are ready, they'll click the Next button to advance to the question slide. The question slide should include the question, the answer choices as text (and with graphics, if desired), and the audio clips.

To use audio clips as answer choices:

1. Create an introduction slide as described above using a blank slide. Remember to include the question text that will also appear on the question slide. (Chapter 13, "Pumping Up Your Quizzes," describes how to use blank slides.)

2. Create the question slide (typically Multiple Choice) and add the question text.

3. Create answer choices using text, such as Bob, Maria, and Sue. You can also include images in the answer choices, such as pictures of Bob, Maria, and Sue. (The section titled "Adding and Formatting Images" earlier in this chapter explains how to use images as answer choices.)

4. In Slide view, add three audio clip files to the slide.

5. Using the timeline, time the first answer choice (and image if included) and audio clip combination to appear/play a few seconds after the slide is displayed. This gives the viewer a chance to adjust to the new slide for a moment. (By including the question text in the previous introduction slide, you don't have to worry about giving the viewer time to read and comprehend the question. They've already seen it in the previous slide.) (The section titled "Working with the Timeline" later in this chapter explains how to time answer choices, images, and audio clips.)

6. Time the next answer choice/image/audio clip combination to appear/play a few seconds after the previous clip finishes. Repeat this step for the remaining answer choice/image/audio clip combinations.

7. To turn off answer shuffling, click the **Options** tab in Slide view, and select **None** from the Shuffle list. (It's important to turn off answer shuffling because the answers are timed to appear at specific intervals. If this is hard to understand, just try it with answer shuffling on and you'll immediately see the issue!)

8. Preview the question and adjust the timings if necessary.

Practice 2

Now's your chance to practice importing an audio clip and recording your own narration. If you need an audio clip, search for the file chimes.wav, which comes with Windows. Note that this practice relies on your knowledge of how to create a new question (this is covered in Chapter 9, "Quizmaker Basics").

▶ Importing and Recording Audio

1. Create a new Multiple Choice question in Form view by adding a question and several answer choices.

2. Click the **Sound** button on the Home tab of the ribbon.

3. From the Sound menu, select **Import Sound**.

4. In the Insert Sound dialog box, browse to the sound file and then double-click it.

5. Click the **Sound** button on the Home tab of the ribbon again.

6. From the Sound menu, select **Play Sound** to preview the sound.

7. In the Set Feedback and Branching section, click the **More** button next to the incorrect feedback.

8. Prepare a short narration to add to the incorrect feedback.

9. In the Audio pane of the Question Feedback dialog box, click the **Record** button ⦿ and speak into the microphone.

10. When you have finished recording, click the **Stop** button ⦿.

11. To verify that the audio is correct, click the **Play** button ⦿.

12. Click **OK** to close the Question Feedback dialog box.

13. Click the **Slide View** button on the Home tab of the ribbon to switch to Slide view.

14. Click the icon representing the audio clip you imported 🔊, located to the left of the content slide. (Note that audio attached to the feedback is not accessible from Slide view.)

15. Click the **Options** tab under Sound Tools on the ribbon. (If the Options tab is not available, make sure the audio clip icon is selected.)

16. Click the **Sound Volume** button on the ribbon and select **High**.

17. Preview the slide by clicking the **Preview** button in the Preview group on the ribbon.

Adding Animation Effects

Animations can help you liven up a slide by "building" the slide components in the player instead of displaying them all at once. Following are some ideas for using animations in your quizzes:

- Animate the question text by fading it in.

- Animate the answer choices to fade in as a group or one at a time.

- Animate multiple images on an introduction slide to appear one at a time using various entrance effects. (This involves using the timeline, which is covered later in this chapter.)

- Animate a text box on a slide to grow for emphasis.

- Add a very subtle transition effect from one slide to the next.

A Warning about Using Animations

Using animation effects can frustrate or overwhelm viewers, so these must be chosen wisely. What is acceptable for second-graders will not be acceptable for a certification exam. For graded questions, it is generally inappropriate to include elements that compete for attention with the task at hand. Not sure? Think subtle. Having answer choices fade into the slide in succession is subtle. Having those questions flying around the screen isn't.

Animation effects are applied to specific objects on a slide, and transitions are applied to entire slides. Both animations and transitions can be added only in Slide view, and the procedures to add them are similar to adding animations and transitions in PowerPoint 2007. (However, Quizmaker offers a smaller group of animation effects than PowerPoint.) We'll cover just the basics here. For more details on working with animations and transitions, we suggest you refer to your favorite PowerPoint 2007 book.

Animating Slide Objects

To animate any object on a slide, you first need to select it. For example, to animate the question text, you select the question text box. However, keep in mind that some objects are part of a larger object, which will affect how the animations are applied. For example, each answer choice in a Multiple Choice question is contained in a separate text box. These text boxes are all contained within a larger text box for the answer choice group. If you select one answer choice text box (Figure 12.17), the animation effect will apply only to that answer choice. If you select the answer choice group text box (Figure 12.18), the animation effect will apply to the answer choices as a group. (As you'll see, you can still animate individual answer choices within the group if you want.)

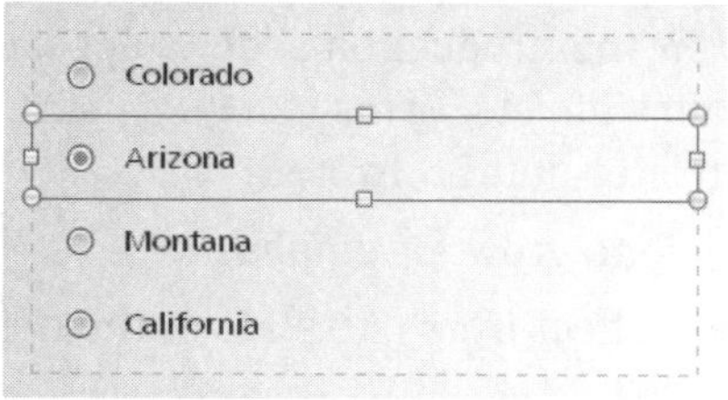

Figure 12.17. Single answer choice text box selected

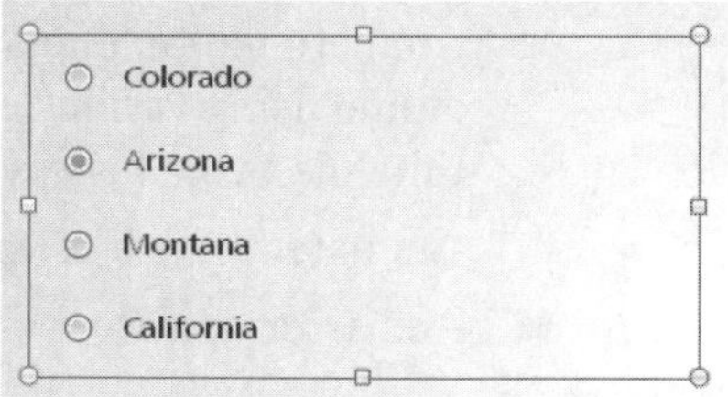

Figure 12.18. Answer choice group text box selected

Once you select the object you want to animate, you can add and customize the animation effect using the Animations tab on the ribbon (Figure 12.19). The following instructions describe how to animate a single object and a group of related objects.

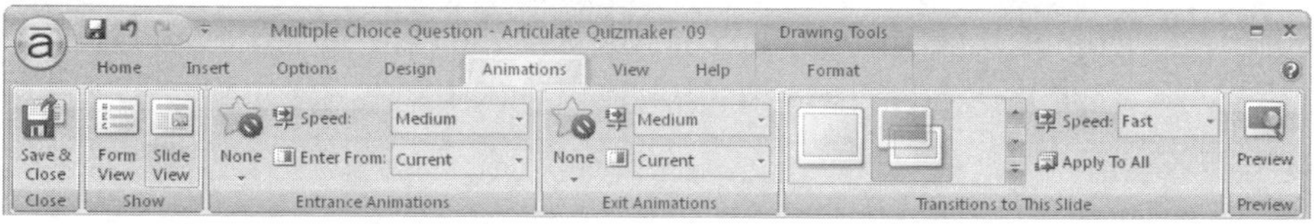

Figure 12.19. Slide view Question window ribbon, Animations tab

To animate a single object:

1. Open the slide in Slide view.

2. Select the object (e.g., the question text box).

3. Click the **Animations** tab on the ribbon.

4. To animate the object to enter the slide, click the **None** button in the Entrance Animations group and select an effect (Figure 12.20). (Note that the button is labeled None because no animations have been applied. After you select an animation, the button label will change.)

5. To animate the object to exit the slide, click the **None** button in the Exit Animations group and select an effect (Figure 12.21).

6. Customize the animation effects, if desired, by using the tools on the ribbon:

   ■ The **Speed** option determines how fast or slow the object is animated.

   ■ The **Enter From** option in the Entrance Animations group determines from which direction the object enters the slide (if applicable). A value of **Current** means that the object is animated using its current location.

   ■ The **Exit** option in the Exit Animations group (not shown) determines in which direction the object leaves the slide (if applicable).

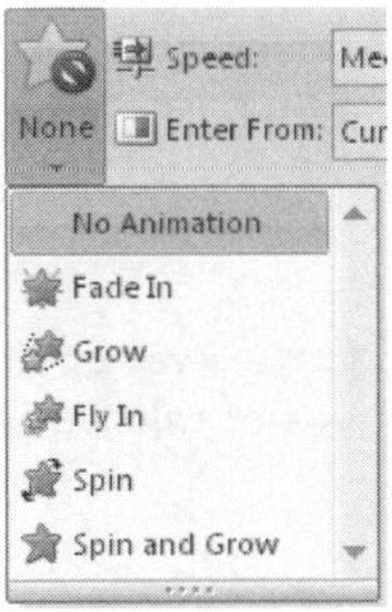

Figure 12.20. Entrance Animations group, Single object

Figure 12.21. Exit Animations group, Single object

To animate a group of related objects:

1. Open the slide in Slide view.

2. Select the group box containing the objects (e.g., the Answer choice text box as indicated in Figure 12.18).

3. Click the **Animations** tab on the ribbon.

4. To animate the object to enter the slide, click the **None** button in the Entrance Animations group to display the menu of animation options. (Note that the button is labeled None because no animations have been applied. After you select an animation, the button label will change.)

5. The menu lists the effects along with two options for each effect (Figure 12.22):

    ■ To apply the effect to all objects in the group at once, select **All At Once**. For example, Fade In All At Once will result in all answer choices fading in to the slide at once.

    ■ To apply the effect to each object, one at a time, select **By First Level Paragraph**. For example, Fade In By First Level Paragraph will result in each answer choice fading in to the slide one at a time. Note that if you select this option, answer shuffling will be automatically disabled.

6. Customize the animation effects, if desired, by using the tools on the ribbon. (See step 6 of the instructions to animate a single object.)

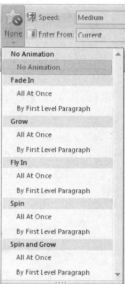

Figure 12.22. Entrance Animations, related objects

 Note: Exit animations are not available for answer choices. However, they are available for other groups of related objects, such as bulleted list items in a text box.

Timing Animated Objects

If you're familiar with PowerPoint 2000-2003 or 2007, you know that you can control when animations appear on the slide. For example, you can trigger an animated object with a mouse click or configure it to appear several seconds after the previous animation. In Quizmaker, you can control the timing of animated objects using the timeline. However, timing options are limited compared to PowerPoint. For details about timing animated objects, refer to the section titled "Working with the Timeline" later in this chapter.

Adding Transitions to Slides

A transition is a special effect that is applied as the slide is displayed in the Quizmaker player. By default, Quizmaker applies the Fade Smoothly transition to all slides. This is a subtle effect that softly fades the slide into view. Especially for graded questions, subtle is appropriate because it is less distracting.

You can add a different transition to specific slides or to all slides using the Transitions to This Slide group on the Animations tab on the ribbon (Figure 12.23). You can also remove the transition from one or more slides.

By default, the left side of the Transitions to This Slide group displays an icon to apply No Transition to the slide and an icon representing the currently applied transition. However, when you select a different transition, both of these icons will change.

Figure 12.23. Slide view Question window ribbon, Transitions to This Slide group on the Animations tab

To add a transition:

1. Open the question in Slide view.

2. Click the **Animations** tab on the ribbon.

3. Click the down-arrow button ⊟ next to the transition icons in the Transitions to This Slide group.

4. Select a different transition from the Transition effects menu (Figure 12.24). Note that transitions are grouped by type, such as Wipes.

5. If desired, select a different speed from the Speed list on the ribbon. Options are Very Slow, Slow, Medium, Fast, and Very Fast.

6. If you want to apply this transition to all slides in the quiz, click the **Apply To All** button on the ribbon.

7. To preview the transition effect, you need to preview the entire quiz. If you preview just the question from the Question window, the transition effect will not be displayed.

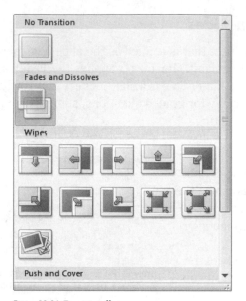

Figure 12.24. Transition effects menu

Note: A transition applied to the very first slide in the quiz will not be displayed because transitions happen when moving from a previous slide.

To remove a transition, use either of these two methods:

■ Click the **No Transition** icon *if* it is still displayed on the ribbon.

■ Click the down-arrow button ▾ next to the transition icons in the Transitions to This Slide group and click **No Transition**.

Then, if you want to remove the transitions from all slides in the quiz, click the **Apply To All** button.

Practice 3

In this exercise, you'll add animation effects to a Multiple Choice question so that the question fades in and the answer choices fade in one at a time. Note that this practice relies on your knowledge of how to create a new question (covered in Chapter 9, "Quizmaker Basics").

1. Create a new Multiple Choice question in Form view by adding a question and several answer choices.

2. Click the **Slide View** button on the Home tab of the ribbon to switch to Slide view.

3. Click anywhere on the question text to select it.

4. Click the **Animations** tab on the ribbon.

5. Click the **None** button in the Entrance Animations group and select **Fade In**.

6. Select **Fast** from the **Speed** list in the Entrance Animations group.

7. Select the group of answer choices:
    a. Click any answer choice.
    b. You'll see a dashed border surrounding all the answer choices. Click the left, right, or lower border.

---

66 **Note:** If you're already familiar with the timeline, you can select all answer choices by selecting the Multiple Choice Question layer in the timeline.

8. Click the **None** button in the Entrance Animations group and select **By First Level Paragraph** under the Fade In group.

9. Click the **Preview** button on the ribbon to preview the slide.

Quizmaker

Adding Shapes and Text Boxes

As we've discussed in this chapter, Quizmaker provides loads of tools to help you build creative and engaging slides. In addition to adding pictures, movies, sounds, and animations, you can create your own works of art using shapes and text boxes. These tools let you add and format a variety of shapes, lines, and arrows, with or without text. Figure 12.25 shows a slide using a text box, two arrow shapes, and a callout shape.

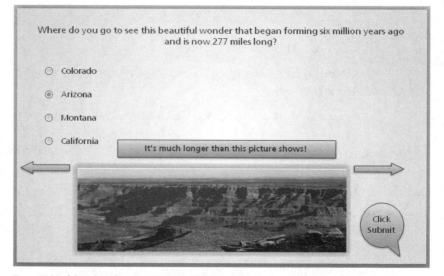

Figure 12.25. Slide with text box, arrow shapes, and callout shape

Following are just a handful of other ideas for using these items in your slides:

- Add a formatted text box to provide a hint for the question.
- Use a callout shape to serve as a talking balloon.
- Create simple diagrams using arrows, lines, and text boxes. These diagrams can complement the question or serve as answer choices.
- Use a formatted text box or shape to create a banner at the top of the slide.

- Use callouts, text boxes, or arrows to provide navigational support for the viewer.

- Use a shape as a background for answer choices. For example, create an oval and place the answer choices on top.

The Shapes and Text Box tools are located on the Insert tab of the Slide view ribbon (Figure 12.26). The procedures for adding and formatting these items are very similar to those for Office 2007 applications, so we won't go into too much detail here.

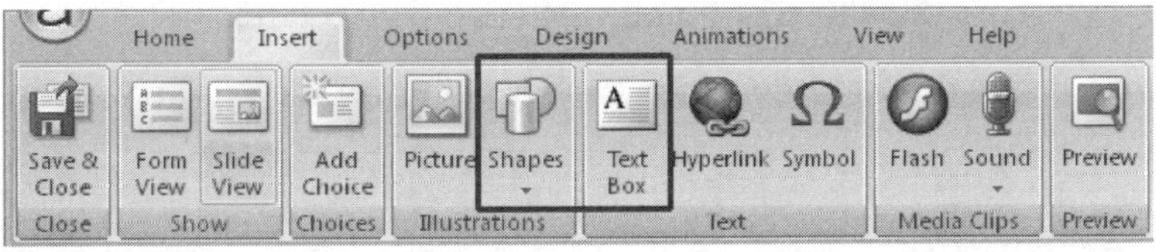

Figure 12.26. Slide view Question window ribbon with Shapes button and Text Box button highlighted on the Insert tab

Adding a Shape

To add a shape to a slide:

1. Open the slide in Slide view.

2. On the Insert tab of the ribbon, click the **Shapes** button.

3. From the Shapes menu, select a shape (Figure 12.27).

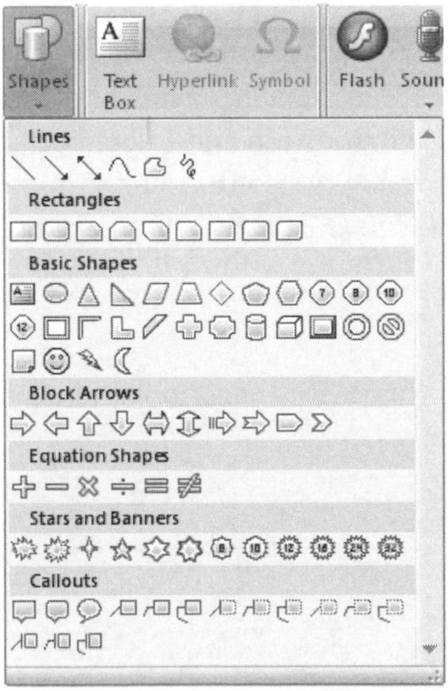

Figure 12.27. Shapes menu

4. Either click the slide to insert the shape using the default size *or* drag the mouse to draw the shape.

5. The Drawing Tools Format tab becomes available. Click the **Format** tab and select options to format the shape, if desired. (These options are covered in the section titled "Formatting Objects" in Chapter 9, "Quizmaker Basics.")

6. To add text to a shape, make sure the shape is selected and type the text. (Alternatively, right-click the shape, select **Edit Text** from the shortcut menu, and then type the text.)

7. If necessary, reposition the shape anywhere on the slide by dragging it.

Adding a Text Box

The procedures to add a text box are similar to those to add a shape:

1. Open the slide in Slide view.

2. On the Insert tab of the ribbon, click the **Text Box** button.

3. Either click the slide to insert the text box using the default size *or* drag the mouse to draw the text box.

4. By default, the text box will have no borders. However, a selection border will surround the text box, indicating its boundaries. The insertion point will be blinking inside the text box. Type the desired text.

5. The Drawing Tools Format tab becomes available when the text box is selected. Click the **Format** tab and select options to format the shape, if desired. (These options are covered in the section titled "Formatting Objects" in Chapter 9, "Quizmaker Basics.")

6. If necessary, reposition the text box anywhere on the slide by dragging it.

Once you get the hang of working with these tools, you'll find many creative uses for them on your slides!

Adding Hyperlinks

What if you want your viewers to have access to resources outside the quiz as they are taking the quiz? By using hyperlinks in question slides, feedback text, and other quiz slides, you can enable viewers to quickly access a web page or email address while still working with the quiz. Following are some of the best uses of hyperlinks in quizzes:

- **Question slide or information slide:** Provide a link to a web page to help viewers answer the question (Figure 12.28).

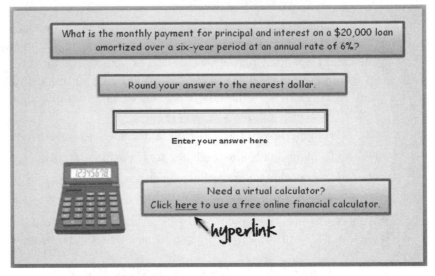

Figure 12.28. Question slide with hyperlink

- **Results slide:** Provide a link to a web site containing additional information related to the quiz. Provide a link to download a certificate of achievement. Provide a link to an email address so viewers can submit feedback.
- **Feedback text:** Provide a link to a web site that shows the correct answer or offers additional information. Provide a link to a web site that shows why the incorrect answer is incorrect.

Hyperlinks vs. Branching

It's important to remember that a hyperlink in Quizmaker is used only to link to a web page or to an email address. Hyperlinks are *not* used to branch to other questions in the quiz. To do that, you'll need to use the Branching pane in the Question Feedback dialog box. Information about branching is covered in the section titled "Setting Feedback and Branching" in Chapter 9, "Quizmaker Basics," and in the section "Creating a Branched Scenario" in Chapter 13, "Pumping Up Your Quizzes."

A hyperlink is created using text or an object on the slide, such as a picture. (However, hyperlinks cannot be created from text in answer choices.) Depending on the type of text or object used for the hyperlink, you may be restricted to adding the hyperlink using Slide view or Form view. At the risk of making this more confusing than it needs to be, here's a quick summary:

- Add a hyperlink to the question text: Slide view or Form view.
- Add a hyperlink to the feedback text: Form view only.
- Add a hyperlink to any other object, such as a graphic or text in an additional text box: Slide view only.

We'll briefly describe how to add a hyperlink to any content in Slide view, and how to add a hyperlink to feedback text in Form view.

Adding Hyperlinks to Content in Slide View

To add a hyperlink to content:

1. Open the slide in Slide view.
2. Select the object to serve as the hyperlink. For example:
   - Select existing text.
   - Select an object, such as a shape or picture.
   - Place the insertion point anywhere in a text box (which includes the question text box).
3. On the Insert tab on the ribbon, click the **Hyperlink** button.

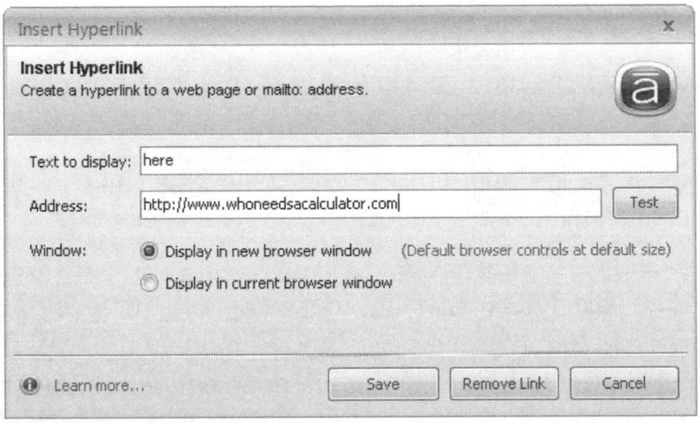

Figure 12.29. Insert Hyperlink dialog box

4. In the Insert Hyperlink dialog box (Figure 12.29), enter the following information as needed:

    ■ **Text to display:** If you selected text, the text will appear here by default. You can change it, but this will also change the text on the slide. If you selected an object, this option is not applicable. If you didn't select text or an object, enter the text to be used for the hyperlink.

    ■ **Address:** Quizmaker enters the protocol http:// by default. To include a link to a web page, type the web address, and then click the **Test** button to make sure the link works. To include a link to an email address, replace http:// with **mailto:** and then type the email address.

    ■ **Window:** Select one of the following options:

        ■ **Display in new browser window:** This option displays the web page in a browser window that is separate from the quiz's browser window. Click the **(Default browser controls at default size)** link to customize how the new browser appears.

        ■ **Display in current browser window:** This option displays the web page using the same browser window used by the quiz. To return to the quiz, your viewers will need to click the Back button on the browser window. If you choose this option, make sure you provide instructions to the viewer.

5.   Click the **Save** button.

If you used text as the hyperlink, the text will appear underlined by default.

Following are a few additional points about hyperlinks. These apply to hyperlinks added to slide content and to feedback text:

■   To change or rcmove the hyperlink, just right-click the hyperlink text or object. The shortcut menu contains options to Edit, Open, Copy, and Remove the hyperlink. Removing the hyperlink removes the link association but does not delete the original text or object.

■   The hyperlink functionality is not active when you preview the slide. To test the hyperlink, you need to *publish* the quiz.

■   When the question is displayed in the Quizmaker player, the mouse pointer changes to a hand when the viewer moves the mouse over the hyperlink.

■   And, just another reminder: If you configure the destination web page to open in the current browser window, be sure to include instructions to your viewers about how to return to the quiz. If they close the browser, they'll lose the quiz!

Adding Hyperlinks to Feedback Text in Form View

Adding a hyperlink to feedback text is similar to adding a hyperlink to content on a slide. The Insert Hyperlink dialog box is used to create the hyperlink, but you can only access the feedback text in Form view. There are a couple of ways to add hyperlinks in Form view, but we'll focus on one method.

To add a hyperlink to feedback text:

1.   Open the question in Form view.

2.   Click the **More** button next to the feedback response that will contain the hyperlink.

3.   In the Question Feedback dialog box (Figure 12.30), select existing text to be used as the hyperlink *or* position the insertion point where new hyperlink text will be inserted.

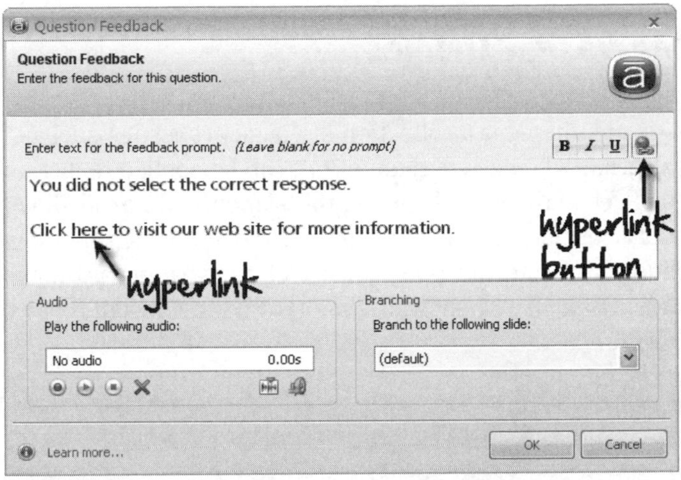

Figure 12.30. Question Feedback dialog box in Form view with hyperlink added

4. Click the **Hyperlink** button 🔗.

5. Complete the information in the Insert Hyperlink dialog box. (For details, see the instructions in the section "Adding Hyperlinks to Content in Slide View.")

6. Click the **Save** button and close the Question Feedback dialog box.

Tip: Here's another way to add a hyperlink in Form view: Select the text you want in the Question window (e.g., question text or feedback text) and then click the Hyperlink button on the Home tab of the ribbon. Then complete the information in the Insert Hyperlink dialog box.

Applying Design Themes

A design theme is a collection of visual properties such as background pattern, text colors, and fonts that can be applied to just one slide or to all slides in the quiz. Applying the same theme to all slides gives your quiz a consistent look and feel. The default design theme applied to slides is a white background with a bit of shading at the bottom of the slide. Figure 12.31 shows a slide that uses a design theme named Dots.

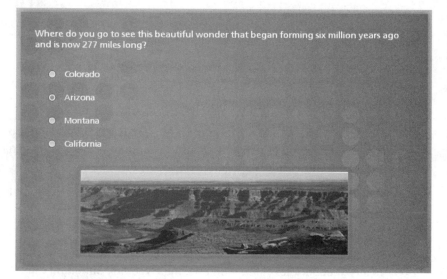

Figure 12.31. Slide using the Dots design theme

The Design tab on the ribbon in Slide view (Figure 12.32) offers a variety of built-in design themes as well as tools to customize the colors, fonts, and background used by the theme (thereby letting you effectively create your own theme). If you're familiar with PowerPoint 2007, you'll notice that these tools are the same as those on the Design tab on the PowerPoint ribbon. Because the tools are so similar, we'll cover just the basics of applying design themes here. For more details on working with themes, we suggest you refer to a good PowerPoint 2007 book. Quizmaker '09 Help also includes a topic on applying design themes.

Selecting a Theme

The Themes group on the Design tab of the ribbon in Slide view displays a sample of the themes you can apply to all slides in the quiz. Figure 12.32 shows this group with the default theme selected as the current theme. Once you select a different theme, the icons on this group will change. You can click the down arrow on the group's scroll bar to see additional built-in themes (Figure 12.33).

Figure 12.32. Question window ribbon Design tab in Slide view

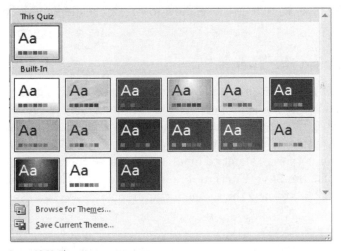

Figure 12.33. Themes menu

Although the process of applying a theme is simple enough, you want to think about what design elements will work best for your quiz. For example, if you're planning to use the quiz in a Presenter project, make sure the design theme is consistent with the design theme used by the PowerPoint slides.

To apply a theme to all slides:

1. Open any slide from the quiz in Slide view.

2. Click the **Design** tab on the ribbon.

3. To view all available design themes, click the down-arrow button ⏷ in the scroll bar next to the design icons.

4. Click a theme on the menu (Figure 12.33). If you have created and saved other themes (or you know that other themes are stored on your computer), you can use the **Browse for Themes** item to apply a theme not listed here.

To apply a theme to just the current slide, follow steps 1-3 above. In step 4, right-click the theme you want and select **Apply Only to This Question** from the shortcut menu (Figure 12.34).

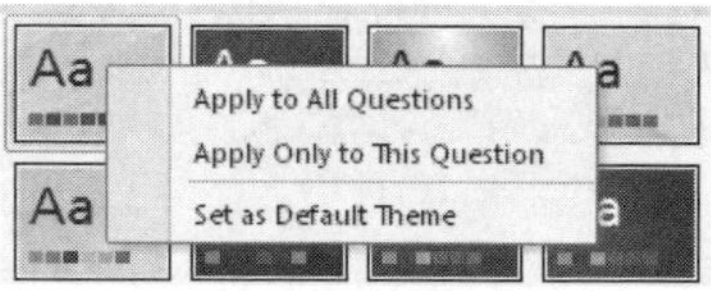

Figure 12.34. Theme shortcut menu

The next section discusses how to customize elements of the theme.

Customizing the Theme

The built-in themes provided by Quizmaker use specific sets of colors, fonts, and background properties. You can modify any of these elements to create your own custom theme. For example, you can customize the theme so it matches your corporate color scheme and uses your corporate standard fonts. Once you've customized the theme, use the **Save Current Theme** item on the Themes menu (Figure 12.33) to save the theme for future use.

Colors

Clicking the **Colors** button in the Themes group displays the sets of colors that can be used in a theme (Figure 12.35). A color set affects the text, background, accent, inserted shapes, and hyperlink colors. The color set used by the current theme is outlined on the list. Just click another color set to apply it. You can also create your own color scheme using the **Create New Theme Colors** item at the bottom of the menu.

Fonts

Clicking the **Fonts** button in the Themes group displays the fonts that can be used for text in the theme (Figure 12.36). The theme font affects heading text and body text in your slides. Select a font from the list, or click **Create New Theme Fonts** to create a customized theme font, such as using one font for heading text and another font for body text.

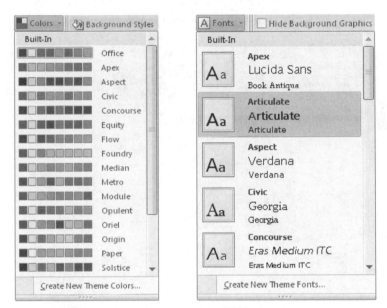

Figure 12.35. Colors menu   Figure 12.36. Fonts menu

> **66   Note:** The theme font does not affect the font used by the text in the Quizmaker prompts, such as the feedback pop-up box. To change the prompts font globally, use the Quiz Properties dialog box, which is covered in Chapter 9, "Quizmaker Basics."

Background

The Background group on the Design tab contains tools to modify the style of the background. This is a good option if you don't necessarily want to apply an entirely new theme. For example, you can use the default theme and just apply a different background. Of course, you can still use the Background tools to customize a theme.

Clicking the Background Styles button on the ribbon displays the available styles. You can select one of these styles, or choose from many other options by clicking Format Background at the bottom of the Background Styles menu. This opens the Format Background dialog box (Figure 12.37), which offers other types of background elements. For example, you can use a picture as the background or apply a texture (like pebbles!). We highly recommend playing around with the options in the Format Background dialog box—you'll be amazed at the fun types of backgrounds you can create.

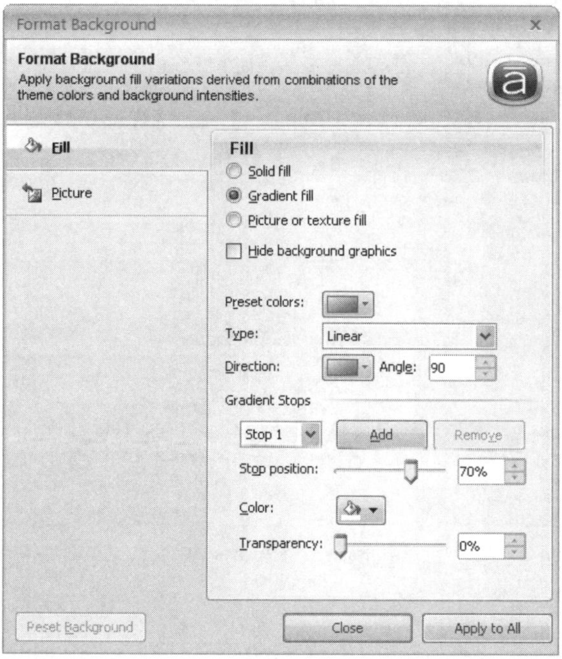

Figure 12.37. Format Background dialog box

Working with the Slide Master

As we've just discussed, design themes let you apply a consistent look and feel to all of your slides. You can also use the Quizmaker slide master (Figure 12.38) to apply consistent colors, fonts, and backgrounds to slides, as well as to insert objects that appear on every slide. Changes you make to the slide master are automatically incorporated into every slide in the current quiz, so it's a great tool for

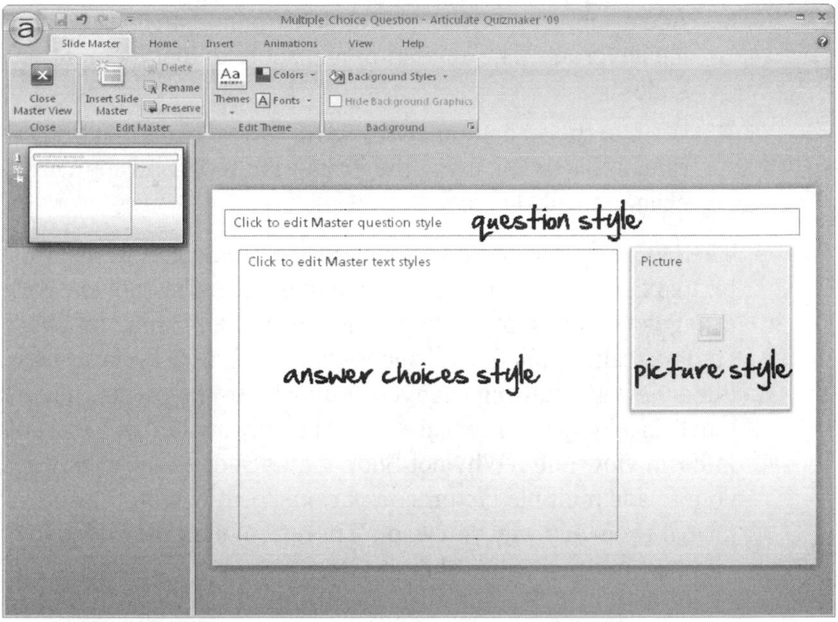

Figure 12.38. Default slide master

applying global properties. Following are some examples of how you can use the slide master in Quizmaker:

■ Change the font properties of the question text, such as font style, size, and color. The font properties will be applied to the question text on every slide.

■ Change the font properties of the answer choices text, such as font style, size, and color. The font properties will be applied to the answer choices on every slide.

■ Add an image that appears on every slide, such as a corporate logo.

■ Add a text box to serve as a header or footer on every slide.

■ Add other objects to appear on every slide, such as a hyperlink to a web site.

■ Modify the design theme or elements of the theme, such as the font color of all text or the background. Note that you can also do this in Slide view by modifying the theme and applying the change to all slides.

- Add a subtle animation to a slide element, such as the answer choice group. The animation will apply to that element on all slides.

- Change the transition effect on all slides. Note that you can also do this in Slide view using the Transition tools and applying the change to all slides.

The Quizmaker slide master contains three default items: the question text box, answer choice text box, and picture placeholder. Formatting changes you make to the question and answer choice text boxes are automatically applied to all slides that you create in Form view and Slide view. Formatting changes you make to the picture placeholder (such as adding a border) are automatically applied to a picture added in Form view only. (Why not Slide view? Slide view gives you the freedom to add multiple pictures in various locations on the slide and to format them any way you want. Therefore, pictures added in Slide view are not tied to the slide master.)

Note: When building non-question "blank" slides, the slide master's question text box affects the title of the blank slide, and the answer choice text box affects the main text box in the blank slide.

You can also add new objects to the slide master and position them anywhere on the slide stage. The new objects will appear on every slide in the quiz. Figure 12.39 shows a customized slide master in which the font size for the question has been increased and a company logo added to the lower-right corner.

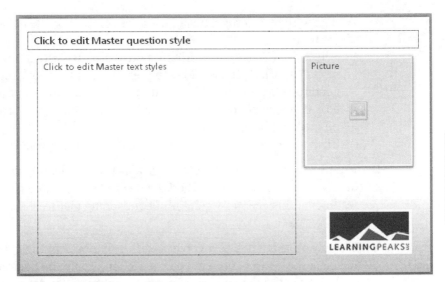

Figure 12.39. Slide master customized to include logo and larger font for question text

Modifying the Slide Master

Following are the basic steps for modifying the Quizmaker slide master to apply global properties to your slides.

1. Open any slide in Slide view.

2. Click the **View** tab on the ribbon and then click the **Slide Master** button. The slide master is displayed (Figure 12.39), and the ribbon changes to include the Slide Master tab and five other tabs from the Slide View ribbon (Figure 12.40).

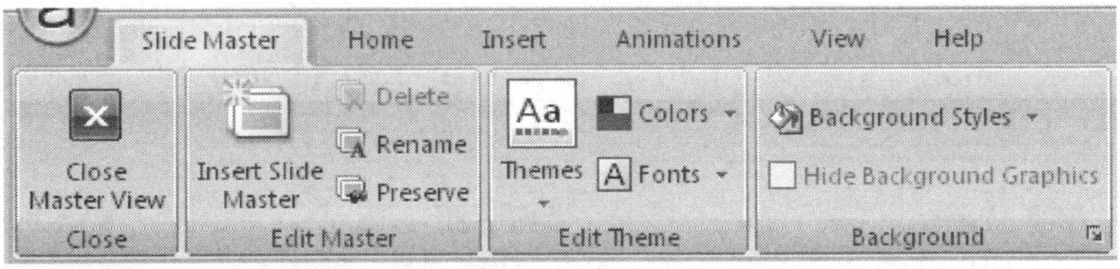

Figure 12.40. Slide view Question window Slide Master tab

3. To change the font properties of the question text or the answer choice text:

    a. Select the **Click to edit Master question style** text box or select the **Click to edit Master text styles** text box. You need to select the text box itself by clicking a border of the text box. If you select only the text inside the text box, the properties will not be applied to the slides.

    b. Click the **Home** tab on the ribbon and apply font properties.

4. To add an object to the slide (such as a picture or shape), click the **Insert** tab on the ribbon and add the desired object. (See previous sections in this chapter for details about adding pictures, shapes, text boxes, etc.)

5. To apply an animation to an object on the slide, select the object and click the **Animations** tab on the ribbon. Apply the desired animation. (See the previous sections in this chapter for details about animating slide objects.)

6. To edit the theme or background of the slide, select the appropriate options from the Slide Master tab of the ribbon. (See the previous sections in this chapter for details about working with themes.)

7. When you are finished editing the slide, click the **Close Master View** button on the ribbon to return to Slide view.

The changes made to the slide master are automatically applied to all slides in the quiz. The properties will also be applied automatically to new slides. Note, however, that any changes you make directly to a slide in Slide view will override the slide master properties. For example, if the slide master question text font is Arial, you can change the font to Calibri for a question on a single slide in Slide view.

66 **Note:** The revised slide master also appears as an option in the Themes group of the Design tab on the ribbon.

Adding New Slide Masters

Quizmaker enables you to create additional slide masters that you can apply to specific slides or to all slides. For example, you might create an additional slide master if you want a specific picture or question text style applied to several slides but not all slides. Following are the basic steps to add a new slide master:

1. Open any slide in Slide view.

2. Click the **View** tab on the ribbon and then click the **Slide Master** button. The ribbon changes to include the Slide Master tab and five other tabs from the Slide View ribbon (Figure 12.40).

3. Click the **Insert Slide Master** button on the ribbon.

4. Quizmaker creates a duplicate of the current slide master and displays a thumbnail in the left pane of the window.

5. Modify the new slide master as desired. (See the steps in the previous section, "Modifying the Slide Master.")

6. By default, Quizmaker names the new slide master **Custom Design Slide Master.** (This name appears as a tooltip when you move the mouse pointer over the thumbnail.) If you want to change the name, click the **Rename** button on the ribbon, enter a new name in the Rename dialog box, and then click the **Rename** button in the dialog box.

7. By default, Quizmaker *preserves* the new slide master, meaning that the slide master will always be available, even if it is not applied to any questions. (You can tell that the slide master is preserved by the highlighted Preserve button on the ribbon.) If a slide master is *not* preserved, Quizmaker automatically removes it if it is not being used by any questions. If you don't want to preserve the new slide master, click the **Preserve** button on the ribbon to remove the highlight.

8. Click the **Close Master View** button on the ribbon to return to Slide view.

Quizmaker

9. The new slide master appears as an option in the Themes group of the Design tab on the ribbon (Figure 12.41). To apply the new slide master to the current slide, right-click its icon and select **Apply Only to This Question**. To apply it to all questions in the current quiz, select **Apply to All Questions**.

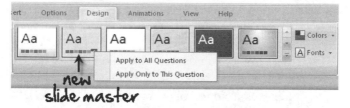

Figure 12.41. New slide master in the Themes group of the Design tab

PowerPoint 2007 Slide Master vs. Quizmaker '09 Slide Master

The Quizmaker slide master feature is similar to the slide masters used in PowerPoint 2007, but there are some differences between the two. Whether or not you're familiar with PowerPoint 2007, keep the following points in mind:

■ Although you can create multiple slide masters in Quizmaker, they are not applied to slides the way PowerPoint slide masters are applied to slides. As discussed earlier, use the Design tab to apply a new slide master to one or more slides.

■ The layout (positioning) feature for the default items in the Quizmaker slide master is locked. Any changes you make to the layout of the default items will not be reflected in the slides. For example, if you move the image placeholder to a new location, the new location will not be reflected in the slides. However, you can control the layout of any *new* objects you add to the slide master.

■ The Quizmaker slide master does not offer the page number, date, header, and footer options. However, you can easily add a static header or footer to slides by inserting a text box.

Working with the Timeline

We think the timeline is one of the coolest features in Quizmaker. By controlling when objects appear on the slide, you can change a static ho-hum slide into an engaging question. And although the primary function of the timeline is to let you time objects on the slide, there are some other helpful tools for working with your slides. In a nutshell, you can use the timeline to:

■ Control when objects on the slide appear (and/or disappear) and when audio starts playing.

■ Control the layered order of objects so that they appear in front of or behind other objects.

■ Hide and show objects.

■ Lock objects so they can't be edited.

■ Select and rename objects.

The callouts in Figure 12.42 point out the features of the timeline as it appears when you first open a new Multiple Choice question. Each slide object is listed in the timeline. Timeline objects are also referred to as *layers*, because the objects appear in the timeline in the order they are layered on the slide. Layering affects whether an object appears behind (beneath) or in front of (on top of) another object. The topmost layered object on the slide is listed at the top of the timeline.

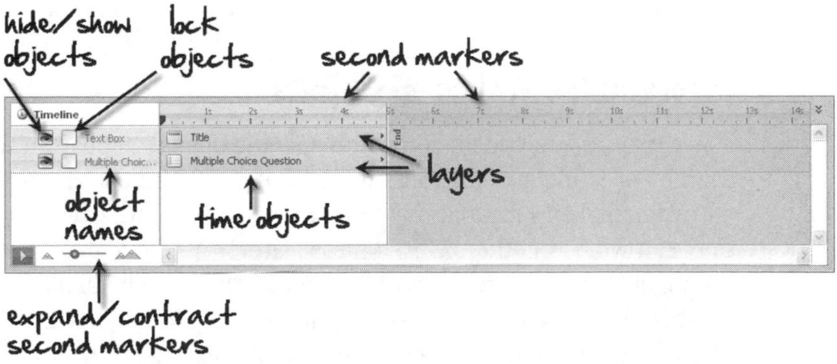

Figure 12.42. Timeline in Slide view

The object names are listed in the far left column. In the example in Figure 12.42, Text Box refers to the text box that will contain the Title of the slide, which is the question text for this question. The second column contains the tools to time each object, which is labeled by its description. (Once you add the question text, the Title label in the second column will change to the question text.) By default, all objects are timed to appear immediately when the slide is displayed and to remain in place as long as the slide displays.

> **Tip:** If the timeline is not displayed on the slide, click the View tab and then select the Timeline check box. If the timeline bar appears but is not fully expanded, click the double up-arrow button ▲ on the right side of the bar.

We'll discuss each of these features next, starting with the most fun feature—timing your objects.

> **Play Around with the Timeline ASAP**
>
> We strongly recommend that you play around with the timeline. Although we certainly tried to come up with the right words to explain how the timeline works, the best way to really "get it" is to use it. Some of what we describe here will make much more sense after you've had a few trial and error sessions of your own.

Controlling the Timing of Objects

The timeline lets you decide when specific objects appear on the slide, thereby creating an animated effect. (But don't confuse the timeline with Quizmaker's Animations tab—they are separate tools, although they can work together. More on that later!) A simple example using timing is to create the effect of "building" the slide by displaying one component at a time. For example, an introduction slide can display the title of the quiz first, then a graphic, then instruction text. Once you get the hang of timing your objects, you'll find many creative ways to present your slides. But, on the flip side, don't get too carried away.

There's a very fine line between making the question more "interesting" and making it confusing. If your audience wants to get through a quiz quickly and easily, don't bog your questions down with timings that might become irritating.

Following are just a few examples of how you can time your objects on slides. Although we won't go into the details of creating all of these examples, they'll give you an idea of what you can do with the timeline once you're up to speed:

- For a Multiple Choice or Multiple Response question, show just the question (and maybe a graphic) when the slide is displayed. Let the viewer read and think about the question for a few seconds. Then display the answer choices. This encourages learners to think about the question before "dealing" with the answers. If you decide to use this approach, we think it makes sense to use it on *all* questions so viewers won't be concerned that something is wrong when a question does not appear in this manner.

- Time a graphic to appear after the question and answer choices are displayed.

- Time an audio clip to play a few seconds after the slide is displayed. If you have multiple audio clips, time the clips to play one after the other.

- For a slide with several graphics (such as the quiz introduction), time each graphic to appear on the slide one at a time. This would make the most sense when using graphics to tell a story. Create an audio clip for each graphic and time the audio to play at the same time the graphic appears.

Now let's look at the steps to time objects. Although you can create very complex timings using the timeline, we'll cover just the basic steps.

1. Select the object to be timed.

2. Move the object on the timeline.

3. Change the duration of the object (optional).

Selecting the Object to be Timed

Your first step is to select the object you want to time. If you want several objects to share the same timing (such as all the graphics appearing together after three seconds), select those objects as a group. There are several ways to select an object:

- Click the object on the slide.
- Click the object name in the first column of the timeline.
- Click the object description in the second column of the timeline.
- To select multiple objects, use any of the above methods and hold down the Ctrl key as you click each object.

Figure 12.43 shows a simple Multiple Choice question with the graphic Picture 1 (Calendar.jpg) selected for timing. As you add objects to the slide, Quizmaker puts the new objects at the top of the timeline, which is why the picture object appears above the others.

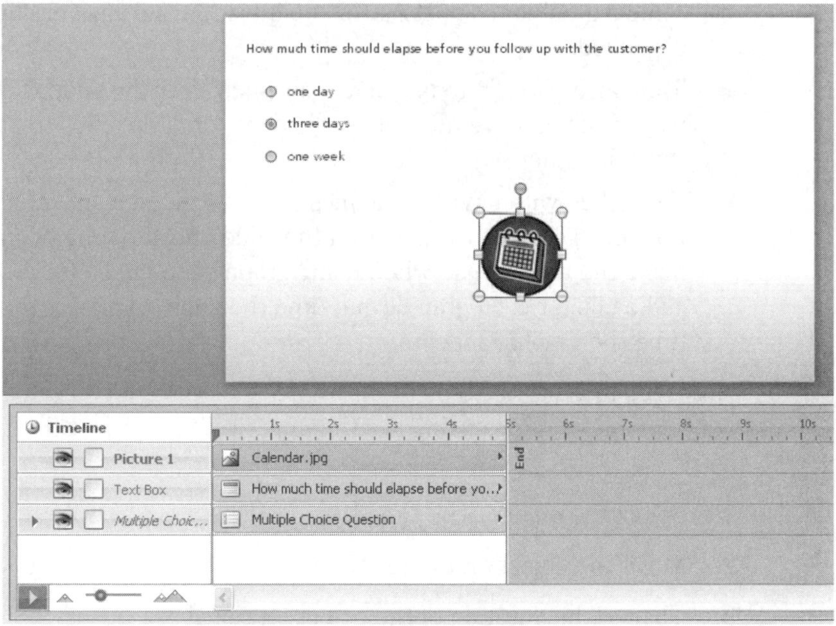

Figure 12.43. Timeline with selected object

Depending on the slide you are working with, an object may have "subobjects" associated with it. In the example in Figure 12.43, the Multiple Choice Question object represents the answer choices for this question. Clicking the arrow to the left of the object in the left column expands the object to display all of its subobjects, as seen in Figure 12.44. You may then select one or more of the subobjects to time. Clicking the arrow again collapses the subobjects.

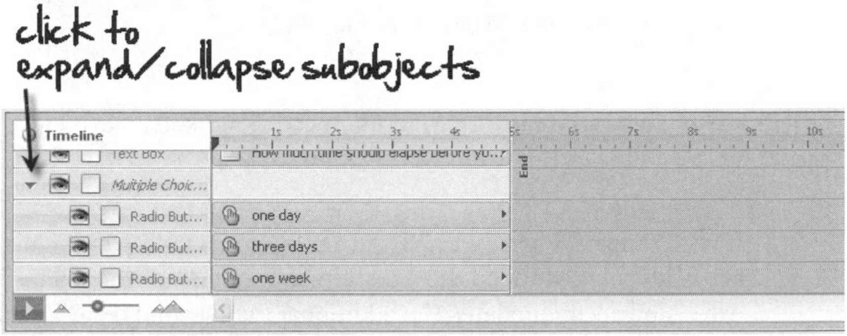

click to expand/collapse subobjects

Figure 12.44. Timeline with Multiple Choice Question subobjects (answer choices) expanded

Moving the Object on the Timeline

Your next step is to position the object to the marker (identified in seconds) that represents when the object should appear on the slide. To do this, just use your mouse to drag the object along the timeline. The example in Figure 12.45 shows the Picture 1 object aligned under the 2s (two seconds) marker. This means that the picture will appear on the slide two seconds after the slide is displayed. The overall effect is that the Text Box object (question text) and Multiple Choice Question object (answer choices) will appear immediately, two seconds will elapse, and then the picture will appear.

playhead   *2 second marker*

end line

play button (preview)

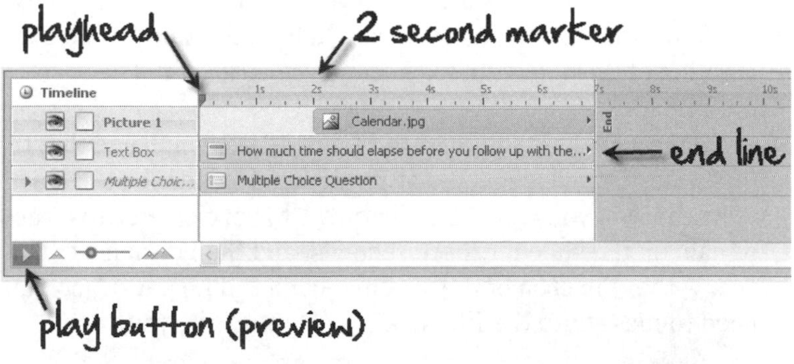

Figure 12.45. Timeline specifying Picture 1 (Calendar.jpg) to appear two seconds after slide is displayed

To preview the new timing effect in Slide view, you can click the **Play** button in the lower-left corner of the timeline. The playhead will then move along the timeline, indicating the elapsed time of the slide. When the playhead reaches the 2s marker in this example, the picture will appear on the slide. You can also preview the new timing by simply dragging the playhead along the timeline.

Tip: To expand the display of the seconds markers, move the slider in the lower-left corner of the timeline.

If you compare Figures 12.43 and 12.45, you'll notice that Quizmaker automatically extended the End line of the objects from 5s to 7s. This extension accommodates the additional two-second delay of Picture 1. We'll discuss the End line in more detail next.

Controlling the Duration of the Object

Just as you can control when an object appears on the slide, you can control how long it stays on the slide. By default, all objects stay on the slide until the "end" of the slide. The "end" of the slide is indicated by the End line on the timeline. However, it's important to understand that the End line does *not* represent the time when all objects (or the slide) will magically disappear. *The End line simply represents the end of the period in which objects are timed.* Once the End line is reached, the current state of each object becomes "frozen" until the viewer moves to the next slide. As you'll see next, you can extend the End line if additional time is needed to control the timing of specific objects.

To explain how to control the duration of an object, we'll present two common scenarios using the Multiple Choice question example. In the first scenario, you don't need to adjust the End line to control the duration of the object. In the second scenario, you'll need to work with the End line.

Scenario 1: If you refer to Figure 12.45, you'll see that the end of the timing period is marked at 7s (seven seconds) by the End line. In this scenario, you would like Picture 1 to appear after two seconds, remain on the slide for three seconds, and then disappear. This activity falls within the span of the seven-second timing period, so you don't need to mess with the End line. To achieve this, you:

1. Select the **Picture 1** object (in this example, **Calendar.jpg**).

2. Drag the arrow marker on Calendar.jpg to the left to align the end of the object with the 5s marker. (Hint: Make sure the mouse pointer is a double horizontal arrow. Otherwise, you'll end up dragging the End line and not the object.)

Figure 12.46 shows the result of these steps. When the slide is displayed, two seconds will elapse before the calendar picture is displayed, then the picture will be displayed for three seconds, and then the picture will be removed from the slide. The other objects will remain on the slide.

Figure 12.46. Scenario 1: Picture 1 timed to appear after two-second delay, then disappear three seconds later

Scenario 2: Referring again to Figure 12.45, suppose you would like Picture 1 to appear after two seconds, remain on the slide for five seconds, and then disappear. In this scenario, you'll need to extend the End line because once the End line is reached, the current state of each object is "frozen." So right now, Picture 1 would remain on the slide. To remove Picture 1 after its five-second display:

1. Drag the End line past the current 7s point, for example to 8s. The durations of *all* objects are extended along with the End line.

2. Select the **Picture 1** object (in this example, **Calendar.jpg**).

3. Drag the arrow marker on Calendar.jpg to the left to align the end of the object back to the 7s marker.

Figure 12.47 shows the result of these steps. When the slide is displayed, two seconds will elapse before the calendar picture is displayed, then the picture will be displayed for five seconds, and then the picture will be removed from the slide. The other two objects will remain on the slide because their current states will be frozen at the End line.

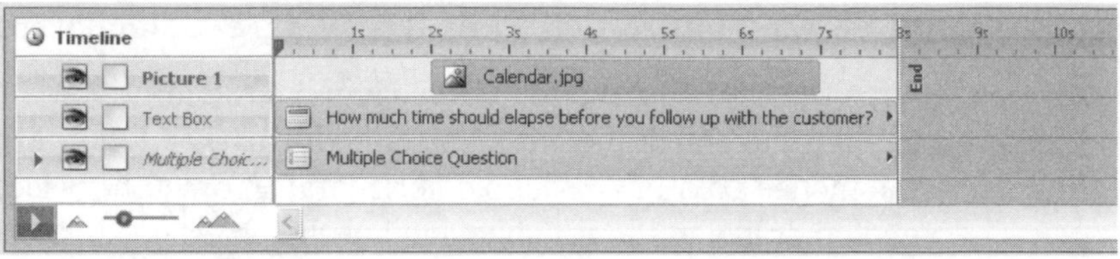

Figure 12.47. Scenario 2: Picture 1 timed to appear after two-second delay, then disappear five seconds later

If this is starting to sound confusing, don't worry. The best way to wrap your head around the End line and timing objects is to start playing around with them. After a few trial and error experiences, you'll probably reach the "aha" stage too.

Using the Timing Dialog Box

Quizmaker offers another tool to control objects on the timeline. The Timing dialog box enables you to manually enter the timings for each object. To open the dialog box, right-click the desired object and then select **Timing** from the shortcut menu (more on the shortcut menu later...).

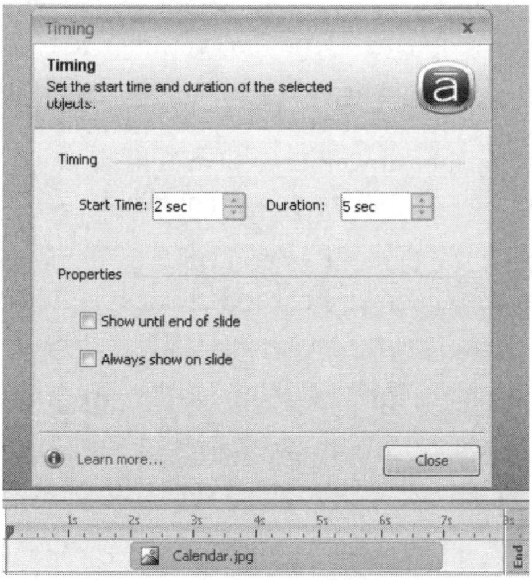

Figure 12.48. Timing dialog box

Figure 12.48 shows the dialog box with the timing of the Picture 1 (Calendar.jpg) example. As you can see, you can use the Start Time box to enter the time the object appears on the slide. The Duration box lets you specify how long the object will appear. Selecting the Show until end of slide check box ensures that the object is displayed from its start point until the end of the slide. Selecting the Always show on slide check box ensures that the object is displayed from the beginning of the slide to the end.

Timing Sounds

Controlling the timing of sounds is very similar to controlling other objects on the slide. An audio clip is considered a slide object, so you can control it in the timeline just as you would any other object. There are a couple of things to consider, however, as you time audio clips:

■ If the audio clips appear in the same position on the timeline (e.g., at the beginning), then the clips will be played at the same time. If you want clips to play at different times, just adjust their layers on the timeline.

■ The duration of each audio clip is automatically determined by the length of the clip. In other words, you can't increase or decrease the duration of an audio clip using the timeline. You can only determine when it starts playing. (However, you can use the Audio Editor to edit the audio clip if it needs to be shorter.)

Figure 12.49 shows an example of two audio clips on a slide. Sound 2 is a short narrated recording, and Sound 1 is a sound effect. Sound 1 has been moved along the timeline so that it is synchronized to play at the same time that Picture 1 (Calendar.jpg) is displayed.

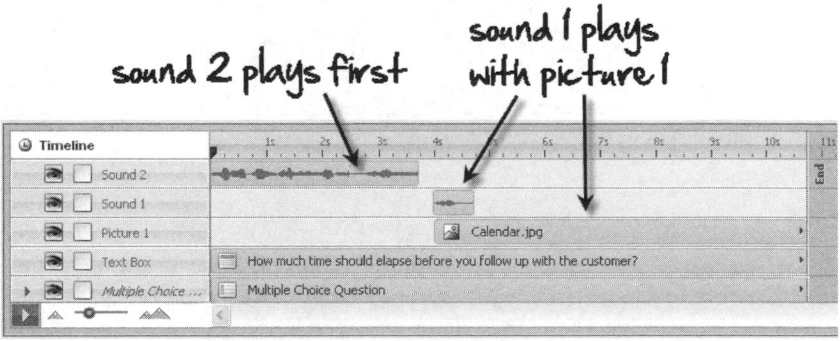

Figure 12.49. Timeline with sound clips

Timing Animated Objects

If you're familiar with PowerPoint 2000-2003 or 2007 animations, you may be used to creating an animation *and* controlling its timing using the tools in the PowerPoint 2007 Animations tab or the PowerPoint 2000-2003 Custom Animation task pane. Quizmaker is a bit different, as you use two different tools to create and time animations. First, you add an animation effect to an object using the Animations tab, and then you use the timeline to time its appearance and/or disappearance, if desired. The process to control the timing of animated objects on the Quizmaker timeline is exactly the same as the process to control the timing of any other object.

Figure 12.50 shows the timeline for three answer choices in a Multiple Choice question example. The answer choices happen to be animated using the Fade In By First Level Paragraph animation effect. In this example, the first answer choice will fade in when the slide is first displayed, the second answer choice will fade in one second later, and the third answer choice will fade in two seconds after the slide is displayed. It's important to keep in mind, however, that the timeline here would look exactly the same if the answer choices did *not* have animation effects. In that case, they would simply appear on the slide using the timings specified here. As you can see, there is nothing on the timeline that shows that these objects have animation effects.

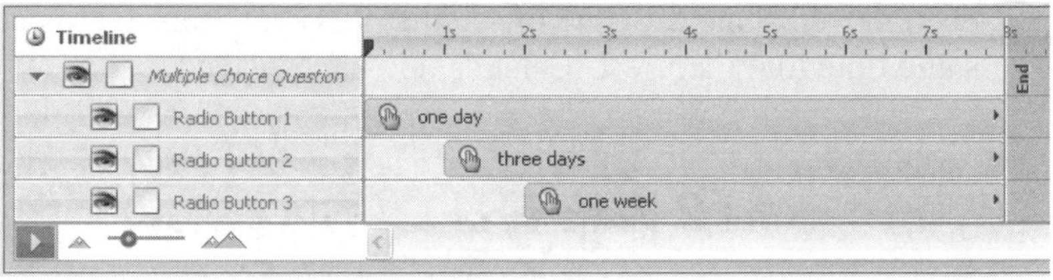

Figure 12.50. Timeline showing three timed answer choices

Tip: The section titled "Adding Animation Effects" earlier in this chapter describes how to add animation effects to objects.

Mouse Click Triggers for Animations

If you're wondering if you can control the timing of Quizmaker animations (or any other object) with a mouse click trigger, the answer is *no*. PowerPoint 2007 offers that capability because it makes sense for presenters who want to control when objects (like bullets) appear on the slide. But Quizmaker viewers are using a quiz rather than presenting information.

Controlling the Layered Order of Objects

Each object on a slide is *layered* in a default order. You can think of a layer as one item in a stack—an item can be in front of another item, obscuring part of that item, or behind an item, obscured by that item. These layers may not be apparent on the slide, because most objects have their own space on the slide—they are not stacked on top of each other. But as you design your slides, you may want some of your objects to overlap. For example, you might want to place the answer choice text boxes on top of a graphic. In that case, you need to make sure that the graphic layer is behind the text box layers.

As mentioned earlier, the objects in the timeline are also referred to as layers. The order of the layers in the timeline reflect how the objects are layered on the slide, such that objects added later display over items added previously. You can change the order of object layers by arranging the order in which they appear in the timeline. (Note that you can also order layers using the Bring to Front and Send to Back options on the Align tools on several ribbon tabs.)

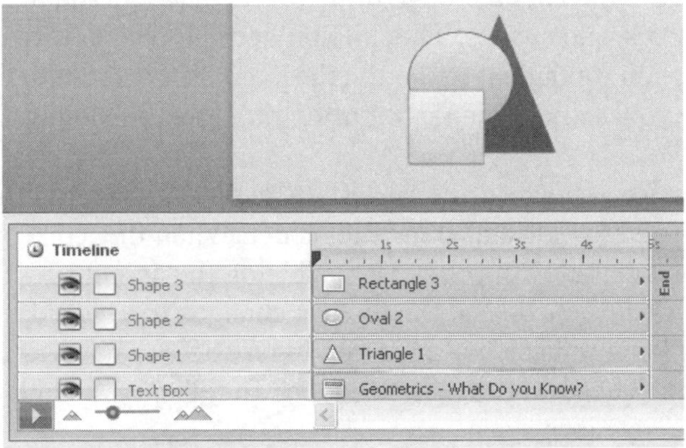

Figure 12.51. Timeline showing the layered order of three shapes

Figure 12.51 shows three shapes that were added to an introduction slide. The triangle was added first, then the oval, and finally the rectangle. As each object is added to a slide, Quizmaker puts the newest object on top of the other layers. You can change this order using several different methods. One way is to simply drag the object in the second column of the timeline to a new location. Figure 12.52 shows the result of dragging the Oval 2 object up to the top of the timeline. Notice that the oval now appears on top of the other shapes on the slide.

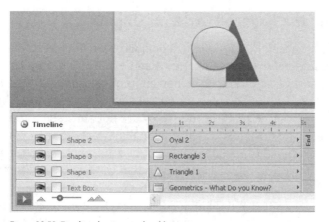

Figure 12.52. Timeline showing reordered layers

Hiding, Showing, and Locking Objects

As you build your slides, you may want to hide specific objects. For example, you can create a "rough draft" of the slide by adding text boxes, graphics, and shapes. Then, if you decide you don't want one of the objects, you can hide it without deleting it from the slide. Later, if you change your mind again (as we often do), you can simply show it again.

The eye icon shown at the far left on an object's layer in the timeline is used to hide and show the object. When the icon contains a picture of an open eye, the object is visible on the screen. To hide the object, just click the icon and the picture changes to a closed eye. The object is no longer visible on the slide. Figure 12.53 shows a slide with three shapes. The Oval 2 shape is hidden. To redisplay a hidden shape, just click the eye icon again.

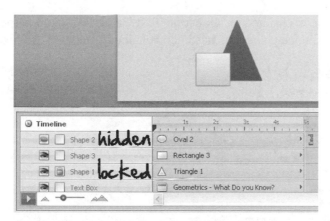

Figure 12.53. Timeline showing hidden Oval 2 and locked Triangle 1

Quizmaker also lets you lock an object on the slide, so that no changes can be made to it. This is handy when you're manipulating a number of objects and you want to ensure that an object doesn't accidentally get changed or moved. To lock an object, click the box immediately to the left of the object's name in the first column of the timeline. A lock icon appears in the box, as indicated in Figure 12.53. As long as the object is locked, you cannot select it on the slide or make any changes to it. To unlock the object, simply click the box again.

Selecting and Renaming Objects

If you've read any part of the section "Working with the Timeline," you've already learned that you can select an object by clicking its name in the timeline. This feature comes in handy even if you don't plan to use the timeline to manipulate the object. For example, you might have accidentally covered a text box with a graphic on the slide. You can't click the text box on the slide without moving the graphic out of the way. But you can quickly select the text box by clicking its name in the timeline.

Quizmaker also lets you rename objects using the timeline. By default, Quizmaker assigns "generic" names to each layer, such as Text Box and Shape 1. Although the object description in the second column is helpful, you may want to assign more descriptive names to the object layers. To rename an object, double-click its name in the first column of the timeline and then type the new name. Figure 12.54 shows two objects that have been renamed. The default name "Text

Box" has been changed to "Question Text," and the default name "Multiple Choice Question" has been renamed "Answer Choices."

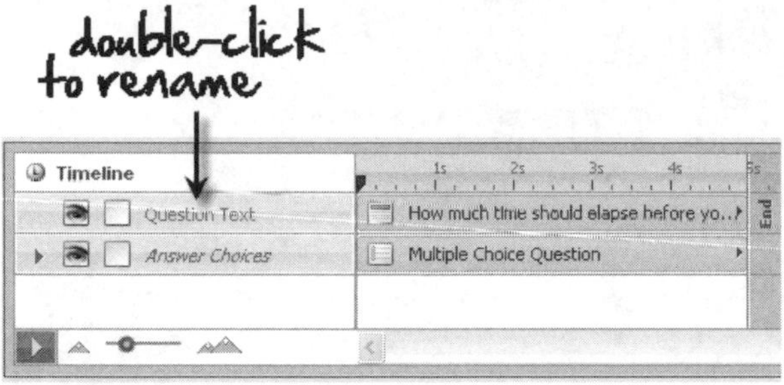

double-click to rename

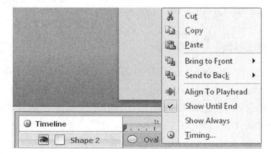

Figure 12.54. Timeline showing renamed object layers

Using the Timeline Shortcut Menu

We'll wrap up this section on the timeline by pointing out the handy shortcut menu that's available by right-clicking anywhere on an object layer. Figure 12.55 shows the shortcut menu options that are available for each object layer. Table 12.6 provides a brief description of these options.

Figure 12.55. Timeline layer shortcut menu

Table 12.6. Timeline layer shortcut menu options

Option	Description
Cut, Copy, Paste	Moves or copies the selected layer to a different layer position (order) on the slide
Bring to Front	This options leads to a submenu with two options: Bring to Front: Positions the layer so that the object is in front of (on top of) all other objects on the slide. No part of the object will be hidden by another object. Bring Forward: Positions the layer so that the object is placed in front of (on top of) the adjacent layer on the slide. In other words, this option "bumps up" the object by just one layer level.
Send to Back	This options leads to a submenu with two options: Send to Back: Positions the layer so that the object is behind (beneath) all other objects on the slide. Send Backward: Positions the layer so that the object is placed behind (beneath) the adjacent layer on the slide. In other words, this option "bumps down" the object by just one layer level.
Align To Playhead	Moves the object on the timeline so that it is aligned to the current location of the playhead. You can use this option by previewing the timeline in Slide view and then pausing the playhead at the desired time. Then select this option to move the object to the time indicated by the playhead. This is helpful when you're not quite sure when you want an object to appear/disappear. By previewing and using the playhead, you can get a better idea of when to start/stop the object.
Show Until End	Extends the duration of the object from its current start time to the End line (until the viewer moves to the next slide)
Show Always	Extends the duration of the object from the beginning of the slide to the End line. In other words, the object is always there!
Timing	Opens the Timing dialog box, where you can manually enter the start time and duration of the object

Is It a Quiz or Something Else?

Articulate's Tom Kuhlmann uses Quizmaker to build branched scenarios that can be used for discovery and practice content. When using Quizmaker this way, you can get away with far fewer constraints on pumping up your questions and quizzes. Find his demos on the Articulate site for lots of ideas.

Practice 4

||||▶ **Timing Three Graphic Objects**

As you've gathered, you can create many sophisticated effects using the timeline. In this practice, you'll create a basic effect of three graphics appearing on the slide at different times. (If you want to pump up this practice slide even more, you can apply an animation effect to each graphic.) To help you visualize the way the timeline should look after completing these steps, refer to Figure 12.56 at the end of the practice. Note that this practice relies on your knowledge of how to create a new question (covered in Chapter 9, "Quizmaker Basics") and add graphics (covered in the section "Adding Media" in this chapter).

1. Create a new Multiple Choice question in Form view by adding the question and answer choices.

2. Click the **Slide View** button on the Home tab of the ribbon to switch to Slide view.

3. Add three graphic files to the bottom of the slide. Position them so that they overlap each other. (If you don't have any graphic files to insert, use the **Shapes** tool on the Insert tab to create three different shapes.)

4. If the timeline is not displayed, click the **View** tab on the ribbon and select the **Timeline** check box. If the timeline appears as just a horizontal bar, click the double up-arrow button ⬆ on the right side of the bar.

5. The graphics should be labeled Picture 3, Picture 2, and Picture 1 in the first column of the timeline. (If you inserted shapes instead of pictures, the labels will be Shape 3, Shape 2, and Shape 1.) The graphic file names should be listed in the second column. Using the mouse, drag the file name of Picture 1 in the second column of the timeline to the **1s** marker.

6. Now use the Timing dialog box to change the timing of Picture 2:
   a. Right-click the file name of Picture 2 in the second column of the timeline.
   b. From the shortcut menu, select **Timing**.
   c. In the Timing dialog box, change the Start Time to two seconds by typing **2** and pressing **Tab**.
   d. Click the **Close** button.

7. Using the mouse, drag the file name of Picture 3 in the second column of the timeline to the **3s** marker.

8. Now change the duration of Picture 2 so that it is displayed for only five seconds:
   a. Select the file name of Picture 2 in the second column of the timeline.
   b. Using the mouse, drag the arrow on the object to align with the **7s** marker.

9. Preview the timing by clicking the **Play** button ▶ in the lower-left corner of the timeline. (Note that the slide will reset itself after the preview.)

10. Change the layering order so that Picture 1 appears in front of Picture 2. You can drag the layer (the object name in the second column) using the mouse or:
    a. Right-click anywhere on the Picture 1 layer.
    b. From the shortcut menu, select **Bring to Front**, and then select **Bring Forward**.

11. Preview the timing again by dragging the playhead from the beginning of the timeline to the End line.

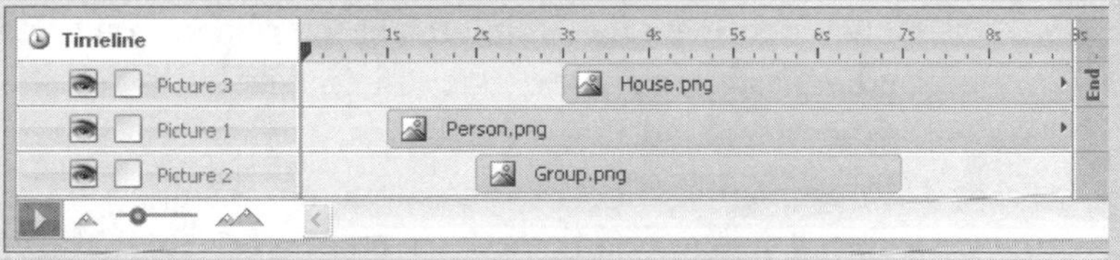

Figure 12.56. Timeline showing results of the practice

Chapter Recap

Here's our list of the most important things to remember from this chapter:

- Many of the things you can do with questions that are discussed in this chapter should be toned down for graded tests because they can be distracting or frustrating or worse.

- Not sure if the media and animations will be distracting? Err on the side of caution. And unless your viewers will love lots of things going on in the screen, make sure what you add is subtle.

- Use images and movies on your slides to serve as answer choices or provide required additional information.

- Quizmaker lets you add one image or movie file in Form view using the Media button on the Home tab of the ribbon. You can add multiple images and movies in Slide view using the Picture button and Flash button on the Insert tab of the ribbon.

- Format a picture by selecting it and then working with the tools on the context-sensitive Picture Tools Format tab. Format a movie by selecting it and working with the tools on the context-sensitive Movie Tools Options tab.

- Use audio on your slide to expand on the question, narrate an introduction, or complement the feedback text. But don't use audio gratuitously.

- You can record your own audio in Quizmaker or import an existing audio file. Quizmaker lets you import .wav and .mp3 files.

- Quizmaker lets you add one audio file in Form view using the Sound button on the Home tab of the ribbon. You can add multiple audio files in Slide view using the Sound button on the Insert tab of the ribbon.

- Use animation effects to add motion to the question text, answer choices, images, and other objects. Be careful that transitions don't become confusing or overwhelming.

- To animate an object, switch to Slide view, select the object(s), and use the tools in the Animations tab on the ribbon. You can select from a variety of entrance and exit effects.

- You can animate related objects (such as answer choices) as a group. When applying animation effects to a group, you have the option to animate all objects in the group at once (All At Once) or one at a time (By First Level Paragraph).

- Add shapes and text boxes to your slides by switching to Slide view and using the tools on the Insert tab on the ribbon.

- Use hyperlinks to link to a web page from a question slide, feedback text, non-question slide, or Results slide. Add hyperlinks using text and other objects in Slide view. Add hyperlinks to feedback text in Form view.

- The Design tab on the Slide View ribbon is similar to the Design tab in PowerPoint 2007. Use these tools to apply and customize a design theme, which affects the colors, fonts, and background of the slide.

- Use the Quizmaker slide master to globally format all slides in your quiz. For example, apply font properties to specific text elements, modify the design theme, and insert objects.

- The Quizmaker timeline lets you control when objects on the slide appear (and/or disappear).

- To change when an object appears on the slide, drag its layer to the appropriate seconds marker in the timeline. To change its duration, shrink or expand the layer in the timeline.

- The timeline also enables you to control the layering of objects, hide, show, and lock objects, select objects, and rename objects.

Chapter 13

Pumping Up Your Quizzes

Chapter Snapshot

In this chapter, you'll learn how to customize various features of your quiz.

Once you've created a quiz and built the questions, it's time to pump up your quiz by organizing those questions and inserting additional slides to help the quiz flow smoothly. Although every task covered in this chapter is optional, working with even a few of these features just might make the difference between a good quiz and a great one.

Revisiting the Quizmaker 1-2-3-4-5 Workflow

This chapter focuses on step 4 of the Quizmaker 1-2-3-4-5 workflow: Customize the quiz. Table 13.1 shows all of the substeps typically completed in this step.

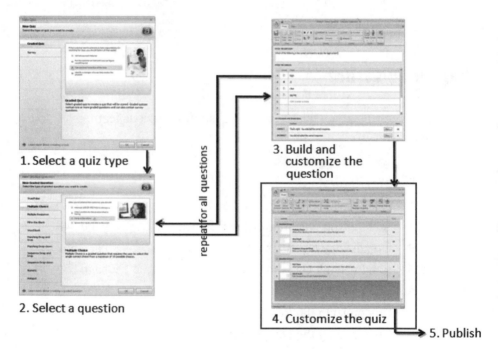

Figure 13.1. Quizmaker 1-2-3-4-5 workflow

Table 13.1. Detailed workflow for step 4

Step	Description
4. Customize the quiz	a) Add non-question (blank) slides, such as an introduction slide, review slides, and transition slides.
	b) Customize features of the quiz, such as by grouping questions, randomizing questions, and modifying the Results slide.
	c) Customize the Quizmaker player, such as by modifying the color scheme and changing navigation options.
	d) Create quiz templates for future use.

Substeps a) and b) basically affect the structure of the slides in the quiz. Substep c) affects how the quiz looks and works in the player, and substep d) is handy when you want to create a new quiz based on features from an existing quiz. In addition to these substeps, we've included a brief section on creating a branched scenario and a final section showing some really creative quiz examples to inspire you to go beyond the basics.

Although we've placed step 4 after step 3 (build and customize questions) in the workflow, keep in mind that you can customize your quiz at the same time as you build your questions. We placed this step after the other steps because you need a few slides in your quiz before performing many of the tasks in this chapter. Also keep in mind that part of customizing your quiz involves setting global properties using the Quiz Properties dialog box. Many developers set these properties before starting a quiz, since many of the options affect the default values in new slides. Chapter 9, "Quizmaker Basics," covers working with the Quiz Properties dialog box.

Let's begin by exploring how to insert additional slides in your quiz.

Quizmaker

Adding Non-Question (Blank) Slides

In addition to creating 20 different types of question slides, you can insert additional "non-question" slides in your quiz using Quizmaker's Blank Slide feature. A blank slide is just that—an empty canvas that you can use however you want. Blank slides give you the opportunity to provide more information to your viewers as they step through the questions.

Figure 13.2. Introduction slide created from a blank slide

Following are a few ideas for using blank slides:

- **Quiz introduction:** Describe the purpose of the quiz (Figure 13.2) and, for surveys, provide a reason to respond.

- **Quiz instructions:** Provide instructions for taking the quiz and describe how to navigate the quiz, if needed.

- **Pre-question content:** Provide content before presenting the question. For example, show a diagram of computer components using a blank slide, and then ask the viewer to recall components on the next question slide. If the content is needed to answer the question (such as a video of a customer service scenario), you should ideally put that content on the slide with the question.

- **Review content:** Reinforce the content covered by a question after the fact. This is especially useful for self-check questions, which help viewers determine if they understand the content but the "score" doesn't count. Using Quizmaker's branching feature, you can even direct viewers to a specific review slide based on whether they answered the question correctly or incorrectly.

- **Group transition:** If you organize your questions into groups (covered later in this chapter), you can insert a slide that provides a transition between one group of questions and the next. This might include an introduction or instructions or other valuable information.

- **Customized feedback:** Instead of using the default feedback pop-up box, display a more robust feedback slide that can include pictures, movies, and hyperlinks.

 Note: In case you're wondering, you cannot develop a new question type using a blank slide. The answer choice (tracking) functionality is not built into a blank slide.

The steps for creating a non-question slide are similar to those for creating a question slide. You can build the slide in Form view and/or Slide view, although Slide view is your best bet if you plan to add more than just simple text and a media file.

To add a non-question slide, click the **Blank Slide** button, which is located on the Home tab of the Quiz window ribbon (Figure 13.3). (Note that if you're creating a survey or if your application window is large, the Blank Slide button will look like this: [Blank Slide] .)

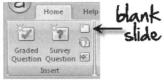

Figure 13.3. Graded Quiz window ribbon, Insert group of the Home tab

After you click the Blank Slide button, the slide is opened in Form view by default (Figure 13.4). This view provides placeholders for a title at the top of the slide, text in the center of the slide, and feedback at the bottom. The feedback placeholder is blank by default, meaning no feedback will be displayed unless you add it.

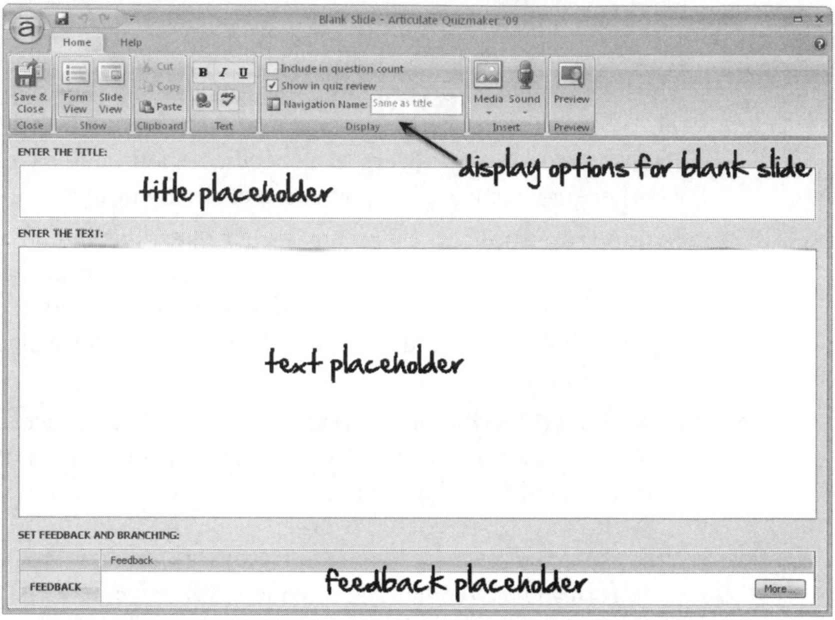

Figure 13.4. Blank slide in Form view Question window

Notice that the Display group on the ribbon contains options that are different from the options for questions. Because blank slides are not used for questions and answers, there are no scoring options. Instead, the following options are included:

- **Include in question count:** Select this option if you want the slide to count as one question in the quiz. The question count is displayed as the label of the Question navigation menu, which appears in the upper-left corner of the Quizmaker player as the viewer takes the quiz. In most cases, you would not include information slides in the question count.

- **Show in quiz review:** Select this option if you want this slide displayed when the viewer chooses to review each slide in the quiz. If the content is needed to answer the quiz question, the information slide should be shown.

- **Navigation Name:** The navigation name identifies the slide in the question navigation menu in the upper-left corner of the Quizmaker player. By default, the text displayed in the Title section of the slide is used as the navigation name. Using the Navigation Name field, you can change this name, if desired.

You can start building the blank slide in Form view by completing the placeholders, if desired. You can also add one picture or movie and one sound clip in Form view. To pump up the slide with animations, additional graphics, and other features, switch to Slide view. The procedures to build a slide in Form view and Slide view are covered in Chapter 9, "Quizmaker Basics," and Chapter 12, "Pumping Up Your Questions." These procedures are basically the same for both non-question blank slides and question slides.

After you save and close the blank slide, the new slide is inserted in the Question list (Figure 13.5). The name of the slide is Blank Slide, although we all know that it's not really blank anymore. You can move the slide to a different location in the list by dragging it with your mouse, using the Move Question button ✥ · on the ribbon, or using the Move Question command on the slide's shortcut menu.

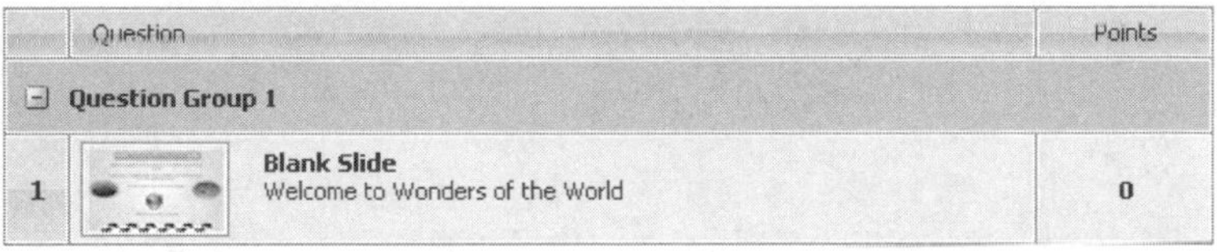

Question	Points
⊟ **Question Group 1**	
1 **Blank Slide** Welcome to Wonders of the World	0

Figure 13.5. Blank slide in the Question list

Now that you know how to create question slides and non-question slides, you can organize them within the quiz. You may want to refer to the section titled "Working with the Question List" in Chapter 9, "Quizmaker Basics," which describes a few ways to organize questions, such as by moving and deleting them. The next few sections in this chapter describe some additional ways to organize your questions and other slides.

Organizing Questions into Groups

As you add questions and other slides to your quiz, Quizmaker auto-matically places them together in one group—the default Question Group 1 in the Quiz window. However, you can organize your slides into multiple groups using Quizmaker's group feature. Grouping lets you divide your quiz into separate sections so that each section can be manipulated separately. For example, you may want the quiz to consist of a set of graded questions and a set of survey questions (Figure 13.6). You want the graded questions to be randomized in the quiz, but you want the survey questions displayed in a specific order. By creating two groups, you can randomize the graded question group and fix the order of the survey question group.

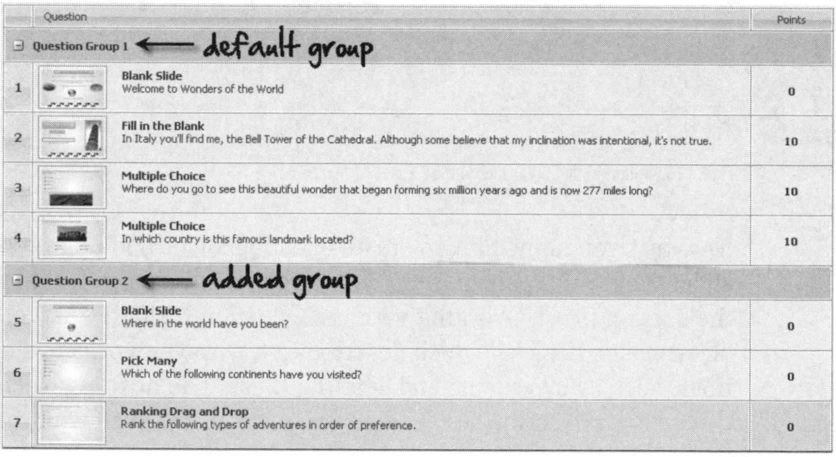

Figure 13.6. Question pane with grouped questions

When you organize and randomize questions in a group, you have the option of including and omitting specific questions and can even lock specific questions into place. Organizing the slides into groups can make it easier to work with the questions, especially for large quizzes. You can copy, move, and preview questions as a group, making editing and testing your quizzes even easier.

Adding Question Pools

The ability to organize and randomize questions in "pools" has very important learning assessment implications. If you group questions by learning objective, you can set the number of questions to be "included" from each group. To do this you will:

1. Create the bank of questions.
2. Group them by learning objective.
3. Select to randomize the questions from each group.
4. Select the number of questions to include from each group.

Because you can determine how many questions to include from each group, you are able to build a question bank and weight certain learning objectives as more important by including more questions from more important learning objectives.

Keep in mind that the group feature in Quizmaker is just a development tool. The grouping of questions is transparent to your viewers, meaning they won't see question groups in the Question navigation panel. You can, however, separate groups using a non-question (blank) slide that provides a transition between the groups. Also keep in mind that you cannot score groups separately. All questions in the quiz, regardless of groups, are scored together. The viewer receives one pass/fail score on the Results slide for all questions in the quiz.

You can add a new group anytime using the **Question Group** button ⚏ on the Home tab of the Quiz window ribbon. (Note that if you're creating a survey or if your application window is large, the Question Group button will look like this: ⚏ Question Group .)

After you click this button, Quizmaker adds a new group to the end of the quiz and assigns it the default title of **Question Group x**, where x is the next group number.

Once you have created a new group, you can use it to organize your questions. Following are some of the ways you can work with groups.

Create a New Question (or Slide) in a Group

To add a new question to the group:

1. Click the group title.

2. Click either the **Graded Question**, **Survey Question**, or **Blank Slide** button on the ribbon.

3. Build the slide. (These tasks are covered in other Quizmaker chapters.)

Move an Existing Question (or Slide) to a Group

You can move an existing question to a different group using several methods:

- Using the mouse, drag the question or slide from one group into another group.

- Right-click the question or slide and use the **Cut** and **Paste** commands or the **Move Question** command on the question's shortcut menu.

Change the Group Name

To change the group title to be more descriptive:

1. Click the group title and then click it again, *or* right-click the group title and select the **Rename Group** command from the group's shortcut menu (Figure 13.7).

2. Type the new group name and press **Enter**.

Figure 13.7. Question pane: Group shortcut menu

Move a Group

To move the group before or after another group in the quiz:

1. Click the group title.

2. Click the **Move Group** button on the ribbon and select **Up** or **Down**. (Note that the Move Group button changes to the Move Question button when a question is selected.)

You can also use the **Move Group** command on the group's shortcut menu to move the group (Figure 13.7).

Delete a Group

Deleting a group deletes *all* of the questions in the group. So if you just want to combine questions into a different group, first move the questions and then delete the empty group.

To delete a group:

1. Click the group title.

2. Click the **Delete Group** button ☒ on the ribbon. (Note that the Delete Group button changes to the Delete Question button when a question is selected.)

You can also use the **Delete Group** command on the group's shortcut menu to move the group (Figure 13.7).

Preview a Group

To preview only one group of questions (instead of all questions in the quiz):

1. Right-click the group title.

2. From the shortcut menu, select **Preview Group** (Figure 13.7).

Collapse and Expand the Question Display

To collapse (hide) the display of the questions in a group, click the ⊟ button to the left of the group title. The button then changes to ⊞, which you can click to expand (show) the display of questions.

Quizmaker also enables you to randomize questions within a group, which is covered in the next section.

Randomizing Questions

Whether your quiz has just one group of questions or several groups, you can randomize the order of questions within a group using the Group tools in the Home tab of the Quiz window. Randomizing displays the questions in a different order each time a viewer takes the quiz. This can be helpful when viewers may take the quiz more than once (for example, they need to pass the quiz before proceeding to the next lesson or module). By default, questions in a group are *not* randomized. When a quiz is previewed or published, the questions are displayed in the order they appear in the Question list. As mentioned earlier, you can choose to randomize questions in one group, and keep the predefined, non-random order in another group.

To randomize questions in a group:

1. Click the group title.

2. Click the **Randomize Group** button on the Home tab of the ribbon. The button becomes highlighted on the ribbon (Figure 13.8) and the message *(Randomize all questions)* is displayed next to the group title (Figure 13.9).

Figure 13.8. Group tab with Randomize Group option selected

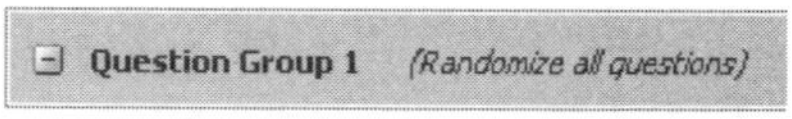

Figure 13.9. Question Group 1 randomized

Once you randomize a group of questions, the Include and Lock Question tools become available on the ribbon. These tools let you work with the questions in the randomized group as follows:

■ To specify the number of questions to be asked, click the **Include** list box and select a number from the list. Each group must include at least one question, so the list will display **All** and the numbers **1** through **x**, where x is one less than the total number of questions in the group (Figure 13.10).

Tip: If you do not see any numbers on the list, drag the lower border [⎯⎯⎯⎯⎯] of the list down.

■ To lock a question so that it is *always included,* first click the question in the Question list, then click the **Lock Question** button and select one of the options (Figure 13.11). These options let you choose where the question appears within the randomized group. For example, you might want an introduction slide (created from a blank slide) to always appear as the first slide in the group. Note that some options may not be available depending on the relative position of the question in the group. After locking a question, you can unlock it by selecting the **Remove Lock** option.

Figure 13.10. Group tab with Include options displayed

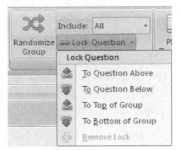

Figure 13.11. Group tab with Lock Question options displayed

After randomizing your questions, it's a good idea to preview the quiz. You may find that some questions don't work well when randomized. If that is the case, you can modify the randomizing features, or turn off randomizing completely.

Importing Questions

As you build your quizzes, you may find that you want to include questions from other quizzes. Quizmaker lets you easily import existing questions from other Quizmaker '09 and Quizmaker 2 quizzes. The Import Questions button on the Insert group of the Quiz window ribbon (Figure 13.12) lets you import individual questions, all questions, or specific groups of questions.

Figure 13.12. Insert Group of the Home tab

To import questions:

1. Open the quiz into which you want to import questions.

2. If your quiz contains more than one group, click the group title into which the question(s) will be imported. Otherwise, the questions will be imported into the first question group.

3. Click the **Import Questions** button on the Home tab of the ribbon. (Note that if you're creating a survey or if your application window is large, the Import Questions button will look like this:  .)

4. In the Open dialog box, browse to and double-click the quiz containing the questions you want to import.

5. The Import Questions dialog box displays all of the questions in the quiz you selected (Figure 13.13). Select the questions you want to import and then click the **OK** button. Note that you can select and deselect questions as follows:

■ Select the check box next to one or more questions.

■ Select the **Include All** check box on a group title to select all of the questions in that group.

■ Click the **Check all questions** button 🔲 to select all of the questions in the quiz.

■ Click the **Uncheck all questions** button ✖ to clear all of the current selections.

■ Clear any selection by clicking its check box again to remove the check.

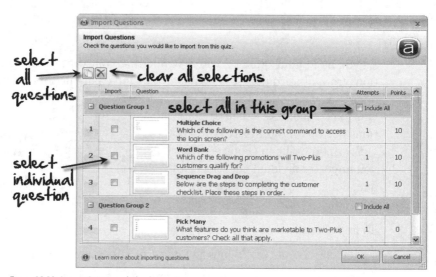

Figure 13.13. Import Questions dialog box

66 **Note:** If you try to import a graded question into a survey, Quizmaker displays a warning message that gives you the option to convert the survey to a graded quiz.

By default, Quizmaker adds the imported question(s) to the end of the group. You can then move the questions to different locations, if desired.

Customizing the Results Slide

After your viewers have completed the required questions in a quiz, the Results slide is displayed as the last slide in the quiz by default. In a graded quiz, either the Pass Result or Fail Result slide is shown, depending on the viewer's score. In a survey, the Survey Result slide is shown, which offers a thank you message. Quizmaker lets you customize the Pass Result, Fail Result, and Survey Result slides by specifying options in Form view and modifying the slide design in Slide view. The options for customizing the Pass Result and Fail Result slides are almost identical, so we'll cover customizing just the Pass Result slide. We'll also take a quick look at how to customize the Survey Result slide.

To customize the Pass Result slide, start by clicking the **Pass Result** button on the Home tab of the Quiz window ribbon. The slide is displayed in Form view by default. Here you can select and clear

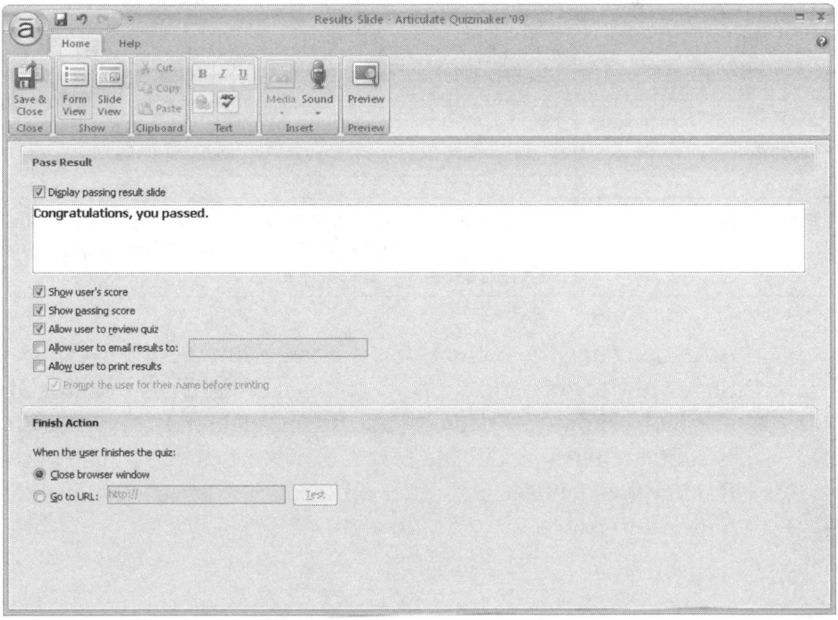

Figure 13.14. Pass Result slide (default settings) in Form view

specific options, as well as customize the text that appears at the top of the slide. Figure 13.14 shows the default settings for the Pass Result slide, and Table 13.2 provides a brief description of each option.

Table 13.2. Pass Result slide options

Option	Description
Display passing result slide	Select this option to display passing results at the end of the quiz. Clear this option if you don't want to display the passing results.
Message text	Use this text box to customize the message displayed to the viewer. You can format the message using the tools in the Text group on the ribbon, or by switching to Slide view and using the formatting tools there.
Show user's score	Select this option to show the viewer's score as a percentage and the number of points scored.
Show passing score	Select this option to include the passing score of the quiz, such as 80%.
Allow user to review quiz	Select this option to include the Review Quiz button on the slide, along with instructions for the viewer. The review displays the correct answer along with the viewer's response.
Allow user to email results to	Select this option to include the Email Results button on the slide, along with instructions for the viewer. The viewer has the option to email the results to the address that you specify here.
Allow user to print results	Select this option to include the Print Results button on the slide, along with instructions for the viewer. The viewer has the option to send a formatted copy of the quiz results to another browser window. The results can then be printed using the browser's print tools. When this option is selected, you can also select or clear the Prompt the user for their name for printing option. This enables the viewer's name to be displayed at the top of the printed results.
Finish action: Close browser window	You can select only one option in the Finish Action section. The default option, Close browser window, closes the Quizmaker player and browser window after the viewer clicks the Finish button.
Finish action: Go to URL	The Go to URL option displays the web page that you enter in the text box to the right of the option. Use the Test button to verify the web page address from the Pass Result slide.

After selecting the options you want in Form view, you can switch to Slide view to customize the appearance of the Pass Result slide. Figure 13.15 shows the default Pass Result slide in Slide view. Each item is contained in a modifiable text box. Note that the Finish button, Review Quiz button, and other optional buttons are not displayed in Slide view.

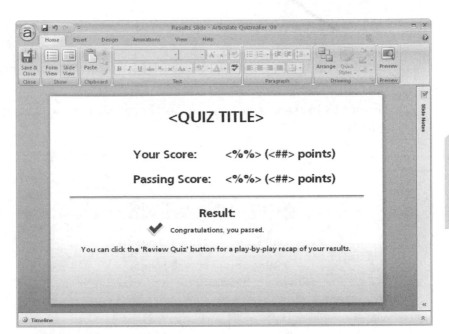

Figure 13.15. Pass Result slide (default settings) in Slide view

You can customize the Pass Result slide in much the same way as you would customize any other slide in Slide view. Following are some ideas for customizing the Pass Result (and Fail Result) slide:

■ Delete any of the items, such as the quiz title.

■ Change the Score display to show only the percentage or only the points.

■ Change the ✔ icon by inserting a different picture.

■ Change the "Congratulations, you passed" text. (Note that you can also change this in Form view.)

■ Change the instructions for additional options text.

■ Add a picture, movie, illustration, and/or sound clip using the Insert tab on the ribbon.

■ Add a hyperlink to a web page.

■ Animate objects using the Animations tab.

- Change the colors, fonts, and/or background using the Design tab on the ribbon.
- Change the layout of the slide, such as showing the score on the left side and the accompanying text on the right side.

Figure 13.16 shows a customized Pass Result slide in the Quizmaker player.

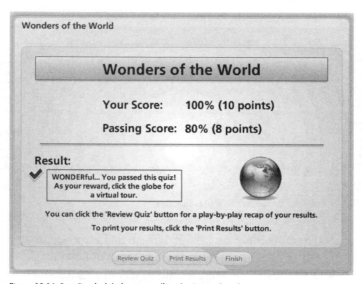

Figure 13.16. Pass Result slide (customized) in the Quizmaker player

The Survey Result slide is similar to the Pass Result and Fail Result slides, except that fewer options are available for surveys. For example, no scores are displayed because surveys are not graded. The Survey Result slide is accessible from the Quiz window of a survey by clicking the **Survey Result** button on the ribbon. Figure 13.17 shows the default options for the Survey Result slide in Form view. These options are also available on the Pass Result slide, which are described in Table 13.2.

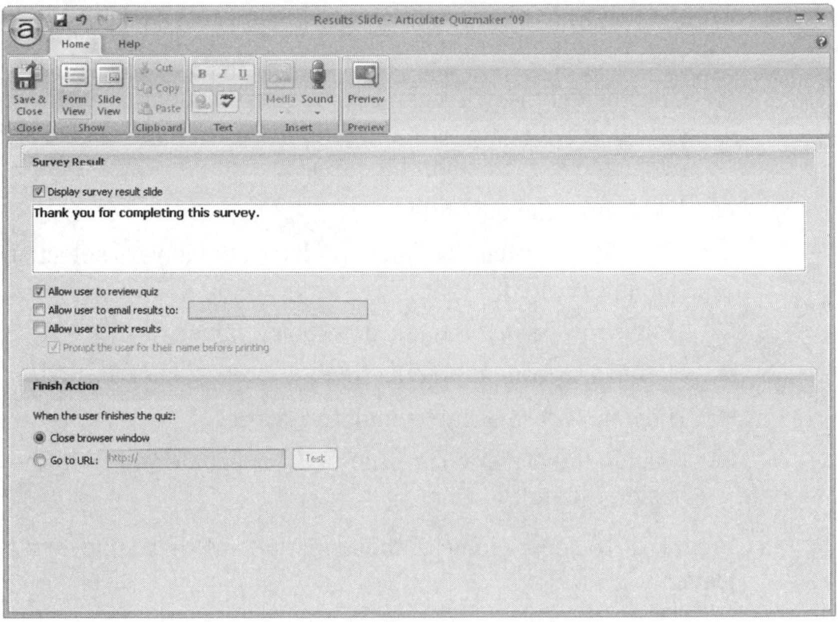

Figure 13.17. Survey Result slide (default settings) in Form view

The procedures for customizing the Survey Result slide are the same as those for customizing the Pass Result and Fail Result slides. After selecting the options you want in Form view, you can switch to Slide view to customize the slide.

Customizing the Quizmaker Player

The Quizmaker player displays the quiz slides and contains the navigation controls for your viewers to use. The way the player looks and acts depends on the player *template* selected for the quiz. The template determines a number of features, such as how the questions are submitted and the color scheme used by the player.

Quizmaker comes with four preconfigured templates, each of which includes (or omits) various player features. By default, the Quiz - Submit one at a time template is applied to all new graded quizzes and surveys. You can keep this default template, select a different template, or customize the template and save it as a new template. Why customize the template? You might want to add features to the player or omit features that are not appropriate for your quiz. For example, you can:

- Control whether viewers submit questions one at a time (feedback can be provided for each question) or all at once (all questions are evaluated at the end of the quiz).

- Hide/show the quiz title.

- Hide/show/format the Question list (lets viewers select any question in the quiz).

- Hide/show/format the question point value.

- Hide/show/format the quiz timer.

- Hide/show/format the cumulative score.

- Change the player color scheme (this is different from the slide design theme).

Figure 13.18 shows some of these features as they appear on the player.

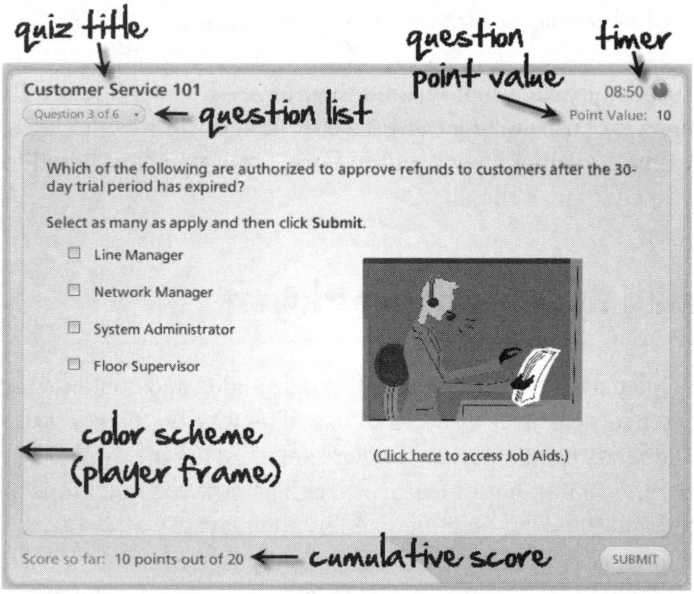

Figure 13.18. Examples of customizable features in the Quizmaker player

In Chapter 9, "Quizmaker Basics," we mentioned that you should take a look at the default template before building your quiz. This is generally a good idea, but keep in mind that you can work with the player template anytime during development. As you build your questions, you might think of features you want to add, remove, or change.

There are three ways you can change the features of the player for the current quiz:

■ Select a different player template, such as one of the four preconfigured player templates.

■ Edit the player template.

■ Create a new player template.

The following sections discuss all three of these methods.

Selecting a Preconfigured Player Template

The four preconfigured Quizmaker player templates are designed for specific types of quizzes. The appropriate feature options for each quiz type are selected or omitted in the associated template, which affects the function and appearance of the player. For example, the Quiz - Submit one at a time player template selects the option for viewers to submit questions one at a time instead of all at once at the end of the quiz.

All player templates are accessible from the Player Template Manager dialog box, as shown in Figure 13.19. Chapter 9, "Quizmaker Basics," describes each preconfigured player template, but Table 13.3 provides a recap of these descriptions.

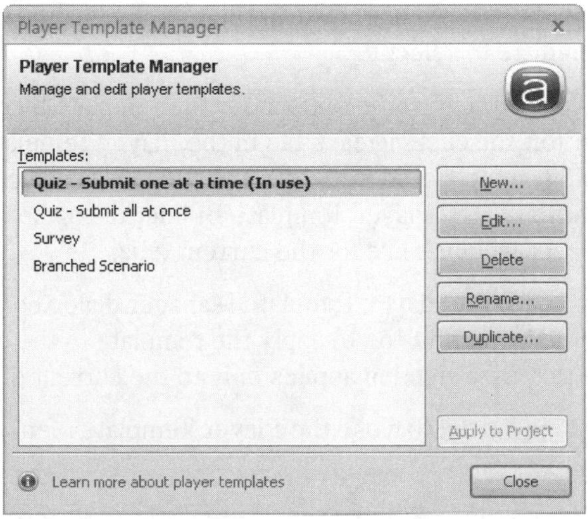

Figure 13.19. Player Template Manager dialog box

Table 13.3. Player Template Manager dialog box preconfigured templates

Template	Description
Quiz - Submit one at a time	Structures the quiz so that viewers answer a question, submit it, and receive feedback (if provided) for each question. The Question list navigation panel is included, allowing viewers to jump to specific questions. A cumulative score for graded quizzes is also included.
Quiz - Submit all at once	Structures the quiz so that viewers answer all questions and submit them together. (No feedback can be displayed for individual questions.) The Question list navigation panel is included, allowing viewers to jump to specific questions. A cumulative score cannot be displayed because the questions are graded together at the end of the quiz.
Survey	Structures the quiz based on the features of a typical survey. Questions are answered and submitted one at a time, but scoring and point values are not included. The Question list navigation panel is not included.
Branched Scenario	Structures the quiz based on the features of a typical branched scenario, which displays specific slides based on how the viewers answer a question. *Note that the branching itself is not part of the template; you implement the branching functionality as you build the slides.* The template structures the player so that viewers answer and submit questions one a time. The Question list navigation panel is omitted so that viewers cannot jump to different questions.

To select a preconfigured player template for the current quiz:

1. In the Quiz window, click the **Player Templates** button on the Home tab of the ribbon.

2. The player templates are displayed in the Player Template Manager dialog box (Figure 13.19). The template currently used by the quiz displays the text (In use) next to the template name. Click a different template to select it.

3. If desired, you can review the options for the template by clicking the **Edit** button and clicking each tab in the Player Template Builder dialog box (covered in the next section). You can click the **Preview** button in the Player Template Builder dialog box to see what the player will look like for the current quiz.

4. After returning to the Player Template Manager dialog box, click the **Apply to Project** button to apply the template to the current quiz. (Note that the selection applies only to the current quiz.)

5. Click the **Close** button to close the Player Template Manager dialog box.

6. It's a good idea to preview the entire quiz in the new template by clicking the **Preview** button on the Home tab of the Quiz window ribbon. If you don't like the way the player works or looks, you can edit specific features; this process is covered in the next section.

---

66 **Note:** If you create new templates later, you can follow the steps above to apply a new template to the current quiz.

Editing a Player Template

Quizmaker lets you edit the settings in any preconfigured template and any new templates you create. (However, if you edit a preconfigured template, Quizmaker prompts you to save the template as a new template. This keeps the preconfigured template intact, so that it is available for other quizzes.) The settings you edit in the template will apply only to the current quiz, although you can apply the revised template to other quizzes if you want.

The process of editing a template is pretty straightforward. The most important part is understanding how all the different settings affect the function and appearance of the quiz. The steps below describe how to edit the template, and then each group of settings is described in detail.

To edit a template:

1. In the Quiz window, click the **Player Templates** button on the Home tab of the ribbon.

2. In the Player Template Manager dialog box, make sure the template you want to edit and apply to the quiz is selected.

3. Click the **Edit** button.

4. In the Player Template Builder dialog box (Figure 13.20), modify the desired settings in each tabbed group. (These settings are described next.)

5. If desired, preview the new settings by clicking the **Preview** button. Then close the Player Template Preview window.

6. In the Player Template Builder dialog box, click the **OK** button to accept the changes or click **Cancel** to discard the changes.

7.   If you made changes to a preconfigured template, you will be prompted to enter a new name for the template. Enter the new name and click **OK**.

8.   The edited template is automatically applied to the current quiz. In the Player Template Manager dialog box, click the **Close** button.

Now let's take a look at the settings you can modify in the Player Template Builder dialog box.

Changing Layout Settings

The Layout tab in the Player Template Builder dialog box contains settings that affect whether certain items appear on the player for the current quiz. Selecting a check box shows the item, and clearing a check box hides the item. Figure 13.20 displays the Layout tab and Table 13.4 describes each setting.

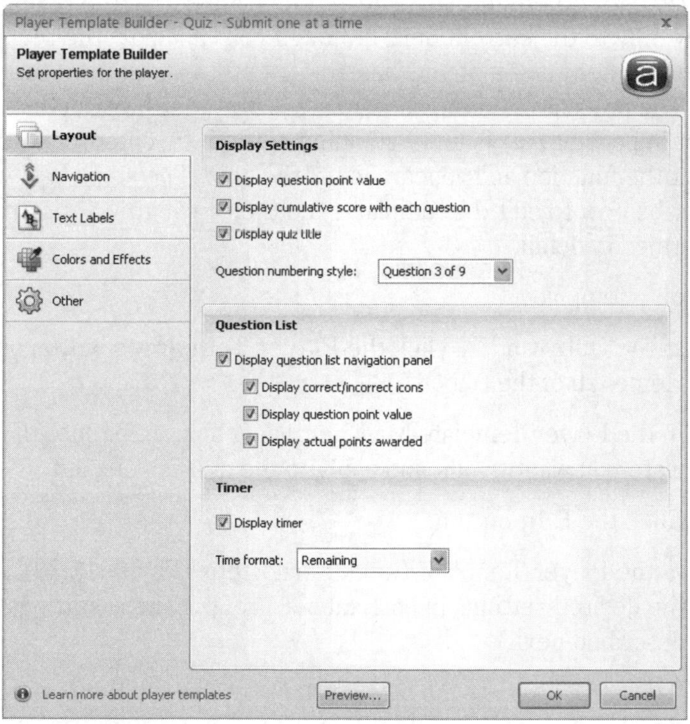

Figure 13.20. Player Template Builder dialog box Layout tab

Table 13.4. Player Template Builder dialog box Layout tab settings

Layout tab sections	Description	
Display Settings	Sets the following items to be visible on the player:	
	Display question point value	Shows/hides the point value assigned to the current question
	Display cumulative score with each question	Shows/hides the total score of the questions answered up to the current question
	Display quiz title	Shows/hides the title of the quiz at the top of the player
	Question numbering style	Sets the format of the question number in the upper-left corner of the player
Question List	Sets properties of the Question list (Figure 13.21), which enables viewers to select a specific question to answer (instead of answering the questions in order).	
	Display Question list navigation panel	Shows/hides the Question list navigation panel. If selected, the remaining options in this section are available.
	Display correct/ incorrect icons	Shows/hides the correct/incorrect icons that are displayed next to each question in the Question list. The icons indicate whether the viewer answered previously viewed questions correctly.
	Display question point value	Shows/hides the point value assigned to the question in the Question list
	Display actual points awarded	Shows/hides the points earned by the viewer for each question in the Question list. This is applicable to previously viewed questions.
Timer	Sets the display of the timer in the upper-right corner of the player. Note that the timer is displayed only when the Time Limit option in the Quiz Properties dialog box is enabled.	
	Display timer	Select to display the timer.
	Time format	Select the format of the timer display, in hours (if applicable), minutes, and seconds.

Quizmaker

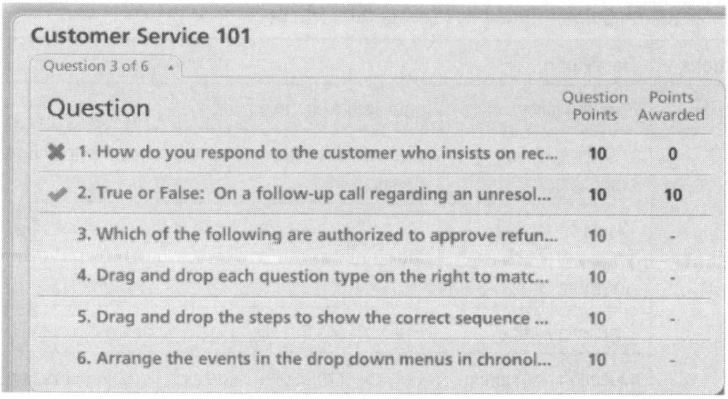

Figure 13.21. Question list navigation panel

Changing Navigation Settings

The Navigation tab in the Player Template Builder dialog box contains settings that let you control how the current quiz functions. Figure 13.22 displays the Navigation tab and Table 13.5 describes each setting.

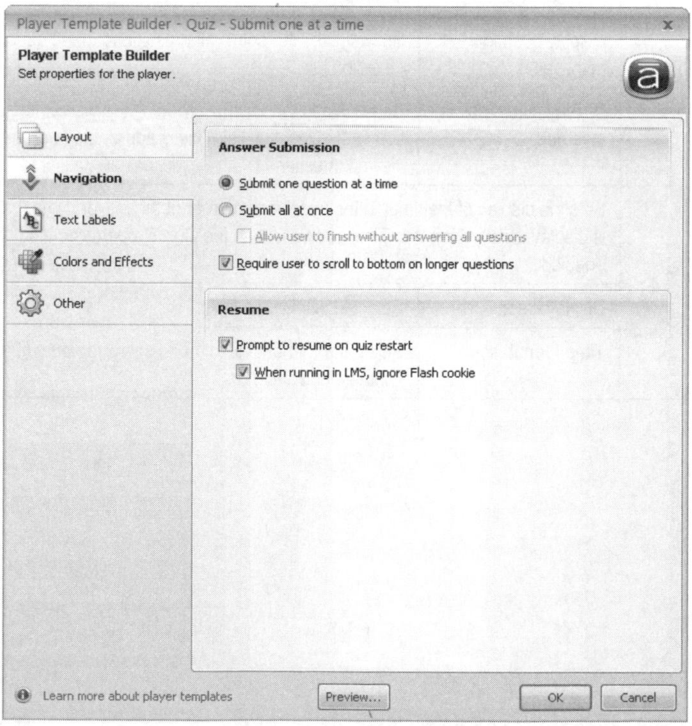

Figure 13.22. Player Template Builder dialog box Navigation tab

Table 13.5. Player Template Builder dialog box Navigation tab settings

Navigation tab sections	Description	
Answer Submission	Determines how the viewer answers the questions:	
	Submit one question at a time	Viewers answer a question and submit it before moving to the next question. Feedback can be provided for each question.
	Submit all at once	Viewers answer all of the questions and then submit them as a group. Feedback and branching cannot be provided for the questions.
	Allow user to finish without answering all questions	If the Submit all at once option is selected, choosing this option allows viewers to skip questions.
	Require user to scroll to bottom on longer questions	If the slide content is long enough to generate scroll bars, viewers must scroll through the entire question before being allowed to answer it.
Resume	Sets the resume feature of the quiz:	
	Prompt to resume on quiz restart	If viewers leave the quiz and return later, they are given the option to resume the quiz where they left off.
	When running in LMS, ignore Flash cookie	If selected, the quiz uses bookmarking from LMS (if supported). If unchecked, the quiz resumes using LMS resume data, if supported. Otherwise, the Flash cookie is used.

Changing Text Labels

The Text Labels tab of the Player Template Builder dialog box (Figure 13.23) lets you change the text that appears on the 60 player buttons and messages for the current quiz. The Buttons/Messages column provides a description of each text label, and the Custom Text column shows the currently assigned text. To change the currently assigned text, click the entry in the Custom Text column and enter the new text. For example, you can change the text that indicates the point value of the current question. Figure 13.24 shows the default text label and Figure 13.25 shows the customized text label.

Figure 13.23. Player Template Builder dialog box Text Labels tab

Figure 13.24. Default Point Value
text label

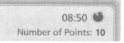

Figure 13.25. Customized Point
Value text label

After making changes to the text labels, you have the option to save the entire revised set of labels for use in another quiz. (Note that this step is not mandatory, as any changes you make here will be applied to the current player template.) Click the **Save** button below the text labels list and then enter a file name for the text label file. All text label files end with the file name extension .labels and are stored by default in the Text Labels subfolder within Articulate's application data folders. After saving a set of revised text labels, you can apply them to any player template. Click the **Load** button below the text labels list and select the text label file (which ends with the file name extension .labels).

Quizmaker also gives you the option to display text labels in other languages. Click the Language list and select one of the following languages:

- English (modified)
- Chinese (simplified)
- Chinese (traditional)
- Dutch
- English
- French
- German
- Italian
- Japanese
- Korean
- Portuguese (Brazil)
- Spanish

After you select a different language, Quizmaker automatically translates each entry in the Custom Text column to that language.

Changing Colors and Effects

The Colors and Effects tab in the Player Template Builder dialog box lets you modify the color scheme, sound effects, and fonts used by the player for the current quiz. Figure 13.26 displays the Colors and Effects tab and Table 13.6 describes each setting.

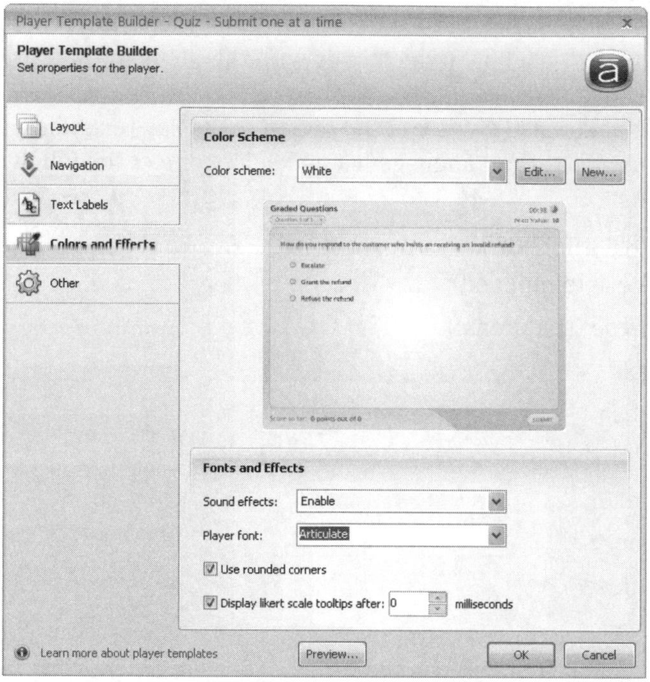

Figure 13.26. Player Template Builder dialog box Colors and Effects tab

Table 13.6. Player Template Builder dialog box Colors and Effects tab settings

Colors and Effects tab sections	Description	
Color Scheme	Lets you select a preconfigured color scheme to apply to the player or customize the color scheme using the Edit and New buttons. (Customizing the color scheme is covered in the next section.) A preview of the selected color scheme is displayed in the slide thumbnail in this section.	
Fonts and Effects	Sets the sound effects and fonts used by the player:	
	Sound effects	Enables or disables the sound effects that are played as certain items are displayed and as viewers click or roll over items
	Player font	Changes the font used in labels on the player, such as the quiz title and point value label. This option does not affect the fonts used by the quiz slides.
	Use rounded corners	If selected, corners of the player are rounded. If not selected, corners are square.
	Display likert scale tooltips after ____ milliseconds	Applies only to Likert Scale survey questions. Specifies when the tooltips that describe the scale values are displayed.

Customizing the Color Scheme

The color scheme affects a number of elements in the Quizmaker player, such as the frame color, text color, and button colors. Keep in mind, however, that the *player color scheme* is different from the *design theme colors* applied to the slides in a quiz. When you apply a design theme, the colors affect the slides and the slide content. When you apply a player color scheme, the colors affect only the Quizmaker player.

Quizmaker provides a set of preconfigured player color schemes that you can apply to the player for the current quiz. The default scheme is White. You can change the color scheme by opening the Player Template Builder dialog box, clicking the Colors and Effects tab, and selecting a different scheme in the Color scheme list (Figure 13.27). The slide thumbnail below the Color scheme list then displays a preview of the selected color scheme.

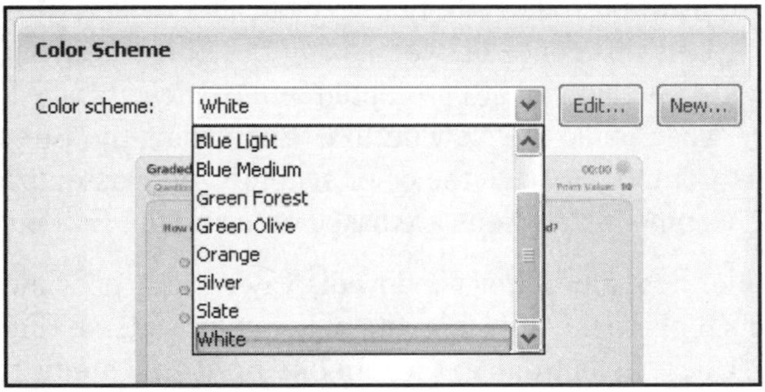

Figure 13.27. Player Template Builder dialog box Color scheme list

Tip: Quizmaker (and Engage) contain many of the preconfigured color schemes that are included in Presenter. So if you plan to incorporate the quiz into a Presenter project, you might consider applying the color scheme used by the Presenter player.

Quizmaker also lets you customize any color scheme (thereby creating a new color scheme) by changing the colors of specific elements in the scheme. For example, suppose you like everything about the default White color scheme, except you want to modify the color of the text that appears on the player buttons and labels. You can change only that element of the color scheme, and then save the modified scheme as a new color scheme. The new scheme is automatically applied to the player for the current quiz and can also be applied to other quizzes, if desired.

To customize a player color scheme:

1. In the Quiz window, click the **Player Templates** button on the Home tab of the ribbon.

2. In the Player Template Manager dialog box, make sure the template you want to edit is selected and click the **Edit** button.

3. In the Player Template Builder dialog box, click the **Colors and Effects** tab.

4. Using the Color scheme list, select the color scheme to use as a basis for the customized color scheme (Figure 13.27).

5. Click the **Edit** button. (Note that you can also click the **New** button. The only difference between using the Edit button and the New button is that you are prompted *immediately* to save the color scheme when using the New button. When using the Edit button, you are prompted to save the color scheme *after* customizing it. The remaining instructions are based on using the Edit button.)

6. The Color Scheme Editor window displays a slide preview and contains tools to modify elements of the color scheme (Figure 13.28). Click the button next to **Choose an item to edit** to select an element to modify (Figure 13.29).

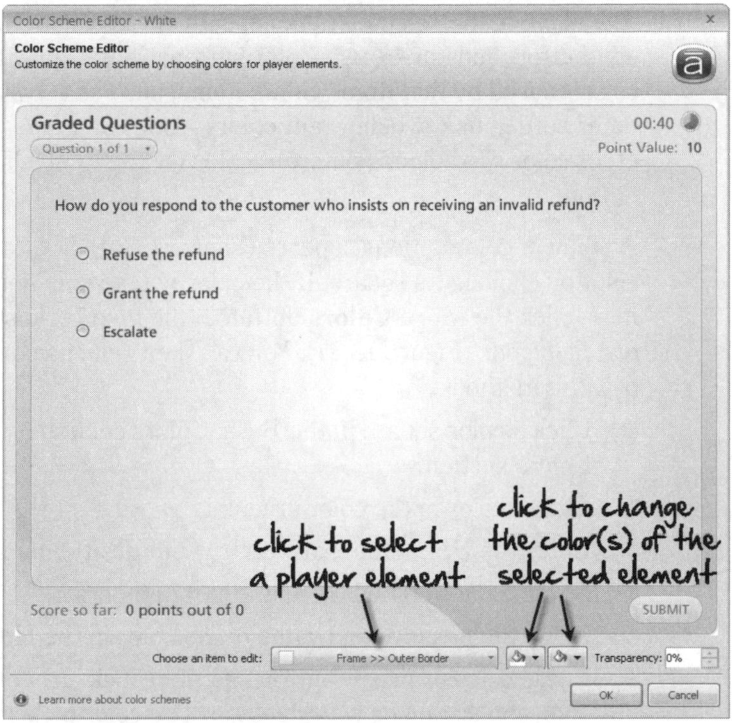

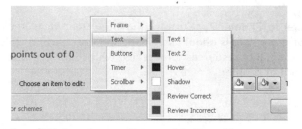

Figure 13.28. Color Scheme Editor window

Figure 13.29. Menu of customizable items in Color Scheme Editor

7. The name of the selected item appears on the Choose an item to edit button, and one or two Color buttons display the current color(s) used by that item. (Some items, such as the player frame's outer border, use two different colors—one color fades into the other color.) To select a different color for the item, click the **Color** button.

8. A menu of color options appears (Figure 13.30). You can select a color by clicking its square. If the color you need is not displayed here, click the **More Colors** button in the menu to display the Colors dialog box (Figure 13.31). You can then select a color using any of these methods:

   ■ Click a color square in the Basic Colors section or the Custom Colors section.

   ■ Click a color in the color gradient.

   ■ Enter the HSL (Hue, Saturation, Luminosity) numbers.

   ■ Enter the RGB (Red, Green, Blue) numbers.

   ■ Enter the hexadecimal value of the color in the Html box.

   ■ Click the color picker button and then click any color on any open application or your desktop. The color picker "grabs" the color.

---

66 **Note:** Refer to Chapter 7, "Customizing Presenter Player Templates," for more details about HSL, RGB, and hexadecimal values of colors. Additional resources for working with colors are also provided in that chapter.

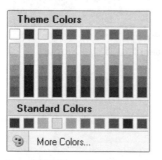

Figure 13.30. Color options menu

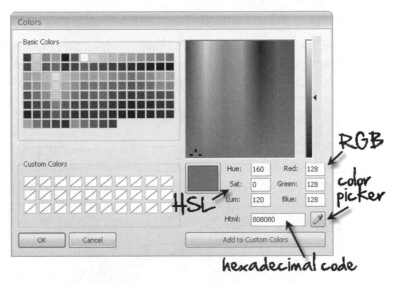

Figure 13.31. Colors dialog box

9. After you've selected a color for the item, the slide in the Color Scheme Editor window displays a preview of the item. You may also choose to change the transparency of the item by entering a percentage value in the **Transparency** box. Transparency affects how "see-through" the color is. A value of 0% is solid and a value of 100% is invisible.

10. Repeat steps 6-9 to change the color of another item.

11. When you're done, click the **OK** button in the Color Scheme Editor.

12. In the New Color Scheme from Master dialog box, type a name for the revised color scheme and click the **OK** button.

Changing Other Settings

The Other tab in the Player Template Builder dialog box lets you make changes to the browser window in which the Quizmaker player is displayed when the quiz is published. Figure 13.32 displays the Other tab and Table 13.7 describes each setting.

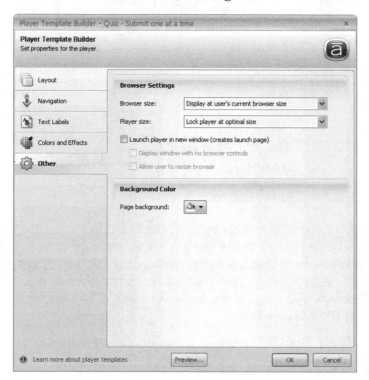

Figure 13.32. Player Template Builder dialog box Other tab

Table 13.7. Player Template Builder dialog box Other tab settings

Other tab sections	Description		
Browser Settings	Determines browser window settings:		
	Browser size	Controls the size of the user's browser, which also affects the player size. Options are: • Display at user's current browser size (default): Browser window remains the same size and player size depends on Player size selection (next option). • Resize browser to optimal size: The browser window will be resized to fit the player's optimal size. • Resize browser to fill screen: Browser window will resize to full screen and player size will depend on Player size selection (same as above).	
	Player size	• Scale presentation to fill browser (default): Player will adjust to the user's browser • Lock presentation at optimal size: Player will resize to 720 pixels wide x 540 pixels tall regardless of the browser size.	
	Launch player in new window	If selected, quiz will launch in a new window via a launch page.	
	Display window with no browser controls	If selected, browser window will open without browser controls (stop, refresh, forward, backward, etc.).	
	Allow user to resize browser	If selected, the browser window can be resized by the viewer.	
Background Color	The Page background button lets you choose the color that is displayed in the background of the browser window when the quiz is published. Clicking the button displays a palette of color options. (These options are the same as those that are available when customizing the player color scheme, discussed in the previous section.)		

I Selected a Setting, but It's Not Showing Up...

When you edit template settings, keep in mind that some of the options cannot be applied to the template if the quiz type does not support them. For example, if the current quiz is a survey, then the option to Display cumulative score will not apply (even if you select it) because survey questions are not scored. In addition, some settings will automatically override other settings. For example, if you choose Submit all (questions) at once, then the option to Display cumulative score will not apply (even if you select it) because questions will be scored at the end of the quiz.

Quizmaker

Previewing the Template

As you edit player template settings (or just view them), you can pre-view the effects of the selected settings by clicking the Preview button at the bottom of the Player Template Builder dialog box. The Player Template Preview window opens (Figure 13.33) and displays the first slide in the quiz in the Quizmaker player. Although not all functionality of the slide is active, you can preview most items, such as the color scheme, the timer, and scoring options, if applicable. To start the pre-view again, click the Replay button at the bottom of the Player Template Preview window. To close the window and return to the Player Template Builder dialog box, click the OK button.

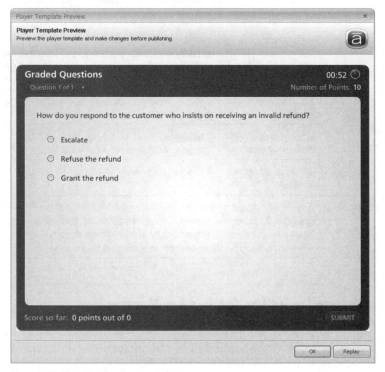

Figure 13.33. Player Template Preview window

Deleting and Renaming Player Templates

Quizmaker lets you delete and rename existing templates (except the four preconfigured templates) using the Player Template Manager dialog box (Figure 13.19).

To rename a player template:

1. Select the player template to rename.

2. Click the **Rename** button.

3. In the Rename Template dialog box, enter the new name and click the **OK** button.

To delete a player template:

1. Select the player template to delete. Note that you cannot delete the player template that is in use by the current quiz.

2. Click the **Delete** button and click the **Yes** button to confirm.

Note: Deleting a player template cannot be "undone."

Creating a New Player Template

Editing a player template and creating a new player template go hand in hand. Essentially, you create a new template by editing an existing one and then saving it using a new name—simple as that. And, as mentioned earlier, if you edit a preconfigured template, you *must* save it as a new template. When you create a new template, it is automatically applied to the current quiz, although you can apply a different template if you want.

The New button and the Duplicate button in the Player Template Manager dialog box offer a starting point for creating a new player template. The New button bases the new template on the default Quiz - Submit one at a time template. The Duplicate button bases the new template on an existing template that you select.

To create a new player template using the New button:

1. In the Quiz window, click the **Player Templates** button on the Home tab of the ribbon.

2. In the Player Template Manager dialog box, click the **New** button.

3. In the New Template dialog box (Figure 13.34), enter the name of the new template and click the **OK** button.

4. Quizmaker opens the Player Template Builder dialog box, where you can edit template settings. Follow the procedures described in the section "Editing a Player Template."

5. After editing the settings, click the **OK** button.

6. The new template is automatically applied to the current quiz. In the Player Template Manager dialog box, click the **Close** button.

Figure 13.34. New Template dialog box highlighted

To create a new template using the Duplicate button:

1. In the Quiz window, click the **Player Templates** button on the Home tab of the ribbon.

2. In the Player Template Manager dialog box, click the template you want to duplicate.

3. Click the **Duplicate** button.

4. In the Duplicate Template dialog box, enter the name of the new template and click the **OK** button.

5. The duplicate template appears in the list of templates in the Player Template Manager dialog box. To edit the template, click the **Edit** button and follow the procedures described in the section "Editing a Player Template."

6. The duplicate template is not automatically applied to the current quiz. If you want to apply it, click the **Apply to Project** button in the Player Template Manager dialog box.

7. Click the **Close** button.

Practice

Now try the following steps to practice customizing the player for a quiz. Note that you'll need to create a quiz with at least one question to perform this practice.

Editing a Player Template

1. Open an existing quiz or create a quiz with at least one question.

2. In the Quiz window, click the **Player Templates** button on the Home tab of the ribbon.

3. Make sure the **Quiz - Submit one at a time** template is selected and click the **Edit** button.

4. In the Player Template Builder dialog box Layout tab, select **Question 3** from the Question numbering style list.

5. Click the **Text Labels** tab.

6. Click the **Score so far:** entry in the Custom Text column and replace it with **Your score so far:**, then press **Enter.**

7. Click the **Colors and Effects** tab.

8. In the Color Scheme section, click the **Edit** button to edit the currently selected color scheme.

9. In the Color Scheme Editor window, click the button next to **Choose an item to edit:**.

10. Move the mouse pointer to **Text** and then select **Text 1** from the submenu.

11. Click the **Color** button ⬛▾ and select another color, such as red. Click the **OK** button.

12. In the New Color Scheme from Master dialog box, type **WhiteRevised** and click the **OK** button.

13. In the Preview Template Builder dialog box, click the **Preview** button.

14. Review the revised items and click the **OK** button.

15. In the Player Template Builder dialog box, click the **OK** button.

16. In the New Template from Master dialog box, type **MyTemplate** and click the **OK** button.

17. In the Player Template Manager dialog box, click the **Close** button.

Creating a Branched Scenario

Chapter 9, "Quizmaker Basics," described how to use the branching feature in Form view when building a slide. The branching feature is easy to use (just select the feedback response and select a slide to branch to), but we thought it would be helpful to present this feature within the context of a simple quiz. Before reading further, you might want to refresh your memory by reviewing the section titled "Setting Feedback and Branching" in Chapter 9.

A branched scenario quiz leads viewers to different slides based on how they respond to a question. For example, you can present a scenario in which the viewers must choose the best "next step" to take. If they choose step 1, they see the next logical step in that path. If they choose step 2, they see a different step for the different path. Needless to say, scenarios can become quite complex. But the process of building them is the same, regardless of the complexity. We recommend starting the process by sketching out the slides and the connections between them. Figure 13.35 shows a simple example that asks follow-up questions to a question answered incorrectly. The feedback for the initial question is eventually displayed, and the viewer is ultimately directed to a new question.

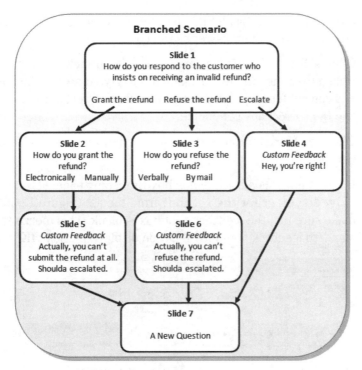

Figure 13.35. Sketch of slides for branched scenario

Following are the steps to build this scenario:

1. Start a new quiz (in this example, graded).

2. Click the **Player Templates** button on the ribbon and select the **Branched Scenario** template. Note that this template does not contain branching functionality, but it includes/omits options that are appropriate for a branched quiz. For example, the Question list navigation panel is not displayed in the quiz (because you don't want to give viewers the option to jump to different slides). Also, questions are submitted one at a time instead of as a group. This option is critical for branched scenarios.

3. Build the slides in the quiz (don't worry about the branching yet). But keep in mind that some question types do not support branching by specific incorrect answer choice. Your best bet is to use the Multiple Choice type of question. In this example, you'll need four question slides (slides 1, 2, 3, 7) and three custom feedback slides

created using the Blank Slide feature (slides 4, 5, 6). For slides 2 and 3, choose either answer as the correct one.

4. Open slide 1 in Form view and use the **Feedback** list box on the ribbon to change the feedback option to **By Answer**. This means you can set feedback/branching for each incorrect answer choice and the correct answer choice.

5. Click the **More** button next to the first answer choice, **Grant the refund**.

6. In the Answer Feedback dialog box Branching pane, select slide **2. How do you grant the refund?** from the list (Figure 13.36). Also make sure that the feedback text box is blank. This means that the standard feedback pop-up will not be displayed. Click **OK**.

Figure 13.36. Answer Feedback dialog box, slide 1, answer choice 1

7. Using the procedures in steps 5 and 6, open the Answer Feedback dialog box for the second answer choice, **Refuse the refund**, and branch to slide **3. How do you refuse the refund?** For the third (correct) answer choice, **Escalate**, branch to slide **4. Hey, you're right!**

8. Save and close the question and open slide 2 in Form view.

9. Slide 2 is a bit tricky because both answers are wrong. However, you still need to select one answer as correct. (Or you could use a Pick One survey question instead, which won't check the answer. But in this example, we used a Multiple Choice graded question.) Regardless of the answer selected by the viewer, you want this slide to branch to slide 6. To do that:

   a. Click the **More** button next to the Correct feedback text in the Set Feedback and Branching pane.

   b. In the Answer Feedback dialog box, delete the feedback text because you don't want the feedback pop-up to appear.

   c. In the Branching pane, select slide **5. Actually, you can't submit the refund at all.** and click **OK**.

   d. Repeat a, b, and c for the incorrect feedback and then save and close the question.

10. Repeat step 9 for slide 3.

11. Using the same procedures, set the branching for slides 4, 5, and 6 so that each branches to slide 7.

12. Preview!

Whew… the instructions might make this process seem more complicated than it really is. The bottom line is that once you've mapped out your quiz, just make sure that each question or answer choice branches to the appropriate slide.

Tips for creating branched scenario questions:

- Create a flowchart of your scenario before building it. Make sure every slide gets the viewer to the right place and all "branches" get to the end.

- Branched scenarios are good for practice and for testing on content that involves decision making. You can build the scenario once and then tweak it so practice and testing operate the same but the content is somewhat different.

- Video, documents (links), and audio can pump up branched scenarios so they can be very realistic.

- Test your branched scenario rigorously to make sure that what you expect to happen actually happens. That is, the viewer gets to the expected slide and completes the scenario as expected.

Creating Quiz Templates

You've just created a great quiz. Your questions have been customized with the perfect design theme, all slides contain your corporate logo, the Pass Result slide includes a cool video, and the Quizmaker player contains just the features you want. You know that you'll need to create several more quizzes with different content, but you want to use all the features that you've worked hard to create for this quiz. One solution is simply to create a copy of the existing quiz and then replace the content with the new questions. Another solution is to create a quiz template.

A quiz template is a special type of Quizmaker file that stores the design features of a quiz, as well as any content you choose to keep. You create a template from an existing quiz and then you can use the template over and over again to create new quizzes. Following is a list of the items that can be retained in a quiz template:

- Quiz properties set in the Quiz Properties dialog box
- Quiz design features, such as the colors, fonts, background, design theme, and any properties set in the slide master
- Quizmaker player template features
- Results slide content and format
- Quiz questions that you always want to include
- Specific slides that contain a layout and design that you want to reuse
- Any other content slides that you want to keep, such as a quiz introduction slide

Quiz Template vs. Player Template

To avoid confusion over the use of the term *template*, let's clarify: The *quiz template* we're describing here is a design template that incorporates all the design (and content) elements of a quiz. A *player template* is a template used to control the features of the Quizmaker player and how the quiz functions. Although they are two separate templates, the quiz template automatically incorporates the player template used by the quiz.

Quizmaker quiz templates are similar to the templates used by
PowerPoint and other Office applications. However, Quizmaker does
not come with predefined templates. You'll need to create the templates yourself or beg/borrow from a colleague. There are several
ways to go about creating a template. You can start from scratch by
putting together a skeleton quiz that contains all the features you want
for future quizzes. Or you can start from an existing quiz and tweak it
down to contain the features you want. Either way, you need to create
a quiz first and then save it as a template. We typically create templates from quizzes we've already developed, so we'll present that
method.

To create a quiz template:

1. Open a quiz containing the design features and content you want
    to reuse.

2. Remove slides that you don't want to reuse. For example, you
    might want to keep one Multiple Choice question that contains the
    layout and graphics you want. If the quiz contains other Multiple
    Choice questions using the same layout, you can delete those
    slides (unless you want to keep the content). You may also want to
    keep a generic instruction slide (created from a blank slide) that
    provides instructions for taking the quiz.

3. Change design features, if necessary. For example, you might want
    the template to contain a different background.

4. Click the **Articulate** button 🅐 and select **Save As** from the File
    menu.

5. In the Save As dialog box, enter a name for the template in the
    File name box. You can also change the location, if desired, using
    the Save in list. By default, Quizmaker stores new quiz templates
    in the My Articulate Projects folder. In Windows XP, this subfolder
    is under the My Documents folder. Figure 13.37 shows the tem-
    plate being saved in the user-created QuizTemplates folder.

6. A quiz template is saved as a *.quiztemplate* file, instead of a *.quiz*
    file. From the Save as type list, select **Quizmaker Template
    (*.quiztemplate)**.

7. Click the **Save** button.

The template is displayed in the Quiz window and is ready to be used for a new quiz. The template is also accessible from the Quizmaker start screen and from the Open dialog box.

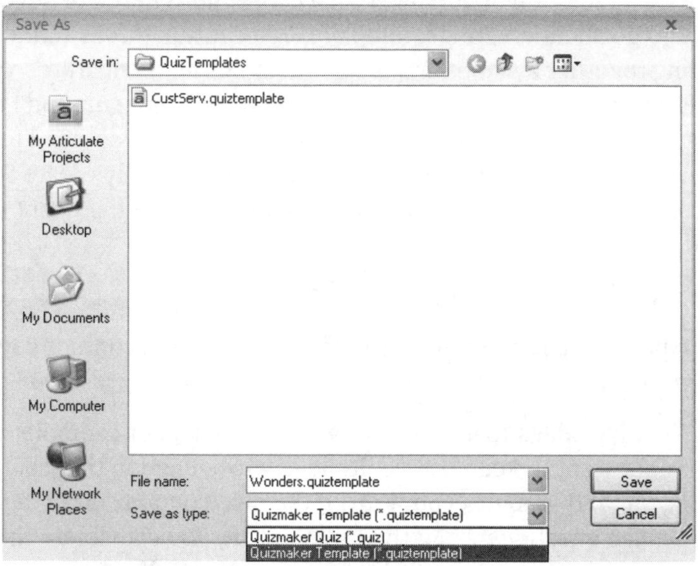

Figure 13.37. Save As dialog box with the Quizmaker Template file type selected

To create a new quiz from a template:

1. Open the template using either of the following methods:

   ■ From the Quizmaker start screen (Figure 13.38), click the name of the template in the New from quiz template section. If the template is not listed, click the **Browse** button to locate it.

   ■ From the Quiz window, select **Open** from the File menu. Quizmaker displays both .quiz and .quiztemplate files. Browse to the template file and double-click it.

2. In the Quiz window, save the template as a new quiz by clicking the **Save** button on the Quick Access toolbar or by selecting **Save** (or **Save As**) from the File menu.

3. Quizmaker automatically opens the Save As dialog box and selects the Quizmaker Quiz (*.quiz) file type. Enter a name for the quiz in the File name box and click the **Save** button.

4. Build the quiz as you normally would. Remember to save often.

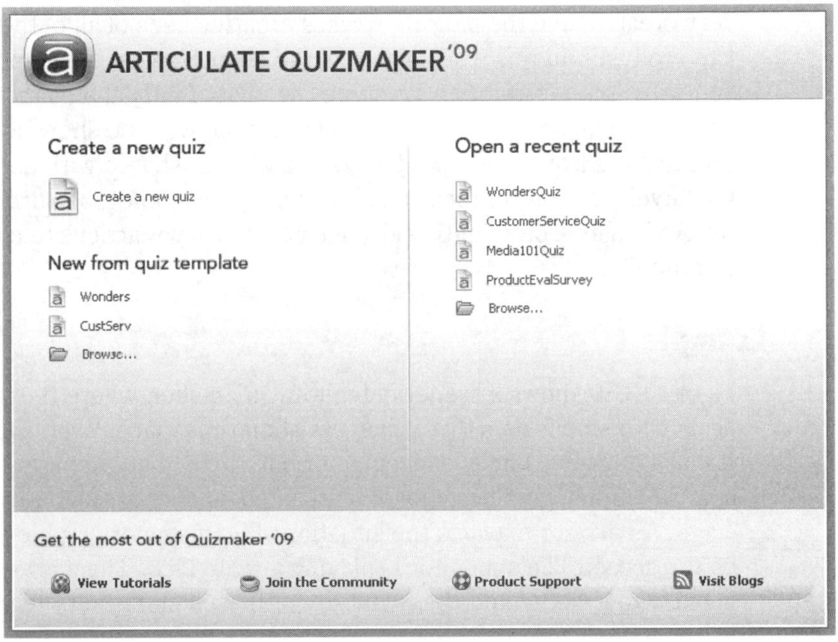

Figure 13.38. Quizmaker start screen with templates

If you want to modify a quiz template, you can open it and make changes. However, to save the template, you need to select the **Save As** command from the File menu and select the **Quizmaker Template (*.quiztemplate)** file type. You can overwrite the original template file or save it as a new template.

Additional Inspiration for Pumping Up Your Quizzes

We've told you in a number of places throughout the book to check out Articulate's Rapid E-Learning blog, written by Tom Kuhlmann. Tom is very creative and the blog showcases creative uses of all of the Articulate products. In this final section of the chapter, we'd like to provide you with some inspiration for doing the kind of nifty things that Tom does with Quizmaker quizzes. In this section, we'll be showing you screenshots from a variety of quizzes that Tom shared with us. To see the "live" versions of these and many other examples, be sure to visit the Articulate Community web page at http://www.articulate.com/community.

Example 1

Figure 13.39 shows a scenerio, built in Quizmaker, where the viewer deals with staff issues that managers sometimes face. What's unique? It looks engaging and *is* engaging, for one thing. The scenarios use quiz questions, graphics, movement, audio, and even video to set the stage. A narrator explains the situation. The manager graphic moves on the screen. Joe's monitor is playing a real video. The answers fade in one at a time. Sounds busy, but it works well and is very engaging.

Figure 13.39. Scenario questions in Quizmaker

Example 2

The quiz shown in Figure 13.40 showcases ways to make quiz slides far more visually interesting. For example, instead of placing a small picture of Einstein on the slide, Tom used the picture as a background. And rather than put the question directions at the top, as is usually done in quiz questions, Tom used a talk bubble to have Einstein "ask" you the question. Too cool!

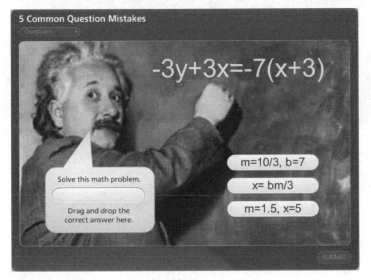

Figure 13.40. Question slides don't need to be boring.

Example 3

In Figure 13.41, the Snail Anatomy information slide (created on a blank slide) opens with the snail picture. Then the callouts to the parts of the snail are added one at a time to the screen. This is a good example of showing information prior to asking a question. The build of callouts, from 1 to 5, helps the viewer figure out what to focus on.

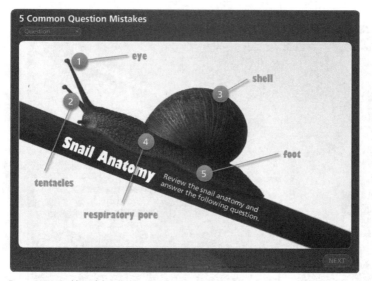

Figure 13.41. Building slide callouts one at a time

Example 4

Figure 13.42 shows an example of a survey built in Quizmaker. Like the other examples, this one is also quite attractive. The slide builds by first showing the picture, and then the question and answer choices appear.

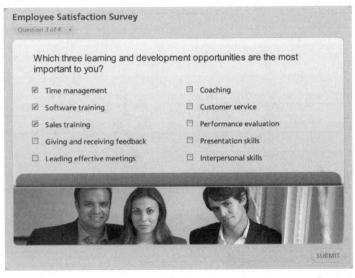

Figure 13.42. Satisfaction survey

Example 5

The example in Figure 13.43 showcases using Slide view to move screen elements around to make the design work better. This question is a Matching Drop-down question. The images and drop-down lists were moved around in Slide view so that the images and drop-down lists were organized to better fit on the slide.

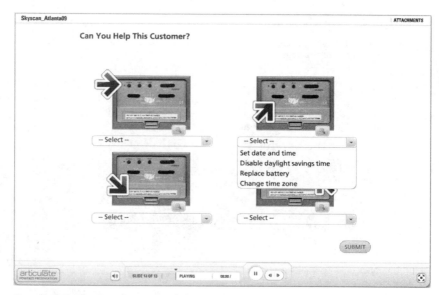

Figure 13.43. Matching Drop-down question with images

Example 6

Figure 13.44 shows another great example of using blank slides to provide or review content before quiz questions. In this example, dinosaur information flies in, and then flies out. This continues (on the same slide) until the viewer clicks the Next button, which starts the quiz.

Figure 13.44. Dinosaur review information

All of these examples have features in common. They are all visually attractive and engaging. They each use media, animations, or the timeline so screens aren't static. They show how Quizmaker can be used to provide quizzes and content that is engaging and fun. And they are all incredibly creative!

Chapter Recap

Here's our list of the most important things to remember from this chapter:

- Use the Blank Slide feature to include non-question slides in your quiz, such as an introduction slide, review slides, feedback slides, and transition slides.

- Building a blank slide is similar to building a question slide. After clicking the Blank Slide button on the ribbon, you can enter basic content in Form view and then switch to Slide view to improve the layout and add media.

- By organizing questions into groups, you can manipulate each set of questions differently. For example, you can randomize one group of questions and set a specific order for another group.

- The ability to organize and randomize questions in "pools" has very important learning assessment implications. Once questions are grouped by learning objective, you can set the number of questions to be "included" from each group.

- To organize your questions into groups, click the Question Group button on the ribbon to add a new group. Then create new questions in the group or move existing questions into the group.

- Whether your quiz has just one group of questions or several groups, you can randomize the order of questions within a group using the Group tools on the ribbon.

- After randomizing a group, you can choose how many questions to be displayed during the quiz. You can also lock certain questions to a specific location in the quiz.

- The Import Questions button on the ribbon enables you to import questions from other Quizmaker '09 and Quizmaker 2 quizzes. You can import all questions, individual questions, or all questions from a specific group.

- Quizmaker lets you customize the Results slide that is displayed at the end of the quiz. For graded quizzes, you can modify the Pass Result slide and the Fail Result slide by selecting options in Form view and customizing other features in Slide view. For surveys, you can modify the Survey Result slide using the same procedures.

- Customize the Quizmaker player by using another player template or by customizing a template. The player template determines a number of features, such as how the questions are submitted and what items are displayed on the player.

- Among the many features on the player you can customize is the color scheme. Using the Color Scheme Editor, you can change the color of many elements of the player, such as the frame border, text, and buttons.

- A branched scenario quiz leads viewers to different slides based on how they respond to a question. Use the Branching pane in the Answer Feedback dialog box to specify the branched slide.

- A quiz template stores all of the design features of a quiz, as well as any content you want to include. To create a quiz template, create or open a quiz that contains the design, layout, and content you want. Then save the quiz using the .quiztemplate file extension in the Save As dialog box.

- To create a new quiz from a template, open the template and then save the quiz using a new file name and the default .quiz file extension. You can then build the content and other features as you would for any other quiz.

- Visit the Articulate web site to explore creative Quizmaker examples!

Chapter 14

Introduction to Engage

Chapter Snapshot

In this chapter, you'll get a flavor of what Engage '09 is all about. What's it good for? How does it work? We try to answer all the fundamental questions here, so that you're ready for some hands-on instruction in the following chapters.

> ? I love the way I can insert an Engage interaction into my Presenter project—it just takes up one slide!

> i But I don't use Presenter... so why should I care about Engage?

> ? Engage doesn't have just one master. Since Engage publishes interactions as Flash output, you can use them anywhere you'd use a Flash file... like on a web site.

What Is Engage?

Engage is a program that lets you create interactive "discovery" experiences for your audience. Or, to use a catchier marketing phrase from Articulate's web site:

> *Looking for compelling learning interaction and stunning visual quality, all without the need for expensive design or programming? That's Articulate Engage.*

Engage interactions enable your viewers to actively examine information by drilling down for details, comparing relationships among components, and exploring different components. Through a combination of graphics, audio, and text, you can create extremely attractive discovery learning experiences for your viewers that look like they took a long time to produce.

You create Engage interactions using prebuilt templates. Each template provides the foundation for a specific interaction type—your job is to fill in the template by adding your own content (text, audio, and graphics). Once you finish the interaction, you *publish* it using one of several delivery methods, all of which use Flash as the output. This Flash format is what gives Engage interactions the flexibility to be used almost anywhere, such as on a web site or in a slide in a Presenter project.

A published Engage interaction file is launched in the Engage *player* (Figure 14.1). The player is simply the vehicle for displaying the interaction. It contains a few controls for the viewer, such as the Next and Previous navigation buttons and an audio control. The player is generally the same, regardless of what interaction you create. However, each interaction type includes additional unique navigation options, such as the step buttons at the bottom of the Process interaction. And you can customize various properties of the player, such as the color scheme, for each interaction.

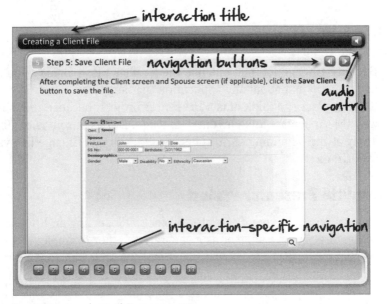

Figure 14.1 Engage player with Process interaction

In fact, what used to take days to create in Flash can now be created in hours using Engage. That's because the templates in Engage already contain many of the features that need to be created manually in Flash. For example, the animated components, hotspot interactivity, and player design have already been created for you. You just add the content and publish. Of course, you can customize the interactions using a variety of Engage tools. But even a plain-vanilla Engage interaction can look like you spent days on it.

> 66 **Note:** If you're familiar with Presenter or Quizmaker, you know that they offer multiple *player templates* that can be applied to a project or quiz, respectively. Engage does not offer multiple player templates. Instead, each interaction contains unique player properties, which can be customized. The range of changes that can be made to each Engage interaction player is smaller than the changes you can make to the Presenter and Quizmaker player templates.

Best Uses of Engage

Because Engage interactions use the familiar Flash format, you can use them in just about any application that supports Flash. Of course, the first place we think of is a Presenter project, because that's really why the Articulate folks invented Engage. But as our invisible friends imply at the beginning of this chapter, you can use Engage in a variety of settings.

Articulate Presenter Project

You can pump up your Presenter project by inserting an Engage interaction directly on a slide or as a separate tab. For example, in a presentation geared for new employees, one slide can contain an Engage interaction stepping through the time tracking process. Instead of each step appearing on a separate PowerPoint slide, all steps are interactively presented on one slide. A presentation tab can be used to store an interactive glossary created in Engage. The tab is accessible all the time—viewers simply click the tab to start working with the glossary.

Web Site

Want to grab the attention of your web site viewers? You can insert an Engage interaction into an existing web page. For example, let your viewers explore all the features of a new product on a page. Or insert an interactive timeline on a page about the company history.

CD

Because a published Engage interaction is a standalone file, you can put it on a CD for viewers to use offline. For example, a set of frequently asked questions (FAQs) or the process to log in to the corporate system can be quickly reviewed from a CD.

Other E-Learning Products

We know that not everyone uses Presenter to develop their e-learning courses, but that doesn't mean they can't use Engage. Inserting an Engage interaction is as easy as inserting a Flash file. Engage interactions can also be published directly to a learning management system (LMS), which enables the tracking of participation and progress of learners.

---

66 **Note:** Stay tuned for Chapter 26, "Publishing." That chapter gives you details about how to create Engage output so that it can be used in the settings described here.

Engage 1-2-3-4 Workflow

Engage is pretty straightforward to use. If you've read the chapters about Presenter, you're familiar with the workflow of creating a Presenter project, which involves both PowerPoint and Articulate Presenter. In Engage, you follow a simpler process of completing the predefined templates and then publishing them to a specific output format. Figure 14.2 shows the typical 1-2-3-4 workflow process for building any Engage interaction. In the next section we'll show examples of the published output. But before you begin development, you'll want to plan your interaction. And throughout the process, you'll be previewing, testing, and fixing your interaction.

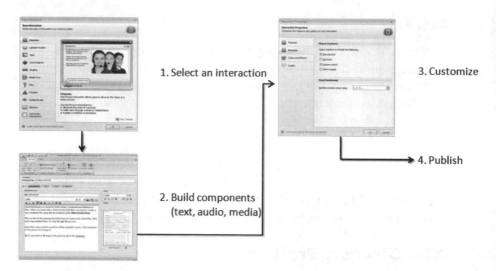

1. Select an interaction

3. Customize

2. Build components
(text, audio, media)

4. Publish

Figure 14.2. Typical Engage high-level workflow

Let's break down this 1-2-3-4 workflow a bit further. Table 14.1 provides a brief description of each step in the process.

Table 14.1. Typical Engage detailed workflow

Step	Description
1. Select an interaction	Determine the best interaction to use based on your content and audience needs. Use the New Interaction dialog box to view samples and start the new interaction.
2. Build components (text, audio, media)	Add text, audio, and media to each component in the interaction. A component is one "content chunk," such as one step in a Process interaction or one label in a Labeled Graphic interaction.
3. Customize	Modify a variety of general interaction features, such as color scheme and viewer navigation options. If applicable, modify features specific to each interaction, such as the marker color on a Labeled Graphic.
4. Publish	Make sure you've previewed, tested, and fixed the interaction appropriately. Determine how you want the viewer to work with the interaction (e.g., web or CD) and create the appropriate output files.

The rest of the Engage chapters are structured around this 1-2-3-4 workflow (kind of). Planning and step 1: Select an interaction are covered in this chapter, where we offer some tips on choosing the right interaction and getting your ducks in a row before building it. Chapter

15, "Engage Basics," covers the essential tasks you need to know to perform all of the steps. Then, each interaction-specific chapter (Chapters 16-25) steps you through the nuts and bolts of creating that interaction from start to finish. Finally, Chapter 26, "Publishing" provides details about step 4 by describing each publishing output option.

Note: If you read all of the interaction chapters, you'll see some redundancy among the chapters. We planned it that way. Our goal is for each interaction chapter to provide just about everything you need to build that interaction, including a performance support practice at the end of each chapter. In fact, if you want a quick start to building an interaction, just jump right to the practice!

Let's start by taking a quick look at the 10 interactions offered by Engage.

A Quick Look at All 10 Interactions

Engage offers 10 interaction templates. Although each interaction is designed for a "specific" purpose, we've found that creative developers don't need to feel constrained by the targeted use—they go outside the box and use the interactions in many different ways. For example, a Process interaction is designed for step-by-step instructions or phases in a process. But you can certainly use this interaction to describe the top 10 features of a new product.

In addition to providing 10 different interactions, Articulate offers the Community Interactions tab. The Engage Software Developers Kit (SDK) lets Flash developers build any type of activity and share it with all Engage users through the Community Interactions tab.

Following is a thumbnail description of each interaction type. Chapters 16-25 describe each interaction in detail and provide more examples of when to use each one.

Process Interaction

A Process interaction is typically used to describe the steps or phases of a linear procedure or process (Figure 14.3). Viewers can navigate the procedure or process from start to finish by clicking each step at the bottom of the player. Examples of content suited for a Process interaction include:

- Step-by-step instructions
- Company procedures
- Project phases

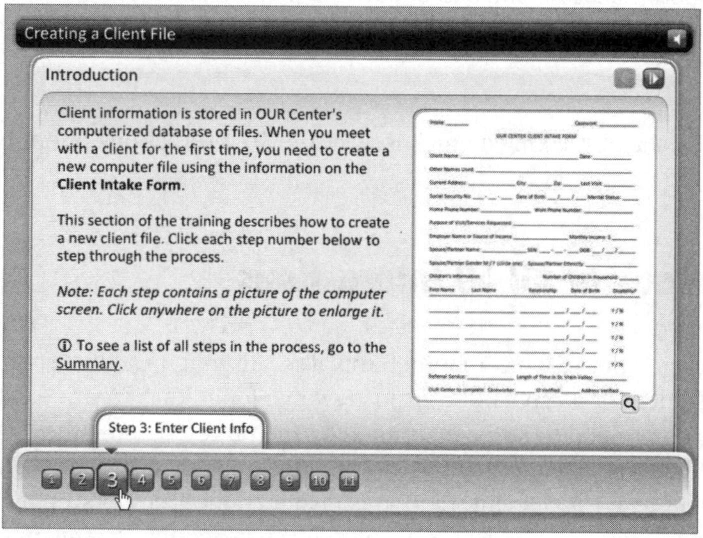

Figure 14.3. Process interaction

Labeled Graphic Interaction

A Labeled Graphic is an interactive image that calls out the key elements of that graphic (Figure 14.4). Viewers can learn about each part of the image by clicking markers that you define on the image. Examples of content suited for a Labeled Graphic interaction include:

- Software application screenshot or photograph
- Form or diagram
- Geographic map

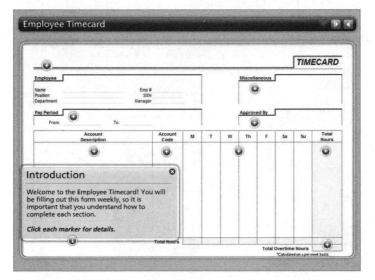

Figure 14.4. Labeled Graphic interaction

Tabs Interaction

A Tabs interaction can be used to describe a set of items that are related in some way, such as a series of concepts, members in a group, or differences among objects (Figure 14.5). Viewers can access descriptions of each item by clicking a tab on the left side of the player. Examples of content suited for a Tabs interaction include:

- Features list
- Company departments
- Product or service offerings

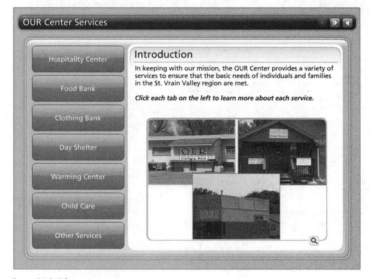

Figure 14.5. Tabs interaction

Circle Diagram Interaction

A Circle Diagram interaction uses a set of concentric circles to depict a hierarchy of core concepts or elements (center) and other elements that radiate around it (Figure 14.6). Viewers explore these concepts or elements by clicking segments of the circle to learn more. Examples of content suited for a Circle Diagram interaction include:

- Philosophies, values
- Problem-solving approaches
- Physical layers of objects

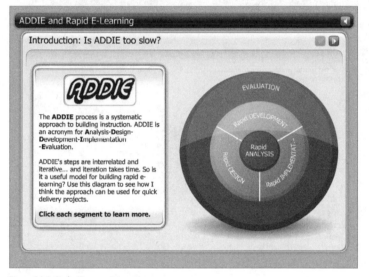

Figure 14.6. Circle Diagram interaction

Timeline Interaction

The Timeline interaction provides a visual way for viewers to move through a timeline of chronological events (Figure 14.7). The events can even be grouped into periods. Examples of content suited for a Timeline interaction include:

- Historical events
- Milestones in a project schedule
- Steps in a process

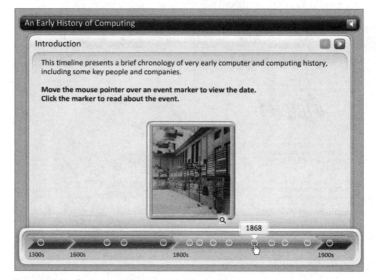

Figure 14.7. Timeline interaction

Media Tour Interaction

A Media Tour interaction is a collection of related images and movie files presented to the viewer linearly (Figure 14.8). Viewers can click forward and back through the presentation, and may have the option of playing and replaying the movies in the interaction. Examples of content suited for a Media Tour interaction include:

- Images of a special event
- Company product categories
- Software screenshots in a process

Figure 14.8. Media Tour interaction

FAQ Interaction

An FAQ interaction is a collection of clickable questions (Figure 14.9). Viewers click a question to display the answer. A "question" does not necessarily need to be in question format. Examples of content suited for an FAQ interaction include:

- Customer/employee questions
- Troubleshooting procedures
- Reviews and self-check questions

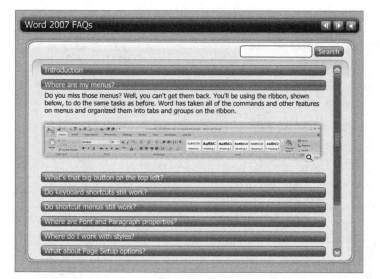

Figure 14.9. FAQ interaction

Pyramid Diagram Interaction

A Pyramid Diagram interaction uses a triangle graphic divided into segments to show a hierarchy of related items (Figure 14.10). Viewers explore the items by clicking segments of the pyramid. Examples of content suited for Pyramid Diagram interactions include:

- Product offerings (by quantity)
- Company departments (by size)
- Tasks (by importance)

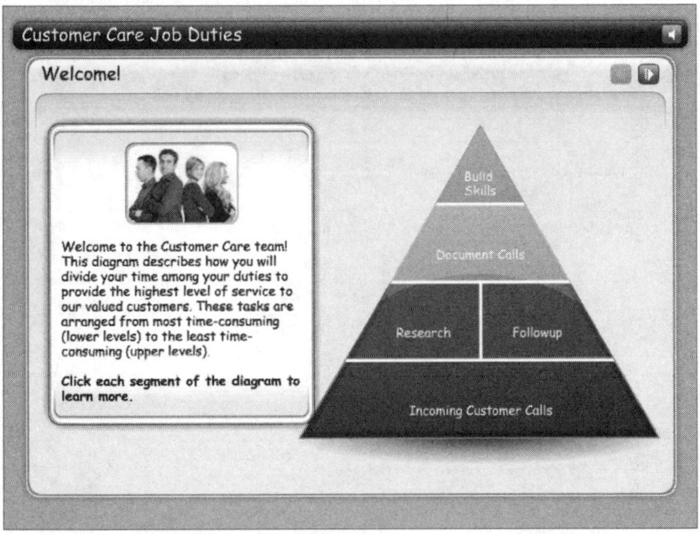

Figure 14.10. Pyramid Diagram interaction

Guided Image Interaction

A Guided Image interaction steps viewers through various components of an image, one component at a time (Figure 14.11). Viewers navigate the components of the image sequentially by clicking the Next button. Examples of content suited for a Guided Image interaction include:

- Installation instructions
- Schedules/calendars following a linear path
- Trip destinations along a map

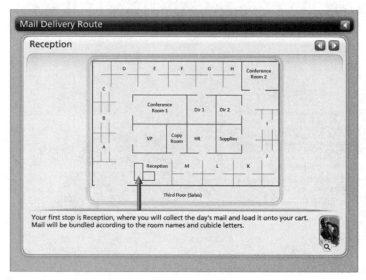

Figure 14.11. Guided Image interaction

Glossary Interaction

A Glossary interaction is a collection of clickable terms displayed alphabetically (Figure 14.12). Viewers click a term to display the definition. Examples of content suited for a Glossary interaction include:

- Terms and technical phrases
- Translations of foreign terms
- Acronyms

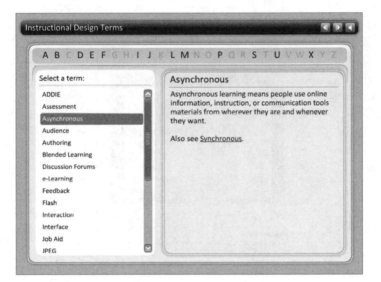

Figure 14.12. Glossary interaction

Community Interactions

Yes, we said there are 10 interactions, but Articulate offers a bonus 11th: Community interactions are developed by your peers in the Engage user community (Figure 14.13). They can include just about any type of activity and can be downloaded and edited directly in Engage '09. In addition to downloading and using an existing community interaction, you can have a Flash developer create a custom interaction that can be published as an Engage interaction.

Figure 14.13. Community Interactions tab in the New Interaction dialog box

As of this writing, Articulate has preinstalled the Flashcards community interaction in Engage. Two additional community interactions are also available for download: Flipbook and Stairstep. Because the Community Interaction feature was implemented right before our publish date, this book does not go into detail about this cool feature. The good news is that you can click the Get more interactions button (accessible after selecting Community Interactions on the New Interaction dialog box), and get all the information you need from the Articulate web site.

Now that you have a general idea of the types of interactions offered by Engage, let's look at how you can plan and use interactions that are specific to the needs of your projects.

Planning Your Interactions

If you've already read any part of this book, you know we're big fans of planning. We will keep bugging you about this. Remember:

Lots of Planning = Faster Development Time

Not Much Planning = Slower Development Time

Each Engage interaction chapter includes a brief section on planning, but we'll give you some general pointers here.

Choosing the Right Interaction

Your very first step is to choose the interaction that will best serve your content. Sometimes this is easy, sometimes not. For example, if you have a technical drawing or a piece of equipment that needs explaining, then the Labeled Graphic or Guided Image interaction is a pretty obvious fit. But content consisting of related "bits and pieces" can fit in several different interactions. For example, a checklist for new employees can be developed using the Process, Tabs, or FAQ interaction. Also keep in mind that some interactions provide more space for content than others. So if you intend to have large images or substantial text, select an interaction that can accommodate those items. For example, a Process interaction offers more real estate for text and graphics than the FAQ interaction offers.

Finally, when choosing an interaction, keep your viewers' best interests at heart. Which interaction will *best* present the information to them? What we're really saying here is that you might be tempted to "show off" using a cool Pyramid interaction, when a straightforward Process interaction is the better fit. When working through this decision, you can view samples of the various interactions using the New Interaction dialog box (Figure 14.14).

Figure 14.14. New Interaction dialog box Process tab

The previous section listed each Engage interaction and a few examples of the types of content that fit well for that interaction. Now let's
turn that inside out and present some content types and the interactions that fit well for each.

Instructions and Processes

Content consisting of step-by-step tasks or phases (such as steps to
log in to a computer) can be presented using these interactions:

■ Process: One step per task/phase

■ Tabs: One tab per task/phase

■ FAQ: One FAQ item per task/phase

■ Media Tour: One image/video per task/phase

■ Timeline: One event per task/phase

■ Guided Image: One label per task/phase, if the task revolves
around one image

Descriptions of Visual Components

Graphic images consisting of different components (such as the buttons on a cell phone) can be described using these interactions:

- Labeled Graphic: One label per component (viewer can pick and choose)

- Guided Image: One label per component (a controlled, guided tour)

- Media Tour: One "zoomed" image per component (same image on each slide, but a different zoomed component)

- Process or Tabs: One "zoomed" image per component (same image on each step/tab, but a different zoomed component)

Hierarchical Relationships

Concepts, ideas, or physical properties that have a hierarchical relationship can be presented using these interactions:

- Pyramid: Layers/segments show largest to smallest concepts, from bottom to top

- Circle Diagram: Layers/segments show central to outlying concepts, from the inside out

- Labeled Graphic: You provide the hierarchical graphic (such as an organizational chart) and use labels to describe each component

Features and Other Lists

Content consisting of a list of features, qualities, departments—you name it!—can be presented using these interactions:

- Process: One step per feature
- Tabs: One tab per feature
- FAQ: One FAQ item per feature
- Media Tour: One image/video per feature
- Timeline: One event per feature
- Glossary: One item per feature (good for alphabetical lists)

Time-Sensitive Events

Content that is historical or time-constrained can be presented using these interactions:

- Timeline: One event per occurrence or several events per period
- Process or Tabs: One step/tab per occurrence
- FAQ: One FAQ item per occurrence
- Media Tour: One image/video per occurrence

Questions, Definitions, Short Bites

Content consisting of many small (and not necessarily related) pieces of information can be presented using these interactions:

- FAQ: One FAQ item per bite
- Glossary: One term per bite (if the bites are alphabetical)
- Timeline: One event per bite

Quizzes and Reviews

Most interactions can be used to present a question/answer format for nongraded quizzes or reviews:

- FAQ: One FAQ item per question/answer
- Process or Tabs: One step/tab per question/answer
- Timeline: One event per question/answer
- Glossary: One term/definition per question/answer

Of course, don't let these suggestions box you in. With creativity, you can present most content using any number of different interactions.

Tip: For a great example of an innovative use of Engage, check out the Word of Mouth blog "Articulate 101: How to Create Mini-Assessments with Engage" (http://www.articulate.com/blog/articulate-101-how-to-create-mini-assessments-with-engage) by Helene Geiger.

Planning the Content

The nice thing about Engage is that most of the interactions consist of the same three content components: text, audio, and media ("still" image or video). Of course, each interaction uses these three components in different ways. But for planning purposes, you will focus on gathering text, audio, and media for all interactions. Chapter 15, "Engage Basics," provides details for working with text, audio, and media in any interaction. Following are a few pointers to remember as you plan each of these elements.

Text

Many interactions use text as the primary way of conveying information. And because most interactions present content in small "chunks," you want to plan the text accordingly. For example, when creating a Process interaction for step-by-step instructions, divide the text into small units of instruction. Figure 14.15 describes the types of text you can include in an interaction.

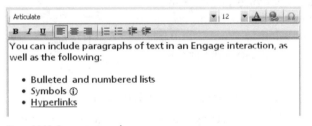

Figure 14.15. Engage text samples

You can create text content on the fly inside an Engage interaction, or copy and paste text from sources outside the interaction.

- **Create Text Inside Engage:** If you have planned your content well and know exactly what you want to include, then it's easy to write and format text within an interaction.

- **Create Text Outside Engage:** Although organizing all of your content beforehand can be time consuming, it's often less time consuming than developing on the fly and then having to rework the content afterward. If you write all the content before starting to build the interaction, you can use another application (such as

Microsoft Word) and then paste the text into an Engage interaction. This approach is helpful if a third party needs to review your content before the interaction is developed. Plus, if you need to recreate your interaction in the future (hey, it happens), you will be thrilled if you have the content easily available elsewhere. And remember that you can format the pasted text in a variety of ways inside the interaction.

66   Note: When copying/pasting text from another source into an Engage interaction, the formatting is generally not retained. You'll need to reapply formatting and preview your interaction to verify.

Audio

All Engage interactions can include one audio clip for each interaction component. For example, each step in a Process interaction can include an audio accompaniment (Figure 14.16). You can record audio from within an interaction or import it from another source. The trick is deciding when to use audio and when to leave it out.

Figure 14.16. Engage Audio pane

Here are a few rules of thumb about including audio:

- If you include audio, it may make sense to use it for every component instead of for just a few. Otherwise, viewers might think the audio is simply not working for some components.

- If you are not going to use audio for every component, consider including audio for the introduction to the interaction. Make sure you point out that there will not be audio in the other components.

- Narration should not read the text on the screen. It should be conversational and concise.

Media

Engage uses the term *media* to refer to both still images and videos. Most components of an Engage interaction can include a media file (Figure 14.17). For example, for each tab in a Tabs interaction, you can include a picture along with the text. However, you're limited to just one media file per component. Also, keep in mind that the ideal graphic element is instructional, not just "eye candy."

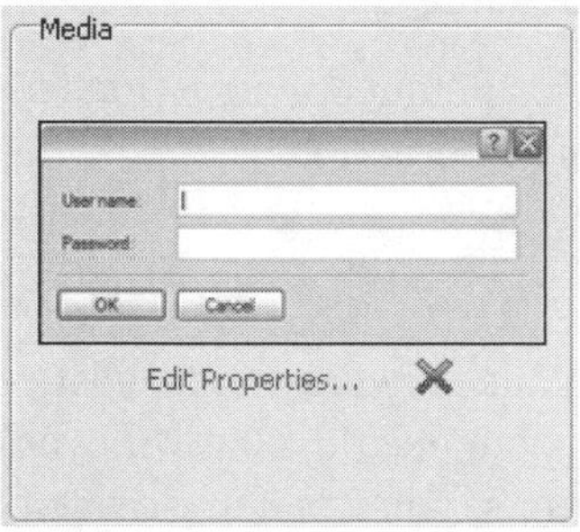

Figure 14.17. Engage Media pane

Engage supports the following media types:

- Images: JPG (or JPEG), BMP, GIF, and PNG
- Videos: SWF (Flash) and FLV (Adobe Flash video)

Note: You cannot create your own media files within Engage. You'll need to create them using another application, buy them, use free media, or hire someone to create them.

Planning the Design Elements

Engage lets you customize many features of an interaction and the player displaying the interaction. As you plan your interaction, keep the following design elements in mind:

- **Layout:** In most cases, you can determine the placement of the media file (image or video) relative to the text. For example, if a step in a Process interaction includes text and an image, you can choose to display the text on the left and the image on the right, or vice versa. In some interactions, such as the Circle Diagram and Pyramid, you can choose whether to place those diagrams on the left or right side of the interaction.

- **Colors:** Engage lets you select a color scheme, which affects components of the interaction (such as color of the tabs in a Tabs interaction) and components of the player (such as the background). You can customize each color scheme and create your own schemes.

■ **Player Features:** For any interaction, you can select player features, such as displaying the audio icon and allowing viewers to resume the interaction where they left off.

Chapter 15, "Engage Basics," provides detailed instructions for working with these design elements in any interaction.

Determining Viewer Control

Engage enables you to control how your viewers can navigate the interaction. As you plan your interaction, decide what will work best for your audience. For most interactions, you can choose one of the following options:

■ **Interactive:** Viewers can select any component of the interaction at any time.

■ **Linear:** Viewers are limited to selecting the components in the order in which they are presented.

■ **Presentation:** Viewers have no control over navigation. The components of the interaction are displayed automatically.

 Note: You may also include hyperlinks within an interaction, which lets viewers jump directly from one component to another.

We are partial to interactive navigation because most adults don't like to be "spoon fed" content. A good rule of thumb is to provide a suggested viewing order but let the audience select the order themselves, especially if they are familiar with the content or will need to refer back to specific parts later to refresh their understanding.

Selecting a Delivery Method

The "Best Uses of Engage" section earlier in this chapter describes some of the ways you can use an Engage interaction. Each of these uses is tied to a delivery method. For planning purposes, it is helpful to know up front how your viewers will be working with an interaction. For example, if the interaction will be delivered as a slide in a Presenter project, then the context for the interaction may have been provided by other slides in the project. This might remove the need to include an introduction to the interaction. On the other hand, if the interaction will be delivered as a standalone piece on a web site, then make sure to include everything the viewer needs to know.

Of course, you can choose any delivery method you want when you publish the interaction, but you should take into account how the interaction will be delivered so you can plan the interaction accordingly. Chapter 26, "Publishing," provides detailed instructions for selecting a delivery method.

Managing Engage Files

When you build and save a new interaction, Engage creates a working file using the extension .intr. This file is usable only by the Engage program—it's the file you work with to create or modify the interaction. After you finish building the interaction, you *publish* the output to a Flash .swf file (plus other supporting files), which is viewable but not modifiable, outside the Engage program.

For example, let's say you start a Pyramid interaction (MyPyramid.intr) and save it in the default My Documents\My Articulate Projects folder, as indicated in Figure 14.18. Every time you want to edit the interaction, you open the MyPyramid.intr file in Engage, make the changes, and then save it. When you're satisfied with the interaction, you publish it so that it can be used on a web site. After you use the Publish to Web option, Engage creates a folder containing a set of files required to display the interaction on the web. Figure 14.19 shows the set of files created. In this example, you could use these files to insert the interaction in a web page. Chapter 26, "Publishing," provides details on different Engage output files.

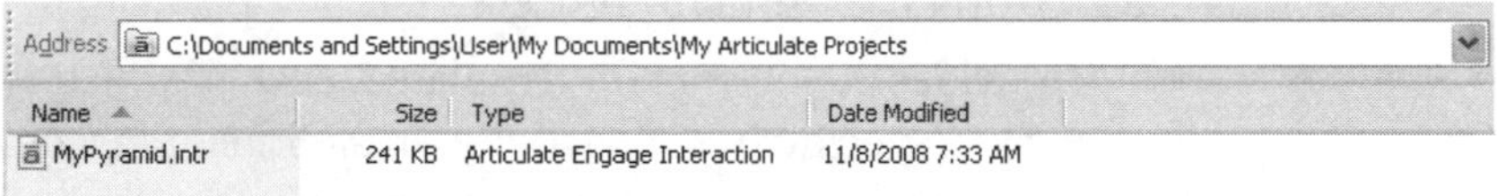

Address	C:\Documents and Settings\User\My Documents\My Articulate Projects		
Name ▲	Size	Type	Date Modified
MyPyramid.intr	241 KB	Articulate Engage Interaction	11/8/2008 7:33 AM

Figure 14.18. Engage working file

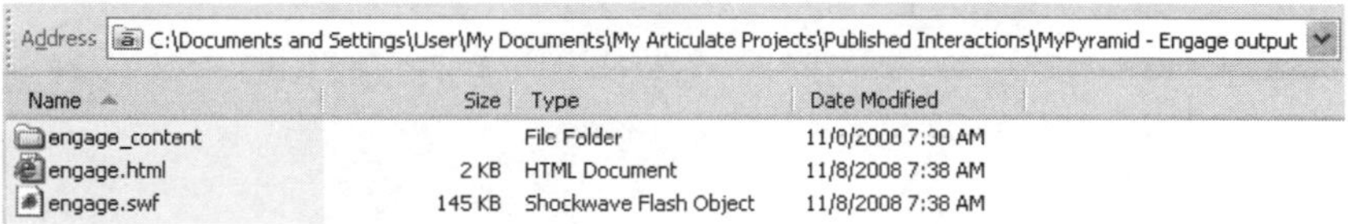

Address	C:\Documents and Settings\User\My Documents\My Articulate Projects\Published Interactions\MyPyramid - Engage output		
Name ▲	Size	Type	Date Modified
engage_content		File Folder	11/0/2000 7:30 AM
engage.html	2 KB	HTML Document	11/8/2008 7:38 AM
engage.swf	145 KB	Shockwave Flash Object	11/8/2008 7:38 AM

Figure 14.19. Engage published files

Keep in mind that you can store your files in other folders besides the default My Articulate Projects folder. In fact, it's a good idea to create an easily recognizable folder for each of your interactions. You can then use that folder to store the .intr file and other files used to create the interaction, such as audio and graphics.

Chapter Recap

Here's our list of the most important things to remember from this chapter:

- Engage is a program that lets you create interactive "discovery" experiences for your audience.

- Engage interactions enable your viewers to actively examine information by drilling down for details, comparing relationships among components, and exploring different components.

- You build an Engage interaction using prebuilt templates. Then you can publish the interaction as Flash output, which can be incorporated into other applications.

- A published Engage interaction file is launched in the Engage player.

- Best uses of Engage include inserting published interactions in Presenter projects, using them on web sites, releasing them on CD, and incorporating them into other e-learning applications.

- The basic workflow for creating all Engage interactions is the same: Select an interaction, build the components with text, audio, and media; customize; and publish. Planning, testing, and fixing are also part of the workflow process.

- Engage provides 10 interaction templates, each of which is designed for a specific type of activity. In addition, the Community Interactions tab enables you to import virtually any type of existing interaction into Engage.

■ Take time to plan your interaction, which includes choosing the right interaction, planning the content (text, audio, media), planning the design elements (layout, colors, player features), determining view control, and selecting a delivery method.

■ Working files in Engage use the file extension .intr. These are the files you create and modify in Engage.

■ Published Engage interaction files result in a Flash .swf file, along with supporting files. These are the files that viewers need to launch the interaction.

Chapter 15

Engage Basics

Chapter Snapshot

In this chapter, you'll learn about the features and procedures that are common to most Engage interactions.

One of the great qualities of Engage is that the interactions share many of the same features, such as text, audio, and media files. Once you learn how to create these items, then you can easily develop any interaction. Some features and procedures in this chapter are more advanced than others, but we've included them because they apply to all interactions. So if you're brand new to Engage, those procedures might make more sense after you've played around with some interactions. But we still recommend starting with this chapter because it provides a good foundation for all 10 interaction types.

If you're eager to jump into a specific interaction, feel free to skip ahead to one of the next 10 chapters and then come back here later for more details. The remaining chapters in this section cover the procedures specific to each interaction type.

Revisiting the Engage 1-2-3-4 Workflow

In Chapter 14, "Introduction to Engage," we discussed the workflow of developing any Engage interaction (Figure 15.1). In this chapter, you'll get a feel for the essential tasks needed to perform all four steps, plus previewing and saving your quiz. Specifically:

- **Step 1:** Selecting an interaction involves identifying the right interaction for your content (discussed in Chapter 14) and then opening it using the New Interaction dialog box.

- **Step 2:** Building the components of any interaction involves entering text, audio, and other media (such as a still image or video).

- **Step 3:** Customizing an interaction involves working with the Interaction Properties dialog box, where you can control player features, color schemes, and more. It may also involve customizing specific features of an interaction, which are covered in later chapters.

- **Step 4:** Publishing an interaction involves creating the final output files that viewers will use to work with the interaction.

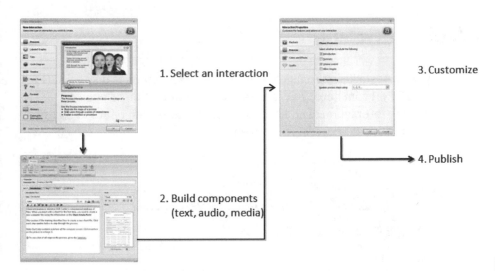

1. Select an interaction

3. Customize

4. Publish

2. Build components
(text, audio, media)

Figure 15.1. Engage 1 2 3 4 workflow

Launching Engage

Engage is a separate application installed on your computer. You can start Engage using any of the following procedures:

- In Windows XP: Click the **Start** button, select **All Programs**, select **Articulate**, and select **Articulate Engage '09**.

- In Windows Vista: Click the **Start** button, select **All Programs**, open the **Articulate** folder, and select **Articulate Engage '09**.

- Double-click the **Articulate Engage '09** shortcut icon on your desktop.

- Double-click an existing interaction file in Windows Explorer.

Tip: You can also open Engage from within Presenter. Just double-click a slide containing an Engage interaction and select Edit in Engage. The Engage program opens and displays the current interaction. Or click the Engage Interaction button on the Articulate tab of the ribbon and click the Create New button.

Selecting an Interaction

After you start the Engage program, the start screen is displayed (Figure 15.2). From here, you can start a new interaction or open an existing interaction. The lower section of the screen offers links to tutorials and resources on the web.

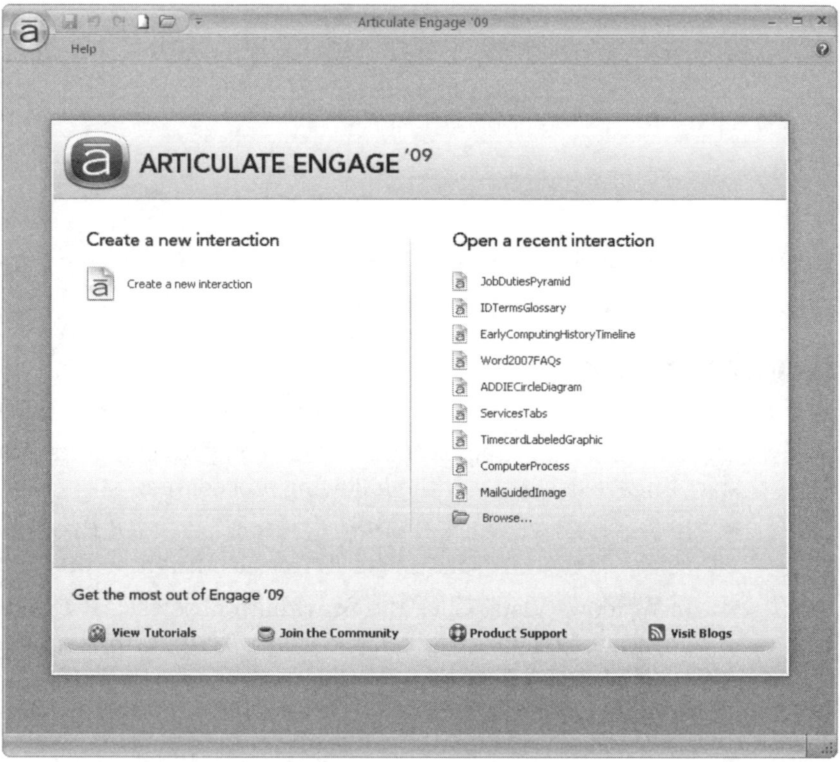

Figure 15.2. Engage start screen

- ■ To start a new interaction, click **Create a new interaction** on the left side.

- ■ To open an existing interaction, click its name in the Open a recent interaction section on the right side. (Note that moving the mouse pointer over an existing interaction name displays a thumbnail preview of the interaction, as well as its file location.) Use the **Browse** button to locate interactions that don't appear in this list.

> IIII▶**Tip:** You can remove an interaction from the Open a recent interaction list by right-clicking the interaction and selecting Remove from List.

Selecting an existing interaction immediately opens the interaction file, where you can make changes. Selecting Create a new interaction opens the New Interaction dialog box (Figure 15.3), where you can select a specific type of interaction to create.

Figure 15.3. New Interaction dialog box

Each interaction type is represented by a tab on the left side of the dialog box. Clicking a tab displays a sample and additional information about the interaction. The View Sample link opens the Articulate web site, where you can view and interact with a real Engage interaction. To start a new interaction, click its tab and then click the **OK** button.

Opening New or Existing Interactions from a Current Interaction

To start a new interaction while working in a current interaction, use any of these methods:

- Click the **New** button on the Quick Access toolbar.
- Click the **Articulate** button and select **New** from the File menu.
- Press **Ctrl+N**.

To open an existing interaction while working in a current interaction, use any of these methods:

- Click the **Open** button on the Quick Access toolbar.
- Click the **Articulate** button and select **Open** from the File menu.
- Press **Ctrl+O**.

Exploring the Engage Interface

The Articulate Engage '09 window (Figure 15.4) contains all the tools you need to build the type of interaction you've selected. Many interaction types use the same tools, so this window is similar for most interactions. Let's take a closer look at the elements of a typical interaction window.

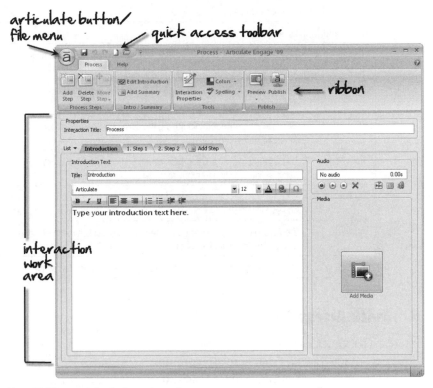

Figure 15.4 Engage window for Process interaction

Articulate Button/File Menu

Clicking the Articulate button opens the File menu (Figure 15.5), which contains commands to work with the interaction file. Table 15.1 describes these commands.

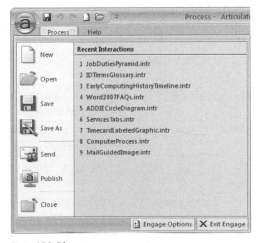

Figure 15.5. File menu

Table 15.1. File menu commands

Command	Description
New	Displays the New Interaction dialog box, where you can select an interaction type (shortcut key — Ctrl+N)
Open	Displays the Open dialog box, where you can select an existing interaction (shortcut key — Ctrl+O)
Save	Saves the current interaction using the current file name and location (shortcut key — Ctrl+S)
Save As	Displays the Save As dialog box, where you can save the interaction using a different file name and location
Send	Displays the message window of your default email program, where you can send the current (unpublished) presentation as an email attachment
Publish	Displays the Publish dialog box, where you can publish the interaction using a specific output format (shortcut key — F10)
Close	Closes the current interaction and displays the Engage start screen

Quick Access Toolbar

The Quick Access toolbar (Figure 15.6) contains buttons that activate common commands. (You can also find most of these commands on the File menu.) Table 15.2 describes each button.

Figure 15.6. Quick Access toolbar

Table 15.2. Quick Access toolbar buttons

Button	Description
Save	Saves the current interaction using the current file name and location (shortcut key — Ctrl+S)
Undo	Reverses the effects of your most recent action. Becomes active only after you perform an action (shortcut key — Ctrl+Z)
Redo	Restores the most recent action that you've undone. Becomes active only after you undo an action (shortcut key — Ctrl+Y)
New	Displays the New Interaction dialog box, where you can select an interaction type (shortcut key — Ctrl+N)
Open	Displays the Open dialog box, where you can select an existing interaction (shortcut key — Ctrl+O)
Customize	Displays a menu of options, where you can hide buttons on the Quick Access toolbar and control the ribbon display

> **Tip:** You can add almost any tool from the Engage ribbon to the Quick Access toolbar. Just right-click the tool (such as the Edit Introduction button) and select Add to Quick Access Toolbar.

Ribbon

Engage '09 uses the Office 2007-type *ribbon* to organize most of the tools used to work with an interaction. The ribbon in all interactions contains two tabs. The first tab is named for the specific interaction you are working with, and it contains most of the tools you need to create the interaction. Figure 15.7 shows the Process tab from the Process interaction. The second tab is named Help, and it contains basically the same options regardless of which interaction you are working with.

> **Tip:** You can hide the ribbon by right-clicking it and selecting Minimize the Ribbon. Just the ribbon tabs are displayed. Redisplay the ribbon by right-clicking a tab and selecting Minimize the Ribbon again.

Interaction Tab

The interaction tab tools consist of buttons and menus and are organized by groups. The groups for many interactions are similar. Table 15.3 describes the groups on the interaction tab.

Figure 15.7. Engage ribbon Process tab

Table 15.3. Interaction tab groups

Group	Description
Process Steps	The name of this group varies, depending on the interaction. It contains tools to add, delete, and move the primary components of the interaction, such as steps in a Process interaction.
Intro/Summary	Contains tools to edit the introduction to the interaction and add/edit a summary for the interaction
Tools	Contains tools to edit features of the interaction, such as properties of the interaction, spelling, and color schemes
Publish	Contains tools to preview the interaction and to publish it using a specific output format

Help Tab

The Help tab in Engage (Figure 15.8) is similar to the Help tab in the Quizmaker ribbon and the Help menu in Presenter. A few items are Engage-specific, such as the tools in the Articulate Engage '09 section. The Documentation button in the Help and Support group leads directly to help topics for Engage. Chapter 1, "Introduction to Articulate Studio," describes how to use the help system from any Articulate Studio '09 program.

Figure 15.8. Engage ribbon Help tab

Interaction Work Area

The interaction work area (Figure 15.9) in the Engage window varies slightly, depending on the interaction. In general, this area is used to build the components of the interaction. Table 15.4 describes the sections of the interaction work area.

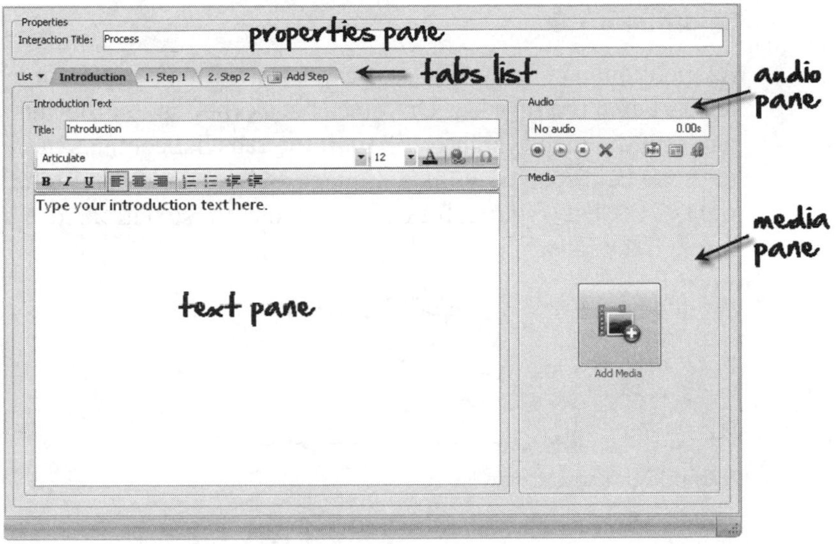

Figure 15.9. Interaction work area for Process interaction

Table 15.4. Interaction work area sections

Section	Description
Properties pane	Contains the customizable title of the interaction
Tabs list	Contains a tab for each component in the interaction. For example, a step is one component of a Process interaction, and a label is one component of a Labeled Graphic interaction. You can select a tab by clicking it or by using the List menu to the left of the first tab.
Text pane	Contains the text for the current component
Audio pane	Contains the tools to record, play, and import audio for the current component
Media pane	Contains the tools to add a media file, such as an image or movie, to the current interaction

Selecting a Tab

As mentioned in Table 15.4, you can work with a component by clicking its tab in the tabs list. Or you can click the List button and select a tab from the menu (Figure 15.10). If the tabs list contains more tabs than can be displayed at once, Engage adds navigation buttons to the right of the list (Figure 15.11). You can use those buttons to scroll through the tabs.

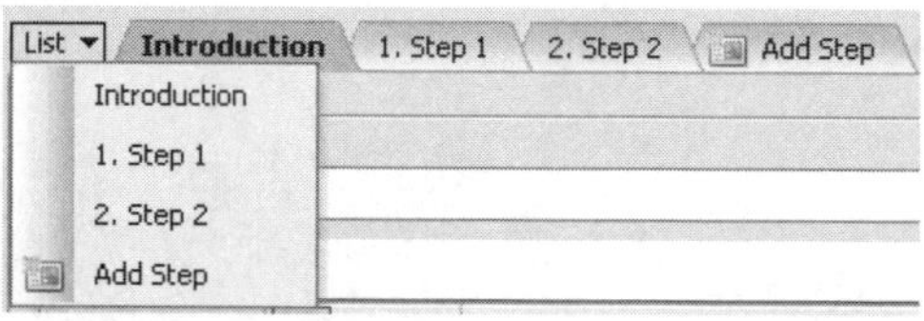

Figure 15.10. List menu on the tabs list

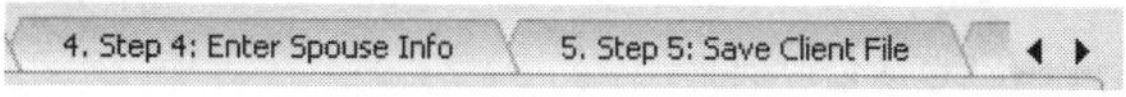

Figure 15.11. Navigation buttons on the tabs list

Now that you have an idea of how to start an interaction, the next section of this chapter focuses on step 2 of the Engage workflow: Build components using text, audio, and media.

Working with Text

Chances are you're going to include text in any Engage interaction. Text will appear in different places, depending on the interaction, but the tools for creating and formatting text are basically the same. Let's use the Process interaction as an example of the many ways you can work with text. Figure 15.12 shows the text used for the introduction to a Process interaction.

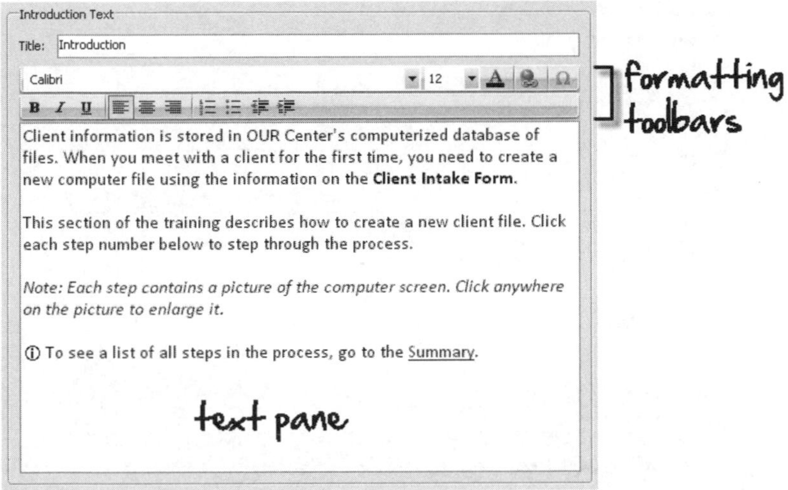

Figure 15.12. Introduction text for a Process interaction

Text Placeholders

Engage tries to make it easy for you to determine where you need to enter text. Every interaction includes text placeholders for each significant component (Figures 15.13 and 15.14). Your job is to replace these placeholders with your own text. Most interactions use text in the following areas:

- **Interaction Title:** The interaction title is displayed in the top horizontal bar when the learner runs the interaction. Your title should give a good indication of what the learner is about to experience. In this example, we've called the Process interaction "Creating a Client File."

- **Component Titles:** Most interactions consist of a group of components, such as steps, tabs, labels, captions, or sections. Each component needs a title that describes that piece of the interaction. For example, the first step in the Creating a Client File interaction is "Step 1: Log On."

- **Component Text:** The component text is the heart and soul of your content. Here you get to say everything you need to say. In the Log On step, the viewers learn how to turn on the computer and log on to the system.

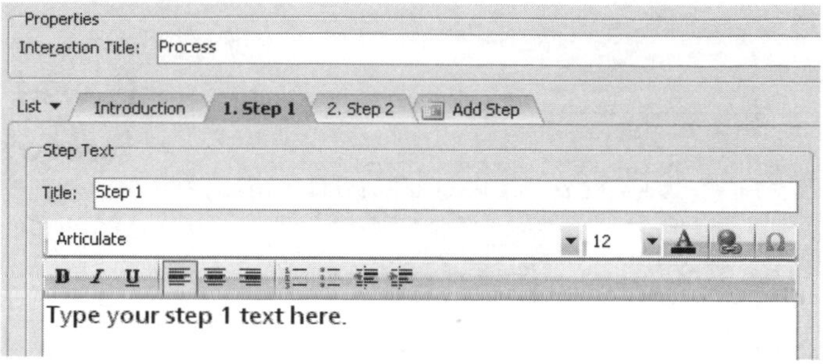

Figure 15.13. Text placeholders

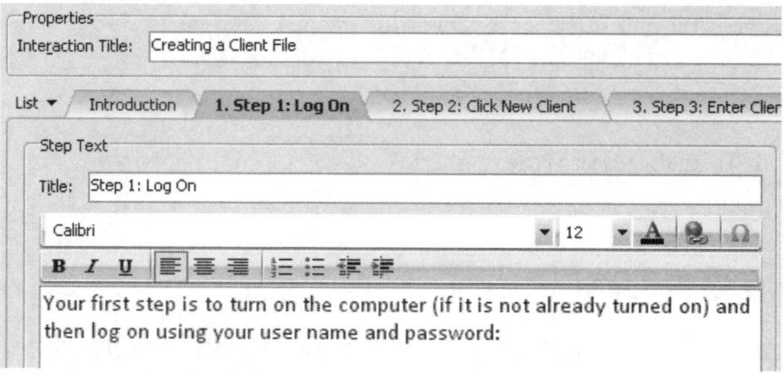

Figure 15.14. Text placeholders populated

Beware of Scrolling Text

The components in most Engage interactions don't accommodate huge amounts of text. If you include more text than can be displayed at once, Engage adds scroll bars. However, we strongly advise you to "chunk" text so that your viewers don't need to scroll. Many people find scrolling annoying, and there's a chance that viewers won't see the scroll bars. (In fact, you won't see the scroll bars either as you develop the interaction. They don't show up until you preview.)

Entering Text

Now that you've figured out where you need to enter text (and what you're going to say), you can enter your text in several different ways.

Typing Text

Okay, this one is too obvious, but we had to say it. You'll probably type text into the Interaction Title and component Title fields. If you are writing content as you go (or prefer not to copy and paste), then you can also type your text into each component text area.

Copying and Pasting Text

Engage supports the standard Cut, Copy, and Paste commands, meaning you can copy text from another application and then paste it into any text area in the interaction. These commands in Engage are accessible from the shortcut menu, which is displayed by right-clicking an area or text selection (Figure 15.15). You can also use the standard shortcut keys: Ctrl+X (Cut), Ctrl+C (Copy), and Ctrl+V (Paste).

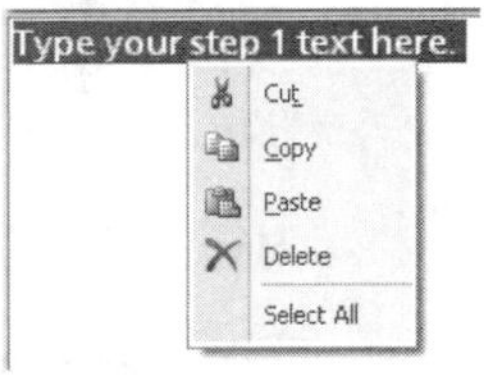

Figure 15.15. Text shortcut menu

Keep in mind that when you paste text into the interaction, the formats from the original source text are not retained. Instead, the currently defined format of the Engage component is applied to the pasted text. An exception to this is that copied bullets are retained. However, text wrapping in copied bullets is unpredictable—your best bet is to remove the bullets and reapply them using the Bullets button in Engage.

Inserting Symbols

Need to include a symbol that is not on your keyboard? Clicking the Insert Symbol button on the Formatting toolbar opens the Symbol menu (Figure 15.16), which enables you to insert just about any symbol offered by most applications, such as © (copyright) or ÷ (divided by).

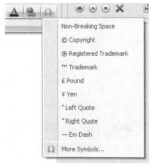

Figure 15.16. Symbol menu

To add a symbol:

1. Position the insertion point where the symbol is to be inserted.

2. Click the **Insert Symbol** button.

3. The Symbol menu appears, which displays a list of commonly used symbols. Click a symbol to insert it, or click the **More Symbols** option to open the Symbol dialog box.

4. In the Symbol dialog box, all of the symbols in the Webdings font and the Basic Latin subset are displayed by default. To view different symbols, select a different font from the Font list or a different subset from the Subset list.

5. Either double-click a symbol *or* click a symbol and click the **Insert** button.

The symbol is inserted using the formats of the existing paragraph.

Using Spell Check

Like any good application that handles text, Engage includes a spell checker. By default, Engage places a wavy red underline below any word it does not recognize. Right-clicking the underlined word displays options for correcting the spelling or ignoring the word. You can also check the spelling of all text in the interaction:

1. Click the **Spelling** button on the ribbon.

2. If Engage does not recognize a word, the Spelling dialog box is displayed:

    ■ Click the **Ignore Once** button or **Ignore All** button to ignore the change.

    ■ Click the **Change Once** button or **Change All** button to replace the word with the selected suggestion.

3. Engage continues to locate unrecognized words and then displays a message box when the spell check process is complete. Click the **OK** button to remove the message.

 Note: The Engage '09 Help docs contain more information about using spell check.

Adding Hyperlinks

A hyperlink in the interaction text gives your viewers the flexibility to open a web site on the fly or jump to a different location within the interaction. Although Engage doesn't support sophisticated branching sequences, the use of hyperlinks offers some elementary branching capabilities. Following are some examples of how to use hyperlinks in an interaction:

- **Open a web resource:** Display a web resource related to the interaction or the current component.

- **Jump or return to the summary:** Although most interactions let you add a summary, it is accessible only by clicking the Next button after the last component is displayed. In other words, there is no component labeled "Summary" for the viewer to click. You can include a link to the summary from any of the components.

- **Return to the introduction:** Just like the summary, there is no component labeled "Introduction" for the viewer to click. It is accessible only by clicking the Previous button at the beginning of the interaction. You can include a link to the introduction from any of the components.

- **Review a related component:** One component in an interaction may be closely related to another component. You can enable the viewer to jump directly to the related item by including a hyperlink. For example, in a Glossary interaction, include a hyperlink to a related term.

Tip: Engage interactions are compact and each template comes with a specific navigation method. Be sure that any hyperlinks that you add don't confuse the viewer or leave them wondering where they are.

To add a hyperlink:

1. Position the insertion point where the link is to be inserted *or* select the text to serve as the hyperlink.

2. Click the **Hyperlink** button on the toolbar.

3. In the Hyperlink dialog box, in the Text to display box, enter the text that will represent the link, such as **Articulate Web Site**. If

you already selected the text to serve as the hyperlink, it will be displayed by default in this box.

4. Engage lets you create a link to either a web site or to another component within the interaction:

   ■ To link to a web site, click the **URL** option and enter the web site address in the lower text box. Make sure you include the protocol http://. Click the **Test Link** button 🔲 to open the web page.

   ■ To link to another component within the interaction, click the component name option, then select a component from the list box. Note that the component name will vary, depending on the type of interaction.

5. Click the **OK** button to create the link.

Figure 15.17. Hyperlink dialog box Link to URL option

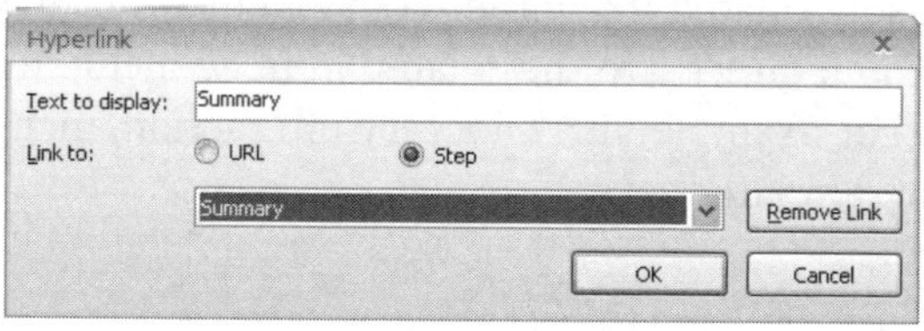

Figure 15.18. Hyperlink dialog box Link to component (step) option

Figures 15.17 and 15.18 show the options for linking to a web site and to another component in a Process interaction.

To remove the hyperlink properties from a link:

1. Click anywhere in the link text.

2. Click the **Hyperlink** button on the toolbar.

3. In the Hyperlink dialog box, click the **Remove Link** button.

4. Click the **OK** button.

A hyperlink appears as underlined text. Keep in mind that you cannot test the link within the text area of the development screen. However, you can test the link when the interaction is in Preview mode.

Formatting Text

Once you've entered text, you can apply a variety of common formats using the two toolbars above the text area (Figure 15.19). The buttons on the toolbars are similar to the formatting buttons found in most word processing programs.

Figure 15.19. Formatting toolbars

To format the appearance of text:

1. Select the text you want to format.

2. Click a format button or select an item from a list box. For example:

   ■ Click the **Bold**, **Italic**, or **Underline** buttons.

   ■ Click the **Font Color** button and then click a color.

   ■ Click the arrow on the Font list box and select a font, such as Arial.

   ■ Click the arrow on the Font Size list box and select a size, such as 14.

To format the alignment of text:

1. Select the text you want to align.

2. Click an alignment button. For example:

   ■ Click the **Align Left**, **Center**, or **Align Right** buttons to justify the text.

   ■ Click the **Numbering** or **Bullets** buttons to create a numbered or bulleted list.

   ■ Click the **Decrease Indent** or **Increase Indent** buttons to shift the text to the left or right.

Engage also lets you globally apply a font to all content text and to all title text using the Colors and Effects tab in the Interaction Properties dialog box (Figure 15.20).

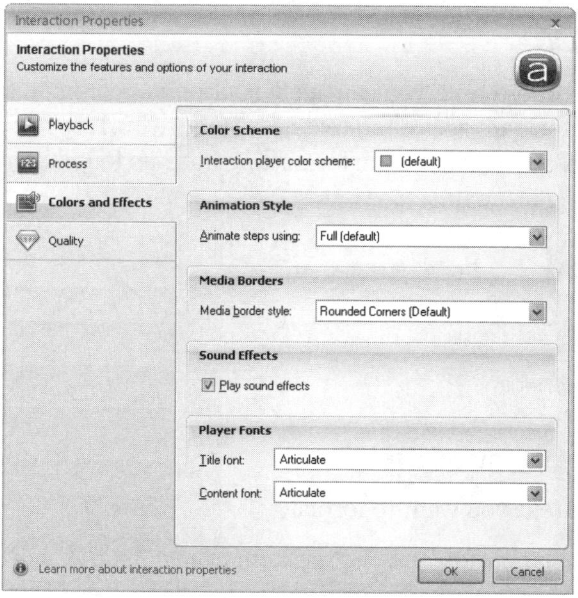

Figure 15.20. Interaction Properties dialog box, Colors and Effects tab

To change the title font and content font globally:

1. Click the **Interaction Properties** button on the ribbon.

2. In the Interaction Properties dialog box, click the **Colors and Effects** tab.

3. To apply a font to the interaction title and all component titles, select a font from the **Title font** list.

4. To apply a font to all content in the interaction, select a font from the **Content font** list.

5. Click the **OK** button.

Practice 1

Want to brush up on your text-entering and formatting skills? Try the following steps to get used to working with the text features in Engage.

Entering and Formatting Text

1. From the Engage start screen, click **Create a new interaction**.

2. Click the **Process** tab and then click the **OK** button.

3. Double-click the text in the Interaction Title box and type **New Employee Checklist**.

4. From another application, copy a paragraph of text to the clipboard.

5. Right-click in the text area of the Introduction, and select **Paste** from the shortcut menu.

6. Click the **1. Step 1** tab.

7. Select **Type your text here** and press the **Delete** key on your keyboard.

8. Type the following text:

   When you meet with your supervisor on your first day of the job, you can expect to go over the following items:

   Work hours

   Daily schedule

   Performance expectations

   Your questions

   Click here to visit the company web site.

9. Select all of the text, click the arrow on the Font list box, and click **Arial**.

10. Click to the left of the last sentence, and then click the **Insert Symbol** button ▣ on the Formatting toolbar.

11. From the Symbol list, select **More Symbols**.

12. Click the information symbol ⓘ, and then click the **Insert** button.

13. Double-click the word **here** in the last sentence, and then click the **Hyperlink** button 🔗 on the Formatting toolbar.

14. Choose the **URL** option, type **www.articulate.com** after http://, and click the **OK** button.

15. Select the four items beginning with **Work hours** and ending with **Your questions**.

16. Click the **Bullets** button on the toolbar.

17. Click in front of the last sentence and then click the **Increase Indent** button.

Once you have a good idea of how the text formatting options work, close and abandon the interaction.

Working with Audio

You can include audio (such as narrations and sound effects) in any Engage interaction. But be careful not to overwhelm the viewer with long audio clips or a barrage of text and audio together.

Once you've decided to use audio in an interaction, you can create the audio in Engage or import existing audio files using the Audio pane (Figure 15.21). Depending on the interaction, the audio can be placed in any component (such as a step in the Process interaction or a tab in the Tab interaction), as well as in the introduction. Let's continue using the Process interaction as an example and take a closer look at how to work with audio.

Figure 15.21. Audio pane

Preparing a Script

If you are going to use audio, it's a good idea to prepare a script. A script simply contains the text to be included in the narration. Although scripts can be written using any word processing program, Engage offers the handy Narration Script window, which enables you to write and view the script within the interaction (Figure 15.22). If you plan to record the audio yourself in Engage, we recommend using this feature.

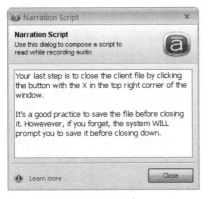

Figure 15.22. Narration Script window

To prepare the script using the Narration Script window:

1. Select the component to contain the audio, such as a step in the Process interaction.

2. In the Audio pane, click the **Narration script** button 📧.

3. In the Narration Script window, type the script for the current component.

4. If you plan to record the script immediately, leave the window open. If you want to close the window, click the **Close** button. Your script will be saved and will appear in the window the next time you click the Narration script button.

Tip: You can adjust the size of the Narration Script window if needed. We reduced the size of the window for the example in this chapter.

Recording and Playing Audio

Once the script is prepared, you can record and then play back the audio from within the interaction. You need a good microphone, speakers, and a quiet environment. Chapter 5, "Presenter Basics," provides information about using microphones.

If an audio recording already exists, the field in the Audio pane displays the word "Ready" and the length of the audio clip in seconds (Figure 15.23). If you record another audio clip, it will replace the existing clip. If the component doesn't have an audio clip, the Audio control field displays the words "No Audio."

Figure 15.23. Audio pane showing Recorded audio

To record the audio:

1. Display the prewritten script. For example, if the script was composed in the Narration Script window, click the **Narration script** button in the Audio pane to open the window.

2. Click the **Record** button in the Audio pane.

3. Narrate the script by speaking clearly into the microphone. The Audio control field displays a running count of the recording time, in seconds.

4. When you have finished, click the **Stop** button in the Audio pane. The Audio control field then displays the word "Ready" and the length of the audio clip in seconds.

To play the audio:

1. Click the **Play** button in the Audio pane.

The Audio control field displays a progress bar, indicating the number of elapsed seconds. If you make a mistake and want to rerecord the script, you can simply click the **Record** button again and rerecord the audio. Engage replaces the old audio with the new. You can also delete the recording entirely by clicking the **Remove/Delete** button .

Importing Audio Files

Although Engage makes it easy for you to record your own audio, you can also import audio files. For example, you might hire a voice talent to narrate audio clips to be used for an Engage interaction. Once you receive the audio files, you can include them in an interaction. Engage supports WAV and MP3 audio file types.

Note: For more details about each of the supported audio file types, refer to the section titled "Importing Audio" in Chapter 5, "Presenter Basics."

To import an audio file:

1. Select the component to contain the audio, such as a step in the Process interaction.

2. In the Audio section, click the **Import audio file** button.

3. In the Open dialog box, do one of the following:

   ■ Type the name of the audio file.

   ■ Browse to the folder containing the audio files and click the file. (In Windows XP, Engage displays the My Articulate Projects folder by default, which is contained in the My Documents folder.)

4. Click the **Open** button.

To play the imported audio file, click the **Play** button in the Audio pane.

Editing Audio Files

Sometimes the audio you record or import isn't perfect. Engage offers a tool that enables you to modify audio files. The Audio Editor enables you to delete and move sections of an audio clip, as well as add silence and change the volume (Figure 15.24). This is the same Audio Editor used by Presenter and Quizmaker.

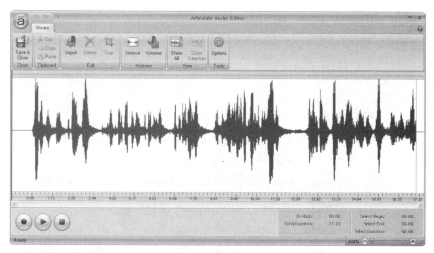

Figure 15.24. Audio Editor window

To open the Audio Editor window:

1. Select the component containing the audio, such as a step in the Process interaction.

2. Click the **Edit audio** button ▦ in the Audio pane.

The Articulate Audio Editor window displays a series of waveforms, which are visual representations of the sound. The waveforms correspond to time intervals, which are marked in seconds and fractions of seconds. Because Chapter 5, "Presenter Basics," covers working with the Audio Editor in detail, we won't cover it again here. You can refer to that chapter as well as the "Editing Audio" topic in the Engage '09 Help documentation.

Practice 2

Got a microphone? Try the following steps to get used to recording and playing audio in Engage.

Recording and Playing Audio

1. From the Engage start screen, click **Create a new interaction**.

2. Click the **Process** tab and then the **OK** button.

3. In the Audio pane of the interaction window, click the **Narration script** button 🔳.

4. In the Narration Script dialog box, type the script to be narrated. For example:

   Your first day on the job is important to us. By completing this check list of items, you will learn everything about your new position.

5. In the Audio pane, click the **Record** button ⊙.

6. Narrate the script by speaking clearly into the microphone.

7. When you are done, click the **Stop** button ⊙ in the Audio pane.

8. To listen to your script, click the **Play** button ⊙ in the Audio pane.

Working with Media Files

Engage lets you insert a variety of media files into interaction components, including still images and videos.

As we discussed in Chapter 14, "Introduction to Engage," the ideal graphic element is instructional and is not just "eye candy." It's okay to make your interaction components pretty, but media should also serve a purpose. Although the procedures for adding an image and a video are the same, Engage offers slightly different customization options for each of these media types. Both types are added using the Media pane (Figure 15.25).

Figure 15.25. Media pane

66 **Note:** When you add a media file, a copy of the original file is embedded in the media item. In other words, the media file in the interaction is not linked to the original source file.

Adding an Image

An image is a "still" graphic and can be created using a variety of graphic programs, resulting in a variety of media file types. Engage supports JPG (or JPEG), BMP, GIF, and PNG graphic file types. You can also insert a .swf file as a static image. For screenshots, the best file type to use in Articulate programs is PNG because it uses *lossless compression*—your file will look the same as the original image. Once you have created or obtained an image for an interaction, you can easily insert it into an interaction component. Keep in mind that you can insert just one media file into each component. If you need more than one image, you can combine them into one image file using a graphics program.

To add an image:

1. Select the component to contain the image, such as a step in a Process interaction.

2. In the Media pane, click the **Add Media** button.

3. In the Open dialog box, browse to the image file and then double-click it.

4. In the Multimedia Properties dialog box, select the options you want. (These options are covered next.)

5.   Click the **OK** button to insert the image into the component.

▌▌▌▌**Tip:** Instead of performing steps 2 and 3, you can drag and drop an image file from Windows Explorer into the Media pane.

After the image has been inserted, an image preview appears in the Media pane (Figure 15.26). Clicking the **Edit Proper-ties** link opens the Multimedia Properties dialog box, where you can modify the image options. Clicking the **Remove** but-ton ✖ deletes the image from the interaction. To see how the image looks in the running interaction, click the **Pre-view** button on the ribbon.

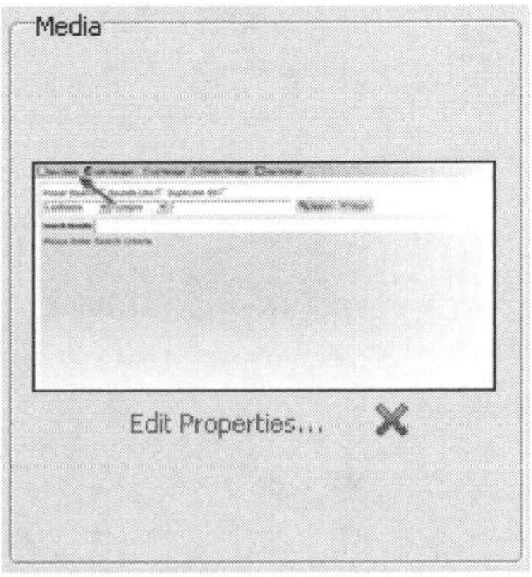

Figure 15.26. Media pane after inserting an image

Tips for Using Images

Avoid using graphics that need to be scaled up or down, even in PNG format. When Engage scales the image and the interaction is published to Flash, quality is reduced. So your best option is to use a graphic or screenshot that does not need to be resized. For example, the total size of the Engage player is 720 x 540 pixels. If you need an image for a step in a Process interaction, consider the amount of text required for the step and then determine the approximate space left for the image. For best quality, use an image that matches the size of the allotted space.

Selecting Media Properties for an Image

When inserting an image, you use the Multimedia Properties dialog box (Figure 15.27) to specify various options that control how the image will look in the final output. Table 15.5 describes these options.

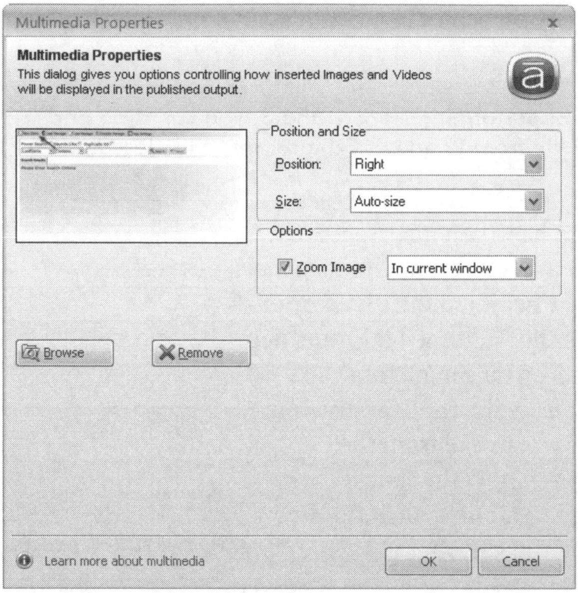

Figure 15.27. Multimedia Properties dialog box

Table 15.5. Multimedia Properties dialog box image options

Option	Description
Position	Determines the location of the image (Top, Bottom, Right, Left) relative to the text within the component. The position options vary, depending on the interaction. For example, in a Process interaction, you can place the image to the right, left, top, or bottom of the text in the current step. In a Labeled Graphic, you can place the image on the top or bottom of the current label.
Size	Determines the size of the image within the component. By default, the Auto-size option is selected. This option automatically scales the image to fit in one section of the component. However, you can set a specific size by selecting the Custom size option from the list box.
Zoom Image	Determines whether the viewer can click the image to enlarge it. Selecting the check box enables the viewer to see a larger version of the image by clicking it within the interaction. The list box to the right of Zoom Image lets you choose where the expanded image is displayed: In current window or In new window. If you don't want the viewer to be able to enlarge the image, then clear the check box. (Note that this option is available only when the image has been reduced to fit the interaction.)
Browse	Displays the Open dialog box, where you can select a different media file to replace the current file
Remove	Removes the current image from the interaction component. You can select another media file using the Browse button.

Customizing the Image Size

If you want Engage to display an image using specific dimensions, you can select the **Custom size** option in the Position and Size section (Figure 15.28). Once you choose Custom size, the pane expands to allow you to enter values into the **Width** and **Height** fields. **The Keep Aspect Ratio** check box tells Engage to resize the image proportionally. For example, if you enter a height, Engage automatically adjusts the width by the same ratio.

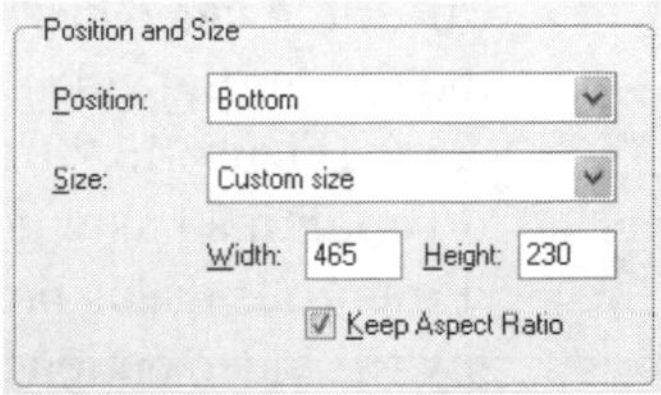

Figure 15.28. Multimedia Properties dialog box Position and Size section

Keep in mind that if the image size is so large that all of the accompanying text cannot be displayed at once, Engage adds scroll bars to the text. If the image is too large for the interaction, you'll get a message informing you of the maximum size allowed for that specific component.

Adding a Video

Engage enables you to insert two types of video files into interactions: SWF (Flash) and FLV (Adobe Flash video). These videos can be produced using the Adobe Flash program, as well as some other programs. If you have Video Encoder, which comes with Articulate Studio '09, you can use it to convert most standard video formats to .flv files. Depending on the type of video you insert, Engage offers slightly different customization options.

To add a video:

1. Select the component to contain the video, such as a step in the Process interaction.

2. In the Media pane, click the **Add Media** button.

3. In the Open dialog box, browse to the video file and then double-click it. (You might see a message informing you of Flash player requirements. Click **Yes**.)

4. In the Multimedia Properties dialog box, select the options you want and click **OK**. (These options are covered next.)

Tip: Instead of performing steps 2 and 3, you can drag and drop a video file from Windows Explorer into the Media pane.

After the video has been inserted, a place-holder for the video appears in the Media panc (Figure 15.29). Clicking the **Edit Properties** link opens the Multimedia Properties dialog box, where you can mod-ify the video options. Clicking the **Remove** button ✖ deletes the video from the inter-action. Clicking the **Play** button ▶ and **Stop** button ◉ lets you preview the video in the Media section. To see how the video looks in the running interaction, click the **Preview** button on the ribbon.

Figure 15.29. Media pane after inserting a video

Selecting Media Properties for a Video

When inserting a video, you use the Multimedia Properties dialog box (Figure 15.30) to specify various properties of the video. The options in the dialog box vary, depending on the video type. For .swf files, all of the options listed in Table 15.6 are available. For .flv files, all but the Display and Thumb-nail options are available.

Figure 15.30. Multimedia Properties dialog box

Table 15.6. Multimedia Properties dialog box video options

Option	Description
Position	Determines the location of the video (Top, Bottom, Right, or Left) relative to the text within the component. For example, in a Process interaction, you can place the video to the right, left, top, or bottom of the text in the current step.
Size	Determines the size of the video within the component. By default, the Auto-size option is selected. This option automatically scales the video to fit in one section of the component. However, you can set a specific size by selecting the Custom option from the list box.
Include Playbar	Adds a playbar to the video display. Select this option if you want to enable the viewer to pause and restart the video file while it is running in the interaction.
Auto Start	Select this option if you want the video to begin immediately when the interaction is loaded. Note that this option is available only if you select the Include Playbar option. If a playbar is not included, then the interaction always starts automatically.
Display	*For .swf files only.* Enables you to choose how the video is displayed: Full size: The full size of the original video is displayed in the center of the Engage interaction after the viewer clicks the Play button. Note that this option overrides the Position option. In new window: The video is displayed in a separate browser window after the viewer clicks the Play button. (Note that if the playbar is included, the viewer must also click the Play button in the new window.) Embedded: The video is displayed in the location indicated by the Position field.
Thumbnail	*For .swf files only.* Enables you to choose the initial image seen by the viewer. Note that if a thumbnail option is selected, then the viewer must click the Play button to start the video. Also note that this option is not available for embedded .swf files. Flash icon: Displays the Adobe Flash icon 1st frame of Flash movie: Displays the first frame of the movie as a still image Custom image: Displays the image you select. Choose an image by using the button to the right of the Thumbnail list box.
Browse	Displays the Open dialog box, where you can select a different media file to replace the current file
Remove	Removes the current video from the interaction component. You can select another media file using the Browse button.

Customizing the Video Size

The procedures for customizing the video size are the same as those for customizing the image size. You can use the Position and Size section to enter a new height and width. Refer to Figure 15.28 in the section titled "Customizing the Image Size."

Practice 3

Got an image and Flash (SWF) video clip? Try the following steps to get used to adding media files in Engage. (If you only have a .flv file, you can still perform the practice—just skip the second part of step 11.)

Adding Media Files

1. From the Engage start screen, click **Create a new interaction**.

2. Click **Process** and click the **OK** button.

3. Add some text to the Introduction step.

4. In the Media pane of the interaction window, click the **Add Media** button.

5. In the Open dialog box, browse to the location of an image file and double-click it.

6. In the Multimedia Properties dialog box, select **Left** from the Position list box.

7. Click the **OK** button.

8. In the interaction window, click the **1. Step 1** tab.

9. In the Media pane, click the **Add Media** button.

10. In the Open dialog box, browse to the location of a .swf file and double-click it.

11. In the Multimedia Properties dialog box, keep the default options except for the following:

    ■ Select **Include Playbar.**

    ■ Select **1ˢᵗ Frame of Flash movie** from the Thumbnail list.

12. Click the **OK** button.

13. To preview the interaction, click the **Preview** button on the ribbon.

14. In the Interaction Preview window, click the image in the introduction to expand it, and then click it again to restore its size.

15. Click the **1** button 🔳 to display the first step in the interaction.

16. Click the **Play** button ▶ on the video placeholder.

17. Click the **Play** button on the new window containing the video.

18. Close the Interaction Preview window and then close and abandon the new interaction.

Customizing Interaction Properties

Building an Engage interaction is a wonderful blend of using predefined elements (so you don't have to create them) and then customizing those elements. Previous sections in this chapter described how to add and customize text, audio, and media files. Engage also enables you to customize the general *properties* of an interaction, which is step 3 of the Engage workflow. You can think of a property as a characteristic of the interaction, such as the color of the window or how the viewer can navigate the interaction.

To customize the interaction, start by clicking the **Interaction Properties** button on the ribbon. This opens the Interaction Properties dialog box (Figure 15.31), which contains four tabs of customization options. The Playback, Colors and Effects, and Quality tabs are common to all interactions—the options are the same whether you are building a Process interaction or a Labeled Graphic. The second tab in the dialog box, however, is specific to the interaction you are currently building. For example, when you open the Interaction Properties dialog box while developing a Process interaction, the Process tab is included. That tab contains options that are applicable to Process interactions. However, the Player Feature options in this tab are the same for every interaction, with a couple of exceptions.

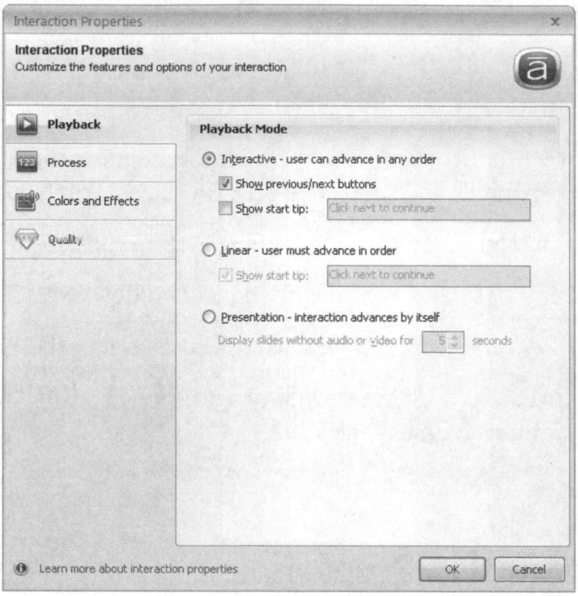

Figure 15.31. Interaction
Properties dialog box
Playback tab for Process
interaction

Let's examine the three tabs that are common to all interactions, as
well as the Player Feature options. You can learn about the interaction-specific options by referring to the chapter about that particular
interaction (Chapters 16-25).

Controlling Playback

The Playback tab in the Interaction Properties dialog box (Figure
15.31) lets you specify how the viewer navigates the interaction. In
essence, you are determining how much control to give your viewers.
For most interactions (and for most adults!), it's preferable to let the
viewers work with any part of the interaction whenever they want. For
example, a Process interaction might be presented as a series of linear
steps, but your viewers can access the steps in any order. Table 15.7
describes the options in the Playback tab.

Table 15.7. Interaction Properties dialog box Playback tab options

Option	Description
Interactive	Selecting this option enables the viewer to select and work with any component of the interaction at any time. You can also include Previous and Next buttons so that the viewer can advance and return to one component at a time. Selecting the Show start tip check box displays a tooltip prompting the viewer to click Next to continue (this message is editable). *Note that the Interactive option is not available for some interactions.*
Linear	Selecting this option forces the viewer to select and work with the components in the order in which they are designed. Previous and Next buttons are automatically included in the interaction when you choose linear navigation.
Presentation	Selecting this option removes all control from the viewer. The components of the interaction are displayed automatically. If a component contains audio or video, the length of the media file determines how long the component remains visible. For components that do not contain audio or video, you can specify how long they should be displayed.

For the Circle Diagram and Pyramid interactions, the Playback tab also includes options to control the order in which the diagram segments are presented during navigation. These options are covered in Chapters 19 and 23.

Changing Player Features

Each interaction-specific tab contains a Player Features section (Figure 15.32). This section contains options to show and hide elements in the Engage player. These options are the same for just about every type of interaction. The lower section of the interaction-specific tab contains options specific to the interaction. (As mentioned earlier, these options are covered in later chapters.) Table 15.8 describes the options in the Player Features section.

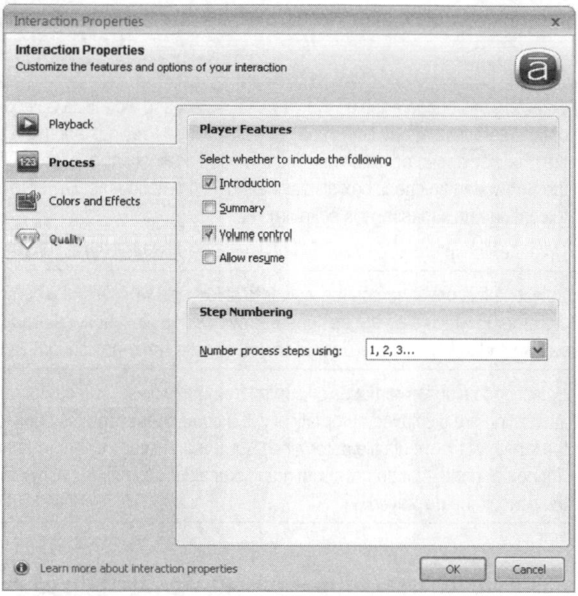

Figure 15.32. Interaction Properties dialog box Process tab for Process interaction

Table 15.8. Interaction Properties dialog box Player Features options

Option	Description
Introduction	Selecting this check box displays the introduction at the beginning of the interaction. By default, an introduction is included in most interactions. Clearing the check box deletes the introduction.
Summary	Selecting this check box displays the summary at the end of the interaction. By default, a summary is not included in an interaction. Clearing the check box deletes the summary after you have added one.
Volume control	Selecting this check box displays an audio icon on the Engage player, which viewers can use to increase and decrease the audio volume. Clearing the check box hides the audio icon from the player.
Allow resume	Selecting this check box enables viewers to leave the interaction and then return to the interaction where they left off.

Changing Colors and Effects

All Engage interactions are initially designed using a default color scheme with default animation and sound effects. The Colors and Effects tab lets you customize these items (Figure 15.33). For example, you might want the colors of the Engage player to match your corporate colors. During the design phase of developing an interaction, you should think about the colors, fonts, and effects that are best suited to the content and your audience. And you can use these settings across all interactions in a given set of training modules.

Figure 15.33. Interaction Properties dialog box Colors and Effects tab for Process interaction

The following sections describe the options in the Colors and Effects tab.

Color Scheme

The color scheme affects a variety of elements that make up the interaction, such as the background, buttons, tooltips, callouts, and text. You can use the Color Scheme section (Figure 15.34) to select a predefined color scheme, as well as create your own custom color schemes. For example, applying the

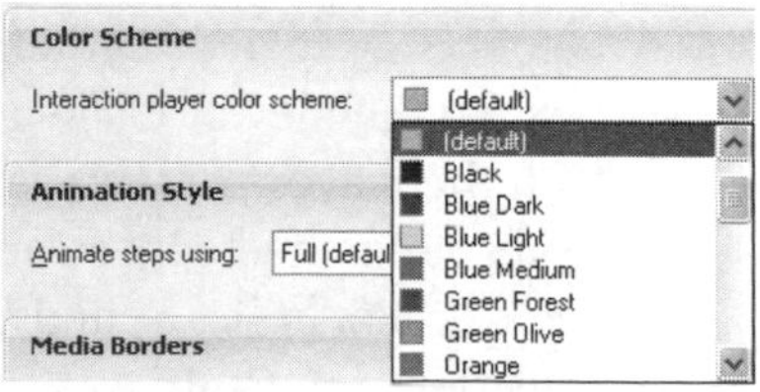

Figure 15.34. Color Scheme list

predefined Green Forest color scheme to a Process interaction changes the interaction background, navigation buttons, and step buttons to green.

> **Tip:** Most interactions contain a Colors button on the ribbon, which you can also use to change the color scheme.

> **Tip:** The Articulate Studio '09 products come with many of the same default color schemes for easy integration.

Animation Style

When the viewer opens and works with an interaction, various elements are displayed by default using full animation effects. For example, the player elements are swiped in one at a time. You can remove these animation effects by selecting the Appear option in the Animation Style section (Figure 15.35), or you can change the animation style to the fade effect by selecting the Fade option.

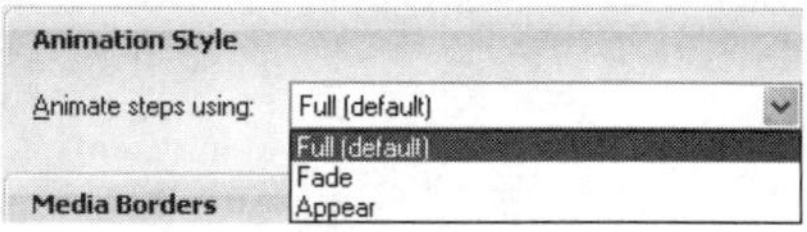

Figure 15.35. Animation Style list

Media Borders

If an interaction component contains an image or a video, Engage places a rounded border around it by default. You can remove these borders by selecting the None option or change the borders to a drop shadow using the Drop Shadow option in the Media Borders section (Figure 15.36).

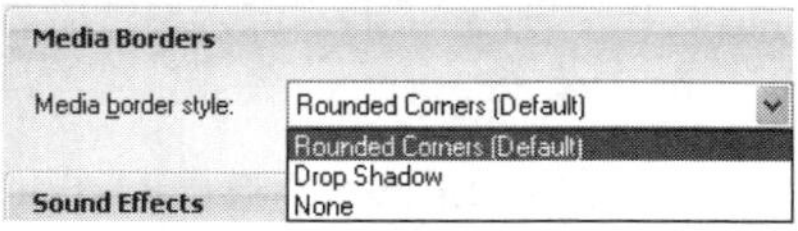

Figure 15.36. Media Borders list

Sound Effects

When the viewer opens and works with an interaction, various sound effects are played by default. For example, a clicking sound is played when the viewer clicks a button on the player. You can remove all sound effects by clearing the check box in the Sound Effects section (Figure 15.37).

Figure 15.37. Sound Effects check box

Player Fonts

The text used in interaction titles and the content of all components appears in the Articulate font by default. Although you can format content text using the Formatting toolbars, you can also apply a global font style to the title text and content text using the options in the Player Fonts section (Figure 15.38). The Title font is applied to the title of the interaction and to the titles of each component, such as the steps in a Process interaction. The Content font is applied to all content in the interaction components.

Figure 15.38. Player Fonts section Content font list

Note: If you use a custom font type and then share your unpublished interaction file with another author who does not have that font installed, Engage will revert to the default font type. Also, if you use a commercial font, make sure you have a license for it if you plan to share your files.

Creating a Custom Color Scheme

If the predefined color schemes don't quite work for your interactions, you can create a custom scheme by selecting specific colors for specific elements, such as the background, buttons, and tooltips. You can even assign custom colors to these elements. (This is good news if you need to use your corporate colors in your interactions!) Once you create a color scheme, you can then apply it to any interaction.

You can create a custom color scheme while any interaction is open. However, the color scheme of the current interaction will be used as the basis for the new color scheme, and the new scheme will be automatically applied to the interaction. So it may be helpful to open an interaction that uses the colors that most closely match what you're looking for. If you don't want the new color scheme applied to the interaction, no problem. Just reapply the original color scheme when you're done.

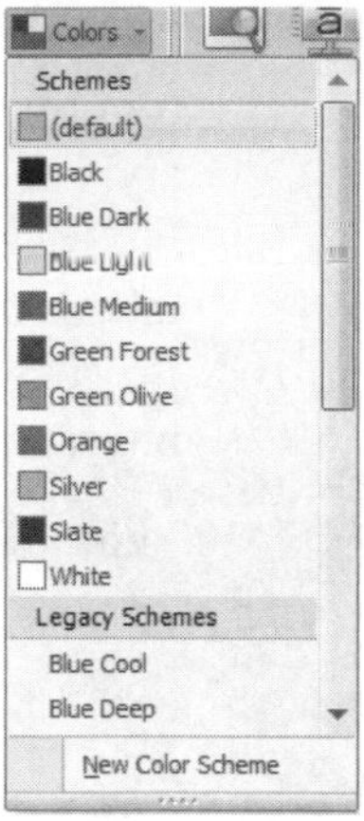

You begin creating a new color scheme by displaying the Colors menu (Figure 15.39) using the **Colors** button on the ribbon in the interaction window. (At this time, the Colors and Effects tab in the Interaction Properties dialog box does not include an option to create a new color scheme.) Then, you use the Color Scheme Editor window to customize the color scheme (Figure 15.40). The general steps to customize the color scheme are presented next, followed by a description of the Color Scheme Editor.

Figure 15.39. Colors menu

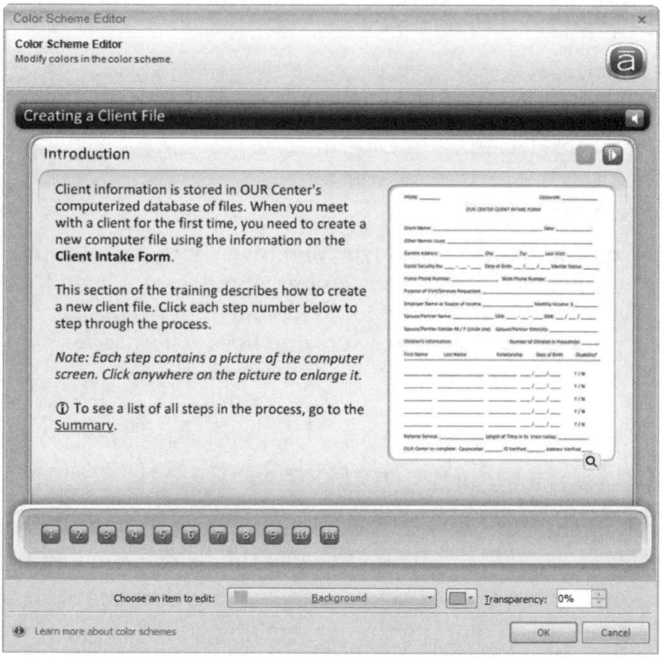

Figure 15.40. Color Scheme Editor for Process interaction

To create a custom color scheme:

1. Click the **Colors** button on the ribbon.

2. Select **New Color Scheme** from the bottom of the menu.

3. The Color Scheme Editor is displayed using the color scheme for the current interaction. Select an item to edit using the **Choose an item to edit** menu.

4. Select the color for the item by clicking the **Color** button ⬛▾ and selecting a color.

5. If you are editing the background color, you may choose a transparency level from 0% to 100% using the Transparency box.

6. Click the **OK** button.

7. Enter a name for the new color scheme and click the **OK** button.

The new color scheme is automatically applied to the current interaction. If you open the Colors menu again, you'll see the new color scheme at the top of the menu.

───────

IIII▶ **Tip:** You can edit an existing color scheme by right-clicking the color scheme on the Colors menu and selecting Edit. This opens the Color Scheme Editor again. To delete a color scheme, just right-click the color scheme on the Colors menu and select Delete.

Now let's take a closer look at the items and color options available in the Color Scheme Editor (Figure 15.40). This window displays a preview of the current interaction component along with options to change various color components.

Color Scheme Editor: Editable Items

Clicking the arrow in the Choose an item to edit menu displays a list of all the items whose colors you can modify (Figure 15.41). Items are grouped into submenus. For example, the Background and Text option contains items for four types of backgrounds and two text items (Figure 15.42). A sample of the current color for each item appears to the left of the item name. After you select an item, its name and current color appear in the Choose an item to edit box (Figure 15.43).

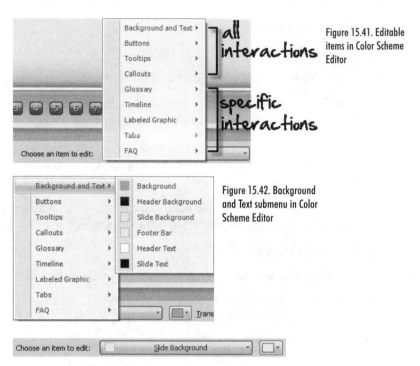

Figure 15.41. Editable items in Color Scheme Editor

Figure 15.42. Background and Text submenu in Color Scheme Editor

Figure 15.43. Slide Background item selected in Color Scheme Editor

Note that some items are applicable only to specific interactions. The Glossary, Timeline, Labeled Graphic, Tabs, and FAQ items apply only to those interactions. For example, the Period Text item in the Timeline submenu is used to change the text that is used to label periods in the timeline (Figure 15.44).

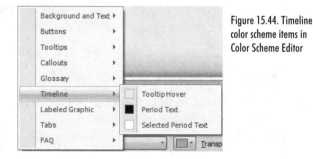

Figure 15.44. Timeline color scheme items in Color Scheme Editor

Color Scheme Editor: Color Options

Clicking the Color button [▣▾] in the Color Scheme Editor displays a window of color options, as shown in Figure 15.45.

To select a color to apply to the item, you can:

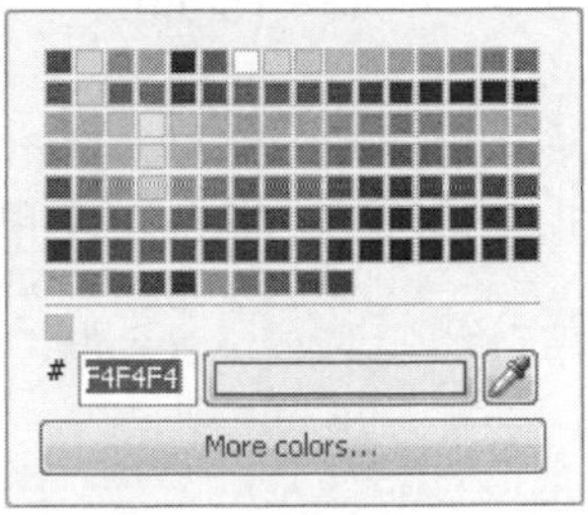

- Click a color square.

- Enter the hexadecimal code for a color in the # box.

- Click the eyedropper and then click a color that exists anywhere on your screen. For example, click the Windows taskbar if you want to "grab" that color for the selected Engage item.

- Click the **More Colors** button to display the Color dialog box, as shown in Figure 15.46. Here you can create custom colors by entering RGB (Red, Green, Blue) values, as well as Hue, Sat (Saturation), and Lum (Luminescence) values.

Figure 15.45. Color options for interaction items

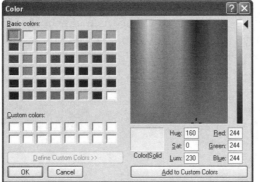

Figure 15.46. Color dialog box

Color Scheme Editor: Transparency Options

An interaction's background color refers to the color appearing behind the major components of the interaction. You can think of *transparency* as how invisible you want the background color to be when you place it on top of another background. The Transparency box (Figure 15.47) enables you to control the transparency level of the background color. A setting of 0% results in a solid (no transparency) background

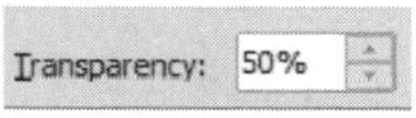

Transparency: [50%] ↕

Figure 15.47. Transparency box in Color Scheme Editor

and a setting of 100% results in an invisible (complete transparency) background.

Background transparency comes into play if you are planning to display the Engage interaction in an item that already has a background. For example, you might want to make the interaction background transparent if you are planning to insert the interaction in a Presenter slide. That way, the interaction will blend seamlessly with the slide.

Tip: Check out Tom Kuhlmann's great article on the Word of Mouth blog: "Create Custom Color Schemes in Engage '09" (http://www.articulate.com/blog/create-custom-color-schemes-in-engage-09).

Defining Quality Levels

The Quality tab in the Interaction Properties dialog box lets you decide how to compress the graphics and audio in the interaction so that it can be properly displayed on the web or a CD (Figure 15.48). If you don't know anything about compression, that's okay; the Engage program takes care of that for you. The main idea here is for you to specify whether your interaction will be viewed on the web or from a CD. Table 15.9 describes the options in the Quality tab.

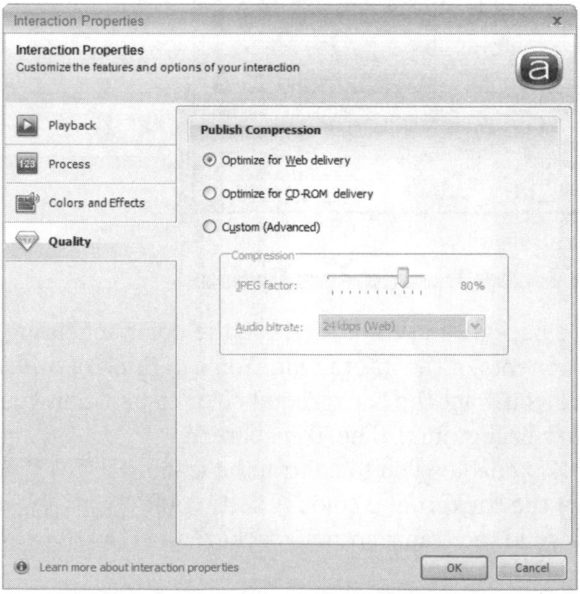

Figure 15.48. Interaction Properties dialog box Quality tab for Process interaction

Table 15.9. Interaction Properties dialog box Quality tab options

Option	Description
Optimize for Web delivery	Select this option if you plan to deliver the interaction locally, on the Internet or an intranet. This option creates good quality audio and .jpg files, and at the same time maintains a smaller file size.
Optimize for CD-ROM delivery	Select this option if you plan to deliver the interaction on a CD-ROM. This option results in higher quality but also creates larger audio files than the Web delivery option.
Custom (Advanced)	This option is recommended only for developers with advanced knowledge of compression settings. Select this option to specify custom audio and JPEG settings. Remember that the higher the bitrate and JPEG settings used, the larger the output file size will be.

Practice 4

If you're not sure what you want an interaction to look like, it can be helpful to experiment with some of the different interaction properties. Try the following steps to get used to customizing your interactions.

Customizing Interaction Properties

1. From the Engage start screen, click **Create a new interaction**.

2. Click **Process** and click the **OK** button.

3. Click the **Interaction Properties** button on the ribbon.

4. In the Interaction Properties dialog box, click the **Playback** tab.

5. Select the **Linear** option.

6. Click the **Colors and Effects** tab.

7. Select **Green Forest** from the Interaction player color scheme list.

8. Select **Fade** from the Animate steps using list.

9. Select **Broadway** from the Title font list.

10. Click the **OK** button.

11. To preview the interaction, click the **Preview** button on the ribbon.

12. In the Interaction Preview window, click the **Next** button ▶.

13. Close the Interaction Preview window and then close and abandon the new interaction.

Previewing and Saving Interactions

As you develop the components of an interaction, you can preview what it will look like inside the Engage player. We also recommend that you save the interaction frequently. You can preview and save the interaction at any time.

Previewing Interactions

By previewing an interaction, you can see it the way your viewers will. Well, almost... Some features are not active until after you publish the interaction, but you can still get a pretty good idea of how the interaction will look and behave. You don't need to save an interaction before previewing it, but you should, unless you are just experimenting with different options.

To preview an interaction:

1. Click the arrow on the Preview button on the ribbon.

2. A menu with two options appears (Figure 15.49):

   ■ To preview the interaction from the first component (such as the first step in a Process interaction), click **From Beginning**.

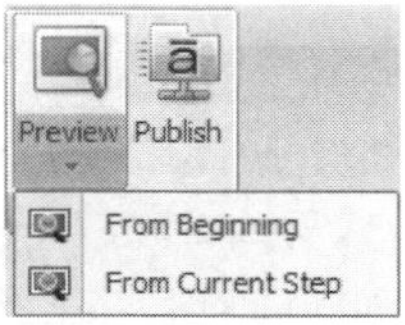

Figure 15.49. Preview button options

||||▶**Tip:** You can also just click the top part of the Preview button to preview the interaction from the beginning.

   ■ To preview the interaction from the currently selected component, click **From Current Step**. Note that this command is specific to the current interaction. For example, when you are working with a Labeled Graphic interaction, this command will appear as From Current Label.

The interaction is then displayed in the Interaction Preview window (Figure 15.50), which behaves like the Engage player. You can interact with most features, just as your viewers will. The menu bar of the Preview Interaction window contains the Close Preview button and the Edit button. Clicking the Edit button (named Edit Step for a Process interaction, Edit Tab for a Tabs interaction, etc.) closes the preview window and displays the selected component in the interaction window, where you can edit it.

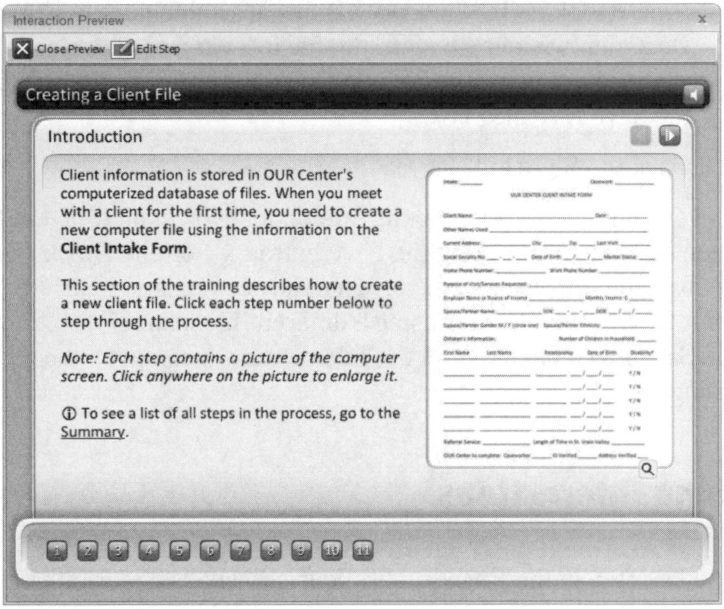

Figure 15.50. Interaction Preview window

Saving Interactions

When you create a new interaction, Engage assigns a default file name based on the type of interaction. For example, a new Process interaction is named Process.intr. You should save the interaction using a different file name, and you can also choose a folder location in which to store the file.

Although other programs enable you to save files using different formats, Engage interactions are all saved in one format. The file name extension for interaction files is .intr. This is the only option available on the Save as type list. Keep in mind, however, that you can *publish* the interaction using a variety of delivery modes.

To save a file for the first time:

1.   Click the **Save** button 🖫 on the Quick Access toolbar *or* click the **Articulate** button ⓐ and select **Save** or **Save As**.

2.   In the Save As dialog box, enter a new name in the File name box.

3.   By default, Engage stores new interactions in the My Articulate Projects folder. In Windows XP, this is a subfolder under the My Documents folder. To store the file in a different location, browse to the folder using the Save in list or the icons on the left side of the Save As dialog box.

4.   Click the **Save** button.

As you continue developing the interaction, you should save it frequently by simply clicking the Save button 🖫 on the Quick Access toolbar. You can also use the shortcut key combination Ctrl+S. If you want to save the file later using a different file name or location, select the Save As command from the File menu, which opens the Save As dialog box.

Publishing Interactions

The last step in the Engage workflow is to *publish* your interaction. Publishing means creating the output files that viewers use to work with the interaction. Chapter 26, "Publishing," provides details on the various output file formats you can create. But here's a quick explanation of publishing to the web, in case you want to create an interaction from start to finish by the end of this chapter.

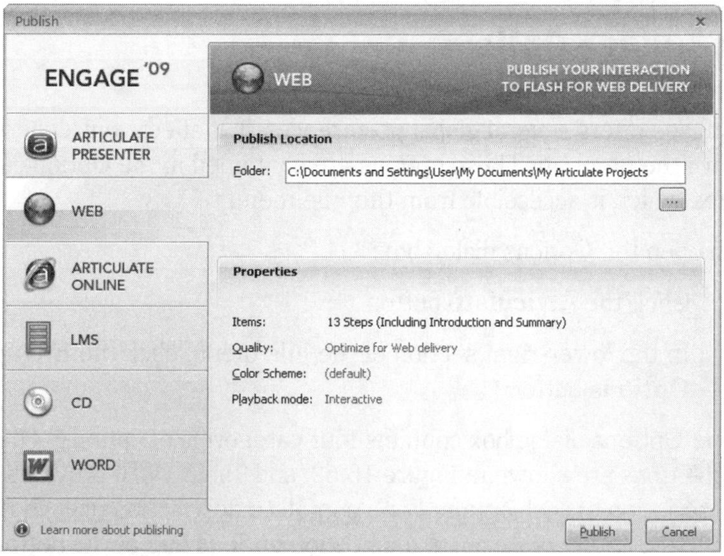

Figure 15.51. Publish dialog box Web tab

To publish an interaction to the web:

1. Click the **Publish** button on the ribbon.

2. In the Publish dialog box, click the **Web** tab (Figure 15.51).

3. In the Publish Location section, use the Folder box to enter the full path name of the folder to contain the published interaction.

4. In the Properties section, verify that the properties are appropriate for the interaction. You may change the Quality, Color Scheme, and Playback Mode properties by clicking the current value (blue text link). Note that the Quality value should be set to Optimize for Web delivery or a custom setting.

5. At the bottom of the Publish dialog box, click the **Publish** button.

6. In the Publish Successful dialog box, choose whether to view the interaction, send as email, send to an FTP site, create a Zip file, or open the folder containing the published files.

When you publish an interaction to the web, Engage creates a folder called [Name of Interaction] - Engage output. This folder contains all of the files required to post the interaction to a web site.

Setting Engage Options

Engage offers several global preferences that affect your experience with the program. These options are contained in the Options dialog box, which is accessible from the File menu.

To open the Options dialog box:

1. Click the **Articulate** button a .

2. In the lower-right section of the File menu, click the **Engage Options** button ⬚ Engage Options .

The Options dialog box contains four categories of options. The default selections are shown in Figure 15.52, and Table 15.10 provides a brief description of each option. For a complete description of each item, click the Learn more about application options link at the bottom of the Options dialog box.

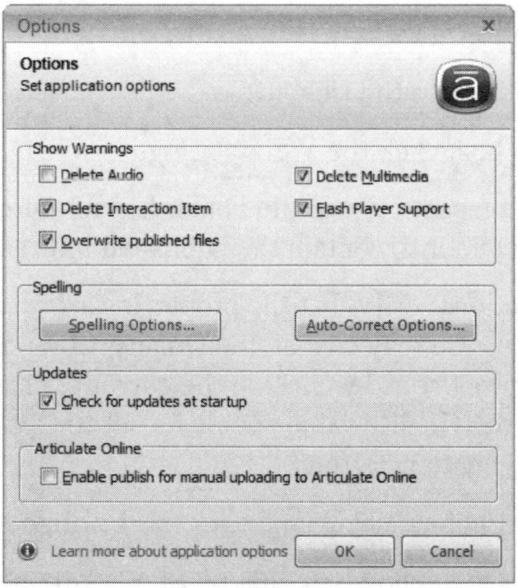

Figure 15.52. Options dialog box: default selections

Table 15.10. Options dialog box options

Option	Description
Show Warnings	If you want Engage to display a warning message when you delete any of these items, add a check mark to the item.
Spelling	Click the Spelling Options button to configure how you want Engage to check the spelling in an interaction. Click the Auto-Correct Options button to configure how you want Engage to automatically enter or correct text entries. Note that both of these options are similar to the Spelling and AutoCorrect options used in Microsoft Office 2007 applications.
Updates	Check this option if you want Engage to look for program updates every time you open the program. (You can always manually check for updates using the Check for Updates button on the ribbon's Help tab.)
Articulate Online	Check this option if you want to manually upload a published interaction to your Articulate Online account.

Chapter Recap

Here's our list of the most important things to remember from this chapter:

- The procedures for adding text, audio, and media files are basically the same for any interaction.

- All of the tools you need for building an interaction are on the ribbon and the File menu.

- Engage helps identify where you need to enter text by including placeholders. For most interactions, you'll enter an interaction title, component title, and component text.

- Use hyperlinks to enable viewers to open a web site or jump to the interaction introduction or summary.

- You can include audio in any component by recording it in Engage, or by importing an existing audio file.

- Engage lets you add one still image or one video to each component in an interaction. Supported image file types are JPG (or JPEG), BMP, GIF, and PNG. Supported video file types are SWF and FLV.

- Don't be afraid to customize! Explore all the different ways to control the playback, display features on the player, change colors, and change effects. Remember, you can even create your own color scheme.

- Preview your interaction at any point in development by clicking the Preview button on the ribbon.

- Save your interaction often by clicking the Save button on the Quick Access toolbar. Interaction files are saved with the file name extension .intr.

- Check out the Options dialog box to tell Engage how you like to experience the program. Do you want warnings and reminders, or do you just want to be left alone?

- Publish your interaction using the Publish dialog box. After you select the type of output (e.g., web), the location of the files, and properties, Engage creates an output folder containing the appropriate files to run the interaction.

- Bookmark this chapter! The remaining chapters build on what you've learned here by explaining how to create each of the 10 interaction types. You might need to come back here to refresh your memory on the basics, such as adding media files.

Chapter 16

Creating a Process Interaction

Chapter Snapshot

In this chapter, you'll learn how to use the Process interaction to show your viewers step-by-step instructions, present the phases in a process, or simply walk through a list of related items.

If you're an e-learning developer, there's a good chance you've had to develop training that demonstrates how to perform a specific task. The Process interaction provides a handy structure for presenting a series of task steps or the phases in a process. Once you determine the steps or phases of the process, you can make the content of each step come alive by adding text, audio, and media.

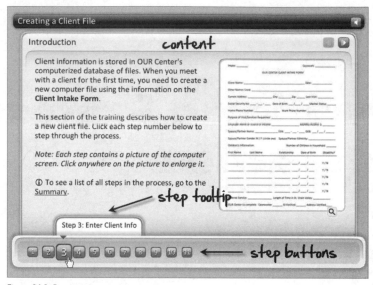

Figure 16.1. Process interaction

What Is a Process Interaction?

A Process interaction is often used to describe the steps or phases of a linear procedure or process. Most procedures and processes can be broken down into manageable stages or phases, which Engage refers to as steps. A Process interaction presents these steps from start to finish. Each step can consist of text, audio, graphics, and other media files to demonstrate one piece of the overall process. Your viewers can even go back and revisit steps, if you want them to.

How the Process Interaction Works

The first screen of a Process interaction generally provides an introduction to the procedure being demonstrated (Figure 16.1). Viewers can then navigate the interaction using several different methods (which *you* get to determine). For example, viewers can:

- Click the Next or Previous buttons to move ahead or back to a step.

- Click the step buttons at the bottom of the interaction to view the steps in any order. Moving the mouse pointer over a step button displays the name of the step.

- Click a hyperlink to the introduction or summary, which you may include when you build the interaction.

If you don't want viewers to click their way through the process, you can configure the interaction as a presentation. In that case, each step is displayed for a specific number of seconds.

Real-Life Examples

As we've discussed, the Process interaction is a great tool for demonstrating linear procedural steps or phases in a process. But keep in mind that you can use the Process interaction for almost anything, even if there are no steps or phases involved. For example, you may have a list of the top 10 features of your new product. You can let your viewers "step" through each feature, one at a time. Here are some of our favorite examples of this type of interaction:

- Call center procedures
- Building a product
- Using a software application
- Stepping through a checklist
- Department workflow

The example used in this chapter steps the viewer through the process of creating a new client computer file for a nonprofit social services agency.

Planning the Process Interaction

Planning the design of a Process interaction involves determining the steps in the process or procedure, gathering the content for each step (which can include text, audio, and a media file), and deciding on other features of the interaction, such as content layout and the color scheme.

Planning the Steps

Since a Process interaction revolves around the steps in a procedure or the phases in a process, think carefully about how many steps to include. How simple do you want the steps to be? Can several small steps be combined into one larger step? If you find that an interaction is growing out of control, consider dividing the process into two separate interactions. A rule of thumb when breaking down a task into subtasks is to divide it into logical groups or sequential categories. Engage limits interactions to 20 steps.

Gathering Step Content

Once you've determined the steps to include in the interaction, you can plan the content elements of the steps (Figure 16.2). Each step can consist of text, one audio file, and one media file.

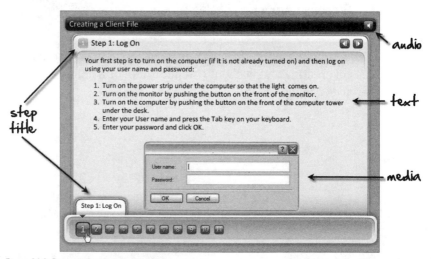

Figure 16.2. Process interaction step content

Following are the content elements for the steps in a Process interaction:

- **Step title:** Assign a title to each step. Keep it short, but meaningful. The step title is displayed at the top of the step, as well as in the tooltip that appears when the viewer moves the mouse pointer over the step number. Keep in mind that you cannot modify the content in the buttons containing the step *numbers*, but you can change the number format.

- **Text:** Describe the step using paragraphs and/or bullet points, and try to be concise. You can include links to more information and to other steps in the interaction. If you are including audio in a step, make sure the text complements the audio but does not repeat it verbatim.

- **Audio:** Each step can include one audio clip. You can use audio to narrate the description of the step or to add descriptive sound effects. In general, if one step is narrated, then all steps should be. Otherwise, the viewer might think that the audio is not working for specific steps. If you choose not to include audio in the steps, you might consider narrating just the introduction.

- **Media:** Each step can include one media file. Many processes are best demonstrated through visual elements, such as pictures, graphs, videos, screen captures, diagrams, or checklists. Consequently, your Process interaction should have an image or animation for most steps, if possible. In many cases, you can also enable the viewer to enlarge (zoom into) the image by clicking it.

Determining Step Order and Viewer Control

The order of steps is generally important in a Process interaction. For a linear process, steps should, of course, be in order. For processes where order isn't critical, present items in the order that will make the most sense to your viewers, such as importance, alphabetical order, or logical categorization.

If step order is important for your interaction, then you also need to consider how much navigation control to give viewers. If you want viewers to be forced to complete one step before moving on to the next, choose *linear* navigation. If you want to allow viewers to pick and choose among various steps, choose *interactive* navigation. To remove all control from your viewers and automatically display the steps for them, choose *presentation* navigation. Typically we recommend that you give viewers as much control as possible when navigating interactions.

Planning Additional Features

Following are a few additional features you may want to consider as you plan your Process interaction.

- **Introduction:** Optional. Appears as the first screen when the interaction is launched.

- **Summary:** Optional. Appears as the last screen.

- **Color Scheme:** Affects the colors of the interaction player's components, such as the background and the navigation buttons. For a Process interaction, the color scheme also affects the step buttons at the bottom of the player.

- **Layout:** Determines the placement of the text relative to the media file in a specific step (e.g., text left/graphic right). However, the placement of the step buttons (at the bottom of the player) cannot be changed.

- **Step button style:** Affects the type of number appearing in the step buttons.

Starting a New Process Interaction

Opening a New Interaction

Now that you have planned your interaction, it's time to dive into the development tool. Your first step is to open a new Process interaction.

1. Double-click the **Articulate Engage '09** icon on your desktop *or* select **Articulate Engage '09** from the appropriate folder on the Start menu.

2. Click **Create a new interaction** on the start screen.

3. In the New Interaction dialog box, click the **Process** tab and then click **OK**.

The Process interaction window contains features standard to most interactions, such as the ribbon, Audio pane, and Media pane (Figure 16.3). The tabs list contains a series of tabs; each tab is used to build a separate step component. By default, Engage provides placeholders for the introduction and two steps.

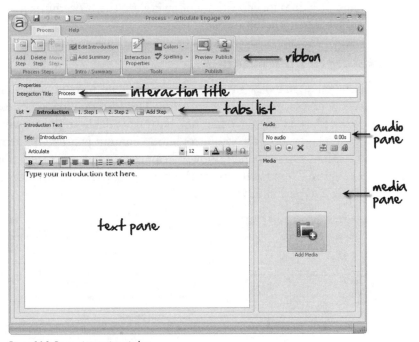

Figure 16.3. Process interaction window

Entering the Interaction Title

The interaction title appears at the top of the Engage player when the interaction is running. By default, Engage enters the placeholder title "Process." This title should be replaced to describe the purpose of the interaction, such as "Creating a Client File." Keep in mind that you cannot format the text of the interaction title using the Formatting toolbar. However, the Colors and Effects tab in the Interaction Properties dialog box enables you to select a different font style for the title.

Building the Steps

As you've learned, the foundation of the Process interaction consists of steps. Each component tab contains the text, audio, and media file (image or video) for one step. Following are the procedures for building the steps in the interaction.

Creating the Introduction

When you open a new Process interaction, the Introduction tab is displayed with placeholder text selected. The Introduction is not exactly a step, as there is no "Introduction" button available to the viewer in the Engage player. Instead, the introduction content is presented when the interaction is first opened. Viewers can return to the introduction by clicking the Previous button at the beginning of the interaction or by clicking a hyperlink if you provide one.

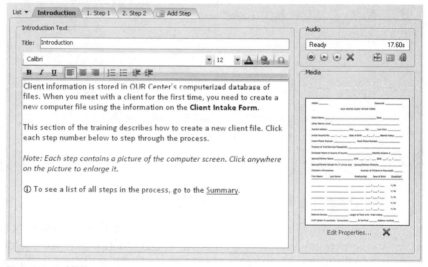

Figure 16.4. Introduction completed

To create the introduction:

1.   If desired, replace the "Introduction" placeholder in the Title field with a meaningful description.

2. Replace the "Type your introduction text here" placeholder in the text pane with your content. Remember, you can format the text using the toolbars above the text area.

3. Use the Audio pane to record or select an audio file, if desired.

4. Use the Media pane to add an image or video file, if desired.

See Figure 16.4 for an example of a completed Introduction.

Note: Chapter 15, "Engage Basics," provides detailed instructions for working with text, audio, and media.

Tip: After completing the introduction and moving on to other steps, you can quickly return to the Introduction tab by clicking the Edit Introduction button on the ribbon.

Creating Steps

Engage includes placeholders for two steps. To create the first step, open the 1. Step 1 tab and edit the default content:

1. Click the **1. Step 1** tab.

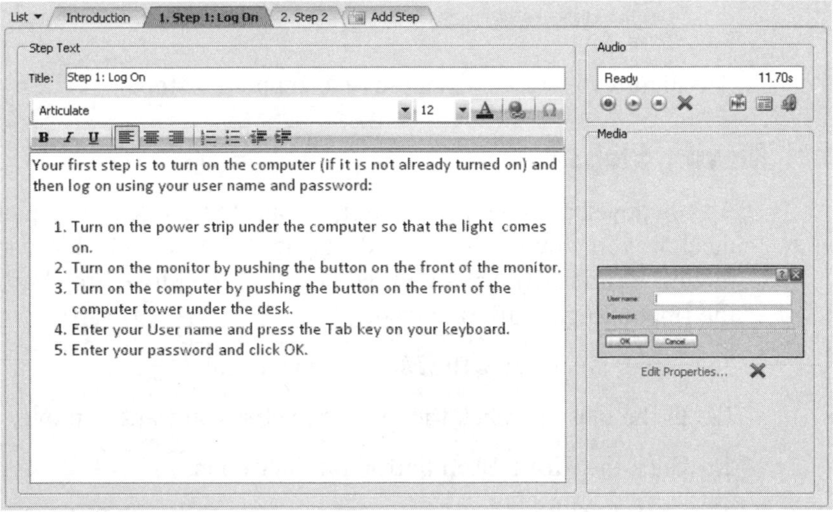

Figure 16.5. Step 1 completed

2. Replace the Step 1 placeholder in the Title field with a meaningful description, such as **Step 1: Log On**. The title text will appear at the top of the step in the running interaction when the step is selected. The step number will appear as a graphic icon to the left of the title. (For the example in this chapter, we chose to include the text "Step 1:" because the graphic is not always obvious.) The step title will also appear as a tooltip when the viewer positions the mouse pointer over the step 1 button ▣ in the running interaction.

3. Add text, audio, and a media file, as appropriate.

Now you can create the remaining steps using the same procedures as above:

4. Click the **2. Step 2** tab and enter your content.

5. To add more steps, click the **Add Step** tab on the tabs list or the **Add Step** button on the ribbon (Figure 16.6). A new tab will be inserted at the end of the steps.

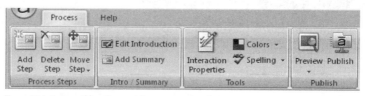

Figure 16.6. Engage ribbon Process tab

See Figure 16.5 for an example of a completed step.

Moving Steps

As you develop the steps, you might want to change the step order. A quick way to move a step is by dragging the step tab with the mouse to its new location. Alternatively, you can use the Move Step button on the ribbon (Figure 16.6).

To reorder steps using the Move Step button:

1. In the tabs list, click the tab of the step you want to move.

2. Click the **Move Step** button on the ribbon.

3. Click **Left** to move the step one position to the left. Click **Right** to move the step one position to the right.

4.   To move the step more than one position, repeat steps 2-3 above.

Engage will automatically update the step number that appears on the step button when the interaction is published. If you included a step number in the customizable step title, remember to change it according to its new position.

Deleting Steps

You can easily remove a step if it is no longer needed. However, you cannot remove steps as a group. Only one step at a time can be deleted.

To remove a step from the interaction:

1.   In the tabs list, click the step you want to delete.

2.   Click the **Delete Step** button on the ribbon (Figure 16.6).

3.   The Engage dialog box asks you to confirm the deletion. Click the **Yes** button.

If you change your mind and want to restore a step immediately after deleting it, click the **Undo** button 🔄 on the Quick Access toolbar.

Adding a Summary

A summary is optional for all interactions. You may choose to include one for a Process interaction to list all of the step names on one screen. Keep in mind, however, that the summary is accessible to the viewer only by clicking the Next button after the last step is displayed (or by clicking a hyperlink if you provide one). A summary step is not included with the other step buttons in the interaction.

To add a summary:

1.   Click the **Add Summary** button on the ribbon (Figure 16.6). By default, the Summary tab is added to the end of the steps.

2.   Add text, audio, and a media file using the same procedures as for building any other step.

▶**Tip:** After the summary is completed, the Add Summary button on the ribbon changes to Edit Summary. You can use this button to make changes to the summary at any time.

Customizing the Process Interaction

In addition to customizing general interaction properties, you can customize the format of the step numbers that are used to navigate the Process interaction. The Interaction Properties dialog box contains these options.

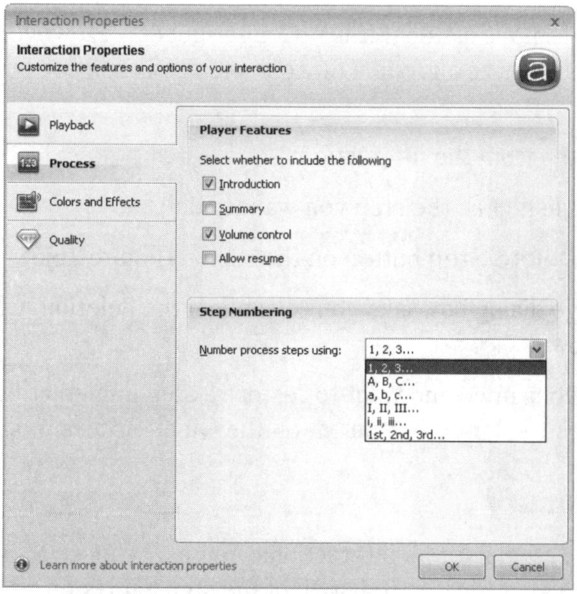

Figure 16.7. Interaction Properties dialog box Process tab

Customizing the Step Number Format

The default format of the step numbers in the navigation section is 1, 2, 3, etc. You can easily change the number format to something else, such as 1st, 2nd, 3rd (Figure 16.7). However, you cannot create your own custom number formats.

To format the step numbers:

1. Click the **Interaction Properties** button on the ribbon.

2. In the Interaction Properties dialog box, click the **Process** tab, if it is not already displayed.

3. In the Step Numbering section, select a number format from the Number process steps using list.

The new format will be visible when you preview or publish the interaction.

Customizing General Interaction Properties

The Interaction Properties dialog box offers standard ways to customize all interactions, including the Process interaction. These standard options are covered in detail in Chapter 15, "Engage Basics." We suggest that you review these options and decide which features work best for your Process interaction. For example, you can include the start tip "Click Next to continue" on the Next button on the player.

Practice

Now's your chance to create a Process interaction using your own content. If you need an idea, think of a simple task that can be divided into a few steps, such as placing a conference call. Then, describe the procedures for each step.

|||| ▶ **Building a Process Interaction**

1. Plan your interaction and gather content.

2. From the Engage start screen, click **Create a new interaction**.

3. In the New Interaction dialog box, click **Process** and click the **OK** button.

4. In the Process interaction window, replace the text in the Interaction Title box with the title of your interaction.

5. Enter the text in the Introduction tab:
   a. Enter a title in the Title box (or keep the default text).
   b. Enter text in the Introduction Text area.

6. Add an image to the introduction:
   a. In the Media pane, click the **Add Media** button.
   b. In the Select Image or Video File dialog box, browse to the folder containing your media files and double-click the desired file.
   c. In the Multimedia Properties dialog box, use the Position list to change the location of the image, if desired, and then click the **OK** button.

7. Add an audio narration to the introduction:
   a. In the Audio pane, click the **Record** button ⊙.
   b. Using your computer's microphone, narrate the audio for the introduction. Click the **Stop** button ⊙ when you are finished.
   c. Review the audio by clicking the **Play** button ⊙.

8. Click the **Step 1.** tab and repeat steps 5-7 above to create the first step.

9. Create additional steps using the above procedures. (Click the **Add Step** tab to insert a new step.)

10. After completing the steps, click the **Interaction Properties** button on the ribbon.

11. In the Interaction Properties dialog box, click the **Process** tab.

12. From the Number process steps using list box, select **1st, 2nd, 3rd** and click the **OK** button.

13. Preview the interaction by clicking the **Preview** button on the ribbon.

14. Close the Interaction Preview window.

15. Save the interaction:
    a. Click the **Save** button ▣ on the Quick Access toolbar.
    b. In the Save As dialog box, enter a file name and location for the interaction.
    c. Click the **Save** button.

Engage

Chapter Recap

Here's our list of the most important things to remember from this chapter:

■ A Process interaction can be used to describe the steps or phases of a linear procedure or process. (But feel free to be creative in using this interaction!)

■ The introduction in a Process interaction generally describes the procedure or process. Viewers may then navigate the interaction by clicking each step button.

■ When planning a Process interaction, think about how to break the interaction into manageable steps.

■ Decide how much navigational control to give your viewers: Interactive (complete freedom), Linear (in order), or Presentation (no control at all).

■ Remember that the introduction and summary are not represented by step buttons. Viewers need to use the Previous and Next buttons (or a hyperlink you provide) to revisit these screens.

■ Build your steps by including text, audio, and/or a media file.

■ Use the tools on the ribbon to add, move, and delete steps.

■ Use the Customize Interaction Properties dialog box to customize features such as navigation control, the color scheme, and the number format of the step buttons.

Chapter 17

Creating a Labeled Graphic Interaction

Chapter Snapshot

In this chapter, you will learn how to use the Labeled Graphic interaction to describe specific areas of an image.

Although a picture might be worth a thousand words, often you want to use both a picture and a thousand words (okay, maybe less) to present information. A Labeled Graphic interaction offers a simple yet effective way to describe various components of an image, such as a screenshot of a software application, an online form, a map, or a photograph.

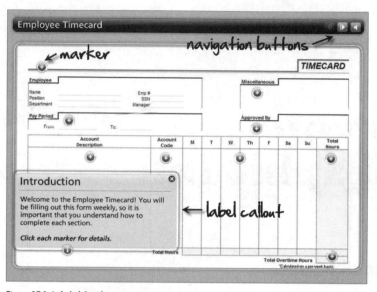

Figure 17.1. Labeled Graphic interaction

What Is a Labeled Graphic?

A Labeled Graphic is an interactive image that calls out the key elements of that graphic, such as a map, software application screenshot, or photograph. Viewers can learn about each part of the image by clicking markers that you define on the image.

How the Labeled Graphic Works

When the viewer first sees the Labeled Graphic, the Introduction label callout is fully displayed (Figure 17.1). This label describes the image and also provides instructions for viewing the other labels on the image. The viewer can then move the mouse pointer over a marker to display the label title (Figure 17.2). The label title is typically the name of the area identified by the marker. To see the full label callout (which can include text, audio, and a media file), the viewer clicks the marker (Figure 17.3). As each marker is clicked, the callout for that marker is fully displayed and the previous label is hidden. In other words, only one fully displayed label callout appears at a time.

Figure 17.2. Mouse pointer over label

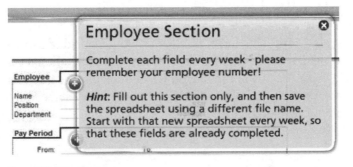

Figure 17.3. Clicked label

Viewers can also click the Next and Previous navigation buttons to view labels. As you develop the Labeled Graphic, you can determine the order in which the labels appear if the navigation buttons are used. However, this navigation approach is not as popular as simply clicking the markers, so you probably won't need to stress too much over label order.

Real-Life Examples

The Labeled Graphic is a great tool for providing details about an image. Here are some of our favorite examples of this type of interaction:

- Software application screenshot
- Online or paper form
- Photograph, such as a group of employees
- Geographic map
- Foreign language signs, with audio translations
- Musical instrument collage, with audio samples

The example used in this chapter is an online employee timecard. Each section of the timecard is labeled with instructions.

How Is a Labeled Graphic Different from a Guided Image?

A Labeled Graphic interaction and a Guided Image interaction are similar, but they serve different purposes and function in a different way. As this chapter shows, a Labeled Graphic enables viewers to learn about areas of an image by clicking markers. In a Guided Image, viewers do not have the option of clicking any part of the image; the parts of the image are presented step-by-step, using linear navigation. And instead of using labels, the Guided Image displays text, audio, and an additional graphic in a separate area of the player. Guided Images are good for teaching procedures that are based around one image, such as configuring electrical equipment.

Planning the Labeled Graphic

Planning the design of a Labeled Graphic involves selecting the appropriate graphic and deciding which areas of the graphic to label. You should also determine the content for each label, which can include text, audio, and a media file.

Planning the Background Image

A Labeled Graphic consists of just one graphic, which is referred to as the *background image* (Figure 17.4). Other images can be included in the labels, but they are visible to the viewer only when the label is displayed. When creating or selecting the background image, keep the following in mind:

- Engage supports JPG, BMP, GIF, and PNG graphic file types.
- The optimal size for a background image is 690 x 470 pixels.
- Engage will scale down images larger than 690 x 470, but will not scale up smaller images. Remember that scaling down the image and publishing to Flash will reduce the quality of the image. One way to work around this for large screenshots is to include the full shot, but include "zoomed in" pieces of the screenshot as images in the labels.

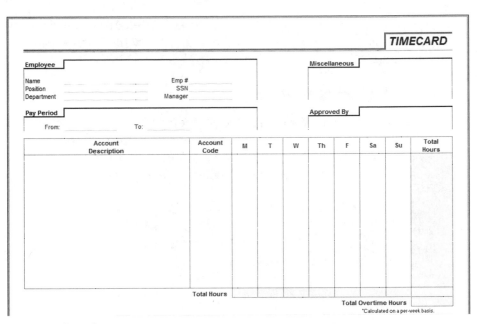

Figure 17.4. Background image

- Select an image that can be divided into a reasonable number of areas. Although the number of labels on the image is not limited, you want to avoid an image that is cluttered with too many label markers. Consider dividing the graphic into two parts and creating two different interactions if the image size and number of markers are unmanageable.

Planning the Labels

Each label in a Labeled Graphic provides a description of a specific component of the background image. A label consists of a marker and its associated callout. The callout consists of a title (text only) and a description. The description can contain text, audio, and/or a media file. There is no limit to the number of labels you can include in the interaction.

Your first step is to identify which sections of the image should be labeled. Try to avoid "over labeling" the graphic. If necessary, you can provide one label for a group of related items, such as a group of options on an application screenshot. Also, keep in mind that when the viewer expands a label by clicking it, the resulting label window might cover other labels on the image. So you want to arrange the labels in a

way that provides lots of space between each label. As you build the
interaction, use the Preview feature to check how the labels expand on
the graphic.

Gathering Label Content

The content for a Labeled Graphic is generally less comprehensive
than the content for other interactions, such as a Process interaction.
Since the purpose of each label is to provide a brief description, the
operative word when developing content is *brevity*.

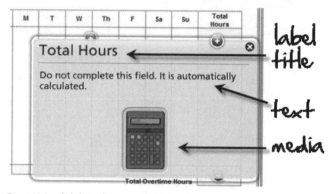

Figure 17.5. Labeled Graphic interaction label content

Following are the content elements for the Labeled Graphic (Figure
17.5):

- **Label title:** Assign a short title to each label. The title should
  clearly identify the area of the graphic and will appear when the
  viewer moves the mouse pointer over the label marker.

- **Text:** Most labels rely heavily on text descriptions. Describe the
  section of the graphic using paragraphs and/or bullet points. You
  can also include links to more information and to other labels in
  the interaction.

- **Media:** Each label can contain one media file, such as a picture,
  photo, or video. Depending on the purpose of the Labeled Graphic,
  media files may not be necessary. An appropriate use of a media
  file in a label is to provide a picture of a related component, either
  within the current image or from another image. For example,
  include a picture of the menu that appears when you click a button
  that is labeled on the graphic.

- **Audio:** Audio is an option for each label, but we recommend using narration sparingly. Remember that the viewer wants a quick description of one section of an image—a brief text description and/or a complementary graphic can generally provide this. (Narrations can take longer to present than text.) However, including narration in the introduction is generally okay. Another appropriate use of audio in a Labeled Graphic is to provide sound effects or foreign language translations. For example, the labels on an image of a symphony orchestra can provide an audio sample of each instrument.

Tip: For Labeled Graphics, Engage enables you to hide the text in the label and play just the audio portion. This feature is helpful when you want to include a large amount of information in one label. Instead of displaying lots of text (making the label very large), suppress the text and use audio to describe the labeled area (or introduction).

Determining Label Order and Viewer Control

The visual order of the labels in a Labeled Graphic is obviously determined by the placement of each label on the graphic. However, you also need to plan the "internal" order of the labels, which affects the display order of the labels when the viewer chooses to use the Next and Previous buttons to navigate the interaction. Although you can control the navigation to be *interactive*, *linear*, or in *presentation* format, the best option for a Labeled Graphic is interactive. Most viewers prefer to click labels in the order they choose.

Planning Additional Features

Following are a few additional features you may want to consider as you plan your Labeled Graphic interaction.

- **Introduction label:** Optional. Automatically displayed when the viewer opens the Labeled Graphic. It explains what the viewer is about to learn or see, and can also include instructions about navigating the interaction. In most cases, you should include the introduction label.

■ **Summary label:** Optional. Many Labeled Graphics don't include a summary because the idea is for the viewer to explore a variety of components within one image.

■ **Color scheme:** Affects the colors of the interaction player's components, such as the background and the navigation buttons. For a Labeled Graphic, the color scheme also affects the callout background. (The marker colors are customized separately, and are not part of the color scheme itself.)

■ **Marker color and style:** Determines the colors of the markers and the icon that appears on each marker.

Starting a New Labeled Graphic

Opening a New Interaction

After you have planned the background image and the accompanying labels, you can start developing your Labeled Graphic. Your first step is to open a new Labeled Graphic interaction:

1. Double-click the **Articulate Engage '09** icon on your desktop *or* select **Articulate Engage '09** from the appropriate folder on the Start menu.

2. Click **Create a new interaction** on the start screen.

3. In the New Interaction dialog box, click the **Labeled Graphic** tab and click **OK**.

The Labeled Graphic interaction window contains features standard to most interactions, such as the ribbon, the interaction title, and the interaction work area (Figure 17.6). The component tabs, tabs list, Audio pane, and Media pane are contained in the Edit Labels dialog box, which is available when editing a label.

By default, Engage provides placeholder markers for the introduction and three labels. The Change Image button is used to select the background image for the Labeled Graphic.

Figure 17.6. Labeled Graphic interaction window

Entering the Interaction Title

The interaction title appears at the top of the Engage player when the interaction is running. By default, Engage enters the placeholder title "Labeled Graphic." This title should be replaced to describe the purpose of the interaction, such as "Employee Timecard." Keep in mind that you cannot format the text of the interaction title. However, the Colors and Effects tab in the Interaction Properties dialog box enables you to select a different font style for the title.

Changing the Background Image

When you start a Labeled Graphic, Engage provides a background image by default. Your first step is to change the default background image by selecting your own picture. Engage supports images in JPG, BMP, GIF, and PNG formats.

To change the background image:

1. Click the **Change image** button on the background image *or* click the **Change Image** button on the ribbon.

2. In the Change Background Image dialog box, browse to the folder containing your media files and double-click the desired file.

The new image appears in the interaction area and the Change image button is removed (Figure 17.7). If necessary, you can change the image again by clicking the **Change Image** button on the ribbon.

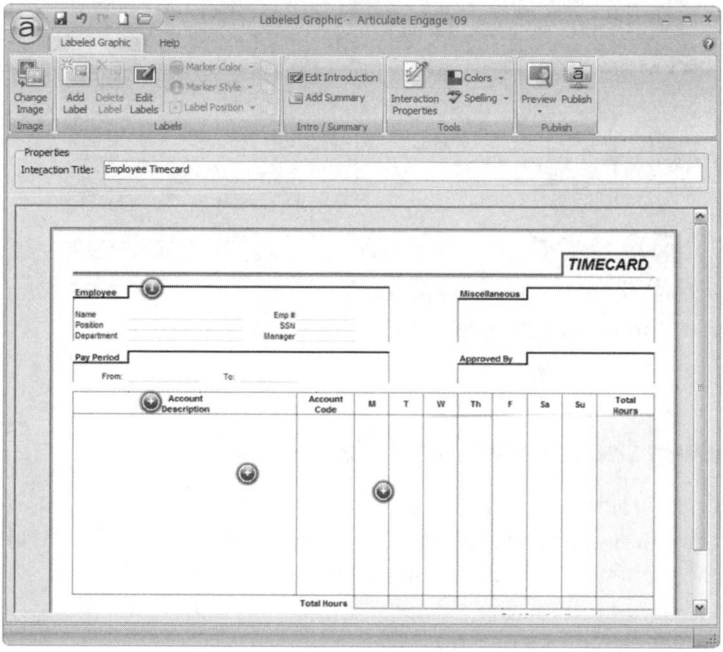

Figure 17.7. Background image selected (default label marker positions)

Note: When you change the background image, the random label marker positions will not be accurate. You'll learn how to move these markers later in this chapter.

Building the Labels

Engage provides four label placeholders (Figure 17.7). You can use these placeholders to create the introduction and your first three labels. A label *title* can be modified directly in the interaction work area by clicking the marker and then entering different text in the title field. However, to modify the label *description*, you need to double-click the marker, which opens the Edit Labels dialog box (Figure 17.8). This dialog box provides a central place to create everything you need for the interaction.

Before learning how to create the labels and the introduction, let's explore the Edit Labels dialog box.

Exploring the Edit Labels Dialog Box

The Edit Labels dialog box enables you to build and customize the current label. You can also work with another label by selecting it from the tabs list.

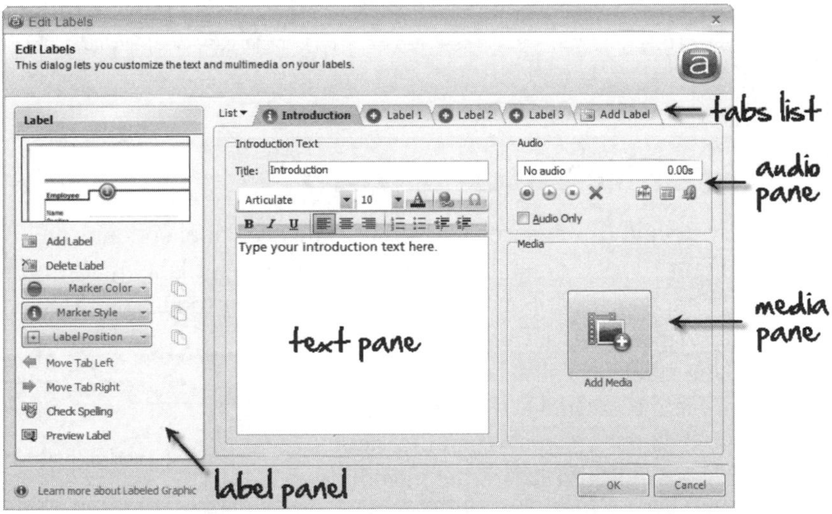

Figure 17.8. Edit Labels dialog box

This dialog box is accessible using several different methods:

- Double-click a marker on the background image.
- Click the **Edit Labels** button on the ribbon.

- Click the **Edit Introduction** button on the ribbon.
- Click the **Add Summary** button on the ribbon.

When you open the dialog box, the tab of the current label (or introduction or summary) is displayed in the tabs list. Table 17.1 describes each section of the dialog box.

Table 17.1. Edit Labels dialog box sections

Section	Description
Tabs list	Each tab represents a label in the interaction. Click a tab to work with that label. Click the Add Label tab to insert a new label.
Text pane	This section is labeled "Introduction Text," "Label Text," or "Summary Text," depending on the label type. Use this section to enter the label title (which the viewer sees when moving the mouse pointer over a label) and the text for the label description (which the viewer sees when clicking the marker).
Audio pane	Record an audio clip for the current label or import an existing audio clip. The audio is played when the viewer clicks the label marker. Selecting the Audio Only check box hides the label description text and plays just the audio clip.
Media pane	Click the Add Media button to insert a media file (picture, photo, or video) into the current label. Engage enables you to position the media file at the top or bottom of the label description.
Label panel	These options enable you to add, delete, customize, and move the selected label. A "close-up" of the label's position on the image is displayed at the top of the panel.

Creating the Introduction Label

By default, the marker for the Introduction label contains an "i" ⓘ (Figure 17.9), which is different from the other label markers. When the viewer first opens the interaction, the introduction title and description are automatically displayed.
This label typically explains the purpose of the interaction and provides instructions to the viewer. When the viewer clicks a different label, the introduction label text is hidden.

Figure 17.9. Introduction label on background image

To create the introduction:

1. Double-click the **Introduction** marker ⓘ on the interaction work area.

2. In the Edit Labels dialog box, on the Introduction tab (Figure 17.10), replace the "Introduction" placeholder in the Title field with a meaningful description, if desired.

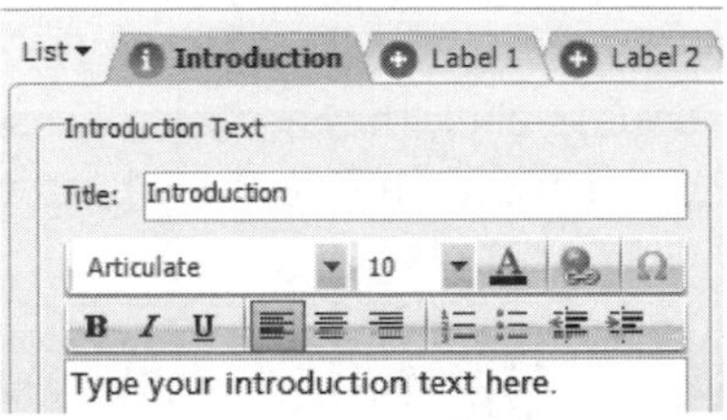

Figure 17.10.
Introduction tab in Edit Labels dialog box

3. Replace the "Type your introduction text here" placeholder with your content. Remember, you can format the text using the toolbars above the text area.

4. Use the Audio pane to record or select an audio file, if desired. Selecting the **Audio Only** check box hides the label description text and plays just the audio clip.

5. Use the Media pane to add a picture, photo, or video, if desired.

6. Move or customize the label using the options in the Label panel. These options are covered in the section titled "Customizing the Labeled Graphic" later in this chapter.

7. Preview the appearance of the fully displayed label by clicking **Preview Label** in the Label panel.

8. Close the Interaction Preview window and the Edit Labels dialog box.

Note: Chapter 15, "Engage Basics," provides detailed instructions for working with text, audio, and media.

Tip: After completing the introduction and moving on to other labels, you can quickly return to the Introduction tab by clicking the Edit Introduction button on the ribbon.

Creating the Interaction Labels

The three other label placeholders are used to identify specific sections of the image. By default, Engage uses a red marker with a "+" sign ⊕ (Figure 17.11) to represent these labels. If the Edit Labels dialog box is not already open, double-click the marker representing the label in the interaction area or click the **Edit Labels** button on the ribbon. Then, select a label by clicking its tab (Figure 17.12).

Figure 17.11. Label 1 on background image

Figure 17.12. Label 1 tab in Edit Labels dialog box

The procedures for building these labels are similar to those for building the Introduction label, which we listed earlier. Here are a few things to keep in mind as you create the remaining labels:

- The label tab order in the Edit Labels dialog box indicates the order in which the labels will be displayed if the viewer uses the Next button to navigate the interaction.

- When the viewer clicks a label marker in the interaction, the small window containing the label title, text, and media files covers a portion of the image. Make sure that the covered portion is not related to the label. For example, if the label describes a section of an online form, ensure that the section being described is not covered by the label. The Label Position option in the Label panel enables you to modify the position. This option is covered in the section "Customizing the Labeled Graphic" later in this chapter.

- You can add a Summary label by clicking the **Add Summary** button on the ribbon. But keep in mind that the marker for the Summary label is no different from the markers for the interaction labels. Consequently, your viewers have no way of knowing where the Summary label is until they move the mouse pointer over the label. However, a Summary label can be useful if you know the viewers will be navigating the interaction using the Next button. The Summary label will be the last label displayed.

Adding New Labels

Chances are you'll need more labels than the placeholders provided by Engage. You can add as many new labels as you need, but try to avoid cluttering the image. Labels can be added from the interaction window or from the Edit Labels dialog box.

Figure 17.13. Engage ribbon Labeled Graphic tab

- To add a new label from the interaction window, click the **Add Label** button on the ribbon (Figure 17.13). Engage places a new marker on the image and displays the text box for the label title.
- To add a new label from the Edit Labels dialog box, click the **Add Label** tab at the end of the tabs list or click **Add Label** in the Label panel. Engage adds a tab for the new label.

New labels are automatically placed at the end of the tabs list. That means the new label is the last label the viewer will see when navigating the interaction using the Next button. You can change the order of labels and also move the marker on the image if necessary. These steps are covered in the next section, "Moving Labels."

Moving Labels

In a Labeled Graphic, moving a label can mean two different things:

- Moving the marker and label on the image
- Changing the order of the labels in the tabs list

Moving the marker and label on the image does exactly that—positions the marker on the image so it lies on the area described by the label (Figure 17.14). Moving a label tab in the tabs list changes the order of the labels (Figure 17.15). This affects the order in which the

Figure 17.14. Moving a marker and label on the image

Figure 17.15. Moving a label tab to change the label order

labels are displayed when the viewer navigates the interaction using the Next button.

To move the marker and label on the image:

1. Click the marker of the label you want to move.

2. Using the mouse, drag the marker to another location on the image.

The label order remains the same after you drag a marker. In other words, if the viewer uses the Next button to navigate the interaction, all labels will be displayed in the original order.

To change the order of labels in the tabs list:

1. Click the **Edit Labels** button on the ribbon (Figure 17.13).

2. In the tabs list in the Edit Labels dialog box, click the tab of the label you want to move.

3. Use one of the following methods to move the label tab:
    - Drag the label tab using the mouse.
    - In the Label panel, click **Move Tab Left** to move the label one position to the left. Click **Move Tab Right** to move the label one position to the right.

Deleting Labels

Deleting a label removes the label content and the label marker on the image. You can delete labels using either the interaction window or the Edit Labels dialog box. Note that you cannot delete labels as a group.

To delete a label using the interaction window:

1. Click the marker of the label you want to delete.

2. Click the **Delete Label** button on the ribbon (Figure 17.13) *or* press the **Delete** key on your keyboard.

3. The Engage dialog box asks you to confirm the deletion. Click the **Yes** button.

4. To delete additional labels, repeat the above steps.

To delete a label using the Edit Labels dialog box:

1. Click the **Edit Labels** button on the ribbon.

2. In the Edit Labels dialog box, click the tab of the label you want to delete.

3. Click **Delete Label** in the Label panel.

4. The Engage dialog box asks you to confirm the deletion. Click the **Yes** button.

5. To delete additional steps, repeat steps 2-4 above.

If you change your mind and want to restore a deleted label, click the **Undo** button ⟳ on the Quick Access toolbar.

Customizing the Labeled Graphic

So far you've learned how to build the basic elements of a label by adding a title, descriptive text, an audio clip, and a media file. Engage enables you to customize various characteristics of each label, such as the marker color and style. To do this, you can use the options in the Edit Labels dialog box or buttons in the Labels group on the ribbon. We prefer using the Edit Labels dialog box because the preview area lets you see how your changes will affect the interaction before you commit the changes. Additionally, you can use the Interaction Properties dialog box to customize the marker animation and some global features of the Labeled Graphic.

Customizing the Label Position

The label position refers to the placement of the label in relation to the marker on the image. For example, the Bottom Left position option always displays the label below and to the left of the label marker (Figure 17.16). By default, Engage uses the Auto position for all labels, which automatically adjusts the position of the label so that it is always fully displayed within the space allotted in the Engage player. For the example in Figure 17.17, we changed the Auto position for the Employee Section label to Right.

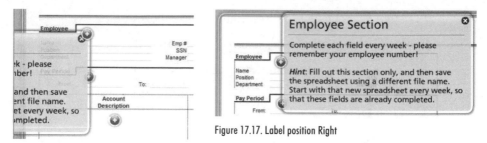

Figure 17.17. Label position Right

Figure 17.16. Label position Bottom Left

You can modify the position of a label, but make sure that the label remains within the borders of the player window. As you can see in Figure 17.16, an absolute position of Bottom Left does not work well for markers near the left or lower border. The label box is truncated if there is not enough room between the marker and the window border.

To customize the label position:

1. Double-click the label marker ⊚ on the background image.

2. In the Label panel of the Edit Labels dialog box, click the **Label Position** button.

3. Select one of the position options. The red circle on each option represents the location of the marker relative to the label.

4. The preview section at the top of the Label panel does not display the new label position, but you can test the new position by clicking **Preview Label** in the Label panel.

5. To apply the same position to all labels in the interaction, click the **Apply position to all** button ⬓ to the right of the Label Position button.

6. To modify the position of a different label, click the label's tab and repeat the above steps.

7. Click the **OK** button in the Edit Labels dialog box.

Customizing the Marker Color

By default, Engage uses a green marker for the Introduction label and red markers for the interaction labels.

To customize the marker color:

1. Double-click the marker of the label you want to change ☺ on the background image.

2. In the Label panel of the Edit Labels dialog box, click the **Marker Color** button.

3. Select one of the color options. Note that you cannot create your own custom color.

4. The marker in the preview section at the top of the Label panel (and the marker on the label tab) displays the new color. To apply the same color to all markers in the interaction, click the **Apply color to all** button ▣ to the right of the Marker Color button.

5. To modify the color of a different label marker, click the label's tab and repeat the above steps.

6. Click the **OK** button in the Edit Labels dialog box.

---

66   **Note:** You can change the entire color scheme of the interaction (or create a new color scheme) using the Colors button on the ribbon. These procedures are covered in Chapter 15, "Engage Basics."

Customizing the Marker Style

The marker style refers to the icon that is displayed inside the marker. By default, Engage uses the letter "i" for the Information marker ☺ and the "+" sign for interaction markers ☺.

To customize the marker style:

1. Double-click the marker of the label you want to change ☺ on the background image.

2. In the Label panel of the Edit Labels dialog box, click the **Marker Style** button.

3. Select one of the style options. Note that you cannot create your own custom style.

4. The marker in the preview section at the top of the Label panel (and the marker on the label tab) displays the new icon. To apply

the same icon style to all markers in the interaction, click the **Apply style to all** button 🗇 to the right of the Marker Style button.

5.   To modify the style of a different label marker, click the label's tab and repeat the above steps.

6.   Click the **OK** button in the Edit Labels dialog box.

Customizing the Callout Background Color

The color scheme you have chosen for the interaction affects many items, including the callout background. (This is the color of the label callout that appears when the viewer double-clicks the label marker.) When you choose a color scheme, these and other items are automatically affected. However, Engage enables you to choose specific colors for specific items by modifying those elements in the color scheme using the Color Scheme Editor (Figure 17.18). The procedures to create and edit color schemes are covered in detail in Chapter 15, "Engage Basics."

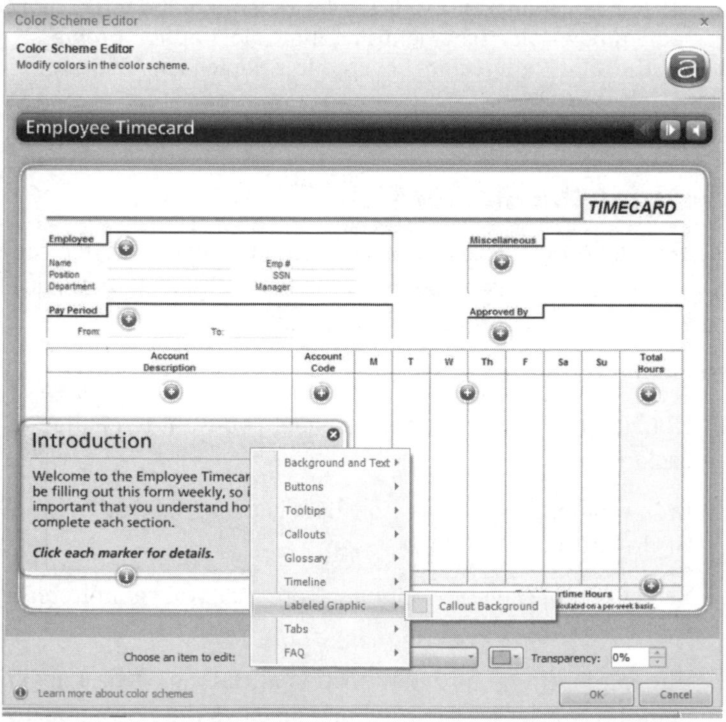

Figure 17.18. Labeled Graphic option in the Color Scheme Editor

Customizing the Marker Animation

The animation style refers to how the markers are animated on the background image. The default animation is Swirl, which shows a comet-like light swirling around each marker. You can change this style using the Labeled Graphic tab in the Interaction Properties dialog box (Figure 17.19).

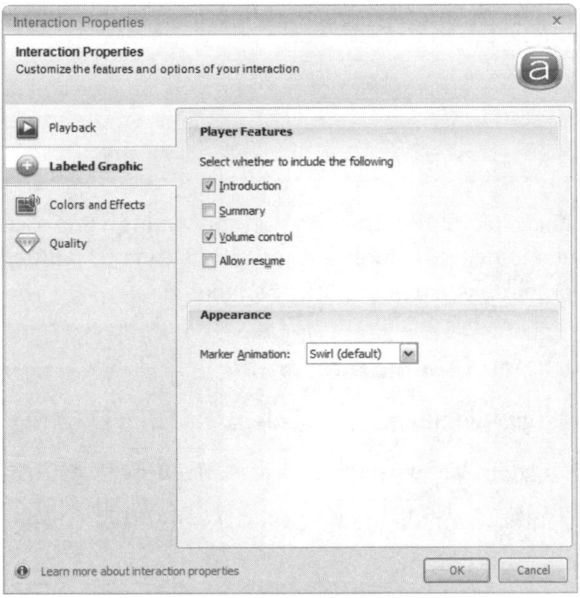

Figure 17.19. Interaction Properties dialog box Labeled Graphic tab

To customize the marker animation style:

1. Click the **Interaction Properties** button on the ribbon.

2. In the Interaction Properties dialog box, click the **Labeled Graphic** tab, if it is not already selected.

3. In the Appearance section, use the Marker Animation list box to select the animation style (**Swirl** or **Pulse**). Selecting **None** removes all animation effects from the markers.

You will see the new style when you preview or publish the interaction.

Customizing General Interaction Properties

The Interaction Properties dialog box offers standard ways to customize all interactions, including the Labeled Graphic. These standard options are covered in detail in Chapter 15, "Engage Basics." We suggest that you review these options and decide which features work best for your Labeled Graphic interaction. For example, if you don't want to include the Introduction label, you can clear the check mark in the Labeled Graphic tab to hide it.

Practice

Now's your chance to create a Labeled Graphic using your own content. If you need an idea, just look for any image in your collection (or on the Internet) that has parts that can be labeled.

Building a Labeled Graphic Interaction

1. Plan the background image and labels, and gather content.

2. From the Engage start screen, click **Create a new interaction**.

3. In the New Interaction dialog box, click **Labeled Graphic** and click the **OK** button.

4. In the Labeled Graphic interaction window, replace the text in the Interaction Title box with the title of your interaction.

5. Click the **Change image** button on the background image.

6. In the Change Background Image dialog box, browse to the folder containing your media files and double-click the desired file.

7. In the interaction window, double-click the **Introduction** marker ⊙.

8. In the Edit Labels dialog box, enter the text in the Introduction tab:
    a. Enter a title in the Title box.
    b. Enter text in the Introduction Text area.

9. Add an audio narration to the introduction:
    a. In the Audio pane, click the **Record** button ⊙.

b. Using your computer's microphone, narrate the audio for the introduction. Click the **Stop** button ⊙ when you are finished.

c. Review the audio by clicking the **Play** button ⊙.

10. In the Label panel, click the **Marker Color** box and select a different color.

11. Create the first label:
   a. Click the **Label 1** tab.
   b. Enter a short description of the label in the Title box.
   c. Enter text in the Label Text area.
   d. In the Label panel, click the **Marker Style** box and select a different icon.
   e. Click the **Apply style to all** button ⧉ to the right of the Marker Style button.
   f. Close the Edit Labels dialog box by clicking the **OK** button.

12. In the interaction window, drag the Label 1 label (which now contains the title you specified) to the correct location on the background image.

13. Create additional labels using the above procedures. (Click the **Add Label** button on the ribbon to insert a new label.)

14. After completing the labels, click the **Interaction Properties** button on the ribbon.

15. In the Interaction Properties dialog box, click the **Labeled Graphic** tab.

16. From the Marker Animation list, select **Pulse** and click the **OK** button.

17. Preview the interaction by clicking the **Preview** button on the ribbon.

18. Close the Interaction Preview window.

19. Save the interaction:
   a. Click the **Save** button 🖫 on the Quick Access toolbar.
   b. In the Save As dialog box, enter a file name and location for the interaction.
   c. Click the **Save** button.

Chapter Recap

Here's our list of the most important things to remember from this chapter:

- A Labeled Graphic is an interactive image that calls out key elements of the graphic. Viewers can learn about each part of the image by clicking labels.

- Each label consists of a marker and a callout. The marker indicates the part of the image being described. The callout consists of the label title and description.

- Viewers move the mouse pointer over a marker to view the label title. Clicking the label displays the full callout description.

- When planning the Labeled Graphic, avoid putting too many labels on the image and be aware that the label callouts might cover other portions of the graphic (including the portion the label is describing).

- You can control where the labels appear on the image and the order in which the labels are displayed when the viewers use the Next and Previous buttons.

- Before creating the labels, use the Change image button to select the background graphic.

- To work with all features of the labels on the graphic, double-click a label to open the Edit Labels dialog box.

- Each label description can contain text, audio, and a media file. If desired, you can hide the text and play just the audio when a marker is clicked.

- You can customize many features of the Labeled Graphic, including the marker color, callout background color, marker style, marker animation effect, and label position (relative to the marker).

- Use the Interaction Properties dialog box to customize standard player features, such as the navigation mode and the color scheme.

Chapter 18

Creating a Tabs Interaction

Chapter Snapshot

In this chapter, you'll learn how to build a Tabs interaction to enable viewers to explore related items in a group.

By now you've learned that Engage offers many interactive alternatives to simply reading paragraphs, pages, or bulleted lists of information. The Tabs interaction is a great tool for describing a group of related items, such as company departments or physical components of an object. If you're familiar with the Process interaction, you'll find that the procedures to create a Tabs interaction are similar. Instead of creating *steps*, you create *tabs*, each of which contains information about one item in a group. Its simple layout and ease of use make the Tabs interaction a perfect vehicle for providing information to your viewers.

Figure 18.1. Tabs interaction

What Is a Tabs Interaction?

A Tabs interaction is used to describe a set of items that are related in some way, such as a series of concepts, members in a group, or differences among objects. The content for each item in the set is contained in what Engage calls a *tab*.

The Tabs interaction is similar to the Process interaction, except that the order in which the viewers see the tabs is generally not important. A Process interaction is typically used to present linear, step-by-step procedures, whereas a Tabs interaction presents an unordered group of items.

How the Tabs Interaction Works

The first screen of a Tabs interaction provides an introduction to the set of items being described (Figure 18.1). The tab names are listed on the left side of the Engage player. If the interaction is published in *interactive* mode, viewers can click any tab to display the content related to that tab. The active tab changes to a different color and the related content is displayed in the right side of the player. If navigation buttons are included in the interaction, viewers can click the Next button to view the tabs from top to bottom.

Real-Life Examples

Here are some of our favorite examples of this type of interaction:

- Departments in a company
- Components of an object
- Different concepts, such as "schools of thought"
- Product or service offerings
- Features list
- Team member "bios"

The example used in this chapter describes the services offered by a nonprofit social services agency.

Planning the Tabs Interaction

Planning the design of a Tabs interaction involves deciding what items (tabs) will be included in the interaction, determining the content for each item, and selecting the tab order. Each tab can include text, audio, and a media file.

Planning the Tabs

Each tab in the interaction contains content for one item in a group. For example, in an interaction describing an organization's services, each tab could describe one service. So your first step is to divide the group into logical items. Engage enables you to create up to 20 tabs in the interaction. The tab labels are sized according to how many tabs you've created.

Gathering Tab Content

Once you've determined the tabs to include in the interaction, you can plan the content elements of the tabs (Figure 18.2). Each tab can consist of text, one audio file, and one media file.

Figure 18.2. Tabs interaction tab content

Following are the content elements for the tab items in a Tabs interaction:

- **Tab title:** Assign a title to each tab. The title should represent the item being described; the example above uses "Clothing Bank." This title is displayed inside its respective tab on the left side of the Engage player. Depending on the number of characters in the title, Engage adjusts the font to ensure that the title fits inside the tab.

- **Text:** Descriptive text for each tab is displayed when the tab is selected by the viewer. Describe the tab item using paragraphs and/or bullet points, and try to be concise. You can include links to more information and to other steps in the interaction. If you are including audio in a tab, make sure the text complements the audio.

- **Audio:** Each tab can include one audio clip. You can use audio to narrate the description of the tab or to add sound effects. In general, if one tab is narrated, then all tabs should be. Otherwise, the viewer might think that the audio is "not working" for specific tabs. If you choose not to include audio in the tabs, you might consider narrating just the introduction.

■ **Media:** Each tab can include one media file, such as a picture, graph, video, screen capture, or diagram. When you add a media file to a tab, you can select its location relative to the text. In most cases, you can also enable the viewer to enlarge (zoom into) the image by clicking it. Depending on the nature of your content, each tab may or may not need a media file.

Determining Tab Order and Viewer Control

Order is not necessarily important in a Tabs interaction, but you should still decide on a logical order of the tabs—from top to bottom. Remember that viewers have the option to use the Next and Previous buttons to navigate the tabs, unless you configure the interaction as a *presentation*. Although you can control the navigation to be *interactive*, *linear*, or in *presentation* format, the most common option for a Tabs interaction is interactive. Most viewers prefer to click tabs in the order they choose.

Planning Additional Features

Following are a few additional features you may want to consider as you plan your Tabs interaction.

■ **Introduction:** Optional. Appears as the first screen when the interaction is launched.

■ **Summary:** Optional. Appears as the last screen.

■ **Color scheme:** Affects the colors of the interaction player's components, such as the background and the navigation buttons. For a Tabs interaction, the color scheme also affects the graphic tabs on the left side of the player, the background of the tabs, and the background of the slide (content) area.

■ **Layout:** Determines the placement of the text relative to the media file in a specific component (e.g., text left/graphic right). However, the placement of the tabs (on the left side of the player) cannot be changed.

■ **Tabs width:** Determines how much space the tabs on the left use. Default is 30%.

Starting a New Tabs Interaction

Opening a New Interaction

After dividing the interaction into tabs and gathering the content, you are ready to develop the interaction. Your first step is to open a new Tabs interaction.

1. Double-click the **Articulate Engage '09** icon on your desktop *or* select **Articulate Engage '09** from the appropriate folder on the Start menu.

2. Click **Create a new interaction** on the start screen.

3. In the New Interaction dialog box, click the **Tabs** tab and click **OK**.

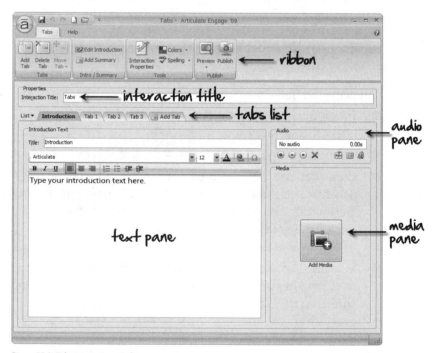

Figure 18.3. Tabs interaction window

The Tabs interaction window contains features standard to most inter-actions, such as the ribbon, Audio pane, and Media pane (Figure 18.3). The tabs list contains a series of tabs; each tab is used to build a sepa-rate tab component in the interaction. By default, Engage provides placeholders for the introduction and three tabs.

Entering the Interaction Title

The interaction title appears at the top of the Engage player when the interaction is running. By default, Engage enters the placeholder title "Tabs." This title should be replaced to describe the purpose of the interaction, such as "OUR Center Services." Keep in mind that you cannot format the text of the interaction title using the Formatting toolbar. However, the Colors and Effects tab in the Interaction Proper-ties dialog box enables you to select a different font style for the title.

Building the Tabs

As you've learned, the foundation of the Tabs interaction consists of a group of specific items, called tabs. You develop each tab using the tabs in the tabs list. Each tab contains the text, audio, and graphic for one interaction tab. The order of the tabs in the tabs list represents the order in which the tabs will appear in the Engage player (from top to bottom). Following are the procedures for building the tabs in the interaction.

Creating the Introduction

When you open a new Tabs interaction, the Introduction tab is dis-played with placeholder text selected. However, the introduction is not exactly an interaction tab, as there is no "Introduction" tab available to the viewer in the Engage player. Instead, the introduction content is presented when the interaction is first opened. Viewers can return to the introduction by clicking the Previous button to the beginning of the interaction or by clicking a hyperlink if you provide one.

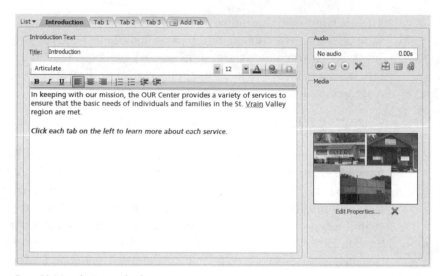

Figure 18.4. Introduction completed

To create the introduction:

1. If desired, replace the "Introduction" placeholder in the Title field with a meaningful description.

2. Replace the "Type your introduction text here" placeholder with your content. Remember, you can format the text using the toolbars above the text area.

3. Use the Audio pane to record or select an audio file, if desired.

4. Use the Media pane to add a picture, photo, or video, if desired.

See Figure 18.4 for an example of a completed introduction.

---

66 Note: Chapter 15, "Engage Basics," provides detailed instructions for working with text, audio, and media.

Tip: After completing the introduction and moving on to other steps, you can quickly return to the Introduction tab by clicking the Edit Introduction button on the ribbon.

Creating Tabs

Engage includes placeholders for three tabs. To create the first tab, just open Tab 1 and edit the default content:

1. Click the **Tab 1** tab.

2. Replace the "Tab 1" placeholder in the Title field with a meaningful description, such as **Hospitality Center.** The title text will appear in the tab icon on the left side of the Engage player when the interaction is launched.

3. Add text, audio, and a media file, as appropriate.

Now you can create the remaining tabs using the same procedures as above:

4. Click the **Tab 2** tab and enter your content.

5. To add more tabs, click **Add Tab** at the end of the tabs list or click the **Add Tab** button on the ribbon. A new tab will be inserted at the end of the tabs list.

See Figure 18.5 for an example of a completed tab.

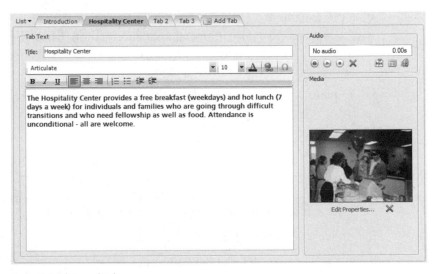

Figure 18.5. Tab 1 completed

Moving Tabs

The order of the tabs in the tabs list represents the order in which the tabs will appear in the Engage player (from top to bottom). As discussed earlier, if the viewer chooses to navigate the interaction using the Next button, the tabs will be displayed in this order. You can quickly change the order of tabs by dragging a tab with the mouse to its new location. Alternatively, you can use the Move Tab button on the ribbon (Figure 18.6).

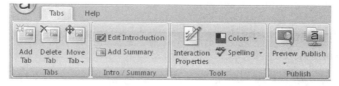

Figure 18.6. Engage ribbon Tabs tab

To reorder tabs using the Move Tab button:

1. In the tabs list, click the tab you want to move.

2. Click the **Move Tab** button on the ribbon.

3. Click **Left** to move the tab one position to the left. (This results in moving the tab *higher* in the running interaction). Click **Right** to move the tab one position to the right. (This results in moving the tab *lower* in the running interaction).

4. To move a tab more than one position, repeat steps 2-3 above.

Deleting Tabs

You can easily remove a tab if it is no longer needed. However, you cannot remove tabs as a group. Only one tab at a time can be deleted. Keep in mind that the sizes of the remaining tabs in the Engage player will expand to accommodate the space left by the deleted tab.

To remove a tab from the interaction:

1. In the tabs list, click the tab you want to delete.

2. Click the **Delete Tab** button on the ribbon (Figure 18.6).

3. The Engage dialog box asks you to confirm the deletion. Click the **Yes** button.

4. To delete additional tabs, repeat the above steps.

If you change your mind and want to restore a tab immediately after deleting it, click the **Undo** button ↰ on the Quick Access toolbar.

Adding a Summary

A summary is optional for all interactions. You may choose to include one for a Tabs interaction to recap the content of all tabs on one screen. Keep in mind, however, that the summary is accessible to the viewer only by clicking the Next button after the last tab is displayed (or by clicking a hyperlink if you provide one). A summary tab is not displayed in the Engage player.

To add a summary:

1. Click the **Add Summary** button on the ribbon (Figure 18.6). By default, the Summary tab is added to the end of the tabs list. It cannot be moved.

2. Enter the title, text, audio, and media file using the same procedures as those for building any other tab.

⫸ **Tip:** After the summary is completed, the Add Summary button on the ribbon changes to Edit Summary. You can use this button to make changes to the summary at any time.

Customizing the Tabs Interaction

You can customize several properties of the Tabs interaction, including the tab width, the color of the tabs background area, and the color of the slide (content) area. As with other Engage interactions, you can also customize general properties of the Tabs interaction.

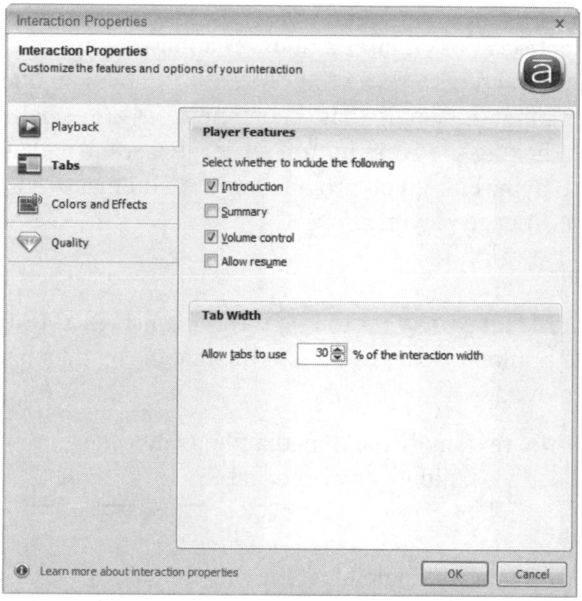

Figure 18.7. Interaction Properties dialog box Tabs tab

Customizing Tab Width

Engage enables you to control how much space the tabs occupy on the left side of the Engage player. The default is 30% of the player's width, but you can increase or decrease this amount.

To format the tab width:

1. Click the **Interaction Properties** button on the ribbon.

2. In the Interaction Properties dialog box, click the **Tabs** tab, if it is not already active (Figure 18.7).

3. In the Tab Width section, use the increase and decrease arrows to change the width percentage. Or just type a new percentage.

You will see the new width format when you preview or publish the interaction.

Customizing Tabs Background and Slide Background Colors

The color scheme you have chosen for the interaction affects many items, including the color used in the background area of the Tabs interaction and the background color of the slide (content) area. When you choose a color scheme, these and other items are automatically affected. However, Engage enables you to choose specific colors for these items by modifying those elements in the color scheme using the Color Scheme Editor (Figure 18.8). The procedures to create and edit color schemes are covered in detail in Chapter 15, "Engage Basics."

Figure 18.8. Tabs options in the Color Scheme Editor

Customizing General Interaction Properties

The Interaction Properties dialog box offers standard ways to customize all interactions, including the Tabs interaction. These standard options are covered in detail in Chapter 15, "Engage Basics." We suggest that you review these options and decide which features work best for your Tabs interaction. For example, you can allow viewers to resume where they left the interaction by selecting the Resume check box in the Tabs tab.

Practice

Now's your chance to create a Tabs interaction using your own content. If you need an idea, think of the various products offered by a company. Then, develop a tab for each product.

Building a Tabs Interaction

1. Plan your interaction and gather content.

2. From the Engage start screen, click **Create a new interaction**.

3. In the New Interaction dialog box, click **Tabs** and click the **OK** button.

4. In the Tabs interaction window, replace the text in the Interaction Title box with the title of your interaction.

5. Enter the text in the Introduction tab:
   a. Enter a title in the Title box (or keep the default Introduction text).
   b. Enter text in the Introduction Text area.

6. Add an image to the introduction:
   a. In the Media pane, click the **Add Media** button.
   b. In the Select Image or Video File dialog box, browse to the folder containing your media files and double-click the desired file.

c. In the Multimedia Properties dialog box, use the Position list box to change the location of the image, if desired, and then click the **OK** button.

7. Add an audio narration to the introduction:
   a. In the Audio pane, click the **Record** button ⊙ .
   b. Using your computer's microphone, narrate the audio for the introduction. Click the **Stop** button ⊙ when you are finished.
   c. Review the audio by clicking the **Play** button ⊙ .

8. Click the **Tab 1** tab and repeat steps 5-7 above to create the first tab.

9. Create additional tabs using the above procedures. (Click the **Add Tab** tab to insert a new tab, if needed.)

10. After completing the tabs, click the **Interaction Properties** button on the ribbon.

11. In the Interaction Properties dialog box, change the following properties:
    ■ In the Tabs tab, change the Tab Width to **40%** of the interaction width.
    ■ In the Colors and Effects tab, change the color scheme to **Blue Dark**.
    ■ Click the **OK** button to save the changes.

12. Preview the interaction by clicking the **Preview** button on the ribbon.

13. Close the Interaction Preview window.

14. Save the interaction:
    a. Click the **Save** button ▦ on the Quick Access toolbar.
    b. In the Save As dialog box, enter a file name and location for the interaction.
    c. Click the **Save** button.

Chapter Recap

Here's our list of the most important things to remember from this chapter:

- A Tabs interaction can be used to describe a group of related items, such as company departments or physical components of an object.

- The introduction in a Tabs interaction generally describes the procedure or process. Viewers may then navigate the interaction by clicking each tab.

- Remember that the introduction and summary do not have tab labels. Viewers need to use the Previous and Next buttons (or a hyperlink you provide) to revisit these screens.

- Although you can control how viewers navigate the interaction, the interactive mode is generally the best choice for Tabs interactions.

- You can create up to 20 tabs in the interaction. Engage automatically adjusts the size of each tab to accommodate the player size.

- Tabs always appear on the left side of the running interaction. However, you can control the layout of the text and graphics in the description area of each tab.

- Use the tools on the ribbon to add, move, and delete tabs.

- You can customize several features of the Tabs interaction, including the width of the tabs, background color of the tabs, and background color of the slide (content) area.

- Use the Interaction Properties dialog box to customize standard player features, such as the navigation mode and the color scheme.

Chapter 19

Creating a Circle Diagram Interaction

Chapter Snapshot

In this chapter, you'll learn how to use the Circle Diagram interaction to depict relationships among items using circular layers.

A lot of knowledge-based content lends itself to being represented graphically. Engage offers several interactive diagrams to help your viewers visualize a hierarchical set of concepts or physical properties of an object. If you need to present content that can be described as "layers of an onion," then the Circle Diagram interaction is the perfect tool for you.

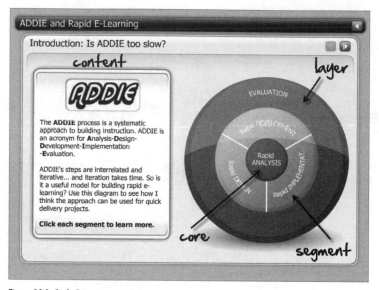

Figure 19.1. Circle Diagram interaction

What Is a Circle Diagram?

A Circle Diagram uses a set of concentric circles to depict a hierarchy of core concepts or elements (center) and other elements that radiate around it. It's a great tool for presenting concepts and values, and can also be used to describe the physical properties of an object. (Yes, you *will* be tempted to use it to describe the various flavor layers of a jaw-breaker.) The center of the diagram represents the "core" concept, and each layer around the core represents the next level in the hierarchy.

Many of us tend to think of a *hierarchy* as represented by a traditional corporate flowchart: the president in the top box, vice presidents in the second row of boxes, managers in the third row of boxes, and so forth. This "top-down" perception isn't wrong, but hierarchies can be represented using many different models. The hierarchy in a Circle Diagram is different from that in a flowchart because the circle shows that each level is *encompassed* by other levels. This arrangement shows a greater connectedness than that of a typical top-down hierarchical flowchart. So as you plan your hierarchical interactions, remember to "think outside the flowchart" and consider other visual models.

How the Circle Diagram Works

When the viewer opens the Circle Diagram interaction, the diagram and introduction are displayed on the screen (Figure 19.1). The introduction describes the purpose of the interaction and provides instructions for exploring the diagram. Viewers can then click a *segment* of the diagram, which displays related content in a callout. A segment is one section of a *layer*, which represents a major hierarchical level in the diagram. The segments comprising the layers contain the "chunks" of information for the viewer. The *core* lies at the center of the diagram and can also be clicked for more information.

In addition to clicking the core and segments, viewers can click the Next and Previous buttons to navigate each section of the diagram. As you develop the Circle Diagram, you can determine the order in which the segments appear if the navigation buttons are used.

Real-Life Examples

The Circle Diagram is an effective tool for presenting both conceptual and physical hierarchies. Here are some of our favorite examples of this type of interaction:

- Description of a philosophy
- Corporate value structure
- Problem-solving approach
- Psychological "layers" of the human mind
- Physical properties of a planet

The example in this chapter depicts the Rapid ADDIE Instructional Design model.

Planning the Circle Diagram

Planning the design of a Circle Diagram interaction involves determining the core, layers, and segments comprising the diagram, gathering the content for each segment, and deciding on other features of the interaction, such as layout and color scheme.

Planning the Core, Layers, and Segments

As we've discussed, the Circle Diagram consists of the *core*, *layers*, and *segments* (Figure 19.1). The core lies at the center of the diagram. Layers surround the core and can contain one or multiple segments. Viewers click the core and the segments to view information. A Circle Diagram may contain up to 10 layers outside the core layer. A layer may consist of up to 20 segments. As you plan your interaction, you need to decide what to include in the core, layers, and segments. Table 19.1 provides a description of these elements.

Table 19.1. Circle Diagram elements

Element	Description
Core	The core represents the central concept of the diagram, around which all other concepts are based. For example, in the ADDIE example, the core of the model is Rapid Analysis.
Layers	When planning the layers, think about how they should be arranged around the core. One approach is to build layers based on their importance or relativity to the core; the most closely related layers are found closer to the core. In the ADDIE example, the Evaluation layer is on the outside of the circle because it encompasses the other elements of the model.
Segments	The diagram's layers consist of at least one segment. In some cases, that's all you need. In other cases, it is more descriptive to divide a layer into several segments. In the ADDIE example, the Rapid Design, Rapid Development, and Rapid Implementation elements are performed concurrently "outside" the Rapid Analysis core. In that case, it makes sense to divide the layer into three segments.

Gathering Segment Content

The content for a Circle Diagram consists of the content for each segment (and the core), which can include text, audio, and one media file. Each segment must include a title, which is displayed on the diagram. When the viewer clicks a segment, the related content is displayed next to the diagram (Figure 19.2).

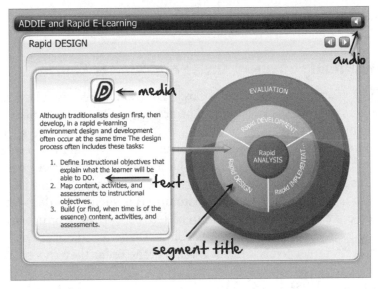

Figure 19.2. Circle Diagram content

Following are the basic content components you'll want to think about when planning a Circle Diagram:

- **Segment/core title:** Assign a short title to each segment (and the core). This title appears directly on the diagram and should clearly identify the item being represented.

- **Text:** Write a text description for each segment (and the core). Remember that the viewer gets information by clicking a segment, not a layer. Consequently, there are no text descriptions (or audio or media) for layers as a whole. Describe the segment using paragraphs and/or bullet points. You can also include links to more information and to other segments in the interaction.

- **Audio:** You can use audio to narrate the description of the segments or to add descriptive sound effects. In general, if one segment is narrated, then all steps should be. Otherwise, the viewer might think that the audio is "not working" for specific segments. If you choose not to include audio in the segments, you might consider narrating just the introduction.

- **Media:** Each segment can include one media file, such as a picture, graph, video, screen capture, or diagram. In most cases, you can also let the viewer enlarge (zoom into) the image by clicking it. Depending on the nature of your content, each segment may or may not need a media file.

Determining Segment Order and Viewer Control

As you plan the design of the Circle Diagram, think about how the segments within each layer should be arranged. This arrangement affects the display of the diagram, as well as the order in which the segment content is presented when viewers use the Next and Previous buttons to navigate. When the navigation buttons are used, Engage presents the segments from the inside of the circle outward, and in a clockwise direction. (However, you can customize this segment order.) Although you can control the navigation to be *interactive*, *linear*, or in *presentation* format, the best option for a Circle Diagram is interactive. Most viewers prefer to click the segments in the order they choose.

Planning Additional Features

Following are a few additional features you may want to consider as you plan your Circle Diagram.

- **Introduction:** Optional. Appears as the first screen when the interaction is launched.
- **Summary:** Optional. Appears as the last screen.
- **Color scheme:** Affects the colors of the interaction player's components, such as the background and the navigation buttons. (The colors of the core and layers are controlled separately and are not part of the color scheme itself.)
- **Diagram colors:** Determines the colors that will be used for the core and the layers in the diagram. By default, each layer in the diagram appears in a different color, and the segments appear in different shades of that color.
- **Interaction layout:** Determines whether the diagram appears on the left or right side of the player.
- **Segment layout:** Determines the placement of the text relative to the media file in a specific segment (e.g., text left/graphic right).

Starting a New Circle Diagram

Opening a New Interaction

After you have planned the diagram components and gathered content, you can start developing your Circle Diagram. Your first step is to open a new Circle Diagram interaction:

1. Double-click the **Articulate Engage '09** icon on your desktop *or* select **Articulate Engage '09** from the appropriate folder on the Start menu.

2. Click **Create a new interaction** on the start screen.

3. Click **Circle Diagram** on the left side of the New Interaction dialog box, and click the **OK** button.

Figure 19.3. Circle Diagram interaction window

The Circle Diagram window contains features standard to most interactions, such as the ribbon, Audio pane, and Media pane (Figure 19.3). The Select Layer pane enables you to select a layer to build. After you select a layer, the component tabs for the segments within the layer are displayed.

By default, Engage provides placeholders for the introduction, the diagram core, two layers, and two segments within each layer.

Entering the Interaction Title

The interaction title appears at the top of the Engage player when the interaction is running. By default, Engage enters the placeholder text "Circle Diagram." This title should be replaced to describe the purpose of the interaction; in Figure 19.2 we used "ADDIE and Rapid E-Learning." Keep in mind that you cannot format the text of the interaction title; however, the Colors and Effects tab in the Interaction Properties dialog box enables you to select a different font style for the title.

Building the Diagram Components

Building the diagram components involves modifying the existing placeholders for the introduction, core, layers, and segments. You can also add new layers and segments, and customize layer properties. Clicking a layer (or segment) in the Select Layer pane enables you to work with all the segments in that layer.

Creating the Introduction

When you open a new Circle Diagram interaction, the Introduction tab is displayed with the default placeholder text selected. The introduction is not part of the graphic circle. Instead, the introduction content is presented when the interaction is first opened. Keep in mind that once viewers start interacting with the graphic, they can redisplay the introduction only by clicking the Previous button until they reach the beginning of the interaction. Or you can include a hyperlink to the introduction in one or more of the segments.

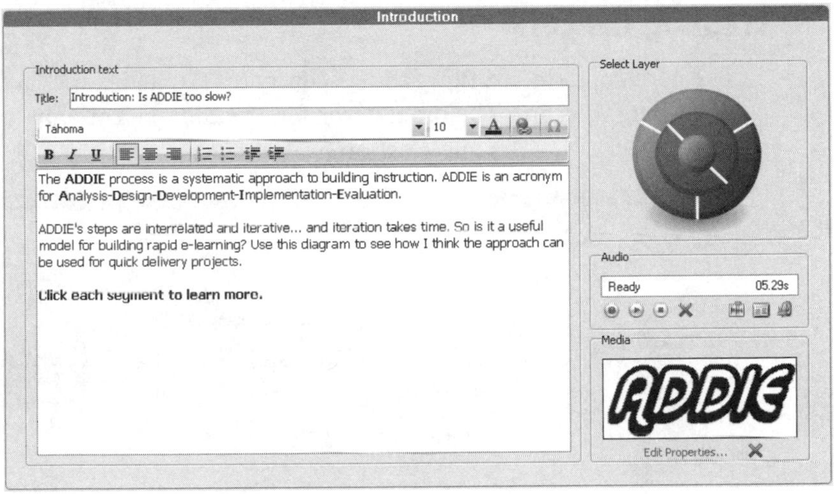

Figure 19.4. Introduction completed

To create the introduction:

1. Replace the "Introduction" placeholder text in the Title field with a meaningful description, such as **Introduction: Is ADDIE too slow?**

2. Replace the "Type your introduction text here" placeholder with your content. Remember, you can format the text using the toolbars above the text area.

3. Use the Audio pane to record or select an audio file, if desired.

4. Use the Media pane to add a picture, photo, or video, if desired.

See Figure 19.4 for an example of a completed introduction.

Note: Chapter 15, "Engage Basics," provides detailed instructions for working with text, audio, and media.

Tip: After completing the introduction and moving on to other steps, you can quickly return to the Introduction tab by clicking the Edit Introduction button on the ribbon.

Creating the Core

The core consists of a title and the content (text, audio, media file) describing the core. The procedures for creating the core are similar to those for creating the introduction.

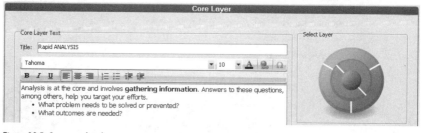

Figure 19.5. Core completed

To create the core:

1. In the Select Layer pane, click the core.

2. Replace the "Core" placeholder text in the Title field with a meaningful description, such as **Rapid ANALYSIS**.

3. Replace the "Type your core layer text here" placeholder with your content. Remember, you can format the text using the toolbars above the text area.

4. Use the Audio pane to record or select an audio file, if desired.

5. Use the Media pane to add a picture, photo, or video, if desired.

See Figure 19.5 for an example of a completed core.

Creating Layers and Segments

As mentioned earlier, a layer can consist of just one segment or multiple segments. The actual content presented to the viewer is always contained in a segment. So you can think of segments as your building blocks for the layer content. When you select a layer to work with, tabs for each segment are displayed in the interaction work area. You can then add content to each segment tab.

Engage numbers the layers from the inside of the circle outward. In other words, the layer closest to the center is labeled Layer 1, the next layer is Layer 2, and so forth. These numbers are not visible to the viewer—they are for development use only and serve to identify the layer you are working with. The segments in a layer are initially numbered from the left side of the layer clockwise. However, these numbers are part of the default title text—you should change the titles as you develop your content.

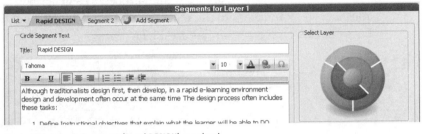

Figure 19.6. Layer 1, Segment 1 (Rapid DESIGN) completed

To create the segments in Layer 1:

1. In the Select Layer pane, click any segment in the layer closest to the core.

2. In the tabs list, click the **Segment 1** tab if it is not already selected.

3. Replace the "Segment 1" placeholder text in the Title field with a meaningful description, such as **Rapid DESIGN**. The title text will appear in that segment of the diagram when the interaction is launched.

4. Add text, audio, and a media file, as appropriate. Figure 19.6 shows a completed segment.

5. Click the **Segment 2** tab and follow steps 3 and 4 above to create the second segment.

To add more segments to the current layer, use one of the following methods:

- ▪ Click **Add Segment** at the end of the tabs list (Figure 19.6).
- ▪ Click the **Add Segment** button on the ribbon (Figure 19.7).

A new segment will be inserted at the end of the tabs list. Note that the other segments in the layer will be resized to accommodate the new segment. The diagram in the Select Layer panel gives a preview of the segment sizes. The example displayed at the beginning of the chapter (Figure 19.1) shows the completed circle with an additional segment in Layer 1.

Once you have created all the segments for Layer 1, click the next layer in the circle diagram in the Select Layer panel. Then create the segments for that layer using the same procedures described above. You can add more layers to the diagram, if needed, by clicking the Add Layer button on the ribbon (Figure 19.7).

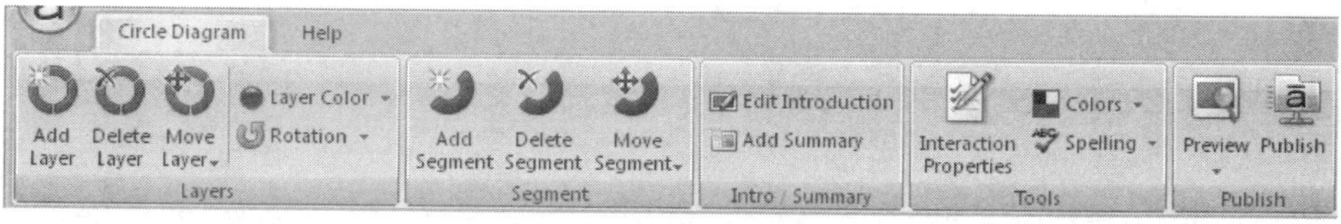

Figure 19.7. Engage ribbon Circle Diagram tab

Deleting Layers and Segments

You can remove a layer from the circle diagram if it is no longer needed—the segments in the layer and all associated content will be deleted. You can also remove just one or several segments from a layer without deleting the layer. When you remove a segment, the remaining segments are resized to accommodate the deleted segment.

To delete a layer:

1. In the Select Layer pane, click the layer you want to delete.

2. Click the **Delete Layer** button on the ribbon (Figure 19.7).

3. The Engage dialog box asks you to confirm the deletion. Click the **Yes** button.

If you change your mind and want to restore a layer immediately after deleting it, click the **Undo** button ↰ on the Quick Access toolbar.

To delete a segment:

1. In the Select Layer pane, click the layer containing the segment you want to delete. (You can also click the specific segment in the diagram, although the segments are not labeled.)

2. Click the tab of the segment you want to delete.

3. Click the **Delete Segment** button on the ribbon (Figure 19.7).

4. The Engage dialog box asks you to confirm the deletion. Click the **Yes** button.

If you change your mind and want to restore a segment immediately after deleting it, click the **Undo** button 🔄 on the Quick Access toolbar.

Moving Layers and Segments

You can change the order of concentric layers in the diagram by moving them in or out from the center of the diagram. Engage also enables you to change the order of segments within a layer, as well as move a segment from one layer into another layer.

To move a layer:

1. In the Select Layer pane, click the layer you want to move.

2. Click the **Move Layer** button on the ribbon (Figure 19.7).

3. Select **In** to move the layer closer to the center, or select **Out** to move the layer farther from the center.

The layers are automatically renumbered to reflect their new positions in the diagram.

To move a segment within a layer:

1. In the Select Layer pane, click the layer containing the segment you want to move. (You can also click the specific segment in the diagram, although the segments are not labeled.)

2. In the tabs list, click the tab of the segment you want to move.

3. You can move the segment using either of the following methods:

    ■ Using the mouse, drag the segment's tab in the tabs list to a different location.

    ■ Click the **Move Segment** button on the ribbon (Figure 19.7), and then select **Counterclockwise** or **Clockwise**.

To move a segment to a different layer:

1. In the Select Layer pane, click the layer containing the segment you want to move. (You can also click the specific segment in the diagram, although the segments are not labeled.)

2. In the tabs list, click the tab of the segment you want to move.

3. Click the **Move Segment** button on the ribbon (Figure 19.7).

4. Select **In** to move the segment to the adjacent layer that is closer to the center, or select **Out** to move the segment to the adjacent layer that is farther from the center.

Engage resizes the segments in the affected layers to accommodate the change.

Adding a Summary

A summary is optional for all interactions. You may choose to include one for a Circle Diagram interaction to recap all of the segments in one screen. Keep in mind, however, that the summary is accessible to the viewer only by clicking the Next button after the last segment is displayed, unless you include a hyperlink to it within a segment. A Summary layer or segment is not displayed in the diagram itself.

To add a summary:

1. Click the **Add Summary** button on the ribbon (Figure 19.7).

2. Add text, audio, and a media file using the same procedures as for building a segment.

Tip: After the summary is completed, the Add Summary button on the ribbon changes to Edit Summary. You can use this button to make changes to the summary at any time.

Customizing the Circle Diagram

So far you've learned how to build the basic components of a Circle Diagram by creating the core, layers, and segments. Engage enables you to customize each layer by selecting a different color and changing the rotation of the segments. For example, you might want to change the colors of the layers to match your company colors or to better represent the content of each layer. Rotating the layers enables you to display the segment titles at different angles, and to provide a contrast between the segments in different layers.

Customizing Layer Colors

Engage uses default colors for the core and layers in the Circle Diagram. The segments within each layer appear in a different shade of the layer color. You can change the color of any layer, but you cannot change segment colors individually.

To change the layer color:

1. In the Select Layer pane, click the layer you want to customize.

2. Click the **Layer Color** button on the ribbon.

3. Select one of the color options. Note that you cannot create your own custom color.

The diagram in the Select Layer panel (and the title bar of the interaction work area) displays the new color. To modify the color of a different layer, select another layer and repeat the above steps.

---

66 **Note:** You can change the entire color scheme of the interaction (or create a new color scheme) using the Colors button on the ribbon. These procedures are covered in Chapter 15, "Engage Basics."

Customizing Layer Rotation

The layer rotation refers to the clockwise positioning of each segment. The rotation is offset in degrees from the start of the first segment in the current layer. By default, Engage rotates the two placeholder layers as pictured on the left in Figure 19.8. You can rotate any layer to shift the positions of the segments as desired. This feature is helpful if you don't want the segment edges between layers to line up with each other.

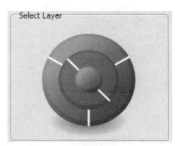 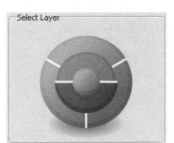

Figure 19.8. Default rotation of segments in Layer 1 (left) and custom rotation (right)

To change the layer rotation:

1. In the Select Layer pane, click the layer you want to rotate.

2. Click the arrow next to **Rotation** on the ribbon (Figure 19.7) and select a rotation degree. Rotation options are available in increments of 45 degrees.

The circle diagram in the Select Label pane displays the new rotation. To modify the rotation of a different layer, select another layer and repeat the above steps.

Customizing Circle Placement

The Circle Placement section of the Interaction Properties dialog box (Figure 19.9) lets you place the circle diagram on the right or left side of the Engage player while the interaction is running. The content appears on the opposite side of the diagram.

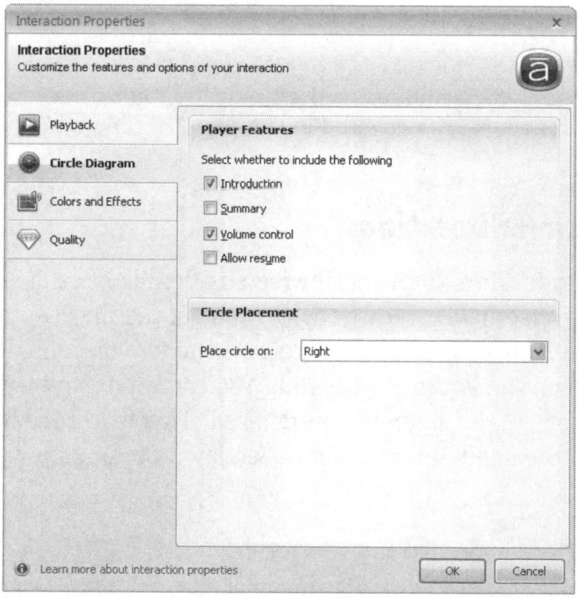

Figure 19.9. Interaction Properties dialog box Circle Diagram tab

To change the circle placement:

1. Click the **Interaction Properties** button on the ribbon.

2. In the Interaction Properties dialog box, click the **Circle Diagram** tab, if it is not already selected.

3. Use the Place circle on list box to select **Left** or **Right**.

You will see the new placement when you preview or publish the interaction.

Customizing Segment Order

You can control the order in which the segments of the Circle Diagram are presented for viewers using the Next button to navigate the interaction. (This order also applies to presentation mode, when the Next button is not available.) By default, the segments are presented from the inside to the outside, in a clockwise direction.

To change the segment order:

1. Click the **Interaction Properties** button on the ribbon.

2. In the Interaction Properties dialog box, click the **Playback** tab.

3. In the Segment Order section, use the list boxes to change the order:

   ■ Select **Inside** or **Outside**.

   ■ Select **Clockwise** or **Counterclockwise**.

You will see the new placement when you preview or publish the interaction.

Customizing General Interaction Properties

The Interaction Properties dialog box offers standard ways to customize all interactions. These standard options are covered in detail in Chapter 15, "Engage Basics." We suggest that you review these options and decide which features work best for your Circle Diagram interaction. For example, if you want to change the color scheme of the player background and navigation buttons, you can select a new scheme using the Colors and Effects tab.

Practice

Now's your chance to create a Circle Diagram using your own content. If you need an idea, think about the values or concepts of an organization that you belong to. Then, develop a few simple layers and segments for each concept.

Building a Circle Diagram Interaction

1. Plan the core, layers, and segments and gather content.

2. From the Engage start screen, click **Create a new interaction**.

3. In the New Interaction dialog box, click **Circle Diagram** and click the **OK** button.

4. In the Circle Diagram interaction window, replace the text in the Interaction Title box with the title of your interaction.

5. Enter the text in the Introduction tab:
    a. Enter a title in the Title box.
    b. Enter text in the Introduction Text area.

6. Add an image to the introduction:
    a. In the Media pane, click the **Add Media** button.
    b. In the Select Image or Video File dialog box, browse to the folder containing your media files and double-click the desired file.
    c. In the Multimedia Properties dialog box, use the Position list box to change the location of the image, if desired, and then click the **OK** button.

7. Add an audio narration to the introduction:
    a. In the Audio pane, click the **Record** button ◉ .
    b. Using your computer's microphone, narrate the audio for the introduction. Click the **Stop** button ◉ when you are finished.
    c. Review the audio by clicking the **Play** button ◉ .

8. In the Select Layer pane, click the core and enter a title and text.

9. In the Select Layer pane, click the layer closest to the core (Layer 1) and then click the **Segment 1** tab.

10. Enter a title and text to create the first segment. Add audio and a media file, if desired.

11. Create additional segments for Layer 1 using the above procedures. (Click the **Add Segment** tab to insert a new segment, if needed.)

12. In the Select Layer pane, click the outer layer (Layer 2) and use the above procedures to create the second layer. Add additional layers, if desired, by clicking the **Add Layer** button on the ribbon.

13. In the Select Layer pane, click the layer closest to the core (Layer 1), click the **Layer Color** button on the ribbon, and select a different color.

14. In the Select Layer pane, click the outermost layer, click the arrow next to Rotation on the ribbon, and select **90**.

15. Experiment with the Move Layer and Move Segment features. (You can click the **Undo** button ↻ on the Quick Access toolbar after each change if you want to restore the original position.)

   ■ Click the **Move Layer** button on the ribbon and select **In**.

   ■ Click a segment tab, click the **Move Segment** button on the ribbon, and select **Clockwise**.

   ■ Click another segment tab, click the **Move Segment** button on the ribbon, and select **Out**.

16. Preview the interaction by clicking the **Preview** button on the ribbon.

17. Close the Interaction Preview window.

18. Save the interaction:
   a. Click the **Save** button 💾 on the Quick Access toolbar.
   b. In the Save As dialog box, enter a file name and location for the interaction.
   c. Click the **Save** button.

Chapter Recap

Here's our list of the most important things to remember from this chapter:

- A Circle Diagram is a multilayercd circle that you can use to depict hierarchical concepts or physical properties of an item.

- The diagram consists of a central core and several layers surrounding the core. Each layer can consist of multiple segments.

- Each segment can contain text, audio, and a media file.

- The introduction is displayed when the viewer first opens the interaction. Viewers then click a segment of the diagram to get more information, which is displayed in a callout.

- After creating the introduction, click the core of the diagram in the Select Layer diagram and add text, audio, and a media file, if desired.

- Build segments by clicking a layer in the Select Layer panel and then use the tabs list to create each segment.

- Add, move, and delete layers and segments using the tools on the ribbon.

- You can change the color of the layers using the Layer Color button on the ribbon. Segments appear in different shades of the layer color.

- You can change the rotation of a segment using the Rotation tool on the ribbon.

- Use the Interaction Properties dialog box to customize features such as navigation control, the color scheme, and the placement of the circle (left or right).

Chapter 20

Creating a Timeline Interaction

Chapter Snapshot

In this chapter, you'll learn how to create a Timeline interaction to present information about a linear series of events or a set of related items.

Chapter Topics

Many of us are familiar with timelines because they are so frequently used to describe historical events and landmarks, such as major discoveries. The Timeline interaction enables you to present chronological information to your viewers using a familiar visual aid: a time continuum stretching from left (early times) to right (later times). However, this interaction isn't limited to a "time" framework. We've seen some creative uses of this versatile interaction, including product feature/subfeature descriptions and procedural explanations.

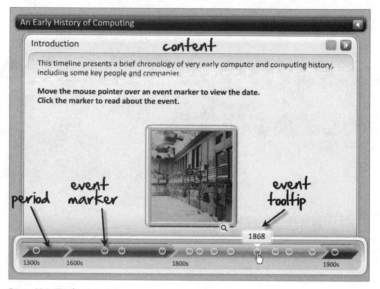

Figure 20.1. Timeline interaction

What Is a Timeline Interaction?

Whether or not time is *really* linear, the Timeline interaction presupposes this theory and provides a visual way for your viewers to click their way through a timeline of chronological events. These events can be divided among different time *periods*, such as past, present, and future. Although commonly used by academic and reference resources to present a "nutshell" visual aid for historical events, the Timeline interaction has worked its way into the corporate world. Any series of events or concepts, whether actual or projected, can be effectively presented using Engage's colorful and intuitive timeline.

How the Timeline Interaction Works

The first screen of a Timeline interaction provides an introduction to the series of *events* being presented (Figure 20.1). Events are represented by *markers*, and are grouped on the timeline graphic by *periods*. A period is simply a visual reference to give context to the events; viewers do not interact with the periods. Viewers can move the mouse pointer over an event marker to see the name of the event. Clicking the event marker displays the content for that event, replacing the introduction content.

Viewers can also click the Next and Previous buttons to navigate the timeline. If you don't want viewers to click their way through the timeline at all, you can configure the interaction as a presentation. In that mode, each event is displayed for a specific number of seconds.

Real-Life Examples

The Timeline interaction is a simple but effective way to present a series of chronological events. Keep in mind that the timeline can incorporate future events as well as past events. It can also be used to chronologically order events that are ongoing, such as a standard company process. If you really want to go outside the box, you can use the Timeline interaction as a substitute for the Process or Tabs interactions.

Here are some of our favorite examples of this type of interaction:

- Tasks that should be performed in a specific time frame (present, ongoing)
- Projected client contracts over the next three years (future)
- Company milestones (past, present, future)
- Progression of student achievement (past, present)
- Events leading up to and causing a current situation (past)
- Steps and substeps in a simple process
- Product features and subfeatures
- Historical/evolutionary events

For the example in this chapter, we took the simple route and put together a brief history of early computing.

Planning the Timeline Interaction

Planning the design of a Timeline interaction involves determining the periods and events comprising the timeline, gathering the content for each event, and deciding on other features of the interaction, such as content layout and the color scheme.

Planning the Events and Periods

As we've discussed, the Timeline interaction consists of *events* and *periods*. Events contain the content (text, audio, and media file) describing a specific item on the timeline. Periods are visual "containers" for one or more events. An interaction may contain up to 12 periods. There is no limit to the number of events in each period. As you plan the timeline, you need to decide what elements make up the events and how to arrange these events among periods.

- **Events:** Determine the overall timeframe of the timeline and decide how many events to include. If your list of events grows out of control, consider combining smaller events into one. Also consider the proper order of events (which is usually not a challenge for the Timeline interaction!).

- **Periods:** Determine the periods used to group events. For example, 1st, 2nd, 3rd, and 4th quarters of a fiscal year or the archeological eras of the Stone Age. Make sure the periods are meaningful, and not just random divisions among events. Keep in mind that your viewers do not interact directly with the periods—they serve only as a visual reference.

Gathering Event Content

The content for a Timeline interaction consists of the content for each event, which can include text, audio, and one media file (Figure 20.2). Each event must also include a title. When the viewer clicks an event marker, the related content is displayed above the timeline.

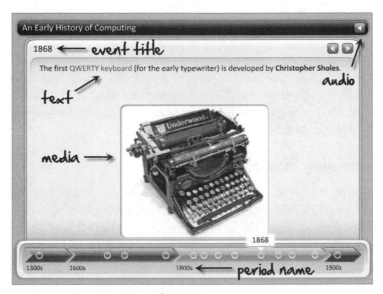

Figure 20.2. Timeline interaction content for 1868 event

Following are the basic content components you'll want to think about when planning a Timeline interaction:

- **Title:** Assign a short title to each event. The title should clearly identify the event being represented. It can be as simple as a date, or it can include more information, such as the name of an event. The event title is displayed as a tooltip when the viewer moves the mouse over the event marker, and is also displayed at the top of the event content section. Also assign a name to each period, such as 1300s, 1600s, 1800s, etc. Period names are displayed on the graphic timeline.

- **Text:** Write a text description for each event. Remember that the viewer gets information by clicking an event, not a period. Consequently, there are no text descriptions (or audio or media) for periods as a whole. Describe the event using paragraphs and/or bullet points. You can also include links to more information and to other events in the interaction.

- **Audio:** Each event can include one audio clip. You can use audio to narrate the description of the event or to add descriptive sound effects. In general, if one event is narrated, then all events should be. Otherwise, the viewer might think that the audio is "not working" for specific events. If you choose not to include audio in the events, you might consider narrating just the introduction.

■ **Media:** Each event can include one media file, such as a picture, graph, video, screen capture, or diagram. In most cases, you can also enable the viewer to enlarge (zoom into) the image by clicking it. Depending on the nature of your content, each event may or may not need a media file.

Determining Viewer Control

After planning the events and periods, think about how you want viewers to navigate the events in the timeline. If you want viewers to be forced to review one event before moving on to the next, then choose *linear* navigation. If viewers can pick and choose among various events, then choose *interactive* navigation. To remove all control from your viewers and automatically display the events for them, choose *presentation* navigation. Typically we recommend that you give viewers as much control as possible when navigating interactions.

Planning Additional Features

Engage offers a number of additional features and properties that you can customize for almost all interactions. Following are a few specific features you may want to consider as you plan your Timeline interaction.

■ **Introduction:** Optional. Appears as the first screen when the interaction is launched.

■ **Summary:** Optional. Appears as the last screen.

■ **Color scheme:** Affects the colors of the interaction player's components, such as the background and the navigation buttons. For the Timeline interaction, the color scheme also affects the tooltips, period text, and selected period text. (The background colors of the periods are controlled separately.)

■ **Layout:** Determines the placement of the text relative to the media file in a specific event (e.g., text left/graphic right). However, the placement of the timeline graphic (at the bottom of the player) cannot be changed.

■ **Period colors:** Determines the colors that will be used for the periods in the timeline. By default, each period in the timeline appears in a different color, and the event markers use the color of the period in which they are contained.

Starting a New Timeline Interaction

Opening a New Interaction

After you have planned the components and gathered content, you can start developing your timeline. Your first step is to open a new Timeline interaction:

1. Double-click the **Articulate Engage '09** icon on your desktop *or* select **Articulate Engage '09** from the appropriate folder on the Start menu.

2. Click **Create a new interaction** on the start screen.

3. In the New Interaction dialog box, click the **Timeline** tab and click **OK**.

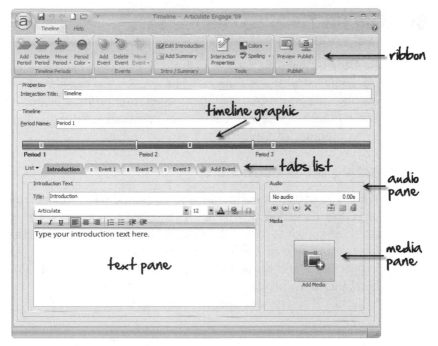

Figure 20.3. Timeline interaction window

The Timeline interaction window contains features standard to most interactions, such as the ribbon, Audio pane, and Media pane (Figure 20.3). The tabs list contains a series of tabs; each tab is used to build a separate event. By default, Engage provides placeholders for the introduction and three events (one event for each of three periods). A graphic representation of the timeline appears above the tabs list. You can use this timeline to select and move event markers, which are represented by tabs in the tabs list.

Entering the Interaction Title

The interaction title appears at the top of the Engage player when the interaction is running. By default, Engage enters the placeholder title text "Timeline." This title should be replaced to describe the purpose of the interaction, such as "An Early History of Computing." Keep in mind that you cannot format the text of the interaction title. However, the Colors and Effects tab in the Interaction Properties dialog box enables you to select a different font style for the title.

Building the Timeline Components

Building the timeline components involves modifying the existing placeholders for the introduction and events. You can also add new events and periods, and customize event properties. Clicking a marker in the timeline graphic or clicking an event tab enables you to create the content for that event.

Creating the Introduction

When you open a new Timeline interaction, the Introduction tab is displayed with the default "Introduction" placeholder text selected. The introduction is not part of the graphic timeline during the running interaction. Instead, the introduction content is presented when the interaction is first opened. It's also available by clicking the Previous button until the beginning of the interaction is reached or by clicking a hyperlink if you include one.

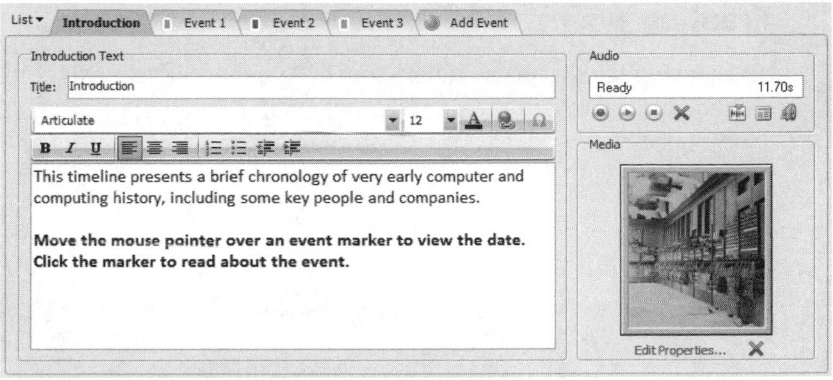

Figure 20.4. Introduction completed

To create the Introduction:

1. If desired, replace the "Introduction" placeholder text in the Title field with a meaningful description.

2. Replace the "Type your introduction text here" placeholder with your content. Remember, you can format the text using the toolbars above the text area.

3. Use the Audio pane to record or select an audio file, if desired.

4. Use the Media pane to add a picture, photo, or video, if desired.

See Figure 20.4 for an example of a completed introduction.

Note: Chapter 15, "Engage Basics," provides detailed instructions for working with text, audio, and media.

Tip: After completing the introduction and moving on to other steps, you can quickly return to the Introduction tab by clicking the Edit Introduction button on the ribbon.

Creating Events

Engage includes placeholders for three events. Each event tab is color coded to represent the period in which it is located. For example, the default title on the Event 1 tab contains a green square to match the color of Period 1.

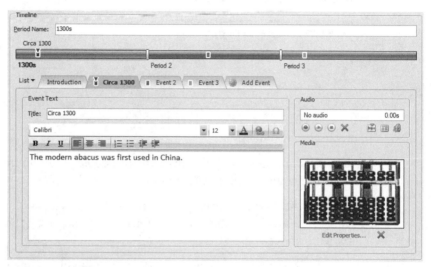

Figure 20.5. Event 1 completed

To create the first event, just open the Event 1 tab and edit the default content:

1. Click the **Event 1** tab in the tabs list *or* click the event marker in **Period 1** of the timeline graphic.

2. Replace the "Event 1" placeholder text in the Title field with a meaningful description, such as **Circa 1300**. The title text will appear at the top of the event in the Engage player when the event is selected. It will also appear as a tooltip when the viewer positions the mouse pointer over the event marker.

3. Add text, audio, and a media file, as appropriate.

Now you can create the remaining events using the same procedures as above:

4. Click the **Event 2** tab and enter your content.

5. To add more events, click the **Add Event** tab or the **Add Event** button on the ribbon. A new event tab will be inserted at the end of the tabs list, and the event will be positioned in the last period of the timeline by default.

See Figure 20.5 for an example of a completed event.

Moving Events

As you create and add events, you may need to move them to different locations on the timeline. Events can be moved within the same period and to other periods. If you move an event to a different time period, the color-coded square on the event tab is automatically changed to match the corresponding time period.

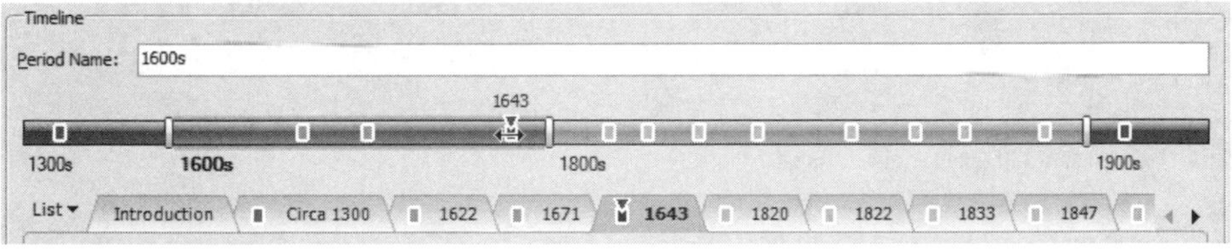

Figure 20.6. Moving an event by dragging its marker

Engage offers several ways to move an event:

- Drag the event marker on the timeline graphic to a new location (Figure 20.6).

- Drag an event tab in the tabs list to a new location.

- Click an event tab, click the **Move Event** button on the ribbon (Figure 20.7), and select **Left** or **Right**.

Naming Periods

As we've discussed, the periods in the timeline serve as containers for the events—they enable events to be grouped within a smaller time section of the timeline. However, periods do not contain any content, except for the period name. As you build the interaction, you will probably want to change the default period names to something more meaningful, such as 1300s, 1600s, and 1800s. The period names are displayed on the timeline graphic.

To name a period:

1. On the timeline graphic (above the tabs list), click anywhere on the period you want to name.

2. Replace the placeholder text in the Period Name field with a meaningful description, such as **1300s**.

If your interaction requires more than the three default periods, you can easily add more periods by clicking the **Add Period** button on the ribbon (Figure 20.7). A new period is then added to the end of the timeline, and the original periods are resized to accommodate the new one. You can move the new period to a different location, if desired.

Figure 20.7. Engage ribbon Timeline tab

Moving and Resizing Periods

Engage enables you to rearrange periods along the timeline using the Move Period button on the ribbon (Figure 20.7). When you move a period, all of the associated events are moved with it. You can also increase and decrease the length or "duration" of a period to accommodate the event markers.

To move a period:

1. In the timeline graphic above the tabs list, click the period you want to move.

2. Click the **Move Period** button on the ribbon, and select **Left** or **Right**.

3. To move the period more than one place on the timeline, repeat step 2 above.

The event tabs in the tabs list are automatically rearranged to match the new position of the period.

To resize a period:

In the timeline graphic above the tabs list, drag the vertical spacer between two periods.

Note that the size of the entire timeline is fixed. Consequently, expanding the duration of one period automatically reduces the duration of the adjacent period.

Deleting Periods and Events

You can remove a period from the timeline if it is no longer needed—the events in the period and all associated content will be deleted. When a period is removed, the remaining periods are resized to accommodate the deleted period.

You can also remove one or more events from a period. When an event is removed, the remaining event markers stay in their original positions.

To delete a period:

1. In the timeline graphic (above the tabs list), click the period you want to delete.

2. Click the **Delete Period** button on the ribbon (Figure 20.7).

3. The Engage dialog box asks you to confirm the deletion. Click the **Yes** button.

If you change your mind and want to restore a period immediately after deleting it, click the **Undo** button 🔄 on the Quick Access toolbar.

To delete an event:

1. Click the tab of the event you want to delete. (You can also click the event marker in the timeline graphic, but markers are not labeled when they are not selected.)

2. Click the **Delete Event** button on the ribbon (Figure 20.7).

3. The Engage dialog box asks you to confirm the deletion. Click the **Yes** button.

If you change your mind and want to restore an event immediately after deleting it, click the **Undo** button 🔄 on the Quick Access toolbar.

Adding a Summary

A summary is optional for all interactions. You may choose to include one for a Timeline interaction to recap all of the segments in one screen. However, the summary is accessible to the viewer only by clicking the Next button after the last event is displayed, unless you include a hyperlink to the summary from within an event. A summary period or event is not displayed in the diagram itself, just as the introduction is not displayed in the diagram.

To add a summary:

1. Click the **Add Summary** button on the ribbon (Figure 20.7).

2. Add text, audio, and a media file using the same procedures as for building an event.

Tip: After the summary is completed, the Add Summary button on the ribbon changes to Edit Summary. You can use this button to make changes to the summary at any time.

Customizing the Timeline Interaction

Engage enables you to customize the period colors, tooltip colors, and period text colors, as well as the standard interaction properties.

Customizing Period Colors

Engage uses default colors for the periods in the timeline. The event markers use the color of the period in which they are contained. You can easily modify the color of any period using the Period Color button on the ribbon (Figure 20.7). The colors of the associated event markers are automatically changed, too. (You cannot change the event marker color separately.)

To customize the period color:

1. In the timeline graphic (above the tabs list), click the period whose color you want to change.

2. Click the **Period Color** button on the ribbon (Figure 20.7).

3. Select one of the color options. Note that you cannot create your own custom color.

4. The timeline graphic (and the squares in the Event tabs) displays the new color. To modify the color of a different period, repeat the above steps.

66 **Note:** You can change the entire color scheme of the interaction (or create a new color scheme) using the Colors button on the ribbon.

Customizing the Tooltip and Period Text Colors

The color scheme you have chosen for the Timeline interaction affects many items, including the color of the tooltip that appears when the viewer moves the mouse over an event marker. The color of the text that appears inside the period label is also affected—one color is used for the static period text and another color is used for the text of the period that is selected. When you choose a color scheme, these and other items are automatically affected; however, Engage enables you to choose specific colors for these items by modifying those elements in the color scheme using the Color Scheme Editor (Figure 20.8). The procedures to create and edit color schemes are covered in detail in Chapter 15, "Engage Basics."

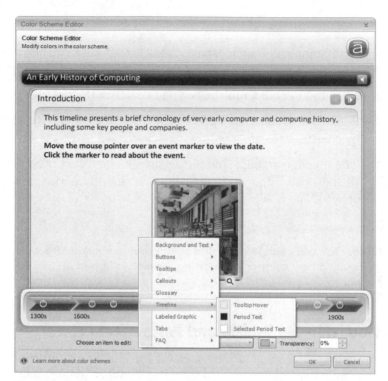

Figure 20.8. Timeline options in the Color Scheme Editor

Customizing General Interaction Properties

The Interaction Properties dialog box offers standard ways to customize all interactions, including the Timeline interaction. These standard options are covered in detail in Chapter 15, "Engage Basics." We suggest revisiting this dialog box to review its options. Unlike other Engage interactions, the Timeline tab in the Interaction Properties dialog box contains no options specifically for the Timeline interaction, other than the Player Features options.

Practice

Now's your chance to create a Timeline interaction using your own content. If you need an idea, think about the development stages of your company, or of your own professional growth. Each stage is a period on the timeline. Then, think of at least two major events for each period.

Building a Timeline Interaction

1. Plan the periods and events, and gather content.

2. From the Engage start screen, click **Create a new interaction**.

3. In the New Interaction dialog box, click **Timeline** and click the **OK** button.

4. In the Timeline interaction window, replace the text in the Interaction Title box with the title of your interaction.

5. Enter the text in the Introduction tab:
   a. Enter a title in the Title box.
   b. Enter text in the Introduction Text area.

6. Add an image to the introduction:
   a. In the Media pane, click the **Add Media** button.
   b. In the Select Image or Video File dialog box, browse to the folder containing your media files and double-click the desired file.
   c. In the Multimedia Properties dialog box, use the Position list box to change the location of the image, if desired, and then click the **OK** button.

7. Add an audio narration to the introduction:
   a. In the Audio pane, click the **Record** button ⊙.
   b. Using your computer's microphone, narrate the audio for the introduction. Click the **Stop** button ⊙ when you are finished.
   c. Review the audio by clicking the **Play** button ⊙.

8. In the timeline graphic, click **Period 1** and enter a period name.

9. Click the **Event 1** tab.

10. Enter a title and text to create the first event. Add audio and a media file, if desired.

11. In the timeline graphic, drag the event marker in Period 2 to the first period.

12. Enter a title and text to create the second event. Add audio and a media file, if desired.

13. In the timeline graphic, click **Period 2**, click the **Delete Period** button on the ribbon, and then click the **Yes** button.

14. In the timeline graphic, click **Period 3** and enter a period name.

15. Enter a title and text for Event 3.

16. Click the **Add Event** button on the ribbon, and then enter a title and text for Event 4.

17. If desired, use the **Add Period** and **Add Event** buttons on the ribbon to add more periods and events.

18. In the timeline graphic, click the first period, click the **Period Color** button on the ribbon, and select a different color.

19. Click the **Colors** button on the ribbon, and select a different color scheme for the player features.

20. Preview the interaction by clicking the **Preview** button on the ribbon.

21. Close the Interaction Preview window.

22. Save the interaction:
    a. Click the **Save** button 🖫 on the Quick Access toolbar.
    b. In the Save As dialog box, enter a file name and location for the interaction.
    c. Click the **Save** button.

Chapter Recap

Here's our list of the most important things to remember from this chapter:

- The Timeline interaction provides a visual way for viewers to click their way through a timeline of chronological events.

- The Timeline interaction can also be used as a replacement for simple Process and Tabs interactions.

- The graphic representing the timeline is divided into periods. Each period contains one or more events, which are identified by markers.

- Events contain the content (text, audio, and media file) describing a specific item on the timeline. Periods are visual "containers" for one or more events.

- Viewers click a marker to obtain information about that event.

- The introduction and summary are not clickable areas on the timeline. They are accessible using the Previous and Next buttons or by including a hyperlink in an event.

- Build the timeline by selecting a period on the timeline graphic and then entering information into each Event tab in the tabs list.

- Add, move, and delete periods and events using the tools on the ribbon.

- You can customize the color of any period using the Period Color button on the ribbon. The color of the event markers within that period are automatically changed.

- You can customize the color of the tooltip and period text by modifying the color scheme.

- Use the Interaction Properties dialog box to customize standard player features, such as navigation control and the color scheme.

Chapter 21

Creating a Media Tour Interaction

Chapter Snapshot

In this chapter, you'll learn how to create a presentation of images and videos using the Media Tour interaction.

The concept of presenting a series of images and video files is nothing new. For years, viewers have been able to click their way through pictures and videos using a variety of players and applications, such as Flash and PowerPoint. The beauty of the Media Tour interaction is that the format and structure of an image/video presentation has already been created for you. By simply selecting media files, writing a caption, and (optionally) including audio, you can create beautiful presentations with lightning speed.

Figure 21.1. Media Tour interaction

What Is a Media Tour?

A Media Tour is a collection of related images and movie files presented to the viewer linearly. Viewers can click forward and back through the presentation and may have the option of playing and replaying the movies in the interaction. Although the Media Tour is the least "interactive" of all Engage interactions, it is a valuable tool for compiling a quick and simple series of media files.

Once you've built a Media Tour interaction, you can easily place it on a web page or insert it into a Presenter project. When you insert it into a Presenter project, you are effectively providing a "presentation within a presentation." One slide in the project contains an entire series of related images and movies.

How the Media Tour Works

When the Media Tour interaction is launched, the first media item is displayed (Figure 21.1). A caption appears below the media file, and audio can also be included. Viewers can then click the Next and

Previous buttons to view each media item (*linear* navigation mode), or you can change the navigation mode to *presentation* (which removes navigation control from the viewer). By default, Engage adds the *Click next to continue* tooltip when the tour is configured using linear mode. If a media item contains a .swf (Flash) file, the movie plays automatically. If a media item contains a .flv (Flash video) file, then either the movie plays automatically or the viewer must click a Play button to start it (that's your call).

Unlike other Engage interactions, such as the Process and Tabs interactions, viewers do not have the option to navigate the Media Tour by selecting a media item (like selecting a step in a Process interaction). Instead, the viewer navigates by clicking the Next and Previous buttons. If the Media Tour is configured in presentation mode, then the screens advance automatically. Also, unlike many other Engage interactions, the Media Tour does not contain a formal introduction item and a formal summary item. To provide this type of content, you use a regular media item template—the first media item is the introduction and the last media item is the summary.

Real-Life Examples

The Media Tour is a great tool for providing a rich visual presentation about a specific subject. Here are some of our favorite examples of this type of interaction:

- Highlights of a new software application using representative screenshots
- Photographs and videos of a geographical area
- Corporate events and projects
- An image-based "how to" manual, with limited text
- A pictorial "story" of a journey
- Company product categories
- An employee recognition presentation

The example used in this chapter presents a slide slow of a company's community service project.

Planning the Media Tour

Planning the design of a Media Tour interaction involves deciding on the images and movie files you want in the presentation, as well as the accompanying captions and audio. Remember that the primary content mechanism is pictorial, not textual. So as you select each graphic file, make sure that it provides a rich representation of the event, place, or idea you want to convey. Captions and audio clips can complement each media file, but the graphics themselves should be telling the story.

Planning the Media Files

Each screen in the Media Tour is referred to as an *item* in Engage. The focus of each item is the media file (Figure 21.2), which takes up most of the real estate on the screen. You can insert only one media file per item. (If you want more than one image, then consider creating a collage of images that are saved as one image file.) Before jumping into the development tool, you should take some time to select, size, and organize the media files.

00:02 / 00:16

Change Media...
☐ Include Playbar   ☐ Auto Start

Change Media...

Figure 21.2. Image file (left) and video file (right)

Selecting Images

Images are centered vertically and horizontally within the Engage player. When creating or selecting an image file for a media item, keep the following in mind:

- Engage supports JPG, BMP, GIF, and PNG graphic file types.

- The optimal size for an image in the Media Tour interaction (with a caption) is 690 x 470 pixels.

- Engage will scale down images larger than 690 x 470, but will not scale up smaller images.

- You cannot resize images within Engage. If an image is the wrong size for the interaction, you need to resize the original image and then reinsert it into the media item.

- By default, Engage adds a drop shadow border around all images. You do not need to add them yourself to the images you select. However, if your images already contain borders or if you just don't want borders, you can turn off the default border.

Selecting Videos

Video files are also centered vertically and horizontally within the Engage player. When creating or selecting a movie file for a media item, keep the following in mind:

- Engage supports FLV (Flash video) and SWF (Flash) movie file types.

- The optimal size for a movie in the Media Tour interaction (with a caption) is 690 x 470 pixels.

- Engage will scale down movies larger than 690 x 470, but will not scale up smaller movies.

- You cannot resize the movie size within Engage. If a movie is the wrong size for the interaction, you need to resize the original movie and then reinsert it into the media item.

- When you insert a .flv (Flash video) file, you can choose to include a playbar for the viewer. This option allows viewers to control the playback, and so can be very helpful if you include longer movie files in the tour.

- When you insert a .swf (Flash) file, no playbar option is provided. The movie plays automatically when the media item is displayed and cannot be paused or stopped during the presentation. However, the viewer can simply click Next to move to the next screen.

Organizing the Media Files

Once you have selected the images and movies for the Media Tour, your next step is to decide how to arrange them. The media files will be viewed from beginning to end (or end to beginning), so it's important to arrange the files in a logical, meaningful order.

At some point, you'll need to decide whether to let the viewer navigate the tour using the Next and Previous buttons (*linear*), or to remove control from the viewer and display each item automatically (*presentation*). Unlike other Engage interactions, the Media Tour does not include an *interactive* navigation option, where the viewer can select any component of the interaction at any time. Although we are generally in favor of interactive and linear navigation, the Media Tour is a good candidate for an automatic presentation. If timed correctly and accompanied by quality audio, the presentation offers a valuable way to control the viewers' experience as you take them through your graphical journey.

Planning the Captions

Each media item can contain an optional caption, which is displayed below the media file (Figure 21.3). The purpose of the caption is to provide a brief snippet of information about the image or movie—it should *not* be used to provide detailed information about the media file. If you want a longer explanation, an accompanying audio clip is probably preferable. In a perfect world, the media file itself should do most of the "talking."

Enjoy the highlights of our annual community service project!

Figure 21.3. Media Tour caption

Planning the Audio

Audio is an optional feature for all Engage interactions, and some interactions are more conducive to audio than others. The Media Tour is a good candidate for audio because many people use the tour as a presentation. Just as someone showing slides from a visit to China wants to talk about each slide, the developer of a Media Tour (i.e., you) generally likes to provide an audio accompaniment for each image. But remember: If you insert a video file that already has audio, don't add additional audio via Engage. Both will play together, which is probably not the result you want!

Each media file can contain one audio clip. This means separate audio files are required for each media item. But what about playing one continuous audio file throughout the interaction? You can do this if you import the interaction (without any audio) into Presenter and add the audio to the slide containing the interaction. As you plan the audio for each media item, keep the following in mind:

- If you plan to offer the tour in presentation mode, make sure that the audio clip is not longer than the time you have selected to display each item.

- If a media item contains a movie file with sound, an audio accompaniment may not be necessary. However, an audio introduction (with instructions for playing the movie) might be appropriate.

Starting a New Media Tour

Opening a New Interaction

After you have selected and organized your media files, you can start developing the tour. Your first step is to open a new Media Tour interaction:

1. Double-click the **Articulate Engage '09** icon on your desktop *or* select **Articulate Engage '09** from the appropriate folder on the Start menu.

2. Click **Create a new interaction** on the start screen.

3. In the New Interaction dialog box, click the **Media Tour** tab and then click **OK**.

The Media Tour interaction window contains features standard to most interactions, such as the ribbon, the interaction title, and tabs list (Figure 21.4). By default, Engage provides placeholders for two media items, which are represented by tabs in the tabs list. The names of the media files are used for the tab names—these names do not appear when the interaction is running.

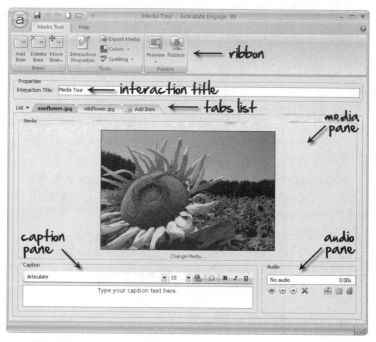

Figure 21.4. Media Tour interaction window

The Media pane is used to select the image or movie file. The Caption pane enables you to enter and format the text caption. The Audio pane lets you add an audio clip to accompany the media file.

Entering the Interaction Title

The interaction title appears at the top of the Engage player when the interaction is running. By default, Engage enters the placeholder title text "Media Tour." This title should be replaced to describe the purpose of the interaction, such as "Community Service Project." Keep in mind that you cannot format the text of the interaction title. However, the Colors and Effects tab in the Interaction Properties dialog box enables you to select a different font style for the title.

Building the Media Items

A media item consists of three major elements: the media file, caption, and audio clip. The only mandatory element is the media file. Engage provides placeholders for two media items, which contain sample media files. After replacing this file with your own image or movie, you then enter the caption and audio, if desired. Assuming your Media Tour needs more than two items, you add more items using the Add Item tab or the Add Item button on the ribbon.

In the running interaction, Engage displays the media items in the order they appear in the tabs list. So as you build media items, remember to position the items in the order you want them to appear.

Selecting a Media File

Each media item placeholder contains a sample image. Your first step is to replace this image with your own image or movie.

To select a media file:

1.   Click the **Change Media** link below the current image.

2.   In the Select Image or Video File dialog box, browse to the folder containing your media files. Note that you can use the Files of type list to display specific file types, such as .jpg or .flv files.

3.   Select the media file by double-clicking it.

4.   In the Engage dialog box, click **Yes** to confirm the selection.

The new media file appears in the tab in the interaction area, as shown in Figure 21.5. If necessary, you can replace the media file again by clicking the **Change Media** link. Note that the tab name changes to match the name of the media file. This name is not displayed during the running interaction.

Figure 21.5. Media file (image) inserted

Figure 21.6. Media file (video) inserted

If you select a .flv or .swf file, Engage includes small Play and Stop buttons to the right of the media file (Figure 21.6). These buttons are for development purposes only—they enable you to preview the movie file from within the media item tab.

If you select a .flv file, Engage includes two check box options below the file:

- **Include Playbar:** Select this check box to display a playbar (with Play/Pause button) for the viewer.

- **Auto Start:** If the Include Playbar check box is selected, then select the Auto Start option to have the movie file play automatically when the media item is displayed.

Note that if neither check box is selected, Engage plays the movie file automatically. The viewer has no control over the display.

Adding a Caption

When the Media Tour interaction is running, the caption appears in a horizontal box below the media file. If you leave the Caption text box blank, then the box is not displayed.

After replacing the "Type your caption text here" placeholder with your own content, you can format the text using the Formatting toolbar in the Caption pane (Figure 21.7).

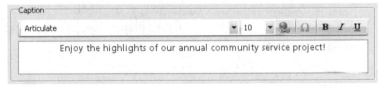

Figure 21.7. Caption completed

Note that you can also include symbols, as well as a link to other content. And although the Formatting toolbar does not contain alignment buttons, you can change the alignment using the following keyboard shortcuts:

- ▓ Ctrl+L — Left align
- ▓ Ctrl+E — Center align
- ▓ Ctrl+R — Right align

Chapter 15, "Engage Basics," provides detailed information about each button on the Formatting toolbar.

Adding Audio

As we discussed in the section "Planning the Media Tour," the Media Tour is a good candidate for audio. Each media item can be accompanied by one audio clip, which plays automatically when the media item is displayed during the interaction. Chapter 15, "Engage Basics," describes the details of recording, importing, and editing audio using the Audio pane (Figure 21.8).

Figure 21.8. Audio recorded

Adding New Items

Most Media Tour interactions need more media items than the two placeholders provided by Engage. By default, new items are added at the end of the interaction; you can then move the item to a different location, if needed.

To add a new item:

1. Click the **Add Item** tab in the tabs list *or* click the **Add Item** button on the ribbon (Figure 21.9).

2. Engage automatically opens the Select Image or Video File dialog box. Browse to the folder containing your media files. Note that you can use the Files of type list to display specific file types, such as .jpg or .flv files.

3. Select the media file by double-clicking it.

A new item tab is added at the end of the tabs list and the media file appears in the tab. The remaining procedures for creating the new media item are the same as those described earlier. Simply add a caption and audio, if desired, and the media item is done.

Figure 21.9. Engage ribbon Media Tour tab

Adding Several Items at Once

You can add several items at once by clicking the Add Item tab, then Ctrl+clicking each media file you want from the Select Image or Video File dialog box. Engage automatically creates a new item tab for each media file you select. For example, if you Ctrl+click three images in the dialog box and click Open, Engage creates three new item tabs—one for each of the images you selected.

Moving Items

During the running interaction, Engage displays the media items in the order they appear in the tabs list. Since all new items are automatically added to the end of the list, you'll probably need to move some items. A quick way to move an item is by using the mouse to drag the item's tab in the tabs list to its new location. Alternatively, you can use the Move Item button on the ribbon (Figure 21.9):

1. Click the tab of the item you want to move.

2. Click the **Move Item** button on the ribbon.

3. Click **Left** to move the item one position to the left. Click **Right** to move the item one position to the right.

4. To move the item more than one position, repeat steps 2-3 above.

Deleting Items

You can easily remove an item if it is no longer needed. However, you cannot remove items as a group. Only one item at a time can be deleted.

To remove an item from the interaction:

1. Click the tab of the item you want to delete.

2. Click the **Delete Item** button on the ribbon.

3. The Engage dialog box asks you to confirm the deletion. Click the **Yes** button.

4. To delete additional items, repeat the above steps.

If you change your mind and want to restore a deleted item, click the **Undo** button on the Quick Access toolbar.

Exporting Media Files

The Media Tour interaction offers an Export Media feature, which lets you create a copy of a media file in a media item, and store it outside the interaction. Why use this feature? For starters, if you happen to lose the source file you inserted into an item, you can easily create a copy of it. Also, after inserting a media file into an item, you might want to customize the image or movie. Instead of customizing the original source file, you can export a copy of the media file, make changes, and then reinsert it into the media item. That way, you don't need to change the original source file.

To export and modify a media file without changing the original source file:

1. Click the **Export Media** button on the ribbon (Figure 21.9).

2. In the Export File dialog box, browse to the folder to contain the file copy.

3. Enter a new file name in the File name box and click the **Save** button.

4. Open the file copy in a compatible editing program and make the desired changes.

5. In the Engage window, click the **Change Media** link in the media item tab and select the revised image.

Customizing the Media Tour

You can customize several properties of the Media Tour, including the caption height and caption background color. As always, you can also customize general properties of the interaction.

Customizing the Caption Height

Engage automatically adjusts the height of the caption area in the Media Tour interaction, depending on the number of lines and/or font size of the caption text. By default, the maximum height is 60 pixels, but you can adjust this height restriction to anywhere between 40 and 100 pixels. If the caption text requires more space than the defined maximum height, then Engage adds a vertical scroll bar to the caption area (not very attractive).

You can use the Interaction Properties dialog box (Figure 21.10) to change the maximum height restriction. Just make sure that the maximum caption height will not interfere with the displayed media file. Although the caption area background is somewhat transparent (thus allowing part of a covered media file to show), the best design practice is to prevent the media file and the caption area from overlapping.

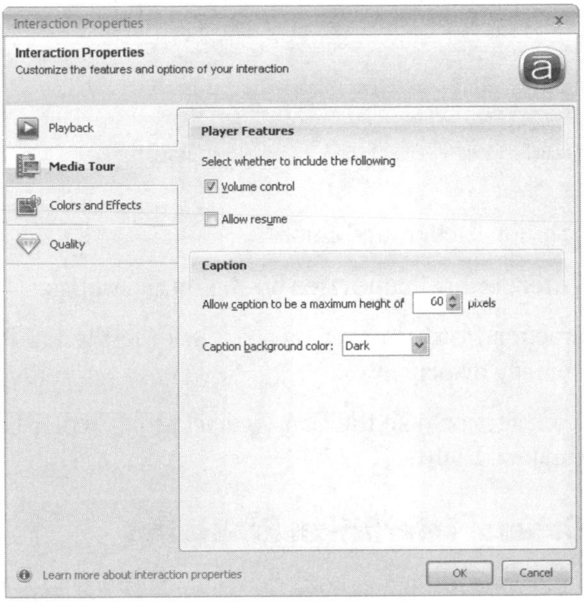

Figure 21.10. Interaction Properties dialog box Media Tour tab

To modify the caption height:

1. Click the **Interaction Properties** button on the ribbon.

2. In the Interaction Properties dialog box, click the **Media Tour** tab, if it is not already displayed.

3. In the Caption section, use the increase and decrease arrows to change the height in pixels, or just type a new number.

Customizing the Caption Background Color

The background of the caption area is dark (and somewhat transparent) by default. Engage offers two options for the background color: Dark (with light text) and Light (with dark text). Yes, dark and light aren't really "colors," but Figure 21.11 should give you a general idea of what we're talking about. The light background is a good choice when you can't avoid an overlap between the media file and the caption area. The transparency is greater in a light background, and thus the "covered" part of the media file is more visible.

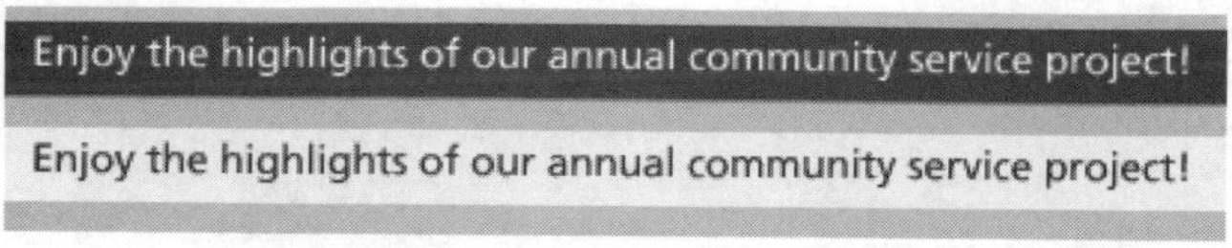

Figure 21.11. Setting the caption background color to Dark (top) and Light (bottom)

To modify the caption background color:

1. Click the **Interaction Properties** button on the ribbon.

2. In the Interaction Properties dialog box, click the **Media Tour** tab, if it is not already displayed.

3. In the Caption section, use the Caption background color list box to select **Dark** or **Light**.

Customizing General Interaction Properties

The Interaction Properties dialog box offers standard ways to customize all interactions, including the Media Tour. These standard options are covered in detail in Chapter 15, "Engage Basics." We suggest that you review these options and decide which features work best for your interaction. For example, you can change the interaction to *presentation* mode, which automatically advances each screen.

Practice

Now's your chance to create a Media Tour using your own content. If you need an idea, gather some stock photos and video files from a company's public relations department. Then, plan a presentation introducing the company to potential employees.

Building a Media Tour Interaction

1. Select and organize the media files, and plan the captions.

2. From the Engage start screen, click **Create a new interaction**.

3. In the New Interaction dialog box, click **Media Tour** and click the **OK** button.

4. In the Media Tour interaction window, replace the text in the Interaction Title box with the title of your interaction.

5. In the first placeholder tab, click the **Change Media** link.

6. In the Select Image or Video File dialog box, browse to the folder containing your media files and double-click an image file. (If prompted to overwrite the existing file, click the **Yes** button.)

7. In the Caption pane, replace the caption placeholder with your caption text.

8. Format the caption text by changing the font size to **12** and choosing **Bold**.

9. Add an audio narration to the item:
   a. In the Audio pane, click the **Record** button.
   b. Using your computer's microphone, narrate the audio for the introduction. Click the **Stop** button ⊙ when you are finished.
   c. Review the audio by clicking the **Play** button.

10. Click the second media item placeholder tab.

11. Repeat steps 5-8, except select a .flv (Flash video) file instead of an image file.

12. Click the **Play** button ⊙ to the right of the video file to preview the movie.

13. Select both the **Include Playbar** check box and the **Auto Play** check box.

14. Click the **Add Item** tab, and repeat steps 5-8 to create another media item. Add more items, if needed.

15. Using the mouse, drag one of the media item tabs to a new location in the tabs list.

16. After completing the labels, click the **Interaction Properties** button on the ribbon.

17. In the Interaction Properties dialog box, change the following properties:
    a. In the Media Tour tab, change the caption maximum height to **40** pixels.
    b. In the Media Tour tab, change the caption background color to **Light**.
    c. In the Colors and Effects tab, change the media border style to **Rounded Corners**.
    d. In the Playback tab, change the playback mode to **Presentation**.
    e. Click the **OK** button to save the changes.

18. Close the Interaction Properties dialog box and then preview the interaction by clicking the **Preview** button on the ribbon.

19. Close the Interaction Preview window.

20. Save the interaction:
    a. Click the **Save** button 🖫 on the Quick Access toolbar.
    b. In the Save As dialog box, enter a file name and location for the interaction.
    c. Click the **Save** button.

Chapter Recap

Here's our list of the most important things to remember from this chapter:

- A Media Tour is a collection of related images and movie files presented to the viewer linearly.

- Viewers can click forward and back through the presentation, and may have the option of playing and replaying the movies in the interaction. However, they cannot select specific items to view.

- The Media Tour interaction does not contain a formal introduction or summary. You may create them using a standard media item.

- Each media item consists of a media file (.jpg, .bmp, .gif, or .png image or .flv or .swf video), an optional caption, and an optional audio file. Add these elements using the tools in the media item's tab.

- Add, move, and delete media items using the tools on the ribbon.

- The Export Media button lets you create a copy of the media file in a media item. That way, you can modify it and reinsert it without changing the original source file.

- Use the Interaction Properties dialog box to customize features such as navigation control, color scheme, maximum caption height, and caption background color.

Chapter 22

Creating an FAQ Interaction

Chapter Snapshot

In this chapter, you'll learn how to create an FAQ (Frequently Asked Question) interaction, as well as explore the dos and don'ts of writing FAQs.

If you've surfed the Internet, you've probably experienced the sometimes helpful (sometimes not) FAQ page. The idea is to provide quick answers to questions that web page visitors ask most often, thereby offloading those pesky telephone calls to customer service. The FAQ interaction provides an easy way for viewers to scan a group of questions and then get answers with one mouse click. FAQs are also

803

searchable. But remember to think outside the interaction box—FAQs can also be used for "non-questions," such as a features list.

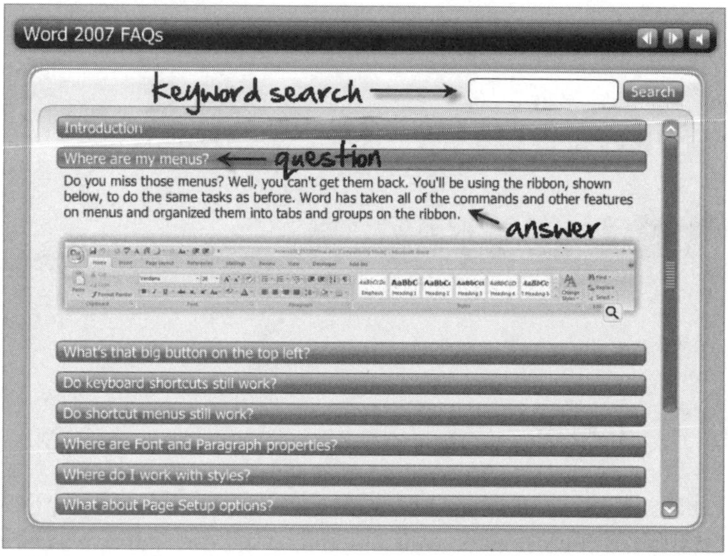

Figure 22.1. FAQ interaction

What Is an FAQ Interaction?

An FAQ interaction is a collection of clickable questions—clicking a question displays the answer. In Engage, each question typically consists of one short sentence, and each answer can consist of text, media, and an audio clip.

Developing an FAQ interaction in Engage is pretty straightforward. The real trick is figuring out what questions are "most frequently asked" by your viewers! In other words, an effective FAQ relies on your ability to get inside your viewers' heads and try to predict what they want to know. Sometimes this is just a matter of compiling a list of questions that your audience has really asked. More often, however, it's a matter of analyzing your content and the projected needs of your audience. You then come up with a "best guess" list of questions that addresses those needs. Later in the chapter, we'll give you some tips for coming up with really *useful* questions.

How the FAQ Interaction Works

The FAQ interaction screen displays a set of horizontal bars, with each bar containing one question (Figure 22.1). An optional Introduction bar may also be included at the top of the screen. Answers to the questions are not initially displayed (except for the introduction). If the interaction is published in *interactive* mode, viewers can click any question to display the answer. The answer is hidden when the viewer clicks another question bar.

If navigation buttons are included in the interaction, viewers can click the Next button to view the tabs—from top to bottom. If the search feature is included in the interaction, viewers can enter a keyword to search for questions addressing specific topics. As shown in Figure 22.2, the search results filter the FAQ list to display questions that contain the search text in *either* the question *or* the answer. Viewers can redisplay all questions by clicking the small close button ⊗ to the left of the search results text.

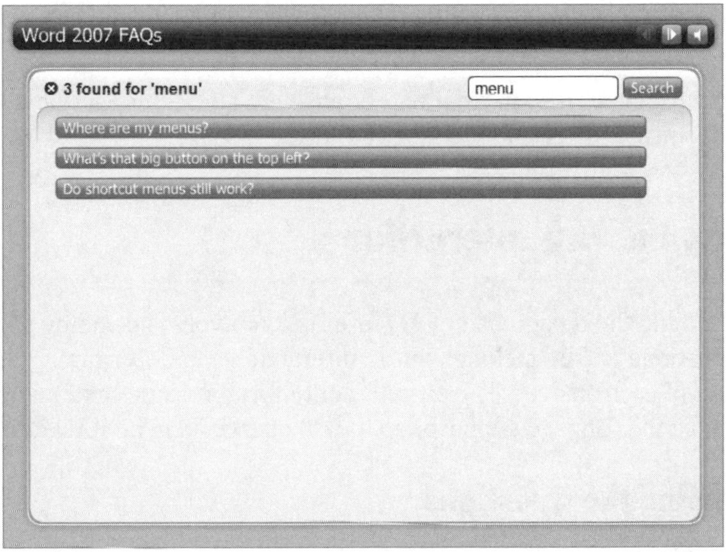

Figure 22.2. FAQ interaction search results

Real-Life Examples

As we've discussed, the FAQ interaction is a perfect tool for providing quick answers to simple questions. Keep in mind, however, that a "question" doesn't necessarily have to be in question format. This interaction has also been used as a creative alternative to the Process, Tabs, and Glossary interactions. Since the FAQ template contains placeholders for an item of interest and a description of that item, you can use this interaction for a variety of purposes.

Here are some of our favorite examples of this type of interaction:

- Troubleshooting procedures for a tech support team
- "Flashcard" review for corporate terminology
- Riddles and jokes (just for fun)
- Questions and answers about an employee benefits package
- Top 10 product features
- Self-check quiz
- Introduction to a course (Objectives, Audience, etc., are each a "question")

The example used in this chapter answers questions that new Word 2007 users often ask. We kept it short!

Planning the FAQ Interaction

Planning the design of an FAQ interaction involves deciding which questions will be included in the interaction and determining the content of each answer. The answer content can include text, audio, and a media file. Engage supports up to 500 questions in an FAQ interaction.

Planning the Questions

As mentioned earlier, the toughest part about planning an FAQ is deciding what questions to include. You might already have a list started, based on real questions from your audience. But if you're at a loss for where to start, think about questions that answer the *who*, *what*, *when*, *where*, *how*, and *why* of your content. For example, "Where do I go to sign in?" and "How do I find out how many hours I've logged?" Once you answer these basic questions, then it's just a matter of putting yourself in your audience's shoes and anticipating the more subtle questions they might have. For example, a frequently overlooked topic is "Why *can't* I [do so-and-so]?" One of the best gifts you can give your viewers is a clarification of the *cannots*, such as a nonexistent software feature or a company regulation.

Question Order and Viewer Control

Question order comes into play if you enable viewers to use the Next button to navigate the interaction—the answers to questions are displayed in sequence from top to bottom. As discussed in earlier chapters, you determine how the viewer can navigate the interaction by configuring the navigation mode as *interactive, linear,* or *presentation*. For a set of FAQs, interactive navigation is really the only way to go. Viewers are looking for something specific and need the freedom to select what they want. Linear and presentation modes are too restrictive for the purposes of an FAQ interaction.

Question Content

The content for the question component of an FAQ item consists of one sentence of text, usually in question format. From a technical standpoint, the question text can consist of up to 100 characters; from a design standpoint, questions should be concise, yet meaningful. Also keep in mind that Engage automatically shrinks the font size of questions that are longer than about 85 characters (Figure 22.3). So if you have some long questions and some shorter questions, the font sizes will be different on the interaction, which might not appeal to your sense of design.

How do I divide the current window so that I can scroll down one while the other window stays put?

Additional Resources

Figure 22.3. Long question (smaller font) vs. short question (regular font)

Planning the Answers

After you've determined the questions (or while you are determining them), you can plan the elements for the answers. Each answer can contain text, an audio clip, and a media file (Figure 22.4).

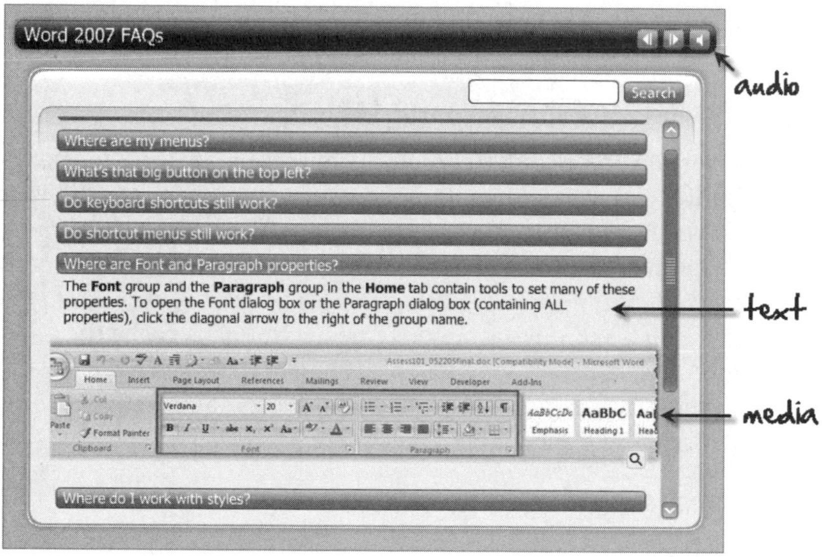

Figure 22.4. FAQ interaction answer content

Following are some guidelines for planning the answer content:

- **Text:** Don't be afraid to provide detailed explanations. After all, the reason most viewers are visiting the FAQ interaction is that they can't find the information they need elsewhere. You can arrange your content using paragraphs and/or bulleted and numbered lists. You can also include links to other information.

- **Media:** An image or a video can often help describe the answer or solution to a problem. Smaller images are preferable for FAQ answers, although Engage does make room for larger media files. Each answer can contain just one media file.

- **Audio:** Most FAQ answers don't need to be "narrated," but definitely include an audio accompaniment if your content calls for it. For example, an audio clip can identify the noise made by a broken piece of equipment or can serve as a guide for pronunciation. You may also consider using audio to narrate the introduction.

Planning Additional Features

Following are a few additional features you may want to consider as you plan an FAQ interaction.

- **Introduction:** Optional. Uses the same format as question/answer and is automatically displayed when the interaction is launched.

- **Summary:** Optional. Appears at the end of the FAQ list, but viewers typically aren't interested in a summary.

- **Color scheme:** Affects the colors of the interaction player's components, such as the background and the navigation buttons. For an FAQ interaction, the color scheme also affects the color of the question buttons and the question text. When planning a color scheme, note that each scheme consists of two colors: a dominant color and a complementing color. When the viewer clicks a question button, the color of the button changes from the dominant color to the complementing color.

- **Search capability:** Determines whether viewers can search for questions/answers based on keywords.

Starting a New FAQ Interaction

Opening a New Interaction

After planning your questions and answers, you're ready to develop the FAQ interaction. Your first step is to open a new FAQ interaction:

1. Double-click the **Articulate Engage '09** icon on your desktop *or* select **Articulate Engage '09** from the appropriate folder on the Start menu.

2. Click **Create a new interaction** on the start screen.

3. In the New Interaction dialog box, click the **FAQ** tab and click **OK**.

The FAQ interaction window contains features standard to most interactions, such as the ribbon, Audio pane, and Media pane (Figure 22.5). The tabs list contains a series of tabs; each tab is used to build a separate question/answer combination. By default, Engage provides placeholders for the introduction and two questions, as seen on the tabs list.

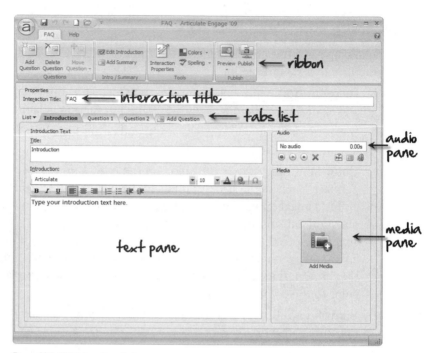

Figure 22.5. FAQ interaction window

Entering the Interaction Title

The interaction title appears at the top of the Engage player when the interaction is running. By default, Engage enters the placeholder title text "FAQ." This title should be replaced to describe the purpose of the interaction, such as "Word 2007 FAQs." Keep in mind that you cannot format the text of the interaction title using the Formatting toolbar. However, the Colors and Effects tab in the Interaction Properties dialog box enables you to select a different font style for the title.

Building the Questions

Building the questions involves completing a question tab for each question and answer set. Each tab enables you to enter the question text and the answer components, which can include text, media, and audio. You may also include an introduction and summary to the interaction. After completing the placeholder tabs provided by Engage, you can add more questions using the Add Question tab in the tabs list.

In the running interaction, Engage displays the questions from top to bottom, in the order they appear in the tabs list. So as you build the questions, remember to position them in the order you want them to appear.

Creating the Introduction

When you start developing a new FAQ interaction, the Introduction tab is displayed with placeholder text selected. In the running interaction, the introduction content is initially displayed in full at the top of the screen. It behaves the same way as other questions—when the viewer clicks another question bar, the introduction is hidden and the answer content for the selected question is displayed. It is generally helpful to include an introduction, although you can omit it.

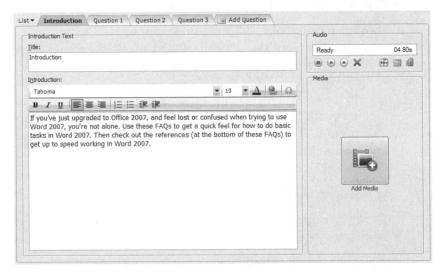

Figure 22.6. Introduction completed

To create the introduction:

1. If desired, replace the "Introduction" placeholder text in the Title field with a meaningful description.

2. Replace the "Type your introduction text here" placeholder with your content. Remember, you can format the text using the toolbars above the text area.

3. Use the Audio pane to record or select an audio file, if desired.

4. Use the Media pane to add a picture, photo, or video, if desired.

See Figure 22.6 for an example of a completed introduction. Note that we did not include a media file.

---

66 **Note:** Chapter 15, "Engage Basics," provides detailed instructions for working with text, audio, and media.

 Tip: After completing the introduction and moving on to other steps, you can quickly return to the Introduction tab by clicking the Edit Introduction button on the ribbon.

Creating Questions

Engage includes placeholders for two questions. To create the first question, just open the Question 1 tab and edit the default content:

1. Click the **Question 1** tab.

2. In the Question Text box, replace the "Question 1" placeholder text with the text for the first question, such as **Where are my menus?** The tab name then changes to reflect the question text, although the name might be truncated if the question contains more than about 40 characters.

3. Add text, audio, and a media file, as appropriate.

Now you can create the remaining questions using the same procedures as above:

4. Click the **Question 2** tab and enter your content.

5. To add more questions, click the **Add Question** tab at the end of the tabs list or click the **Add Question** button on the ribbon (Figure 22.8). A new question tab will be inserted at the end of the tabs list.

See Figure 22.7 for an example of a completed question.

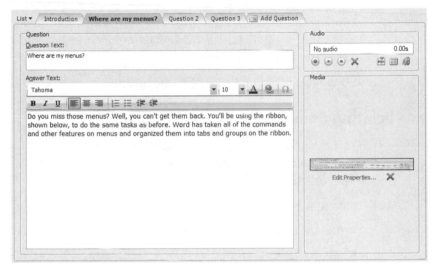

Figure 22.7. Question 1 completed

Figure 22.8. Engage ribbon FAQ tab

Moving Questions

The order of the questions in the tabs list represents the order in which the questions will appear in the Engage player (from top to bottom). You can quickly change the order of questions by dragging a question tab to its new location. Alternatively, you can use the Move Question button on the ribbon (Figure 22.8).

To reorder questions using the Move Question button:

1. In the tabs list, click the tab of the question you want to move.

2. Click the **Move Question** button on the ribbon.

3. Click **Left** to move the question one position to the left in the tabs list. (This results in moving the question *higher* in the list in the running interaction). Click **Right** to move the question one position to the right. (This results in moving the question *lower* in the list in the running interaction).

4. To move a question more than one position, repeat steps 2-3.

Deleting Questions

You can easily remove a question and all of its content if it is no longer needed. However, you cannot remove questions as a group. Only one question at a time can be deleted.

To remove a question from the interaction:

1. In the tabs list, click the tab of the question you want to delete.

2. Click the **Delete Question** button on the ribbon.

3. The Engage dialog box asks you to confirm the deletion. Click the **Yes** button.

4. To delete additional questions, repeat the above steps.

If you change your mind and want to restore a question immediately after deleting it, click the **Undo** button ↺ on the Quick Access toolbar.

Adding a Summary

A summary is optional for all interactions. Most FAQ interactions do not require a summary because viewers are generally focused on retrieving specific information. However, if your FAQ interaction calls for a summary, the steps for creating one are similar to those for creating the introduction.

To add a summary:

1. Click the **Add Summary** button on the ribbon. By default, the Summary tab is added to the end of the tabs list. It cannot be moved.

2. Enter the title, text, audio, and media file using the same procedures as those for building the introduction.

Tip: After the summary is completed, the Add Summary button on the ribbon changes to Edit Summary. You can use this button to make changes to the summary at any time.

Customizing the FAQ Interaction

You can customize several properties of the FAQ interaction, including the search feature and the color of the text on the FAQ buttons. As always, you can also customize general properties of the interaction.

Figure 22.9. Interaction Properties dialog box FAQ tab

Customizing the Search Feature

Engage lets you enable and disable the search feature. By default, this feature is enabled because most viewers like to search for specific topics. The search functionality is built into the interaction. After the viewer enters a keyword or phrase, Engage searches both the question text and the answer text for matches. It then displays a search results screen containing just the questions whose content matches the keyword or phrase. If you want to disable this feature, simply clear the Enable search check box in the FAQ tab of the Interaction Properties dialog box (Figure 22.9).

If the search feature is enabled, you can customize the search-related text that the viewer sees during the running interaction. The Search text refers to the label on the button that appears next to the search box. The default label is "Search," but you can change this to something else, such as "Find." The Result text refers to the phrase used to describe the results of the search. The default phrase is "found for" (as in 3 found for [keyword]), but you can modify or expand this. For example, "matching" (as in 3 matching [keyword]) (Figure 22.10).

To customize the Search text and Result text:

1. Click the **Interaction Properties** button on the ribbon.

2. In the Interaction Properties dialog box, click the **FAQ** tab, if it is not already displayed.

3. Use the Search text box and the Result text box to enter your customized text.

You will see the customized text when you preview or publish the interaction. Figure 22.10 compares the default and customized search text.

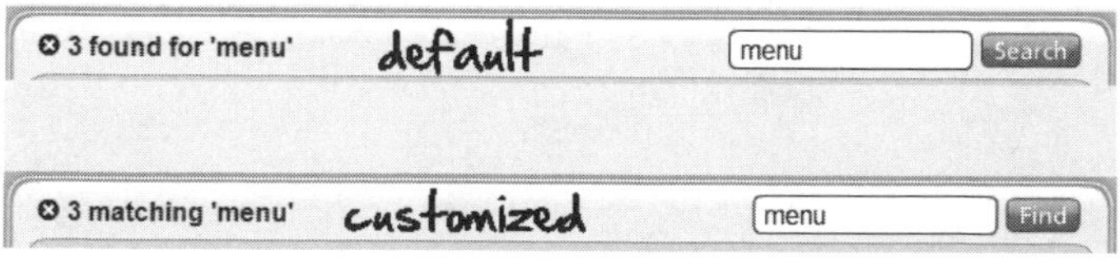

Figure 22.10. Default and customized search text

Customizing the FAQ Button Text Color

The color scheme you have chosen for the interaction affects many items, including the text inside the FAQ buttons. When you choose a color scheme, this and other items are automatically affected. However, Engage enables you to choose a specific color for the FAQ button text by modifying that element in the color scheme using the Color Scheme Editor (Figure 22.11). The procedures to create and edit color schemes are covered in detail in Chapter 15, "Engage Basics."

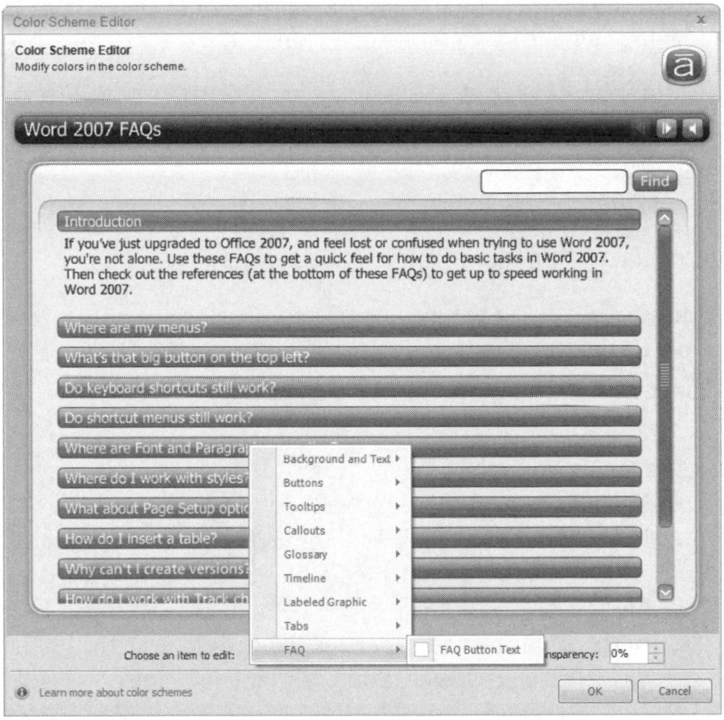

Figure 22.11. FAQ option in the Color Scheme Editor

Customizing General Interaction Properties

The Interaction Properties dialog box offers standard ways to customize all interactions, including the FAQ interaction. These standard options are covered in detail in Chapter 15, "Engage Basics." We suggest that you review these options and decide which features work best for your FAQ interaction. For example, you can change the entire color scheme using the Color Scheme list in the Colors and Effects tab.

Practice

Now's your chance to create an FAQ interaction using your own content. If you need an idea, think of the questions that a new employee in your department might ask.

Building an FAQ Interaction

1. Plan the interaction and gather content for the questions (text) and answers (text, audio, media files).

2. From the Engage start screen, click **Create a new interaction**.

3. In the New Interaction dialog box, click **FAQ** and click the **OK** button.

4. In the FAQ interaction window, replace the text in the Interaction Title box with the title of your interaction.

5. Enter the text in the introduction:
   a. Enter a title in the Title box (or keep the default, "Introduction").
   b. Enter text in the Introduction area.

6. Add an image to the introduction:
   a. In the Media pane, click the **Add Media** button.
   b. In the Select Image or Video File dialog box, browse to the folder containing your media files and double-click the desired file.
   c. In the Multimedia Properties dialog box, use the **Position** list box to change the location of the image, if desired, and then click the **OK** button.

7. Add an audio narration to the Introduction:
   a. In the Audio pane, click the **Record** button ⊙.
   b. Using your computer's microphone, narrate the audio for the introduction. Click the **Stop** button ⊙ when you are finished.
   c. Review the audio by clicking the **Play** button ⊙.

8. Create the first question:
    a. Click the **Question 1** tab.
    b. In the Question Text box, enter the text for the question (maximum of 100 characters).
    c. In the Answer Text box, enter the text for the answer.
    d. If desired, add a media file and/or audio clip by following steps 6-7.

9. Create additional questions using the **Question 2** tab and the **Add Question** tab.

10. After completing the questions, modify some of the interaction properties:
    a. Click the **Interaction Properties** button on the ribbon.
    b. In the Interaction Properties dialog box, click the **FAQ** tab if it is not already selected.
    c. In the Search section, change the Search text to **Look for.**
    d. Click the **Colors and Effects** tab.
    e. In the Color Scheme section, change the color scheme to **Green Forest.**
    f. In the Player Fonts section, change the Title font to **Arial.**
    g. Modify other properties, if desired, and click the **OK** button.

11. Preview the interaction by clicking the **Preview** button on the ribbon.

12. Close the Interaction Preview window.

13. Save the interaction:
    a. Click the **Save** button ▣ on the Quick Access toolbar.
    b. In the Save As dialog box, enter a file name and location for the interaction.
    c. Click the **Save** button.

Engage

Chapter Recap

Here's our list of the most important things to remember from this chapter:

- An FAQ interaction is a collection of clickable questions—clicking a question displays the answer.

- Although useful for "question and answer" types of content, the FAQ interaction is also a creative alternative to the Process, Tabs, and Glossary interactions.

- Each question consists of one text sentence up to 100 characters. Each related answer can consist of text, audio, and a media file.

- When planning your FAQ interaction, think about questions that answer the *who*, *what*, *when*, *where*, *how*, and *why* of your content.

- If navigation is set to interactive, viewers can browse the list of questions.

- By default, viewers can search the FAQs by entering a keyword. Entries containing the keyword in either the question or the answer are displayed.

- Use the tabs list to enter the content for each question and answer.

- Add, move, and delete questions using the tools on the ribbon.

- You can customize the labels used for the search feature, which includes the search text and the result text.

- You can customize the color of the FAQ button text by modifying the color scheme.

- Use the Interaction Properties dialog box to customize standard player features, such as navigation control and the color scheme.

Chapter 23

Creating a Pyramid Diagram Interaction

Chapter Snapshot

In this chapter, you'll learn how to use the Pyramid Diagram interaction to show the hierarchical relationships among objects or concepts.

The Pyramid Diagram interaction might trigger visions of the traditional food guide pyramids, released in various forms over the years by the United States Department of Agriculture. The food guides are a classic example of the visual power of the pyramid for depicting and quantifying hierarchical relationships. As you'll see in this chapter, however, the pyramid is a versatile tool for exploring a variety of concepts.

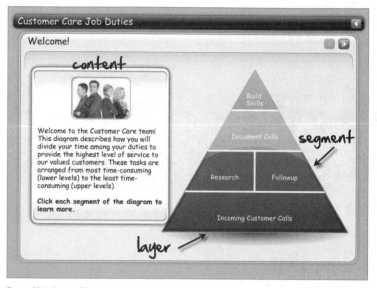

Figure 23.1. Pyramid Diagram interaction

What Is a Pyramid Diagram?

A Pyramid Diagram interaction uses a triangle graphic divided into segments to show the hierarchy of related items. If you've already read our chapter on the Circle Diagram interaction, you know that hierarchical items can also be depicted in circular layers. The main difference between the Pyramid Diagram and the Circle Diagram is that the Pyramid typically shows relationships among *quantities* of related items. Using the old food guide pyramid as an example, foods that should be consumed in the greatest quantities are represented by the base of the pyramid (the widest part). Quantities are then reduced as they move higher in the pyramid, with the really tasty stuff (meaning mostly off-limits) at the top.

The "quantity" representation offered by the pyramid is also useful for nonphysical models. For example, the varying levels of the pyramid can be used to compare levels of importance among related concepts. The levels can also be used to show steps in a process, similar to the Process interaction. In the Pyramid Diagram, steps that are more time-consuming (or more important) can be shown in the lower levels of the pyramid and steps that are less time-consuming (or less important) shown in the upper levels. Categories or departments can also be depicted using the pyramid if relative size or importance is significant—a viable alternative to the Tabs interaction. So as you plan your interactions for hierarchies, processes, and categories, we recommend weighing the benefits of the Pyramid Diagram interaction against the Circle Diagram, Process, and Tabs interactions.

How the Pyramid Diagram Works

When the viewer opens the interaction, the pyramid diagram and introduction are displayed on the screen (Figure 23.1). The introduction describes the purpose of the interaction and provides instructions for exploring the pyramid. Viewers can then click a *segment* of the pyramid to display the content callout related to that segment. A segment is one section of a *layer*, which represents a major hierarchical level in the pyramid. Each layer (except the top layer) can consist of one or multiple segments. The segments comprising the layers contain the "chunks" of information for the viewer.

In addition to clicking segments, viewers can click the Next and Previous buttons to navigate the pyramid. The top layer is displayed first, followed by the second highest layer, and down to the lowermost layer. If a layer has more than one segment, the segments are displayed from left to right.

Real-Life Examples

As we've discussed, the Pyramid Diagram interaction is an effective tool for presenting hierarchies in which quantities or levels of importance are significant. Here are some of our favorite examples of this type of interaction:

- Job duties performed by an employee (according to time spent or importance)
- Products offered by a company (according to quantity)
- Departments within a company (according to size or importance)
- Steps or procedures for performing a task (according to time spent or importance)

The example used in this chapter describes the job duties of a customer care representative according to time spent performing each duty.

Planning the Pyramid Diagram

Planning the design of a Pyramid Diagram involves determining the layers and segments comprising the pyramid, gathering the content for each segment, and deciding on additional features, such as layout and color scheme.

Planning the Layers and Segments

As we've discussed, the Pyramid Diagram consists of *layers* and *segments*. Each layer represents a hierarchical level in the pyramid and may be divided into multiple segments. A pyramid may contain a maximum of 10 layers below the top layer. A layer may consist of up to 20 segments. As you plan the pyramid, you need to decide what to include in the layers and segments. Table 23.1 provides a description of these elements.

Table 23.1. Pyramid Diagram elements

Element	Description
Layers	When planning the layers, think about the order in which they should appear in the pyramid. The largest (or most important) items should appear at the bottom of the diagram. The smallest (or least important) item should appear in one layer at the top of the diagram. For example, a pyramid describing the job duties of a new customer care associate might include Incoming Customer Calls in the bottom layer and Build Skills in the top layer.
Segments	Each of the pyramid's layers consist of at least one segment. (The top layer can contain *only* one segment.) In some cases, that's all you need. In other cases, it is more descriptive to divide a layer into several segments. In the customer care example, the time spent performing the job duties Research and Followup is about equal. In that case, it makes sense to divide the layer into two segments.

Gathering Segment Content

The content for a Pyramid Diagram interaction consists of the content for each segment callout, which can include text, audio, and one media file (Figure 23.2).

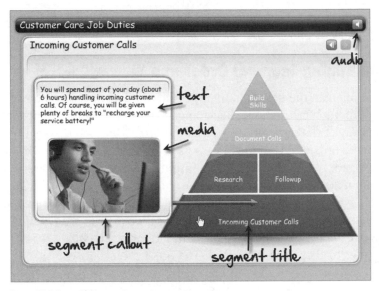

Figure 23.2. Pyramid Diagram interaction segment content

Following are the basic content components you'll want to think about when planning a Pyramid Diagram:

- **Segment title:** Assign a short title to each segment. This title appears directly on the pyramid (and at the top of the slide) and should clearly identify the item being represented.

- **Text:** Write a text description for each segment. Remember that the viewer clicks a segment for information, not a layer. Consequently, there are no text descriptions (or audio or media) for layers as a whole. Describe the segment using paragraphs and/or bullet points. You can also include links to more information and to other segments in the interaction.

- **Audio:** You can use audio to narrate the description of the segments or to add descriptive sound effects. In general, if one segment is narrated, then all steps should be. Otherwise, the viewer might think that the audio is "not working" for specific steps. If you choose not to include audio in the segments, you might consider narrating just the introduction.

- **Media:** Each segment can include one media file, such as a picture, graph, video, screen capture, or diagram. In most cases, you can also enable the viewer to enlarge (zoom into) the image by clicking it. Depending on the nature of your content, each segment may or may not need a media file.

Determining Segment Order and Viewer Control

As you plan the design of the pyramid, think about how the segments within each layer should be arranged. This arrangement affects the display of the pyramid, as well as the order in which the segment content is presented when viewers use the Next and Previous buttons to navigate. When the navigation buttons are used, Engage presents the segments from top to bottom, and from left to right within a layer. (However, you can customize this segment order.) Although you can control the navigation to be *interactive*, *linear*, or in *presentation* format, we recommend keeping the default interactive mode. Most viewers prefer to click the segments in the order they choose.

Planning Additional Features

Following are a few additional features you may want to consider as you plan your Pyramid Diagram.

- **Introduction:** Optional. Appears as the first screen when the interaction is launched.
- **Summary:** Optional. Appears as the last screen.
- **Color scheme:** Affects the colors of the interaction player's components, such as the background and the navigation buttons. (The colors of the layers are controlled separately and are not part of the color scheme itself.)
- **Diagram colors:** Determines the colors that will be used for the layers in the diagram. By default, each layer in the diagram appears in a different color, and the segments appear in different shades of that color.
- **Interaction layout:** Determines whether the diagram appears on the left or right side of the player.
- **Segment layout:** Determines the placement of the text relative to the media file in a specific segment (e.g., text left/graphic right).

Starting a New Pyramid Diagram

Opening a New Interaction

After you have planned the diagram components and gathered content, you can start developing your pyramid. Your first step is to open a new Pyramid Diagram interaction:

1. Double-click the **Articulate Engage '09** icon on your desktop *or* select **Articulate Engage '09** from the appropriate folder on the Start menu.

2. Click **Create a new interaction** on the start screen.

3. Click **Pyramid** on the left side of the New Interaction dialog box, and click the **OK** button.

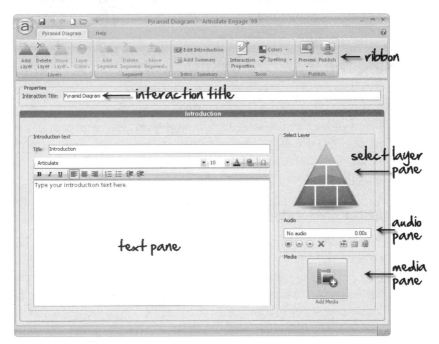

Figure 23.3. Pyramid Diagram interaction window

The Pyramid Diagram interaction window contains features standard to most interactions, such as the ribbon, Audio pane, and Media pane (Figure 23.3). The Select Layer pane enables you to select a layer to build. After you select a layer, the component tabs for the segments within the layer are displayed. By default, Engage provides placeholders for the introduction, the top layer, two lower layers, and segments within the two lower layers.

Entering the Interaction Title

The interaction title appears at the top of the Engage player when the interaction is running. By default, Engage enters the placeholder title text "Pyramid Diagram." This title should be replaced to describe the purpose of the interaction, such as "Customer Care Job Duties." Keep in mind that you cannot format the text of the interaction title. However, the Colors and Effects tab in the Interaction Properties dialog box enables you to select a different font style for the title.

Building the Pyramid Components

Building the pyramid components involves modifying the existing placeholders for the introduction, top layer, lower layers, and segments. You can also add new layers and segments, and customize layer properties. Clicking a layer (or segment) in the Select Layer pane enables you to work with all the segments in that layer.

Creating the Introduction

When you open a new Pyramid Diagram interaction, the Introduction tab is displayed with placeholder text selected. The introduction is not part of the graphic pyramid. Instead, the introduction content is presented when the interaction is first opened. Keep in mind that once viewers start interacting with the graphic, they can redisplay the introduction only by clicking the Previous button until they reach the beginning of the interaction. Or you can include a hyperlink to the introduction in one of the segments.

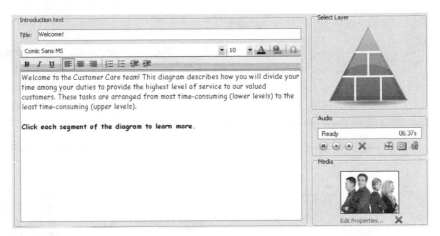

Figure 23.4. Introduction completed

To create the Introduction:

1. If desired, replace the "Introduction" placeholder text in the Title field with a meaningful description, such as **Welcome**.

2. Replace the "Type your introduction text here" placeholder with your content. Remember, you can format the text using the toolbars above the text area.

3. Use the Audio pane to record or select an audio file, if desired.

4. Use the Media pane to add a picture, photo, or video, if desired.

See Figure 23.4 for an example of a completed introduction.

Note: Chapter 15, "Engage Basics," provides detailed instructions for working with text, audio, and media.

Tip: After completing the introduction and moving on to other steps, you can quickly return to the Introduction tab by clicking the Edit Introduction button on the ribbon.

Creating the Top Layer

The top layer consists of a title and the content (text, audio, media file). This layer is slightly different from the lower layers because it consists of just one segment (Figure 23.5). You can't split the top layer into multiple segments. The procedures for creating the top layer are similar to those for creating the introduction.

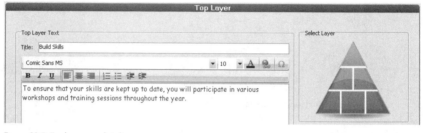

Figure 23.5. Top layer completed

To create the top layer:

1. In the Select Layer pane, click the top layer.

2. Replace the "Top Layer" placeholder text in the Title field with a meaningful description, such as **Build Skills**. This title will appear on the top layer of the pyramid diagram when the interaction is launched.

3. Add text, audio, and media, as appropriate.

See Figure 23.5 for an example of a completed layer.

Creating Lower Layers and Segments

As mentioned earlier, the lower layers of the pyramid can consist of just one segment or multiple segments. The actual content presented to the viewer is always contained in a segment. So you can think of segments as your building blocks for the layer content. When you select a layer to work with, tabs for each segment are displayed in the interaction work area. You can then add content to each segment tab.

Engage numbers the layers from the second highest layer of the pyramid down (keep in mind that the top layer is not numbered). In other words, the layer below the top layer is labeled Layer 1, the next layer is Layer 2, and so forth. These numbers are not visible to the viewer—they are for development use only and serve to identify the layer you are working with. The segments in a layer are initially numbered from left to right. However, these numbers are part of the default title text—you should change the titles as you develop your content.

To create the segments for Layer 1:

1. In the Select Layer pane, click any layer or segment.

2. In the interaction work area, click the **Segment 1** tab if it is not already selected.

3. Replace the "Segment 1" placeholder text in the Title field with a meaningful description, such as **Research**. The title text will appear in that segment of the pyramid when the interaction is launched.

4. Add text, audio, and media, as appropriate. See Figure 23.6 for an example of a completed segment.

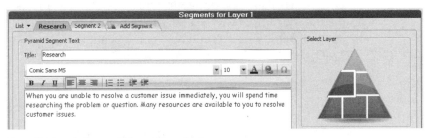

Figure 23.6. Layer 1, Segment 1 (Research) completed

5. Click the **Segment 2** tab and follow steps 3 and 4 above to create the second segment.

To add more segments to the current layer, do one of the following:

■   Click **Add Segment** at the end of the tabs list

■   Click the **Add Segment** button on the ribbon (Figure 23.7).

A new segment will be inserted at the end of the tabs list. Note that the other segments in the layer will be resized to accommodate the new segment. The diagram in the Select Layer pane gives a preview of the segment sizes.

Once you have created all the segments for Layer 1, click the next layer in the pyramid diagram in the Select Layer panel. Then create the segments for that layer using the same procedures described above. You can add more layers to the pyramid, if needed, by clicking the **Add Layer** button on the ribbon (Figure 23.7). Engage adds each new layer to the bottom of the pyramid. The example displayed at the beginning of the chapter (Figure 23.1) shows the completed pyramid with an additional layer.

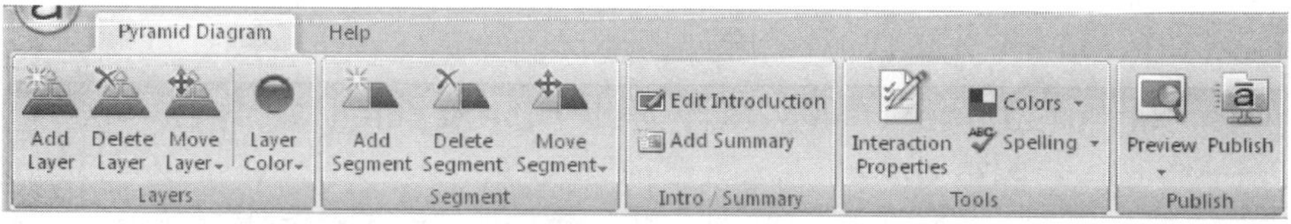

Figure 23.7. Engage ribbon Pyramid Diagram tab

Deleting Layers and Segments

You can remove a layer from the pyramid diagram if it is no longer needed—the segments in the layer and all associated content will be deleted. You can also remove one or more segments from a layer without deleting the entire layer. When you remove a segment, the remaining segments are resized to accommodate the deleted segment. Note that you cannot delete the top layer.

To delete a layer:

1.   In the Select Layer pane, click the layer you want to delete.

2.   Click the **Delete Layer** button on the ribbon (Figure 23.7).

3.   The Engage dialog box asks you to confirm the deletion. Click the **Yes** button.

If you change your mind and want to restore a layer immediately after deleting it, click the **Undo** button ↜ on the Quick Access toolbar.

To delete a segment:

1.   In the Select Layer pane, click the layer containing the segment you want to delete. (You can also click the specific segment in the diagram, although the segments are not labeled.)

2.   Click the tab of the segment you want to delete.

3. Click the **Delete Segment** button on the ribbon (Figure 23.7).

4. The Engage dialog box asks you to confirm the deletion. Click the **Yes** button.

If you change your mind and want to restore a segment immediately after deleting it, click the **Undo** button ↰ on the Quick Access toolbar.

Moving Layers and Segments

You can change the order of layers in the pyramid by moving them up or down in the diagram. Engage also enables you to change the order of segments within a layer, as well as move a segment from one layer into another layer. Note that you cannot move the top layer.

To move a layer:

1. In the Select Layer pane, click the layer you want to move.

2. Click the **Move Layer** button on the ribbon (Figure 23.7).

3. Select **Up** to move the layer closer to the top, or select **Down** to move the layer closer to the bottom.

The layers are automatically renumbered to reflect their new positions in the diagram.

To move a segment within a layer:

1. In the Select Layer pane, click the layer containing the segment you want to move. (You can also click the specific segment in the diagram, although the segments are not labeled.)

2. In the tabs list, click the tab of the segment you want to move.

3. You can move the segment using either of the following methods:

   ■ Using the mouse, drag the segment's tab in the tabs list to a different location.

   ■ Click the **Move Segment** button on the ribbon (Figure 23.7), and then select **Left** or **Right**.

To move a segment to a different layer:

1. In the Select Layer pane, click the layer containing the segment you want to move. (You can also click the specific segment in the diagram, although the segments are not labeled.)

2. In the tabs list, click the tab of the segment you want to move.

3. Click the **Move Segment** button on the ribbon (Figure 23.7), and then select **Up** or **Down**.

Engage resizes the segments in the affected layers to accommodate the change.

Adding a Summary

A summary is optional for all interactions. You may choose to include one for a Pyramid Diagram interaction to recap all of the segments in one screen. Keep in mind, however, that the summary is accessible to the viewer only by clicking the Next button after the last segment is displayed, unless you include a hyperlink to it within a segment. A summary layer or segment is not displayed in the diagram itself.

To add a summary:

1. Click the **Add Summary** button on the ribbon (Figure 23.7).

2. Add text, audio, and a media file using the same procedures as for building a segment.

Tip: After the summary is completed, the Add Summary button on the ribbon changes to Edit Summary. You can use this button to make changes to the summary at any time.

Customizing the Pyramid Diagram

So far you've learned how to build the basic components of a Pyramid Diagram interaction by creating the top layer, lower layers, and segments. Engage enables you to customize each layer by selecting a different color. For example, you might want to change the colors of the layers to match your company colors or to better represent the content of each layer.

Customizing Layer Colors

Engage uses a default color scheme for all the layers in the diagram. The segments within each layer appear in a different shade of the layer color. You can change the color of any layer, but you cannot change segment colors individually.

To change the layer color:

1. In the Select Layer pane, click the layer you want to customize.

2. Click the **Layer Color** button on the ribbon (Figure 23.7).

3. Select one of the color options. Note that you cannot create your own custom color.

The diagram in the Select Layer pane (and the title bar of the interaction work area) displays the new color. To modify the color of a different layer, select another layer and repeat the above steps.

---

66 **Note:** You can change the entire color scheme of the interaction (or create a new color scheme) using the Colors button on the ribbon. These procedures are covered in Chapter 15, "Engage Basics."

Customizing Pyramid Placement

The Interaction Properties dialog box contains standard options for customizing the interaction, as well as an option for customizing the position of the pyramid (Figure 23.8). The Pyramid Placement section lets you place the diagram on the right or left side of the Engage player while the interaction is running. The content appears on the opposite side of the diagram.

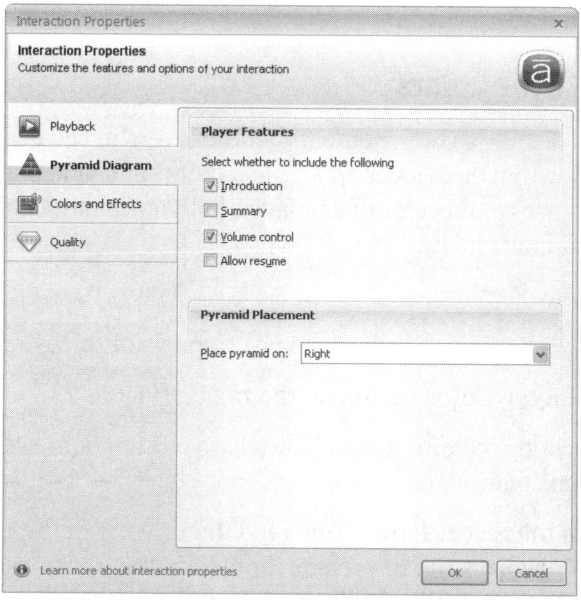

Figure 23.8. Interaction Properties dialog box Pyramid Diagram tab

To change the pyramid placement:

1. Click the **Interaction Properties** button on the ribbon.

2. In the Interaction Properties dialog box, click the **Pyramid Diagram** tab, if it is not already selected.

3. Use the Place pyramid on list box to select **Left** or **Right**.

You will see the new placement when you preview or publish the interaction.

Customizing Segment Order

You can control the order in which the segments of the pyramid are presented for viewers using the Next button to navigate the interaction. (This order also applies to presentation mode, when the Next button is not available.) By default, the segments are presented from top to bottom, and from left to right.

To change the segment order:

1. Click the **Interaction Properties** button on the ribbon.

2. In the Interaction Properties dialog box, click the **Playback** tab.

3. In the Segment Order section, use the list boxes to change the order:

   ■ Select **Top** or **Bottom**.

   ■ Select **Left to Right** or **Right to Left**.

You will see the new placement when you preview or publish the interaction.

Customizing General Interaction Properties

The Interaction Properties dialog box offers standard ways to customize all interactions, including the Pyramid Diagram interaction. These standard options are covered in detail in Chapter 15, "Engage Basics." We suggest that you review these options and decide which features work best for your interaction. For example, you can change the navigation mode or the color scheme.

Practice

Now's your chance to create a Pyramid Diagram interaction using your own content. If you need an idea, think about the duties you perform at your job. Then, develop a few simple layers and segments for each duty, using the lower layers of the pyramid for the most time-consuming or important duties.

▶ Building a Pyramid Diagram Interaction

1. Plan the top layer, lower layers, and segments and gather content.

2. From the Engage start screen, click **Create a new interaction**.

3. In the New Interaction dialog box, click **Pyramid** and click the **OK** button.

4. In the Pyramid Diagram interaction window, replace the text in the Interaction Title box with the title of your interaction.

5. Enter the text in the Introduction tab:
    a. Enter a title in the Title box.
    b. Enter text in the Introduction Text area.

6. Add an image to the introduction:
    a. In the Media pane, click the **Add Media** button.
    b. In the Select Image or Video File dialog box, browse to the folder containing your media files and double-click the desired file.
    c. In the Multimedia Properties dialog box, use the **Position** list box to change the location of the image, if desired, and then click the **OK** button.

7. Add an audio narration to the introduction:
    a. In the Audio pane, click the **Record** button ⦿ .
    b. Using your computer's microphone, narrate the audio for the introduction. Click the **Stop** button ⦿ when you are finished.
    c. Review the audio by clicking the **Play** button ⦿ .

8. In the Select Layer pane, click the top layer and enter a title and text.

9. In the Select Layer pane, click the layer directly below the top layer (Layer 1) and then click the **Segment 1** tab.

10. Enter a title and text to create the first segment. Add audio and a media file, if desired.

11. Create additional segments for Layer 1 using the above procedures. (Click the **Add Segment** tab to insert a new segment, if needed.)

12. In the Select Layer pane, click the next layer (Layer 2) and use the above procedures to create the second layer. Add additional layers, if desired, by clicking the **Add Layer** button on the ribbon.

13. In the Select Layer pane, click the layer directly below the top layer (Layer 1), click the **Layer Color** button on the ribbon, and select a different color.

14. Experiment with the Move Layer and Move Segment features (click the **Undo** button ⤺ on the Quick Access toolbar after each change if you want to restore the original position):

    ▪ Click the **Move Layer** button on the ribbon and select **Down**.

    ▪ Click a segment tab, click the **Move Segment** button on the ribbon, and select **Left**.

    ▪ Click another segment tab, click the **Move Segment** button on the ribbon, and select **Up**.

15. Preview the interaction by clicking the **Preview** button on the ribbon.

16. Close the Interaction Preview window.

17. Save the interaction:
    a. Click the **Save** button 🖫 on the Quick Access toolbar.
    b. In the Save As dialog box, enter a file name and location for the interaction.
    c. Click the **Save** button.

Chapter Recap

Here's our list of the most important things to remember from this chapter:

- A Pyramid Diagram interaction uses a triangle graphic divided into segments to show the hierarchy of related items.

- The Pyramid Diagram interaction typically shows relationships among *quantities* of items, both physical and nonphysical.

- The diagram consists of several layers. Each layer (except the top layer) can consist of multiple segments.

- Each segment can contain text, audio, and a media file.

- The introduction is displayed when the viewer first opens the interaction. Viewers then click a segment of the diagram to get more information, which is displayed in a callout.

- After creating the introduction, build segments by clicking a layer in the Select Layer pane and then using the tabs list to create each segment.

- Add, move, and delete layers and segments using the tools on the ribbon.

- You can change the color of the layers using the Layer Color button on the ribbon. Segments appear in different shades of the layer color.

- Use the Interaction Properties dialog box to customize features such as navigation control, the color scheme, and the placement of the pyramid (left or right).

Chapter 24

Creating a Guided Image Interaction

Chapter Snapshot

In this chapter, you'll learn how to use the Guided Image interaction to guide your viewers step-by-step through the components of a picture.

If you've ever tried to follow the "1-2-3" installation instructions that come with hardware equipment, then you'll appreciate the value of the Guided Image interaction. This interaction provides a simple, linear, and really cool way to point out significant features in one picture, one feature at a time. And with some imagination, you can take your viewers on a variety of journeys using one image—from a mail delivery route to a cross-country trip.

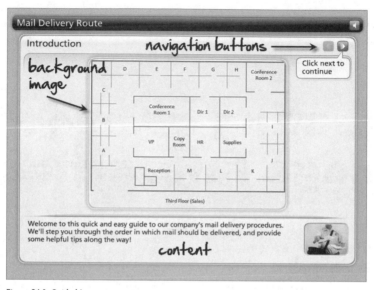

Figure 24.1. Guided Image interaction

What Is a Guided Image?

A Guided Image interaction steps viewers through various components of an image, one component at a time. Each component is identified by an animated arrow and is accompanied by a description, which can include text, audio, and a media file.

If you're familiar with other Engage interactions, you can think of a Guided Image as a cross between a Process interaction and a Labeled Graphic—but with a few unique characteristics. Like the Process interaction, the Guided Image presents content in a linear, step-by-step format. Like the Labeled Graphic, the Guided Image identifies parts of one background image. But unlike these other two interactions, the Guided Image is *not* designed for viewers to pick and choose what they want to see. Instead, viewers navigate the interaction from beginning to end. For this reason, the Guided Image is a good tool for controlling the delivery of a step-by-step procedure (or a process flow) that is centered around one image.

How the Guided Image Works

When the Guided Image interaction is launched, the background image and an introduction to the interaction (if included) are displayed (Figure 24.1). Viewers can then click the Next button to view the first component, or *label*, of the image. The label describes one area of the image and can consist of text, audio, and a media file. Unlike labels in a Labeled Graphic, the label content of a Guided Image appears in a separate section of the Engage player. An animated arrow marks the labeled area.

Viewers continue stepping through the image by clicking the Next button. Although they can return to previous labels using the Previous button, viewers cannot go directly to any label in the image. At the end of the interaction, a summary screen may be displayed.

Real-Life Examples

The Labeled Graphic is a great tool for stepping viewers through an image. Although this interaction is frequently used to describe procedures, Engage developers have come up with some pretty creative ideas. Here are some of our favorite examples of this type of interaction:

- Detailed explanation of a project schedule
- Step-by-step procedures for installing hardware
- Travel route on a map, with points of interest described
- Highlights of chronological events on a calendar
- Features of a new product
- Guided tour of a facility

The example used in this chapter steps the viewer through the mail delivery route using an office floor plan.

Planning the Guided Image

Planning the design of a Guided Image interaction involves selecting the appropriate background image, deciding which components of the graphic to describe or "label," determining the descriptive content of the labels, and planning the layout of the image, label content, and arrows.

Planning the Background Image

A Guided Image consists of just one graphic, which is referred to as the background image (Figure 24.2). This graphic forms the basis of the interaction—all labels are designed around the image components. Other images can be included in the label content, but they are visible to the viewer only when the label is displayed.

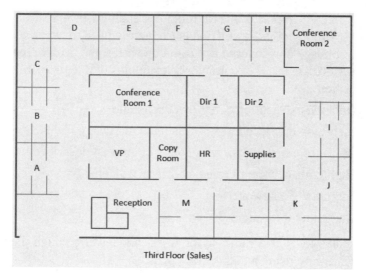

Figure 24.2. Background image

When creating or selecting the background image, keep the following in mind:

- Engage supports JPG, BMP, GIF, and PNG graphic file types.

- The optimal size for a background image is 690 x 470 pixels.

- Engage will scale down images larger than 690 x 470, but will not scale up smaller images.

- Select an image whose components are clearly visible. Although you can include an enlarged picture of a component in the label content, viewers should not have to strain to see the component on the background image.

Planning the Labels

Engage refers to the descriptions of image components as *labels*. However, don't confuse these labels with those used in a Labeled Graphic interaction. Labels in a Labeled Graphic appear as small "pop-up" windows directly on the background image. In contrast, labels in a Guided Image appear in a separate section of the Engage player—similar to the layout of a Circle Diagram or Pyramid Diagram interaction. Consequently, Guided Image labels can contain more content than their counterparts in a Labeled Graphic.

As you plan the interaction, consider which components of the diagram should be described. In step-by-step procedures, the procedures themselves usually determine what components of the image need to be highlighted. For other uses of the Guided Image, you might need to make some subjective decisions. For example, when tracing a journey using a picture of a map, which cities or points of interest should be included? Although it's okay if you don't cover every part of an image, some viewers might wonder why some components are described and others are not. Keep this in mind as you plan the component labels.

Gathering Label Content

Each label in the Guided Image can consist of a title, text description, audio clip, and media file (Figure 24.3).

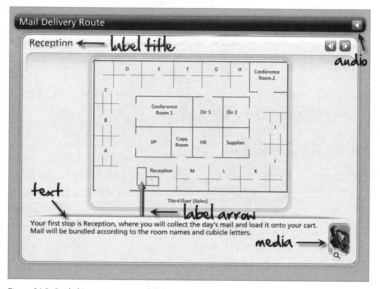

Figure 24.3. Guided Image interaction label content

Following are the content elements for the Guided Image labels:

■ **Label title:** Assign a short title to describe the image component or the step in the procedure. This title will appear in the upper-left corner of the content area when the interaction is running. Note that the label title does *not* appear directly on the background image. Instead, a label arrow automatically points to the labeled area.

■ **Text:** Most labels rely heavily on a text description. Describe the component or procedural step using paragraphs and/or bullet points. You can also include links to more information and to other labels in the interaction.

■ **Audio:** Each label can include one audio clip. You can use audio to narrate the description of the component or to add descriptive sound effects.

■ **Media:** Each label can include one media file, such as a picture, photo, or video. A good use of media in a Guided Image label is to provide a "zoomed" version of the component being described. The example shown in Figure 24.3 shows a picture of the receptionist in the reception area. Viewers can click the magnifying glass on the picture to enlarge the image.

Determining Label Order and Viewer Control

Because viewers are limited to navigating the Guided Image from start to finish, the order of the labels is important. For most Guided Images, the content drives the order, such as steps in a procedure or the chronological events in a process. When the order of labels is not important, consider the most logical order for your audience. For example, for a new product description, order the labels from the most important features to the least important.

When you develop a Guided Image interaction, you can keep the default *linear* navigation mode or change to *presentation* mode. *Interactive* mode is not an option for the Guided Image because the labels are not collectively displayed, as they are in a Labeled Graphic.

Planning Additional Features

Following are a few additional features you may want to consider as you plan your Guided Image interaction.

■ **Introduction:** Optional. Automatically displayed when the viewer opens the Guided Image. Although Engage refers to it as a label, the introduction does not reference a specific component on the background image. It explains what the viewer is about to learn or see, and can also include instructions about navigating the interaction.

■ **Summary:** Optional. Appears at the end of the interaction, but does not reference a specific component of the image.

■ **Color scheme:** Affects the colors of the interaction player's components, such as the background and the navigation buttons. (The colors of the arrows are controlled separately.)

Starting a New Guided Image

Opening a New Interaction

After you have planned the background image and the accompanying labels, you can start developing your Guided Image. Your first step is to open a new Guided Image interaction:

1. Double-click the **Articulate Engage '09** icon on your desktop *or* select **Articulate Engage '09** from the appropriate folder on the Start menu.

2. Click **Create a new interaction** on the start screen.

3. In the New Interaction dialog box, click the **Guided Image** tab and click **OK**.

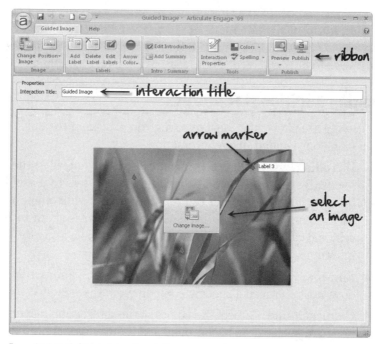

Figure 24.4. Guided Image interaction window

The Guided Image window contains features standard to most interactions, such as the ribbon, the interaction title, and the interaction work area (Figure 24.4). The Audio pane and Media pane are contained in the Edit Labels dialog box, which is available when editing a label.

By default, Engage provides placeholders for the introduction and three labels. Each label is marked by a small arrow on the background image. These markers do not appear on the image when the interaction is running. Instead, an animated arrow from the content to the marked area is displayed. The Change Image button is used to select the background image for the interaction.

Entering the Interaction Title

The interaction title appears at the top of the Engage player when the interaction is running. By default, Engage enters the placeholder title text "Guided Image." This title should be replaced to describe the purpose of the interaction, such as "Interaction Tour." Keep in mind that you cannot format the text of the interaction title. However, the Colors and Effects tab in the Interaction Properties dialog box enables you to select a different font style for the title.

Changing the Background Image

When you start a Guided Image interaction, Engage provides a background image by default. Your first step is to change the default background image by selecting your own picture. Engage supports images in JPG, BMP, GIF, and PNG formats.

To change the background image:

1. Click the **Change Image** button on the background image *or* click the **Change Image** button on the ribbon.

2. In the Change Background Image dialog box, browse to the folder containing your media files and double-click the desired file.

The new image appears in the interaction area and the Change Image button is removed (Figure 24.5). If necessary, you can change the image again by clicking the **Change Image** button on the ribbon.

 Note: When you change the background image, the random arrow marker positions will not be accurate. You'll learn how to move these markers later in this chapter.

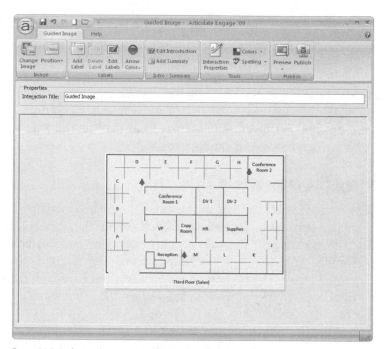

Figure 24.5. Background image selected (default arrow marker positions)

Setting Image Placement and Arrow Direction

The placement of the background image affects the layout of the label content and the direction of the arrows. For example, if the background image appears on the right side of the Engage player, then the label content will appear on the left side. This means that the arrows will automatically point to the right. It also means that any media files you insert in the label content will look best positioned at the top or bottom of the label content area. By default, the background image appears at the top of the Engage player, label content appears at the bottom, and arrows are pointing up. You can change this layout, if desired.

Figure 24.6. Position menu

To change the placement of the background image:

1. Click the **Position** button on the ribbon (Figure 24.6).

2. Select the background image placement: **Top, Left, Right,** or **Bottom.**

Engage automatically changes the direction of the arrows, based on the position of the background image. For example, if the image is placed on the right, then the animated arrows point to the right from the label content. Although you can change the placement of the background, you cannot modify the arrow direction associated with that placement.

 Note: You can also change the background image placement using the Guided Image tab in the Interaction Properties dialog box.

Building the Labels

The three arrow markers that initially appear on the background image represent the three placeholder labels provided by Engage. (The introduction is a special type of "label." It appears at the beginning of the interaction and contains a title and description, but no arrow.) You can use these placeholders to create your first three labels. A label *title* can be modified directly in the interaction work area by clicking the arrow marker and then entering different text in the title field. However, to modify the label *description*, you double-click the marker or click the Edit Labels button, which opens the Edit Labels dialog box. This dialog box provides a central place to create everything you need for the interaction.

Before learning how to create the labels and the introduction, let's explore the Edit Labels dialog box.

Exploring the Edit Labels Dialog Box

The Edit Labels dialog box enables you to create the introduction, create labels using the existing placeholders, and add new labels (Figure 24.7).

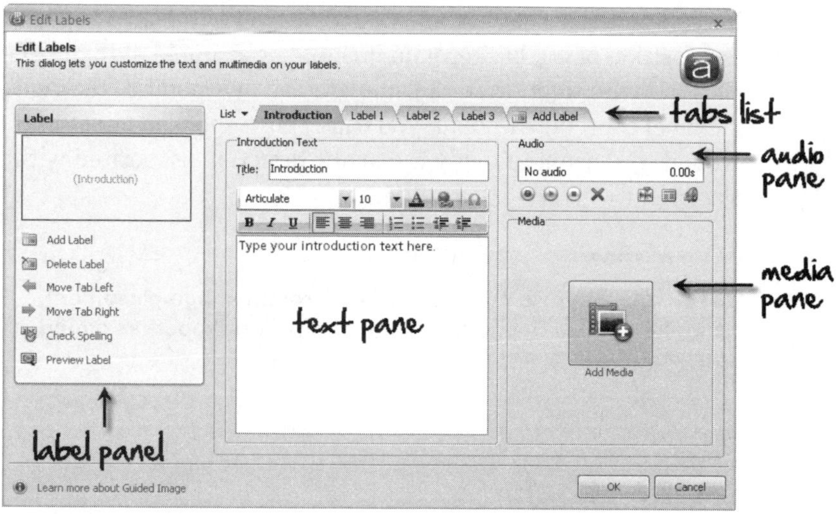

Figure 24.7. Edit Labels dialog box

You can access it using several different methods:

- Double-click an arrow marker on the background image.
- Click the **Edit Labels** button on the ribbon.
- Click the **Edit Introduction** button on the ribbon.
- Click the **Add Summary** button on the ribbon.

When you open the dialog box, the tab of the current label (or introduction or summary) is displayed in the tabs list. Table 24.1 describes each section of the dialog box.

Table 24.1. Edit Labels dialog box sections

Section	Description
Tabs list	Each tab represents a label in the interaction. Click a tab to work with that label. Click the Add Label tab to insert a new label.
Text pane	This section is labeled "Introduction Text," "Label Text," or "Summary Text," depending on the label type. Use this section to enter the label title (which will be displayed in the top-left corner of the content area when the interaction is running) and the text for the label description (which will be displayed in the label content area when the interaction is running).
Audio pane	Record an audio clip for the current label or import an existing audio clip. The audio is played when the label content is displayed.
Media pane	Click the Add Media button to insert a media file (picture, photo, or video) into the current label. Engage enables you to position the media file at the top, bottom, left, or right of the label description.
Label panel	These options enable you to add, delete, and move the selected label. A "close-up" of the label's position on the image is displayed at the top of the panel.

Creating the Introduction

As mentioned earlier, the introduction appears as the first screen when the interaction is first opened. You can use the introduction to describe the purpose of the Guided Image, as well as to provide instructions for navigating it.

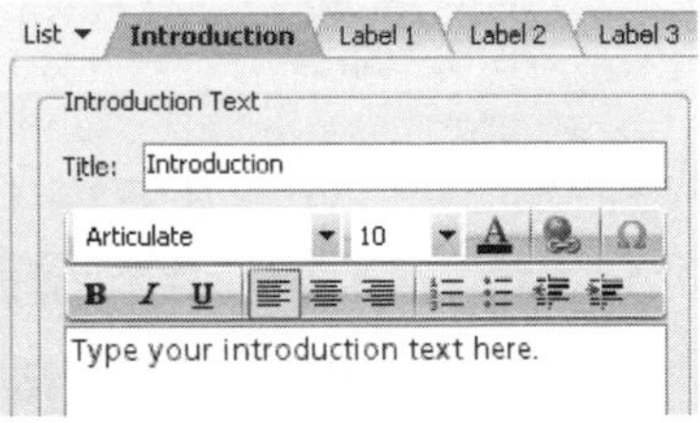

Figure 24.8. Introduction tab in the Edit Labels dialog box

To create the introduction:

1. If the Edit Labels dialog box is not already open, click the **Edit Introduction** button on the ribbon.

2. In the Introduction tab (Figure 24.8), replace the "Introduction" placeholder text in the Title field with another description, if desired.

3. Replace the "Type your introduction text here" placeholder with your content. Remember, you can format the text using the toolbars above the text area.

4. Use the Audio pane to record or select an audio file, if desired.

5. Use the Media pane to add a picture, photo, or video, if desired. Position the media file (top, bottom, left, or right) based on the orientation (horizontal or vertical) of the introduction content.

> **Note:** Chapter 15, "Engage Basics," provides detailed instructions for working with text, audio, and media.

> **Tip:** After completing the introduction and moving on to other steps, you can quickly return to the Introduction tab by clicking the Edit Introduction button on the ribbon.

Creating the Labels

The procedures for building the labels are similar to those for building the introduction. Keep in mind that the order of the labels in the Edit Labels dialog box indicates the order in which the labels will be displayed during the interaction.

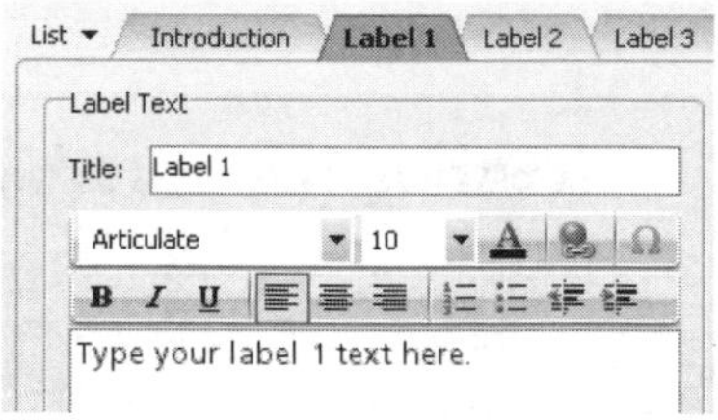

Figure 24.9. Label 1 tab in Edit Labels dialog box

To create a label using an existing placeholder:

1. If the Edit Labels dialog box is not already open, click the **Edit Labels** button on the ribbon *or* double-click an arrow marker in the interaction work area.

2. Select a label placeholder by clicking its tab in the tabs list (Figure 24.9). The Label panel then displays a close-up of the section of the background image that is referenced by the label.

3. Replace the "Label 1" placeholder text in the Title field with a brief description of the label.

4. Add text, audio, and a media file, as appropriate.

5. If desired, preview the label by clicking **Preview Label** in the Label panel.

Figure 24.10. Engage ribbon Guided Image tab

Adding New Labels

Chances are you'll need more labels than the placeholders provided by Engage. Once you add a new label, you can build the label using the procedures covered earlier. Labels can be added from either the interaction window or the Edit Labels dialog box:

■ To add a new label from the interaction window, click the **Add Label** button on the ribbon (Figure 24.10). Engage places a new marker on the image and displays the text box for the label title.

■ To add a new label from the Edit Labels dialog box, click the **Add Label** tab at the end of the tabs list or click **Add Label** in the Label panel. Engage adds a tab for the new label.

New labels are automatically placed at the end of the tabs list in the Edit Labels dialog box. That means the new label is the last label the viewer will see when navigating the interaction. You can change the order of labels and also move the arrow marker on the image if necessary. These steps are covered next.

Moving Arrow Markers

The arrow markers indicate the area of the background image that the animated arrows will point to when the interaction is running. Since Engage randomly positions the placeholder markers and new markers on the background image, you'll probably need to move them. Note that moving an arrow marker does *not* change the order in which the corresponding label will be displayed. If you want to change the order of the label content, you'll need to move the label tabs (covered in the next section).

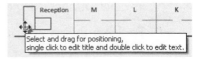

Figure 24.11. Moving an arrow marker on the image

To move an arrow marker on the background image:

1. Click the arrow marker you want to move.

2. Using the mouse, drag the marker to another location on the image (Figure 24.11).

Changing Label Order

Because the Guided Image interaction is completely linear, you need to specify the order in which the label content is displayed. The order of the label tabs in the tabs list (in the Edit Labels dialog box) reflects this order. To change the order, you just move the tabs. You can use the mouse to drag a tab to any posi-tion in the tabs list, as shown in Figure 24.12. You can also use the tabs list to change the label order.

Figure 24.12. Moving a label tab to change the label order

To change the order of labels in the tabs list:

1. Click the **Edit Labels** button on the ribbon (Figure 24.10).

2. In the tabs list in the Edit Labels dialog box, click the tab of the label you want to move.

3. In the Label pancl, click **Move Tab Left** to move the label one position to the left. Click **Move Tab Right** to move the label one position to the right.

4. To move a label more than one position, repeat step 3 above.

Deleting Labels

Deleting a label removes the label content and its associated arrow marker. You can delete labels from the interaction window or from the Edit Labels dialog box. Note that you cannot delete labels as a group.

To delete a label using the interaction window:

1. Click the arrow marker of the label you want to delete.

2. Click the **Delete Label** button on the ribbon (Figure 24.10) *or* press the **Delete** key on your keyboard.

3. The Engage dialog box asks you to confirm the deletion. Click the **Yes** button.

To delete a label using the Edit Labels dialog box:

1. Click the **Edit Labels** button on the ribbon.

2. In the Edit Labels dialog box, click the tab of the label you want to delete.

3. Click **Delete Label** in the Label panel.

4. The Engage dialog box asks you to confirm the deletion. Click the **Yes** button.

If you change your mind and want to restore a deleted label, click the **Undo** button 🔄 on the Quick Access toolbar.

Adding a Summary

If you choose to add a summary, keep in mind that it is accessible to the viewer only by clicking the Next button after the last label is displayed or by clicking a hyperlink if you provide one. The summary is not a component on the background image.

To add a summary:

1. Click the **Add Summary** button on the ribbon. By default, the Summary tab is added to the end of the tabs list in the Edit Labels dialog box.

2. Add text, audio, and a media file using the same procedures as for building any other step.

Tip: After the summary is completed, the Add Summary button on the ribbon changes to Edit Summary. You can use this button to make changes to the summary at any time.

Customizing the Guided Image

Engage enables you to customize several features of the Guided Image, including the image placement, arrow color, and size of the background image area. Earlier in this chapter, in the section "Setting Image Placement and Arrow Direction," we discussed how to change the placement of the image. (This decision often drives the layout of the content, so we thought we better mention it up front!) Now let's take a look at the other customization options.

Customizing the Arrow Color

By default, the animated arrows that appear during the interaction are blue. Note that this color is *not* tied to the color scheme of the interaction; you can customize the arrow color independently. Changing the arrow color changes the color of *all* arrows; you cannot use different colors for different arrows.

To customize the arrow color:

1. Click the **Arrow Color** button on the ribbon (Figure 24.10).

2. Select one of the color options. Note that you cannot create your own custom color.

The arrow markers on the background image change to match the selected color. To preview the animated arrows, you can click the **Preview** button on the ribbon.

Customizing the Background Area Size

By default, Engage allows the background image to occupy 75% of the interaction area. That means 25% of the interaction area can be used for label content. You can adjust these percentages (anywhere from 30% to 85%) using the Allow image to use box in the Appearance section of the Interaction Properties dialog box (Figure 24.13). For example, if your background image is relatively small and simple but the label descriptions are pretty hefty, you can allow the image to use 60% of the interaction size, thereby freeing up 40% of space for your content.

Figure 24.13. Interaction Properties dialog box Guided Image tab

To customize the background area size:

1. Click the **Interaction Properties** button on the ribbon.

2. In the Interaction Properties dialog box, click the **Guided Image** tab, if it is not already selected.

3. In the Appearance section, use the increase and decrease arrows in the **Allow image to use** box to change the percentage. Or just type a new number.

Note: Engage automatically increases or decreases the size of the background image so that it fits in the background area.

Customizing General Interaction Properties

The Interaction Properties dialog box offers standard ways to customize all interactions, including the Guided Image interaction. These standard options are covered in detail in Chapter 15, "Engage Basics." We suggest that you review these options and decide which features work best for your Guided Image interaction. For example, you can change the navigation mode or the color scheme.

Practice

Now's your chance to create a Guided Image using your own content. If you need an idea, take a screenshot of a calendar. Then, create labels describing major events that took place, in chronological order.

|||||▶ **Building a Guided Image Interaction**

1. Plan the background image and labels, and gather content.

2. From the Engage start screen, click **Create a new interaction**.

3. In the New Interaction dialog box, click **Guided Image** and click the **OK** button.

4. In the interaction window, replace the text in the Interaction Title box with the title of your interaction.

5. Click the **Change Image** button on the background image.

6. In the Change Background Image dialog box, browse to the folder containing your media files and double-click the desired file.

7. Change the position of the background image:
   a. Click the **Position** button on the ribbon.
   b. Select **Right**.

8. In the interaction window, click the **Edit Labels** button on the ribbon.

9. In the Edit Labels dialog box, enter the text in the Introduction tab:
   a. Enter a title in the Title box.
   b. Enter text in the Introduction Text area.

10. Add an audio narration to the introduction:
    a. In the Audio pane, click the **Record** button ◉.
    b. Using your computer's microphone, narrate the audio for the introduction. Click the **Stop** button ◉ when you are finished.
    c. Review the audio by clicking the **Play** button ◉.

11. Close the Edit Labels dialog box.

12. In the interaction window, drag the arrow marker for **Label 1** (far left) to its correct location on the background image.

13. Create the first label:
    a. Double-click the arrow marker for **Label 1**.
    b. In the Edit Labels dialog box, enter a short description of the label in the **Title** box.
    c. Enter text in the **Label Text** area.
    d. In the Media pane, click the **Add Media** button.
    e. In the Select Image or Video File dialog box, browse to the folder containing your media files and double-click the desired file.
    f. In the Multimedia Properties dialog box, use the **Position** list box to change the location of the image to **Bottom**, and then click the **OK** button.
    g. Use the Audio pane to include an audio clip, if desired.
    h. Close the Edit Labels dialog box.

14. Create additional labels using the above procedures. (Click the **Add Label** button on the ribbon to insert a new label.)

15. If necessary, change the order of the labels by dragging a label tab in the tabs list (Edit Labels dialog box).

16. Click the **Color** button on the ribbon and select a different color scheme.

17. Preview the interaction by clicking the **Preview** button on the ribbon.

18. Close the Interaction Preview window.

19. Save the interaction:
    a. Click the **Save** button 🖫 on the Quick Access toolbar.
    b. In the Save As dialog box, enter a file name and location for the interaction.
    c. Click the **Save** button.

Chapter Recap

Here's our list of the most important things to remember from this chapter:

- A Guided Image interaction steps viewers through various components of an image, one component at a time.

- Each component is identified by an animated arrow and a label. The label describes the component and is displayed in a separate section of the interaction.

- Viewers click the Next and Previous buttons to view the labels in linear sequence. They cannot go directly to a specific label.

- When planning the Guided Image, determine the content of each label and decide on the best placement for the background image.

- Before creating the labels, use the Change Image button to select the background graphic.

- If desired, use the Position button to change the placement of the background graphic. The arrow direction will automatically change based on the graphic placement.

- To work with all features of the labels on the graphic, double-click a label to open the Edit Labels dialog box.

- Each label description can contain text, audio, and a media file. Use the tabs list in the Edit Labels dialog box to create each label and the optional introduction and summary.

- Change the order in which the labels will be displayed by changing the order of the tabs in the tabs list. Move an arrow marker by dragging the marker on the image.

- You can customize many features of the Guided Image, including the arrow color and background area size.

- Use the Interaction Properties dialog box to customize standard player features, such as the navigation mode and the color scheme.

Chapter 25

Creating a Glossary Interaction

Chapter Snapshot

In this chapter, you'll learn how to create a set of terms and definitions using the Glossary interaction.

The glossary is a mainstay of technical and informational documentation. Whether it appears in one section at the end of a book or is scattered throughout a presentation, the glossary is an essential reference tool for your viewers. The Glossary interaction in Engage enables you to bring technical terms and acronyms to life, as you can include pictures, formatted text, and even audio in each entry. You can even use this interaction for other purposes, such as presenting short questions and answers.

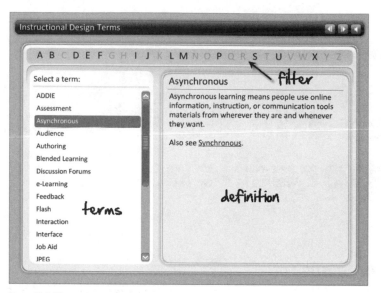

Figure 25.1. Glossary interaction

What Is a Glossary Interaction?

A Glossary interaction is a collection of clickable terms, such as technical jargon, acronyms, and cultural phrases. Clicking a glossary term displays the definition. In Engage, each term consists of a word or short phrase, and each definition can consist of text, media, and an audio clip. The definition can also include links to other glossary terms, web sites, and other resources. A great use of the Glossary interaction is to include it as a tab in a Presenter project. Viewers can easily access the tabbed glossary without leaving the current slide in the presentation. (For more information, refer to Chapter 6, "Pumping Up Your Presenter Projects.")

How the Glossary Interaction Works

When the Glossary interaction is launched, the set of terms is displayed in alphabetical order on the left, and an introduction to the interaction (if included) is displayed on the right. Viewers can then click a term on the left to view its definition on the right (Figure 25.1). Optionally, an alphabet bar that viewers can use to filter the terms may appear at the top of the interaction. For example, clicking the letter S filters the term list so that only entries beginning with the letter S are displayed (Figure 25.2). After filtering the term list, viewers can redisplay the entire list by clicking the Clear Results button.

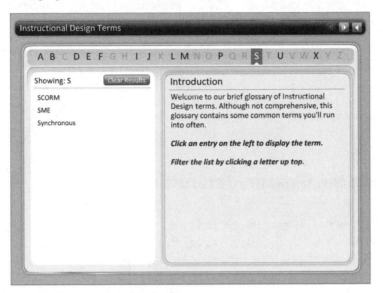

Figure 25.2. Glossary interaction filtered on S

If navigation buttons are included in the interaction, viewers can click the Next button to view the terms from the top of the list to the bottom. A summary screen may also be included at the end of the interaction, which is accessible only by clicking the Next button after the last term is displayed or from a hyperlink within a glossary item.

Real-Life Examples

A common use of the Glossary interaction is to provide a list of terms with associated definitions. However, with some imagination, you can create a glossary for other uses. Here are some of our favorite examples of this type of interaction:

- Short questions and answers
- Terms with associated antonyms and synonyms (like a thesaurus)
- Definitions of military/government acronyms
- Translation guide from one language to another
- Definitions of technical terms, with pictures and examples

- Definitions of stock market abbreviations
- Popular subjects with a list of links to related web sites

The example used in this chapter presents a brief list of instructional design terms and definitions.

||||▶ **Tip:** Check out Tom Kuhlmann's great article on the Word of Mouth blog: "Power Up Your Engage '09 Glossary Interactions by Using Hyperlinks" (http://www.articulate.com/blog/power-up-your-engage-09-glossary-interactions-by-using-hyperlinks).

Planning the Glossary Interaction

Planning a Glossary interaction requires some creative thinking. What terms should be included? (Engage supports up to 500 terms.) What terms *don't* need to be included? How can you make the best use of text, media files, and audio clips to define the terms? In addition to planning the glossary entries, you should also think about the general properties of the interaction, such as the color scheme and whether to include the filter feature.

Planning the Terms

Your first step in designing a Glossary interaction is to decide which terms to include. Of course, your content will drive these decisions, but here are a few tips to keep in mind:

- Keep the terms or phrases short. Although Engage accepts up to 100 characters, only 30 characters can be displayed in the term list (using the default term list width).
- If using the glossary to describe acronyms, consider spelling out the acronym in the term itself. That way, viewers can quickly get the general meaning of an acronym without having to click the term. The definition content can contain an expanded explanation of the acronym. However, do not spell out the acronym in the term if it will exceed the character limit accommodated by the term list width.

- It's okay to include a mix of one-word terms, phrases, and acronyms in one glossary.

Unlike other Engage interactions, you don't have to worry about what order to present the terms because Engage automatically sorts them alphabetically (Figure 25.3). No other sort options are available. And although you can change the default navigation from *interactive* to either *linear* or *presentation*, interactive navigation is the most logical choice for a Glossary interaction. In most cases, viewers need the freedom to choose specific terms.

Figure 25.3. Glossary terms

Planning the Definitions

After you've determined the terms (or while you are determining them), you can plan the elements for the definitions. Each definition can contain text, an audio clip, and a media file (Figure 25.4).

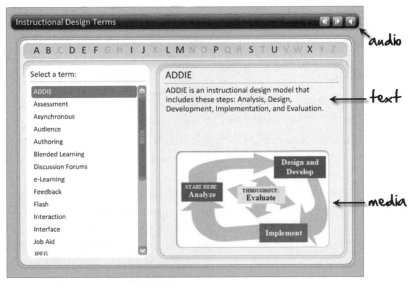

Figure 25.4. Glossary interaction definition content

Following are some guidelines for planning the definition content.

- **Text:** Glossary definitions are often formal and succinct, but they don't have to be. Often, a lengthier description is necessary, so don't limit yourself to a "one sentence or less" definition. You can arrange your content using paragraphs and/or bulleted and numbered lists. You can also include links to other glossary entries and to files outside the interaction.

- **Audio:** You can implement audio for a variety of purposes. For example, include an audio clip to repeat the term (for pronunciation), or to use the term in a sentence, or both. Sound effects can also be helpful, such as in a glossary of musical instruments. Each definition can contain just one audio clip.

- **Media:** An image or a video can often help describe the term, especially for technical nouns. Smaller images are preferable for definitions, and you can enable the viewer to enlarge, or zoom into, the image by clicking on it. Each definition can contain only one media file.

Planning Additional Features

Following are a few additional features you may want to consider as you plan a Glossary interaction.

- **Introduction:** Optional. Appears as the first screen when the interaction is launched.

- **Summary:** Optional. Appears as the last screen, although a glossary typically does not use a summary of terms.

- **Color scheme:** Affects the colors of the interaction player's components, such as the background and the navigation buttons. For a Glossary interaction, the color scheme also affects the rollover state of a term and the selected state of a term. When planning a color scheme, note that each scheme consists of several colors: a dominant color and complementing colors. For example, the Orange color scheme changes the background and navigation buttons to orange, the rollover state of a term to light blue, and the selected state of a term to dark blue.

- **Filter capability:** Determines whether viewers can filter the term list so that only terms beginning with a specific letter are displayed.

Starting a New Glossary Interaction

Opening a New Interaction

After planning your terms and definitions, you're ready to develop the Glossary interaction. Your first step is to open a new Glossary interaction:

1. Double-click the **Articulate Engage '09** icon on your desktop *or* select **Articulate Engage '09** from the appropriate folder on the Start menu.

2. Click **Create a new interaction** on the start screen.

3. In the New Interaction dialog box, click the **Glossary** tab and click **OK**.

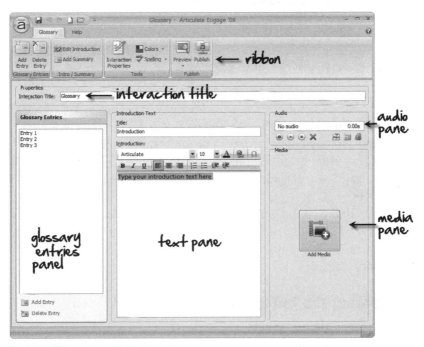

Figure 25.5. Glossary interaction window

The Glossary interaction window contains features standard to most interactions, such as the ribbon, Audio pane, and Media pane (Figure 25.5). The Glossary Entries panel lists placeholders for three glossary entries. New entries will also appear in this panel. The Text pane in the center of the window is used to add the text for the selected glossary entry, the introduction, or the summary.

Entering the Interaction Title

The interaction title appears at the top of the Engage player when the interaction is running. By default, Engage enters the placeholder title text "Glossary." This title should be replaced to describe the purpose of the interaction, such as "Instructional Design Terms." Keep in mind that you cannot format the text of the interaction title using the Formatting toolbar. However, the Colors and Effects tab in the Interaction Properties dialog box enables you to select a different font style for the title.

Building the Glossary Entries

Building the glossary entries involves entering the text for each term and adding content for each definition, which can include text, media, and audio. You may also include an introduction and summary to the interaction. After completing the placeholder entries provided by Engage, you can add more entries using the Add Entry button on the ribbon.

In the running interaction, Engage displays the terms in alphabetical order. So as you build the terms, Engage automatically sorts them in the Glossary Entries panel. You cannot rearrange the order of glossary entries.

Creating the Introduction

When you start developing a new Glossary interaction, the introduction is displayed with placeholder text selected. In the running interaction, the introduction content is initially displayed in the definition area. It is generally helpful to include an introduction, although you can omit it. If you omit the introduction, then the first term in the glossary is displayed when the viewer launches the interaction.

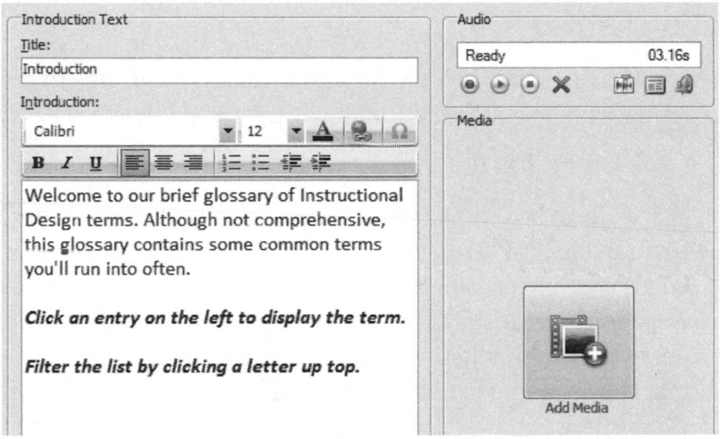

Figure 25.6. Introduction completed

To create the introduction:

1. If desired, replace the "Introduction" placeholder text in the Title field with another name.

2. Replace the "Type your introduction text here" placeholder with your content. You can format the text using the toolbars above the text area.

3. Use the Audio pane to record or select an audio file, if desired.

4. Use the Media pane to add a picture, photo, or video, if desired.

See Figure 25.6 for an example of a completed introduction. Note that this example does not contain a media file.

Note: Chapter 15, "Engage Basics," provides detailed instructions for working with text, audio, and media.

Tip: After completing the introduction and moving on to other steps, you can quickly return to the Introduction pane by clicking the Edit Introduction button on the ribbon.

Creating Entries

Engage includes placeholders for three glossary entries. To create the first entry, just select Entry 1 and edit the default content:

1. Click **Entry 1** in the Glossary Entries panel.

2. In the Term box, replace the "Entry 1" placeholder text with the text for the first term, such as **ADDIE**. The entry name in the Glossary Entries panel then changes to match the term text. Engage automatically sorts the entries in alphabetical order, so the entry's position might change in the list. (Note that you cannot format the appearance of the term text.)

3. In the Definition section, replace the "Type your entry 1 text here" placeholder with the content for the definition of the term. You can format the text using the toolbars above the text area.

4. Use the Audio pane to record or select an audio file, if desired.

5. Use the Media pane to add a picture, photo, or video, if desired.

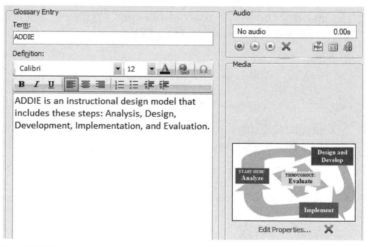

Figure 25.7. Entry 1 completed

Now you can create the remaining entries using the same procedures as above:

6. Click **Entry 2** in the Glossary Entries panel and enter your content.

7. To add more entries, click **Add Entry** at the bottom of the Glossary Entries panel or click the **Add Entry** button on the ribbon (Figure 25.8). A new entry will be inserted in its respective alphabetical position in the Glossary Entries list.

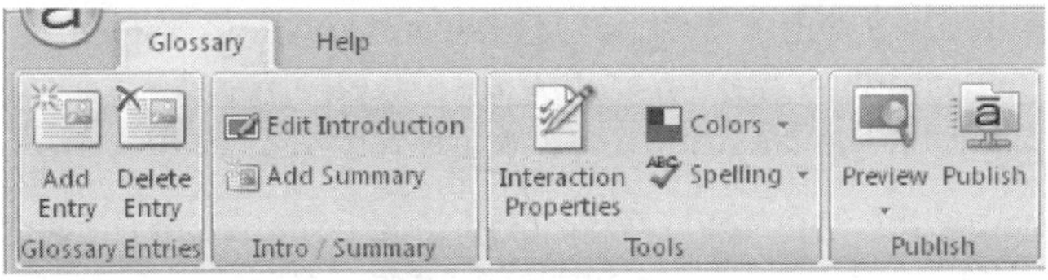

Figure 25.8. Engage ribbon Glossary tab

See Figure 25.7 for an example of a completed entry.

Deleting Entries

You can easily remove an entry if it is no longer needed. However, you cannot remove entries as a group. Only one entry at a time can be deleted.

To remove an entry from the interaction:

1. In the Glossary Entries panel, click the entry you want to delete.

2. Click **Delete Entry** at the bottom of the Glossary Entries panel *or* click the **Delete Entry** button on the ribbon (Figure 25.8).

3. The Engage dialog box asks you to confirm the deletion. Click the **Yes** button.

If you change your mind and want to restore an entry immediately after deleting it, click the **Undo** button ↺ on the Quick Access toolbar.

Adding a Summary

A summary is optional for all interactions. Most Glossary interactions do not require a summary because viewers are generally focused on retrieving specific information. However, if your Glossary interaction calls for a summary, the steps for creating one are similar to those for creating the introduction.

To add a summary:

1. Click the **Add Summary** button on the ribbon (Figure 25.8). A Summary entry does not appear in the Glossary Entries panel, but the Summary screen will be displayed after the last term is displayed if the Next button is used to navigate.

2. Enter the title, text, audio, and media file using the same procedures as those for building the introduction.

After the summary is completed, the Add Summary button on the ribbon changes to Edit Summary. You can use this button to make changes to the summary at any time. You can also hide or show the summary using the Glossary tab in the Interaction Properties dialog box.

Customizing the Glossary Interaction

You can customize several properties of the Glossary interaction, including the width of the term list, the search filter, and the color of a term based on its rollover state. As always, you can also customize general properties of the interaction.

Customizing the Term List Width

The term list width refers to the width of the area containing the terms, located on the left side of the running Glossary interaction. By default, Engage allows the term list to occupy 40% of the interaction area. That means 60% of the interaction area can be used for definition content. You can adjust these percentages using the **Allow terms to use** box in the Term List Width section of the Interaction Properties dialog box (anywhere from 20% to 60%) (Figure 25.9). For example, if your terms are relatively long (such as multiword phrases), but the descriptions are short and simple, you can allow the term list to use

55% of the interaction area. Consequently, the description content will occupy 45% of the interaction area.

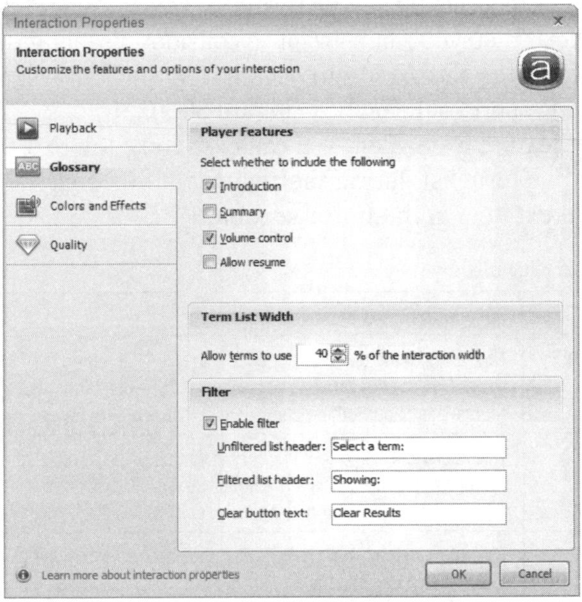

Figure 25.9. Interaction Properties dialog box Glossary tab

To customize the term list width:

1. Click the **Interaction Properties** button on the ribbon.

2. In the Interaction Properties dialog box, click the **Glossary** tab, if it is not already selected.

3. In the Term List Width section, use the increase and decrease arrows in the **Allow terms to use** box to change the percentage. Or just type a new number.

66 **Note:** Engage automatically increases or decreases the size of the media file (if used) in the description content area, so that it fits in the allotted space.

Customizing the Filter Feature

The filter feature enables viewers to click a letter in the alphabet bar so that only terms beginning with that letter are displayed. (Compare Figures 25.1 and 25.2 at the beginning of this chapter.) Engage allows you to enable and disable this feature. By default, filtering is enabled because it eliminates the need for viewers to scroll through the entire glossary term list to locate a specific term. However, if your term list is relatively short, then you might want to consider disabling this feature—simply clear the Enable filter check box in the Glossary tab of the Interaction Properties dialog box (Figure 25.9).

If the filter feature is enabled, you can customize the text that the viewer sees in the term list during the running interaction. Table 25.1 describes each text item in the Filter section.

Table 25.1. Filter text options

Option	Description
Unfiltered list header	This refers to the text that appears at the top of the term list if the viewer has not filtered the list. The default text is "Select a term:", but you can change this to something else, such as "Click a term below:".
Filtered list header	This refers to the text that appears at the top of the term list after the viewer has filtered the list. The default text is "Showing:", but you can change this to something else, such as "Filter results:".
Clear button text	This refers to the label on the button that viewers use to remove the filtered list and redisplay all entries in the glossary. The default text is "Clear Results", but you can change this to something else, such as "Show All Terms".

To customize the filter text:

1. Click the **Interaction Properties** button on the ribbon.

2. In the Interaction Properties dialog box, click the **Glossary** tab, if it is not already displayed.

3. Use the three text boxes in the Filter section to enter your customized text (Table 25.1).

Figure 25.10. Customized Filtered list header and Clear button text entries

You will see the customized text when you preview or publish the interaction. Figure 25.10 shows an example of customized filter text.

Customizing the Colors of Selected/Hovered Terms

The color scheme you have chosen for the interaction affects many items, including the color of the terms. The color of a term changes when it is selected and when the viewer moves the mouse pointer over it. The color scheme refers to these items as Item Selected and Item Hover. When you choose a color scheme, these and other items are automatically affected. However, Engage enables you to choose specific colors for the selected and hovered states of a term using the Color Scheme Editor (Figure 25.11). The procedures to create and edit color schemes are covered in detail in Chapter 15, "Engage Basics."

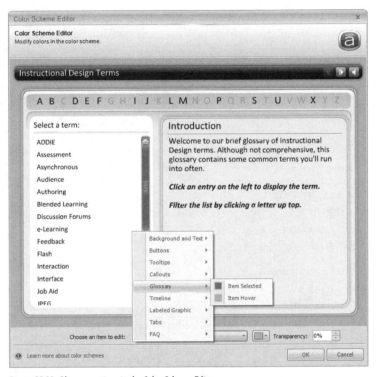

Figure 25.11. Glossary options in the Color Scheme Editor

Customizing General Interaction Properties

The Interaction Properties dialog box offers standard ways to customize all interactions, including the Glossary interaction. These standard options are covered in detail in Chapter 15, "Engage Basics." We suggest that you review these options and decide which features work best for your Glossary interaction. For example, you can change the navigation mode or remove sound effects.

Practice

Now's your chance to create a Glossary interaction using your own content. If you need an idea, think of 10 terms that you use in your job. Then, create a description and locate images to represent them.

Building a Glossary Interaction

1. Plan the interaction and gather content for the terms (text) and definitions (text, audio, media files).

2. From the Engage start screen, click **Create a new interaction**.

3. In the New Interaction dialog box, click **Glossary** and click the **OK** button.

4. In the Glossary interaction window, replace the text in the Interaction Title box with the title of your interaction.

5. Enter the text in the introduction:
    a. Enter a title in the Title box (or keep the default **Introduction** text).
    b. Enter text in the Introduction area.

6. Add an image to the introduction:
    a. In the Media pane, click the **Add Media** button.
    b. In the Select Image or Video File dialog box, browse to the folder containing your media files and double-click the desired file.
    c. In the Multimedia Properties dialog box, use the **Position** list box to change the location of the image, if desired, and then click the **OK** button.

7. Add an audio narration to the introduction:
    a. In the Audio pane, click the **Record** button ⊙.
    b. Using your computer's microphone, narrate the audio for the introduction. Click the **Stop** button ⊙ when you are finished.
    c. Review the audio by clicking the **Play** button ⊙.

8. Create the first term:
   a. Click **Entry 1** in the Glossary Entries panel.
   b. In the Term box, enter the text for the term (maximum of 100 characters).
   c. In the Definition box, enter the text for the answer.
   d. Select the text and change the font size to **12** using the Font Size box on the Formatting toolbar.
   e. If desired, add a media file and/or audio clip by following steps 6-7.

9. Create additional terms using the **Entry 2** and **Entry 3** placeholders, and the **Add Entry** button.

10. After completing the questions, modify some of the interaction properties:
    a. Click the **Interaction Properties** button on the ribbon.
    b. In the Interaction Properties dialog box, click the **Glossary** tab if it is not already selected.
    c. In the Filter section, change the Clear button text to **Show All Entries**.
    d. Click the **Colors and Effects** tab.
    e. In the Color Scheme section, change the color scheme to **Turquoise Cool**.
    f. In the Animation Style section, change the animation style to **Fade**.
    g. Modify other properties, if desired, and click the **OK** button.

11. Preview the interaction by clicking the **Preview** button on the ribbon.

12. Close the Interaction Preview window.

13. Save the interaction:
    a. Click the **Save** button 🖫 on the Quick Access toolbar.
    b. In the Save As dialog box, enter a file name and location for the interaction.
    c. Click the **Save** button.

Chapter Recap

Here's our list of the most important things to remember from this chapter:

- A Glossary interaction is a collection of clickable terms. Clicking a term displays the definition.

- Each term consists of a word or short phrase, and each definition can consist of text (including hyperlinks), media, and an audio clip.

- Terms are always displayed in alphabetical order. However, the viewer can filter the list using the alphabet bar at the top of the interaction.

- Building the glossary entries involves entering the text for each term and adding content for each definition.

- Use the tools on the ribbon to add and delete glossary entries.

- You can customize several features of the Glossary interaction, such as the width of the terms and the filter feature.

- You can customize the color of the rollover state of a term and the selected state of a term by modifying the color scheme.

- Use the Interaction Properties dialog box to customize standard player fcatures, such as the navigation mode and the color scheme.

Chapter 26

Publishing

Chapter Snapshot

In this chapter, you will learn how to complete your development and make your project viewable by intended users. You'll also learn how to test your files, both before and after publishing.

This chapter includes quite a lot of repeated material, specifically the settings that can be chosen in the Publish dialog box for each tool and output type. We recommend that you read the sections "Introduction to Publishing," "Exploring the Publish Dialog Box," "Tracking," and "Published Output Files" first and then skip to whatever additional sections you need.

> ? What kind of published output should I use?

> i   Whatever type of published output you need! Really though, this chapter should help you answer that question.

Introduction to Publishing

After you've developed the desired content using Presenter, Quizmaker, Engage, or Video Encoder, that content needs to be put into a format that viewers can see and use. Before publishing, the content is still in development and can only be viewed using the authoring tool that created it. After the content is published, it becomes published output, which typically includes a Flash output file (.swf) plus supporting files.

Revisiting the Presenter, Quizmaker, and Engage Workflows

Throughout the book, we have discussed workflows for developing content with Presenter, Quizmaker, and Engage. Figures 26.1a-c recap the workflow diagrams for these three Articulate applications. You can see that the last step of the workflows for all three tools is Publish, the topic of this chapter.

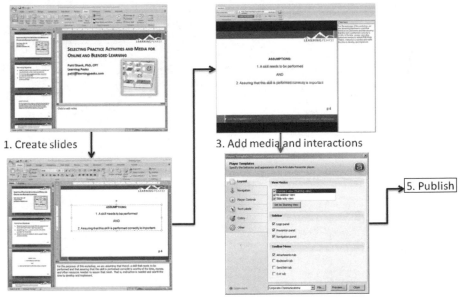

PowerPoint

1. Create slides

2. Write narration script

Presenter

3. Add media and interactions

4. Customize the player

5. Publish

Figure 26.1a. Workflow diagram for Presenter

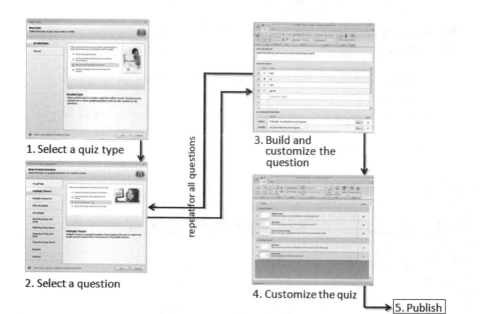

1. Select a quiz type

2. Select a question

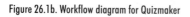
repeat for all questions

3. Build and customize the question

4. Customize the quiz

5. Publish

Figure 26.1b. Workflow diagram for Quizmaker

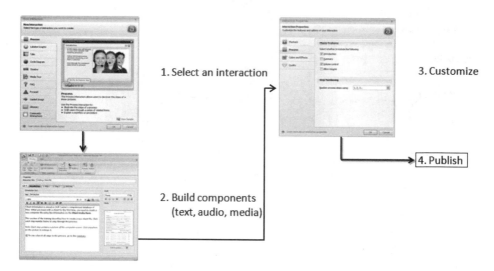

1. Select an interaction

2. Build components (text, audio, media)

3. Customize

4. Publish

Figure 26.1c. Workflow diagram for Engage

Publishing Output Types

Presenter, Quizmaker, and Engage allow you to publish to a variety of output types. Table 26.1 shows the publishing output types that are available for each tool.

Table 26.1. Available publishing formats by tool

Publish to	Presenter	Quizmaker	Engage
Presenter		√	√
Web	√	√	√
Articulate Online	√	√	√
LMS	√	√	√
CD	√	√	√
Word	√	√	√
Podcast	√		
Mobile	√		

Your output type selection depends on how you plan to use the published output. For example, you can incorporate an Engage interaction into a Presenter project, include the interaction on a web page, or put the interaction on a CD. We'll describe each of these output types next.

Presenter

Publishing to Presenter means that the published output (a Quizmaker quiz or an Engage interaction) will be incorporated in a Presenter project. The interaction or quiz can be inserted as a slide in the presentation or as a player tab, which is always accessible to the viewer.

Web

Publishing to the web means the published output will be viewed in a web browser. Publishing will produce a variety of files that allow the output to be viewed in a web browser. This typically means that you want to make the files freely available (over a network or the Internet) and you don't need to track anything.

Articulate Online

Publishing to Articulate Online means that the output will be viewed in Articulate's hosted tracking service, Articulate Online. For more information about subscribing to Articulate Online, go to www.articulate.com and click the Products tab.

LMS

Publishing to LMS means that the output will be viewed in a learning management system. In many cases, the files will be given to the LMS administrator so that he or she can upload and test the files before they are made available to viewers.

CD

Publishing to CD means that viewers will view the output from a CD. This option is often chosen to provide copies of the output to testers (to find and fix problems before the content is made available to viewers), but may also be chosen when viewers do not have Internet access or when the content contains media files that are too large to be viewed easily over a network or the Internet.

Word

Publishing to Word creates a Word document that shows content and other information. This is especially useful when collecting input from subject matter experts or others. Word output can serve as a storyboard and as an alternate means of viewing slide content for viewers who use screen readers or who would otherwise benefit from a printable version.

Podcast

Publishing to podcast is only available for Presenter content. This publishing option packages slide audio files (narration and other slide audio but not audio from inserted multimedia) used in a Presenter project as an audio file for viewers to listen to online or as an .mp3 file that can be listened to with an MP3 player. This can be especially valuable when the content needs to be studied or when the ability to listen to content outside of the Presenter player makes sense.

Mobile

Publishing to mobile is only available for Presenter content and the files can only be used with Adobe Flash Lite 3-enabled mobile devices (see http://www.adobe.com/mobile/supported_devices for more information).

Testing and Fixing Before Publishing

Although this chapter is called "Publishing," we'd like to start with something you should do *before* you publish, which is to thoroughly test what you have built. You can do this by reviewing the materials one last time in the Articulate application in which they were built. In other words, you should preview them to see how they look, sound, and work. You're likely to find a few things that don't work as expected.

Actually, testing what you are building should be ongoing throughout the development process so that when you are ready to publish, the kinks have been worked out. But our years of experience have taught us that there are often a few issues to address, even at this stage.

Table 26.2 lists some testing options. This list isn't meant to be exhaustive (and simple projects, quizzes, and interactions may not require more than quick testing), but should give you a good idea of the kinds of things that should be tested along the way and then once again, before publishing.

Table 26.2. Testing options

What to test	What to test for	Who should test
Design	Good use of real estate Not crowded Consistency (by page type or across page types) Not confusing or frustrating	Designer/developer Tester (QA) Potential users
Player/Navigation	Textual content is easy to read Viewer control is adequate (unlocked in most cases) Player controls are intuitive Navigation is intuitive and not confusing Viewer can find/return to previous content easily	Designer/developer Tester (QA) Potential users

What to test	What to test for	Who should test
Graphics	Useful (not gratuitous) Clear Callouts, if needed Clear explanations, if needed (narration)	Designer/developer Potential users
Media	Accuracy Useful (not gratuitous) Works as expected Viewer can start/pause/stop Clear explanations, if needed (narration)	Designer/developer Subject matter expert Tester (QA) Potential users
Interactions (Engage Interactions, Quizmaker Quizzes, Presenter Learning Games, etc.)	Accuracy Directions for use, if needed Adequate feedback Branching, if used, is not confusing	Designer/developer Subject matter expert Tester (QA) Potential users
Content	Accuracy Sequencing Printable version, if viewer will want to print Right reading level Spelling and grammar	Designer/developer Subject matter expert Potential users
Accessibility*	Text is readable Content is accessible (alternate formats, narration transcript, etc.) Narration available in transcript Background/foreground contrast is adequate Keyboard shortcuts are activated Navigation with Tab and Space keys works as expected Downloadable attachments are accessible	Designer/developer Tester (QA) Potential users
Platforms, browsers	Works in platforms and browsers available to viewers	Designer/developer Tester (QA) Potential users

* A search of discussion boards shows developer concerns about the accessibility of all Flash output. This may be a good place to start for considering the accessibility of Articulate Studio Flash output: http://files.articulate.com/files/Articulate-Presenter-VPAT.pdf.

This kind of testing will take too much time. I'm in a hurry.

Like they say, there's never time to do it right but there's always time to explain why it doesn't work right. And then fix it...

Obviously, the more critical and complex the project, quiz, or interaction, the more important it is to test it thoroughly. Simple, linear projects with little media and few interactions can often be tested and published very quickly.

A major plus of building Flash output is that it generally behaves similarly across browsers. That is, it will likely work in Internet Explorer, Firefox, Opera, Safari, Chrome, and so on. However, there are some Articulate Studio '09 functionalities that don't work in certain browsers*, as follows:

- The Exit button (in Presenter) and the Finish button (in Quizmaker), which close the browser window, don't function in Firefox because of Firefox security restrictions. A workaround involves launching the player in a new browser window: http://www.articulate.com/support/presenter09/kb/?p=317.

- In Quizmaker, the email results functionality doesn't work in some browsers and email clients. This is because of security restrictions in those browsers and email clients.

- In Presenter, Web Objects will launch in a new browser window in some older Safari browsers. This is because Safari doesn't adequately execute embedded Web Objects, which slows player performance.

Articulate tools support Flash Player 6 and up for playback. Most Flash players *after* Flash Player 8 are very similar and will behave similarly.

---

* This information is courtesy of Dave Mozealous, Articulate QA Manager.

Publishing

Exploring the Publish Dialog Box

The process of publishing for all formats is basically the same, even though each output type may produce different published output folders and files. Presenter, Quizmaker, and Engage make use of the Publish dialog box for selecting and inputting publishing settings. Immediately after publishing, you'll see the Publish Successful dialog box, which allows you to choose what to do next. Before getting into the specifics of each of the publishing formats, let's look at these two dialog boxes and what you will be doing with them.

Publish Dialog Box

When you have completed developing your content in Presenter, Quizmaker, or Engage and are ready to publish it, you'll click the **Publish** button on the Articulate tab or menu (Presenter) or the **Publish** button on the Quizmaker or Engage ribbon. The Publish dialog box for Presenter, Quizmaker, or Engage (Figures 26.2 , 26.3, and 26.4, respectively) will open and you will select the desired *output type* tab (Web, Articulate Online LMS, CD, etc.) and then decide if the settings need to be changed. If they do, you can change them. Notice that the tabs on the left side of each Publish dialog box correspond to the output formats discussed earlier. We'll discuss each of these output options in more depth shortly.

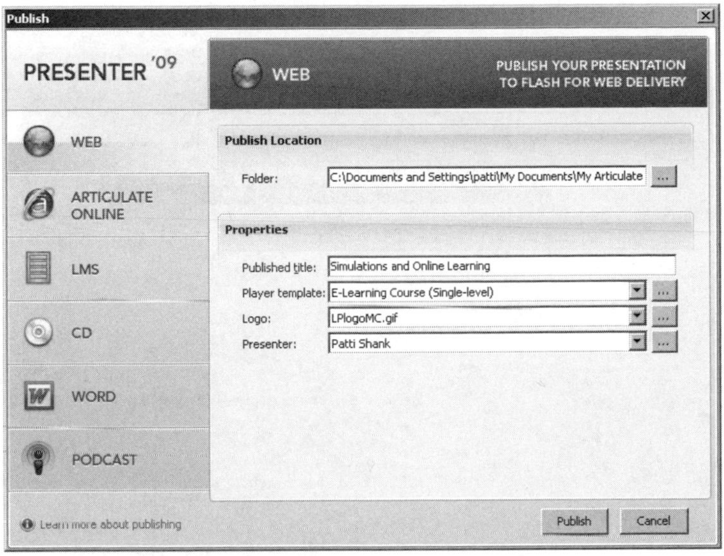

Figure 26.2. Presenter Publish dialog box

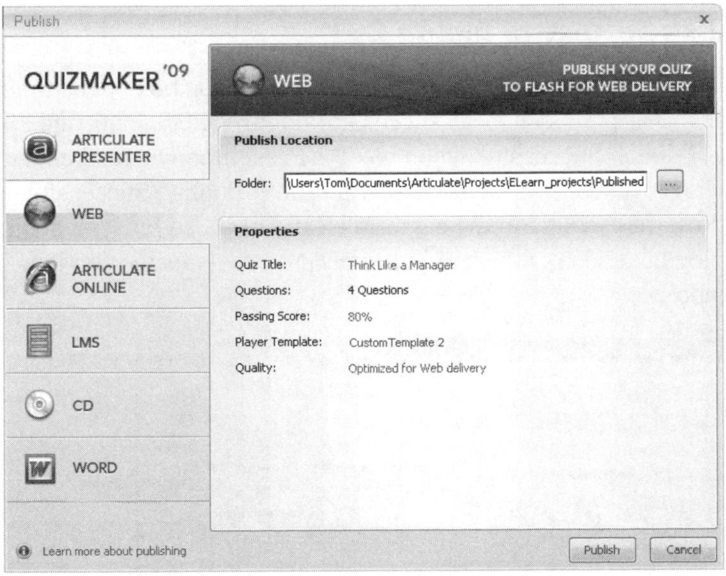

Figure 26.3. Quizmaker Publish dialog box

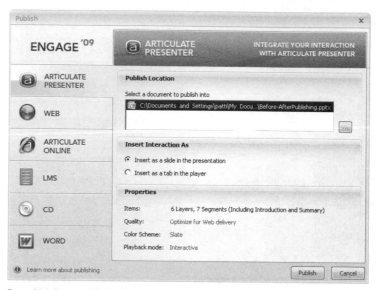

Figure 26.4. Engage Publish dialog box

Publish Successful Dialog Box

After you publish, the Publish Successful dialog box opens to let you know that publishing was successful. Figures 26.5, 26.6, and 26.7 show the Publish Successful dialog box for Presenter, Quizmaker, and Engage, respectively. Notice that all three Publish Successful dialog boxes are essentially the same. We call out those few cases where the dialog boxes look different in the output type-specific sections of this chapter.

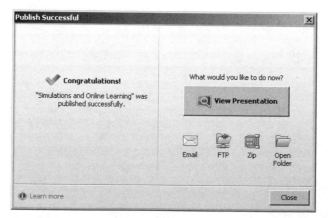

Figure 26.5. Presenter Publish Successful dialog box

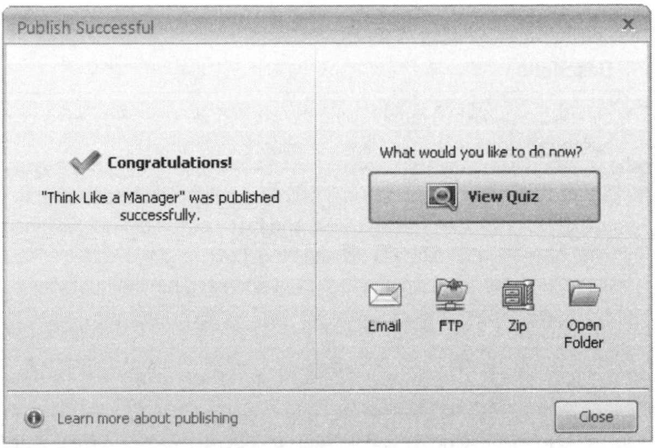

Figure 26.6. Quizmaker Publish Successful dialog box

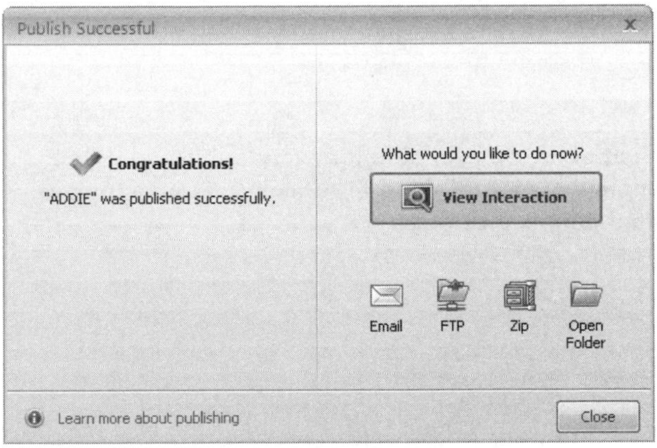

Figure 26.7. Engage Publish Successful dialog box

When the Publish Successful dialog box opens, you can typically choose from the options described in Table 26.3. The table provides a brief description of each option that is available in the Publish Successful dialog box.

Table 26.3. Publish Successful dialog box options

Option	Description
View	Opens the published output using the published output files. For example, if published to the web, it will open in your default browser.
Email	Sends the published output via email. This option combines all of the published output files into one .zip file (folder) and then opens your default email program. The .zip file is automatically attached to a new message. The message body contains generic instructions for how to open and run the published output.
FTP	Uploads the output files to an FTP site. Opens the FTP Published Content dialog box, where you can input server information, test the connection, and send the files.
Zip	Creates a .zip (compressed) file of all output files. Opens a New Zip File dialog box, where you can choose the location and name of the .zip file.
Open Folder	Opens the folder that contains the published output files
Close	Closes the Publish Successful dialog box

 Note: Not all options are available for every published output type. For example, when publishing to Articulate Online, only a Manage Content item is included.

Tracking

Some of the readers of this book will be publishing to a learning management system, using hosted or purchased infrastructure to track learners (such as Articulate Online). The main reason for using an LMS is to track learners' use and completion of courses. In the "Publishing to an LMS" section of this chapter, we discuss what can be tracked from Presenter, Quizmaker, and Engage. But what can be tracked is more complicated than what data Presenter, Quizmaker, and Engage can send to your LMS. Although Articulate products produce SCORM- and AICC-compliant content that should work with a SCORM-/AICC-compliant LMS, LMSs vary significantly. Check with your LMS administrator to learn how to upload and test the tracking of your Articulate content. Your LMS may or may not support capturing all of the data that Presenter, Quizmaker, and Engage can send.

The takeaway here is that you should read the tracking topic in the LMS section of this chapter if this issue is important to you. But you should also determine what your LMS can do with the data that

Presenter, Quizmaker, and Engage can send. And if you are considering purchasing an LMS, the ability to support all of the data sent by
Presenter, Quizmaker, and Engage may be an important factor.

In addition to using an LMS and Articulate Online for tracking,
there are numerous folks in the Quizmaker Community Forums
(http://www.articulate.com/forums/articulate-quizmaker) talking about
custom programming to send Quizmaker tracking data to a database.
For example, there is information about using .NET and PHP code to
take Quizmaker data in this thread: http://www.articulate.com/forums/
articulate-quizmaker/4317-quiz-database-instructions-code.html. If you
aren't a programmer or reasonable facsimile thereof, you may need
programming assistance.

Published Output Files

Publishing from Presenter, Quizmaker, and Engage to any of the available output types (Web, CD, and so on) creates a folder (in the location
that you specify or in the default My Articulate Projects folder) that
contains the published output. Figures 26.8, 26.9, and 26.10, show
examples of the published output folders and files created for a Presenter project (published to Web), a Quizmaker quiz (published to CD),
and an Engage interaction (published to LMS), respectively.

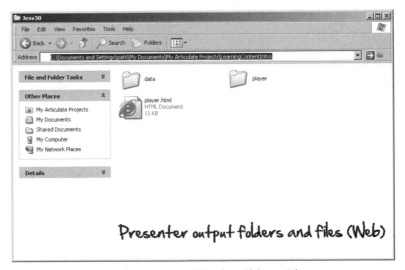

Figure 26.8. Presenter published output folders and files after publishing to Web

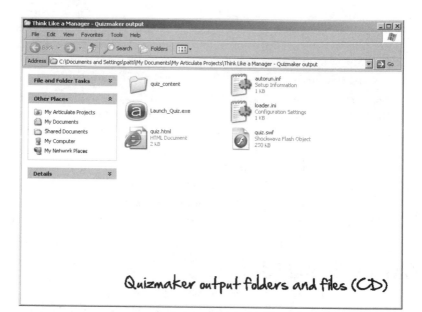

Figure 26.9. Quizmaker published output folders and files after publishing to CD

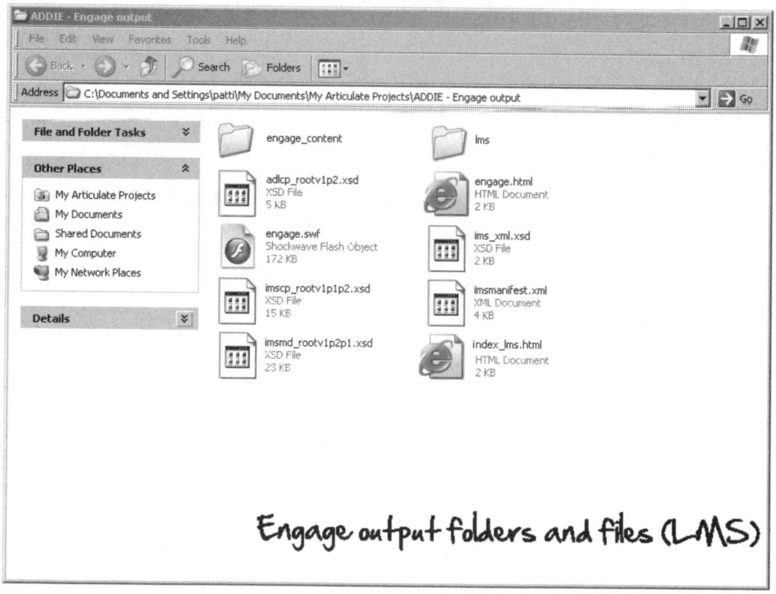

Figure 26.10. Engage published output folders and files after publishing to LMS

The actual output files created during publishing for each output type (Web, CD, LMS, and so on) are discussed in the output type sections of this chapter, but the process is the same. You publish content and the Presenter, Quizmaker, or Engage application produces a folder that contains all of the output files needed to view the content for that output type.

Publishing to Articulate Presenter

Publishing to Articulate Presenter means that the output (a Quizmaker quiz or an Engage interaction) will be incorporated into a Presenter project. This option is available only for Quizmaker and Engage, meaning you can't publish a Presenter project to another Presenter project. When you include a Quizmaker quiz or an Engage interaction in a Presenter project, you can add the quiz/interaction as a slide in the presentation or as a tab in the Presenter player.

- **As a slide:** Adding the quiz or interaction as a slide places it on a new slide in the PowerPoint presentation. If the presentation is currently open when you publish the quiz or interaction, the new slide is added immediately after the currently selected slide.

- **As a player tab:** Adding a quiz or interaction as a tab creates a tab (which really looks like a "button") on the Presenter player. Since the player tab is separate from the presentation slides, viewers can click the tab at any time to access the quiz or interaction. The tab option is good for reference interactions, such as a glossary or FAQs.

> 66 **Note:** In addition to publishing a quiz or interaction from Quizmaker or Engage *to Presenter,* you can also insert a quiz or interaction *from within Presenter* by using the Quizmaker Quiz or Engage Interaction buttons on the Articulate tab (Figure 26.11). The final result is the same. (Chapter 6, "Pumping Up Your Presenter Projects," provides details about inserting quizzes and interactions from Presenter.)

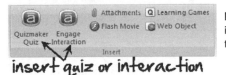

Fiigure 26.11. Insert a quiz or interaction from the Articulate tab in PowerPoint.

insert quiz or interaction

Figures 26.12 and 26.13 show the Publish dialog box with the Articulate Presenter tab open for Quizmaker and Engage, respectively. Tables 26.4 and 26.5 describe the settings available when the Articulate Presenter tab for that tool is selected.

Quizmaker—Publish to Articulate Presenter

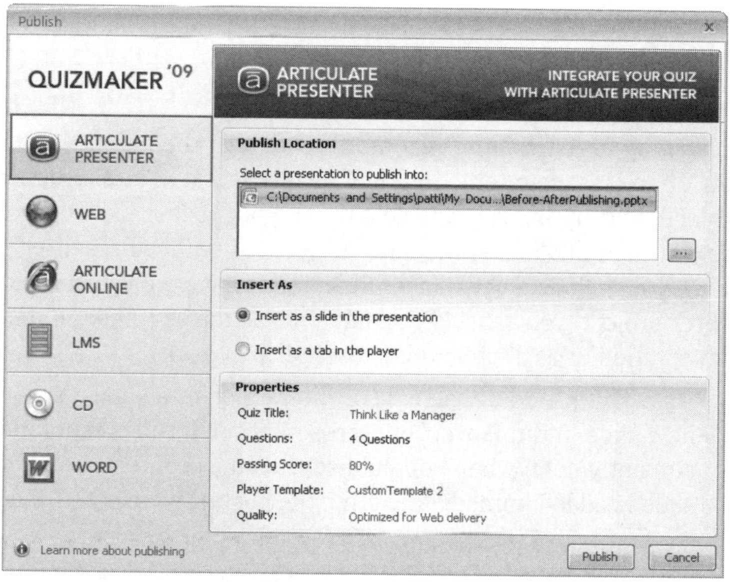

Figure 26.12. Quizmaker publish to Articulate Presenter tab

Table 26.4 describes the publishing settings on the Articulate Presenter tab of the Quizmaker Publish dialog box.

Table 26.4. Quizmaker Publish dialog box settings

Property/setting	Description
Publish Location	This box displays the names of all open Presenter projects. Select the project to contain the Quizmaker quiz. If the project is not open, you can click the ellipsis button ([...]) to browse for the project file or type a directory path to select the file.
Insert As	Select Insert as a slide in the presentation to insert the quiz in a new slide. Select Insert as a tab in the player to create a player tab that contains the quiz.

Property/setting	Description
Quiz Title	Quiz title is the title of the published quiz as it is seen by viewers on the title bar of the player. The title can be changed by clicking the Quiz Title link and entering a new title in the Quiz Properties dialog box.
Questions	This is the number of questions in the quiz.
Passing Score	The default passing score is 80%. The passing score default can be changed by clicking the Passing Score link. This opens the Quiz Properties dialog box, where the passing score can be changed. (The passing score can also be set by inputting a score percentage in the Quiz Properties dialog box during development of a graded quiz.)
Player Template	This option lets you select a template to use for the current quiz from the preconfigured templates that come with Quizmaker or from custom templates you have created and saved previously. Custom player templates are created using the Player Template Manager dialog box.
Quality	The default Quality setting is Optimized for Web delivery. The quality can be changed by clicking the Quality link. This opens the Publish Compression dialog box, where the quality setting can be changed. **Note:** Higher quality means larger file sizes and more bandwidth needed to view and interact with the quiz.

Engage—Publish to Articulate Presenter

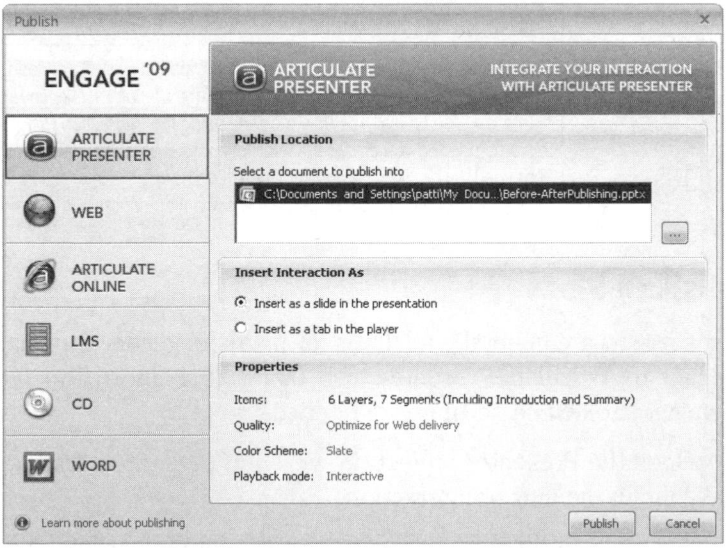

Figure 26.13. Engage publish to Articulate Presenter tab

Table 26.5 describes the publishing settings on the Articulate Presenter tab of the Engage Publish dialog box.

Table 26.5. Engage Publish dialog box settings

Property/setting	Description
Publish Location	This box displays the names of all open Presenter projects. Select the project to contain the Engage interaction. If the project is not open, you can click the ellipsis button (⊡) to browse for the project file or type a directory path to select the file.
Insert As	Select Insert as a slide in the presentation to insert the interaction in a new slide. Select Insert as a tab in the player to create a player tab that contains the interaction.
Items	The Items property shows how many items comprise the current interaction, including the introduction and summary, if applicable. You can think of an item as the screen that is displayed when the viewer clicks the Next button.
Quality	The default Quality setting is Optimize for Web delivery. The quality can be changed by clicking the Quality link. This opens the Publish Compression dialog box, where the quality setting can be changed.
Color Scheme	The color scheme refers to the colors used by general components of the interaction, such as the screen background and navigation buttons. You typically set this property using the Interaction Properties dialog box when you create the interaction. However, you can modify it here, if needed, by clicking the current value. This opens the Interaction Properties dialog box, where you can change the color scheme in the Colors and Effects tab.
Playback mode	The playback mode refers to the type of navigation control provided to the viewer. The three options for most interactions are *interactive, linear,* and *presentation.* You typically set this property using the Interaction Properties dialog box when you create the interaction. However, you can modify it here, if needed, by clicking the current value. This opens the Interaction Properties dialog box, where you can change the navigation control in the Playback tab.

Publishing Steps

These steps are general guidelines for publishing from Quizmaker and Engage to Articulate Presenter. Use Tables 26.4 and 26.5 to determine if changes to default settings are needed.

1.   Open the Presenter project (PowerPoint presentation) that will contain the quiz or interaction.

2.   Click the **Publish** button on the Engage or Quizmaker ribbon.

3. In the Publish dialog box, select the **Articulate Presenter** tab.

4. In the Publish Location section, select or browse to the Presenter project that will contain the quiz or interaction.

5. In the Insert Interaction As section, select whether to add the quiz or interaction as a slide or as a tab.

6. Input desired settings in the Properties section.

7. Click the **Publish** button.

8. Once finished, the Publish Successful dialog box opens (Figure 26.14) and then the Quizzes and Interactions dialog box in Presenter is displayed. You can then customize properties of the quiz or interaction as it appears in the Presenter project. These properties are covered in Chapter 6, "Pumping Up Your Presenter Projects."

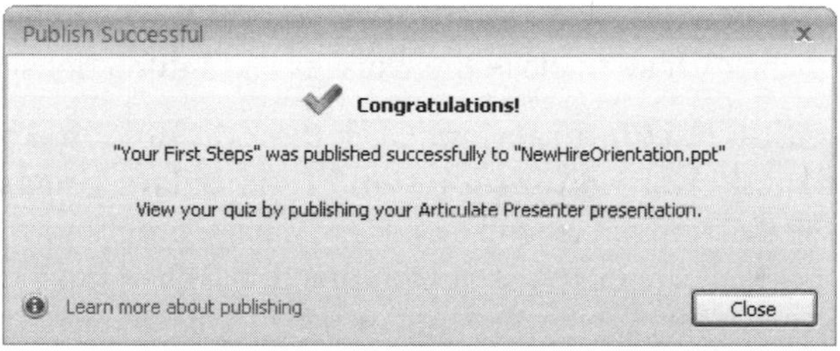

Figure 26.14. Publish Successful dialog box

Output Files

After you publish a quiz or an interaction to a Presenter project, the information required to run the quiz or interaction is "rolled into" the project's .ppta file. After you publish the entire Presenter project, the supporting files for the quiz or interaction are stored in the project's output files data folder.

Deleting or Editing a Quiz or Interaction Published to Presenter

To delete or edit an interaction or quiz *after* it has been published to Presenter:

1. Click the **Quizmaker Quiz** or the **Engage Interaction** button on the Articulate tab or the **Quizmaker Quiz** or **Engage Interaction** menu selection on the Articulate menu.

2. In the Quizzes and Interactions dialog box, select **Quizmaker Quizzes** or **Engage Interactions** if the quiz/interaction is a slide, or select **Player Tabs** if the quiz/interaction is a tab.

3. Select the quiz/interaction to be deleted or edited from the Quiz Slides or Interaction Slides list (for slides) or the Player Tabs list (for tabs).

4. **To remove a quiz/interaction:** Click the **Remove** button and then click **Close** to close the Quizzes and Interactions dialog box.

   To edit a quiz/interaction: Click the **Edit quiz in Articulate Quizmaker** or **Edit interaction in Articulate Engage** button. Presenter opens the Quizmaker or Engage program, where you can make changes to the quiz/interaction. When finished, click the **Save and Return to Presenter** button that appears on the ribbon. The quiz/interaction will be saved and reinserted into your presentation. Then click the **Close** button.

Tip: You can also remove quizzes or interactions that were inserted as slides by deleting the slide itself while working inside PowerPoint.

Publishing to the Web

Publishing to the web means that the tool you are publishing from, whether Presenter, Quizmaker, or Engage, will produce the folders and files needed to view the published output via the Internet. This option is typically chosen if the published output will be viewed on a web site and you want to make it freely available.

Figures 26.15, 26.16, and 26.17 show the Publish dialog box with the Web tab open for Presenter, Quizmaker, and Engage, respectively. Tables 26.6, 26.7, and 26.8 describe the settings available when the Web tab for that tool is selected.

Presenter—Publish to Web

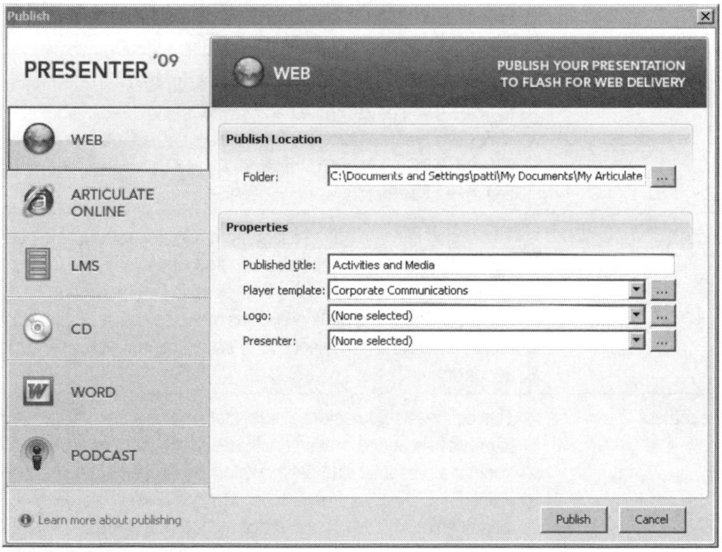

Figure 26.15. Presenter publish to Web tab

Table 26.6 describes the settings and properties on the Web tab of the Presenter Publish dialog box.

Table 26.6. Presenter Publish dialog box settings

Property/setting	Description
Publish Location Folder	Select the location where the published output files will be created. The default location is My Documents\My Articulate Projects. You can click the ellipsis button (⬚) to browse for the location or type a directory path to select the location where the published output should reside. Saving the published output files to your hard disk is a good idea for backing up the files, but it doesn't put the published output files in a place that others can view unless they are using your computer. If you are publishing to a company location, you may need help from your company's IT department or your LMS administrator to find out where to put your files and how to get them there. They may need to create a directory and permissions to allow you to upload the files or they may want to do the uploading themselves.
Published title	The Published title is the title of the published project as it is seen by viewers on the title bar of the player. The title can be changed by clicking the link and entering a new title. We recommend that the Published title setting match the title page of your slides.
Player template	This option lets you select a template to use for the current project from the preconfigured templates that come with Presenter or from custom templates you have created and saved previously. Custom player templates are created using the Player Template Manager dialog box. (See Chapter 7, "Customizing Presenter Player Templates," for more information about this topic.)
Logo	This option lets you select a logo from a list of previously added logos to use for the current project. You can add logos using the Presentation Options dialog box (using the Presentation Options button on the Articulate tab or the Presentation Options menu selection on the Articulate menu). You can also select (None selected), in which case no logo will appear.
Presenter	This option lets you select a presenter (typically the narrator) from a list of previously added presenters to use for the current project. Information about the presenter can be shown on the Presenter player. You can add presenters using the Presentation Options dialog box (using the Presentation Options button on the Articulate tab or the Presentation Options menu selection on the Articulate menu). You can also select (None selected), in which case no presenter will appear. If you have multiple presenters (for example, Patti presents slides 1-10 and Jennifer presents slides 11-20), presenters can be set up at the slide level in Slide Properties. (They need to be set up in Presentation Options first.)

Quizmaker—Publish to Web

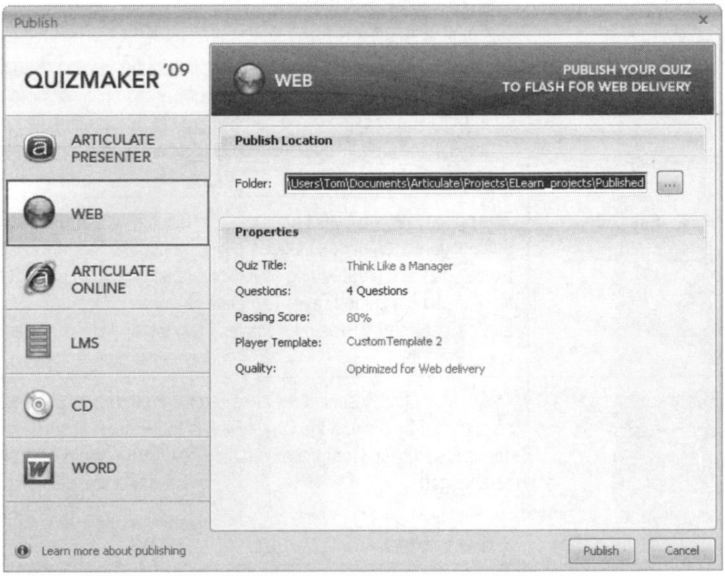

Figure 26.16. Quizmaker publish to Web tab

Table 26.7 describes the settings and properties on the Web tab of the Quizmaker Publish dialog box.

Table 26.7. Quizmaker Publish dialog box settings

Property/setting	Description
Publish Location Folder	Select the location where the published output files will be created. The default location is My Documents\My Articulate Projects. You can click the ellipsis button ( ) to browse for the location or type a directory path to select the location where the published output should reside.
	Saving the published output files to your hard disk is a good idea for backing up the files, but it doesn't put the published output files in a place that others can view unless they are using your computer.
	If you are publishing to a company location, you may need help from your company's IT department or your LMS administrator to find out where to put your files and how to get them there. They may need to create a directory and permissions to allow you to upload the files or they may want to do the uploading themselves.
Quiz Title	Quiz Title is the title of the published quiz as it is seen by viewers on the title bar of the player. The title can be changed by clicking the Quiz Title link and entering a new title in the Quiz Properties dialog box.

Property/setting	Description
Questions	This is the number of questions in the quiz.
Passing Score	The default passing score is 80%. The passing score default can be changed by clicking the Passing Score link in the Publish dialog box. This opens the Quiz Properties dialog box, where the passing score can be changed. (The passing score can also be set by inputting a score percentage in the Quiz Properties dialog box during development of a graded quiz.)
Player Template	This option lets you select a template to use for the current quiz from the preconfigured templates that come with Quizmaker or from custom templates you have created and saved previously. Custom player templates are created using the Player Template Manager dialog box. (See Chapter 7, "Customizing Presenter Player Templates," for more information about this topic.)
Quality	The default Quality setting is Optimized for Web delivery. The quality can be changed by clicking the Quality link in the Publish dialog box. This opens the Publish Compression dialog box, where the quality setting can be changed. **Note:** Higher quality means larger file sizes and more bandwidth needed to view and interact with the quiz.

Engage—Publish to Web

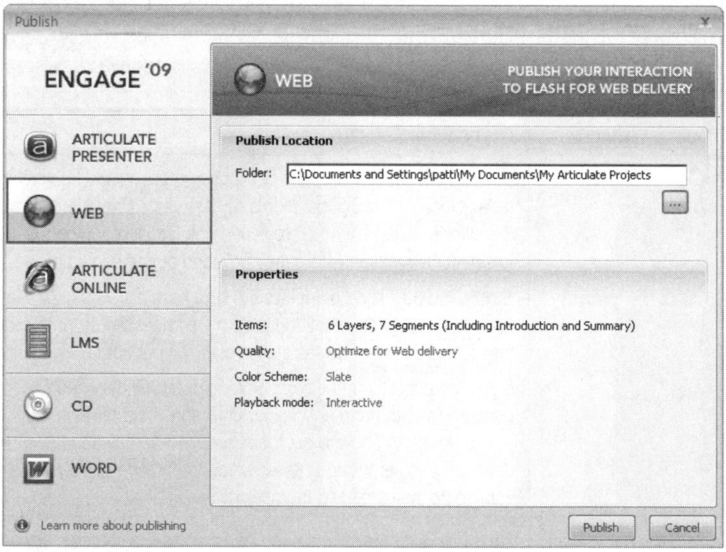

Figure 26.17. Engage publish to Web tab

Table 26.8 describes the settings and properties on the Web tab of the Engage Publish dialog box.

Table 26.8. Engage Publish dialog box settings

Property/setting	Description
Publish Location Folder	Select the location where the published output files will be created. The default location is My Documents\My Articulate Projects. You can click the ellipsis button (⬚) to browse for the location or type a directory path to select the location where the published output should reside.
	Saving the published output files to your hard disk is a good idea for backing up the files, but it doesn't put the published output files in a place that others can view unless they are using your computer.
	If you are publishing to a company location, you may need help from your company's IT department or your LMS administrator to find out where to put your files and how to get them there. They may need to create a directory and permissions to allow you to upload the files or they may want to do the uploading themselves.
Items	The Items property shows how many items comprise the current interaction, including the introduction and summary, if applicable. You can think of an item as the screen that is displayed when the viewer clicks the Next button.
Quality	The default Quality setting is Optimize for Web delivery. The quality can be changed by clicking the Quality link in the Publish dialog box. This opens the Publish Compression dialog box, where the quality setting can be changed.
Color Scheme	The color scheme refers to the colors used by general components of the interaction, such as the screen background and navigation buttons. You typically set this property using the Interaction Properties dialog box when you create the interaction. However, you can modify it here, if needed, by clicking the current value. This opens the Interaction Properties dialog box, where you can change the color scheme in the Colors and Effects tab.
Playback mode	The playback mode refers to the type of navigation control provided to the viewer. The three options for most interactions are *interactive*, *linear*, and *presentation*. You typically set this property using the Interaction Properties dialog box when you create the interaction. However, you can modify it here, if needed, by clicking the current value. This opens the Interaction Properties dialog box, where you can change the navigation control in the Playback tab.

Publishing

Publishing Steps

These steps are general guidelines for publishing from Presenter, Quizmaker, and Engage to Web. Use Tables 26.6, 26.7, and 26.8 to determine if changes to default settings are needed.

1. Click the **Publish** button from the Articulate tab, the **Publish** menu selection from the Articulate menu (Presenter), or the **Publish** button on the Quizmaker or Engage ribbon. The Publish dialog box opens.

2. Select the **Web** tab in the Publish dialog box.

3. Specify a folder in the Publish Location area.

4. Input the desired settings in the Properties area (see Tables 26.6, 26.7, and 26.8 for Presenter, Quizmaker, and Engage).

5. Click the **Publish** button.

6. When the final output files are published, the Publish Successful dialog box will open. Choose whether to view the published output, send the published output as email, send to an FTP site, create a Zip file, or open the folder containing the published files. You can also close the dialog box without selecting any of these options.

7. Test the final output by viewing all pages, all media (such as audio and video), and all interactions (such as Engage interactions and Quizmaker quizzes). Make note of any problems that need to be fixed and fix them in the development files (not the published output files), as needed. Then republish and retest, if necessary.

8. Upload the final output folders and files to the web (typically this is done with a web development tool such as Dreamweaver or an FTP program).

Video Compression Settings

If you plan to use large Flash video (.flv) files, you need to make sure that the video compression setting adequately accounts for viewer bandwidth. Most of the programs that create Flash video allow you to specify a compression setting, so you can select more compression for audiences with lower bandwidth (dial-up or slow DSL connection). Dave Mozealous, Articulate QA Manager, has more information on this topic in his blog: http://www.mozealous.com/?p=59.

Output Files

When publishing to the web, the following output folders and files are created.

Launch File (Presenter/Quizmaker/Engage)

The launch file for Presenter, Quizmaker, and Engage (player.html, quiz.html, and engage.html, respectively) pulls together the player and all other files needed to view the Presenter project, Engage interaction, or Quizmaker quiz. You can double-click the player.html file to view the published project as viewers will see it.

If you chose Launch Presentation in new window in the Presenter Player Templates dialog box, a launcher.html file will also be created that launches the file in a new window. In this case, the launcher.html file is technically considered to be the launch file.

Flash File(s) (Presenter/Quizmaker/Engage)

Flash output files (slide.swf, quiz.swf, engage.swf) contain the Flash output of the project/quiz/interaction.

Data Folder (Presenter)

The data folder contains:

- A swf folder, which contains individual .swf files for each slide in the project.
- A playerproperties.xml file, which gives the player property information such as color scheme, navigation restrictions, tabs, and so on.

- A presentation.xml file, which contains slide-specific information including slide notes, slide view, timings, and so on.

Content Folder (Quizmaker/Engage)

The quiz_content folder and the engage_content folder contain supporting files required to run the quiz or interaction.

Player Folder (Presenter)

This folder contains pieces of the Presenter player, including .swf files, .html files, .gif files, and .js files. These files contain all the information the player needs to "play" the project.

Publishing to Articulate Online

Publishing to Articulate Online means that the tool you are publishing from, whether Presenter, Quizmaker, or Engage, will publish the folders and files needed to view the published output through Articulate Online, Articulate's subscription-based, hosted tracking service. When you publish to Articulate Online, you may also want to publish a backup copy on your hard drive or other storage medium so that you have a "local" copy of the files as well.

 Note: Information about tracking is in the section "Publishing to an LMS."

Figures 26.18, 26.19, and 26.20 show the Publish dialog box with the Articulate Online tab open for Presenter, Quizmaker, and Engage, respectively. Tables 26.9, 26.10, and 26.11 describe the settings available when the Articulate Online tab for that tool is selected.

Presenter—Publish to Articulate Online

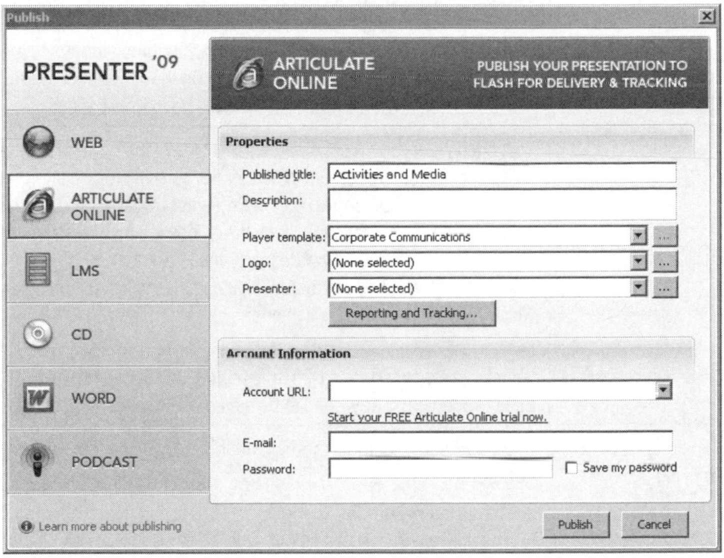

Figure 26.18. Presenter publish to Articulate Online tab

Table 26.9 describes the settings and properties on the Articulate Online tab of the Publish dialog box for Presenter.

Table 26.9. Presenter Publish dialog box settings

Property/setting	Description
Published title	Published title is the title of the published project as it is seen by viewers. The title can be changed by clicking the link and entering a new title. We recommend that the title match the title page of your slides.
Description	Use the Description field to enter the description that will appear with the published project in your Articulate Online account.
Player template	This option lets you select a template to use for the current project from the preconfigured templates that come with Presenter or from custom templates you have created and saved previously. Custom player templates are created using the Player Template Manager dialog box. (See Chapter 7, "Customizing Presenter Player Templates," for more information about this topic.)

Property/setting	Description
Logo	This option lets you select a logo from a list of previously added logos to use for the current project. You can add logos using the Presentation Options dialog box (using the Presentation Options button on the Articulate tab or the Presentation Options menu selection on the Articulate menu). You can also select (None selected), in which case no logo will appear.
Presenter	This option lets you select a presenter (typically the narrator) from a list of previously added presenters to use for the current project. Information about the presenter can be shown on the Presenter player. You can add presenters using the Presentation Options dialog box (using the Presentation Options button on the Articulate tab or the Presentation Options menu selection on the Articulate menu). You can also select (None selected), in which case no presenter will appear.
	If you have multiple presenters (for example, Patti presents slides 1-10 and Jennifer presents slides 11-20), presenters can be set up at the slide level in Slide Properties. (They need to be set up in Presentation Options first.)
Reporting and Tracking	Click the Reporting and Tracking button to modify the following options, if desired:
	• Report status as: Choose the label to describe the completion status. The viewer will see this status label when they have completed the project. The default value is Passed/Incomplete, which means the status Passed will be displayed if the viewer has viewed the required minimum number of slides in the project. The status Incomplete will be displayed for fewer than the required minimum number of slides.
	• Minimum number of slides viewed to complete: Specify how many slides must be viewed in order to receive a "completed" or "passed" status. The default value is the total number of items in the interaction.
Account Information	Enter the URL of the web site in the Account URL box, and complete the E-mail and Password boxes. This information is provided to you when you set up an Articulate Online account.

Quizmaker—Publish to Articulate Online

Figure 26.19. Quizmaker publish to Articulate Online tab

Table 26.10 describes the settings and properties on the Articulate Online tab of the Publish dialog box for Quizmaker.

Table 26.10. Quizmaker Publish dialog box settings

Property/setting	Description
Title	This is the title of the quiz in Articulate Online.
Description	Use the Description field to enter the description that will appear with the published interaction in your Articulate Online account.
Questions	This is the number of questions in the quiz.
Passing Score	The default passing score is 80%. The passing score default can be changed by clicking the Passing Score link in the Publish dialog box. This opens the Quiz Properties dialog box, where the passing score can be changed. (The passing score can also be set by inputting a score percentage in the Quiz Properties dialog box during development of a graded quiz.)
Player Template	This option lets you select a template to use for the current project from the preconfigured templates that come with Quizmaker or from custom templates you have created and saved previously. Custom player templates are created using the Player Template Manager dialog box.

Property/setting	Description
Quality	The default Quality setting is Optimized for Web delivery. The quality can be changed by clicking the Quality link in the Publish dialog box. This opens the Publish Compression dialog box, where the quality setting can be changed. Note: Higher quality means larger file sizes and more bandwidth needed to view and interact with the quiz.
Reporting	Click the Reporting button and select the desired option. The viewer will see the report status after working with the quiz. The default value is Completed/Incomplete, which means the status Completed will be displayed if the viewer has viewed the required minimum number of items in the interaction. The status Incomplete will be displayed for fewer than the required minimum numbers of items. You can change the default label to another option, such as Passed/Failed.
Account Information	Enter the URL of the web site in the Account URL box, and complete the E-mail and Password boxes. This information is provided to you when you set up an Articulate Online account.

Engage—Publish to Articulate Online

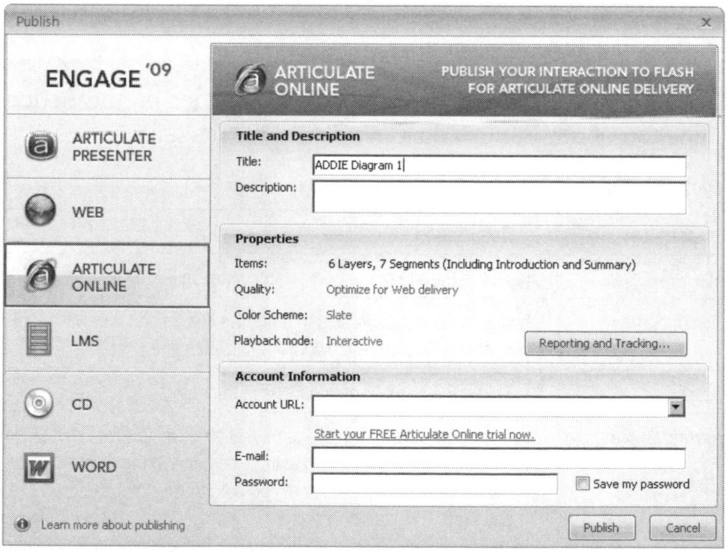

Figure 26.20. Engage publish to Articulate Online tab

Table 26.11 describes the settings and properties on the Articulate Online tab of the Publish dialog box for Engage.

Table 26.11. Engage Publish dialog box settings

Property/setting	Description
Title	If you want to modify the title, input a new title here.
Description	Use the Description field to enter the description that will appear with the published interaction in your Articulate Online account.
Items	The Items property shows how many items comprise the current interaction, including the introduction and summary, if applicable. You can think of an item as the screen that is displayed when the viewer clicks the Next button.
Quality	The default Quality setting is Optimize for Web delivery. The quality can be changed by clicking the Quality link in the Publish dialog box. This opens the Publish Compression dialog box, where the quality setting can be changed.
Color Scheme	The color scheme refers to the colors used by general components of the interaction, such as the screen background and navigation buttons. You typically set this property using the Interaction Properties dialog box when you create the interaction. However, you can modify it here, if needed, by clicking the current value. This opens the Interaction Properties dialog box, where you can change the color scheme in the Colors and Effects tab.
Playback mode	The playback mode refers to the type of navigation control provided to the viewer. The three options for most interactions are *interactive*, *linear*, and *presentation*. You typically set this property using the Interaction Properties dialog box when you create the interaction. However, you can modify it here, if needed, by clicking the current value. This opens the Interaction Properties dialog box, where you can change the navigation control in the Playback tab.
Reporting and Tracking	Click the Reporting and Tracking button to modify the following options, if desired: • Report status as: Choose the label to describe the completion status. The viewer will see this status after working with the interaction. The default value is Completed/Incomplete, which means the status Completed will be displayed if the viewer has viewed the required minimum number of items in the interaction. The status Incomplete will be displayed for fewer than the required minimum number of items. You can change the default label to another option, such as Passed/Failed. • Minimum number of items viewed to complete: Specify how many items in the interaction must be viewed in order to receive a "completed" or "passed" status. The default value is the total number of items in the interaction.
Account Information	Enter the URL of the web site in the Account URL box, and complete the E-mail and Password boxes. This information is provided to you when you set up an Articulate Online account.

Publishing Steps

These steps are general guidelines for publishing from Presenter, Quizmaker, and Engage to Articulate Online. Use Tables 26.9, 26.10, and 26.11 to determine what settings are needed.

1. Click the **Publish** button from the Articulate tab, the **Publish** menu selection from the Articulate menu (Presenter), or the **Publish** button on the Quizmaker or Engage ribbon.

2. In the Publish dialog box, select the **Articulate Online** tab.

3. Input a Title and Description (the description is not required).

4. Input the desired settings in the Properties area (see Tables 26.9, 26.10, and 26.11 for Presenter, Quizmaker, and Engage).

5. Click the **Reporting and Tracking** button (Presenter and Engage) or the **Reporting** button (Quizmaker) and select desired options.

6. Input information in the Account Information area fields for the account URL, email, and password.

7. Click the **Publish** button.

8. When the final output files are published, the Publish Successful dialog box will open.

---

66 **Note:** The Publish Successful dialog box shows only one option, Manage Content, when publishing to Articulate Online (Figure 26.21). If you click the Manage Content button, the content you just published will be launched.

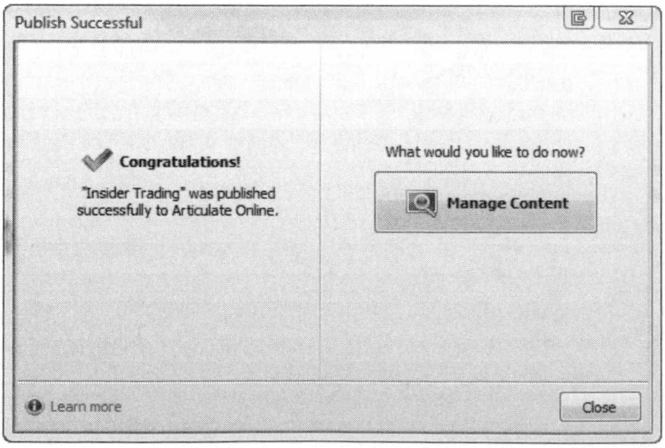

Publish Successful

Congratulations!

"Insider Trading" was published successfully to Articulate Online.

What would you like to do now?

Manage Content

Learn more   Close

Figure 26.21. Publish Successful dialog box

|||| ▶**Tip:** Consider publishing to web on your hard drive (or other storage location) to test your project before uploading to Articulate Online. Publishing to Articulate Online can be time consuming because the content has to be uploaded to the Articulate Online server, so it makes sense to make sure everything works first.

Video Compression Settings

If you plan to use large Flash video (.flv) files, you need to make sure that the video compression setting adequately accounts for viewer bandwidth. Most of the programs that create Flash video allow you to specify a compression setting, so you can select more compression for audiences with lower bandwidth (dial-up or slow DSL connection). Dave Mozealous, Articulate QA Manager, has more information on this topic in his blog: http://www.mozealous.com/?p=59.

Publishing to an LMS

Publishing to LMS means that the tool you are publishing from, whether Presenter, Quizmaker, or Engage, will produce the folders and files needed to view the published output through your learning management system. When you publish to LMS, you may also want to publish a backup copy on your hard drive or other storage medium. If you have an LMS administrator, it is common practice to provide the development files (pre-publishing) or published output files to him or her for loading into the LMS.

---

66 **Note:** LMSs are quite often tricky to work with. The information we are providing is generic, and you may need help from your LMS administrator to upload published output into your LMS.

Tracking

The main reason for using an LMS is to track learners' use and completion of courses. Use is typically tracked by the LMS itself. It may be able to tell you whether the viewer opened the course and what pages he or she opened. Completion, though, is typically tracked by sending data (such as a quiz score) from the course to the LMS.

When you publish to an LMS, you need to select the method you want to use to track completion.

Presenter lets you track one of the following:

- The number of slides viewed (default is number of slides in the project)
- The score from *one* Quizmaker quiz
- The score from *one* Choices Learning Game

Quizmaker lets you track any or all of the following:

- **Score:** The total quiz score is tracked as a percentage. For example, if the viewer scored 40 out of 50 points, the score is tracked as 80%.
- **Status:** The quiz status (Pass/Complete or Fail/Incomplete) is based on whether the viewer's score met the minimum passing score. For example, if the passing score is 80% and the viewer scored 75%, then the status is tracked as Fail or Incomplete. Note that you can decide which status terms to use (Pass, Fail, Complete, Incomplete) when publishing to an LMS or to Articulate Online.
- **Question Detail:** Question details show how the viewer answered each question. For example, the answer choice selected or the short answer entered.

---

66 Note: Quizmaker tracks how each viewer answered each question. This is important data that can be used to continually improve your questions. Unfortunately, not all LMSs can capture and report question details. If you are considering purchasing an LMS, I (Patti) feel strongly that you *should* be able to capture question details. Then *use those details to improve your questions.*

Engage lets you track any or all of the following:

■ **Number of items viewed:** An item is a screen that is displayed when the viewer clicks the Next button. For example, if a Process interaction consists of 10 steps, the interaction consists of 10 items. Each step that is displayed counts as one item viewed.

■ **Status:** The interaction status (Pass/Complete or Fail/Incomplete) is based on the minimum number of items that the viewer must work with to complete the interaction. You can specify the minimum number when publishing to an LMS or to Articulate Online. For example, if you specify a minimum 12 (out of 14) items, then the viewer must work with at least 12 items to receive a Pass/Complete score. Note that you can decide which status terms to use (Pass, Fail, Complete, Incomplete) when publishing to an LMS or to Articulate Online.

So what should you track? We think the answer, in most cases, should be to track something meaningful, such as a Quizmaker quiz score or Choices Learning Game score. It seems silly to track number of pages viewed in most cases because the number of pages viewed isn't very meaningful. But in "compliance" courses, tracking page views may be necessary. Tracking a quiz or Learning Game at least provides some information about each viewer's understanding. (We realize that the decision of what to track is sometimes based on pragmatics, not on what makes sense instructionally.)

Figures 26.22, 26.23, and 26.24 show the Publish dialog box with the LMS tab open for Presenter, Quizmaker, and Engage, respectively. Tables 26.12, 26.13, and 26.14 describe the settings available when the LMS tab for that tool is selected.

Publishing

Presenter—Publish to LMS

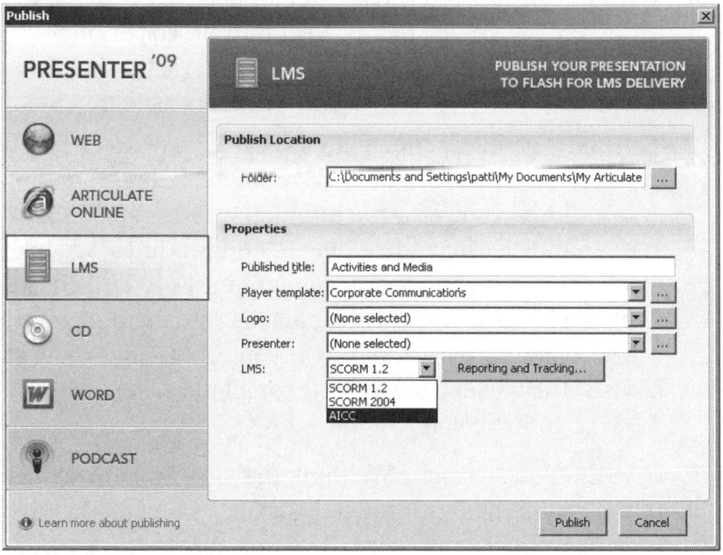

Figure 26.22. Presenter publish to LMS tab

Table 26.12 describes the settings and properties on the LMS tab of the Presenter Publish dialog box.

Table 26.12. Presenter Publish dialog box settings

Property/setting	Description
Publish Location Folder	Select the location where the published output files will be created. The default location is My Documents\My Articulate Projects. You can click the ellipsis button ([...]) to browse for the location or type a directory path to select the location where the published output should reside.
	Saving the published output files to your hard disk is a good idea for backing up the files, but it doesn't put the published output files in a place that others can view unless they are using your computer.
	When publishing to an LMS, you may need help from your company's IT department or your LMS administrator to find out where to put your files and how to get them there. They may need to create a directory and permissions to allow you to upload the files or they may want to do the uploading themselves.

Property/setting	Description
Published title	Published title is the title of the published project as it is seen by viewers on the title bar of the player. The title can be changed by clicking the link and entering a new title. We recommend that the title match the title page of your slides.
Player template	This option lets you select a template to use for the current project from the preconfigured templates that come with Presenter or from custom templates you have created and saved previously. Custom player templates are created using the Player Template Manager dialog box. (See Chapter 7, "Customizing Presenter Player Templates," for more information about this topic.)
Logo	This option lets you select a logo from a list of previously added logos to use for the current project. You can add logos using the Presentation Options dialog box (using the Presentation Options button on the Articulate tab or the Presentation Options menu selection on the Articulate menu). You can also select (None selected), in which case no logo will appear.
Presenter	This option lets you select a presenter (typically the narrator) from a list of previously added presenters to use for the current project. Information about the presenter can be shown on the Presenter player. You can add presenters using the Presentation Options dialog box (using the Presentation Options button on the Articulate tab or the Presentation Options menu selection on the Articulate menu). You can also select (None selected), in which case no presenter will appear.
	If you have multiple presenters (for example, Patti presents slides 1-10 and Jennifer presents slides 11-20), presenters can be set up at the slide level in Slide Properties. (They need to be set up in Presentation Options first.)
LMS	Select the industry standard to use from the LMS list (your LMS vendor or administrator should be able to provide you with this information): SCORM 1.2, SCORM 2004, or AICC.
	Information about selecting reporting and tracking settings for all tools is provided later in this section.

Quizmaker—Publish to LMS

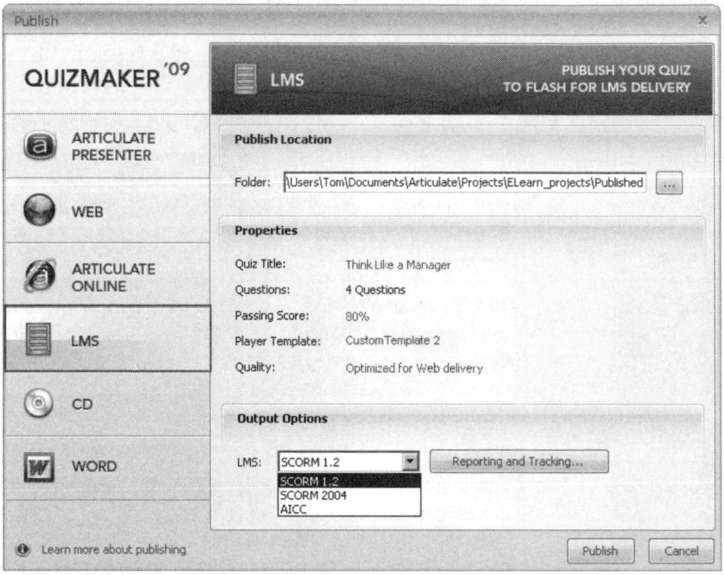

Figure 26.23. Quizmaker publish to LMS tab

Table 26.13 describes the settings and properties on the LMS tab of the Quizmaker Publish dialog box.

Table 26.13. Quizmaker Publish dialog box settings

Property/setting	Description
Publish Location Folder	Select the location where the published output files will be created. The default location is My Documents\My Articulate Projects. You can click the ellipsis button (⬚) to browse for the location or type a directory path to select the location where the published output should reside.
	Saving the published output files to your hard disk is a good idea for backing up the files, but it doesn't put the published output files in a place that others can view unless they are using your computer.
	When publishing to an LMS, you may need help from your company's IT department or your LMS administrator to find out where to put your files and how to get them there. They may need to create a directory and permissions to allow you to upload the files or they may want to do the uploading themselves.
Quiz Title	Quiz Title is the title of the published quiz as it is seen by viewers on the title bar of the player. The title can be changed by clicking the Quiz Title link and entering a new title in the Quiz Properties dialog box.
Questions	This is the number of questions in the quiz.

Property/setting	Description
Passing Score	The default passing score is 80%. The passing score default can be changed by clicking the Passing Score link in the Publish dialog box. This opens the Quiz Properties dialog box, where the passing score can be changed. (The passing score can also be set by inputting a score percentage in the Quiz Properties dialog box during development of a graded quiz.)
Player Template	This option lets you select a template to use for the current quiz from the preconfigured templates that come with Quizmaker or from custom templates you have created and saved previously. Custom player templates are created using the Player Template Manager dialog box.
Quality	The default Quality setting is Optimized for Web delivery. The quality can be changed by clicking the Quality link in the Publish dialog box. This opens the Publish Compression dialog box, where the quality setting can be changed. **Note:** Higher quality means larger file sizes and more bandwidth needed to view and interact with the quiz.
LMS	Select the industry standard to use from the LMS list (your LMS vendor or administrator should be able to provide you with this information): SCORM 1.2, SCORM 2004, or AICC. Information about selecting reporting and tracking settings for all tools is provided later in this section.

Engage—Publish to LMS

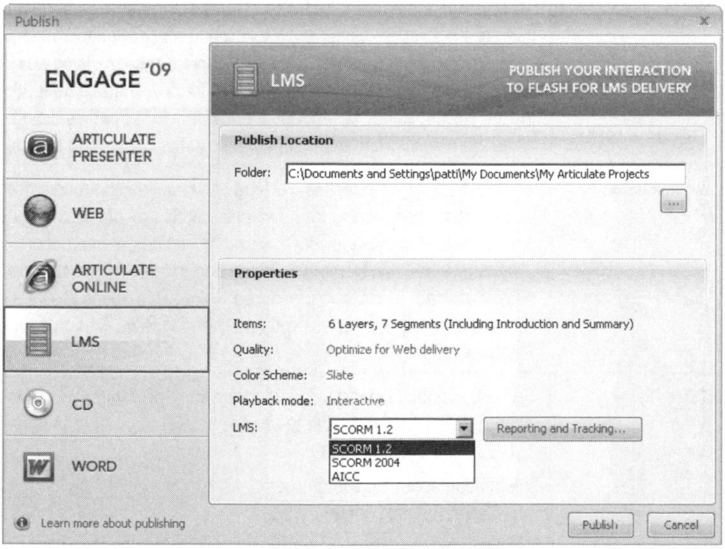

Figure 26.24. Engage publish to LMS tab

Table 26.14 describes the settings and properties on the LMS tab of the Engage Publish dialog box.

Table 26.14. Engage Publish dialog box settings

Property/setting	Description
Publish Location Folder	Select the location where the published output files will be created. The default location is My Documents\My Articulate Projects. You can click the ellipsis button (⬚) to browse for the location or type a directory path to select the location where the published output should reside.
	Saving the published output files to your hard disk is a good idea for backing up the files, but it doesn't put the published output files in a place that others can view unless they are using your computer.
	When publishing to an LMS, you may need help from your company's IT department or your LMS administrator to find out where to put your files and how to get them there. They may need to create a directory and permissions to allow you to upload the files or they may want to do the uploading themselves.
Items	The Items property shows how many items comprise the current interaction, including the introduction and summary, if applicable. You can think of an item as the screen that is displayed when the viewer clicks the Next button.
Quality	The default Quality setting is Optimize for Web delivery. The quality can be changed by clicking the Quality link in the Publish dialog box. This opens the Publish Compression dialog box, where the quality setting can be changed.
Color Scheme	The color scheme refers to the colors used by general components of the interaction, such as the screen background and navigation buttons. You typically set this property using the Interaction Properties dialog box when you create the interaction. However, you can modify it here, if needed, by clicking the current value. This opens the Interaction Properties dialog box, where you can change the color scheme in the Colors and Effects tab.
Playback mode	The playback mode refers to the type of navigation control provided to the viewer. The three options for most interactions are *interactive*, *linear*, and *presentation*. You typically set this property using the Interaction Properties dialog box when you create the interaction. However, you can modify it here, if needed, by clicking the current value. This opens the Interaction Properties dialog box, where you can change the navigation control in the Playback tab.
LMS	Select the industry standard to use from the LMS list (your LMS vendor or administrator should be able to provide you with this information): SCORM 1.2, SCORM 2004, or AICC.
	Information about selecting reporting and tracking settings for all tools is provided in the next section.

Reporting and Tracking

When using the LMS tab of the Publish dialog box for Presenter, Quizmaker, and Engage, you'll see a Reporting and Tracking button. This is where you will select applicable reporting and tracking settings. The information in this section should be considered as guidelines only, because each LMS has its own idiosyncrasies. If you have an LMS administrator, he or she will likely provide you with a list of reporting and tracking settings to use or will handle this part of the publishing process for you.

Figures 26.25, 26.26, 26.27, and 26.28 show the Reporting and Tracking Options dialog box for Presenter (Reporting tab), Presenter (Tracking tab), Quizmaker, and Engage, respectively. Note that these figures show the reporting and tracking options available when SCORM 1.2 is chosen. The options are different for SCORM 2004 and AICC.

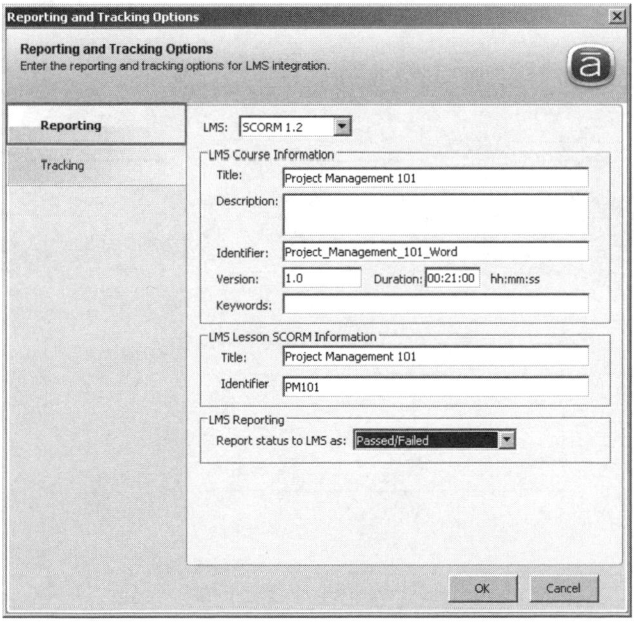

Figure 26.25. Presenter Reporting and Tracking Options dialog box, Reporting tab

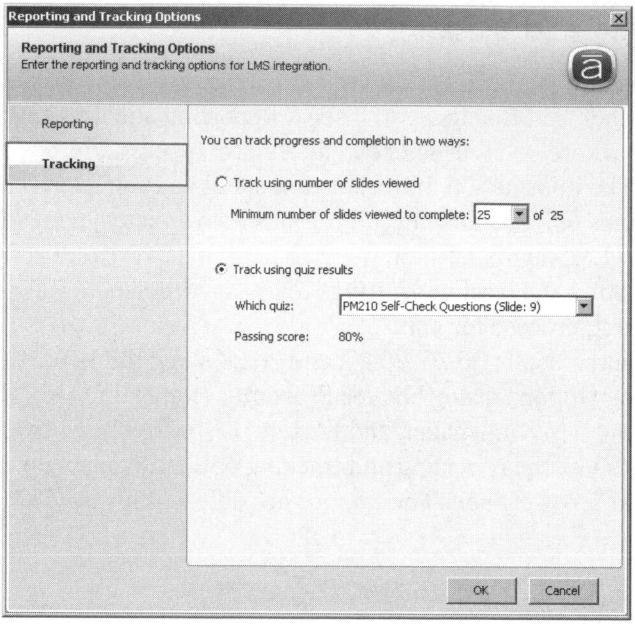

Figure 26.26. Presenter Reporting and Tracking Options dialog box, Tracking tab

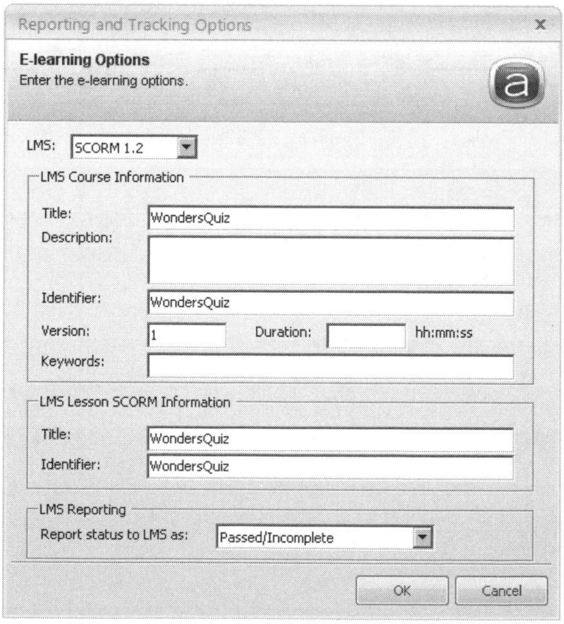

Figure 26.27. Quizmaker Reporting and Tracking Options dialog box

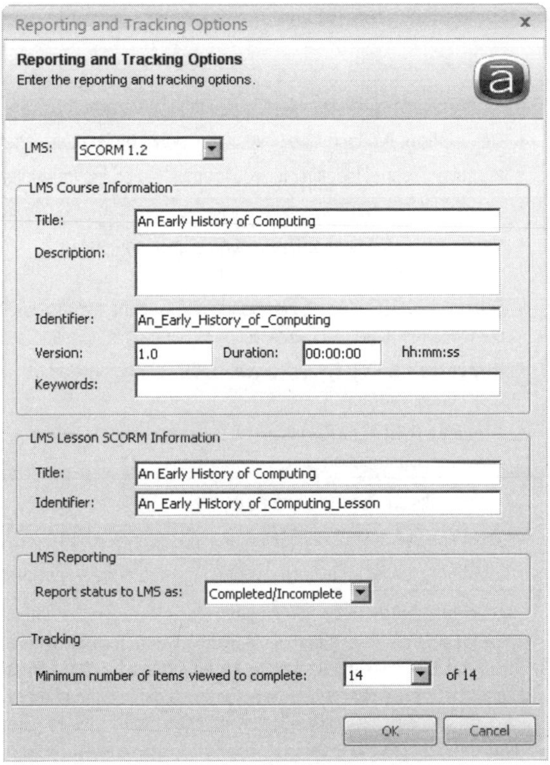

Figure 26.28. Engage Reporting and Tracking Options dialog box

Table 26.15 describes reporting and tracking options that can be input or edited on the Presenter (Reporting tab and Tracking tab), Quizmaker, and Engage Reporting and Tracking Options dialog boxes. Not all settings apply to all tools or all LMS standards.

Table 26.15. Reporting and Tracking Options dialog box settings

Options	Settings	
Reporting options	LMS Course Information	• **Title**: The title of the completed project/quiz/interaction • **Description**: A description of your completed project/quiz/interaction • **Identifier**: A brief identifier for your completed project/quiz/interaction • **Creator** (*AICC only*): The author's name • **Version** (*SCORM only*): The version of your completed project/quiz/interaction, if applicable • **Duration** (*SCORM only*): How long it will take the average user to complete the project/quiz/interaction in hours, minutes, and seconds • **Keywords** (*SCORM only*): Keywords for your completed project/quiz/interaction • **Filename (URL)** (*AICC only*): The location of the published project/quiz/interaction
	LMS Lesson SCORM Information	(*SCORM only*, can be the same as above) • **Title**: The title of your completed project/quiz/interaction • **Identifier**: A brief identifier for your completed project/quiz/interaction
	LMS Reporting	Choose the label to describe the completion status. The viewer will see this status label when he or she has completed the project/quiz/interaction. The default value is Passed/Incomplete, which means the status Passed will be displayed if the viewer has viewed the required minimum number of items. The status Incomplete will be displayed for fewer than the required minimum number of items. **Tip:** If the completed project includes a graded quiz or choices game, it may make sense to use Passed/Failed and track the score. If the project does *not* include a graded quiz or choices game, it may make sense to use Completed/Incomplete and track the slides. In that case, completion should be set by having learners view all slides. (Yes, we did say this was not terribly useful earlier in the chapter, but it doesn't make sense tracking Complete/Incomplete any other way if there isn't a graded quiz or choices game.)
Tracking options	Presenter	Track number of slides viewed and quiz results. • **Number of slides viewed**: Viewer must view a specific number of slides before the completion status is set to Passed (or whatever label you selected for completed). The default is the total number of slides in the project. • **Quiz results**: Viewer must complete a Quizmaker quiz or choices Learning Game with a minimum of the set passing score before the completion status is set to Passed (or whatever label you selected for completed). The Passing score is defined in your quiz or Learning Game.

Options	Settings	
	Quizmaker	Track score and completion, and view question details.
		• **Score:** The minimum passing score is set in the Quiz Properties dialog box. (Setting this passing score is discussed in Chapter 9, "Quizmaker Basics.")
		• **LMS Reporting:** As discussed earlier, the reporting status (Pass/Complete or Failed/Incomplete) is based on whether the viewer's score met the set minimum passing score. For example, if the passing score is 80% and the viewer scored 75%, the status is tracked as either Failed or Incomplete.
		• **Question Detail:** If your LMS supports tracking question data, you can query your LMS to see how each viewer answered each question. This can be used to improve your questions.
	Engage	Track number of items viewed.
		Viewer must view a certain number of items in the interaction to receive a Pass or Complete status. The default value is the total number of items in the interaction. Status (Pass/Complete or Fail/Incomplete) is based on the minimum number of items that the viewer must view to complete the interaction. You can specify the minimum number of items to view. Note that you can decide which status terms to use (see the LMS Reporting section of this table).

In SCORM 2004 there are two types of status—Completion and Success. "Completion" refers to whether the viewer has *finished* the learning object (Complete/Incomplete). Completion is tracked using number of pages/items/questions viewed or answered. Success refers to whether the viewer's *score is high enough* (Pass/Fail). Success is tracked using the percentage correct score on a test or Learning Game.

Completion status can provide one of the following values to the LMS: Complete, Incomplete, not_attempted, and unknown. Complete means that the viewer has viewed enough of the content to consider the learning object completed. Incomplete means that the viewer has *not* viewed enough of the content to consider the learning object completed.

Success status can provide one of these values to the LMS: Passed, Failed, or unknown. Passed means the viewer has mastered the content. Failed means that the viewer has *not* mastered the content. Mastery is calculated as a percentage score on a test or Learning Game. To pass, the viewer must achieve a minimum of a certain percentage correct.

In SCORM 1.2 and AICC, there is only one "Status," but using two statuses allows the LMS to track finishing the content separately from mastering the content. It's easy to see that viewers could have a completion status of "Complete" because they viewed all of the slides or items, but also have a success status of "Failed" because they did not get a high enough score on the test.

If you select SCORM 2004, the status Articulate sends to the LMS is based on a formula, which is partially based on your selection in the LMS Reporting section of the Reporting and Tracking Options dialog box (where you select Passed/Incomplete, Passed/Failed, Completed/Incomplete, or Completed/Failed). For example, if you select Passed/Failed, here's what is sent to the LMS:

- If viewer doesn't do what is necessary to pass:
  - The Success status is set to "Failed."
  - The Completion status is set to "Complete" because "Failed" means viewer has finished.

- If viewer does do what is necessary to pass:
  - The Completion status is set to "Completed."
  - The Success status is set to "Passed."

The takeaway here is that reporting and tracking are complex issues. Understanding how learning standards work and how Articulate applications work with the standards and learning management systems is beyond the scope of this book. But it's good to have a smidgen of understanding about what is going on "behind the scenes."

Publishing Steps

These steps are general guidelines for publishing from Presenter, Quizmaker, and Engage to LMS. Use Tables 26.12, 26.13, and 26.14 to determine what settings are needed.

1. Click the **Publish** button from the Articulate tab, the **Publish** menu selection from the Articulate menu (Presenter), or the **Publish** button on the Quizmaker or Engage ribbon. The Publish dialog box opens.

2. Select the **LMS** tab in the Publish dialog box.

3. Specify a Publish Location.

4. Input the desired properties and output options (see Tables 26.12, 26.13, and 26.14).

5. Click the **Reporting and Tracking** button. The Reporting and Tracking Options dialog box opens. (See the reporting and tracking options in Table 26.15.)

6. Input or select reporting and tracking options.

7. Click **OK** to save your LMS metadata.

8. Click the **Publish** button. When the final output files are published, the Publish Successful dialog box will open.

9. In the Publish Successful dialog box, choose whether to view the project/quiz/interaction, send as email, send to an FTP site, create a Zip file, or open the folder containing the published files.

10. Test the final output by viewing all pages, all media (such as audio and video), and all interactions (such as Engage interactions and Quizmaker quizzes). Make note of any problems that need to be fixed and fix them in the development files (not the published output files), as needed. *Then republish and retest, if necessary.*

11. Provide the files to the LMS administrator or publish them to your LMS.

Tip: Consider publishing to web on your hard drive (or other storage location) to test your project before uploading to the LMS.

Note: If your LMS administrator has to upload your files, he or she may ask you to also send the SCORM zip file. Select Zip file from the Publish Successful dialog box to launch a dialog box where you can save the SCORM zip file in a selected location.

Video Compression Settings

If you plan to use large Flash video (.flv) files, you need to make sure that the video compression setting adequately accounts for viewer bandwidth. Most of the programs that create Flash video allow you to specify a compression setting, so you can select more compression for audiences with lower bandwidth (dial-up or slow DSL connection). Dave Mozealous, Articulate QA Manager, has more information on this topic in his blog: http://www.mozealous.com/?p=59.

> **Note:** Articulate has a helpful blog posting about troubleshooting Articulate and LMS issues (original posting: http://www.articulate.com/blog/9-ways-to-troubleshoot-articulate-lms-issues).

Output Files

When publishing to LMS, a variety of file types are produced. Output files will vary, based on the learning standard (SCORM 1.2, SCORM 2004, or AICC) selected.

SCORM 1.2-Specific Files

imsmanifest.xml: This file tells the LMS about the SCORM package (what files are included, how the content is organized, what the passing score is, etc.).

.xsd documents: These files describe the schema or structure of the imsmanifest.xml file.

SCORM 2004-Specific Files

imsmanifest.xml: This file tells the LMS about the SCORM package (what files are included, how the content is organized, what the passing score is, etc.).

.xsd documents: These files describe the schema or structure of the imsmanifest.xml file.

metadata.xml: This file describes the content package and the characteristics of the content package, and in some LMSs, makes search and discoverability of the content package possible.

AICC-Specific Files

course.* files (course.au, course.crs, course.cst, course.des): These four files tell the LMS about the content (location of the content, passing score, time limit of the content, etc.)

HTML Files

player.html (Presenter only): This file displays the presentation SWF.

quiz.html (Quizmaker only): This file displays the quiz SWF.

engage.html (Engage only): This file displays the interaction SWF.

index_lms.html (all): This file launches the presentation/quiz/interaction and manages the communication with the LMS.

Folders

The quiz_content folder and the engage_content folder contain supporting files required to run the quiz or interaction.
 The lms folder contains the files that communicate with the LMS.
 The common folder, extend folder, unique folder, and vocab folder (SCORM 2004 only) contain control documents.

Publishing to CD

Publishing to CD lets you provide electronic copies of published output to testers or viewers. For example, you may not have a development server (typically used to stage and test content before it is put on a server to which viewers can have access), but may want testers to see if there are any problems with the published output before going live. You may want to use large media files and not tie up bandwidth on your network. Or you may want to distribute promotional materials to prospective clients at trade shows. Publishing to CD is also helpful when viewers do not have network or Internet access, or when access to the network or Internet is sporadic or slow.

 Figures 26.29, 26.30, and 26.31 show the Publish dialog box with the CD tab open for Presenter, Quizmaker, and Engage, respectively. Tables 26.16, 26.17, and 26.18 describe the settings available when the CD tab for that tool is selected.

Presenter—Publish to CD

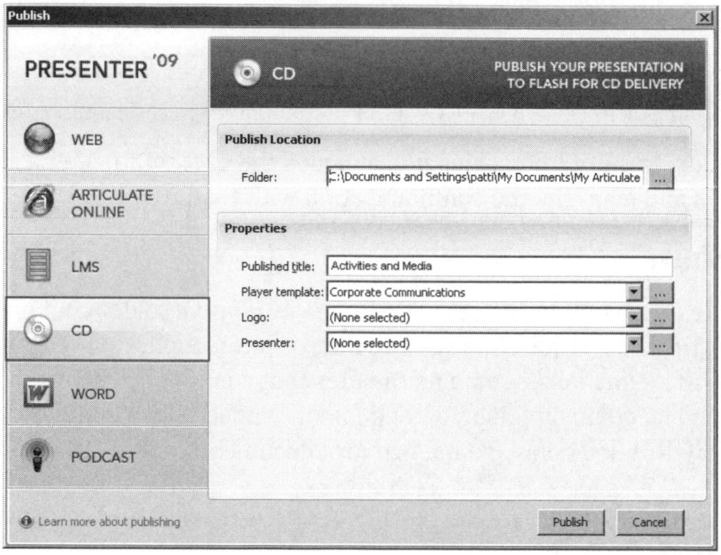

Figure 26.29. Presenter publish to CD tab

Table 26.16 describes the settings and properties on the CD tab of the Presenter Publish dialog box.

Table 26.16. Presenter Publish dialog box settings

Property/setting	Description
Publish Location Folder	Select the location where the published output files will be created. The default location is My Documents\My Articulate Projects. You can click the ellipsis button ( ) to browse for the location or type a directory path to select the location where the published output should reside.
Published title	This is the title of the published project as it is seen by viewers on the title bar of the player. The title can be changed by clicking the link and entering a new title. We recommend that the title match the title page of your slides.
Player template	This option lets you select a template to use for the current project from the preconfigured templates that come with Presenter or from custom templates you have created and saved previously. Custom player templates are created using the Player Template Manager dialog box. (See Chapter 7, "Customizing Presenter Player Templates," for more information about this topic.)

Property/setting	Description
Logo	This option lets you select a logo from a list of previously added logos to use for the current project. You can add logos using the Presentation Options dialog box (accessed by clicking the Presentation Options button on the Articulate tab or by choosing the Presentation Options menu selection on the Articulate menu). You can also select (None selected), in which case, no logo will appear.
Presenter	This option lets you select a presenter (typically the narrator) from a list of previously added presenters to use for the current project. Information about the presenter can be shown on the Presenter player. You can add presenters using the Presentation Options dialog box (accessed by clicking the Presentation Options button on the Articulate tab or the Presentation Options menu selection on the Articulate menu). You can also select (None selected), in which case, no presenter will appear. If you have multiple presenters (for example, Patti presents slides 1-10 and Jennifer presents slides 11-20), presenters can be set up at the slide level in Slide Properties. (They need to be set up in Presentation Options first.)

Quizmaker—Publish to CD

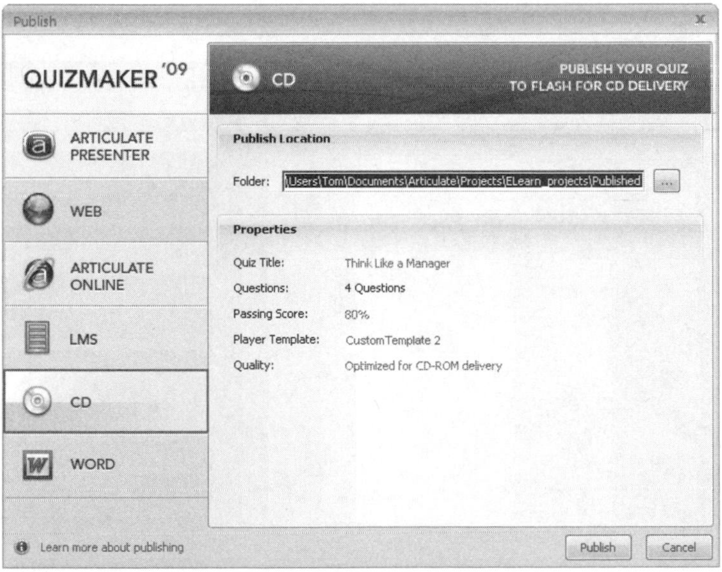

Figure 26.30. Quizmaker publish to CD tab

Table 26.17 describes the settings and properties on the CD tab of the Quizmaker Publish dialog box.

Table 26.17. Quizmaker Publish dialog box settings

Property/setting	Description
Publish Location Folder	Select the location where the published output files will be created. The default location is My Documents\My Articulate Projects. You can click the ellipsis button (⬚) to browse for the location or type a directory path to select the location where the published output should reside.
Quiz Title	This is the title of the published quiz as it is seen by viewers on the title bar of the player. The title can be changed by clicking the Quiz Title link and entering a new title in the Quiz Properties dialog box.
Questions	This is the number of questions in the quiz.
Passing Score	The default passing score is 80%. The passing score default can be changed by clicking the Passing Score link in the Publish dialog box. This opens the Quiz Properties dialog box, where the passing score can be changed. (The passing score can also be set by inputting a score percentage in the Quiz Properties dialog box during development of a graded quiz.)
Player Template	This option lets you select a template to use for the current quiz from the preconfigured templates that come with Quizmaker or from custom templates you have created and saved previously. Custom player templates are created using the Player Template Manager dialog box.
Quality	The default Quality setting is Optimized for CD-ROM delivery. The quality can be changed by clicking the Quality link in the Publish dialog box. This opens the Publish Compression dialog box, where the quality setting can be changed.

Engage—Publish to CD

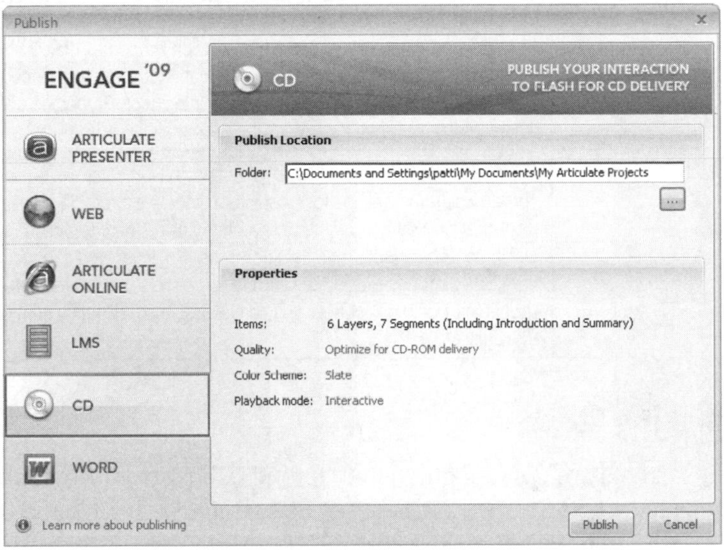

Figure 26.31. Engage publish to CD tab

Table 26.18 describes the settings and properties on the CD tab of the Engage Publish dialog box.

Table 26.18. Engage Publish dialog box settings

Property/setting	Description
Publish Location Folder	Select the location where the published output files will be created. The default location is My Documents\My Articulate Projects. You can click the ellipsis button (⬚) to browse for the location or type a directory path to select the location where the published output should reside.
Items	The Items property shows how many items comprise the current interaction, including the introduction and summary, if applicable. You can think of an item as the screen that is displayed when the viewer clicks the Next button.
Quality	The default Quality setting is Optimize for CD-ROM delivery. The quality can be changed by clicking the Quality link in the Publish dialog box. This opens the Publish Compression dialog box, where the quality setting can be changed.

Property/setting	Description
Color Scheme	The color scheme refers to the colors used by general components of the interaction, such as the screen background and navigation buttons. You typically set this property using the Interaction Properties dialog box when you create the interaction. However, you can modify it here, if needed, by clicking the current value. This opens the Interaction Properties dialog box, where you can change the color scheme in the Colors and Effects tab.
Playback mode	The playback mode refers to the type of navigation control provided to the viewer. The three options for most interactions are *interactive*, *linear*, and *presentation*. You typically set this property using the Interaction Properties dialog box when you create the interaction. However, you can modify it here, if needed, by clicking the current value. This opens the Interaction Properties dialog box, where you can change the navigation control in the Playback tab.

Publishing Steps

These steps are general guidelines for publishing from Presenter, Quizmaker, and Engage to CD. Use the settings in Tables 26.16, 26.17, and 26.18 to determine what settings are needed.

1. Click the **Publish** button from the Articulate tab, the **Publish** menu selection from the Articulate menu (Presenter), or the **Publish** button on the Quizmaker or Engage ribbon. The Publish dialog box opens.

2. Select the **CD** tab on the Publish dialog box.

3. Specify a publish location.

4. Input the desired properties settings (see Tables 26.16, 26.17, and 26.18).

5. Click the **Publish** button.

6. In the Publish Successful dialog box, choose whether to view the published output, send as email, send to an FTP site, create a Zip file, or open the folder containing the published files.

7. Test your project by viewing all pages and all media. Make note of any problems that need to be fixed and fix them in the development files (not the published output files), as needed. Republish and retest, if necessary.

8. Copy the final output folders and files to a CD using any CD burning program.

Output Files

When you publish to CD, a folder is created that contains that project's published output. The following output folders and files are created.

Launch File (Presenter/Quizmaker/Engage)

The launch file for Presenter, Quizmaker, and Engage (Launch_Presentation.exe, Launch_Quiz.exe, and Launch_ Engage.exe, respectively) is a self-contained executable/player for launching the project's published output without a web browser. The launch file is ideal for CDs since it avoids Flash security and other issues.

Tip: If you want to customize the .exe icon, there is a support article on this topic at http://www.articulate.com/support/presenter09/kb/?p=519.

The .html file can launch the project through a web browser, but it is preferable to use the .exe file because it gets around browser security issues. A developer can specify which file should be launched by editing the file name entry in the loader.ini file. (By default, the.html file is used.)

Flash File(s) (Presenter/Quizmaker/Engage)

Flash output files (slide.swf, quiz.swf, engage.swf) contain the Flash output of the project/interaction/quiz.

Data Folder (Presenter)

The data folder contains:

- A swf folder, which contains individual .swf files for each page of the project.
- A playerproperties.xml file, which gives the player properties information such as color scheme, navigation restrictions, tabs, and so on.
- A presentation.xml file, which contains slide-specific information including slide notes, slide view, timings, and so on.

Content Folder (Quizmaker/Engage)

The quiz_content folder and the engage_content folder contain supporting files required to run the quiz or interaction.

Player Folder (Presenter)

This folder contains pieces of the Presenter player, including .swf files, .html files, .gif files, and .js files. These files contain all the information the player needs to "play" the project.

Other Files (Presenter/Quizmaker/Engage)

- autorun.inf: Instructs the computer to launch the project/interaction/quiz when the viewer inserts the CD into the CD drive.
- load.ini: Contains information used by the executable file (Launch_Presentation.exe, Launch_Quiz.exe, and Launch_Interaction.exe).

 Note: Presenter projects that are published to CD publish with higher quality settings than Presenter projects published to web. As a result, Presenter CD output file sizes are likely to be bigger than if you publish the same project to web.

Make Sure It Works

When you publish to CD, make sure to completely test the development files and then the published output files *before* distribution. Once your files are distributed on CD, you cannot easily get them back to make changes. For this same reason, it's a good idea to label CD output with the date published so newer CD versions can be easily distinguishable from older CD versions.

Publishing to Word

Publishing to Word creates a Microsoft Word document that displays content and information about the content. Publishing to Word allows you to share content with others without having to upload the actual files. This is especially useful when collecting input from subject matter experts, stakeholders (such as your boss or client), or others on the design team. Although you can provide the content on a CD, providing it in Word allows these individuals to comment directly, either on a printed copy or electronically (for example, using Track Changes).

You can also use publish to Word functionality as a project storyboard. If you are thinking "So what?" consider how much of a pain it is to maintain a storyboard that matches the associated on-screen content. Mary makes a change to slide 6 and Toby edits the tables on slides 3, 16, 27, and 30. Now the slides and the storyboard don't match. If you publish to Word (as a storyboard), the content *is* the storyboard. Figure 26.32 shows a section of the storyboard for a specific Presenter project. The left column provides slide information. The middle column shows a thumbnail of the slide, and the right column shows the narration script from the slide notes pane. Figure 26.33 shows a page from a Quizmaker quiz published to Word.

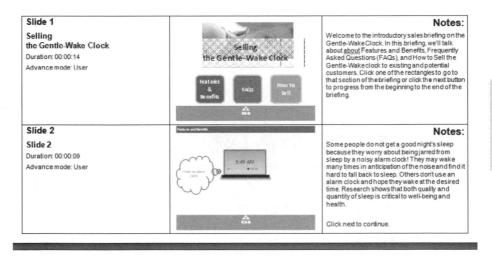

Figure 26.32. Presenter project published to Word (storyboard)

Questions

Question Group 1

1. Why are technology-related risks hard to specify on long (12+ months) projects?

(Multiple Choice Question, 10 points, 1 attempt permitted)

Why are technology-related risks hard to specify on long (12+ months) projects?

○ Some team members may be less comfortable with technology. They may resist using it.

◉ Technologies can change over time. It's hard to specify risks on less known elements.

○ Technology costs are likely to go down over time so calculated risks may be too high.

Correct	Choice
	Some team members may be less comfortable with technology. They may resist using it.
X	Technologies can change over time. It's hard to specify risks on less known elements.
	Technology costs are likely to go down over time so calculated risks may be too high.

Figure 26.33. Quizmaker quiz published to Word

Here are a few other uses for publish to Word functionality.

- **Changes, approvals and sign-offs:** You can publish to Word and send the published Word file electronically to anyone who needs to provide changes, approvals, and sign-offs. Stakeholders can input changes and questions in the document.

Tip: The file size of these documents can be quite large. If it gets too large, you can often reduce the file size by saving as a PDF document. (But using a PDF may make it harder to provide input unless reviewers have a tool that allows them to mark up PDF files.)

- **Archiving:** An electronic or print-based copy of the finalized content in Word format makes it easy to get information about the project in the future (without having to open the actual project).
- **Maintenance:** A copy of the storyboard can be sent to stakeholders and subject matter experts to solicit needed updates.
- **Accessibility:** Published to Word files can be useful for viewers who use screen readers or those who would benefit from a printable version.
- **Handouts:** A printable version of your project, quiz, or interaction can be used as a handout or takeaway.

> Got it! Publish to Word can make my life easier!

Figures 26.34, 26.35, and 26.36 show the Publish dialog box with the Word tab open for Presenter, Quizmaker, and Engage, respectively. Tables 26.19, 26.20, and 26.21 describe the settings available when the Word tab for that tool is selected.

Presenter—Publish to Word

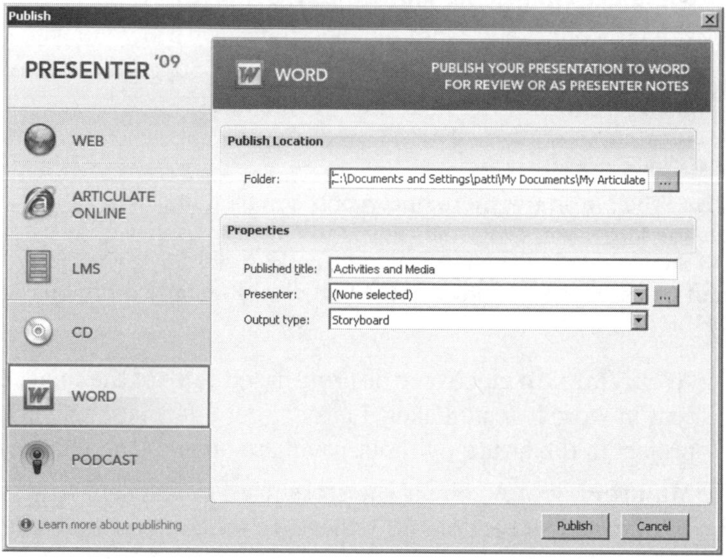

Figure 26.34. Presenter publish to Word tab

Table 26.19 describes the settings and properties on the Word tab of the Presenter Publish dialog box.

Table 26.19. Presenter Publish dialog box settings

Property/setting	Description
Publish Location Folder	Select the location where the published output files will be created. The default location is My Documents\My Articulate Projects. If you want to save it elsewhere, you can click the ellipsis button (⬚) to browse for the location or type a directory path to select the location where the published output should reside.
Published title	This is the title of the published project.
Presenter	This option lets you select a presenter (typically the narrator) from a list of previously added presenters to use for the current project. Information about the presenter can be shown on the Presenter player. You can add presenters using the Presentation Options dialog box (using the Presentation Options button on the Articulate tab or the Presentation Options menu selection on the Articulate menu). You can also select (None selected), in which case, no presenter will appear.
	If you have multiple presenters (for example, Patti presents slides 1-10 and Jennifer presents slides 11-20), presenters can be set up at the slide level in Slide Properties. (They need to be set up in Presentation Options first.)

Property/setting	Description
Output type	Storyboard is the default output type. Storyboard output contains the most detailed information, and includes slide thumbnails and slide notes, Web Object information, and other media information. Choosing Presenter Notes creates output that contains the Slide Notes (narration script) only.

Quizmaker—Publish to Word

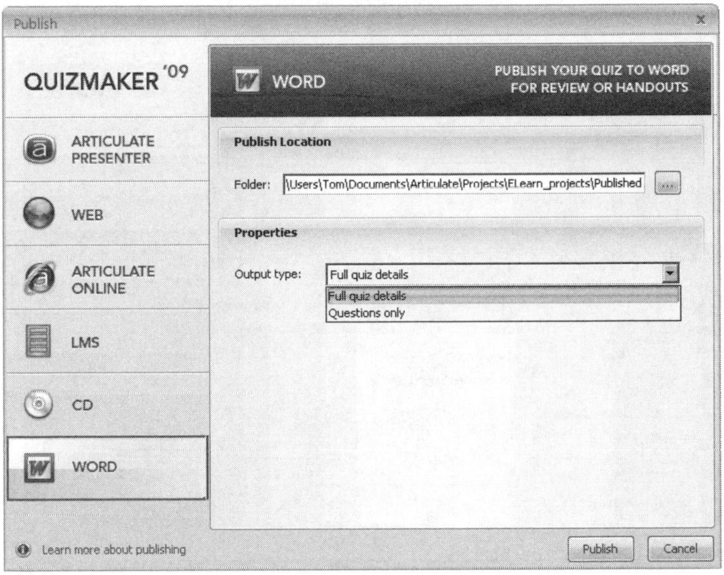

Figure 26.35. Quizmaker publish to Word tab

Table 26.20 describes the settings and properties on the Word tab of the Quizmaker Publish dialog box.

Table 26.20. Quizmaker Publish dialog box settings

Property/setting	Description
Publish Location Folder	Select the location where the published output files will be created. The default location is My Documents\My Articulate Projects. If you want to save it elsewhere, you can click the ellipsis button ( ) to browse for the location or type a directory path to select the location where the published output should reside.
Output type	Full quiz details is the default output type and creates a Word document with all quiz details. Questions only creates a Word document with questions only (which is useful for producing a paper-based quiz).

> **Note:** Publishing to Word is the *only* way to print a quiz. If you select the Print command from the File menu in Quizmaker, the Publish dialog box automatically opens with the Word tab selected.

Engage—Publish to Word

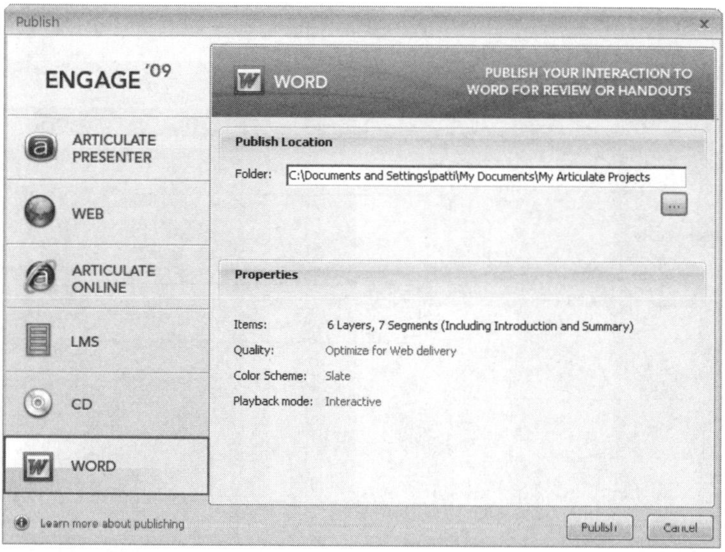

Figure 26.36. Engage publish to Word tab

Table 26.21 describes the settings and properties on the Word tab of the Engage Publish dialog box.

Table 26.21. Engage Publish dialog box settings

Property/setting	Description
Publish Location Folder	Select the location where the published output files will be created. The default location is My Documents\My Articulate Projects. If you want to save it elsewhere, you can click the ellipsis button (![...]) to browse for the location or type a directory path to select the location where the published output should reside.
Properties	The published output will show the color scheme, so make sure the selected color scheme is correct.

Publishing Steps

These steps are general guidelines for publishing from Presenter, Quizmaker, and Engage to Word. Use Tables 26.19, 26.20, and 26.21 to determine what settings are needed.

1. Click the **Publish** button from the Articulate tab, the **Publish** menu selection from the Articulate menu (Presenter), or the **Publish** button on the Quizmaker or Engage ribbon. The Publish dialog box opens.

2. Select the **Word** tab on the Publish dialog box.

3. Specify a publish location.

4. Input the desired properties (see Tables 26.19, 26.20, and 26.21).

5. Click the **Publish** button.

6. When the final output files are published, the Publish Successful dialog box will open. You can choose whether to view the Presenter project published output (a Word document), send as email, send to an FTP site, create a Zip file, or open the folder containing the published file. You can also close the dialog box without selecting one of these options.

Output Files

When publishing to Word, the following file is created.

Word (.doc) File

The Word document contains the content from your project/interaction/quiz. The content included in the document depends on the output type chosen (for Presenter and Quizmaker).

Publishing to Podcast

You can package the audio files used in a Presenter project as an audio-only file for viewers to listen to online (in a small player) or as an .mp3 file that can be listened to using MP3 players.

If you are developing complex content or building courses with critical tests (as part of a certification process, for example), learners may wish to listen to the content to review or study it. And, in case this isn't obvious, Presenter can produce the podcasts that you wish to provide, regardless of whether they are part of a presentation or course.

Figure 26.37 shows the Publish dialog box Podcast tab for Presenter.

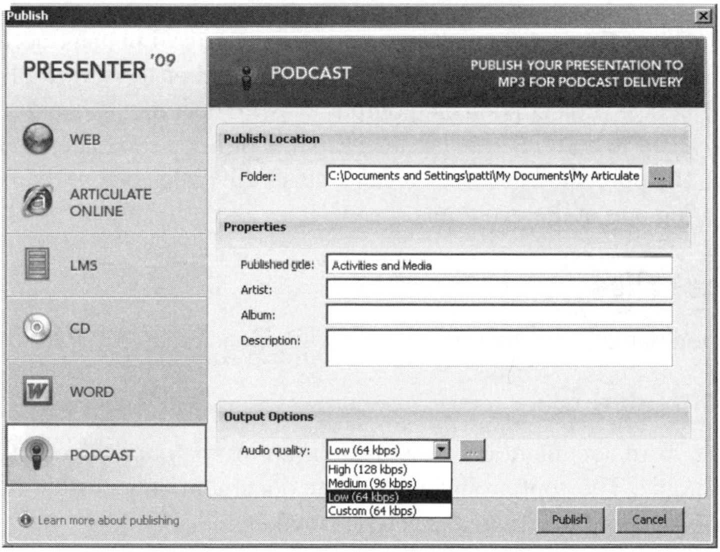

Figure 26.37. Presenter publish to Podcast tab

Publish to Podcast—Steps

1. Click the **Publish** button from the Articulate tab or the **Publish** menu selection from the Articulate menu. The Publish dialog box opens.

2. Select the **Podcast** tab on the Publish dialog box.

3. Specify a publish location for your presentation. The default location is My Documents\My Articulate Projects. Click the ellipsis button (⬚) to browse for the location or type a directory path to input a different location.

4. Input the desired Properties settings:

   ◾ If you wish to modify the title, input a new name in the Published title field.

   ◾ Input the artist's name. This is typically the speaker.

   ◾ Input the album name if this is part of a series of podcasts that belong to the same "album."

   ◾ Input a description of the podcast content.

❝❝ **Note:** These properties are embedded in the .mp3, so when the .mp3 file is opened in your MP3 player, these properties will display.

5. For the Output Options settings, select the audio quality you'd like to use for your podcast:

   ◾ High (128 kbps)

   ◾ Medium (96 kbps)

   ◾ Low (64 kbps)

   ◾ Custom: Click the ellipsis button (⬚) to choose a quality setting within the range 16 kbps to 160 kbps

---

▐▐▐▶**Tip:** Most iTunes, .mp3 files, and podcasts are around 128 kbps. The higher the quality, the bigger the file size.

6. Click the **Publish** button.

7. When the final output files are published, the Publish Successful dialog box will open. You can choose whether to play the podcast, send as email, send to an FTP site, create a Zip file, or open the folder containing the published files. You can also close the dialog box without selecting one of these options.

Output Files

When you publish your Presenter project to Podcast, a folder is created that contains the project's published output. Inside this folder are the folders and files created during the publishing process. They include:

- A podplayer.html file, which contains the podplayer.swf and, in the source code, information on how to embed the podplayer.swf file in another HTML page.

- A podplayer.js file, which contains code to display the podplayer.swf in an HTML page and configuration options.

- A podplayer.swf file, which is the podcast player that plays the podcast (Figure 26.38)

Figure 26.38. Presenter's podcast player

- A [filename]-podcast.mp3 file, which is the actual audio file.

Publishing to Mobile

You can also publish your Presenter project so that it can be viewed on a Flash Lite 3-enabled mobile device (see http://www.adobe.com/mobile/supported_devices for more information).

Preparing a Project for Playback on a Flash Lite-Enabled Mobile Device

1. Publish your project to web or open the published output folder for a published project.

2. Navigate to C:\Program Files\Articulate\Presenter\players\mobile and copy **mobile-player.swf** from the players folder to the data folder of your published presentation.

3. Copy the data folder (containing mobile-player.swf) to your mobile device.

4. Launch **mobile-player.swf** via your mobile device to view your presentation.

Testing Playback on Your Computer in Quasi-Emulation Mode

1. Navigate to the data folder of your published presentation where you've copied the mobile-player.swf file.

2. Drag **mobile-player.swf** into your web browser to view your presentation.

3. Resize your browser (really small) to match the screen size of your Flash Lite-enabled mobile device.

4. Resizing the browser taller than it is wide will automatically rotate the player to maximize playback size and will allow you to view the presentation either tall or wide on your mobile device.

5. Your mobile device controls will control playback, but you can use your computer's keyboard to emulate those commands:

   ■ Enter: Play/Pause

   ■ Left/Right Arrows: Previous/Next

   ■ Up/Down Arrows: Volume Up/Volume Down

Testing Published Output Files

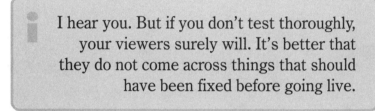

? I'm really getting sick of testing.

I hear you. But if you don't test thoroughly, your viewers surely will. It's better that they do not come across things that should have been fixed before going live.

After you publish, you should test the published output as your viewers will use it. So if learners will view the content through an LMS, make sure that it not only works locally, but it also works on the LMS. In some cases, you will find that you need to do some additional tweaking, so don't be surprised if this occurs.

So what's left to test at this point? (Drum roll...) The published output! Publishing prepares the files for viewing outside of the Presenter application. You'll want to make sure that published output works as expected before providing it to viewers. That means once again testing the pages, player, graphics, media, interactions, and so on, using the published output in the browsers and platforms that viewers will be using.

You will also want to see if anything loads too slowly. If it does, you may want to further compress inserted .swf and .flv files or change quality settings. Do any security messages appear? You may need to add text to tell viewers to expect this and what to do. (For example, "If the pop-up warning displays, you should click the..."). Also, if you have bandwidth-intensive files that start immediately, they won't have time to preload and it will seem as if the content is very slow to load. In that case, you may wish to rearrange files so media has time to load or let viewers know that media is loading.

If you are the person who designed and built the content, it's a good idea to include a tester or three who do not know the content the way that you do. Watch them try to use the project (while you stay quiet and provide no direction). This is a great way to learn what doesn't work, from the viewer's perspective. And having that information (and using it to make the viewer's experience more positive) is priceless. We have described ways to make your content more compelling throughout the book, but if you do all of that and the published output doesn't work well or as expected, viewers will have a negative view of the materials you built and the potential impact will be lessened.

 Note: After testing the published output, you may need to make some changes. You cannot change the published output files directly, so you will need to open and edit the development files and then publish again.

Tip: Develop a process for expediting changes to the content after it has been published. For example, many developers can't directly access their organization's LMS for loading and testing. When you test the content after it has been loaded (by others) into the LMS and find some glitches (not unlikely), you need to have a process in place that expedites getting needed changes made. Expect these problems up front so you have a process in place to deal with them.

Practice

To practice publishing, we recommend that you complete a small set of slides (Presenter) or build a small Quizmaker quiz or one Engage interaction. Then narrate the slides (Presenter) and add desired media to the Quizmaker quiz or Engage interaction. If you want to do a quick practice, publish to web, CD, and Word (storyboard). For more in-depth practice, add an Engage interaction, a Quizmaker quiz, or a Learning Game to a Presenter project and then publish the project. Then test the published output. Does everything work as expected? If not, troubleshoot the problems and fix them (incredibly useful skills when using any application).

||||▶**Tip:** As you test your projects/quizzes/interactions before pub-
lishing and test the published output after publishing, begin (or
add to) a checklist to use when testing.

Chapter Recap

Here are some of the most important points made in this chapter:

■ Publishing a Presenter project, Quizmaker quiz, or an Engage
interaction creates a set of output files that viewers can use and
interact with outside of the Presenter, Quizmaker, and Engage
applications.

■ Prior to publishing, you should test all of your pages, navigation,
graphics, media, and interactions and should also check the content for accuracy, spelling, and grammar.

■ The Publish dialog box lets you select or input options for creating
published output files. Although different publishing output types
(web, CD, LMS, and others) may ask for different information,
most output types ask for similar information.

■ The Articulate Presenter publishing option lets you insert a
Quizmaker quiz or Engage interaction as a new slide in a
PowerPoint presentation or as a standalone tab in the Presenter
player.

■ The Web publishing option creates published output files that can
be viewed through a web browser.

■ The Articulate Online publishing option lets subscribers upload
published output files to their Articulate Online subscription-based
tracking service.

■ The LMS publishing option produces files for delivering published
output files through an LMS.

■ The CD publishing option creates published output files that can
be launched directly from a CD.

■ The Word publishing option creates a Word document that
includes the content included in the published output files.

■ If you are developing complex Presenter projects or building courses that have critical tests (as part of a certification process, for example), learners may wish to listen to the content to review or study it. You can publish the audio in Presenter projects as podcasts.

■ The published output files will include the files needed to view and interact with the content. They typically include one or more Flash (.swf) files and other files, depending on the output type.

■ After publishing to most output types, you can select from several options in the Publish Successful dialog box. For example, you can view the published content (using the published output files) or package it to be sent via email.

■ If you are publishing to a company location, you may need help from your company's IT department or your LMS administrator to find out where to put your files and how to get them there. He or she may want to take your files and upload them to the LMS.

■ After publishing, you'll want to make sure that the published output works as expected before viewers access it.

Chapter 27

Video Encoder

Chapter Snapshot

In this chapter, you'll learn how to use Articulate Video Encoder to convert most digital video formats to the popular FLV format. Then you can use the full-motion video in your Articulate and web projects.

If you're an e-learning developer or frequent web user, you are probably already aware of the increasing popularity of video content on web sites ranging from commercial sites to online newspapers, magazines, and, of course, YouTube. Thanks to high-speed broadband connectivity and almost universal Flash player support, most people can view Flash video on their computer. Video Encoder allows you to take advantage of the new and almost limitless audience for online video.

> **?** I can't use video—it's too expensive and technical.

> **i** Not anymore! I just used Video Encoder to convert a video so I can use it in an Articulate Presenter presentation and then converted a video of my cat and placed it on our family web page—all in the time it took to have a pizza delivered for lunch.

Articulate Video Encoder '09 converts most common video formats to the FLV Flash video format, which can be easily inserted into Articulate Presenter, Engage, and Quizmaker or displayed on a web page. Video Encoder also allows you to record video using your webcam. After video files are converted, you can tweak them by trimming the length, cropping and resizing, and adjusting the volume.

Launching Video Encoder

Video Encoder is a separate application that comes with Articulate Studio '09. It is installed on your computer like the other Articulate Studio '09 applications. You can start Video Encoder using any of the following procedures.

- In Windows XP: Click the **Start** button, select **All Programs**, select **Articulate**, and select **Video Encoder '09**.
- In Windows Vista: Click the **Start** button, select **All Programs**, open the **Articulate** folder, and select **Video Encoder '09**.
- Double-click the **Video Encoder '09** shortcut icon on your desktop.

Importing or Opening a Video File

After you start the Video Encoder program, the start screen is displayed (Figure 27.1). From here, you can import a new video file to be converted, open a video file you worked with previously, or record a video using your webcam.

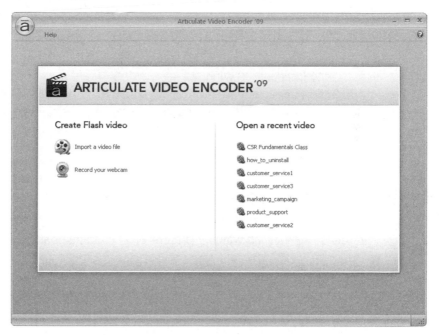

Figure 27.1. Articulate Video Encoder start screen

66 Note: "Importing" and "opening" a file in Video Encoder means working with a video file to edit (if desired) and convert it to the FLV format.

The Open a recent video section on the right side of the start screen provides links to videos that you have opened recently.

⫸ Tip: You can remove a video from the Open a recent video list by right-clicking the file name and selecting Remove from List.

What Video Formats Can I Convert?

Video Encoder converts the following video formats to FLV Flash video: AVI files (.avi), Windows Media files (.wmv, .asf), QuickTime files (.mov, .qt), MPEG files (.mpg, .mpe, .m1v, .m2v, .m4v, .mp4), Digital Video files (.dv), and 3G Video files (.3gp, .3g2).

To open an unconverted video file you worked with previously, click any file name in the Open a recent video section. The video file opens in the Video Encoder '09 window.

To import an unconverted file that you have not opened previously, click **Import a video file** and then browse in the Open dialog box to select any video file. The video file opens in the Video Encoder '09 window.

Exploring the Video Encoder Interface

The Video Encoder '09 window (Figure 27.2) contains tools to:

- Convert or publish video files to the FLV Flash format.
- Edit and format video files.
- Record video using a webcam.

Let's take a closer look at some of the elements of the Video Encoder window. Figure 27.2 shows the Video Encoder window with an open video file.

In the middle of the Video Encoder window is the video pane, which displays video content while you work with it. A timeline displays below the video pane with a playhead that allows you to jump to various points to select sections of video for editing. Player control buttons on the bottom left allow you to play, pause, and stop the video. Video properties on the bottom right show information about video position, size, and duration.

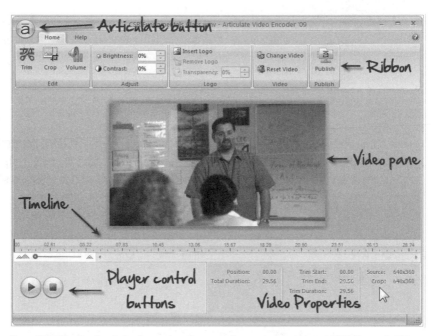

Figure 27.2. Video Encoder window (source: http://www.articulate.com/community/tutorials09/videoencoder09/Edit/player.html)

Video Encoder uses an Office 2007-type *ribbon* to organize most of the tools used to work with the video file. The ribbon contains two tabs. The first tab is the Home tab (Figure 27.3), which contains editing and formatting tools and a button to publish the video file, converting it to the FLV Flash format.

Figure 27.3. Video Encoder ribbon Home tab

The Help tab in Video Encoder (Figure 27.4) is similar to the Help tab in the Engage and Quizmaker ribbons. A few items are Video Encoder-specific, such as the tools in the Articulate Video Encoder '09 group.

Figure 27.4. Video Encoder ribbon Help tab

The Articulate button in the top-left corner opens the File menu (Figure 27.5), which provides redundant ways to import, record, publish, or close a video file. A menu of recently opened video clips is also shown.

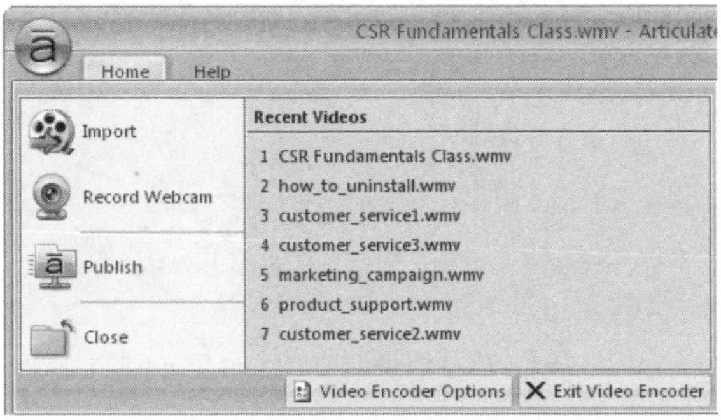

Figure 27.5. File menu

Recording Video from Your Webcam

Using Video Encoder you can create your own video clips using any computer that is equipped with a webcam (Figure 27.6).

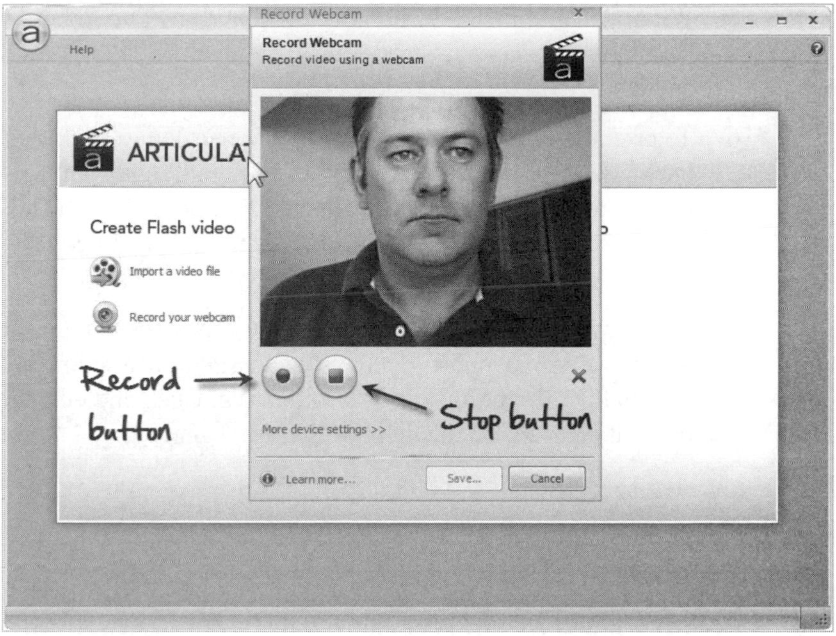

Figure 27.6. Record Webcam widow

To begin, make sure your webcam and a microphone are plugged in and functional. Set up any background that will show in your video.

To record webcam video:

1. Launch Video Encoder. The Video Encoder start screen opens.

2. Click **Record your webcam** in the Create Flash video section on the left side of the start screen. The Record Webcam window opens, showing the output from your webcam in the video pane.

3. If you need to select the video device or audio device to be used or adjust the size of the video image, click the **More device settings** link. The More device settings link changes to **Less device settings** and fields display at the bottom of the window, allowing you to make these adjustments.

4. When you are ready to begin, click the **Record** button. When the countdown timer reaches zero, recording starts.

5.   When you are finished, click the **Stop** button. The Record button becomes the Play button and the gray X to the right of the Play and Record buttons becomes a red X.

6.   To preview your video after you have recorded it, click the **Play** button. If you are not satisfied with the result and want to delete the file and begin again, click the red X to delete the clip. Then repeat steps 4 and 5 as many times as necessary to get the result you want.

7.   When you are satisfied with your video, click the **Save** button. The Save As dialog box opens. If necessary, browse for the folder in which you want to save your video file. Click and edit the file name if desired. Then click the **Save** button.

> 66   **Note:** After you click Save, Video Encoder saves your video in the Windows Media format (WMV) and your video opens automatically in Video Encoder. Then you can edit and enhance the video clip, if desired, and publish it to the FLV Flash video format.

Switching to Another Video

If you have one video open and want to switch to a different video, you can do so by clicking the **Change Video** button on the ribbon (Figure 27.7). In the Open dialog box, navigate the video file you want to work on, select it, and then click **Open**.

Figure 27.7. Change Video button

The new video appears in the video pane.

Editing Video

Video Encoder is not a video editing program, but it will allow you to tweak the video you bring into the program. The tools used to edit your videos can be found on the Home tab of the ribbon. You can use these tools to make changes in the video file that become permanent when you publish the file and convert it to FLV format.

Note: Prior to publishing the video file, Video Editor does not allow you to save the file and make your changes permanent in the file's original format. The only way to make your changes permanent is to publish the file to FLV format. However, if you close and reopen the file, Video Editor remembers the changes you have made and displays the file with your changed settings intact from the previous session.

Trimming Length

The Trim button on the Home tab of the ribbon (Figure 27.8) allows you to change the beginning and end points of the video, which shortens the duration of the video by removing content you do not want to include when the video is published.

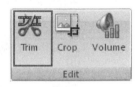

Figure 27.8. Trim button

To trim the length of a video that is open in Video Encoder:

1. Click the **Trim** button. Start and end points appear on the timeline (Figure 27.9).

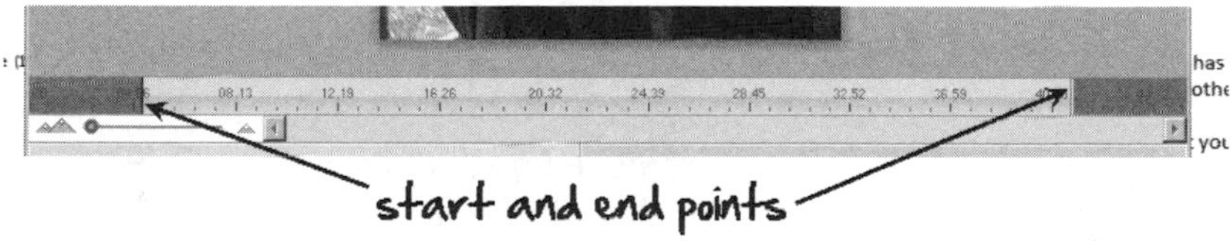

start and end points

Figure 27.9. Video start and end points

2. Drag the start and/or end points to move them. You will see the video frames as you move the start and end points, which can help to pinpoint the exact frame you want to start and end on.

You can also set the start and end points by playing the video and clicking the **Pause** button at the desired start point. Then drag the start point to this place on the timeline. Finish playing the video and click the **Pause** button at the desired end point. Then drag the end point to this place on the timeline.

Video Encoder

If you want to be very precise about setting start and end points, use the zoom slider below and to the left side of the timeline (Figure 27.10) to expand the scale of the timeline. The timeline scale is expanded and you can more easily set the start and end points to more exact locations.

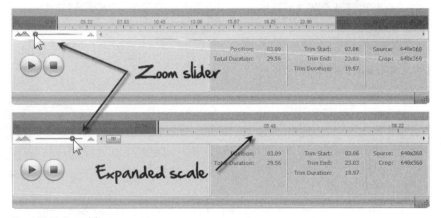

Figure 27.10. Zoom slider

Cropping Video

The Crop button on the Home tab of the ribbon (Figure 27.11) lets you remove unwanted space on any or all of the four sides of the video.

Figure 27.12 shows cropping a video. The area outside of the rectangle will be deleted.

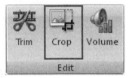

Figure 27.11. Crop button

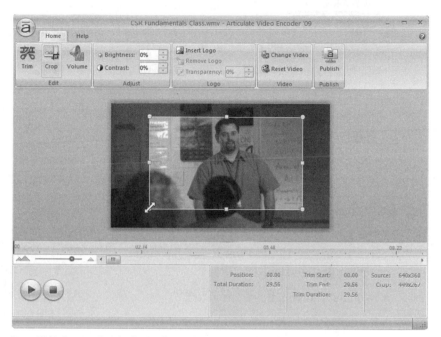

Figure 27.12. Cropping the video (source: http://www.articulate.com/community/tutorials09/videoencoder09/Edit/player.html)

To crop a video clip that is open in the Video Encoder window:

1. Click the **Crop** button. The crop window appears on the video display in the video pane.

2. Adjust the crop window to the desired size or position by dragging the edges. You can resize the video by dragging the corners, which maintains the aspect ratio. You can also drag the sides to add space to or remove space from that side, changing the aspect ratio. To recap, there are three ways to crop the video:

    ■ Drag the corners of the crop window to resize the window while keeping the original aspect ratio intact.

    ■ Drag any of the four sides of the crop window to move the sides, changing the aspect ratio.

    ■ Hover over the border of the crop window until your mouse pointer appears as a four-pointed arrow, then drag to move the crop window while keeping its dimensions intact.

> **Tip:** Keep in mind the maximum size available to display video in the player you will be using (Table 27.1).

Table 27.1. Maximum area usable for video in Presenter, Quizmaker, and Engage

Area	Size in pixels
Presenter slide area	720 x 540 when optimal
Quizmaker slide area	686 x 424 when optimal
Background graphics area in Engage interaction	690 x 470 (optimal maximum)

Adjusting Video Audio Volume

The Volume button on the Home tab of the ribbon (Figure 27.13) lets you adjust the audio volume of the video.

To adjust the volume of the video:

Figure 27.13. Volume button

1. Click the **Volume** button on the ribbon. The Change Volume dialog box (Figure 27.14) opens.

Figure 27.14. Change Volume dialog box

2. Click and drag the sliders to increase or decrease volume by the desired percentage value.

3. Click **OK**.

---

66 **Note:** Unfortunately, there's no way to preview how the new setting will sound. You will be able to hear the new volume only after the file is published. If you are unhappy with the new volume, re-edit the volume of the audio clip.

Adding a Logo

Video Encoder lets you brand or decorate your video with a logo or image that displays on top of the video image. The Insert Logo button on the Home tab of the ribbon (Figure 27.15) is used to insert a logo or other image.

Figure 27.15. Insert Logo button

To add a logo or image:

1. Click the **Insert Logo** button on the ribbon. The Open dialog box opens.

2. In the Open dialog box, navigate to the logo or other image file, select it, and then click **Open**. The image appears superimposed over the video image in the video pane (Figure 27.16).

Video Encoder

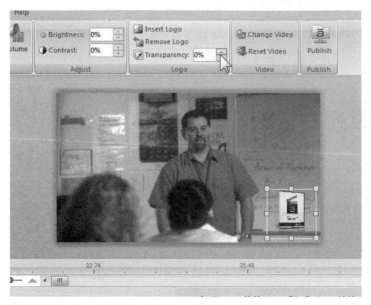

Figure 27.16. Logo superimposed on video (source: http://www.articulate.com/community/
tutorials09/videoencoder09/Edit/player.html)

3. Click and drag to size and place your logo—typically in one of the
    corners of the video screen.

Making Your Logo Semi-transparent

To make the logo semi-transparent (like
the network logos on television programs), select the logo, and set the
transparency percentage (Figure 27.17).

A setting of 100% is completely transparent, and 0% is completely opaque. The
logo will become more or less transparent
according to the setting (Figure 27.18).

Figure 27.17. Logo Transparency
percentage

Figure 27.18. Semi-transparent logo

Removing a Logo

The Remove Logo button (Figure 27.19) will remove the inserted logo or other image.

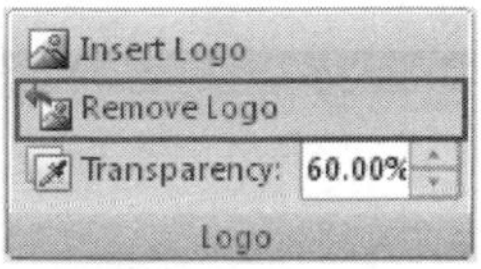

To remove a logo or image:

1. Select the logo or image to be removed.

2. Click the **Remove Logo** button. The logo or image is removed.

Figure 27.19. Remove Logo button

Changing Brightness and Contrast

The Brightness and Contrast settings (Figure 27.20) can improve the quality of the video if the picture looks too dark or not quite sharp.

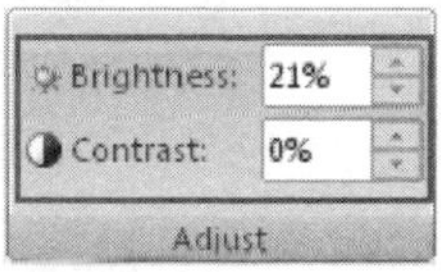

To change the video brightness or contrast settings:

Figure 27.20. Brightness and Contrast settings

1. Click the up and down arrows on the Brightness and Contrast controls or input the desired percentage values.

2. Notice how the video changes and continue to make changes until you are satisfied with the results.

Removing Changes

If you want to remove all of the changes you have made and return to the original settings from before the video was opened, click the **Reset Video** button (Figure 27.21).

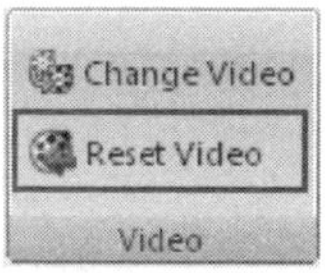

Figure 27.21. Reset Video button

Converting Videos to the FLV Format

The Publish button on the Home tab of the ribbon (Figure 27.22) is used to publish the video file, converting the video to FLV format.

To publish video to the FLV format:

Figure 27.22. Publish button

1. Click the **Publish** button. The Publish dialog box opens (Figure 27.23).

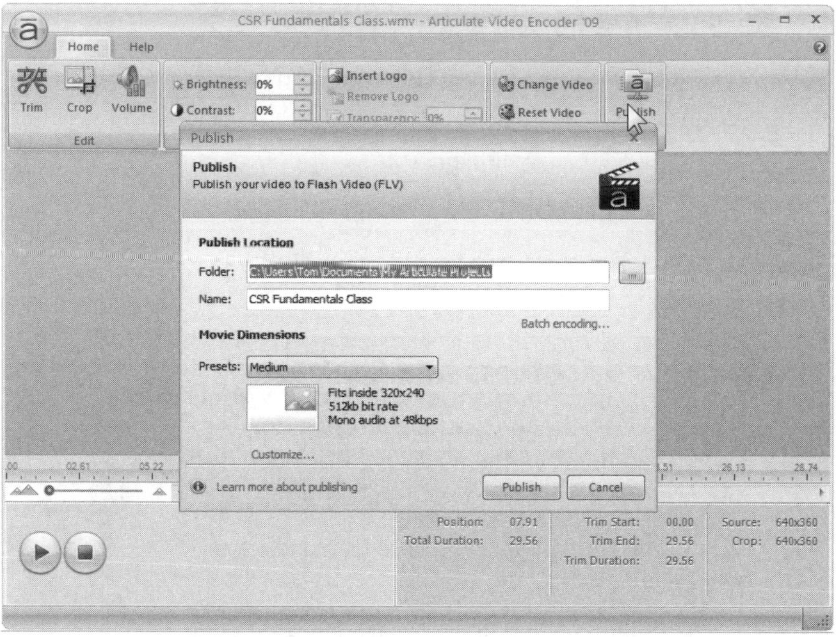

Figure 27.23. Publish dialog box

2. Change the output name that displays in the Name field if desired (this is the name that will display on the title bar of the video player).

3. Change the movie dimensions, if desired, by selecting the dimensions from the Presets menu (see Table 27.2 in the next section).

You can also select custom video and audio settings by clicking the **Customize** link. Once the Custom Encoding dialog box is open (Figure 27.24), you can further tweak video settings by clicking on the **Advanced Video** link.

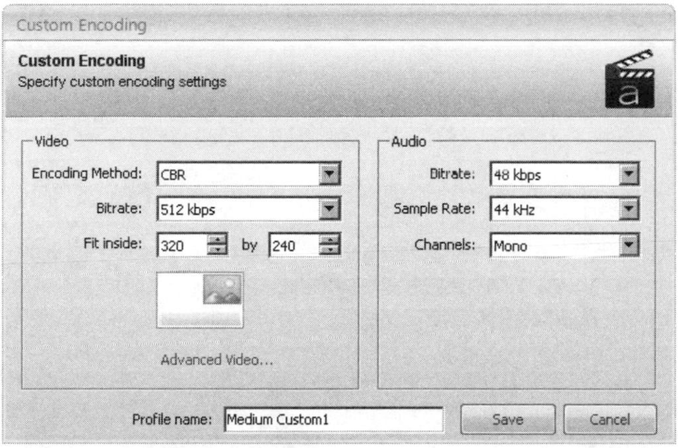

Figure 27.24. Custom Encoding dialog box

 Note: You should check with your network administrator for recommended settings. It's important to determine if your network
has the bandwidth to view video at the selected settings. If the
settings are too high, the video can impede the operation of the
project, interaction, or quiz in which the video is used.

4. Click the **Publish** button to convert the video to FLV format (Fig-
    ure 27.25). The conversion typically takes anywhere from a few
    seconds to a minute or longer, depending on the length of the
    video clip.

5. When the conversion is complete, the Publish Successful dialog
    box opens (Figure 27.26).

6. From the Publish Successful dialog box, you can click the **View
    Flash Video** button to see the .flv video, click the **Open output
    folder** link to open the folder in which the output file is located, or
    click the **Close** button to close the dialog box.

When you publish, the output file for your video will be in FLV Flash
format and will display the file extension .flv. This file can be used
inside Presenter, Quizmaker, or Engage. You can also display it on a
web page or send it to others as is.

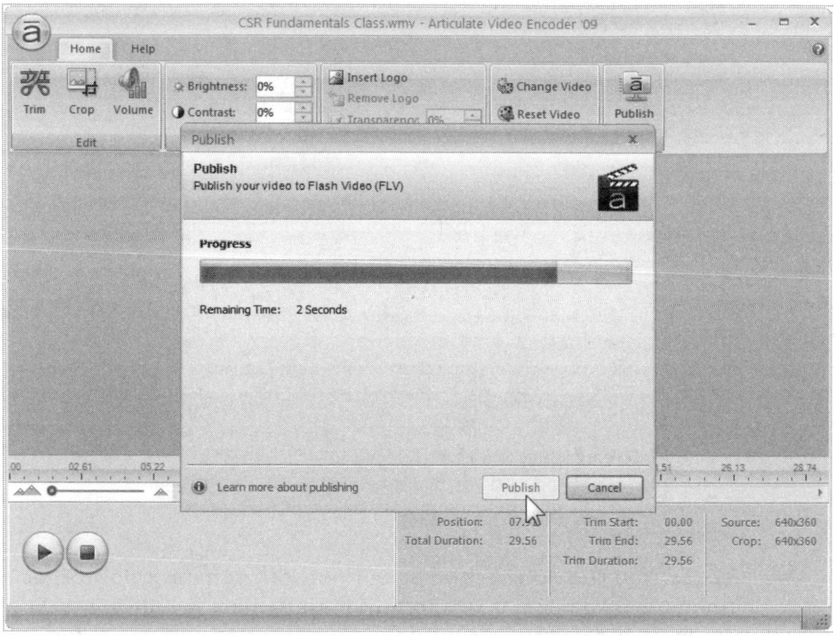

Figure 27.25. Converting to the FLV format

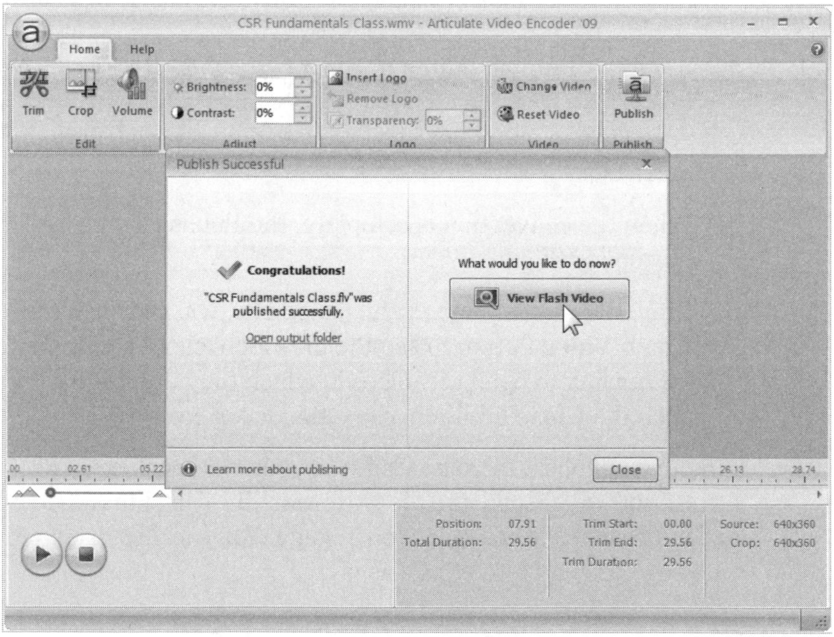

Figure 27.26. Publish Successful dialog box

> **66** **Note:** If you published this video previously (same title and same file location), you'll be prompted about whether you want to overwrite the existing video with the same name. Click Yes to overwrite it or No to cancel publishing.

Batch Converting Videos to the FLV Format

Video Encoder's batch encoding feature allows you to import and convert multiple videos at the same time.

To perform a batch conversion:

1. Open one video from the batch in Video Encoder.

2. In the Video Encoder window, click the **Publish** button. The Publish dialog box opens (Figure 27.27).

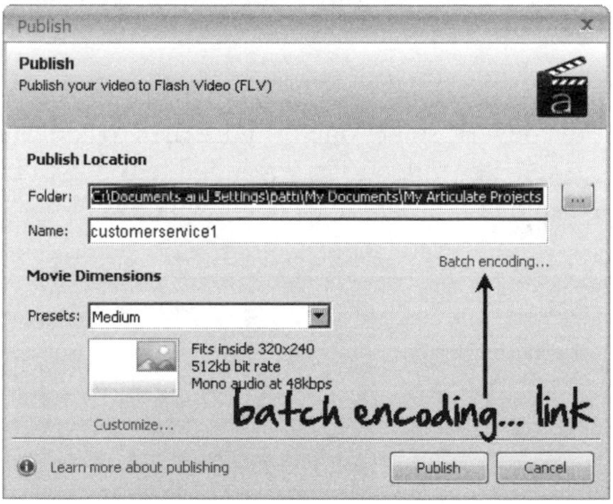

Figure 27.27. Publish dialog box

3. Click the **Batch encoding** link. The Batch Encoding window opens (Figure 27.28).

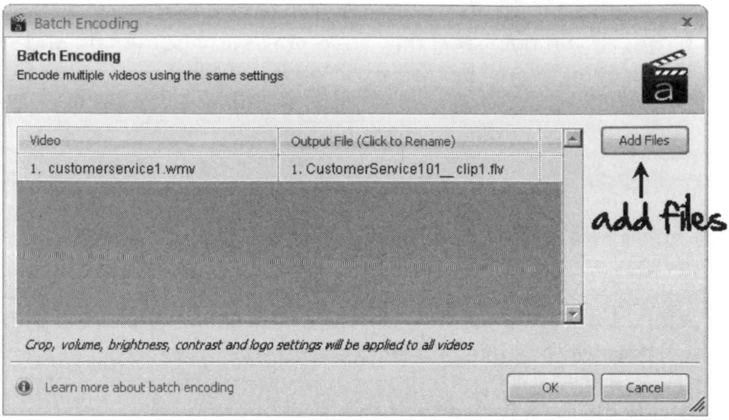

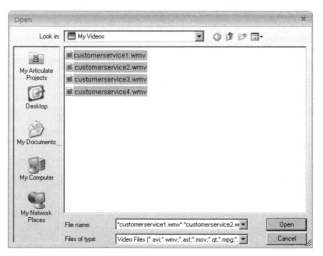

Figure 27.28. Batch Encoding window

4. The open video appears in the Batch Encoding window. To add
    more video files, click the **Add Files** button. The Open dialog box
    opens.

5. In the Open dialog box (Figure 27.29), navigate to the video files
    you want to convert, select one or more files to add, and then click
    Open. The selected video(s) is/are added to the list of video files
    to be converted in the Batch Encoding window.

Figure 27.29. Open dialog box

To add more videos from other file locations, click the **Add** button again, navigate to the video files you want to convert, select one or more files to add, and then click **Open.**

6. In the Batch Encoding window (Figure 27.30), rename some or all videos if desired by selecting and editing the values in the Output File column. Then click **OK** to return to the Publish dialog box.

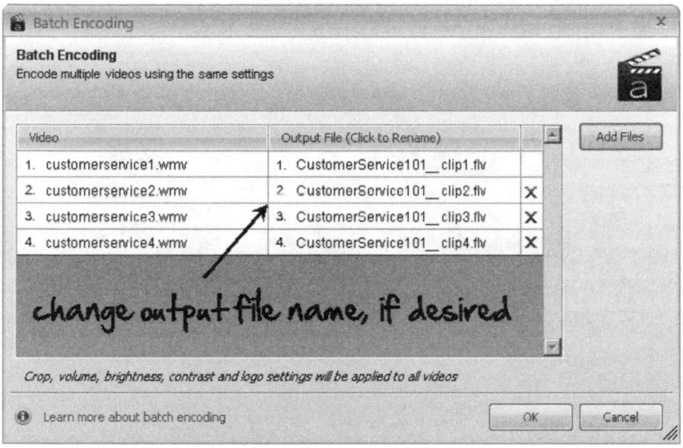

Figure 27.30. Changing the output file name

7. Change the movie dimensions, if desired, by selecting the dimensions from the Presets menu (Table 27.2).

Table 27.2. Movie dimensions size and bit rate

Movie dimensions	Size	Bit rate
Small	240 × 180	256 kb bit rate; mono audio at 48 kbps
Medium	320 × 240	512 kb bit rate; mono audio at 48 kbps
Large	480 × 360	768 kb bit rate; mono audio at 48 kbps

You can also select custom video and audio settings by clicking the **Customize** link. Once the Custom Encoding dialog box is open (Figure 27.24), you can further tweak video settings by clicking on the **Advanced Video** link.

> **66 Note:** You should check with your network administrator for rec-
> ommended settings. It's important to determine if your network
> has the bandwidth to view video at the selected settings. If the
> settings are too high, the video can impede the operation of the
> project, interaction, or quiz in which the video is used.

8. Click the **Publish** button to convert the batch. The Publish dialog
    box opens (Figure 37.31).

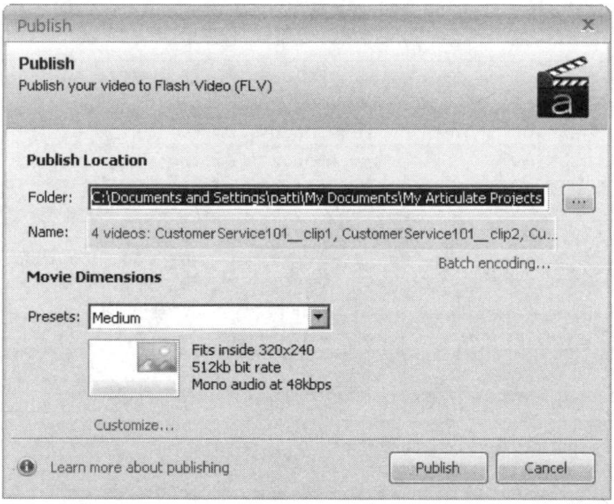

Figure 27.31. Publish dialog box

9. When the conversion is complete, the Publish Successful dialog
    box opens.

10. From the Publish Successful dialog box, you can click the **Open
    Output Folder** button to access the video files (which will display
    the file extension .flv) or click the **Close** button to close the dialog
    box.

Authoring and Viewing Requirements

To run the Video Encoder '09 application, developers will need the following hardware and software.

Hardware

- CPU: 500 MHz processor or higher (32- or 64-bit)
- Memory: 256 MB minimum
- Available disk space: 100 MB minimum
- Display: 800 x 600 screen resolution (1,024 x 768 or higher recommended)

Software

- Operating system: Microsoft Windows 2000 SP4 or later, XP SP2 or later, 2003, or Vista (32- or 64-bit)
- .NET Runtime: .NET 2.0 or later (gets installed if not present)
- Adobe Flash Player: Adobe Flash Player 6.0.79 or later

To view video that has been encoded by Video Encoder, viewers will need Flash Player 6.0.79 or later (http://www.adobe.com/go/getflash) (Flash Player 7 or later recommended) and one of the following browsers:

- Windows: Internet Explorer 6 or 7, Firefox 1.x and later, Safari 3, Google Chrome, Opera 9.5
- Macintosh: Firefox 1.x and later, Safari 3
- Linux: Firefox 1.x

Chapter Recap

Here's our list of the most important things to remember from this chapter:

- Video Encoder is an application that allows you to convert video clips to the FLV Flash video format. These files can be inserted into Presenter, Quizmaker, and Engage and into web projects.

- Video Encoder is not a video *editing* application, but you can use it to tweak your video files before converting them to the FLV Flash video format.

- Video Encoder lets you trim, crop, and resize videos, as well as adjust the volume level, add a logo, and adjust the brightness and contrast before publishing.

- Video Encoder allows you to record video clips using a webcam.

- After tweaking existing video files, you can convert them to the FLV format.

- Video Encoder allows you to convert multiple videos at the same time by using the batch encoding feature.

Index

On the CD

The companion CD-ROM includes a 30-day trial version of Articulate Studio '09, Articulate Studio documentation, and links to helpful content on the Articulate Studio web site. The files are organized as follows:

- Studio-09-Update-4.exe: The 30-day trial version of Articulate Studio '09.

- Articulate-REL-Blog-ebook-8-page-excerpt.pdf: An excerpt from *The Insider's Guide to Becoming a Rapid E-Learning Pro* in PDF format.

- links.doc: Contains links to various articles on the Articulate Studio web site.

- Documentation: Articulate documentation files for the Articulate Studio authoring tools in PDF format.

By opening the CD package, you accept the terms and conditions of the CD/Source Code Usage License Agreement. Additionally, opening the CD package makes this book nonreturnable.

CD/Source Code Usage License Agreement

Please read the following CD/Source Code usage license agreement before opening the CD and using the contents therein:

1. By opening the accompanying software package, you are indicating that you have read and agree to be bound by all terms and conditions of this CD/Source Code usage license agreement.

2. The compilation of code and utilities contained on the CD and in the book are copyrighted and protected by both U.S. copyright law and international copyright treaties, and is owned by Wordware Publishing, Inc. Individual source code, example programs, help files, freeware, shareware, utilities, and evaluation packages, including their copyrights, are owned by the respective authors.

3. No part of the enclosed CD or this book, including all source code, help files, shareware, freeware, utilities, example programs, or evaluation programs, may be made available on a public forum (such as a World Wide Web page, FTP site, bulletin board, or Internet news group) without the express written permission of Wordware Publishing, Inc. or the author of the respective source code, help files, shareware, freeware, utilities, example programs, or evaluation programs.

4. You may not decompile, reverse engineer, disassemble, create a derivative work, or otherwise use the enclosed programs, help files, freeware, shareware, utilities, or evaluation programs except as stated in this agreement.

5. The software, contained on the CD and/or as source code in this book, is sold without warranty of any kind. Wordware Publishing, Inc. and the authors specifically disclaim all other warranties, express or implied, including but not limited to implied warranties of merchantability and fitness for a particular purpose with respect to defects in the disk, the program, source code, sample files, help files, freeware, shareware, utilities, and evaluation programs contained therein, and/or the techniques described in the book and implemented in the example programs. In no event shall Wordware Publishing, Inc., its dealers, its distributors, or the authors be liable or held responsible for any loss of profit or any other alleged or actual private or commercial damage, including but not limited to special, incidental, consequential, or other damages.

6. One (1) copy of the CD or any source code therein may be created for backup purposes. The CD and all accompanying source code, sample files, help files, freeware, shareware, utilities, and evaluation programs may be copied to your hard drive. With the exception of freeware and shareware programs, at no time can any part of the contents of this CD reside on more than one computer at one time. The contents of the CD can be copied to another computer, as long as the contents of the CD contained on the original computer are deleted.

7. You may not include any part of the CD contents, including all source code, example programs, shareware, freeware, help files, utilities, or evaluation programs in any compilation of source code, utilities, help files, example programs, freeware, shareware, or evaluation programs on any media, including but not limited to CD, disk, or Internet distribution, without the express written permission of Wordware Publishing, Inc. or the owner of the individual source code, utilities, help files, example programs, freeware, shareware, or evaluation programs.

8. You may use the source code, techniques, and example programs in your own commercial or private applications unless otherwise noted by additional usage agreements as found on the CD.

By opening the CD package, you accept the terms and conditions of the CD/Source Code Usage License Agreement. Additionally, opening the CD package makes this book nonreturnable.